prediction = data if baseline continu[...]
verification = proof that if baselin[...]
it would have been same as prediction
Replication = Repeating results to show strength
of results.

Single-Case
Research Designs

Methods for
Clinical and Applied Settings

SECOND EDITION

Alan E. Kazdin

Yale University

New York   Oxford
OXFORD UNIVERSITY PRESS
2011

Oxford University Press, Inc., publishes works that further Oxford University's
objective of excellence in research, scholarship, and education.

Oxford New York
Auckland   Cape Town   Dar es Salaam   Hong Kong   Karachi
Kuala Lumpur   Madrid   Melbourne   Mexico City   Nairobi
New Delhi   Shanghai   Taipei   Toronto

With offices in
Argentina   Austria   Brazil   Chile   Czech Republic   France   Greece
Guatemala   Hungary   Italy   Japan   Poland   Portugal   Singapore
South Korea   Switzerland   Thailand   Turkey   Ukraine   Vietnam

Published by Oxford University Press, Inc.
198 Madison Avenue, New York, New York 10016
http://www.oup.com

Oxford is a registered trademark of Oxford University Press

Library of Congress Cataloging-in-Publication Data
Kazdin, Alan E.
   Single-case research designs : methods for clinical and applied settings / Alan E. Kazdin.—2nd ed.
      p. cm.
Includes bibliographical references and index.
ISBN 978-0-19-534188-1
1. Single subject research. 2. Case method. 3. Psychology—Research. 4. Psychotherapy—Research.
5. Social sciences—Research. 6. Experimental design. 7. Single subject research. I. Title.
BF76.6.S56.K39   2011
616.890072′4—dc22   2009046998

Printing number: 9 8 7 6 5

Printed in Canada
on acid-free paper

To Nan Taylor, PhD

CONTENTS

Single-case research—is that an oxymoron or an effort to legitimize an uncontrolled case study? Also, what can one learn from studying one person? And if one can learn anything, it is limited to information about just that one person? More generally, can one really do experiments—real science—with the single case? By the end of this book, I hope these and other questions are fully answered and that you view single-case and group research in a slightly different light. Both single-case and between-group research methods have goals, methods of achieving them, and strengths and limitations. They share the goals, but their different methods, strengths, and limitations underscore their complementary roles in uncovering knowledge. The purpose of this book is to provide a concise description of single-case methodology as well as to convey its contribution to science more generally.

Single-case research has played an important role in developing and evaluating interventions that are designed to alter some facet of human functioning. Many disciplines and professions provide interventions. Prominent among these are education, medicine, psychology, counseling, social work, occupational and physical rehabilitation, nursing, and others. Public and private agencies through policies, legislation, advertising, and public appeals too are always intervening to foster health, safety, and welfare. Most interventions and programs are not evaluated systematically. When they are, the usual method is based on between-group designs. These are the very familiar designs with such characteristics as comprising groups that receive different conditions (e.g., treatment, placebo, or no-treatment), carefully standardizing the interventions (e.g., in relation to duration or dose), testing the null hypothesis, and using statistical significance as a criterion to draw inferences about the effects of the intervention. The randomized controlled trial, which begins with randomly assigning participants to the different conditions of the study, is the ideal and considered to be the "gold standard" for research. Between-group research has made and continues to make enormous contributions to a range of basic and applied questions. As any methodological approach, it has its own limitations and sources of debate, but two of these in particular are related to this book.

First, evaluation is needed in many applied or everyday situations in which controlled between-group experiments are not feasible. Virtually every school, community, hospital, prison, college, and large business has one or more interventions designed to help people or change some facet of human functioning. Are these interventions effective or worth the cost or effort, and are they having the desired impact? Using random assignment, forming a comparison group, withholding the intervention, and securing a sample size sufficient to detect group differences (when such differences exist) preclude mounting a randomized controlled trial to test the impact of most interventions in most settings. Some interventions, such as individual psychotherapy or counseling, in principle cannot be subjected to a controlled trial because only one or a few individuals are being treated or counseled. In these and a myriad of other situations, programs go unevaluated because the gold standard of a randomized trial is not possible. There is no reason to go from a gold standard to no or shoddy evaluation. Single-case designs can evaluate interventions in ways that more are compatible with the demands of programs in applied contexts such as classrooms, hospitals, clinics, businesses, and the community. Like the randomized controlled trial, single-case designs are true experiments. That means they can lead to causal knowledge about the impact of the intervention.

Second, the unique facet of single-case designs is the capacity to evaluate interventions with one or a few individuals. We want the conclusions that are obtained from randomized trials about the effects of interventions and the relative effects of various interventions. The findings from group data are essential. In addition, we very much care, as scientists but also as regular citizens, about the impact of interventions on the individual. Results from between-group studies typically do not address the individual. We want to know if individuals change and to what extent. Single-case designs are remarkably well suited to evaluating interventions with the individual and in providing information that can be used to improve the effects if the intervention is not working or working very well.

Single-case designs provide a range of options for researchers, whether or not between-group designs are feasible. The designs provide a novel set of research tools to answer critical questions, particularly in relation to the effect of interventions. By training, many of us have learned that if the research is not between groups there are inherent flaws. Two flaws, that might also be called myths, come to mind quickly to illustrate the point: (1) one cannot have a true experiment with just one case, and (2) even if it were possible, one cannot generalize any finding from the individual to others. These two myths and others like them are addressed because they raise important problems for both between-group and single-case research. This book is not at all about one research strategy *versus* another. Just the opposite. Multiple methodologies are needed because of their strengths and weaknesses and because of their complementary contributions to knowledge.

Beyond investigation of individual subjects, the single-case designs greatly expand the range of options for conducting research. The designs provide a methodological approach that is well suited to the investigation of groups. Indeed, "single-case" designs have been used to study interventions applied to hundreds and thousands of subjects all in a given study. Hence, even in cases where investigation of the individual subject is not of interest, the designs greatly expand the available methods for research.

Although single-case designs have enjoyed increasingly widespread use, the methodology is rarely taught in undergraduate, graduate, or postdoctoral training. Moreover, relatively few texts are available to elaborate the methodology. Consequently, the designs are not used as widely as they might be in situations that could greatly profit from their use. This book elaborates the methodology of single-case research and illustrates its use in many areas of application including education; school, clinical, and counseling psychology; medicine; speech and language; rehabilitation; and other areas.

A central goal of scientific research is to draw valid inferences, that is, conclusions that result from minimizing, ruling out, or making implausible any alternative explanations that would obscure interpretation of the findings. Single-case methods, as between-group methods, encompass three broad topics: assessment, experimental design, and data evaluation. These are the components of research methodology and act in concert to draw valid inferences. The central goal of this book is to convey the logic of single-case designs and to illustrate precisely how the methodology achieves the purpose. Assessment methods, different experimental design options, and methods of data evaluation are covered in detail. Although not all options and design strategies are elaborated, certainly the main designs are illustrated. For each design, the goal is to convey the underlying rationale, the logic in relation to the goals of scientific research, and strengths and limitations.

Between-group designs often are pre-planned before the first participant enters the study. Such features as the design, characteristics of the sample to be included, how many subjects, and the duration of the intervention are salient pre-planned features to illustrate the point. This pre-planned feature is a strength because many issues that can interfere with drawing valid inferences (e.g., too heterogeneous a sample, low statistical power) can be anticipated and addressed. Aspects of single-case designs are pre-planned as well (e.g., which design, what the intervention focus will be); yet, in single-case designs key decisions about the intervention and its impact influence decisions during the study itself, and in relation to the intervention and the design. Single-case designs require a deep appreciation of what we are trying to accomplish in research in order to understand when and how to make changes while a study is underway. Such changes can greatly strengthen the quality of the inferences that are drawn about the intervention, as examples throughout the book will convey.

The first edition of this book was published almost 30 years ago (I was 2 years old). Needless to say, many changes have transpired in the ensuing years. First, application of single-case designs has expanded along multiple dimensions including the range of disciplines in which they are used, the problem domains that are studied, and the measures used to assess individual functioning. The revision of the book reflects expansion in the description of methods (e.g., assessment) as well as in the range of examples.

Second and related, single-case designs have proliferated in basic and applied behavioral research. An area in psychology known as *applied behavior analysis* focuses on interventions in many applied settings. The area has firmly established the utility of single-case designs. It is still the case that research in this area continues to use single-case designs. Yet, the methodology is applicable to a variety of areas of research well beyond the initial emphases and uses. The designs specify a range of conditions that need to be met; these conditions do not necessarily entail a commitment to a particular conceptual approach, procedures, or a particular discipline. For example, many practices that in the prior edition were viewed as essential or central (e.g., assessment of overt behavior) to single-case designs have expanded without sacrificing the strength of the designs or the quality of the inferences that can be drawn. Although some people may view such changes with ambivalence, if not heresy, this expansion is an enormous advance for science and for the quality of care of individuals who receive interventions. The book makes an effort to convey the expanded applications by clarifying the central and associated features of the designs and by illustrating the expanded options for assessment and evaluation.

Third, the book has been written to incorporate several recent developments within single-case experimental research. In the area of experimental design, new design options and combinations of designs are presented that expand the range of questions that can be asked about alternative interventions. In the area of data evaluation, the underlying rationale and methods of evaluating intervention effects through visual inspection are detailed. In addition, the use of statistical tests for single-case data, controversial issues raised by these tests, and alternative statistics are presented as they were in the first edition. Each of these areas has advanced remarkably. Research on visual inspection and statistical evaluation of the single case has expanded. Although data evaluation of the single case is a core chapter, an appendix is included at the end of the book to permit an expanded discussion of the challenges, advances, and dilemmas of data evaluation in the designs.

In addition to recent developments, several topics are covered in this book that are not widely discussed in currently available texts. The topics include the use of social validation techniques to evaluate the applied importance or significance of intervention effects, quasi-single-case experimental designs as techniques to draw scientific inferences, and experimental designs to study maintenance and generalization of the changes. Many of these have emerged from behavioral research but have broad application and have been adopted more widely in education, clinical psychology, and rehabilitation, for example. In addition, the limitations and special problems of single-case designs are elaborated. The book not only seeks to elaborate single-case designs but also to place the overall methodology into a larger context. Thus, the relation of single-case and between-group designs is also discussed.

There is a new timeliness to the topic of single-case designs. In the period since the first edition, there has been a proliferation of evidence-based interventions. These are interventions that have controlled studies in their behalf and where the effects have been clearly replicated. Many disciplines have delineated evidence-based interventions (e.g., education, medicine and its many branches, psychology, social work, nursing, dentistry, policy, and economics).

How could evidence-based interventions possibly relate to single-case designs? First, among the issues in evidence-based interventions are extending such interventions from the well-controlled settings in which they have been studied, invariably in between-group designs, to individuals and to applied settings (e.g., the classroom). Will the interventions work in the many different contexts to which they could be applied? Single-case designs provide multiple opportunities for such extensions well beyond what between-group research could accomplish.

Second, there is an increased accountability in many domains of intervention including education and psychotherapy as two examples. Some of the accountability concerns (e.g., from insurance companies, third-party payers, local and federal governments) result from uncontrolled costs and little outcome benefit to show for these costs. The strength of single-case design is evaluation and assessment of individuals and groups and use of the information to improve ongoing interventions. The designs can provide information about change or lack of it in novel ways that can determine what gains we are achieving with an intervention.

Finally, single-case designs can establish whether interventions are evidence-based. In evaluation of what interventions are effective (e.g., in education, counseling, child care, parenting practices), between-group research usually is the exclusive method that "counts." Single-case experiments are as rigorous as between-group designs, but they are not usually integrated into a larger body of findings. Science and care of individuals are not served by excluding data from a particular a methodological approach. The reasons why single-case research is often omitted, and options to rectify this, are addressed in this book.

Single-case designs provide a range of options for evaluating interventions in feasible ways and for the purpose of helping people in everyday settings. The careful assessment that the designs use can make a difference in not only extending evidence-based interventions but also in improving the quality of care and services. Single-case designs represent a fascinating union of attention to client care (e.g., educational or clinical services) and systematic evaluation. Research methodology is not at odds with sensitive care but in some way it is the only way to ensure that care, a topic addressed in this edition.

In preparing a book on research methods, it is important to note what is not included. Several critical topics in scientific research are not covered. Examples include ethical issues for the protection of clients (e.g., informed consent, privacy protections), critical issues of scientific integrity (e.g., conflict of interest, fraud), and publication and communication (e.g., making data available, writing up research so it can be added to the accumulating body of knowledge). These topics are shared with the tradition of between-group methods. Not covering the topics does not gainsay their importance, but rather rests on the likelihood that with scientific training in the between-group tradition the reader has had exposure to the topics and the obligations they raise.

ACKNOWLEDGMENTS

It is not possible to list the many people who have contributed to this book, although if reviews of the book are negative and sales plummet and we enter the finger-pointing phase, I have a list ready to go. The book benefitted enormously from the comments and suggestions of Drs. Richard R. Bootzin, Thomas R. Kratochwill, and Thomas H. Ollendick, who reviewed the manuscript. I am very fortunate to have the input of such colleagues who have made major contributions to research and research methodology and who have influenced my work.

Many others have influenced this book, spanning from advisors in graduate school to current students who participate in methodology discussions. I am grateful to Oxford University Press, with whom I have been privileged to work over the years and specifically with Patrick Lynch, Executive Editor, who helped develop this project. Also, my work has been supported in part by various grants and funding agencies (e.g., Research Scientist Award, MERIT Award, and projects from the National Institute of Mental Health, The Robert Wood Johnson Foundation, William T. Grant Foundation, Rivendell Foundation of America, and the Leon Lowenstein Foundation). I am deeply grateful for the support.

Alan E. Kazdin
New Haven, Connecticut
June 2009

ABOUT THE AUTHOR

Alan E. Kazdin is the John M. Musser Professor of Psychology and Child Psychiatry at Yale University and Director of the Yale Parenting Center and Child Conduct Clinic, an outpatient treatment service for children and families. He was 2008 President of the American Psychological Association. He received his PhD in clinical psychology from Northwestern University. Prior to coming to Yale, he was on the faculty of The Pennsylvania State University and the University of Pittsburgh School of Medicine. In 1989, he moved to Yale University, where he has been Chairman of the Psychology Department, Director and Chair of the Yale Child Study Center at the Yale School of Medicine, and Director of Child Psychiatric Services at Yale-New Haven Hospital.

Dr. Kazdin is a licensed clinical psychologist, a Diplomate of the American Board of Professional Psychology (ABPP), and a Fellow of the Association for the Advancement of Science, the American Psychological Association (APA), and the Association for Psychological Science. His honors include Research Scientist Career and MERIT Awards from the NIMH and Awards for Distinguished Scientific Contribution to Clinical Psychology and Distinguished Professional Contribution to Clinical Child Psychology (APA), Outstanding Research Contribution by an Individual (Association for Behavioral and Cognitive Therapies), Distinguished Service Award (ABPP), Joseph Zubin Award for Lifetime Contributions to Understanding Psychopathology (Society for Research in Psychopathology), and Awards for Lifetime Contributions to Psychology (APA; Connecticut Psychological Association). He has served as editor of various professional journals: *Journal of Consulting and Clinical Psychology, Psychological Assessment, Behavior Therapy, Clinical Psychology: Science and Practice,* and *Current Directions in Psychological Science.*

Currently, he teaches and supervises graduate and undergraduate students and runs a clinical-research program on the treatment of oppositional, aggressive, and antisocial behavior among children and adolescents. He has authored or edited over 650 articles, chapters, and books. His 45 books focus on methodology and research design, child and adolescent psychotherapy, parenting and child rearing, and conduct problems among children. His other books with Oxford University Press include *Psychotherapy for Children and Adolescents: Directions for Research and Practice* (2000), *The Encyclopedia of Psychology* (Vols. 1–8) (2000), and *Parent Management Training: Treatment for Oppositional, Aggressive, and Antisocial Behavior in Children and Adolescents* (2005; Reprinted 2009).

Introduction

Study of the Individual in Context

CHAPTER OUTLINE

Single-case designs have been used in many areas of research, including psychology, medicine, education, rehabilitation, social work, counseling, and other disciplines. The designs have been designated by different terms, such as "intrasubject-replication designs," "N = 1 research," "intensive designs," and so on.[1] The unique feature of these

---

[1] Although several terms have been proposed to describe the designs, each is partially misleading. For example, "single-case" and "N = 1" designs imply that only one subject is included in an investigation. Often this is true, but more often multiple subjects are included. Moreover, "single-case" research occasionally includes very large groups of subjects (e.g., thousands). The term "intrasubject" is a useful term because it implies that the methodology focuses on performance of the same person over time, which it often does. The term is partially misleading because some of the designs depend on looking at the effects of interventions across subjects. "Intensive designs" has not grown

designs is the capacity to conduct experimental investigations with the single case, that is, one subject. Of course, the designs can evaluate the effects of interventions with large groups and address many of the questions posed in between-group research; however, the methodology is distinguished by including an approach and multiple designs that rigorously evaluate interventions with one or a small number of cases.

Single-case research methods are rarely taught to students or utilized by investigators in the social and biological sciences. The dominant views about how research should be done still include many misconceptions about single-case research. For example, a widely held belief is that single-case investigations cannot be "true experiments" and cannot reveal "causal relations" between variables, as that term is used in scientific research. Among those who grant that causal relations can be demonstrated in such designs, a common view is that the designs cannot yield conclusions that extend beyond the one or few persons included in the investigation, leave generalizability of any effect unclear, or are inferior to group designs in establishing generality. By the end of the book, the reader can judge whether any of these concerns is just between-group methodology propaganda or has merit, but please wait until the end of the book. If you cannot make it that far—even I have trouble reading my own writing—these concerns are somewhere between flatly false and unequivocally unclear.

Consider three research methodologies, for example, including quantitative between-group research, single-case research, and qualitative research. Each of these is a rather large area of study, with books, journals, and historical traditions. Results from each type of research are scientific findings, subject to replication, and so on. If you, as the reader, have training that is traditional within the social or biological sciences, you would be the informed exception if you did not think ever so slightly that single-case research and qualitative research are poor substitutes for "real" science, that is, research in the group tradition of null hypothesis testing, random assignment, group designs, and statistical evaluation. There is no methodology that is "better" than another in some abstract sense; the methodologies are all to be viewed in the context of how they contribute to our overall goals of acquiring knowledge and our ability to use them to draw valid inferences. Single-case designs are important methodological tools that can be used to evaluate a number of research questions with individuals or groups. It is a mistake to discount them without a full appreciation of their unique characteristics and their similarities to more commonly used experimental methods. The designs should not be proposed as flawless alternatives for more commonly used research design strategies. Like any type of methodology, single-case designs have their own limitations, and it is important to identify these.

A little clarification of terminology is needed before we begin. Single-case designs are used heavily in applied research, and that will be the emphasis in the examples. By applied research I refer to research in everyday life settings including schools, the

---

[1] (Continued) out of the tradition of single-case research and is used infrequently. Also, the term "intensive" has the unfortunate connotation that the investigator is working intensively to study the subject, which probably is true but is beside the point. For purposes of conformity with many existing works, "single-case designs" is used in this book because it draws attention to the unique feature of the designs, that is, the capacity to experiment with individual subjects, and because it enjoys the widest use. (Of course, by referring to the single case, there is no intention of slighting married or cohabiting cases.)

home, in an office (e.g., dentist, physician, psychotherapist), institutions, and business and industry, and for any population in need of care, assistance, or treatment, in ways that reduce behaviors associated with impairment or that increase behaviors that improve functioning. The goal in applied research is to develop, treat, educate, change, help, or have impact in some immediate way. This is distinguished from basic research in laboratory settings where the goal is to understand, conduct tests of principle, and elaborate theory. Applied and basic research are related, and it is easy to show that some of the best clinical care, as in the context of psychotherapy, for example, can derive from basic laboratory research (e.g., see Kazdin, 2007). I emphasize applied settings because single-case designs have broad applicability to evaluating programs in settings where the usual group designs are not possible, or if possible are not feasible. For example, evaluating the effect of a program devoted to altering the reading of two special education students, preventing unprotected sex in a high school, or reducing crime in a neighborhood are areas to which single-case designs can be applied. With increased accountability and interest in evaluation, strategies are needed to help evaluate many programs that are well intentioned but will never see their way into a group design.

Also, I refer to quantitative research in the tradition of null hypothesis testing, random assignment, and statistical significance testing as "between-group research." This term better captures the difference from single-case research. Both methodologies can focus on groups of subjects and evaluate results quantitatively (with statistical analyses). However, the key difference in the methodology includes comparing groups rather than evaluating interventions within the same subject or group over time. There are ambiguities, combined designs, and opportunities to get lost in nuances. Let us not begin there.

The purpose of this book is to elaborate the methodology of single-case experimentation, to detail major design options and methods of data evaluation, and to identify problems and limitations. Single-case designs can be examined in the larger context of applied research in which various methodologies, including single-case designs and between-group designs, make unique as well as overlapping and complementary contributions. In the present text, single-case research is presented as a methodology in its own right and not necessarily as a replacement for other approaches. I also address strengths and limitations of single-case designs and the relationship of single-case to between-group designs.

In this introductory chapter, I would like to place single-designs in four contexts: (1) the study of individuals nonrigorously (e.g., traditional uncontrolled case studies); (2) historical overview of research with single case; (3) contemporary development of single-case research; and (4) current issues in intervention research that make the designs more useful and relevant than ever before.

THE UNCONTROLLED CASE STUDY

The uncontrolled case study serves as an important backdrop for experimental methods with the single case and for scientific research more generally. Historically, the term "case study" has broad use across multiple disciplines, and there is no single definition (Bolgar, 1965; Dukes, 1965; Robinson & Foster, 1979; Sechrest, Stewart, Stickle, & Sidani, 1996). The case study is a generic term that indicates a focus on the individual. Depending on the discipline, that can be an individual person, group, organization, institution, culture, or society. Any instance in which one of some "thing" is studied in depth or used as an example can be a case and hence a case study. There are some general commonalities or characteristics of what a case study is, and these are highlighted in Table 1.1. As noted there, the case study refers to the intensive study of the individual. Within psychology, particularly clinical and counseling psychology, the term has been used mostly to refer to an individual client. Case studies focus on the rich details and usually make an effort to describe details, offer explanations, and make connections (e.g., early experience and current functioning).

The case study is not only defined by the focus on the individual but also has come to encompass a methodological approach. This approach is reflected in the term "anecdotal case study," which refers to descriptions of the case that use anecdotes or narrative and literary statements to describe the case (e.g., details of who, what, where, and when) and draw inferences and connections (e.g., *why* the person is this or that way and *how* some experiences led to the current situation). Systematic measures (e.g., questionnaires, direct observations, archival records) are not used in a way that would allow anyone to draw the same conclusions about the case.

The case study as a methodology has been recognized to be a weak basis for drawing inferences, in part because of the absence of any controls, systematic assessment, and procedures to corroborate what actually transpired (e.g., what happened, what caused an outcome). The relations or connections among events of the case could be in the mind of the beholder, that is, the person who wrote the case description, as much as they are in the actual characteristics of the case. The unsystematic and subjective nature of the descriptions makes the case study generally unacceptable as a way of drawing valid inferences. Methodologists have this lesson more poignantly taught in childhood and learn that if they go to methodology heaven, they have unlimited access to H-net (Internet in heaven) and audio and reading materials that describe randomized controlled trials, those carefully controlled studies that are adored. When methodologists go to the other place, they have to listen to and sit in the audience with an infinitely long (literally) symposium and set of speakers describing and drawing conclusions from anecdotal case studies.

Strengths and Value of the Case Study

The lack of controlled conditions and failure to use measures that that are objective (e.g., replicable, reliable, valid) have limited the traditional case study as a research

Table 1.1 Major Characteristics of Case Studies

Key Characteristics

- The intensive study of the individual. However, this could be an individual person, family, group, institution, state, country, or other level that can be conceived as a unit;

- The information is richly detailed, usually in narrative form rather than as scores on dependent measures;

- Efforts are made to convey the complexity and nuances of the case (e.g., contexts, influence of other people) special or unique features that may apply just to this case; and

- Information often is retrospective; past influences are used to account for some current situation, but one begins with the current situation.

Note: Among diverse sciences, case studies have taken many different forms so that exceptions to these characteristics can be readily found. For a broad and comprehensive view of case studies, see Sechrest et al. (1996).

tool. Yet the naturalistic and uncontrolled characteristics also have made the case a unique source of information that complements and contributes to theory, research, and practice. Case studies, even without serving as formal research, have made important contributions. First, case study has served as a *source of ideas and hypotheses* about human performance and development. For example, case studies from quite different conceptual views such as psychoanalysis and behavior therapy (e.g., case of Little Hans [Freud, 1933]; case of Little Albert [Watson & Rayner, 1920]) were remarkably influential in suggesting how fears might develop and in advancing theories of human behavior that would support these views.

Second, case studies have frequently served as the *source for developing therapy techniques*. Here too, remarkably influential cases within psychoanalysis and behavior therapy might be cited. In the 1880s, the treatment of a young woman (Anna O.) with several hysterical symptoms (Breuer & Freud, 1957) marked the inception of the "talking cure" and cathartic method in psychotherapy. Within behavior therapy, development of treatment for a fearful boy (Peter) followed by evaluation of a large number of different treatments to eliminate fears among children (Jones, 1924a, 1924b) exerted great influence in suggesting several different interventions, many of which remain in use in some form in clinical practice.

Third, case studies permit the *study of rare phenomena*. Many problems seen in treatment or of interest may be so infrequent as to make evaluation in group research impossible. The individual client with a unique problem or situation can be studied intensively with the hope of uncovering material that may shed light on the development of the problem as well as effective treatment. For example, the study of multiple personality, in which an individual manifests two or more different patterns of personality, emotions, thoughts, and behaviors, has been elaborated greatly by the case study. A prominent, historically early illustration is the well-publicized report and subsequent movie of the "Three Faces of Eve" (Thigpen & Cleckley, 1954, 1957). The intensive study of Eve revealed quite different personalities, mannerisms, gait, psychological test performance, and other characteristics of general demeanor. The analysis at the level of the case provided unique information not accessible from large-scale group studies. Also, this was not just an anecdotal description; the investigators were systematic in collecting a range of objective measures, and video tapes, which made this case description novel and quite informative.

Fourth, the case is valuable in *providing a counter instance* for notions that are considered to be universally applicable. For example, in traditional forms of treatment such as psychoanalysis, treatment of overt symptoms was discouraged based on the notion that neglect of motivational and intrapsychic processes presumed to underlie dysfunction would be ill-advised, if not ineffective. Without treating the supposed (but never demonstrated) root or underlying cause, there might be other symptoms that emerge. This was referred to as *symptom substitution*. Yet, decades ago repeated case demonstrations that overt symptoms could be effectively treated without the emergence of substitute symptoms cast doubt on the original caveat (see Kazdin, 1982). Although a case can cast doubt upon a general proposition, it does not itself allow affirmative claims of a very general nature to be made. By showing a counter instance, the case study does provide a qualifier about the generality of the statement. With repeated cases, each showing a similar pattern, the applicability of the original general proposition is increasingly challenged.

Finally, case studies have *persuasive and motivational value*. From a methodological standpoint, uncontrolled case studies generally provide a weak basis for drawing inferences. However, this point is often academic. Even though cases may not provide strong causal knowledge on methodological grounds, a case study often provides a dramatic and persuasive demonstration and makes concrete and poignant what might otherwise serve as an abstract principle. "Did that person my age, with 30 lbs (13.6kg) he would like to get rid of, really lose all that weight on the North Beach Dandelion Diet? Of course, I am skeptical but the TV photos can't be wrong and even though he does not have my looks, charm, head of hair suspiciously thick for his age, or other appeal, he was a lot like me." Even without photos, seeing is believing even though research in cognitive psychology and neuroscience continue to teach us that perception and memory are limited in ways that interfere with drawing valid inferences and accurately perceiving connections among events in the world (e.g., Gilovich, Griffin, & Kahneman, 2002; Pohl, 2004; Roediger & McDermott, 2000). More simply stated, we see many things clearly even when they are not there.

Another reason that cases are often so dramatic is that they are usually selected systematically to illustrate a particular point. Presumably, cases selected randomly from all those available would not illustrate the dramatic type of change that typically is evident in the particular case provided by an author or advertising agency. Nor do the cases convey the relation of the alleged intervention to the alleged outcome. So our dandelion diet chap may have been 1 of 500 who agreed to the diet and the only one who showed change. Even if the illustrated case were accurately presented, it is likely to be so highly selected as to not represent the reaction of most individuals to the program. Also, no conclusions can be drawn about the causal agent—the dandelion guy— I just sent and received a text message—he vomited for 2 years straight and is now 6 inches shorter than he was. The diet did not quite work the way we were led to believe. Notwithstanding reason, logic, and methodology, the selection of extreme cases does not merely illustrate a point, but rather often compels us to believe in causal relations that reason and data would refute.

The example of losing weight conveys what might well be the four main functions that case studies often serve, namely, to *inform, intrigue, inspire, and incite* (Sechrest et al., 1996). Seen in this context, there is nothing like a case to convey the points, to provoke thought, to motivate others, and to move to action. It is not that the case will invariably accomplish any of these, but it will often do so better than a wonderful finding from a study with a large sample (N) and excellent controls. Large studies may not accomplish what a well-placed case study can do. Indeed, a routine failing of science is to take findings and translate them in such a way that they might have broader influence (e.g., on health, climate). For example, in relation to climate changes, conveying to the public in concrete ways with cases (e.g., in relation to continents, non-human animals, and residents of a coastal city) what global warming can do trumps the persuasive appeal of all of the constituent studies that established the problem (e.g., see Gore, 2006). In general, case studies and stories about what has happened or can happen in a given instance might be a more systematic part of that translation effort in conveying "real" research findings to help benefit the public.

Brief Illustrations

Case studies can be quite useful. Indeed, even the single aspect of generating hypotheses for research would make the case study quite valuable. In clinical psychology, there have been a few dominant anecdotal case studies (e.g., some of the key cases of Freud) that have become classics in the mental health professions. The cases make wonderful sense and are cohesive (internally consistent). Yet, in many instances, in-depth analyses refute or undermine the very basis for presenting the case.

For example, recall the case of from the 1880s in which Joseph Breuer (1842–1925), a Viennese physician and collaborator of Sigmund Freud (1856–1939), treated Anna O. (Breuer & Freud, 1957). Anna was 21 years old at the time and had several symptoms including paralysis and loss of sensitivity of the limbs, lapses in awareness, distortions of sight and speech, headaches, and a persistent nervous cough. These symptoms were considered to be due to anxiety rather than to medical or physical problems. As Breuer talked with Anna and used a little hypnosis, she recalled early events in her past and discussed the circumstances associated with the onset of each symptom. As these recollections were made, the symptoms disappeared. This case has had enormous impact and is credited with marking the beginning of the "talking cure" and cathartic method of psychotherapy.

Actually, this case is a wonderful illustration about the mixed blessing of cases. First, we have no really systematic information about the case, what happened, and whether and when the symptoms changed. Second, essential details of the case that readily controvert or weaken the conclusions are rarely noted. For example, talk therapy was combined with hypnosis and rather heavy doses of medication (chloral hydrate, a sleep-inducing agent), which was used on several occasions and when talk did not seem to work (see Dawes, 1994). Thus, the therapy was hardly just talk, and indeed whether talk had any impact cannot really be discerned. Also, the outcome of Anna O., including her very serious symptoms and subsequent hospitalization, raises clear questions about the effectiveness of the combined talk-hypnosis-medication treatment. Cases such as these, while powerful, engaging, and persuasive, do not permit inferences about what happened and why. Talk was not the only intervention, and the impact of treatment was not at all clear in the short and long term.

There are more compelling instances that show what a case can yield with better observations and reporting than those of the previously mentioned case. The well-known case of Phineas Gage is a better example of what an uncontrolled case study can show (Macmillan, 2009). Mr. Gage was a 25-year-old man working on the railroad (in Vermont, USA) and was going to use an explosive to fracture a rock. An accident occurred and caused a large metal bar (a tamping iron, 3 ft, 7 in. long [1.09 meters]) to blast entirely through his skull and to land some 20 meters away (for photos and further details of the story, see www.hbs.deakin.edu.au/gagepage). A physician who treated Mr. Gage within 90 minutes of the accident recorded that he spoke rationally and described what had happened. Follow-up of the case indicated that his personality had changed. Before the accident, he was regarded as capable, well balanced, and very efficient as a foreman. After the accident, he was impatient, obstinate, grossly profane, and showed little deference to others. Also, he seemed to lose his ability to plan the future. His friends noted that he was no longer like the person they knew.

This was a tragic experiment in nature that has become a classic case within neuropsychology. The case is used to reflect the impact of a disastrous intervention on cognitive and personality functioning. The case is compelling because of the abruptness and scope of the accident, so that the causal agent is fairly clear. Also, permanent changes seemed to be induced by the accident so that other influences were not likely. Later we discuss the role of the latency between implementation of an intervention and change as a way of drawing inferences about cause in case studies and in clinical work. The circumstances of Mr. Gage made drawing inferences from the case among the clearest one might expect without formal investigation.

Case studies have played a strong role in elaborating the relation of brain and behavior. The reason is that a variety of special injuries, diseases, and interventions occur that could not be conducted experimentally. As these are carefully documented, one can examine emotional, cognitive, and behavioral functioning over time and the resulting consequences. For example, in one case a young boy had one half of his brain (one hemisphere) removed as part of treatment to control epilepsy. Tracking his development over the course of childhood revealed that several functions thought to be specific to the lost hemisphere still developed. The boy was functioning well in several spheres (e.g., academic, language learning), all of which were reasonably well documented (Battro, 2001) and suggest the brain's ability to compensate and how with training the boy could overcome significant deficits.

The careful assessment of a case can make the results quite persuasive. For example, a report of a 25-year-old man with stroke revealed that he had damage to specific areas of the brain (insula and putamen) suspected to be responsible for the emotion of disgust (Calder, Keane, Manes, Antoun, & Young, 2000). The damage could be carefully documented (by fMRI [functional magnetic resonance imaging]) and hence shows an advance in specification of the assault in comparison to the Phineas Gage example noted previously. His damage could be located to these areas. The man was systematically tested during which he observed photos of people experiencing different emotions (happiness, fear, anger, sadness, and surprise). He had no difficulty identifying these emotions. However, he could not identify the photos of disgust. Disgusting photos or ideas presented to him (e.g., friends who change underwear once a week or feces-shaped chocolate [remember, I am just the messenger here; I am not making this up]) were also difficult for him to identify as disgusting. This is an interesting example, because the case was systematically evaluated and hence the strengths of the inferences that were drawn are commensurately increased. Also, the investigators compared this case to male and female control subjects without brain injury to provide a baseline on each of the tasks. The demonstration becomes even more interesting by falling somewhere between a case study and a between-group (case-control) design.

Methodological Limitations

We know that there are many limitations of the uncontrolled case study. In clinical work, the usual way in which cases are described leads to their many limitations. First, case reports *rely heavily on anecdotal information* in which clinical judgment and interpretation play a major role. Many inferences are based upon reports of the clients; these reports are the "data" upon which interpretations are made. The client's reconstructions of the past, remembered events from one's past, particularly those laden with emotion, are likely to be distorted and highly selective. To this is added interpretation and judgment of the therapist in which unwitting (but normal human) biases operate to weave a coherent picture of the client's predicament and the change of events leading to the current situation.

Second, *many alternative explanations usually are available* to account for the current status of the individual other than those provided by the clinician. The next chapter codifies the alternative explanations and the reasons that case studies often can be seriously challenged. Postdictive or retrospective accounts try to reconstruct early events and show how they invariably led to contemporary functioning. Although such accounts frequently are persuasive, they are scientifically indefensible.

Third, a major concern about the information derived from a case study is the *generalizability to other individuals or situations*. Scientific research attempts to establish general "laws" of behavior that hold without respect to the identity of any individual. Can a case do this? Probably not an anecdotal case study, but we have more to say on this topic later. For now, an anecdotal case is not flawed because the findings may not be generalizable—not at all. More likely, the "findings" may not even apply or apply well to the case itself, as discussed in relation to Anna O. and the putative "talking cure." It is not so much that the anecdotal description is "wrong" but that it may omit critical details that would change the conclusions. In science, we do not talk about generality of a finding until we have a finding.

All that said, I invite the reader to consider the case at a broader level of abstraction. We do research to rule out alternative explanations of findings. For example, I had a cold, started using soap when I bathe, and got better in a week. The implied causal connection is a problem because alternative explanations abound. Yes, given my history, the shock and novelty of using soap may have jolted my system, but processes in time (healing processes within the body) might have led to getting better even without soap. In fact, this case study is so flawed we cannot tell if the soap actually impeded rather than aided recovery. The point here: methodology is not about details of design as much as it is about drawing valid inferences. My little soap case study really allows no valid inferences to be drawn. But there are cases in which inferences could be drawn that are scientifically valid or very close to it (e.g., the 25-year-old male mentioned previously). Also, there are many things one can do with a case to make it so that valid inferences can be drawn (Sechrest et al., 1996). Using single-case designs is one of these, but approximations of the designs, and better observation of cases, can accomplish this as well.

General Comments

It is important to situate single-case designs in the context of the uncontrolled case study for several reasons. First, the uncontrolled case study, especially the anecdotal case study, has very little in common with single-case experimental designs, and eliminating that confusion is valuable at the outset. Second, the study of individuals, even when as an anecdotal case, can contribute to research. Hypothesis generation is not trivial in science, and the meticulous observation of individuals can help generate new ideas to be tested more rigorously. Third, research is about drawing scientifically valid inferences, that is, conclusions about relations between and among variables that can be replicated. Case studies, when uncontrolled, occasionally can suggest causal relations and make implausible other alternatives explanations of the outcome. Later in the book, I talk about systematic ways of drawing inferences from instances when the single-case experimental designs cannot be used.

When we teach research design we often begin with the designs and procedures of design (e.g., randomly assigning subjects to groups, holding things constant, keeping observers naïve). It is more helpful to begin with why we do research in the first place, and the specific sources of artifact, bias, and confound we are trying to combat by going through all these rituals. We engage in methodological practices, such as using control conditions (single-case) or control groups (between-group studies), to persuade ourselves and others that critical variables cannot account for findings we observed. We are trying to draw inferences and rule out competing interpretations. Once this is grasped, as discussed in the next chapter, we have many more options for research and for drawing conclusions. One does not know merely from the fact that there is a case, or a group, or a few groups, whether valid inferences can be derived. The extremes of this are very easy to show, that is, one thoroughly documented and evaluated case that is the strongest scientific demonstration of a causal relation versus a between-group study that provides the weakest or no decent basis for demonstrating causal relations (e.g., my dissertation). Throughout the book I emphasize not only the designs that form single-case methodology but also how they accomplish what we are trying to do in science, that is, draw valid inferences.

HISTORICAL OVERVIEW OF RESEARCH
WITH THE SINGLE CASE

Single-case research is often viewed as a radical departure from tradition in psychological research. The tradition rests on the between-group research approach that is deeply engrained in the biological and social sciences. Interestingly, one need not trace the history of psychological research very far to learn that much of traditional research was based on the careful investigation of individuals rather than on comparisons between groups.

Experimental Psychology

In the late 1880s and early 1900s, most investigations in experimental psychology utilized only one or a few subjects as a basis of drawing inferences. This approach is illustrated by the work of several prominent psychologists working in a number of core research areas. Wundt (1832–1920), the father of modern psychology, investigated sensory and perceptual processes in the late 1800s. Like others, Wundt believed that investigation of one or a few subjects in depth was the way to understand sensation and perception. One or two subjects (including Wundt himself) reported on their reactions and perceptions (through introspection) based on changes in stimulus conditions presented to them. Similarly, Ebbinghaus' (1850–1909) work on human memory using himself as a subject is widely known. He studied learning and recall of nonsense syllables while altering many conditions of training (e.g., type of syllables, length of list to be learned, interval between learning and recall). His carefully documented results provided fundamental knowledge about the nature of memory.

Pavlov (1849–1936), a physiologist who contributed greatly to psychology, made major breakthroughs in learning (respondent conditioning) in non-human animal research. Pavlov's experiments were based primarily on studying one or a few subjects at a time, work that apparently did not demean his research or dissuade the Nobel committee from awarding him their prize (in Physiology, 1904). An exceptional feature of Pavlov's work was the careful specification of the independent variables (e.g., conditions of training, such as the number of pairings of various stimuli) and the dependent variables (e.g., drops of saliva).

Using a different paradigm to investigate learning (instrumental conditioning), Thorndike (1874–1949) produced work that is also noteworthy for its focus on a few subjects at one time. Thorndike experimented on a variety of animals. His best-known work is the investigation of cats' escape from puzzle boxes. On repeated trials, cats learned to escape more rapidly with fewer errors over time, a process dubbed "trial and error" learning.

The preceding illustrations list only a few of the many prominent investigators who contributed greatly to early research in experimental psychology through research on one or a few subjects at a time. Other key figures in psychology could be cited as well (e.g., Bechterev, Fechner, Köhler, Yerkes). The small number of persons mentioned here should not imply that research with one or a few subjects was delimited to a few investigators. Investigation with one or a few subjects was once common practice. Analyses of publications in psychological journals have shown that from the beginning of the 1900s through the 1920s and 1930s research with very small samples (e.g., one to five subjects) was the rule rather than the exception (Robinson & Foster, 1979). Research typically *excluded* the characteristics currently viewed as essential to experimentation, such as large sample sizes, control groups, and statistical evaluation of data.

The accepted method of research soon changed from the focus on one or a few subjects to larger sample sizes. Although this history is extensive in its own right, certainly among the events that stimulated this shift was the development of statistical methods. Advances in statistical analysis accompanied greater appreciation of the between-group approach to research. Studies examined intact groups and obtained correlations between variables as they naturally occurred. Thus, interrelationships between variables could be obtained without experimental manipulation.

Statistical analyses came to be increasingly advocated as a method to permit group comparisons and the study of individual differences as an alternative to experimentation. Dissatisfaction with the yield of small sample size research and the absence of controls within the research (e.g., Chaddock, 1925; Dittmer, 1926) as well as developments in statistical tests (e.g., Gosset's development of the Studentized t test in 1908) all played a role in the move to group methods. Certainly, a major impetus to increase sample sizes was R. A. Fisher, whose book on statistical methods (R. A. Fisher, 1925) demonstrated the importance of comparing groups of subjects and presented the now familiar notions underlying the analyses of variance. By the 1930s, journal publications began to reflect the shift from small sample studies with no statistical evaluation to larger sample studies utilizing statistical analyses (Boring, 1957; Robinson & Foster, 1979). Although investigations of the single case were reported, it became clear that they were a small minority and possibly on their way out (Dukes, 1965).

With the advent of larger-sample-size research evaluated by statistical tests, the rules for research became clear. The basic control-group design became the paradigm for psychological research: one group that received the experimental condition was compared with another group (the control group) that did not. Also, the groups should be comprised in a way that will optimize the likelihood of their equivalence and the absence of a systematic bias, that is, random assignment of subjects to groups before the experimental condition is administered. Most research consisted of variations of this basic design. Whether the experimental condition produced a reliable effect was decided by statistical significance, based on levels of confidence (probability levels) selected in advance of the study. Thus larger samples became a methodological virtue. With larger samples, experiments are more powerful, that is, better able to detect an experimental effect if there truly is one. Also, larger samples were implicitly considered to provide greater evidence for the generality of a relationship. If the relationship between the independent and dependent variables was shown across a large number of subjects, this suggested that the results were not idiosyncratic. (The idea that larger samples or between-group experiments lead to findings with greater generality than the findings from small sample or even N = 1 research has an illusory feature to which we return later in this book.) The basic rules for between-group research have not really changed, although the methodology has become increasingly sophisticated in terms of the number of design options and statistical techniques for data analysis.

Clinical Research

Substantive and methodological advances in experimental psychology usually influence the development of clinical psychology. The anecdotal case study, already covered in the discussion of uncontrolled cases, is the most prominent use of the case in clinical psychology. Leaving aside uncontrolled cases, the role of the individual was specifically identified as critical to the acquisition of knowledge. The study of individual cases has been more important in clinical psychology than in other areas of psychology. At one time, the definition of clinical psychology explicitly included the study of the individual (e.g., Korchin, 1976; Watson, 1951). Information from group research is important but excludes vital information about the uniqueness of the individual. Thus, information from groups and information from individuals contribute separate but uniquely important sources of information. This point was underscored in distinguishing two approaches to research: the intensive study of the individual (the *idiographic approach*) as a supplement to the study of groups (called the *nomothetic approach*) (Allport, 1961). The rationale was to discover the uniqueness of each individual by investigating them intensively. Uniqueness, as an argument, is a two-edged sword. Yes, individuals are different from each other, but science seeks the general laws first and then how groups or subgroups may vary. The evaluation of uniqueness did not catch on within mainstream psychological research. Indeed, the distinction of research approaches may have actually held back single-case research, because it made less clear that single-case research can and does study and is interested in general laws as well.

The investigation of the individual in clinical work has a history of its own that extends beyond one or a few theorists and well beyond clinical psychology. Theories about the etiology of psychopathology, the development of personality and behavior, and treatment techniques have routinely drawn on cases, but these have been mostly anecdotal cases as illustrated by Anna O. and scores of others not mentioned of the same ilk. More well-controlled and systematically evaluated study of the individual played a significant role historically in clinical work. A case study on the development of childhood fear also had important clinical implications. In 1920, Watson and Rayner reported the development of fear in an 11-month-old infant named Albert. Albert initially did not fear several stimuli that were presented to him, including a white rat. To develop Albert's fear, presentation of the rat was paired with a loud noise. After relatively few pairings, Albert reacted adversely when the rat was presented by itself. The adverse reaction appeared in the presence of other stimuli as well (e.g., a fur coat, cotton-wool, Santa Claus mask). This case was interpreted as implying that fear could be learned and that such reactions generalized beyond the original stimuli to which the fear had been conditioned.[2] The preceding cases do not begin to exhaust the dramatic instances in which intensive study of individual cases had considerable impact on clinical work. As I mentioned, individual case reports have been influential in elaborating relatively infrequent clinical disorders, such as multiple personality (Prince, 1905; Thigpen & Cleckley, 1954, 1957), and in suggesting viable clinical treatments (e.g., Jones, 1924a).

Case studies occasionally have had remarkable impact when several cases were accumulated. Although each case is studied individually, the information is accumulated to identify more general relationships. For example, modern psychiatric diagnosis, or the classification of individuals into different diagnostic categories, began with the analysis of individual cases. Kraepelin (1855–1926), a German psychiatrist, identified specific "disease" entities or psychological disorders by systematically collecting thousands of case studies of hospitalized psychiatric patients. He described the history of each patient, the onset of the disorder, and its outcome. From this extensive clinical material, he elaborated various types of "mental illness" and provided a general model for contemporary approaches to psychiatric diagnosis (Zilboorg & Henry, 1941).

As these brief comments note, experimental work, including research and more rigorous studies of basic and applied topics, has a considerable history involving one or a few subjects. Scientific insights into critical phenomena regarding perception, memory, learning, and psychiatric disorders are a few of the examples. This is important to recognize in order to convey that the study of the individual was not invariably uncontrolled case studies with anecdotes and no clear ability to draw inferences of any kind.

CONTEMPORARY DEVELOPMENT OF SINGLE-CASE METHODOLOGY

Current single-case designs have emerged from specific areas of research within psychology. The designs and approach can be seen in bits and pieces in historical antecedents of the sort mentioned previously. However, the full emergence of a distinct methodology and approach has more direct lineage.

---

[2] Interestingly, efforts to replicate this demonstration repeatedly failed, with only occasional exceptions. The inconsistent effects obtained among the studies did not limit the enormous influence of this demonstration on interpreting fears and their acquisition (see Kazdin, 1978).

The Experimental Analysis of Behavior

The development of single-case research, as currently practiced, can be traced to the work of Skinner (1904–1990), who developed programmatic non-human animal laboratory research to understand learning and behavior change. Skinner was interested in studying the behavior of individual organisms and determining the antecedent and consequent events that influenced behavior. In Skinner's work, it is important to distinguish between the content or substance of his theoretical account of behavior (a type of learning referred to as *operant conditioning*) and the methodological approach toward experimentation and data evaluation (referred to as the *experimental analysis of behavior*). The substantive theory and methodological approach were and continue to be intertwined. Hence, it is useful to spend a little time on the distinction.

Skinner's research goal was to discover lawful behavioral processes of the individual organism (Skinner, 1956). He focused on animal behavior and primarily on the arrangement of consequences that followed behavior and influenced subsequent performance. His research articulated a set of relationships or principles that described the processes of behavior (e.g., reinforcement, punishment, discrimination, response differentiation) that formed operant conditioning as a distinct theoretical position and area of research (e.g., Skinner, 1938, 1953a).

Skinner's approach toward research, noted already as the experimental analysis of behavior, consisted of several distinct characteristics, many of which underlie single-case experimentation (Skinner, 1953b). First, Skinner was interested in studying the frequency of performance. Frequency was selected for a variety of reasons, including the fact that it presented a continuous measure of ongoing behavior, provided orderly data, reflected immediate changes as a function of changing environmental conditions, and could be automatically recorded. Second, one or a few subjects were studied in a given experiment. The effects of the experimental manipulations could be seen clearly in the behavior of individual organisms. By studying individuals, the experimenter could see lawful behavioral processes that might be hidden in averaging performance across several subjects, as is commonly done in group research. Third, because of the lawfulness of behavior and the clarity of the data from continuous frequency measures over time, the effects of various procedures on performance could be seen directly. Statistical analyses were not needed. Rather, the changes in performance could be detected by changing the conditions presented to the subject and observing systematic changes in performance over time.

Investigations in the experimental analysis of behavior are based on using the subject, usually a rat, pigeon, or other non-human animal, as its own control. The designs, referred to as intrasubject-replication designs (Sidman, 1960), evaluate the effect of a given variable that is replicated over time for one or a few subjects. Performances before, during, and after an independent variable is presented are compared. The sequence of different experimental conditions over time is usually repeated within the same subject.

In the 1950s and 1960s, the experimental analysis of behavior and intrasubject or single-case designs became identified with operant conditioning research. The association between operant conditioning as a theory of behavior and single-case research as a methodology became somewhat fixed, in part because of their clear connection in the various publication outlets and professional organizations. Persons who conducted research on operant conditioning usually used single-case designs, and persons who used single-case designs usually were trained and interested in operant conditioning. The connection between a particular theoretical approach and a research methodology is not a necessary one, as is discussed later, but an awareness of the connection is important for an understanding of the development and current standing of single-case methodology.

Applied Behavior Analysis

As substantive and methodological developments were made in laboratory applications of operant conditioning, the approach was extended to human behavior (see Kazdin, 1978). The initial systematic extensions were designed to demonstrate the utility of the operant approach in investigating human performance and to determine if the findings of non-human animal laboratory research could be extended to humans. The extensions began primarily with experimental laboratory research that focused on adults with psychiatric disorders and children diagnosed with developmental and intellectual disabilities (mental retardation) and autism as well as adults functioning normally in the community (e.g., Bijou, 1955, 1957; Ferster, 1961; Lindsley, 1956, 1960). Systematic behavioral processes evident in non-human animal research were replicated with humans. Indeed, lawful relations generalized across species as well as individuals. For example, manipulating the delivery of reinforcers on a particular lab task (e.g., pressing a level) yielded curves that were similar across rats, pigeons, and monkeys.

In human applications, clinically interesting findings emerged as well, such as reduction of symptoms among patients with a diagnosis of psychoses during laboratory sessions (e.g., Lindsley, 1960) and the appearance of response deficits among individuals with developmental disabilities (e.g., Barrett & Lindsley, 1962). Aside from the methodological extensions, even the initial research suggested the utility of operant conditioning for possible therapeutic applications.

Although experimental work in operant conditioning and single-case research continued, by the late 1950s and early 1960s an applied area of research began to emerge. Behaviors of clinical and applied importance were focused on directly, including stuttering, reading, writing, and arithmetic skills, and the behavior of patients hospitalized because of severe psychiatric disorders (e.g., Ayllon, 1963; Ayllon & Michael, 1959; Goldiamond, 1962; Staats, Staats, Schutz, & Wolf, 1962). By the middle of the 1960s, several programs of research emerged for applied purposes. Applications were evident in education and special education settings, psychiatric hospitals, outpatient treatment, and other environments (Ullmann & Krasner, 1965). By the late 1960s, the extension of the experimental analysis of behavior to applied areas was recognized formally as *applied behavior analysis* (Baer, Wolf, & Risley, 1968, 1987). Applied behavior analysis was defined as an area of research that focused on socially and clinically important behaviors related to matters such as psychiatric disorders, education, retardation, child rearing, crime, and social functioning more generally. Substantive and methodological approaches of the experimental analyses were extended to applied questions and to virtually all settings (e.g., preschools, colleges, military bases, business and industry, institutions and hospitals) and populations (e.g., infants, the elderly; individuals diagnosed with physical disease or psychiatric disorders) (Kazdin, 1977c).

Applied behavior analysis emerged from the extensions of operant conditioning and the experimental analysis of behavior to diverse applied settings and child, adolescent, and adult populations (Cooper, Heron, & Heward, 2007; Kazdin, 2001). In applied behavior analysis, *intervention techniques* used to change behavior draw heavily on operant conditioning; the *methodology* to evaluate these techniques relies on single-case designs. Thus, operant conditioning and a methodology of evaluation continue to be connected. However, single-case designs represent an important methodological approach that extends well beyond any substantive focus, theoretical views, or discipline. The designs have been extended to a variety of interventions removed from the conceptual framework of operant conditioning and used as a methodology to evaluate interventions in diverse contexts and settings (e.g., schools, hospitals, outpatient treatment, business and industry, competitive sports, rehabilitation centers) where behavior change is of interest. This book elaborates single-case designs and draws from the diversity of uses and applications. The expansion of the designs is not merely to new areas but also reflects modifications in key features (e.g., assessments, data-evaluation methods) of how single-case designs are used.

CURRENT ISSUES IN INTERVENTION RESEARCH

Treatment and intervention work raises issues that provide an important and relatively new context for single-case designs. The context pertains to accountability in providing services and greater interest in evaluating programs, therapies, and interventions in applied settings.

Evidence-Based Interventions

There has been heightened interest in identifying treatments or interventions that are based on strong empirical evidence. In the context of "treatments" (e.g., medicine and its many branches, dentistry, nursing, clinical psychology, speech and language training, occupational and recreational therapy, and rehabilitation), evidence-based treatments (EBTs) delineate these interventions. However, the many applications are not "treatment or therapy." Prominent among these are educational and school psychology where there is considerable work in developing and delineating procedures with evidence on their behalf (e.g., Kratochwill, 2006). There are other non-treatment areas as well that are now evidence based, including social policy, law, economics, and morality (each can be easily searched on the web).

"Evidence-based interventions (EBIs)" has been used as the more generic term and applies to an expanding range of disciplines (e.g., social work, speech and language, rehabilitation) that are committed to drawing on their evidence base. Both EBTs and EBIs refer to specific interventions that have outcome studies that attest to their efficacy. The movement toward EBTs or EBIs encompasses many different disciplines, countries, and professional groups, organizations, and agencies within a country.[3]

---

[3] The various efforts have used many different terms and criteria (e.g., Kratochwill et al., 2009). For example, in the context of psychotherapy, the terms have included "evidence-based treatments," "empirically validated treatments," "empirically supported treatments," "evidence-based practice," and "treatments that work." The different terms are not completely interchangeable. For example, EBTs focus on interventions with supportive research. Evidence-based practice refers to clinical

Table 1.2 Criteria Used to Establish a Treatment or Intervention as Evidence Based

- Random assignment of subjects to treatment and control or comparison conditions (e.g., no treatment) routine care, treatment as usual for the setting);
- The sample has been well specified (inclusion and exclusion criteria);
- Treatment manuals specify the intervention procedures that were used;
- Multiple outcome measures (raters, if used, are naïve to conditions);
- Statistically significant differences between treatment and a comparison condition(s);
- Two or more randomized controlled studies attest to the effects of treatment; and
- The studies include replication of the findings beyond the original investigator or originator of the treatment.

Note: As noted in the text, delineating treatments as evidence based reflects a broad movement involving multiple professional groups and organizations and many different countries. There is no single set of criteria, but those selected for this table are among those most commonly invoked.

Understandably, the terminology and definitions have varied widely, and the variation continues to increase. For example, in the United States and Canada, states, provinces, and the agencies for national governments are defining EBTs to guide psychological services; the definitions can vary widely, and therefore so can the interventions that are selected. In research, the criteria to be counted as evidence-based vary; this variation was evident even from early efforts to delineate the criteria (see Chambless & Ollendick, 2001). Table 1.2 includes criteria commonly used or invoked. As evident in the table, the criteria emphasize sound research methodology, including careful specification of who the clients are and the procedures that comprise the intervention, as well as replication of intervention effects.

Establishing EBIs requires rigorous and well-controlled research. Interestingly, early efforts to specify what this research would entail included both between-group studies (randomized controlled trials) and single-case experimental designs (Chambless & Ollendick, 2001). This is remarkable given the general unfamiliarity of single-case designs. Even so, over time and across many efforts to delineate interventions as evidence based, *randomized controlled trials* (RCTs) have emerged as primary and more often than not the sole criterion. An RCT is a between-group study where participants are assigned randomly to one of the conditions (e.g., treatment, variants of a treatment, control). An RCT is viewed by a broad scientific community as the "gold standard" for intervention research and is usually required to establish the effectiveness of a new treatment (e.g., cancer treatment, medication). Such trials address key methodological concerns that can arise in research, as discussed in the next chapter, and can discern whether one intervention is better than another.

---

[3] (Continued) work in which practitioners integrate evidence about interventions, their clinical judgment and experience, and contextual factors about the clients (American Psychological Association, 2005; Institute of Medicine, 2001). As of this writing, it is not clear that there is evidence for "evidence-based practice," that is, that the integration can be done reliably and makes a difference in helping patients when it does, and that it provides an increment in outcome effects that would surpass relying on evidence related to the intervention. I use EBI here as the more general term to encompass any program, treatment, or strategy with evidence that approximates the criteria discussed in this section and many disciplines involved (e.g., education, clinical psychology).

EBIs and RCTs raise interesting challenges and concerns that set the stage for single-case designs. First, there are so many interventions and they could not be subjected to randomized trials. For example, in the context of psychotherapy, there are hundreds of variations in use. The vast majority of these have not been evaluated at all, but they remain in use. Funds, researchers, and other resources are not available to evaluate in an RCT. Are there alternative ways to evaluate interventions that might be feasible?

Second, intervention delivery in RCTs is very carefully controlled to ensure that the data are interpretable at the end of the study. The carefully controlled conditions of such trials have led to concerns about the generality of the results. That is, will the findings (e.g., treatment A is effective) apply to clinical situations where such careful control of who receives and provides the services is not so meticulously regulated (e.g., Hunsley, 2007; Wampold, 2001; Westen, Novotny, & Thompson-Brenne, 2004)? Is there a way to test treatments as they are extended to clinical practice or service situations?

Third, whether one uses an EBT or one's own brand of individualized treatment, one cannot be sure, in principle or practice, that the treatment will be effective. Generalizing from research, experience, and their combination is always probabilistic and does not guarantee an outcome. EBTs of all sorts (e.g., aspirin, by-pass surgery, plastic surgery, chemotherapy, anti-depressant medication) cannot be depended on to produce the desired outcome without exception. We take systematic evaluation as pivotal in research. However, it is no less important in the application of interventions for the individual (Kazdin, 2008b).

In short, the move toward EBIs underscores the importance of using interventions with evidence in their behalf. In the process, concerns about whether the treatments will work in practice has raised the question of how one could know or tell. One needs assessment and design strategies that could be applied to individual cases, whether adults in therapy or students in special education or other classroom programs.

Increased Evaluation and Accountability

EBIs are part of a broader movement of increased accountability in intervention work. Much of this is prompted by cost control and funding agencies—managed care, insurance, third-party payers, government agencies in the context of medical, psychological, and educational interventions but other areas as well (e.g., rehabilitation, services for the elderly). The guiding questions are, "What are we getting for our money?" and "Do any of these interventions (e.g., educational reforms and fads) make any difference?" Third-party payers (e.g., managed-care companies in the United States) are increasingly interested in the use of interventions that have evidence in their behalf, especially if the treatments reduce costs of care. There is also a concern about increased evaluation, that is, obtaining data about what is provided and what effects it is having.

Consider the delivery of psychological services and the practice of psychotherapy to convey concerns about evaluation and accountability. In psychotherapy for children, adolescents, or adults, treatment is delivered by a practicing clinician. Patient progress is usually evaluated on the basis of clinician impressions, as opposed to systematic observations using validated measures. This is the anecdotal case study "methodology" mentioned at the outset of the chapter. There is a notoriously poor record of the poor reliability of such judgments (e.g., Dawes, 1994; Garb, 2005)—no fault of clinicians but rather limits of normal human perception, cognitive processes, and memory and recall.

Advances have been made in developing measures that are feasible, user (clinician, patient) friendly, and well validated in the context of clinical work. For example, one measure (the Outcome Questionnaire 45 [OQ-45]; Lambert et al., 1996), is a self-report scale for adults designed to evaluate client progress (e.g., weekly) over the course of treatment and at termination. The measure requires approximately 5 minutes to complete and provides information on four domains of functioning, including symptoms of psychological disturbance (primarily depression and anxiety), interpersonal problems, social role functioning (e.g., problems at work), and quality of life (e.g., facets of life satisfaction). The measure has been evaluated extensively and applied to over 10,000 patients (see Lambert, Hansen, & Finch, 2001; Lambert et al., 2003).[4]

Obtaining continuous measures over the course of treatment is pivotal for clinical care to ensure that outcomes are being achieved and to make decisions about when to alter or perhaps end treatment. The collection of continuous measures over time in this fashion is a core component of single-case designs. Once such assessment is in place, all sorts of questions can be asked about treatment. In clinical settings, these questions are about how to improve this patient's care, how to evaluate if changes are occurring in the many contexts in which they are needed, and more.

The practicing clinician is confronted with the individual case, and it is at the level of the clinical case that empirical evaluations of treatment need to be made. The problem, of course, is that the primary investigative tool for the clinician has been, and in the majority of instances continues to be, the uncontrolled case study in which anecdotal information is reported and scientifically acceptable inferences cannot be drawn. There has been a lengthy history of researchers and practitioners advocating the study of the individual to improve the quality of clinical work (e.g., Chassan, 1967; Shapiro, 1961a, 1961b; Shapiro & Ravenette, 1959). Much of this history has fallen on deaf ears, which we can tell by viewing how current practice is routinely conducted and by seeing continued pleas to evaluate clinical work by authors who know that pleading is not a very effective intervention (Borckardt et al., 2008; Kazdin, 2008b). Also, as we discuss in a later chapter, there are ways to improve the uncontrolled case study to increase the scientific yield and improve patient care.

At this point in time and in the very immediate future, the primary pressure on practice will be to justify what interventions are being used. It is still the case that an EBI is not necessarily used even when one is available. Pressure is changing on that front. In addition, increased accountability in the form of measurement of patient care and change is more salient than ever before. Single-case designs discussed in this book provide multiple options that would facilitate the evaluation of interventions in applied settings.

General Comments

An important context for considering single-case designs is the increased accountability in intervention work. Whether in the contexts of individual psychotherapy,

---

[4] For a review and update of research on OQ-45, an excellent overview is provided at www.nrepp. samhsa.gov/programfulldetails.asp?PROGRAM_ID=191. Also, the 45-item measure has been reduced to 30 items and also has been validated (Lambert et al., 2004).

classroom programs to prevent or alter some problem, or school- and school-district-wide interventions, some means of evaluation is likely to be requested. Methods of evaluation often used to establish the effectiveness of an intervention (randomized controlled trials) usually are not feasible in applied settings. Also, we want professionals on the everyday battlefields (e.g., clinicians, teachers, program directors) to evaluate what they are doing, to innovate and develop new interventions, and to feed into as well as draw from large-scale controlled studies. Single-case designs represent a broad methodology that not only includes many design options, but also provides a continuum of conditions that vary in their feasibility for implementation in applied settings. This book elaborates experimental designs and approximations that still permit one to draw inferences about intervention effects.

CONTEXTS AND PERSPECTIVE

I have provided four contexts as a way of introducing single-case designs. The contexts convey different points that serve as underpinnings for subsequent chapters. First, the discussion of uncontrolled case study was not designed to lambaste uncontrolled anecdotal case reports. Such reports are an easy methodological target, but there is something more useful and important to convey than their deficiencies. Rather, it is useful to recognize that in principle an uncontrolled case study can be methodologically (not just subjectively) persuasive and can make implausible potentially competing explanations of what caused a change. A case can yield inferences that are valid; how to accomplish this serves as a basis of a later discussion (Chapter 11). The key point was to convey that a case (N = 1) or group (N = 1,000) is not the issue. Rather, the overarching methodological priority is always whether an arrangement (design, circumstance) allows valid inference to be drawn. Even in some case studies, the answer is yes.

Second, I highlighted historical issues related to research with individual subjects. Here the key point was to note that the evaluation of groups, group comparisons, and statistical analyses were not always the norm in psychology. Research with one or a few subjects was the rule and was the basis for many advances. In most graduate training programs in psychology, education, and counseling, for example, history of the field receives diminished emphasis and classroom time. With astounding advances and new information that must be added to any curriculum and a fixed or limited amount of training time, this is understandable. However, we unwittingly convey that how things are now (group research, quantitative tradition) is the way things always were and, perhaps by implication, how they rightfully ought to be for some good, but never specified, reason. Not long ago, research was focused on one or a few subjects. This was not only to be a legitimate research approach but *the* research approach. Focus on single-case designs actually adds rigor to that tradition, a point conveyed in the next chapter.

Third, I discussed the development and proliferation of single-case designs and how they grew out of and were central to the experimental analysis of behavior. The experimental analysis includes a substantive field (basic human and non-human animal research in operant conditioning) and a methodological approach (single-case designs and all that entails). When the field began to apply key findings and techniques to individuals in everyday life, the area of applied behavior analysis emerged, proliferated, and flourished. The content (often techniques based on findings in operant conditioning) and methodology (single-case designs) began close to the basic laboratory ties, and in many ways the ties remain. However, single-case designs and their scope of application have extended remarkably, in the range of settings, populations, and intervention techniques. That said, it is still the case that applied behavior analysis utilizes single-case designs and has delineated an array of design options, assessment strategies, and combinations that are illustrated in this book. Still, the methodology is very widely applicable and the book can convey key methodological points by sampling from the richness beyond any single field or area of research. As I alluded to, these extensions have influenced single-case methods and how they are used.

Last, I discussed contemporary issues that make single-case research especially relevant in applied settings. The emergence of EBIs has raised the question, "Can these interventions be extended to everyday settings?" Randomized controlled trials have done their job to establish these interventions as effective. Now, how can we apply these interventions and evaluate their impact on patient care in everyday settings? The luxury of controls, randomization, and so on are not possible in clinical, educational, rehabilitation, and other settings. Do individuals get better with the interventions, how do we know, and how can we show this? Single-case designs are well suited to testing the application of findings from large-scale randomized controlled trials and addressing these questions.

Single-case research is not merely a handmaiden of controlled trials and a way of testing what other methodologies show. In many applied settings (schools, clinics, camps, recreational and rehabilitation facilities), those in charge innovate creative programs that they believe are effective. The choices for evaluating any program seem to be: a randomized trial, an anecdotal case study, or an open study.[5] This restricted set of choices in part may be why so few programs have any evaluation whatsoever. A randomized controlled trial is rarely feasible; the yield from an anecdotal case study or open study is minimal and scientifically unacceptable. Actually, single-case experimental designs and quasi-experimental single-case designs, all elaborated in subsequent chapters, fill a huge gap. Valid inferences can be drawn about the impact of programs in ways that are more feasible than randomized trials. Moreover, the designs allow for developing more effective programs. Ongoing data within the designs can be, and often have been, used to make programs more effective while they are being implemented.

Apart from EBIs, increased accountability in services in general inadvertently promotes single-case designs. Are the treatments, educational regimens, and policies working in this setting and with this client, patient, or student? There is increased interest in having data-based answers to these questions and weaving evaluation in with service delivery. This is important not for some methodological ideal; rather, the quality of care depends on having information about impact. This leaves aside some of the

---

[5] An "open study," a term often used in medical research, refers to uncontrolled investigations that omit pivotal controls and hence are not true experiments. Two of the more common controls that are suspended are absence of a control group and masking of who receives the intervention. The absence of a control group is reflected in the fact that open studies are often pre–post (before–after) comparisons of patient functioning. All patients receive some treatment (e.g., medicine, psychotherapy), but there is no control group for comparison. "Masking" refers to ensuring that the investigators and treatment administrators do not know who received what condition (e.g., "double blinding"). Masking procedures are routinely used in medical studies to eschew bias in influencing subjects. In an open study all patients receive the intervention, and everyone knows about it.

driving forces behind accountability such as costs (e.g., wasted money) on programs that seem like a good idea at the time but have no data to show that they helped. Single-case experimental designs can make a difference.

OVERVIEW OF THE BOOK

This text describes and evaluates single-case designs and is divided into five units or sections, each with its own chapters: The sections are Background to the Designs, Assessment, Major Design Options, Evaluating Single-Case Data, and Perspectives and Contributions of the Designs. Assessment, design, and data evaluation are the core ingredients of research methodology, whether single-case or more traditional between-group research. It is important to convey the flow of designs and decisions with this organization but also to help relate the underpinnings and practices of research traditions to each other. Single-case designs are not fundamentally different from group designs in terms of the goals and the means through which these are achieved. There are starkly different practices, but it is critical to convey the commonalities.

The purpose of research, whether single case or between groups, is to draw valid inferences. Experimentation consists of arranging the situation in such a way as to rule out or make implausible the impact of extraneous factors that could explain the results. Chapter 2 discusses key factors that experimentation attempts to rule out in order to permit inferences to be drawn about intervention effects.

Single-case designs depend heavily on assessment procedures. Chapters 3, 4, and 5 convey fundamentals of assessment in single-case research, commonly used strategies for observing behavior, and the different conditions and situations in which assessments are obtained. Ways to ensure and evaluate the quality, integrity, reliability, and validity of assessments also are discussed.

The precise logic and unique characteristics of single-case experimental designs are introduced in Chapter 6. The manner in which single-case designs make and test predictions about performance within the same subject underlies all of the designs, and the rationale shares features with the more familiar between-group designs. In Chapters 6 through 10, several different experimental designs and their variations, uses, and potential problems are detailed. Chapter 11 presents quasi-experimental single-case designs and includes multiple options for situations in which the conditions cannot be completely controlled but one wants to draw inferences about intervention effects.

Single-case designs have relied heavily on visual inspection of the data to evaluate the extent to which the intervention has led to and accounts for change. This is in sharp contrast to the more familiar tests of statistical significance commonly used in between-group research. The underlying rationale and methods of visual inspection are discussed and illustrated in Chapter 12. Visual inspection is facilitated by graphing the data. Options for graphing and how these options aid visual inspection serve as the basis of Chapter 13.

Although problems, considerations, and issues associated with specific designs are discussed throughout the text, it is useful to evaluate single-case research critically and more broadly. Chapter 14 provides a discussion of issues, problems, and limitations of single-case experimental designs. Finally, the contribution of single-case research to experimentation in general and the interface of alternative research methodologies are examined in Chapter 15.

Statistical analyses are infrequently used as the basis of drawing inferences about intervention effects. Instructors who teach single-case designs comment that it would be useful to note that such tests exist and to illustrate their application. However, statistical analysis is not central to the methodology as it is in between-group null hypothesis testing. Nevertheless, statistical analyses are occasionally used and readily available. The appendix at the end of the book provides a more in-depth discussion of data evaluation in single-case research to encompass the strengths and weaknesses of both visual inspection and statistical analyses, illustrate statistical analyses, and convey significant advances in statistics for the single case as well as the dilemmas these advances raise.

Underpinnings of Scientific Research

The previous chapter placed single-case designs in different contexts to convey their lineage, roots, and precedents. Before the methodology is detailed, it is critical to provide the key context, namely, why we do research in the first place and what the designs are trying to accomplish. There are all sorts of techniques, practices, and procedures that are used in research (e.g., various control groups, measuring performance on one [post], two [pre–post], or multiple occasions). Learning the practices is the easier part of methodology. It is important to convey the rationale for why these practices have become important. This is not an intellectual exercise. There are many occasions,

especially in applied settings (classroom, school, clinic, rehabilitation center) in which some critical component or two from a between-group or single-case design cannot be implemented. Will this be a disaster in drawing inferences or persuading colleagues that we have an effective intervention? The answer lies in understanding what one is trying to accomplish rather than whether one can do this or that practice. There are many strategies to accomplish the goal even if an often cherished practice cannot be implemented.

For those trained in between-group research, here is a heart-stopping example. Suppose one wants to conduct an experiment and cannot assign subjects to conditions randomly. That is not necessarily a problem or grounds for MAD (methodologist affective disorder). What is randomization for anyway? Two of the answers include decreasing the likelihood that groups will differ on nuisance variables and addressing some of the assumptions for various statistical tests. We can accomplish the goals of randomization or selectively neglect them in ways that will not necessarily make a difference in our final results (Shadish & Ragsdale, 1996). This sounds like methodological heresy—it actually is methodological gospel. (I always have trouble separating these.) I am not "for or against" randomization; I am for drawing valid inferences and having as many methodological arrows in my quiver to shoot at artifacts and biases that are ready to interfere with that. The randomization arrow is wonderful but does not always hit the target, that is, accomplish what it is supposed to (Hsu, 1989), and other arrows can help.

The methodological goal—we must arrange the situation to obtain valid inferences, that is, inferences in which we can be confident that there are no biases and artifacts that could explain the finding. In science, replication is the key protection. Within a given study, ruling out or making implausible competing explanations that could account for our intervention effect is the protection. Experimentation is needed to examine specifically why change has occurred. Through experimentation, extraneous factors that might explain the results can be ruled out to provide an unambiguous evaluation of the intervention and its effects. This chapter discusses the purposes of experimentation and the types of factors that must be ruled out if valid inferences are to be drawn.

DRAWING VALID INFERENCES

The purpose of research in general is to examine relationships between or among variables. The unique feature of experimentation is that it examines the direct influence of one variable (the independent variable) on another (the dependent variable). Experimentation usually evaluates the influence of a small number of variables under conditions that will permit unambiguous inferences to be drawn. Experiments help simplify the situation so that the influence of the variables of interest can be separated from the influence of other factors. Drawing valid inferences about the effects of an independent variable or intervention requires attention to a variety of factors that potentially obscure the findings. Three key concepts serve as a useful guide for designing experiments and interpreting the results of completed studies.

Parsimony

We are guided by concepts that pervade all science and that are central to methodology, not just the substantive areas in which we do research. Parsimony is a guiding principle

that underscores how to select among competing interpretations or explanations of a finding. Other things being equal, we select the simplest explanation among competing alternatives that explains the finding or phenomenon of interest. There are other names for the guideline and they convey the thrust that is intended. Among the other terms are the "principle of economy," "principle of unnecessary plurality," "principle of simplicity," and "Occam's razor." The latter is the more familiar and is a useful place to begin. William of Ockham (ca. 1285–1349) was an English philosopher and Franciscan monk. He applied the notion (that plurality [of concepts] should not be posited without necessity) in the context of writing on epistemology in which he advocated that concepts ought not to be added (plurality) if they are not needed (necessity) in accounting for phenomena. Supposedly, his frequent and sharp invocation of the principle allegedly accounts for why the term "razor" was added to his (Latinized) name to form Occam's razor.

In the context of science, parsimony means that if competing views or interpretations of any phenomena can be proposed, one adopts the simplest one that can explain the data or information. The presumption of parsimony is not tantamount to saying that things are simple or can be explained simply but rather that the simplest account of the data or phenomena is the one we adopt, until there is a need to move to more complex interpretations.

A familiar issue that illustrates parsimony pertains to the existence of unidentified flying objects (UFOs, aka "flying saucers") from extraterrestrial places. Many sightings of UFOs have been reported for centuries with more recent sightings associated with photos and videos. There are many explanations of these sightings, but I only briefly entertain two. First, the "natural" (i.e., earthly) phenomenon view would explain the sightings to be a result of ordinary phenomena in our world that give an appearance of something not so ordinary, namely, UFOs. Special atmospheric conditions, meteors shooting across the sky, weather balloons, and highly secret military aircraft would be among these phenomena and would explain such sightings.

Second, the extraterrestrial view is that beings and their flying objects come from another planet or galaxy and that they periodically visit. All else being equal, the natural phenomenon view provides a more parsimonious explanation because we do not have to introduce new complexities related to the existence of beings (we do not know of beings on other planets), equipment (novel yet-to-be-invented machines), and incomprehensible ways of travel (above land and some allegedly under water). On the other hand, the public does not have access to more information that is kept secret. That information could easily make the natural explanation simply inadequate. For example, if there really were any physical evidence of the flying vehicles (e.g., from abandoned UFOs on the side of the highways, from UFO crashes, or UFOs that were parked illegally, towed and "booted" by the police and never reclaimed) or of the beings that pilot them, or corroborated evidence unequivocally showing that the objects attained speeds and agility that exceed what we can accomplish by our current technology, then the extraterrestrial explanation becomes parsimonious. The natural phenomenon view would not be able to explain this new evidence without all sorts of new concepts and reasons to accommodate each sign of physical evidence. As the "natural" explanation squirms to add many different reasons that the new information requires, we have parsimony and evidence favoring the second explanation. It might be a simpler account

of all the data (requiring fewer explanations) to just state that there must be extraterrestrial life flying around and visiting us.

Some key points: A more parsimonious view is not necessarily true or accurate. Also, parsimony does not mean the explanation is simple. In fact, combined views that are complex may end up being the most parsimonious. In the preceding example, we know for certain that the natural phenomena view explains many sightings that people report, but we do not yet know if all the available evidence (to which we do not have public access) can be explained by that view. Both views combined may be the best explanation of the data. Also, parsimony combined with evidence may or may not make one of the original interpretations implausible. Aside from explaining substantive questions within a given science, parsimony is central to methodology. From the standpoint of interpreting the results of a study, we begin with a nod to parsimony by asking, "Can we explain the data with concepts and phenomena we already know?"

Plausible Rival Hypotheses

Methodology is all about the conclusions that are reached from a study. At the end of the study we find that there are group differences (between-group study) or clear changes in the individual while some intervention was in place (single-case design). There are many possible explanations for that effect (and these are discussed in this chapter). Of all the explanations, the investigator wishes to say, "It was the intervention that explains the findings." However, the rest of the scientific community (one's peers), by their training, is ready to say, "Maybe, but was the study designed and evaluated to handle all of the other reasonable or plausible explanations?"

Central to methodology and conclusions in a particular study is the notion of a *plausible rival hypothesis* (Cook & Campbell, 1979). A plausible rival hypothesis refers to an interpretation of the results of an investigation on the basis of some other influence than the one the investigator has studied or wishes to discuss. The question to ask at the completion of a study is whether there are other interpretations that are plausible to explain the findings. This sounds so much like parsimony that the distinction is worth making explicit. Parsimony refers to adopting the simpler of two or more explanations that account equally well for the data.

Plausible rival hypothesis has a slightly different thrust. At the end of the investigation, are there other plausible interpretations of the findings than the one advanced by the investigator? Simplicity of the interpretation (parsimony) may or may not be relevant. At the end of the study, there could be two or ten equally complex interpretations of the results, so parsimony is not the issue. For example, an investigator wishes to see whether ethnicity contributes to diet (e.g., proportion of fiber, vitamins in their food) of elderly people and how healthy these people are (e.g., instances and duration of illnesses, hospital visits in the past year). Let us say that two different ethnic groups are shown to differ on both diet and health. At the end of the study, the investigator discusses ethnic differences and how these explain the findings. A plausible rival hypothesis might be socioeconomic status (e.g., family income, occupational status, education, and living conditions). That is, if socioeconomic status (SES) was not controlled in this study, then SES becomes a plausible rival hypothesis. Is SES more parsimonious? Maybe, maybe not. The findings might be equally accounted for by posing one influence versus another (an SES or ethnic difference) so that whether one is simpler than another is arguable. Parsimony (the simpler explanation that can account for the data) and plausible rival hypotheses (other interpretations of the data that could readily explain the effect, whether simple or not) often overlap. Yet, a plausible rival hypothesis does not necessarily invoke simplicity as a key feature but rather only asks whether some other interpretation is plausible. Plausibility derives from whether there is a reasonable basis to say that the findings could be explained in some other way. Often plausibility stems from the fact that other, prior studies have shown that a particular influence has an effect very much like the one produced in this new study. In this hypothetical example, we know in advance of this study that income, occupational status, education, and living conditions (e.g., living in crowded neighborhoods, in an area where there are more pollutants in the air) all correlate with illness. Living conditions, as much as diet, might explain any health differences unless they are ruled out.

Methodological practices are intended to rule out or to make competing interpretations of the results implausible. At the completion of a study, the explanation one wishes to provide ought to be the most plausible interpretation. This is achieved not by arguing persuasively, but rather by designing the study in such a way that other explanations do not seem very plausible or parsimonious. The more well designed the experiment, the fewer the alternative plausible explanations that can be advanced to account for the findings. Ideally, only the effects of the independent variable (intervention) could be advanced as the basis for the results.

Threats to Validity

So what are all of these rival interpretations of the data that might plausibly explain the results? They are called *threats to validity* and refer to methodological issues that are likely to rival the explanation that it was the intervention (or experimental manipulation) that explained the effect. Four types of experimental validity address these purposes in different ways: internal, external, construct, and statistical conclusion validity (Cook & Campbell, 1979). These types of validity serve as a useful way to convey and remember several key facets of research and the rationale for many methodological practices. Table 2.1 lists each type of validity and the broad question each addresses. Each type of validity is pivotal. Together they convey many of the considerations that investigators have before them when they design an experiment. These considerations then translate to specific methodological practices (e.g., random assignment, selection of control groups).

Threats to validity have been devised and elaborated in the context of between-group research. Some of these derive from features that are more characteristic of between-group rather than single-case designs or vary in how they emerge in the different design strategies. I have adapted these here to convey the likely methodological issues and rival explanations that can interfere with drawing valid inferences in single-case designs.[1]

---

[1] There is no single fixed list of threats to each type of validity. Methodology advances and evolves just as substantive findings do in an area of science. The threats discussed in this chapter constitute those that are most fundamental and applicable to single-case designs. For a more extensive discussion of the threats to each type of validity, other sources can be consulted (Cook & Campbell, 1979; Kazdin, 2003; Shadish, Cook, & Campbell, 2002).

Table 2.1 Types of Experimental Validity and Questions or Issues They Address

Type of Validity	Question or Issue
Internal Validity	To what extent can the intervention rather than extraneous influences be considered to account for the results, changes, or differences among conditions (e.g., baseline, intervention)?
External Validity	To what extent can the results be generalized or extended to people, settings, times, measures or outcomes, and characteristics other than those included in this particular demonstration?
Construct Validity	Given that the intervention was responsible for change, what specific aspect of the intervention was the mechanism, process, or causal agent? What is the conceptual basis (construct) underlying the effect?
Data-evaluation validity	To what extent is a relation shown, demonstrated, or evident between the intervention and the outcome? What about the data and methods used for evaluation that could mislead or obscure demonstrating or failing to demonstrate an experimental effect?

Note: These threats apply generally to all of research, although they originally were identified and discussed primarily in the context of between-group studies. They are discussed in this chapter in relation to single-case designs and serve as underpinnings for several design options and strategies to strengthen inferences discussed in subsequent chapters.

The purpose of research is to reach well-founded (i.e., valid) conclusions about the effects of a given intervention and the conditions under which it operates. A useful distinction in research is the difference between findings and conclusions. The *findings* are a descriptive feature of the study and include what was found (e.g., when the intervention was in effect, reading went up by 100% in a single-case design, or people who drink wine have fewer heart attacks in a case-control between-group study). The *conclusions* refer to the basis or explanation of the finding. The investigator wishes to say that it was the intervention, but has the demonstration (measures, design, and data evaluation) made implausible threats to validity? We address threats to help our findings and conclusions converge justifiably on the same explanation; it *was* the intervention. Single-case designs have many elegant ways of establishing that.

INTERNAL VALIDITY

Defined

The task for experimentation is to examine the influence of a particular independent variable or intervention in such a way that extraneous factors will not interfere with the conclusions that the investigator wishes to draw. When the results can be attributed, with little or no ambiguity, to the effects of the independent variable, the experiment is said to be internally valid. *Internal validity* refers to the extent to which an experiment rules out alternative explanations of the results. Factors or influences other than the independent variable that could explain the results are called *threats to internal validity*.

Threats to Internal Validity

An experiment ought to be designed to make major threats to internal validity implausible. Even though the changes in performance may have resulted from the intervention

Table 2.2 Major Threats to Internal Validity

Specific Threat	What It Includes
History	Any event (other than the intervention) occurring at the time of the experiment that could influence the results or account for the pattern of data otherwise attributed to the intervention. Historical events might include family crises; change in job, teacher, or spouse; power blackouts; or any other events.
Maturation	Any change over time that may result from processes within the subject. Such processes may include growing older, stronger, healthier, smarter, and more tired or bored.
Instrumentation	Any change that takes place in the measuring instrument or assessment procedure over time. Such changes may result from the use of human observers whose judgments about the client or criteria for scoring behavior may change over time.
Testing	Any change that may be attributed to the effects of repeated assessment. Testing constitutes an experience that, depending on the measure, may lead to systematic changes in performance.
Statistical regression	Any change from one assessment occasion to another that might be due to a reversion of scores toward the mean. If clients score at the extremes on one assessment occasion, their scores may change in the direction toward the mean on a second testing.
Diffusion of treatment	Diffusion of treatment can occur when the intervention is inadvertently provided during times when it should not be (e.g., return-to-baseline conditions) or to persons who should not yet receive the intervention at a particular point. The effects of the intervention will be underestimated if it is unwittingly administered in intervention and nonintervention phases.

or independent variable, the factors listed in Table 2.2 might also explain the results. If inferences are to be drawn about the intervention (independent variable), then the threats to internal validity must be ruled out. To the extent that each threat is ruled out or made relatively implausible, the experiment is said to be internally valid.

History and *maturation*, as threats to internal validity, are relatively straightforward (see Table 2.2). History refers to events in the individual's environment (e.g., at home, at school, a novel event in the news); maturation refers to processes, usually within the individual over time (e.g., maturing, habituating to something in the environment). Administration of the intervention may coincide with special or unique events in the client's life or with maturational processes within the person over time. The design must rule out the possibility that the pattern of results is likely to have resulted from either one of these threats. In single-case designs, the pattern of data over time could be consistent with history or maturation whether there were rapid or gradual changes (e.g., improvement).

The potential influence of *instrumentation* also must be ruled out. It is possible that the data show changes over time not because of progress in the client's behavior but rather because the observers have gradually changed their criteria for scoring client performance. The instrument, or measuring device, has in some way changed. If it is possible that changes in the criteria observers invoke to score behavior, rather than actual changes in client performance, could account for the pattern of the results, instrumentation serves as a threat to internal validity.

Testing refers to completing a measure on more than one occasion. For many measures (e.g., personality measures, intelligence measures), performance on the second occasion is often better than on the first occasion. In much of group research, the assessment devices are administered on two occasions, before and after treatment. Improvements could be due to repeated experience with the measure. In single-case research, performance is assessed on multiple occasions. Testing is a threat if there is any reason to believe that experience and exposure to the measure alone could explain improvement.

Statistical regression refers to changes in extreme scores from one assessment occasion to another. When persons are selected on the basis of their extreme scores (e.g., those who score low on a screening measure of social interaction skills or high on a measure of hyperactivity), they can be expected on the average to show some changes in the opposite direction (toward the mean) at the second testing merely as a function of regression. If treatment has been provided between these two assessment occasions (e.g., pre- and posttreatment assessment) the investigator may believe that the improvements resulted from the treatment. However, the improvements may have occurred anyway as a function of *regression toward the mean*, that is, the tendency of scores at the extremes to revert toward mean levels upon repeated testing.[2] The effects of regression must be separated from the effects of the intervention.

In group research, regression effects are usually ruled out by including a no-treatment group and by randomly assigning subjects to all groups. In this way, if there is regression it would be evident equally in both groups; changes above and beyond those are likely to be due to the intervention. In single-case research, inferences about behavior change are drawn on the basis of repeated assessment over time. Although fluctuations of performance from one day or session to the next may be based on regression toward the mean, this usually does not compete with drawing inferences about treatment. If there is a phase in single-case designs (e.g., baseline or the period before the intervention begins) with only one observation occasion, we do not know if this is a reliable measurement and typical performance or one which might be extreme. If extreme, the next observation might well be in the opposite direction merely due to regression. In single-case research, regression usually cannot account for the pattern of data because of assessment on several occasions over time and across multiple conditions (e.g., intervention, no intervention).

Diffusion of treatment is one of the more subtle threats to internal validity. When the investigator is comparing treatment and no treatment or two or more different treatments, it is important to ensure that the conditions remain distinct and include the intended intervention. Occasionally, the different conditions do not remain as distinct as intended. For example, the effects of parental praise on a child's behavior in the home might be evaluated in a single-case design in which praise is given to the child in some phases and withdrawn in other phases. It is possible that when parents are instructed

---

[2] Regression toward the mean is a statistical phenomenon that is related to the correlation between initial test and retest scores. The lower the correlation, the greater the amount of error in the measure, and the greater the regression toward the mean. It is important to note further that regression does not mean that all extreme scores will revert toward the mean upon retesting or that any particular person will inevitably score in a less extreme fashion on the next occasion. The phenomenon refers to changes for segments of a sample (i.e., the extremes) as a whole and how those segments, on the average, will respond.

to cease the use of praise, they may continue anyway. The results may show little or no difference between treatment and "no-treatment" phases because the treatment was inadvertently administered to some extent in the no-treatment phase. The diffusion of treatment will interfere with drawing valid inferences about the impact of treatment and hence constitutes a threat to internal validity.

General Comments

I have highlighted major threats to internal validity. These form a critical basis for understanding the logic of experimentation in general. The reason for arranging the situation to conform to one of the many experimental designs is to rule out the threats that serve as plausible alternative hypotheses or explanations of the results. Single-case designs can readily rule out the threats to internal validity; they do so just as well but quite differently from the way they are addressed in between-group designs.

Specific single-case designs rule out threats in different ways, as is discussed in subsequent chapters. Also discussed in later chapters are designs where one may need to be innovative to rule out the threats. This is why I emphasize the importance of understanding the threats and how they operate. Research is all about addressing key concepts (plausibility, threats to validity), and the practices we use are only helpful insofar as they address these.

EXTERNAL VALIDITY

Defined

Internal validity refers to the extent to which an experiment demonstrates that the intervention accounts for change. *External validity* addresses the broader question and refers to the extent to which the results of an experiment can be generalized or extended beyond the conditions of the experiment. In any experiment, questions can be raised about whether the results can be extended to other persons, settings, assessment devices, clinical problems, and so on, all of which are encompassed by external validity. Characteristics of the experiment that may limit the generality of the results are referred to as *threats to external validity*.

Threats to External Validity

A summary of the major threats to external validity is presented in Table 2.3. Each pertains to a feature within the experiment that might delimit generality of the results. The factors that actually limit the generality of the results of an experiment may not be known until subsequent research expands on the conditions under which the relationship was originally examined. For example, the manner in which instructions are given, the age of the subjects, the setting in which the intervention was implemented, characteristics of the teachers or trainers, and other factors may contribute to the generality of a given finding. Technically, the generality of experimental findings can be a function of virtually any characteristic of the experiment. Some characteristics that may limit generality of the findings can be identified in advance.

Generality across subjects is a frequently raised concern in research, and especially single-case research, as I discuss later. Even though the findings may be internally valid, it is possible that the results might only extend to persons very much like those included

Table 2.3 Major Threats to External Validity

Specific Threat	What It Includes
Generality across subjects	The extent to which the results can be extended to subjects or clients whose characteristics may differ from those included in the investigation.
Generality across responses or measures	The extent to which the results extend to behaviors or domains not included in the program. These behaviors or domains may be similar to those focused on or may be entirely different areas of functioning.
Generality across settings	The extent to which the results extend to other situations in which the client functions beyond those included in training.
Generality across time	The extent to which the results extend beyond the times during the day that the intervention is in effect and to times after the intervention has been terminated.
Generality across behavior-change agents	The extent to which the intervention effects can be extended to other persons who can administer the intervention. The effects may be restricted to persons with special skills, training, or expertise.
Reactive experimental arrangements	The possibility that subjects may be influenced by their awareness that they are participating in an investigation or in a special program. The intervention effects may not extend to situations in which individuals are unaware of the arrangement.
Reactive assessment	The extent to which subjects are aware that their behavior is being assessed and that this awareness may influence how they respond. Persons who are aware of assessment may respond differently from how they would if they were unaware of the assessment.
Multiple-treatment interference	When the same subjects are exposed to more than one treatment, the conclusions reached about a particular treatment may be restricted. Specifically, the results may only apply to other persons who experience both of the treatments in the same way or in the same order.

in the investigation. For example, cultural, ethnic, or gender identity may somehow make a difference, and the findings might not generalize to a broad range of groups. Other features of the population, including special experiences, intelligence, age, and receptivity to the particular sort of intervention under investigation, may be potential qualifiers of the findings. For example, findings obtained with children might not apply to adolescents or adults, those obtained with individuals functioning well in the community might not apply to those with serious physical or psychiatric impairment; and those obtained with laboratory rats might not apply to other types of animals, including humans.

Generality across responses, settings, and time are potential threats to external validity. Would the same intervention achieve similar effects if other responses (e.g., completing homework, engaging in discussion), settings (e.g., at home), or times (e.g., after school) were included? Any one of the threats may provide qualifiers or restrictions on the generality of the results. For example, the same intervention might not be expected to lead to the same results no matter what the behavior or problem is to which it is applied.

Generality of behavior-change agent is a special feature that is related to the setting and context that warrants mention. As it is stated, the threat has special relevance for intervention research in which some persons (e.g., parents, teachers, hospital staff, peers, and spouses) attempt to alter the behaviors of others (e.g., children, students, psychiatric patients). When an intervention is effective, it is possible to raise questions about the generality of the results across behavior-change agents. For example, when parents are effective in altering behavior, could the results also be obtained by others carrying out the same procedures? Perhaps there are special characteristics of the behavior-change agents that have helped achieve the intervention effects. The clients may be more responsive to a given intervention as a function of who is carrying it out.

Reactivity of the experimental arrangement refers to the possibility that subjects are aware that they are participating in an investigation and that this knowledge may bear on the generality of the results. Reactivity refers to changes in performance resulting from that awareness or knowledge of participating. The experimental situations may be reactive, i.e., alter the behavior of the subjects because they are aware that they are being evaluated. It is possible that the results would not be evident in other situations in which persons do not know that they are being evaluated. Perhaps the results depend on the fact that subjects were responding within the context of a special situation. A familiar example of reactivity of arrangements—we are all wonderful drivers, of course, but we are usually a little more wonderful in the presence of police cars. The environmental stimuli (presence of police) constitute an arrangement that influences our behavior. The external validity question is: Does our very careful driving generalize to situations when these stimuli are not present? (Just try to squeeze into my lane in traffic and you will have my answer in a heartbeat!)

The *reactivity of assessment* warrants special mention even though it could be subsumed under reactivity of the experimental arrangement. If subjects are aware of the observations that are being conducted or when they are conducted, the generality of the results may be restricted. To what extent would the results be obtained if subjects were unaware that their behaviors were being assessed? Alternatively, to what extent do the results extend to other assessment situations in which subjects are unaware that they are being observed? Most assessment is conducted under conditions in which subjects are aware that their responses are being measured in some way. In such circumstances, it is possible to ask whether the results would be obtained if subjects were unaware of the assessment procedures. The reactivity of assessment too is familiar; various movies and television shows take advantage of assessing people under nonreactive assessments, that is, when they are not aware and are less likely to give their more social, guarded, and politically correct responses. The threat to external validity is whether the the results of an experiment will only be evident when the individual is aware of the assessment procedures?

Multiple-treatment interference only arises when the same subject or subjects receive two or more treatments. In such an experiment, the results may be internally valid, that is, by ruling out threats to internal validity. However, the possibility exists that the particular sequence or order in which the interventions were given may have contributed to the results. For example, if two treatments are administered in succession, the second may be more (or less) effective or equally effective as the first. The results might be due to the fact that the intervention was second and followed this particular intervention. A different ordering of the treatments might have produced different results. Hence, the conclusions that were drawn may be restricted to the special way in which the multiple treatments were presented. There will be many examples in later chapters where single-case designs are used to evaluate more than one intervention in the same study and where multiple-treatment interference might emerge.

General Comments

The major threats to external validity do not exhaust the factors that may limit the generality of the results of a given experiment. Any feature of the experiment might be proposed to limit the circumstances under which the relationship between the independent and dependent variables operate. Of course, merely because one of the threats to external validity is applicable to the experiment does not necessarily mean that the generality of the results is jeopardized. It only means that some caution should be exercised in extending the results. One or more conditions of the experiment *may* restrict generality; only further investigation can attest to whether the potential threat actually limits the generality of the findings.

Also, a misunderstanding about the threats, perhaps especially those related to external validity, is their use and abuse. A given threat is pertinent in any given demonstration only insofar as it is a plausible rival hypothesis about restrictions on the generality of the findings. So the superficial statement that begrudgingly acknowledges a finding usually goes like this, "Yes, o.k. that was found, but it may not apply to the children I see in my classroom, students with this or that background, most people, tall people, and so on." This kind of statement is easy to make and is uninformed or superficial when stated in its vacuous form, that is, without a cogent explanation. To pose that there is threat to validity requires a plausible explanation. That is, the consumer (colleague, peer) ought to have in mind precisely why that is a threat to external validity. A finding might not be applicable to all sorts of other conditions, people, and contexts, but one needs a bit more justification than just cavalierly raising it after each finding (especially findings one does not especially care for).

Consider an example. After years of research, we finally have a growing list of psychotherapies with evidence in their behalf (Nathan & Gorman, 2007; Weisz & Kazdin, 2010). Treatments have been studied in very well controlled trials—so well controlled that the issue of generality is of concern. I mention later in this chapter that there can be a trade-off of careful experimental control such as holding as many variables constant as possible and restrictions in generality of the results. Careful control purposely changes conditions so that they resemble the conditions of everyday life less. Once the finding is established, it is reasonable to question whether the finding would hold when critical conditions change.

Sometimes in psychotherapy trials, patients are selected because they meet criteria for a psychiatric disorder (e.g., depression, anxiety) but are excluded if they have multiple disorders or other sources of impairment (e.g., chronic medical condition that requires treatment). Researchers have wisely looked for homogenous and well-described populations in their initial studies to limit variability (and threats to data-evaluation validity noted later in the chapter). So now, with a list of internally valid studies, replications, and a pile of treatments, external validity is raised as a concern. Practitioners, for example, raise the question: "Fine, the results of the studies are internally valid, but will the results apply to my patients in clinical rather than research settings?" Again, merely asking this is not very informed unless there is a plausible reason to suspect that the proposed variable (changes in patient characteristics) might make a difference. One concern has been that patients seen in clinical work often have multiple psychiatric disorders (referred to as comorbidity), not just one that may have served as a basis for recruiting patients for a randomized controlled trial. In other words, practitioners question the external validity of the findings. This is a reasonable, plausible challenge because patients with multiple disorders are likely to be more difficult to treat and may come from more complex personal situations due to the scope of their disorders. The scope of disorders may not merely reflect the complexity of the current situation with such patients—perhaps they have a stronger genetic and environmental "loading" or more untoward underpinnings of their more severe condition. It is plausible to challenge external validity because more severe cases of anything in life often respond less well or not at all to treatments that worked with less severe cases. Much research will be needed to address this challenge in the many contexts (e.g., many disorders, ages of clients) in which the threat could be valid. At this point, studies on the topic in the context of child therapy at least suggest that in fact, comorbidity and complexity of the case do not limit the external validity generality of the findings. Evidence-based treatments tested to this point work was as well with more severe cases and cases with more complex personal and family characteristics as with other cases (e.g., Doss & Weisz, 2006; Kazdin & Whitley, 2006).

CONSTRUCT VALIDITY

Defined

Construct validity has to do with interpreting the basis of the causal relation. Assume that threats to internal validity have been addressed, that is, the causal relation has been identified between an intervention and behavior change. Now we can ask the construct validity question, What *is* the intervention and *why* did it produce the effect? *Construct validity* addresses the presumed cause or the explanation of the causal relation between the intervention or experimental manipulation and the outcome. Is the reason for the relation between the intervention and behavior change due to the construct (explanation, interpretation) given by the investigator? For example, let us say that in an experiment the intervention consisted of a teacher providing praise to a student for increased time working on arithmetic assignments during a free-study period. The intervention caused the change, let us say, but was it the praise, or increased attention in general, or a teacher taking special interest in this student's arithmetic performance? The answer to these questions focuses specifically on construct validity.[3]

Several features within the experiment can interfere with the interpretation of the results. These are often referred to as *confounds*. We say an experiment is confounded or that there is a confound to refer to the possibility that a specific factor varied (or

---

[3] Construct validity also is a commonly used term in the context of test development and validation and refers to evidence that a measure (e.g., anxiety or depression scale) actually measures the construct (concept) it purports to measure. Multiple lines of evidence are brought to bear to evaluate the construct validity of measures (Kazdin, 2003). The resemblance to the present use of the term is in underscoring a question about the explanation: In test development, what *explains* performance on the measure, what concept best represents the items; in methodology and design, what concept *explains* why the intervention worked and how it achieved its effects.

co-varied) with the intervention. That confound could, in whole or in part, be responsible for the results. Some component other than the one of interest to the investigator might be embedded in the intervention and accounts for the findings. There are many examples where construct validity is in question. For example, in adult psychotherapy, cognitive therapy is a well-established, evidence-based treatment for major depression (Hollon & Beck, 2004). We know from the studies that cognitive therapy causes the change, but we do not know how it works or why the change occurs. The proposed interpretation (changes in cognitions lead to changes in depression) has been unsupported as the likely basis for why that treatment works. In short, treatment works, but why (a construct validity issue)?

In applied work (e.g., education, treatment, prevention, skill acquisition, rehabilitation), where single-case designs are often conducted, there is less of an interest in isolating the reason why the intervention produced change. A multi-component treatment package may be designed to improve the reading or speech of children in a special-education class. The challenge is to improve the skills, and that is the goal. There might be little interest in identifying why and how specifically the intervention worked. Even so, knowing precisely why and how change occurs can be important for maximizing the impact of the intervention and extending the intervention to other settings (see Kazdin, 2007).

Construct validity tries to home in on what facet of the intervention explains the change. Consider an example from group research. We know that consuming a moderate amount of wine (e.g., one to two glasses with dinner) is associated with increased health benefits (e.g., reduced risk of heart attack). In studies of this relation, consumption of wine is the variable of interest. A construct validity question is "Is it the wine or some other construct?" This is a reasonable question because we know that wine drinking is associated with (confounded by) other characteristics. People who drink wine, compared to those who drink beer and other alcohol (spirits), tend to live healthier lifestyles, to smoke less, to have lower rates of obesity, to be lighter drinkers (total alcohol consumption), and to come from higher socioeconomic classes (probably with better health care) (e.g., Wannamethee & Sharper, 1999). These characteristics are related to disease and death. Even so, controlling these other factors reduces but does not eliminate the contribution that wine makes to lower the mortality rate. Wine still appears to make a difference. The research has sharpened the focus to remove or evaluate the impact of other influences than wine drinking itself. More construct validity questions might be asked. For example, what specifically about the wine explains the effect? And that too has been studied (e.g., an antioxidant, resveratrol, found in red wine and grape skins is one explanation). One can see that the demonstration of a causal relation or correlation might be the beginning of research that focuses on evaluating the basis of the original finding, that is, the underlying construct that explains the relation.

Threats to Construct Validity

The reason why the independent variable has an effect raises fundamental questions about the construct the variable is designed to reflect. The independent variable may be a package of factors that ought to be broken down into components. In most single-case studies, few factors may emerge that account for and explain the intervention effects. Two threats to construct validity are noted in Table 2.4 and highlighted here.

Table 2.4 Major Threats to Construct Validity

Specific Threat	What It Includes
Attention and contact accorded the client	The extent to which an increase of attention to the client/participant during the intervention phase or lack of attention during nonintervention phases could plausibly explain the effects attributed to the intervention.
Special stimulus conditions, settings, and contexts	The extent to which special conditions in which the intervention is presented or embedded alone or in combination with the intervention could explain the effects attributed to the intervention by itself. The "real" influence might be "intervention x administered by wonderful person y" rather than the "intervention" free from its connection to special conditions.

Attention and contact accorded the client can serve as one of the explanations for an intervention effect. Before the intervention is implemented there is a baseline period in which observations of performance are obtained. Perhaps during baseline there is relative neglect of the client, but during the intervention phase increased attention, contact, monitoring, and feedback are provided. When these facets are not the intervention but are accoutrements, they are potential threats to construct validity. This is kind of a placebo effect in the sense that mere attention is the intervention—not necessarily attention in the form of positive reinforcement (contingent on behavior) but just involving or attending to the client more in a program, class, or intervention. The intervention consists of a package of components the investigator combines to effect change. Accoutrements of that intervention might be responsible for the effects. Attention and increased contact with the client are threats to validity if they are plausible explanations of the findings. If plausible, some phase in the design needs to accommodate the potential confound. A design that does not control for attention and contact is not necessarily flawed. If the investigator wishes to *conclude* why the intervention achieved its effects, attention and contact ought to be ruled out as rival interpretations of the results.

Special conditions, settings, and contexts may also threaten the construct validity of a study. Sometimes an intervention includes features that the investigator considers as irrelevant to the study, but these features may introduce ambiguity in interpreting the findings. The construct validity question is the same as we have discussed so far, namely, was the intervention (as conceived by the investigator) responsible for the outcome or was it some seemingly irrelevant feature with which the intervention was associated? For example, the intervention may have been conducted in a special school or laboratory school affiliated with a university. In such schools, often the teachers, facilities, assistants, equipment, and other conditions are optimal. The construct validity here overlaps with external validity, but they evaluate different facets of the problem. External validity asks, "Will the program effects be generalizable to other settings where optimal conditions of administration are not as feasible?" Construct validity merely is another way to refer to the problem and asks, "Was the effect due to the intervention by itself or the intervention in combination with a very special teacher and setting?" The investigator may discuss the program without acknowledging that the program in combination with other features may have been critical. Some of my research has included special teachers who could administer interventions extremely well and often in seamless and nuanced fashions as part of their everyday behavior. In those demonstrations with only one teacher, it is possible that the effects were a combination of the teacher and intervention, even though I discussed the results as if it were the intervention alone (e.g., Kazdin & Geesey, 1977; Kazdin & Mascitelli, 1980). (In defense of myself, I had not yet read this book and did not know any better.) Any time the intervention is administered under narrow or restricted circumstances (e.g., one behavior-change agent, one classroom, one program or institution) it may be possible to raise the threat that the program-in-special-context was the intervention. When two or more circumstances (e.g., two teachers, two classrooms) are included, one can see or show that the effect was not restricted to one set of conditions.

The use of a narrow range of stimuli and the limitations that such use imposes sounds similar to external validity. It is. Sampling a narrow range of stimuli as a threat can apply to both external and construct validity. If the investigator wishes to *generalize* to other stimulus conditions (e.g., other teachers, classrooms, therapists, types of clients), then the narrow range of stimulus conditions is a threat to *external validity*. To generalize across conditions of the experiment requires sampling across the range of these conditions, if it is plausible that the conditions may influence the results (Brunswik, 1955). If the investigator wishes to *explain why* a change occurred, then the problem is one of *construct validity* because the investigator cannot separate the construct of interest (e.g., treatment or types of description of treatment) from the conditions of its delivery (e.g., teacher, setting, therapist). Whenever possible in a study, it is useful to include more than one experimenter (teacher, therapist, setting) so that at the end of the study one can separate the influence of the person who administered the intervention from the effects of the intervention. Construct validity is clarified if one can show that the intervention exerted its effect under different conditions.

General Comments

In applied settings, interventions often consist of "packages," that is, several distinguishable components that are put together. For example, an intervention to foster compliance with a medication regimen of an elderly adult at home (e.g., taking pills regularly) might consist of three components: (1) special reminders by a spouse or significant other to take the medication, (2) praise by that person if he or she does take the medication without the reminder, and (3) a cutesy ring tone or favorite song that plays whenever the person opens the special pill box to get the medication. The components are not regarded as accoutrements or artifacts or threats to construct validity. Rather, they are the intervention package. It may be useful to ask if one or more components are the key part of the intervention or what the individual contribution is of each one. This is not regarded as a methodological artifact or threat to validity.

Construct validity as a methodological concern is reserved for those instances in which a more pervasive general feature that is of no interest to the investigator may be confounded with the intervention. I have mentioned two of the likely candidates for single-case research. As with other threats, one does not vacuously criticize a study by holding up one of the construct validity threats I have mentioned. They become threats only when they are plausible rival interpretations. In the context of drug trials (e.g., for physical disease or psychiatric symptoms), a long-established threat to construct validity is the placebo effect. Any medication provided to a group might produce the outcome because of the pharmacological properties of the medicine and/or because of the act of taking medication under the supervision of a professional. We know that a placebo effect is not only a threat to construct validity but is now very plausible, is well documented, and has neurobiological underpinnings that are increasingly understood (e.g., Price, Finniss, & Benedetti, 2008).

DATA-EVALUATION VALIDITY

Defined

In group research, data-evaluation issues are referred to as statistical conclusion validity and encompass those facets of the quantitative evaluation of the results that may mislead or misguide the investigator (Cook & Campbell, 1979; Kazdin, 2003; Shadish et al., 2002). As an example, if the investigator is comparing two or more forms of psychotherapy in a between-group study, she is likely to conduct statistical analyses to compare the treatments on posttreatment performance among the different groups. Low statistical power (e.g., having too few subjects in relation to the likely effect size) is very likely to lead her to conclude that the treatments were not different from each other. It may be that the treatments in fact are not different in their effects. However, more likely than not, the way most of psychotherapy research is conducted, the study was not statistically powerful enough to detect differences (Kazdin & Bass, 1989). Small-to-medium effects require relatively large samples to detect a difference if there is one. In other words, in this example, low power is a threat to validity.

Visual inspection criteria rather than statistical tests are the primary means of evaluating single-case data. There are statistical tests that are occasionally used, as I discuss at much greater length (Chapter 13 and the Appendix), but these are not regarded as the primary criteria and are used in the minority of instances of single-case research. Data evaluation issues still emerge and can interfere with drawing inferences about the impact of the intervention. In single-case research, several aspects of the data can interfere with drawing valid inferences, and these are referred to as *threats to data-evaluation validity*.

Threats to Data-Evaluation Validity

I have adapted several threats raised in the context of statistical evaluation to the methods used to evaluate single-case designs. They encompass any facet of the data or the criteria used to evaluate the data (visual inspection) that may obscure identifying an intervention effect. Those facets that can serve as threats to data-evaluation validity are listed in Table 2.5.

Excessive variability in the data is a threat that can encompass different influences. Single-case designs depend on being able to discern patterns in the data within a given phase and discrepant patterns in the data from phase to phase (e.g., baseline to intervention). Much more will be said about this in relation to decision making during the course of a single-case design. The threat to validity stems from obtaining data within, but also across, phases where there is so much fluctuation in performance that a pattern cannot be reliably discerned. Did the intervention have the intended impact? It

Table 2.5 Major Threats to Data-Evaluation Validity

Specific Threat	What It Includes
Excessive variability in the data	Any source of variability that can interfere with detecting a difference when there is one.
Unreliability of the measures	Error in the measurement procedures that introduces excessive variability that obscures an intervention effect. The error might result from a measure that is not a valid index of the domain of interest, a measure that is unreliable, and conditions of measurement (setting, test administrator) that influence the data in some way.
Trends in the data	The extent to which the direction of change in a given phase or a pattern across phases can interfere with drawing inferences about the effects of the intervention.
Insufficient data	Too few data points to permit conclusions about level of performance and its likely level in the near future.
Mixed data patterns	Intervention effects are usually replicated within a study. The effect of the intervention is inferred from the overall pattern. Mixed data patterns across phases or replications within the study can interfere with drawing valid inferences about the impact of the intervention. Previously mentioned data evaluation threats (excessive variability, trend, and insufficient data) in one or more phases may contribute to the mixed data pattern and obscure inferences about the intervention.

may be that variability is so excessive, one cannot tell. In the one-cannot-tell situation, variability is a threat to data-evaluation validity.

Variability can come from many sources including:

- uncontrolled influences in the setting that may change widely each day;
- error in measurement (unreliability);
- sloppy and inconsistent implementation of the intervention;
- genuinely high variability and inconsistency in performance (which might even be the impetus for developing an intervention);
- differences among subjects if more than one is used; and
- cycles or abrupt changes within the individual (e.g., on or off medicine, normal hormonal fluctuation) or the environment (e.g., scheduled changes in who is present in the setting or who oversees the client, or changes in the classroom activity or routine).

Consider one of the preceding sources in further detail, namely, the way in which the intervention is implemented. Ideally, the procedures will be administered in a way that minimizes their day-to-day variation. This means that the procedures will be applied consistently, and those who administer the program will do so consistently. This might mean that consistency has to be part of the intervention if the program is delivered by the teacher and teacher's aide in a classroom; or different staff or attendants in a nursing home on different days or of course the same person on different days. Rigor in the execution of the procedures is not a methodological nicety for the sake of appearance. Consistency in execution of the procedures has direct bearing on data-evaluation validity. A given difference between phases or subjects may not be clear because of the variation or extra variation introduced by inconsistent procedures.

Variation cannot be eliminated, especially in relation to those aspects of research involving human participants (e.g., as students, clients, experimenters, therapists) and in settings outside of the laboratory. However, in any experiment, extraneous variation can be minimized by attention to the details of how the study is actually executed. If variability is minimized, the likelihood of detecting a true difference between baseline and intervention conditions is increased. In general, data-evaluation validity is threatened when variability can interfere with drawing inferences. The source of variability has implications for what the investigator can do about it, but for present purposes, variability that is excessive interferes with identifying an intervention effect when there is one and even clearly identifying no effect when one has not occurred.

How does one define excessive? It is not in standard deviation units, a familiar measure of variability. The definition is relative to performance within a phase and across phases and relative to the impact of the intervention. This is true of between-group research as well. Data evaluation is obscured by excessive variability, but that is a function of variability in relation to other influences in the design (Kazdin, 2003). The more potent the effect of an intervention, the less likely variability is to obscure interpretation of the effect. Even so, it is wise in experimental demonstrations to do what one can to minimize each of the sources of variability bulleted earlier.

Unreliability of the measures is encompassed by the preceding discussion, but it warrants separate discussion. Measurement plays a special role in all scientific research and therefore in single-case research. Also, reliability of measurement is a key part of the design and methodology, as conveyed in subsequent chapters. For these reasons, I delineate this as a separate threat to data-evaluation validity.

Reliability refers to the extent to which the measures assess the characteristics of interest in a consistent fashion (and is taken up again in Chapter 5). Reliability is, of course, a matter of degree and refers to the extent of the variability in scoring or completing the measure. Variability in the results we obtain in the measurement from day to day can be a direct function of multiple influences that impinge on the individual. For example, performance varies from occasion to occasion as a function of mood, experience, context, prior interactions with others, and many other unspecifiable influences. Thus, even if a measure is perfectly reliable, there will still be variability from one occasion to the next because performance is multiply determined and the measure is only one contributing factor.

Unreliability of the measure imposes another source of variation. Consider for a moment that we have a poorly behaved child robot (named Automated Luke or Al for short) that we place in a third-grade classroom. We program Al to have 15 instances of blurting out inappropriate statements to the teacher during the reading and writing period. Al is made to look just like and is dressed like a child; he is carefully programmed, tested, and calibrated, and has "his" battery charged. So assume for this discussion that Al is doing his job—15 randomly timed and blurted statements (e.g., "Hey, teach! When is recess?" "Mr. Jones, the book is a little booooooor-ing—can we stop now?" "When do we get to the unit on single-case designs?"). We also have Al make five additional neutral or appropriate statements (e.g., he raises his hand and says, "May I have some help?" or "Is it ok if my comments on the book take up more than one page?").

We place two observers at the back of the classroom with the assignment of noting each instance of Al's blurting out. Assume they have not mastered the observational codes. For example, they are inconsistent in deciding what constitutes an inappropriate statement versus a good question and when a statement is one statement or two statements because they seem to be separated by a pause. Another way of saying that they are not too consistent is to note that the measurement procedure has low reliability. If we were to graph the data from one or both of the observers, we would see that even though we know Al's performance is at 15 blurts per day, there is fluctuation introduced by the measure—some days are at 10, others at 15, another at 17, two at 11, and so on. The measurement codes and how they are applied may reflect unreliability in the observations. To the extent that the measure is unreliable, a greater portion of the subject's score is due to unsystematic and random variation.

Needless to say, unreliability of the measure is not unique to any specific modality. Often, checklists, rating scales, and self-report measures are used to evaluate the effect of interventions. These measures too, have reliability that can vary as a function of use, sample, and conditions of administration. The fact that they are standardized (e.g., unvarying items on a scale such as the Beck Depression Inventory) does not mean that their reliability is fixed. Reliability (consistency of the measurement) is not a property of a scale alone but also a function of its use and conditions of administration.

Some measures might be especially reliable because they are automated, mechanical, or use equipment in some way that is unvarying and free from the possibility of human bias in adding error variation. With automated equipment there is an occasional catastrophic break down, and everything stops. This is less pernicious than the illusion that all is going well but there is inconsistency in the observations.

In general, one wants to minimize extra, unneeded, and unsystematic variation from the measure or measurement procedure. Any added variation introduces unnecessary fluctuations in performance. If those fluctuations, resulting from the measure, can interfere with evaluation of the data, unreliability or low reliability of the measure becomes a threat to data-evaluation validity.

Trends in the data refer to the slope or the pattern of change over time based on multiple observations. For example, we may observe for 10 days, the social interactions (number of exchanges that involve more than a hi or hello) of an elderly resident who seems isolated from other people in her assisted-living home. For the 10 days, the trend or slope is the line that best represents the pattern (e.g., horizontal line—no trend in one direction rather than another). Single-case designs depend on seeing changes in trends (slope) over time and hence we shall return to this topic.

Occasionally, when baseline observations begin, one identifies a slope in the therapeutic direction. That is, behavior is improving even though the intervention has not yet begun. How could this occur? As with variability, the how is not critical in relation to threats to validity. Yet, it is sometimes the case that observation of performance before the intervention begins exerts a change (a process I mentioned as reactivity), and this change may continue for a while. Others in the environment who interact with the client may change too in many ways that support improved behavior of the client. Trends can serve as data-evaluation threats in other phases than baseline, if there is a pattern (e.g., behavior improves quickly but seems to be deteriorating over the course of treatment) that obscures or makes drawing inferences about treatment difficult. Evaluation of trends is critical in data evaluation, and we shall return to this topic.

Insufficient data can serve as a threat to data-evaluation validity. Single-case designs depend on looking at current performance across phases when different conditions (e.g., no intervention and intervention) are in effect. A "phase" consists of consecutive observations obtained on the client while some condition (e.g., baseline) is in place. A new phase consists of observations obtained when the condition changes (e.g., intervention). Evaluation depends on looking at multiple characteristics of the data within and across phases to see if there is a change. A validity threat occurs if the data are insufficient to characterize current performance and to provide information to project performance in the future. What constitutes insufficient data in a given phase? This question cannot be answered in the abstract but depends on emerging data in the design.

For example, is one data point insufficient? That is difficult to tell. Suppose someone says her spouse has not exercised since they were married (10 years ago) and she wishes to increase his exercise now. Hopefully our intervention is going to increase daily exercise (in minutes). How many days of baseline do we need? One day might be enough to ensure that the observation system is in place and working. For any later data evaluation you will only have one data point, because retrospective report from the wife will not be part of the data in the study. One data point might be enough for this initial baseline. In general, when behavior is never performed in the immediate past (e.g., exercising, attending activities) one or two observations may be sufficient. In addition, when an intervention is withdrawn, sometimes seemingly perfect performance (100% of the target behavior daily) plunges to the depths of baseline in an instant, that is, with one observation day. One day will be fine, and I shall give examples later to convey that. More is invariably better, so one would want more than one day when possible but in principle it is not the number of days but what the phase attempts to accomplish and how many data points it takes to do that.

Single-case designs require a bit more understanding of the methodology because decision making occurs during the study and drawing inferences depends on these decisions. I shall provide guidelines regarding sufficient length of phases for data collection and more importantly the underlying principles on which decisions are based. I only wish to note here that insufficient data in a phase can interfere with the evaluation and serve as a threat to validity.

Mixed data patterns within and across phases too can interfere with evaluation of the data. Consistency in various patterns of the data is important for drawing inferences in a single-case design. In the different designs, usually there are multiple opportunities to evaluate whether the intervention was responsible for changes. For example, in some designs the intervention is presented and withdrawn on two or more occasions (ABAB designs); in other designs, the intervention is tested across multiple behaviors one at a time (multiple-baseline design across behaviors). These and other instances might be considered mini-replications—I add "mini" in recognition that replication usually refers to an independent attempt to repeat the study. But in single-case designs there is usually more than one opportunity to look at the data pattern and draw conclusions about the intervention within the same study. One can look at the overall pattern, but also at each individual occasion in which the intervention is tested. From this overall pattern, inferences are drawn. A threat to data-evaluation validity occurs if the data pattern is mixed and interferes with drawing inferences about the intervention. Any of the previously mentioned data evaluation threats (excessive variability, trend, and insufficient data) at one or more places in the design (e.g., one phase or one individual in multiple-baseline design across individuals) could be the basis for a mixed data pattern.

Another source of a mixed data pattern may stem from who is included in the demonstration. Single-case designs often include more than one subject, no matter what the design. All subjects are different, of course (even the fingerprints and brains of identical twins), so there is inherent variability from individual differences. In principle, the more diverse the subjects are in a given demonstration, the greater the possibility that responses to the intervention will vary. That is, the pattern of the data for the intervention effects might well be mixed due to diversity and variability among the subjects.

I say "mixed data pattern" to capitalize on the more familiar use of mixed messages in everyday life. When someone says the *three* precious words, "I love you," usually that is clear enough. When the person instead says the *five* slightly less precious words, "I love you" (now a silent pause for 3 seconds, and then continues with...) "sort of" it would be wise to view the message as mixed and the interpretation at best is obscured. Mixed love signals are a threat to interpersonal relationships (methodologists can handle these). Mixed data patterns in any research design are a threat to data-evaluation validity (methodologists enter long-term psychotherapy for these).

General Comments

For both basic and applied research, it is critical to select interventions and parameters of their administration that will maximize intervention effects. The goal of maximizing intervention effects is a given in applied research—we wish to make a real difference that helps people. However, consider the methodological aspect of strong interventions. A more potent intervention decreases the likelihood that the threats to data evaluation will emerge. Also, strong interventions not only affect means (i.e., change the average level of performance from what it was before the intervention), but often reduce variability (i.e., fluctuations around that average point) as well. Thus, intervention strength can directly alleviate some of the threats noted previously.

PRIORITIES AND TRADE-OFFS IN VALIDITY

It is not possible to design a study that is perfectly attentive to all the threats of internal, external, construct, and data-evaluation validity. This is in part because goals of the study may change or dictate that some threats are really more important than others. Also, addressing some threats is inversely related to addressing others. Consider key issues.

Internal validity is usually regarded as the highest priority. Obviously, one must first have an unambiguously demonstrated finding or effect before other questions can be raised (e.g., Can this be generalized?, i.e., external validity; What is the underlying explanation?, i.e., construct validity). Yet, the priorities of internal versus external validity in any given instance depend to some extent on the purposes of the research. Internal validity is given greater priority in basic research. Special experimental arrangements are designed not only to rule out threats to internal validity but also to maximize the likelihood of demonstrating a particular relationship between independent and dependent variables. Events in the experiment are carefully controlled, and conditions are arranged for purposes of the demonstration. Whether the conditions represent events ordinarily evident in everyday life is not necessarily crucial. The purpose of such experiments is to show what *can* happen when the situation is arranged in a particular way. These demonstrations are sometimes referred to as a *test of principle*. Early work on stem cells, cloning, and cell reprogramming were of this type and provided demonstrations of new biological tools and processes that were not previously possible, that is, tests of principle. Many questions about generality of the findings can be asked such as whether the findings can be applied to clone a favorite pet, to produce organs or tissues among individuals who need an organ transplant, or to reverse a disease process (e.g., cancer) by giving cells new "instructions."

I have mentioned uncontrolled sources of variability as a potential threat to validity, data-evaluation validity in particular. Working in applied rather than laboratory settings (e.g., schools, clinics, hospitals, homes, and the community) increases variability in data patterns and data collection. In a classroom, the assignments, presence of multiple teachers, and varied classroom activities all add a little bit of error to measurement. This is contrasted with the splendor of the laboratory where much can be the same, automated, and held constant, all to reduce variability. Under the circumstances, the investigator working in an applied setting tries to control carefully or hold constant as many influences as she can. Consider the trade-offs.

On the one hand, very careful control reduces the likelihood of excessive variability and mixed data patterns, and hence serves the Goddess of Data-Evaluation Validity perfectly. Yet, making applied settings like a quasi lab to achieve control now raises the wrath of the Goddess of External Validity. Will this intervention and its effects generalize (external validity) to any other circumstance where control is not so strong or so heavily invoked? This is not a minor question. For example, there are many prevention demonstration projects (e.g., in the schools) where an investigative team funded by a large grant completes a comprehensive assessment, provides an intervention (to some classes or schools), and evaluates the short- and long-term effects years later (e.g., reduced rates of suicide, substance use [drugs, alcohol, cigarettes], unprotected sex, and criminal activity). It is superb to show that such outcomes can be achieved, but a large question is whether any such programs can be extended on a larger scale without the investigative team of researchers introduced into the settings where the first study was implemented. Is there any external validity to the findings? Only further research can establish that, but the threat to external validity may become more plausible the greater the research setting (with all of its constraints and monitoring) departs from real-world settings.

All four types of validity—internal, external, construct, and data-evaluation validity—need to be considered. In between-group research, many of the decisions to address these can be made before the experiment begins, that is, at the design stage. The challenge is slightly greater for single-case designs, because the investigator responds to the data emerging from the study for basic design decisions (e.g., How long should this phase be? When should a new intervention be tried?). Understanding the underpinnings of design and what we are trying to accomplish is much more important than mastering procedures and techniques that constitute the designs. In any research one must selectively neglect and attend to issues that could influence interpretation of the findings. Being informed of what can emerge as problems, when some problems are more relevant or important than others, and what to do about them—this is black-belt level methodology.

EXPERIMENTAL VALIDITY IN CONTEXT

The threats to validity are fundamental reasons we go through design gyrations and make very special arrangements in how the studied is carried out. It is important to place these in the context of research methodology more broadly and in this way also preview the remaining chapters. Single-case designs, but research design more generally, can be conceived as including three interdependent components:

- Assessment: Use of systematic measures to document performance and to reflect changes where changes are sought;
- Experimental Design: Special arrangements of presenting the intervention or conditions to participants that will help establish that the intervention rather than other influences (threats to validity) is likely to be the cause of behavior change; and
- Data Evaluation: Procedures, techniques, and criteria that are used to decide and show that there was a reliable change and that the effect within, between, or among conditions makes a difference.

Threats to validity enter in at many points, and interpretation of the study can be enhanced or undermined by how each of these is addressed. The following chapters address the three topics in turn and provide critical issues, options, and guidelines to strengthen the quality of inferences from conducting single-case research.

SUMMARY AND CONCLUSIONS

The purpose of experimentation is to arrange the situation in such a way that extraneous influences that might affect the results do not interfere with drawing causal inferences about the impact of the intervention. The *internal validity* of an experiment refers to the extent to which the experiment rules out or makes implausible alternative explanations of the results. The factors or influences other than the intervention that could explain the results are called *threats to internal validity*. Major threats include the influence of history, maturation, instrumentation, testing, statistical regression, and diffusion of treatment.

Apart from internal validity, the goal of experimentation is to demonstrate relationships that can extend beyond the unique circumstances of a particular experiment. *External validity* addresses questions of the extent to which the results of an investigation can be generalized or extended beyond the conditions of the original experiment. Several characteristics of the experiment may limit the generality of the results. These characteristics are referred to as *threats to external validity* and include generality across subjects, responses, settings, time, and behavior-change agents; reactivity of experimental arrangements and the assessment procedures; and multiple-treatment interference.

Construct validity pertains to interpreting the basis for the causal relation between the independent variable (e.g., intervention, experimental manipulation) and the dependent variable (e.g., outcome, performance). Factors that may interfere with or obscure valid inferences about the reason for the effect are *threats to construct validity*. Major threats include attention and contact with the client, and special stimulus conditions, settings, and contexts.

Data-evaluation validity refers to those aspects of the data that obscure or mislead in drawing inferences about the impact of the intervention. The factors that can interfere with drawing conclusions are *threats to data-evaluation validity*. Major threats include excessive variability in the data, unreliability of the measures, trends in the data, insufficient data to discern a pattern within a given phase, and mixed-data patterns.

All four types of validity, internal, external, construct, and data-evaluation validity, are important. Clearly internal validity rises to the top of the list and is the raison d'être for doing research. Yet, the types of validity vary in importance as a function of what the investigator is trying to accomplish and what issues emerge during the collection of data. It is not possible in any one experiment to address all threats well or equally well, nor is this necessarily a goal toward which one should strive. Rather, the goal is to address the primary questions of interest in as thorough a fashion as possible so that clear answers can be provided for those specific questions. At the end of that investigation, new questions may emerge or questions about other types of validity may increase in priority.

The obstacles in designing experiments not only emerge from the manifold types of validity and their threats, but also from the interrelations of the different types of validity. Factors that address one type of validity might detract from or increase vulnerability to another type of validity. For example, factors that address data-evaluation validity might involve controlling potential sources of variation in relation to the experimental setting, delivery of interventions, and homogeneity of the subjects. In the process of maximizing experimental control and making the most sensitive test of the intervention variable, the range of conditions included in the experiment become increasingly restricted. Restricting the conditions, such as the type of subjects or measures and standardization of delivering the intervention or independent variable, may commensurately limit the range of conditions to which the final results can be generalized.

Single-case designs provide many options to rule out and make critical threats to validity implausible. They are equally powerful in addressing the threats as are more familiar between-group studies. In the chapters that follow, I elaborate design options and how they address critical threats.

Background and Key Measurement Considerations

As I noted in the previous chapter, single-case methodology includes three interrelated components: assessment, experimental design, and data evaluation. Assessment is pivotal in all research and is the starting point to begin to answer questions about interventions and their effects. Questions about all sorts of interventions (Does eating certain foods prevent cancer? Will this well-intended therapy help the patient? Is this systematic method of teaching [reading, art, music] really effective?) require special arrangements of conditions (experimental designs) to be answered scientifically. However, before one is able to answer what caused the change, one needs to be sure there was a change in the outcome of interest (rate of cancer, improvement in the patient, change in the student). Assessment is a precondition for drawing inferences.

The importance of assessment is often underemphasized. You will recall mention of the anecdotal case study as scientifically bereft in terms of drawing strong inferences. This is not only due to the lack of an experimental design to evaluate some condition but also to the lack of systematic assessment. As discussed much later in this book (Chapter 11), systematic assessment can rescue all sorts situations and help draw inferences even when experiments cannot be done. As a matter of fact, science can make astounding advances, test theory, and draw inferences, sometimes by meticulous assessment and without the opportunity for experiments (e.g., astronomy and meteorology).

In this chapter and the two that follow, several characteristics of assessment in single-case research are elaborated. This chapter focuses on background consideration or requirements of measures for single-case designs. The next two chapters focus on methods and strategies for assessing behavior and insuring the integrity of the assessment procedures. In each chapter, a distinction emerges that is worth underscoring. I mentioned that single-case designs have flourished in an area that is referred to as applied behavior analysis. This area has applied and evaluated interventions broadly—it is difficult to identify a setting (e.g., schools, institutions, business and industry, community life, colleges, nursing homes) in which, or a client population (e.g., preschool to elderly, psychiatric and medical inpatients and outpatients) with whom, interventions have not been developed and evaluated. In the process of developing the substantive field of applied behavior analysis, methodological innovations have been made as well. Some of those relate directly to key assessment considerations, i.e., identifying what to assess and what to change. I include several of these because they provide superb guidelines for assessment and intervention. However, it is important to mention these components as helpful guides but not necessarily central to single-case research designs.

IDENTIFYING THE GOALS OF THE PROGRAM

Frequently Used Criteria

Assessment and intervention require clearly stating the goal and carefully describing how the outcomes will be evident. Identifying the goal of the program in most cases seems obvious and straightforward because of the direct and immediate implications of the behavior for adjustment, impairment, and adaptive functioning of the individual in everyday life. For examples, many interventions have decreased such behaviors as self-injury (e.g., head banging), anxiety and panic attacks, neglectful parenting among adults, and driving under the influence of alcohol and have increased such behaviors as engaging in practices that promote health (e.g., exercise, consumption of healthful foods) and academic performance among individuals performing poorly at school.

Examples are useful, but they do not address the broader issues, namely, what makes a behavior or domain of functioning worthy or in need of intervention? There are several overlapping criteria that serve as guidelines. First, the *setting and institution may dictate the focus and goals that are worthy of intervention* by their very nature and purpose. Schools, for example, are intended to educate youth and develop competencies. Invariably interventions are of interest to identify whether the current educational program in place can be improved. Also, behavior may be focused on in a setting because it relates to or interferes with the goal or main purpose of the setting. Thus, in schools, focusing on vandalism, disruptive classroom behavior, bullying, and drug use may be quite relevant insofar as they relate to the likelihood that the academic goals can be achieved in the setting. The goals of the setting or contexts have frequently served as the basis of intervention and single-case evaluation. Examples include efforts to increase productivity in business, improve athletic performance among individuals, and improve acquisition of a new language.

Second, many of the criteria that guide interventions are based *on dysfunction, maladaptive behavior, or social, emotional, and behavioral problems that are associated with impairment.* Impairment means that the problem interferes with an individual's functioning in everyday life. Examples would be failing to meet role demands at home, at school, and at work; interacting inappropriately with others, which has deleterious impact on one's own functioning; and being restricted in the settings, situations, and experiences in which one can function. Facets of individual functioning (thoughts, feelings, behavior) that lead to or are associated with impairment are likely to warrant intervention. Impairment is a criterion invoked in defining psychiatric disorders (e.g., major depression, schizophrenia, attention deficit/hyperactivity disorder) (American Psychiatric Association, 1994). In addition to multiple symptoms (e.g., anxiety, substance abuse), impairment in functioning is required as well.

There are all sorts of variations of functioning that fall under the broad rubric of maladaptive behavior. Behaviors that are illegal or rule-breaking serve as the impetus for intervention. Illegal behaviors would include driving under the influence of alcohol, using illicit drugs, and stealing. Rule breaking that is not illegal might include a child leaving school repeatedly during the middle of the day or not adhering to a family-imposed curfew. Also, behaviors that are dangerous to oneself or to others, or that place the individual at risk for dangerous or untoward outcomes, often serve as the basis for intervening. Self-injury, fighting at school, and spouse abuse are obvious examples of dangerous behaviors because each involves physical harm; some are life-threatening. Risk behaviors are those that may have harmful consequences and can include unsafe sex practices, cigarette smoking, not wearing seat belts, and driving while intoxicated. Signs of stress or distress are often grounds for intervening. Perhaps the individual was exposed to a natural or personal disaster or trauma (e.g., loss of home, loved one) or unusual stressor in relation to one's situation (work, relationships). The signs of stress are evident in impairment in some sphere of functioning. Perhaps the most extreme variation within the category of clinical dysfunction would be unusual or extreme symptoms that constitute more stark departures from everyday experiences and functioning. Signs that an individual is hearing voices, acting on these voices, seeing things that are not there, and other marked departures in social behavior, communication, and activity would be grounds for evaluation and intervention.

Third, the basis for intervention often reflects *behaviors that are of concern to individuals themselves or to significant others.* For example, parents bring their children to treatment for a variety of behaviors that affect daily life but may or may not be severe enough to reflect significant social, emotional, and behavioral problems, impairment, or rule breaking. Nevertheless, parents wish for some help and may have concerns. Examples include toilet training, school functioning, shyness, and mildly bothersome behaviors that, if severe, might indeed reflect impairment. "Behaviors that are of concern" is a broad, catchall category but is one that is meaningful nonetheless. The goal is to improve adaptive functioning in a particular domain and perhaps in some cases bring individuals up to seemingly normative levels.

There are occasions in which concerns of significant others are of questionable relevance as targets of treatment. For example, a case at the clinic where I work included a very aggressive and antisocial 8-year-old boy. His behavior was clearly impaired, as, for example, reflected in his multiple and repeated expulsions from school for fighting (physically) with children and teachers. The single parent is extremely concerned about other behaviors that are generally annoying (e.g., he leaves his clothes on the floor, does not always flush the toilet, leaves his shoes outside of the closet, occasionally discards candy wrappers on the furniture, forgets to place the cap on the toothpaste tube after brushing). These latter behaviors do not predict long-term child adjustment, criminality, psychiatric disorder, or impairment. The aggressive and antisocial behaviors do predict these outcomes and meet several of the criteria noted previously.

Fourth, behaviors are focused on that may *prevent problems from developing*. The focus is not on a problem but on behaviors that will avert the likelihood of a problem or minimize the occurrence. Often children or adults are at risk for some untoward consequences. For example, premature babies and children from economically disadvantaged environments are at risk for school difficulties. Early intervention with the parents and children to develop pre-academic behaviors at home are designed to prevent later physical, psychological, and educational problems. Also, developing behaviors that promote safety (e.g., in business and industry or in the home) or health would qualify as efforts to prevent problems.

The previously mentioned criteria capture many of the bases for intervening. Although the criteria focus on characteristics of behaviors of the individual, there are critical contextual influences. A given domain of functioning might be context specific rather than reflect pervasive features that individuals show at all times and places. For example, children may show a particular problem only in the classroom or at home, adults with anxiety may show this only in relation to specific situations (e.g., involving socialization with others), and someone who stutters may do so much more in the presence of a group and strangers than with individuals and family. Age and period of development may make something worthy of intervention. For example, enuresis (bedwetting) may be annoying to parents but is normative in early childhood. In middle and later childhood (e.g., > 7 years old), it becomes a departure from normative function and a risk factor for (predictor of) psychiatric disturbance (Feehan, McGee, Stanton, & Silva, 1990; Rutter, Yule, & Graham, 1973). An intervention is likely to be more appropriate for the older rather than younger children.

The issue of what to select for assessment and intervention is not unique to single-case research. For example, social, emotional, and behavioral problems serve as the frequent basis of intervention studies. Fundamental questions invariably arise related to what constitutes "normal" and deviant functioning and at what point one should intervene. The question has been made more salient with research that shows that in "normal" community samples, approximately one in four meet criteria for a psychiatric diagnosis (National Institute of Mental Health, 2008). Also, many psychiatric diagnoses (e.g., depression, anxiety) and social, emotional, and behavioral problems are on continua so there is no necessary cutoff point that says you have "it" or you do not. Thus, when to intervene can be ambiguous.

Social Validation as a Guide

Social validity or *social validation* occasionally has been used as a guide to both assessment and intervention (Foster & Mash, 1999; Kazdin, 1977b; Kennedy, 2002; Wolf, 1978). The notion of "social" validity is designed to ensure that interventions take into account the concerns of society and the consumers of interventions (parents, teachers, clients) (Schwartz & Baer, 1991). Social validity encompasses three questions about interventions:

- Are the goals of the interventions relevant to everyday life?
- Are the intervention procedures acceptable to consumers and to the community at large?
- Are the outcomes of the intervention important, that is, do the changes make a difference in the everyday lives of individuals?

Each of these involves assessment in some way, but for this chapter I emphasize the first question because it relates directly to selection and assessment of the focus or goal of the intervention. Two social validation methods can be used for identifying the appropriate focus of the intervention, namely, the social comparison and subjective evaluation methods. Each is an empirically based method of identifying what the focus of the intervention and hence the assessment ought to be.

Social Comparison. The major feature of the social comparison method is to identify a peer group of the client, that is, those persons who are similar to the client in subject and demographic variables but who differ in performance of the target behavior or characteristic (e.g., depression, anxiety) of interest. The peer group consists of persons who are considered to be functioning adequately with respect to the target behavior. Essentially, normative data are gathered to provide a basis for evaluating the behavior or domain of functioning of the client. The behaviors that distinguish the client from the normative sample or the magnitude of the departure from the normative sample suggest what domains require intervention. There are broad swaths of everyday life in which this is routinely done. For example, in education, extensive data on reading, language, and arithmetic progress of children at different ages and grade levels provide the basis for identifying who is doing well and who is doing poorly. Each of these may be used for decision making about special interventions (e.g., for individuals identified as gifted or lagging behind in a skill area). Similarly, disabilities (e.g., in walking, talking; in social behavior, as in autism) are identified early in life because of the departures from normative information that is readily available. Consequently, normative data are routinely used already and implicitly in decisions about when to intervene.

Normative data occasionally are used in other areas where the scope of the information is not as well developed, but where some benchmarking would help in deciding the focus. This latter use of normative data to identify the intervention focus was nicely illustrated in a program that trained institutionalized women with developmental disabilities to dress themselves and select their own clothing in a way that coincided with current fashion (Nutter & Reid, 1978). Developing skills in dressing fashionably represents an important focus for persons preparing to enter community living situations. The purpose of the study was to train women to coordinate the color combinations of their clothing. To determine the specific color combinations that constituted popular fashion, the investigators observed over 600 women in community settings where the institutionalized residents would be likely to interact, including a local shopping mall, a restaurant, and sidewalks. Popular color combinations were identified, and the residents were trained to dress according to current fashion. The skills in dressing fashionably were maintained for several weeks after training.

In some cases, it may be useful to look at normative samples to determine precisely what ought to be trained. In the preceding example, the investigators were interested in focusing on specific response areas related to dressing but sought information from normative samples to determine the precise behaviors of interest. The behavior of persons in everyday life served as a criterion for the particular behaviors that were trained. When the goal is to return persons to a particular setting or level of functioning, social comparison may be especially useful. The method first identifies the level of functioning of persons performing adequately (or well) in the situation and then uses the information as a basis for selecting the target focus.

Subjective Evaluation. *Subjective evaluation* consists of soliciting the opinions of others who by expertise, consensus, or familiarity with the client are in a position to judge or evaluate the behaviors or characteristics in need of treatment. Many of the decisions about the behaviors that warrant intervention are made by parents, teachers, peers, or people in society at large who identify deviance and make judgments about which social, emotional, behavioral, or learning problems do and do not require special attention. An intervention may be sought because there is a consensus that there is a problem. Often it is useful to evaluate the opinions of experts systematically to identify what specific domains of functioning present a problem.

The term "subjective" is unnecessarily touchy-feely and misrepresents aspects of the method. Although the information is based on self-report and opinion, the information often draws on very special expertise. For example, subjective evaluation has been used to identify behaviors that are critical when children (or others) escape from their homes in case of fire. Opinions of firefighters are sought to identify what behaviors will save their lives. It demeans the source by referring to this as "subjective." The specific skills recommended based on expertise of the source make a difference in saving lives, hardly just an opinion or subjective view. Similarly, one might ask those who train commercial airline pilots what the most important skills are for emergency landings, and use that to provide rigorous training. Here too, subjective evaluation might better be called "expert evaluation."

Two studies nicely illustrate subjective evaluation outside the context of life or death considerations. In the first study, the investigators were interested in identifying problem situations for youths with delinquent behavior, and the responses they should possess to handle these situations (Freedman, Rosenthal, Donahoe, Schlundt, & McFall, 1978). To identify problem situations, psychologists, social workers, counselors, teachers, boys with a history of delinquency, and others were consulted. After the problem situations were identified (e.g., being insulted by a peer, being harassed by a school principal), the investigators sought to identify the appropriate responses to these situations. The situations were presented to boys with and without prior delinquent behavior. They were asked to respond as they typically would. Judges, consisting of students, psychology interns, and psychologists, rated the competence of the responses. For each of the problem situations, responses were identified that varied in their degree of competence. An inventory of situations was constructed that included several problem situations and response alternatives that had been developed through the subjective evaluations of several judges. The input is a useful basis for identifying what to change and develop during an intervention.

In a second example, the investigators were interested in preparing young children in day care in school readiness skills (Hanley, Heal, Tiger, & Ingvarsson, 2007). The behaviors drew on information obtained from early elementary school teachers and from early education experts. In one of the surveys, over 3,000 kindergarten teachers from different regions of the country, and spanning a period of a decade, provided the information. The results reflected a shift in how experts viewed the components of readiness. The shift moved from a focus on academically oriented skills to social skills. The investigators selected those social skills reported to be the most important (e.g., following directions, taking turns and sharing, telling what one needs, being sensitive to others, and reducing disruptive behavior). These categories were then operationalized, assessed, and successfully trained.

In the preceding examples, persons were consulted to help identify behaviors that warranted intervention. The persons were asked to recommend the desired behaviors because of their familiarity with the requisite responses for the specific situations. The recommendations of such persons can then be translated into training programs so that specific performance goals are achieved.

General Comments. Social comparison and subjective evaluation methods provide empirically based procedures for systematically selecting the target focus for purposes of assessment and intervention. Of course, the methods are not without problems. For example, the social comparison method suggests that behaviors that distinguish a community sample ought to serve as the basis for intervention. Yet, it is possible that normative samples and clients differ in many ways, some of which may have little relevance to the functioning of the clients in their everyday lives. Just because clients differ from a community sample in a particular behavior, does not necessarily mean that the difference is important or that ameliorating the difference in performance will solve major problems for the clients. Also, I already mentioned that terms used decades ago such as "normal" sample are hard to say without gulping—I mentioned 25% as an approximate rate of psychiatric disorder among community samples. "Normal" and community samples include a lot of deviance, which means using them as a bar or criterion requires caution.

Similarly, with subjective evaluation, the possibility exists that the behaviors subjectively judged as important may not be the most important focus of treatment. For example, teachers frequently identify disruptive and inattentive behavior in the classroom as a major area in need of intervention. Yet, we have known for decades that improving attentive behavior in the classroom usually has little or no effect on children's academic performance (e.g., Ferritor, Buckholdt, Hamblin, & Smith, 1972; Harris & Sherman, 1974). However, focusing directly on improving academic performance usually has inadvertent consequences on improving attentiveness (e.g., Ayllon & Roberts, 1974; Marholin, Steinman, McInnis, & Heads, 1975). Thus, subjectively identified behaviors may not be the most appropriate or beneficial focus in the classroom.

Notwithstanding the objections that might be raised, social comparison and subjective evaluation can be useful in guiding assessment and identifying the focus of an intervention. The objections against one of the methods of selecting the intervention focus can be overcome by employing both methods simultaneously. That is, normative samples can be identified and compared with a sample of clients (e.g., individuals with a history of delinquent behavior, people who have a developmental disability) identified for intervention. Then, the differences in specific behaviors, skills, or other facets of functioning that distinguish the groups can be evaluated by raters to examine the extent to which these characteristics are viewed as important.

DEFINING THE TARGET BEHAVIOR OR FOCUS

From the criteria noted previously, the general focus of the intervention is delineated. For both assessment and intervention, the general focus (tantrums, aggressiveness, self-injury) is translated into a more concrete definition. The move from concept (characteristic or idea) to operations (ways in which that concept will be measured) is a critical facet for all of the sciences and permits advances, replication of findings, and accumulation of knowledge. *Operational definitions* refer to defining a concept on the basis of the specific operations used for assessment. Paper-and-pencil measures (questionnaires to assess the domain), interviews, reports of others (e.g., parents, spouses) in contact with the client, physiological measures (e.g., measures of arousal, stress), and direct observation are among the most commonly used measures in psychological, educational, and counseling research to operationalize key concepts.

In applied research where single-case designs have been used heavily, emphasis has been placed on direct observation of overt behavior because overt behavior is viewed as the most direct measure of the treatment focus. So, rather than parent or teacher ratings about the severity or frequency of tantrums, investigators have assessed tantrums directly. This requires defining what a tantrum is or at least what will be counted as a tantrum in the study. Parental reports about tantrums, while important, are a step removed from the tantrums themselves. Moreover, reports are subject to special influences and bias (e.g., the more stress the parent is experiencing in other areas of life than the child's tantrums, the greater their perception of defiance in their children) (see Kazdin, 1994). Consequently, if possible and feasible, it is useful to observe the tantrums directly and to see when they occur, under what circumstances, and whether they change in response to intervention. At the same time, the effects of tantrums on others in the environment are not trivial. In an effective program, one would like to see a genuine and marked reduction in tantrums but also a change that is reflected in the perceptions of others who identified the problem. One measure (direct observation of the behavior) does not substitute for the other (peoples' perceptions that the change made a difference).

Operational definitions are essential to begin to assess and evaluate interventions. In defining an abstract concept (e.g., anxiety or tantrums), an operational definition is not likely to capture the entire domain of interest. Operational definitions are ways of working with the concept by taking a slice or two of the conceptual pie to represent critical components. Usually we are interested in the domain in its fullest definition but use operational definitions to represent it. In such cases, we do not merely wish to change functioning on the one measure we assess but hope to change the many components of the larger concept. In other situations, operational definitions may reflect virtually all or most of the components of interest. In the case of tantrums, for example, frequency of the tantrums may be the main aspect of interest, but we still care about how the world sees and perceives the child's tantrums as well.

We begin by specifying the general domain (e.g., tantrums) and then by identifying a specific definition that permits assessment. To make this transition, one ought to ask others (e.g., parents, teachers, and clients) what the desired or undesired behaviors are. Also, it is useful to observe the client or others informally. Descriptive notes of what behaviors occur and which events are associated with their occurrence may be useful in generating specific response definitions. From inquiries and informal observations, one might be able to answer several questions about the target behavior (e.g., when does it occur, what does it look like, under what circumstances do they occur?).

For example, in one program the goal was to train children with autism in helping behaviors (Reeve, Reeve, Townsend, & Poulson, 2007). Children with autism have severe deficits in socializing with others; helping behaviors in a special classroom were selected because helping others tends to lead to longer social interactions than other classes of behavior (e.g., greetings). To identify where to begin, the investigators surveyed parents of typically developing children, asking them to describe instances of helping behavior. Also, another group of children was observed in a local school during many different activities (story time, free play) in order to identify helping acts. From this information, the investigators developed categories of helping activities (e.g., picking up objects, setting up an activity, sorting materials) in relation to the classroom and then moved to highly specific operational definitions of each category.

Initial canvassing of others may not be necessary for many behaviors that will be observed (e.g., completing homework, taking one's medication). However, one must move to an operational definition to specify how the behavior will be assessed for purposes of observation and intervention. As a general rule, a definition should meet three criteria: *objectivity*, *clarity*, and *completeness* (Hawkins & Dobes, 1977). These concepts are defined and illustrated in Table 3.1. Developing a complete definition often creates the greatest difficulty because decision rules are needed to specify how behavior should be scored. If the range of responses included in the definition is not described carefully, observers have to infer whether such a response has occurred. For example, a simple greeting response such as waving one's hand to greet someone may serve as the target behavior for a socially withdrawn child. In most instances, when a person's hand is fully extended and moving back and forth, there would be no difficulty in agreeing that the person was waving. However, ambiguous instances may require judgments on the part of observers. A child might move his or her hand once while the arm is not extended (rather than back and forth), or a child may not move his or her arm at all but simply move all of the fingers on one hand up and down (in the way that infants often learn to say good-bye). These responses are instances of waving in everyday life, because we can often see others reciprocate with similar greetings. For assessment purposes, the response definition must specify how these and related variations of waving should be scored.

Developing clear definitions requires specifying what is and what is not to be included in the behavior. For example, in one program, the focus was on reducing the frequency of talking to oneself for a hospitalized patient with schizophrenia

Table 3.1 Criteria to Be Met When Defining Behaviors for Observation

Criterion	Defined	Example
Objectivity	The measure refers to observable characteristics of the behavior or to events in the environment that can be observed.	The number of times that a child engages in tantrums (as an operational definition of tantrums); the number of cigarette butts in the ashtray or cigarettes remaining in the pack (as an operational definition of cigarette smoking).
Clarity	A definition is so unambiguous that it could be read, repeated, and paraphrased by an observer or someone initially unfamiliar with the measure. Little explanation is needed to begin actual observations of the behavior.	A tantrum includes anytime the child shouts, whines, stomps feet, throw things, or slams a door in response to a comment from his or her mother or father during the hours of 3:30 p.m. to 5:30 p.m., Monday through Friday, when the child and at least one parent are at home.
Completeness	Delineation of the boundary conditions so that the responses to be included and excluded are enumerated.	Not included in a tantrum is a raised voice that is part of excitement while watching TV or playing a game or an initial expression of disappointment when a request (e.g., staying up later for bedtime) is denied. A statement of disappointment that lasts less than a minute without the behaviors noted in the example of clarity (above) is not a tantrum for present purposes.

Note: These are critical assessment requirements for direct observations introduced by Hawkins and Dobes (1977).

(Wong et al., 1987). Self-talk was defined as any vocalization not directed at another person but excluding sounds associated with physiological functions such as coughing. In another report, the assessment focused on academic behaviors for children with learning disabilities including delays in speech, language, and motor skills (Athens, Vollmer, & Pipkin, 2007). The duration of performance was assessed as children performed various tasks (e.g., writing sentences, tracing letters). Performance on the tasks did not count as beginning until after 3 seconds had elapsed. Then the time was recorded. Performance still counted as working if they paused for less than 3 seconds at any time. This allowed for the children to switch papers, erase what they had written, or just to pause. In a study with a 7-year-old child with autism, the goal was to reduce aberrant vocalizations that made him stand out in social interactions and contributed to his not being integrated into a regular education classroom (Pasiali, 2004). Aberrant vocalizations were defined as noises, words, or phrases without specific content or meaning. These were all tallied during dinnertime and used to reflect the effect of the intervention. Finally, in a program for veterans with problems of substance abuse and at least one other psychiatric disorder, one of the goals was to reduce illicit drug use. Abstinence from drugs was defined as a negative result on urine tests provided twice a week (Drebing et al., 2005).

The examples convey the specificity needed to conduct the observations. The specificity maximizes the reliability in observing and coding the behaviors. As observations are conducted, difficult-to-score examples may emerge, and these may be used to make more precise what is and is not to be counted. A clear definition does not eliminate judgments but allows a way to codify these judgments so that they are made relatively consistently.

MEASUREMENT GUIDELINES AND CONSIDERATIONS

Single-case and between-group designs share core features of scientific methods, but many of their procedures are quite different. Assessment is one feature. A useful way to remember the difference is that between-group research usually uses *many subjects and few measurement occasions* (e.g., pre and post), whereas single-case research *uses few subjects and many measurement occasions*. The statement is wonderfully useful and clear, and I would place it on the ceiling of my bedroom if it were not for the fact that it is not quite right. There are so many permutations of between-group and single-case research that the general statement, while often true, is not invariably true. Also, later in this chapter, I mention a few assessment occasions (characteristics of between-group research) that are very useful to integrate into single-case research.

In single-case designs, at least one measure is needed that will allow evaluation of performance over time in an ongoing way. Ongoing assessment is critical to the logic of single-case designs and to the methods for data evaluation, all elaborated in later chapters. Often, more than one measure will be used in a single-case design. Not every measure of interest to the investigator has to be administered in an ongoing way, but generally speaking at least one does. In this section, it is important to clarify key requirements for the primary measure, that is, the main measure that will meet the requirements of the designs. Additional measures, rationale for their use, and timing of their administration are covered separately.

Assessment Requirements for Single-Case Designs

The measure used to evaluate performance and meet the design and data-evaluation requirements of single-case designs must have several characteristics, highlighted in Table 3.2. First, the measure will need to be *administered repeatedly*, that is, on an ongoing basis over time. This means the measure will be administered or collected daily or several times a week. The collection will be over a period before the intervention is implemented (baseline observations) and then again while the intervention is in effect.

Table 3.2 Measurement Guidelines and Considerations: For Single-Case Designs Select Instruments to Evaluate the Intervention that Include These Characteristics

Characteristic of the Measure	Defined
Administered repeatedly	The measure is one that can be administered continuously over time (e.g., daily or several times a week).
Consistency of measurement	Observers or data collection procedures should have minimal error in obtaining the information.
Capacity to reflect change	If the intervention is effective, the measure must be able to show that. This is a function of how the construct is defined and the way in which it is observed.
Dimensional scale	Measures should reflect a continuous dimension or scale rather than a binary category (yes, no; completed not completed) whenever possible.
Relevance of the measure	The measure ought to assess the problem directly or domain of interest or some facet known to be highly correlated with that domain.
Importance of the measure	The construct or domain that is measured ought to make a difference and serve as one that the client or others see as important to functioning in everyday life.

Second, *behaviors or other domains that are assessed must be able to be observed consistently* (reliably). This has to do with the clarity of the definitions of what is observed and the ability of the observers to invoke these definitions consistently. Consistency of measurement is also referred to as reliability. Error or fluctuations in day-to-day measurement as a result of inconsistencies in the measure can interfere with drawing inferences about change and about what caused change (a threat to data-evaluation validity). More is said about reliability and procedures for its evaluation in Chapter 5.

Third, *the measure must be able to reflect change.* If the intervention is effective, will this particular measure be able to show that? The answer may depend on the definition of the behaviors but also on the assessment strategy. A teacher may count the number of 1-hour periods (out of a total of three) in which a child exhibited serious aggressive behavior (e.g., through throwing objects at the teacher or at other children, hitting someone, breaking something). Any hour in which one of these behaviors occurs is marked as an aggressive period, and we graph the number (or percentage) of periods each day with aggression. The measure is not likely to be very good in reflecting change. We do not get to see whether the child went from 100 to just 1 episode of aggression in any 1-hour period—both of these would count as an aggressive period. Also, we might see the number of aggressive periods go from three to two—not a clear change or not a change likely to meet design and data-analytic requirements noted in later chapters. So much aggression would be hidden by these numbers since so many acts could have occurred within a given period. Also, the insensitivity of the measure (scale with a small range) will make it difficult to detect change.

Reflecting change raises the notion of ceiling and floor effects. *Ceiling* and *floor effects* refer to the fact that change in the measure may reach an upper and lower limit, respectively, and that further change cannot be demonstrated because of that limit. There must be room on the measure that allows for evidence of change in the intended direction. If the goal is to improve some skill or to decrease some problem behavior, there must be room on the scale to show movement in that direction. Sometimes this is easy—if the individual never engages in a behavior (e.g., exercise, leisure reading in methodology and statistics), then baseline observations will be zero, and there is great room for improvement. Detecting change is a precondition to identifying what caused the change, so the measure must allow room for change in the direction the intervention is likely to promote.[1] Sometimes an investigator may wish to compare two or more interventions within the same client; here ceiling or floor effects are quite possible. After one intervention leads to change, it may be

---

[1] Ceiling and floor effects are not merely matters of the numerical scale. For example, if the measure ranges from 1 to 50 and performance goes from a mean of 30 during the baseline (no-intervention) phase to a mean of 40 during the intervention phase, it looks like there is still room for further change on the scale and no ceiling effect. Change on a measure is not equally easy across its full scale. There can be a functional limit or a ceiling that is not easily detected even when the numerical upper limit is not approached. The change from 30 to 40 may be much easier than the change from 40 to 50 and no one, perhaps, ever received scores above 45. There could be a ceiling effect even though there appears to be room at the end of the scale. Prior research can be a helpful guide to identify whether the upper (or lower) limits of a measure have been approached.

more difficult for the second intervention to show much more change if the scale has a restricted range.

Fourth, whenever possible (which is almost always), measures should reflect *a continuous dimension or scale rather than a binary category*. This is related to but distinguishable from detecting change. A continuous dimension can range from some low number (e.g., 0) to some higher number on a continuum (e.g., 50). Percent of arithmetic problems solved correctly, number of minutes on an exercise bike, and number of pages read are all dimensions and reflect a range that can vary widely. The same constructs could be measured in a binary fashion (yes, no) by recording whether the person solved 70% of the problems correctly (yes, no each day), got on the exercise bike at all (yes, no), or sat down and read at least five pages (yes, no). Interventions are more easily evaluated when one can see a larger range than just 0 (no) to 1 (yes each day). It is easy to begin with a dimensional scale (e.g., 1–100) and later convert it to a categorical scale (did or did not meet some criterion [≥ 50 or ≤ 49, respectively]) rather than the other way around.

Often people in everyday life are primarily concerned with bottom-line, categorical events. A mother says her adolescent is developing gum problems and the dentist says the adolescent should brush her teeth at least once a day. The mother cares about the binary measure (brush, no brush) each day. From the standpoint of assessment, we will want to be sure our measure is addressing the problem. Yet from the standpoint of assessment and evaluation, we will want a continuous measure too and use that as our primary measure for evaluation. This might be tooth brushing behaviors and include a series of 10 activities or steps evaluated as occurring or not occurring each day so that a score of 10 is possible. In terms of intervention, breaking down the behavior into steps (a dimensional scale) can be very helpful too. More on various strategies for dimensional and categorical measures is presented in the next chapter. At this point, the recommmendation is clear: assess dimensions whenever possible or develop scales that can vary from 0 or 1 to a larger number because these measures can more readily reflect intervention effects than can categorical, binary measures.

Fifth, the measure must be *relevant to the ultimate focus or interest*. This sounds so obvious that there must be a good reason to make this explicit. There is. Huge swaths of interventions in psychology, education, and counseling focus on constructs that are assumed to be a means to an end. Interventions are directed toward these means, but the means are not very relevant. Some examples are programs in schools, wilderness camps, and some institutions that focus on self-esteem and feelings of self-worth as a way of reducing risky behavior, aggressive actions, or eating problems. Similarly, self-help and other programs directed to improve child-rearing practices of parents often emphasize feelings of parental empowerment. Self-esteem and empowerment might be useful as targets of treatment, but they are not very relevant to the goals (reducing the problem behaviors, improving parenting) for which they are often posed. The reason is that key concepts here are not causally connected to the goals of the program—improving self-esteem may be wonderful in its own right, but it is not established as relevant to changing aggressive behavior. I shall return to this in the discussion of validity later in this chapter.

Finally, the focus of the measure is to *make a difference or be important to the client or to others*. Importance and relevance, the requirement noted previously, are different.

Relevance has to do with ensuring that the measure reflects the construct or domain of interest—if we care about changing tics in an adult, focus on tics, not on how one feels about tics, although both would be quite fine to include. Feelings may be important and, indeed, some of my best friends report having them, but the issue is: What are we trying to accomplish in a given project, and how does the measure relate to that goal? In some cases, feelings might be the focus (e.g., happiness, experience of pain) and direct observations may be ancillary or complementary.

To capture importance of the focus, we ask the question, "Why do we care about this domain or measure?" Often the examples are obvious (self-destructive behavior, driving while intoxicated, not completing homework, defacing books on methodology). Yet, in everyday life, parents and teachers often are concerned with problems that are mainly annoying and temporary (e.g., adolescents overusing words "cool," or "like"; wearing odd but allowable combinations of clothing or having red, spiked hair). In research as well as in everyday life, it is not always obvious that a measure is important or will make a difference.

Relevance and importance, as key considerations in selecting measures, are based on an assumption that the single-case demonstration will have an applied purpose. That is, the demonstration focuses on individuals who have been identified based on the criteria mentioned earlier in the chapter and who would profit from some intervention. Consequently, the measure that will be used has relevance and importance as critical criteria. Single-case designs are also used in the context of experimental work and animal laboratory research. In such cases, of course, the goal is to test theoretical hypotheses or to describe some process. Measures are needed that can reflect change, but are not restricted by the applied concerns noted in the present discussion.

The six characteristics of measures (Table 3.2) are central for single-case research in applied settings. There are other considerations in deciding what measure to use, such as the ease and cost of administration and interpretability to consumers of our work, including clients and the public at large. These are important but less central for the moment in conveying design requirements for the methodology of single-case designs. Assessment and design are very much intertwined, and the characteristics noted here are pivotal for evaluating performance over time, that is, on multiple assessment occasions so that change can be detected and so that patterns in the data, required for the various designs, can be discerned, as elaborated in the design and data-evaluation chapters.

Use of Multiple Measures

In any investigation, single-case or otherwise, there is no need to rely on one measure. Also, the primary measure used to meet the design requirements ought to be administered in an ongoing basis, but not all measures need to be. Consider the use of additional measures and how they can be administered.

Several arguments favor the use of multiple measures when possible. First, it is rare that any single measure captures the construct completely. Indeed, operational definitions translate concepts into specific measures or indices, but by their very nature can omit key components. One could readily translate signs of love between a couple into acts or gestures of affection (e.g., smiles, holding hands, touching each other affectionately, and saying "I love you") and all would be reasonable components of a measure that operationalizes love. Yet, there is more, including the subjective feelings of each person, and less obvious, the neurobiology and brain activation (through neuroimaging) that characterizes romantic love. Clearly there is no one measure of operationalizing love that can encompass all of these features. Similarly, an intervention may focus on pain reduction for someone recovering from an injury. Activity, walking, and not grimacing have been used to operationalize pain. Here too, we would want some subjective evaluation by the patient as a supplementary but critically important measure.

Second, the nature of many problems encompasses multiple facets. One might increase reading or number of pages read, but reading may have more components, such as comprehension, enjoyment of reading, and speaking to others about what one has read. These latter indices may not be the primary focus, but they are relevant and potentially important outcomes. Similarly, depression among clinical samples is not merely a matter of sad mood, but rather a package of behaviors, activities, and views (e.g., changes in appetite, loss of interest in activities, negative thoughts). Multiple measures using varied methods are likely to capture and encompass more of the domain.

Third, multiple perspectives are often pertinent. We might want to know if parents, teachers, peers, or the clients themselves believe there is a difference or change and whether that change was very important. Agreement among different informants or raters in social, emotional, and behavioral problems is notoriously low (Achenbach, 2006; De Los Reyes & Kazdin, 2005). For example, when child deviant behavior (tantrums, aggressiveness, shyness) is measured by child, parent, or teacher report, the results yield somewhat different information. Conclusions vary as a function of which informant is used to provide the measure of deviance of the child. Sometimes it may be important to capture the different perspectives.

Fourth, beyond perspectives of different informants, different methods often yield different information. Self-report or parent report, records of performance (e.g., truancy, missed classes, arrests), and direct observations can yield different conclusions even when they are designed to assess the same construct. For example, self-reports of ethnic bias or prejudice, laboratory tasks that ask or subtly assess bias, and actual behaviors in everyday encounters that reflect bias can yield different results. Because the method of assessment can influence conclusions, use of multiple measures is useful. One can "replicate" the effect across measures and show the extent to which a finding is or is not dependent on one method of assessment.

Fifth, interventions, even when they are focused on specific problem domains, in fact often produce a spread of effect that would be important to know or establish. For example, in my own work with children referred for aggressive and antisocial behavior, our intervention focuses on reducing these behaviors at home, at school, and in the community. We also have shown that parental depression and stress decrease, and family relationships improve over the course of treatment, even though these are not our focus (e.g., Kazdin & Wassell, 2000). We assess these because both relate to child-rearing practices. Parental depression and stress in the home can influence child-rearing practices (e.g., harsh parental reactions, attention to more deviant behavior, commands) that help promote child oppositional behavior. Favorable side effects along these dimensions are informative and important to identify.

Whether and when to use multiple measures depend on many considerations, some substantive (e.g., Are there multiple outcomes of interest?), some methodological (e.g., Could the results be confined to one method of assessment?), and some practical (e.g., Are resources available to carry out or administer, code, and evaluate multiple measures?). Often the case can be made that one is interested in one measure or that a domain is well represented by one measure. The comments here are intended to focus on the other side. One should not automatically assume that a single measure is sufficient, adequate, or the most informative. Multiple measures can improve the demonstration by showing that the effects are not restricted to a single way of evaluating the target focus. Also, intervention effects are rarely surgical, that is, narrowly specific to the target focus. Multiple measures can evaluate the spread of effects to other areas that may be related and of interest but not directly focused on. The importance of this latter point is evident in research on medication in which the main outcome is whether the clinical problem (cancer, blood pressure) is altered. However, multiple measures of outcome (immediate change in symptoms, survival) and of other domains or side effects (e.g., impact on memory and other cognitive processes) enrich the evaluation and may actually determine if anyone uses the medication.

When to Administer These Additional Measures

Pre–Post Assessment. As long as there is a primary outcome measure that is continuous and ongoing, other measures do not have to be. It may be the case that the investigator wishes to administer a test of some domain at pre and post, merely two occasions. This is the common strategy in between-group research (e.g., randomized controlled trials) where the primary measures are not ongoing or continuous over time. I shall not illustrate pre- and post-intervention measures; these are central to between-group research and probably very familiar.

In single-case research, the primary measure may be collected daily (e.g., cigarettes smoked, homework completed, delinquent acts in the setting). At the end of the study or periodically within the study, the investigator may include other measures (e.g., subjective feelings of health, teacher report of grades, arrest records). These supplementary measures can be extraordinarily useful and informative even though assessment on one or two occasions would not meet the essential features of the designs.

For example, a class-wide program was used in a child-care setting with 16 children ages 3 to 5 (Hanley et al., 2007). The focus was on various social skills related to their adjustment in class (e.g., communicating their wishes, following directions, and more). Such skills were identified by educators as being critical to school readiness and success. Training with the children was evaluated by ongoing assessment of the skills. In addition, a pre–post assessment was added. At the beginning and end of the program, teachers completed a questionnaire for 14 of the 16 children and rated the likelihood that each child would engage in the prosocial behaviors in diverse situations. The results indicated that 11 children greatly improved from pre to post; 3 did not, with an overall difference from pre to post that was statistically significant. What have we learned from this added assessment? Teachers believed that there were changes in the children based on what they saw before and after treatment. Could this be due to testing or statistical regression (two threats to validity)? Yes, but teacher reports were in keeping with the ongoing observational data that showed changes in the skills. On these latter measures, these threats to validity are implausible. The changes on observational and teacher report measures are parsimoniously and plausibly explained by the intervention effect.

Teacher perspectives are very important as a complement to the direct observational data. One can readily imagine a situation where student behavior change occurs but the teachers do not perceive a change. In such a case, it is possible that the changes were weak or not evident in a classroom. Also, it is easy to imagine teachers believing there is a change (because of expectations) where direct observations show there is no change. It is more reassuring when change is reflected on both types of measures.

Periodic Probes During the Study. Apart from pre and post examples, single-case designs often use periodic assessment to measure how performance is in settings other than those in which intervention is conducted or in relation to responses other than those included in the intervention program. For example, an intervention may focus on child behavior in the classroom. The measure may be ongoing to meet the requirements of the design; yet the investigator may take periodic samples of behavior on the playground to see if the behavior has changed there as well. The measures administered in this way are called probes. A *probe* is an assessment administered occasionally during a single-case investigation. Usually the purpose of the probe is to see whether the behavior carries over to another setting, is maintained over time, or whether another behavior has changed. These measures are not administered on a continuous basis. Rather they may only be administered a few times during or after the intervention phase.

For example, in one study, four children with autism (ages 5 to 6) were trained to give helping responses after instructions from an experimenter (Reeve et al., 2007). Helping behaviors were grouped into several categories based on interviews of the parents about areas to train. The categories included cleaning, picking up objects, sorting materials, putting objects away, and others, each with different behaviors. Although we might be interested in teaching helping behavior in specific categories, the larger interest is teaching a more general repertoire, that is, helping that extends to areas that are not trained. During training, probe assessments were used to evaluate whether the children increased in helping behaviors in categories that were not trained. Indeed, they did. Before the study, little helping behavior was evident. This increased greatly during training (in a multiple-baseline design). The probe assessments showed that the results extended to areas of helping that were not trained specifically.

Another program focused on teaching skills to prevent sexual abuse among persons with mental retardation (Lumley, Miltenberger, Long, Rapp, & Roberts, 1998). Female adolescents with mental retardation are often victims of sexual abuse. Rates of sexual abuse (attempted and coerced intercourse) have ranged from 25% to 80% in different samples. In this project, six women (ages 30 to 42) with varying degrees of disability were trained to refuse requests, leave the situation, report the incident, and other such behaviors in role-playing situations. In training sessions, several situations were presented, the client was asked what she would do, and a score was assigned to the appropriateness of the response. Training was administered in sessions by a male and female trainer and involved instructions, modeling appropriate responses, rehearsal, praise, feedback, and practice.

Probes were used to assess whether the behaviors would carry over beyond training sessions, raising a delicate ethical dilemma (but approved by the Institutional Review Committee of the university). Probes consisted of someone working for the project who approached the client, made conversation for 15 minutes, and inappropriately made a sexual advance (with a prearranged request) to see what the client would do. The probe interactions were audiotaped. The results: training developed the refusal and avoidance skills very well in the sessions. Probe assessments under more naturalistic conditions did not reflect the effects of training. Probes provided critical information. Training did not do what was needed—more is needed to protect these women once they are in naturalistic situations.

These examples illustrate the utility of assessments that go beyond the main measure that is required for the designs. Periodic assessments and assessment of domains of interest can provide very important supplementary information about the scope of the changes, their impact, and indeed their value. The importance of the multiple assessments becomes even more evident in the discussion of validity in the next section.

RELIABILITY AND VALIDITY

In all scientific measurement, reliability and validity are key concepts. Generally, *reliability* refers to the consistency of the measure or measurement procedure. *Validity* refers to the content of the measure and whether the measure assesses the domain of interest. In psychology, evaluation of reliability and validity has focused on a variety of measures, but has focused most often on paper-and-pencil questionnaires, rating scales, and other tests covering an almost endless list of domains of functioning (e.g., personality, motivation, achievement, intelligence, anxiety, depression, marital satisfaction, coping style, quality of life). In this more traditional assessment focus, several different types of reliability and validity have been identified and are used to establish the individual measures. Commonly designated forms of reliability and validity for traditional assessment are in an appendix at the end of this chapter as a point of reference and to make a connection with single-case designs. The discussion highlights key concepts as they relate to assessments usually conducted in single-case research.

Reliability of Observational Measures

Typically, assessment in single-case designs focuses on direct observation of overt behavior. However, this is not a necessary requirement for the designs, as noted further in the next chapter. Measures are devised to assess a target behavior, as already discussed. An advantage is that measures are often individualized to each client and situation so that there is not a "tantrum" scale or "academic deficiency" scale. The measure for a child referred for tantrums or academic deficiency may be individually tailored, as needed. In assessing behavior, the key reliability question is whether the observations are obtained consistently. Consistency here does not mean, "Does the subject perform consistently?" That is another matter and not what is meant by reliability of measurement. Rather, it means, "To what extent do observers looking at the client record in a consistent fashion?" In relation to the types of reliability listed in the appendix, this is interrater or interobserver agreement. We want consistent assessment—that is, we want the assessment not to be a function of who is doing the observing, but rather who is being observed (the client).

There are normal fluctuations in human performance, so even if there is perfectly consistent assessment, there will be variability in performance. Any inconsistencies in measurement will add to that variability in another way. In general, a research goal is to minimize variability that has to do with extraneous features of the test. (In fact, the nasty word "error" is often used to label all sources of variability that the investigator does not really want to analyze but does want to minimize.) Variability is minimized to facilitate evaluation of the intervention effects. As I discuss later in relation to the logic of designs and data evaluation, excessive variability can interfere and obscure veridical intervention effects in both between-group and single-case research.

Interobserver agreement is a major topic within single-case research. Researchers go to great lengths to ensure that the behaviors are well defined, the observation method is well described, and the measures can be obtained consistently. The significance of the topic, how agreement is measured across different types of measures, and sources of bias and artifact in the measurement procedures serve as a basis for a separate discussion (Chapter 5).

Validity of Single-case Measures

The extent to which a measure assesses the construct of interest is the overall focus of validity. Decades ago, when direct observations were coming into widespread use, the dominant view was that one need not be concerned with validity. The usual types of validity (see the appendix) seemed relevant to the psychological measures such as various scales, inventories, and tasks. For example, when one wants to evaluate intelligence with a measure (intelligence tests), it makes great sense to ask about validity, that is, whether the measure relates to performance beyond performance on the test. And we have learned with decades of research that intelligence test performance relates very highly to academic performance (concurrent and predictive validity), that is, is a valid measure of that performance. All this is going on while there is a tsunami of debates about what intelligence really is, the many types of intelligence, and whether any particular measure captures all that is intended. Behavioral observations were thought to be free from, or at least much less subject to, this kind of validity concern because the performance in situ is being observed directly. That is, we do not have to ask about the extent to which a given measure really gets at the child's bullying or tantrums. Behavioral measures are not a questionnaire or paper-and-pencil measure—they sample the bullying or tantrums directly on the battlefields (school and home).

This view has changed in light of deeper appreciation of assessment in general and the special features of direct observations. Five points convey the issue. First, any single measure does not usually capture all of the domains of interest. Thus an operational definition of something like bullying, tantrums, positive family interaction, and compulsive behavior may be a great reflection of the domain, but it is not the entire domain. The investigator and consumer might be concerned with all sorts of related behaviors that are outside of the operational definition. Are all the behaviors of the domain well represented by the operational definition? That is a validity question. In relation to traditional assessment of validity several types of validity (content, concurrent, face, and convergent) address the relation of a given measure of the domain of interest to other samples of behavior from that same or related domains.

Second, behavioral assessments and observations are usually limited to specific situations such as specific times of the day, tasks or situations that are relatively unvarying, and so on. The investigator often tries to control the assessment conditions to ensure that client behavior does not fluctuate widely because of changing conditions. Insofar as the situation is structured or controlled, one can raise the question, "Do the observations reflect performance under slightly less structured or totally unstructured situations or more 'normal' conditions of everyday life?" That too is a validity question. Here traditional types of validity (e.g., concurrent, predictive) focus on the extent to which the performance on the measure relates to performance on other indices either now or at some point in the future.

Third, let us go back to the measure itself. Is the measure getting at the domain or a behavior that is very important? Sometimes this is obvious because the intervention is designed to overcome a significant condition that impairs performance. Yet, sometimes the focus is less clear. To what extent does this measure get at or assess something that is important and that we ought to care about? This is a validity question—in this case social validity. Social comparison and subjective evaluation (discussed previously) are designed to address this concern.

Fourth, observational measures are completed by humans, and the filter of human perception has been very well elaborated. Various filtering processes (e.g., cognition, perceptions, and beliefs) are not artifacts of human observation; they are built into our hardware (brain), our software (learning, experience), and their interactions. Even with reliability that is established among observers, there can be beliefs that influence behavioral observations. For example, observation of family interaction revealed that the ethnicity of the observers was influenced by the ethnicity of the families that were being observed (Yasui & Dishion, 2008). European American raters viewed African American mothers as showing fewer problem-solving skills and poorer relations with their children than they did in their ratings of European American mothers. African American raters did not show this difference. Moreover, independent evaluations revealed that there were no differences in the families being rated. The study conveys that under some circumstances ethnic bias can influence the observations. The measure on which the results were obtained was observing direct interactions for a brief period and then completing ratings. This is standard in the area of research (family interaction) but not quite the direct observational procedures usually used where concrete behaviors are coded. Even so, when human judgment is involved, core features of judgment (e.g., perceptions, bias) can be expected.

Finally, the observational measure may reflect change. However, do the changes make any difference to the clients or to those who are in contact with the clients (e.g., parents, teachers, and peers at work)? Assume that the intervention is effective and made a change in some important behavior (e.g., stuttering), physical condition (e.g., weight, blood pressure), or habit (e.g., cigarette smoking). Now we can ask, "Was the magnitude of change of the order that makes any real difference?" Sometimes the answer can be addressed easily if the measure (e.g., weight, blood pressure, blood sugar, exercise) can be connected to well-established correlates (e.g., risk for heart attack). That is, we can sometimes assess the value of the change by knowing what the outcome means in other terms. Another situation is one in which a particular behavior that is problematic (e.g., panic attacks, fighting, abusing one's child) is completely eliminated.

No one usually asks, "Yes, but getting the parent to stop brutalizing the child—is that really an important outcome?"

More often than not, behavioral measures do not have clear correlates that facilitate interpretation of the magnitude of the change as in some health outcome. Also, the behavior may not be eliminated or indeed even need to be eliminated. In these circumstances, it is appropriate and important to ask the question, "Does the amount of change make a difference?" This too is a question of social validity. Social comparison and subjective evaluation are very pertinent.

Are there cases where the validity of measures could be questioned, or are all of these concerns merely straw men and women? Yes—in the move from the goal of a program to measurement and intervention, occasionally the validity and relevance of the measure can be challenged. For example, consider a program that is designed to reduce the weight of clients who are grossly obese (defined as overweight $\geq$ 100 lbs [45.36 kg]). In such a program, the goal may be to increase the amount of exercise (e.g., minutes walking or jogging). Exercising is not a direct measure of weight, and one can increase exercise without any change in weight. Even calorie consumption is not a direct index because one can reduce calories and still show little or no weight loss (due to change in metabolism). Needless to say, exercise is important and calorie consumption is relevant, but weight or body mass probably is the measure of interest and ought to be included in the assessment in some way, even if not the primary measure that is assessed daily to meet the requirements of the design.

As I noted, sometimes the measures are obviously important insofar as they sample the domain of interest. Even so, it is useful to ask if the measure and the magnitude of change on the measure over the course of the intervention reflect the domain in contexts that are different from those in which the observations are obtained and make a difference either to the clients or those in contact with them. These are slightly different questions from those in relation to traditional validity (see appendix) but are captured well by social validity.

Reliability and validity are central to all measures. Consistency of observation is fundamental to experimental design and data evaluation and is discussed again in those contexts. Validity is more multifaceted and requires greater effort and attention. The reason is that often direct observations are assumed to be the "real thing" and not removed from the actual domain of interest. Even when the direct behaviors are clearly of interest, they may not reflect those same behaviors outside of the carefully controlled program situation, as evident in the discussion of probes. The use of multiple measures, probes, and social validation techniques are aimed to address the validity of the measures, and we shall see samples of that throughout later chapters.

SUMMARY AND CONCLUSIONS

In this chapter, fundamental issues were discussed that pertain to selecting the focus of the intervention and therefore the assessments. Identification of the focus of assessment is often obvious because of the setting and its goals (e.g., education in the schools, rehabilitation of substance abusers) and the nature of the client's problem (e.g., severe deficits or excesses in performance). Several other criteria were discussed including social, emotional, cognitive, or behavior characteristics that reflect impairment (e.g., illegal or rule-breaking behavior, actions that are of danger to oneself or to others, or the behaviors at risk for untoward outcomes, signs of stress, or unusual or extreme symptoms of clinical dysfunction). Behaviors that are not that severe but are of concerns to others (e.g., parents, teachers) or that may prevent the onset of untoward problems also serve as the basis for intervening.

Social validity was introduced to convey other criteria that are pertinent to selection of the target focus. *Social comparison* consists of identifying target behaviors based on normative data that convey what is accepted or common in everyday life. *Subjective evaluation* is used to examine whether the focus is one that makes a difference in the opinions of experts or those in contact with the client. In this chapter we focused on selection of target behaviors. Social comparison and subjective evaluation are also used in evaluating change. We return to these topics in the discussion of data analyses and evaluation.

When direct observations of behaviors are used as the assessment focus, it is important that the definition of the behaviors meet three criteria: *objectivity*, *clarity*, and *completeness*. To meet these criteria not only requires explicit definitions, but also decision rules about what does and does not constitute performance of the target behavior. The extent to which definitions of behavior meet these criteria determines whether the observations are obtained consistently and, indeed, whether they can be obtained at all. These criteria help reduce error (variability) in the measure that is due to the assessment procedures and in that way can increase the sensitivity of detecting changes in performance.

Several measurement requirements were noted for single-case designs. Measures need to be administered repeatedly, should be administered consistently (reliably), be able to reflect change, reflect a continuous dimension or scale rather than a binary category when possible, and the focus or what is measured ought to be relevant to the ultimate focus or goal of the program. A unique feature of single-case designs is the use of *ongoing, continuous assessment*. Many different measures can be used in a given study. At least one of these ought to meet the requirements mentioned previously because these are central to single-case designs and data evaluation. However, other measures (e.g., at pre- and post-intervention or probes) can supplement and do not have to be administered in an ongoing way.

Reliability and validity were discussed. Both are topics of assessment in research in general but have special facets that pertain to single-case research in the context of direct observations of behavior. Consistency of measurement is critical for evaluation in part to minimize variability in the data due to observers and observational procedures. A careful definition of the target behavior is the starting point for consistent observations, but many more issues are involved and taken up in a later chapter. Validity of the measure cannot invariably be assumed. The measure may obviously sample the domain of interest, but obviousness is not equivalent to having data to show that the measure is relevant, makes a difference, and that changes on the measure are important. Social validity indices are often used to address these latter concerns.

This chapter focused on critical considerations of assessment for single-case designs. Determining the focus, defining the target behavior, and using a measure that will meet the special requirements of single-case designs are key features. Ensuring that the measure can be obtained consistently and that the measure is sampling the domain of interest and makes a difference too are fundamental features. The next step is to move to specific procedures and techniques for assessment, the topic of the next chapter.

APPENDIX 3.1

COMMONLY REFERRED TO TYPES OF RELIABILITY AND VALIDITY

Type	Definition and/or Concept
Reliability	
Test–Retest Reliability	The stability of test scores over time; the correlation of scores from one administration of the test with the scores on the same instrument after a particular time interval has elapsed.
Alternative-Form Reliability	The correlation between different forms of the same measure. The items of the two forms are considered to represent the population of items for that measure.
Internal Consistency	The degree of consistency or homogeneity of the items within a scale. Different reliability measures are used toward this end, such as split-half reliability, Kuder–Richardson Formula 20, and coefficient alpha.
Interrater (or interscorer) Reliability	The extent to which different assessors, raters, or observers agree on the scores they provide when assessing, coding, or classifying subjects' performance. Different measures are used to evaluate agreement such as percent agreement, Pearson product-moment correlations, and kappa.
Validity	
Construct Validity	A broad concept that refers to the extent to which the measure reflects the construct (concept, domain) of interest. Other types of validity and other evidence that elaborates the correlates of the measure are relevant to construct validity. Construct validity focuses on the relation of a measure to other measures and domains of functioning of which the concept underlying the measure may be a part.
Content Validity	Evidence that the content of the items reflects the construct or domain of interest. The relation of the items to the concept underlying the measure.
Concurrent Validity	The correlation of a measure with performance on another measure or criterion at the same point in time.
Predictive Validity	The correlation of a measure at one point in time with performance on another measure or criterion at some point in the future.
Criterion Validity	Correlation of a measure with some other criterion. This can encompass concurrent or predictive validity. In addition, the notion is occasionally used in relation to a specific and often dichotomous criterion when performance on the measure is evaluated in relation to disorders (e.g., depressed vs. nondepressed patients) or status (e.g., prisoners vs. nonprisoners).

Continued

Appendix 3.1 continued

Type	Definition and/or Concept
Face Validity	This refers to the extent to which a measure appears to assess the construct of interest. Not regarded as a formal type of validation or part of the psychometric development or evaluation of a measure.
Convergent Validity	The extent to which two measures assess the similar or related constructs. The validity of a given measure is suggested if the measure correlates with other measures with which it is expected to correlate. The correlation between the measures is expected based on the overlap or relation of the constructs. This is a variation of concurrent validity but takes on special meaning in relation to discriminant validity.
Discriminant Validity	The correlation between measures that are expected not to relate to each other or to assess dissimilar and unrelated constructs. The validity of a given measure is suggested if the measure shows little or no correlation with measures with which it is expected not to correlate. The absence of correlation is expected based on the separate and conceptually distinct constructs. This is especially meaningful in a demonstration that also examines convergent validity.

Note: The types of reliability and validity presented here refer to commonly used terms in test construction and validation and in the context of between-group research. They are broadly relevant to measurement and sensitize the researcher to multiple considerations about what will be used to reflect the outcomes of a study.

CHAPTER 4

Methods of Assessment

Assessment of performance in single-case research has encompassed an extraordinarily wide range of measures and procedures that meet the requirements discussed in the previous chapter. Most measures are based on directly observing overt performance. When overt behaviors are observed directly, a major issue is selecting the measurement strategy. Although observation of overt behavior constitutes the vast bulk of assessment in single-case research, other assessment strategies are used, such as psychophysiological assessment, rating scales, and other measures unique to specific target behaviors. This chapter describes and illustrates several measurement options for single-case designs. Emphasis is given to measures of overt behavior because these have been commonly used in single-case research. In addition, overt behavioral measures are less well covered in traditional texts or other resources on assessment. The chapter samples other types of measures rather than covering them comprehensively. The reason is that any assessment modality, method, or format can be used in single-case designs as long as the requirements (e.g., ongoing assessment) mentioned in the previous chapter are met.

STRATEGIES OF ASSESSMENT

Perhaps the most significant point of departure for assessment is to convey that single-case designs do not necessarily entail any particular assessment modality. Rating scales completed by individuals or others, measures of biological processes or outcomes (e.g., blood pressure, breathing rate), automated responding (e.g., movements), and more all are suitable for the designs. The de facto connection of designs with behavioral research has underscored their connection to direct measures of overt behavior, but examples can be provided to convey that the connection is not required. And perhaps the diffusion of single-case designs into many disciplines and areas of work accounts for the expansion to measures that are less committed to direct observations of overt behavior. At the same time, direct behavioral measures have not been selected arbitrarily. They provide direct measures of many domains of interest in applied settings and warrant the bulk of the attention of the present chapter.

Measures of Overt Behavior

Assessment of overt behavior can be accomplished in different ways. In most programs, behaviors are assessed on the basis of discrete response occurrences or the amount of time that the response occurs. However, several variations and different types of measures are available.

Frequency Measures. Frequency counts require simply tallying the number of times the behavior occurs in a given period of time. A measure of the frequency of the response is particularly useful when the target response is discrete and each instance takes a relatively constant amount of time. A discrete response has a clearly delineated beginning and end so that separate instances of the response can be counted. The performance of the behavior should take a relatively constant amount of time so that the units counted are approximately equal. Ongoing behaviors, such as smiling, sitting in one's seat, reading, lying down, and talking, are difficult to record simply by counting because each response may occur for different amounts of time. For example, if a person talks to a peer for 15 seconds and to another peer for 30 minutes, these might be counted as two instances of talking. A great deal of information is lost by simply counting instances of talking, because they differ in duration.

Frequency measures have been used for a variety of behaviors. For example, a program designed to increase the daily productivity of writers of fiction used word count (automatically counted by software on a document file) to measure how much writing was completed each day (Porritt, Burt, & Poling, 2006). Another study evaluated children's compliance to instructions at home and at school (Tarbox, Wallace, Penrod, & Tarbox, 2007). The number of times the child complied (completed the request within two instructions to do so) was simply counted. In another example, a feeding program was provided for a 4-year-old child hospitalized because he could not eat and swallow food (Girolami, Boscoe, & Roscoe, 2007). His food consumption had been restricted to tube feeding placed in his stomach. During the intervention he was fed spoonfuls of food. Each spoonful was a "trial," that is, an opportunity to take the food and swallow. The measure was food expulsion and consisted of expelling the food (visible outside his mouth) after each spoonful. That is, the number of times he expelled food after feeding was counted. There are additional examples of discrete behaviors that can be easily assessed with frequency counts such as the number of times a person attends an activity, says hello or greets someone, assaults another person, throws an object at another person, uses special vocabulary words in speaking or writing, or makes errors of one kind or another (on the job, in school performance).

The examples convey two ways frequency measures are used. One is a situation in which the behavior is free to occur on multiple occasions, that is, there is no fixed limit in the number of times the behavior could occur. For example, how often one child hits another may be measured by frequency counts. How many times the behavior (hitting) may occur has no theoretical limit. The other is a situation in which the opportunities are restricted because of specific discrete trials or in response to stimuli that are presented only a specific number of times. For example, if the child is greeted by the parent or teacher or given an instruction 10 times per day, the frequency of the child's response is restricted. The distinction is not critical, but it can be. If the opportunities are restricted, we want a large range to be possible (e.g., more than 10 opportunities) to permit evaluation of the base rate and to evaluate whether there is change, once an intervention is introduced. A very small range (e.g., two or three opportunities) might make evaluation of the intervention more difficult.

Frequency measures require merely noting instances in which behavior occurs. Usually there is an additional requirement that behavior be observed for a constant amount of time. Of course, if behavior is observed for 20 minutes on one day and 30 minutes on another day, the frequencies are not directly comparable. However, the *rate of response* can be obtained by dividing the frequency of responses by the number of minutes observed each day. This measure will yield frequency per minute or rate of response, which is comparable for different durations of observation. If the frequency measure is based on a fixed number of opportunities to perform the behavior, one can easily convert the frequency data to percentage of times the behavior occurred given all of the opportunities.

A frequency measure has several desirable features for use in applied settings. First, the frequency of a response is relatively simple to score for individuals working in everyday settings. Keeping a tally of the behavior is usually all that is required. Moreover, counting devices, such as wrist counters or calculators, including those on cell phones, are available to facilitate recording by pressing a button to keep the tally for a given observation period. Second, frequency measures readily reflect changes over time. Years of basic and applied research have shown that response frequency is sensitive to a variety of interventions. Third, frequency expresses the amount of behavior performed, which is usually of concern to individuals in applied settings. In many cases, the goal of the program is to increase or decrease the number of times a certain behavior occurs. Frequency provides a direct measure of the amount of behavior.

Discrete Categorization. Often it is very useful to classify responses into discrete categories, such as correct–incorrect, performed–not performed, or appropriate–inappropriate. In some ways, discrete categorization resembles a frequency measure because it is used for behaviors that have a clear beginning and end and a constant duration. Yet there are critical differences. First, with a frequency measure, performances of a particular behavior are tallied. The focus is on a single response (hitting, complying). In discrete categorization, several different behaviors may be included, and each is scored as having occurred or not. The behaviors go together in forming a larger unit or goal (e.g., all the steps related to getting ready for school in the morning or cleaning one's room or apartment). The constituent behaviors are all different. Second, frequency often has no real limit; the person may engage in that behavior (e.g., hitting, swearing) from zero to some higher and varying number. In discrete categorization, there is only a limited number of opportunities to perform the responses as defined by the total number of steps involved or number of component behaviors.

For example, discrete categorization might be used to measure the sloppiness of one's college roommate. To do this, a checklist can be devised that lists several *different* behaviors all related to sloppiness. These might include such items or tasks as putting away one's shoes in the closet, removing underwear from the kitchen table, putting dishes in the sink, putting food away in the refrigerator, and so on. Each morning (or some constant time each day), the behaviors on the checklist are observed; each one is *categorized* as performed or not performed. The total number (or percentage) of behaviors performed correctly constitutes the measure.

Discrete categories have been used to assess behavior in many applied programs. For example, one program focused on special education teachers who sought assistance in managing off-task and disruptive student behavior (e.g., refusing to do work, disruptive verbal statements) (DiGennaro, Martens, & Kleinmann, 2007). The procedures for managing these behaviors have been established for decades; the task is providing skills to teachers and ensuring that the skills are carried out correctly. Effective components of the program were identified and evaluated as performed or not performed correctly. Sample components included: explaining the program to the student, providing praise and stickers correctly, and providing the back-up reward when enough stickers were earned. This is a good example of multiple steps and each one scored as being performed or not performed correctly. The percentage of steps completed correctly (proportion of categories with "yes") was used to evaluate teacher performance.

Discrete categorization is readily adaptable to many different situations, especially related to completion of activities, skills, and other tasks that may include many different components. Cleaning one's room, being prepared for some activity, completing practice (e.g., music, athletic), and completing one's chores or other responsibilities are examples. In each case, the measure is made by defining the step and deciding what constitutes completed/performed or not completed/performed.

A unique feature of the method is noteworthy. The behaviors that form the list need not be related to one another or represent the flow (steps) of a single activity. Performance of one may not necessarily have anything to do with performance of another. For example, room-cleaning behaviors or a set of separate chores are not necessarily related or very similar; performing one correctly (making one's bed) may be unrelated to another (clearing away dishes). Hence, discrete categorization is a very flexible method of observation that allows one to assess all sorts of behaviors independently of whether they are necessarily related to each other. This is important because sometimes the goal of the program is not increasing the occurrence of a behavior (as in frequency counting) but rather developing execution of a task that has many different components, as in the examples noted here.

Number of People Who Perform the Behavior. Occasionally, the effectiveness of the intervention is evaluated on the basis of the number of people who perform the target response. Obviously, this measure is used in group situations such as a classroom, school, or community where the purpose is to increase the overall performance of a particular behavior, such as coming to an activity on time, completing homework, speaking up in a group, recycling waste materials, paying bills on time, and voting. Once the desired behavior is defined, observations consist of noting how many participants in the group have performed the response. As with frequency and categorization measures, the observations require classifying the response as having occurred or not. But here the *individuals* are counted rather than the number of times an individual performs the response.

Several programs have evaluated the impact of interventions on the number of people who are affected. For example, programs are often designed to improve driver safety and evaluate outcomes such as increasing the use of seat belts and decreasing the use of cell phones while driving, or driving in some other way to avoid accidents (e.g., Clayton, Helms, & Simpson, 2006; Van Houten, Malenfant, Zhao, Ko, & Van Houten, 2005). The number of people, cars, or drivers is the relevant metric. In these instances, there is no interest necessarily in the behavior of individuals, and indeed it would be difficult to track individual cars from one day to the next. The issue is one of changing most or all individuals, whoever they may be.

In other instances the identity of the individuals may be known, but still the number who engage in the outcome is of interest. For example, one program in a college class focused on the number (percentage) of students who submitted their homework assignments (Ryan & Hemmes, 2005). A point program was designed to increase assignment completion. One might make the case for a different focus. For example, in a class where the identity of everyone is known, perhaps the focus ought to shift to those individuals who can be identified and who do not turn in homework. However, number of individuals was quite useful in reflecting intervention effects.

Knowing the number of individuals who perform a response is very useful when the explicit goal of a program is to increase performance in a large group of subjects. Developing behaviors in an institution and in society at large is consistent with this overall goal. Increasing the number of people who exercise, give to charity, or seek treatment in early stages of serious diseases, and decreasing the number of people who smoke, overeat, speed as they drive through school zones, and commit crimes are all important goals. The number of people or some other unit (businesses, schools) that engage in behaviors or some other practice is of keen interest. Prominent examples pertain to climate change and promoting a sustainable environment where the goals might be to increase the number of people who carpool and who elect not to have their linens changed daily during a hotel stay (and thereby reduce energy use from laundering) or the number of homes that have at least one energy-efficient appliance and number of businesses in a community that engage in "green practices" (recycle, provide employee incentives for using public transportation). Hence, the number of people or number of other units (e.g., homes, classrooms) that perform a response is of great interest.

Interval Recording.   A frequent strategy of measuring behavior in an applied setting is to measure the behavior based on units of time rather than on discrete response units. Behavior is recorded during short periods of time for the total time that it is performed. The two main versions of time-based measurement are *interval recording* and *response duration*.

With interval recording, usually behavior is observed for a single block of time such as 30 or 60 minutes once per day. A block of time is divided into a series of short intervals (e.g., each interval equaling 10 or 15 seconds). The behavior of the client is observed during each interval. The target behavior is scored as having occurred or not occurred during each interval. If a discrete behavior, such as hitting someone, occurs one or more times in a single interval, then the response is scored as having occurred. Several response occurrences within an interval are not counted separately. If the behavior is ongoing with an unclear beginning or end, such as talking, playing, and sitting, or occurs for a long period of time, it is scored during each interval in which it is occurring.

Intervention programs in classroom settings frequently use interval recording to score whether students are paying attention, sitting in their seats, and working quietly. An individual student's behavior may be observed for 10-second intervals over a 20-minute observational period. For each interval, an observer records whether the child is in her seat working quietly. If the child remains in her seat and works for a long period of time, many intervals will be scored for attentive behavior. If the child leaves her seat (without permission) or stops working, inattentive behavior will be scored. During some intervals, she may be sitting in her seat for half of the time and running around the room for the remaining time. Since the interval has to be scored for either attentive or inattentive behavior, a rule must be devised as to how to score behavior in this instance. Often, getting out of the seat will be counted as inattentive behavior within the interval.

Interval recording for a single block of time has been used in many programs beyond the classroom setting. For example, one program trained parents to interact with their children in ways that would promote positive child behaviors at home (Phaneuf & McIntyre, 2007). The focus was on parent behavior. At home, the mother-child dyad was observed for several minutes during free play, clean-up, and during an activity. Each 30-second interval was evaluated to assess if the mother engaged in inappropriate behaviors (e.g., giving ambiguous commands, unwittingly reinforcing inappropriate child behavior, and criticizing the child). The benefits of training were evident from the decreases in the percentage of intervals with inappropriate parenting behaviors.

Interval recording was used in a study that was designed to evaluate happiness and quality of life of three nursing home residents (over 80 years old) who were diagnosed with Alzheimer's disease and had limited verbal repertoires (Moore, Delaney, & Dixon, 2007). Ten-minute observation periods were divided into 10-second intervals, each of which was scored as reflecting happiness, unhappiness, or neither happiness nor unhappiness. These were operationalized on the basis of facial and vocal expressions (e.g., smiling, laughing vs. frowning, grimacing, crying, or yelling). If no clear affect was present, the interval would be scored as neither. Assessment was completed before, during, and after participants engaged in various activities.

In using an interval scoring method, an observer looks at the client during the interval. When one interval is over, the observer records whether the behavior occurred. If an observer is recording several behaviors in an interval, a few seconds may be needed to record all the behaviors observed during that interval. If the observer recorded a behavior as soon as it occurred (before the interval was over), he or she might miss other behaviors that occurred while the first behavior was being scored. Hence, many investigators use interval-scoring procedures that allow time to record after each interval of observation. Intervals for observing behavior might be 10 seconds, with 2 to 5 seconds after the interval for recording these observations. If a single behavior is scored in an interval, no time may be required for recording. Each interval might be 10 seconds. As soon as a behavior occurred, it would be scored. If a behavior did not occur, a quick mark could indicate this at the end of the interval. Of course, it is desirable to use short recording times, when possible, because when behavior is being recorded, it is not being observed. Recording consumes time that might be used for observing behavior.

A variation of interval recording is *time sampling*. This variation uses the interval method, but the observations are conducted for brief periods at different times rather than in a single block of time. For example, with an interval method, a child might be observed for a 30-minute period. The period would be broken down into small intervals such as 10 seconds. With the time-sampling method, the 30-minute period might be divided into three 10-minute periods throughout the day (e.g., morning, early afternoon, and late afternoon). During the 10-minute periods, the child is still observed for 10-second intervals just like before. Spreading out the observation periods over the entire day is likely to capture a more representative sample of performance than measuring behavior for a single period.

Interval recording has been widely adopted as an assessment strategy. First, the method is very flexible because virtually any behavior can be recorded. The presence or absence of a response during a time interval applies to any measurable response. Whether a response is discrete and does not vary in duration, is continuous, or is sporadic, it can be classified as occurring or not occurring during a brief time period. Second, the observations resulting from interval recording can easily be converted into a percentage. The number of intervals during which the response is scored as occurring can be divided by the total number of intervals observed. This ratio multiplied by 100 yields a percentage of intervals that the response is performed. For example, if social responses are scored as occurring in 20 of 40 intervals observed, the percentage of intervals of social behavior is 50% (20/40 x 100). A percentage is easily communicated to others by noting that a certain behavior occurs a specific percentage of time (intervals). Whenever there is doubt as to what assessment strategy should be adopted, an interval approach is almost always applicable.

Duration. Another time-based method of observation is duration, or amount of time that the response is performed. This method is particularly useful for ongoing responses that are continuous rather than discrete acts or responses of extremely short duration. Programs that attempt to increase or decrease the length of time a response is performed might profit from a duration method. As an example, one investigation focused on academic tasks of school-age children with learning disabilities. Tasks were individualized to the age and goals of the children (e.g., writing time for an essay, tracing letters for a young child) (Athens et al., 2007). In another program, the focus was on six male children and adolescents (ages 8–17) with Fragile X syndrome, an inherited form of developmental disability (Hall, Maynes, & Reiss, 2009). Individuals with this disorder often show an aversion to eye contact with others. The goal of the intervention was to increase eye contact during periods in which an experimenter sat across from a child and tried to engage him in interaction. Duration of eye contact in seconds was recorded by an observer who pressed keys on a laptop computer to note onset and offset of eye contact during the interactions. Other examples include the amount of time engaging in social interaction, remaining in situations that before treatment promoted anxiety, exercising, studying, practicing (a musical instrument, athletic skill), reading, and so on. For many interventions or programs increasing the duration (e.g., of practicing, exercising) is a central goal.

Assessment of response duration is a fairly simple matter. The requirement is that the observer start and stop a stopwatch or note the time when the response begins and ends. However, the onset and termination of the response must be carefully defined. If these conditions are not met, duration is extremely difficult to employ. For example, in recording the duration of a tantrum, a child may cry continuously for several minutes, whimper for short periods, stop all noise for a few seconds, and begin intense crying again. In recording duration, researchers must decide how to handle changes in the intensity of the behavior (e.g., crying to whimpering) and pauses (e.g., periods of silence) so that they can be consistently recorded as part of the response or as a different (e.g., nontantrum) response.

Use of response duration is generally restricted to situations in which the length of time a behavior is performed is a major concern. Yet that may cover many areas of interest. For example, it may be desirable to increase the length of time that students study or practice a skill or to decrease the length of time an adolescent is in the shower while several siblings are waiting their turn. Duration has ease of observation in its favor if the start and stop can be well defined and lengthy pauses are not likely to be an issue. Interval assessment can be used to assess behavior when duration is of interest. For example, the number or proportion of intervals in which studying occurs reflects changes in study time, since interval recording is based on time.

Latency. Latency refers to how long it takes for the client to begin the response. The amount of time that elapses between a cue (some starting point) and the response is referred to as *latency*. It would be easy to group latency with duration, because they both include the sum of the amount of time that elapses (before the behavior occurs or with the behavior occurring), but for ease of reference and presentation the distinction is useful.

Many programs have timed response latency. For example, in one report, a 19-year-old adult diagnosed with Asperger syndrome was referred to a day-treatment center

(Tiger, Bouxsein, & Fisher, 2007).[1] Among the characteristics to be addressed was the long period of time he took to respond to questions (he delayed before even starting his answer). More generally, he took excessive amounts of time to complete many activities during the day (e.g., several minutes to sign his name to a check in the grocery store), all of which limited his independent functioning. Latency was used as a measure in response to answering questions. After a therapist asked a question (e.g., "What is your sister's name?"), the amount of time that elapsed (timed by a stopwatch) until the answer began constituted the measure. When the question was answered, another question was presented until 10 questions were completed or 10 minutes elapsed. The impact of an intervention program was evaluated by showing a decrease in latency (e.g., mean of approximately 20 seconds in baseline to less than 5 seconds and eventually 3 seconds during the intervention).

Latency has many other uses in relation to assessment and intervention. For example, in a classroom, the teacher might count latency from the beginning of the class until a student engages in disruptive or aggressive behavior. The intervention (e.g., praise, feedback, points) can be provided for increases in the time from the start of school to the end of the day without disruptive behavior. Similarly, parents are often frustrated with getting their child up, dressed, fed, and out the door in time to obtain a ride or catch the school bus. Latency from the first reminder until the child gets out of bed or comes to the breakfast table and sits down could be one measure. The goal of the program would be to decrease the latency. An advantage of latency is that it greatly facilitates observation when individuals in applied settings (parents, teachers) do the observation. The start time is usually easy to specify (e.g., breakfast, 10:00 a.m. activity, when a bell rings to denote the start of class). The parent and teacher now only have to keep track when the behavior first occurs.

Duration and latency can be very useful. Often the goal of a program is related directly to time: how much time is spent either engaging or not engaging in a particular behavior. The main constraint is in defining when the behavior does and does not count as being performed, so that when to start and stop the timing is clear. This requirement is similar to the demands in defining observations using other strategies.

Other Strategies Briefly Noted

Most assessment in single-case research has focused on overt behavior, using variations of one of the strategies mentioned previously. Three other general strategies can be delineated, including response-specific measures, psychophysiological measures, and self- and other-report measures. Although the formats of these measures sometimes overlap with the overt behavioral assessment strategies discussed earlier (e.g., frequency, duration), the strategies have unique features.

Response-specific Measures. Response-specific measures are assessment procedures that are unique to the particular behaviors under investigation. Many behaviors have

---

[1] Asperger syndrome is a condition marked by impaired social interactions and communication, and by limited patterns of behavior. It is viewed as being on a continuum or spectrum with autism being at the more severe and extreme end.

specific measures peculiar to them that can be examined directly. For example, in one study, interventions were directed at increasing the eating and weight gain of three children (ages 3 to 4) who were failing to thrive (Patel, Piazza, Layer, Coleman, & Schwartzwelder, 2005). They consumed less food than normally consumed for children their age and were admitted to an intensive pediatric feeding disorders program. The measure to evaluate alternative feeding strategies was grams of food consumed. Ultimately, weight gain was the measure of the success of the program.

In a similar way, interventions designed to reduce overeating or cigarette smoking can be evaluated by assessing the number of calories consumed or cigarettes smoked. Calories and cigarettes could be considered as simple frequency measures in the sense that they are both tallies of a particular unit of performance. However, the measures are distinguished here because they are peculiar to the target behavior of interest and can be used to assess the impact of the intervention directly.

Response-specific measures are of use because they directly assess the response or a product of the response that is recognized to be of obvious clinical, social, or applied significance. For example, efforts to have drivers conserve energy (gasoline) have measured car mileage directly from odometer readings; efforts to have individuals recycle waste or not litter have measured volume of trash. Response-specific measures are often available from existing data systems or records that are part of the ongoing institutional records (e.g., crime rate, traffic accidents, hospital admissions). A cautionary note for some of the measures: data obtained in institutional records such as crime rate or episodes of events in hospitals and schools are not always kept reliably and may not reflect the care that investigators usually invoke when developing a measure for research. Even so, when decisions about assessment are being made, the investigator may wish to consider whether the response can be assessed in a direct and unique way that will be of clear social relevance. Response-specific measures are often of more obvious significance to persons unfamiliar with research to whom the results may need to be communicated than are specially devised overt behavioral measures.

Psychophysiological Assessment. Psychophysiological responses directly reflect many problems of clinical significance or are highly correlated with the occurrence of psychological and medical conditions of interest, such as anxiety, vigilience, and attentiveness. In addition, physiological arousal and other states can be assessed directly and are of interest in their own right.

Some of the more familiar psychophysiological measures include heart or pulse rate, blood pressure, skin temperature, blood volume, muscle tension, and brain wave activity. Measures related to substance use and abuse are readily available for alcohol, drugs, and tobacco. For example, in one program with cigarette smokers, the primary measure was level of carbon monoxide (CO) (Glenn & Dallery, 2007). Individuals breathed into a CO monitor over the course of an intervention study. A useful feature of this measure is that it has been well studied so one can evaluate levels (parts of CO per million) that are known to reflect abstinence from cigarette smoking. Similarly, a study designed to decrease marijuana dependence among three adults used several measures (Twohig, Shoenberger, & Hayes, 2007). Among them was an oral swab to test for marijuana use. The test requires placing a special pad between the lower cheek and gum for 2 to 5 minutes. The results indicate whether marijuana was used within the past 3 days. In another single-case study, the goal was to reduce muscle tension that caused problems in vocalizing and breathing in a 16-year-old Caucasian adolescent with a 2-year history of the problem (Warnes & Allen, 2005). Biofeedback for reduced muscle tension was the intervention and was evaluated directly as measured by electromyographic responses. Electrodes placed on the neck provided the measure of muscle tension (in microvolts).

Many intervention studies focus on evaluating or altering sexual arousal in persons who experience arousal in the presence of socially inappropriate and censured stimuli (e.g., exhibitionistic, sadistic, masochistic stimuli, or stimuli involving children, animals, or inanimate objects). Direct psychophysiological assessment of sexual arousal is possible by measuring vaginal or penile blood volume to evaluate changes in arousal. For example, penile blood volume is measured by a plethysmograph, which includes a band around the penis that registers increases in the diameter of the penis (e.g., Reyes et al., 2006). This is a well-studied and validated measure of sexual arousal and sexual preference.

More generally, psychophysiological measures are quite relevant insofar as many physical disorders and disease processes and their correlates (e.g., blood levels and chemistry) reflect change in response to individual habits and lifestyle. Blood pressure (by sphygmomanometer) or brain activity (electroencephalogram [EEG]) recordings are other examples. Psychophysiological and biological assessments are used more commonly in group research than in single-case designs. Some of the measures to evaluate intervention effects such as neuroimaging, dense array, and scans of various sorts are often expensive, inconvenient, and not feasible in an ongoing way, but of course that could easily change. Thus, it is much more feasible to assess behavior on one (post-intervention) or two (pre- and post-intervention) occasions only.

The preceding examples provide only a minute sample of the range of measures and disorders encompassed by psychophysiological assessment. Diverse clinical problems have been studied in single-case and between-group research, including insomnia, obsessive-compulsive disorders, pain, hyperactivity, sexual dysfunction, tics, tremors, and many others. Depending on the target focus, psychophysiological assessment permits measurement of precursors, central features, or correlates of the problem.

Self-report Measures. Historically, single-case designs have focused heavily and almost exclusively on overt performance, that is, what people do rather than what they say. A major exception has been those situations in which verbal behavior itself is the target focus (e.g., irrational speech, stuttering, threats of aggression). The emphasis on overt behavior is in sharp contrast to the measures more commonly used in between-group research in education, psychology, counseling, and psychiatry, where pre- and post-intervention assessments rely heavily on various paper-and-pencil measures (questionnaires, rating scales, and checklists) completed by the individual or others (therapists, spouses, parents, and teachers). There are many types of "self-report" measures, and some of these reflect overt behavior in important ways. For example, educational research often relies on self-report measures and on paper-and-pencil measures that reflect competence in an area (e.g., reading, comprehension, arithmetic). These are not ratings or personal views but measures of the domain of interest.

Self-report, when rating a problem or target focus, is often held to be rather suspect because it is subject to a variety of response biases and sets (e.g., responding in a socially desirable fashion, agreeing just to be agreeable, lying, and others) that distort one's own account of actual performance. Of course, self-report is not invariably inaccurate, nor is direct behavioral assessment necessarily free of response biases or distortion. When persons are aware that their behavior is being assessed, they can distort both what they say and what they do. Self-report tends to be more readily under the control of the client than more direct measures of overt behavior, however, and hence it is perhaps more readily subject to distortion.

Even when people do not attempt to distort how they present themselves, they are not necessarily good reporters of what they will do, what they have done, or what has happened. Consider an anecdotal and then research example. People who live long or who have been married a very long time occasionally are asked by reporters, "So what is your secret or key to a long life (or marriage)?" Invariably, the person who is asked has something to say, but we cannot take this as knowledge or a statement of what really accounted for the lengthy period. Luck, a package of genetic and environmental influences, and even obscure influences that we now know a little about (e.g., diet of one's grandparents before one was born) might combine in some novel way to explain longevity. Self-report just does not provide the data, even though the report can be interesting.

As for a research example, there are lines of research showing circumstances in which we do not and perhaps cannot report on critical facets of our experience. Here the problem is not ill will or efforts to distort, but characteristics of our reporting limits. For example, people give verbal statements about what attracts them to a mate and what characteristics they prefer, but for both males and females their actual choices are guided by characteristics that differ from what they say (e.g., Todd, Penke, Fasolo, & Lenton, 2007). There is no effort to distort here; self-report is just not up to the task of identifying key factors that may exert influence. Similarly, teenagers who pledge virginity and abstinence from sexual activity no doubt are genuine in their commitment. Yet, in fact their statements do not relate to actual sexual behavior, that is, are not associated with reduced sexual activity (Rosenbaum, 2009). As intriguing, research has now established procedures for inducing false memories, that is, clear recollections people have of events that did not happen (Bjorklund, 2000; Brainerd & Reyna, 2005). Although people do not equivocate about what they remember, their reports can be shown to be completely inaccurate. Concerns about self-report are not objections in principle; but reflect problems that have emerged from careful study.

Over the years, single-case designs have been applied more broadly in terms of the types of domains that are studied as well as many disciplines that draw on the designs. That has led to the expansion of types of assessment to include greater use of self-report and other-report (e.g., clinician), either as a complement to direct behavioral measures or as a modality of assessment valuable in its own right. In many cases self-report may represent the only modality currently available to evaluate treatment. For example, in the case of private events such as obsessive thoughts, uncontrollable urges, or hallucinations, self-report may be the only possible or feasible method of assessment. When the client is the only one with direct access to the event, self-report may be the primary assessment modality.

Private experience may not be private merely because it is the internal experience of the individual. Sometimes the behavior is not easily publicly observable because the behavior is performed privately or at times throughout the day that cannot be monitored by anyone other than the clients themselves. In such cases, self-report measures may play a central role and be complemented by other measures. Mentioned previously was a study to reduce marijuana dependence among three adults (Twohig et al., 2007). A drug test was used to assess use of marijuana in the previous 3 days. The measure was administered at different points throughout the study. However, self-report was used as well, in which each client kept a record of marijuana use and at the end of each day reported the number of times by leaving a telephone or email message. The self-report data provided a daily measure to provide the continuous observations needed for single-case designs but was corroborated by the drug tests administered less often. Similarly, in a report on cigarette use, the drug test (carbon monoxide monitoring) was supplemented with self-report of cigarette smoking (Glenn & Dallery, 2007). The two measures were moderately to highly correlated ($r = .72$); thus reporting was quite related to actual smoking. Of course, one can question if accuracy in reporting was partially increased because participants knew their smoking could be detected no matter what they said. There are many other actions of interest that in principle can be observed by others but end up being private events and available through self-report. Examples include sexual assault, delinquent acts (e.g., vandalism, firesetting), and bullying (e.g., ridicule or physical abuse on a playground). These behaviors may involve others who could report on the actions, but by the nature of these actions, self-report may be the only alternative.

Self-report measures should not be considered as the default modality of assessment when all else fails or when measures free from reporting biases cannot be used. First, self-report is often a critical facet of many problem domains and areas of functioning (e.g., depression, marital satisfaction, quality of life) and important to assess even when direct behavioral measures might be an option. Indeed, from the standpoint of the client or patient, self-report (one's own subjective perception) is often the bottom line and "true" test of the impact treatment. For example, many intervention studies are directed at reducing or eliminating headaches, debilitating muscle tension, stress, and pain, all of which can be assessed through psychophysiological measures (muscle tension, electrical activity of the cortex, skin temperature) or behavioral indices (walking cautiously to avoid pain, no activity, grimacing as if in pain). As superb as these are as measures, there is no substitute for asking if the client in fact is experiencing fewer or no headaches, less muscle tension and stress, and no pain. Perhaps even more clearly, it is not rare for an adult who is very depressed to have a very successful life by all the usual overt signs (e.g., relationships, work, money, leisure, and control over their lives). Self-report or another type of measure (e.g., physiological) is needed here to assess unhappiness in a valid way.

Similarly, many intervention studies focus on altering sexual arousal in persons who experience arousal in the presence of socially inappropriate and censured stimuli (e.g., exhibitionistic, sadistic, masochistic stimuli or stimuli involving children, animals, or inanimate objects). Direct psychophysiological assessment of sexual arousal is possible by measuring vaginal or penile blood volume to evaluate changes in arousal as a function of treatment, as I mentioned previously. Yet it is important as well to measure what persons actually say about what stimuli arouse them, because self-report is a significant response modality in its own right and does not always correlate with physiological arousal. Hence, it is relevant to assess self-report along with other measures of arousal.

Second, self-report measures often have been very extensively studied in ways that establish their reliability and validity, that is, that they yield consistent results and that the scores on the measures relate to other types of indices (e.g., how children are doing in school, how individuals are functioning at work). The value of a measure, in large part, is established by the extent to which the measure passes various methodological hoops. These hoops reflect different types of studies that convey that the measure assesses what it says it does, that the measure relates to other indices of the same construct, and so on. For example, a question with a seemingly obvious answer is, "What is the better or best way to measure the extent to which adolescents engage in delinquent behavior? Should one use arrest records (how many times a youth has been brought to a police station)? Or should one just ask them?" First, this is a trick question. In research one invariably wants to use measures of more than just one type (Kazdin, 2003). So here an institutional record (arrest) and self-report scale should both be used if possible. They have different limitations and if they converge, any conclusion would be greatly strengthened. However, to return to the main point, self-report is a valid way of measuring delinquent acts and has yielded many findings and insights about delinquency (e.g., scope of acts, changes over the course of development, predictors of) that could not have been obtained by either direct observation or institutional records (see Thornberry & Krohn, 2000).

Third, single-case designs require continuous assessment, that is, repeated administration of the measure on a daily or almost daily basis. The vast majority of self-report measures have not been used or validated as ongoing measures and may not be able to reflect changes. More attention has been accorded to this concern and there are now examples that have redressed the concern. A prominent example is a measure used in the context of psychotherapy for adults. The measure is the Outcome Questionnaire 45 (OQ-45), which is a self-report measure designed to evaluate client progress (e.g., weekly) over the course of treatment (see Lambert et al., 1996, 2001, 2003, 2004). The measure requires approximately 5 minutes to complete and provides information on four domains of functioning, including symptoms of psychological disturbance (primarily depression and anxiety), interpersonal problems, social role functioning, (e.g., problems at work), and quality of life (e.g., facets of life satisfaction). Total scores across the 45 items present a global assessment of functioning. The measure has been evaluated extensively and has been applied to thousands of patients and shown to be useful in evaluating and predicting therapeutic changes. There are now other examples of self-report measures used in clinical work and single-case designs (e.g., Borckardt et al., 2008; Clement, 2007).

Finally, self-report measures can be used to code overt behavior in a way that circumvents some of the traditional concerns that such measures are too transparent. Questions can solicit information (self-report) but be evaluated in a way that is slightly different from what is reported. For example, in a study designed to prevent child abuse and to train parents in more effective ways to handle their children, mothers kept daily dairies (Peterson, Tremblay, Ewigman, & Popkey, 2002). The questions were open-ended and did not specifically ask about harsh discipline practices, the use of ignoring of deviant behavior, or time out from reinforcement. The goal of the program was to decrease harsh discipline and to improve the use of ignoring and time out in its place. The diaries were structured so that they could be coded by observers and evaluated for reliability of the observations. The measure yielded information that could be assessed reliably, reflected changes in parenting behavior in the home over time, and reflected the impact of an intervention designed to change parenting behavior.

In light of advances, self-report ought not to be ruled out in single-case designs. The methodology has advanced in part because of the need to address critical facets of functioning that are not easily assessed in other ways and because these facets are important in their own right. Also, even when behavior can be directly assessed, reports of others or the client may be important to evaluate whether the intervention made a difference to those who see or experience the behaviors in everyday life. Real and perceived changes are relevant, and self-report that taps either one of these, especially when supplemented by other measures, can be valuable.

Reports by Others.   Reports by others refer to measures completed by individuals who have access to, observe, and interact closely with the client. Parents, teachers, spouses, partners, and significant others often serve as informants, the name used to describe raters other than the client. As with self-report, reports by others often play a critical role in intervention research. First, in some areas of research (e.g., clinical depression), other reports (ratings by clinicians) are among the standardized measures to evaluate the impact of treatment (e.g., Levesque et al., 2004; Savard et al., 1998). We want the views of experts (e.g., those in a position to make well-based judgments). In addition, significant others (e.g., relatives, peers) in everyday life who are not "experts" but who have close contact with the client provide valuable information as well.

Second, significant others are often the first to identify a problem as in the case of parents and teachers. Ratings on standardized measures can be used to decide whether an intervention is needed or whether an intervention has had impact. We want these views because the informant has close contact with the client and can provide valuable information. Related, ratings by significant others are used as part of the process of social validation. In this context, subjective evaluation is used, as already mentioned. Individuals in contact with the client are asked to judge whether the behavior that is focused on or more commonly whether the changes that have been made with the intervention make a difference. The fact that these reports are subjective, based on perception, and not necessarily isomorphic with observations of behavior is not a deficiency in the measure. Rather, the purpose is to determine if changes that are reflected in observable behavior are such that they make a difference to others.

Many of the concerns about the advances related to self-report are pertinent here. First, reports by others do not invariably reflect actual behavior of the client, which in a given instance may or may not be a concern. For example, in the context of therapy, studies that compare direct observation with clinician ratings (e.g., in studying something as seemingly concrete as tics) note that clinician ratings may not correspond very well to direct observations (Himle et al., 2006). Second, when different informants rate the same person (e.g., a child referred for treatment), agreement among the informants is in the low to moderate range (Achenbach, 2006; De Los Reyes & Kazdin, 2005). For example, if parents, teachers, and children are asked about areas of child functioning (e.g., aggression, social interaction) they do not agree very well (e.g., parent and teacher, $r = \approx .4$). Third, ratings by others are influenced by factors that can be distinguished from the behavior or characteristics that are being rated. For example, parental report of deviance in their children is partially a function of what the child does but also is influenced by the stress, depression, and isolation of the parent who is doing the ratings. A stressed, depressed, and isolated parent (from social contacts) is likely to see the child as more deviant.

On balance, as with other modalities of assessment, it is important to be aware of their limitations and to draw on multiple measures when possible. The perspectives of others are often critical, both in identifying problems or characteristics of an individual and in determining if these characteristics have changed. Indeed, many decisions and choices in life (e.g., job opportunities) are very much determined by the perspectives (ratings) of others. Interventions to be effective often have to ensure those perspectives are part of the evaluation.

Selection of an Assessment Strategy

In most single-case designs, the investigator selects one of the assessment strategies based on overt performance (e.g., frequency, interval measures). Some behaviors may lend themselves well to frequency counts or categorization because they are discrete, such as the number of profane words used, or the number of toileting or eating responses; others are well suited to interval recording, such as reading, working, or sitting; and still others are best assessed by duration, such as time spent studying, crying, or getting dressed. Target behaviors usually can be assessed in more than one way, so there is no single strategy that must be adopted. For example, an investigator working in an institution for delinquents may wish to record a client's aggressive behavior. Hitting others (e.g., making physical contact with another individual with a closed fist) may be the response of interest. What assessment strategy should be used?

Aggressive behavior might be measured by a *frequency* count by having an observer record how many times the client hits others during a certain period each day. Each hit would count as one response. The behavior also could be observed during *interval recording*. A block of time such as 30 minutes could be set aside for observation. The 30 minutes could be divided into 10-second intervals. During each interval, the observer records whether any hitting occurs. A duration measure might also be used. It might be difficult to time the duration of hitting, because instances of hitting are too fast to be timed with a stopwatch unless there is a series of hits (as in a fight). An easier *duration* measure might be to record the amount of time from the beginning of each day until the first aggressive response, that is, a *latency* measure. Presumably, if a program decreased aggressive behavior, the amount of time from the beginning of the day until the first aggressive response would increase.

Although many different measures can be used in a given program, the measure finally selected may be dictated by the purpose of the program. If one is developing complex behaviors that require mastery of a series of steps, *discrete categorization* may be of special use. The steps (performed vs. not performed scored for each step) could be listed and assessed as well as trained over the course of the program. In group situations (e.g., camp, classroom, prison, military, nursing home, day care), trying to get most or all individuals to engage in some behavior (completing a task, showing up for an event, napping) may be the goal of the intervention. Counting the number of individuals who perform the behavior is a direct measure of that goal. Many responses may immediately suggest their own specific measures. In such cases, the investigator need not devise a special format but can merely adopt an existing measure. Measures such as calories, cigarettes smoked, and miles of jogging are obvious examples that can reflect eating, smoking, and exercising, relatively common target responses.

When the target problem involves psychophysiological functioning, direct measures are often available and of primary interest. In many cases, measures of overt behavior can reflect important physiological processes. For example, seizures, ruminative vomiting, and anxiety can be assessed through direct observation of the client. However, direct psychophysiological measures can be used as well and either provide a finer assessment of the target problem or evaluate an important and highly related component.

To a large extent, selection of an assessment strategy depends on characteristics of the target response and the goals of the intervention. In any given situation, several assessment options are likely to be available. Decisions for the final assessment format are often made on the basis of criteria other than the target response, including practical considerations such as the availability of assessment periods and observers.

It is important to mention a point from the previous chapter, namely, multiple measures are to be encouraged. That takes the onus off the investigator for making a decision about the best, most relevant, and near perfect measure. Constructs and domains of interest usually can be represented in multiple ways, and the yield from different measures of assessment can be different and informative. For single-case designs, one of the measures has to be obtained on an ongoing basis, but other measures can be used that are administered periodically or only once or twice to sample other indices of the domains or other domains that may be related to the target focus.

CONDITIONS OF ASSESSMENT
The strategies of assessment refer to the different methods of recording performance. Observations can vary markedly along other conditions, such as the manner in which behavior is evoked, the setting in which behaviors are assessed, whether the persons are aware that their behaviors are assessed, and whether human observers or automated apparatus are used to detect performance. These conditions of assessment can influence how the client responds and one's confidence that the data accurately reflect performance.

Natural Versus Contrived Tasks and Activities
Observations of client behavior can be obtained under a variety of conditions. A broad dimension is the extent to which performance is observed under everyday conditions without structuring the activities or under conditions that are arranged in some way to foster performance of activities so they can be counted. The *performance, task,* or *activity* that is to be observed can be natural (unstructured) or contrived (structured task of some kind). A separate dimension is the *setting* in which the observations are made. These too can be natural settings (e.g., everyday life, at home, in the park) or contrived settings (e.g., laboratory). It is useful to make the distinction in dissecting assessment options for purposes of presentation, but there are all sorts of permutations

and gradations.[2] In this section, the focus is on the tasks or activities presented to the subject that serve as the basis of observation.

With natural or uncontrived tasks and activities, performance is observed without intervening or structuring the situation for the client. Ongoing performance is observed as it normally occurs, and the situation is not intentionally altered by the investigator merely to obtain the observations. For example, observations of interactions among children at school during a free period in class or on the playground would be considered natural in the sense that an ordinary activity was observed during the school day. Similarly, observation of people eating in a cafeteria or restaurant would constitute assessment under natural conditions.

Although direct observation of performance as it normally occurs is very useful, naturalistic observation often is not possible or feasible. Many of the behaviors of interest are not easily observed because they are of low frequency, require special precipitating conditions, or are prohibitively costly to assess in view of available resources (funds, observers). Consider the problem in a different context. TV shows that portray animals in the wild are often interested in the hunt, the kill, or the drama of a disappointing chase—all observations captured with photography. The difficulty is that these are natural rather than contrived activities, so the photographer is sitting in savannah bushes or trees for days to secure these photos. Analogously, interventions often focus on behaviors that rarely occur or do not occur with sufficient frequency to assess or intervene. Consequently, situations are often contrived to evoke responses so that the target behavior can be assessed.

For example, one study was designed to train young children (ages 4 to 7 years) so they would not play with guns and would respond safely if they encountered one (Gross, Miltenberger, Knudson, Bosch, & Breitwieser, 2007). Disabled guns from the police department were used. Each child was trained how to respond (not touch the gun, leave the room, contact an adult) after encountering a gun in a room at his or her home. A camera was placed in the room to watch the child's interaction and to score the child's behavior. Direct assessment of children in their homes with real guns and in natural uncontrolled situations obviously is not a possibility. Hence, a contrived situation was devised to observe and to train the behavior.

Another study focused on training preschool children to avoid abduction by strangers (Johnson et al., 2005). Assessment was conducted in diverse settings near the school and the child's home; the abduction lure was staged (i.e., contrived) by a confederate (i.e., someone working as part of the study) who approached the child to assess if the child would say "no," immediately walk or run away, and tell an adult about the abduction lure. This is another situation where merely observing the child under natural circumstances (noncontrived activities) would, like the savannah photographer, not yield the behaviors—and worse, "real" abduction efforts would need immediate

---

[2] Psychological research has blurred and blended the activity and the setting in fascinating ways. For example, in studies with college students, individuals will enter a waiting room for some appointment. Another student already in the waiting room starts talking to the person who just arrived. This may look like an unstructured *task* or *activity of the subject*, but the person who starts talking (confederate or "actor") is working from a practiced script; the *setting* looks like it is naturalistic— just a waiting room, but in fact it is all planned for observation, maybe even taping.

intervention that would preclude training. We do not need research to make the point. If one wants to teach people not to drown, waiting until they are in the life-threatening situation and firing instructions or techniques at them probably is not going to be helpful ("Stop swallowing water and screaming!" "Stop moving your arms so aimlessly in the air!" "No need to keep screaming 'help'; I'm here." "Calm down—this is a bathtub."). We train under contrived conditions (regular swimming pools) where there are many opportunities to teach and assess the requisite skills.

Naturalistic and contrived conditions of assessment provide different advantages and disadvantages. Assessment of performance under contrived conditions provides information that often would be too difficult to obtain under naturalistic conditions. The response might be seen rarely if the situation were not arranged to evoke the behavior, as in the gun and abduction examples. Demonstrations have, with the approval and aid of parents, contrived situations so children can learn and practice appropriate responses.

In addition, contrived situations provide consistent and standardized assessment conditions. Consistent assessment conditions directly facilitate evaluation of the intervention and analysis of the data. Without structuring the situation, performance may change or fluctuate markedly as a function of the constantly changing conditions in the natural environment. In evaluation of intervention effects, whether in between-group or single-case studies, variability in performance can make evaluation more difficult (and threaten data-evaluation validity). Contrived situations minimize extraneous variability that results from constantly changing contexts and conditions of the natural environment.

The advantage of providing standardization of the assessment conditions with contrived situations bears a cost as well. When the situation is contrived, the possibility exists that performance may have little or no relation to the performance under naturalistic conditions. For example, family interaction may be observed in a clinic situation in which parents and their children are given structured tasks to perform (e.g., decide where to go on a hypothetical vacation or work on a homework problem together). The contrived tasks allow assessment of a variety of behaviors that might otherwise be difficult to observe if families were allowed to interact normally on their own. However, the possibility exists that families may interact very differently under contrived conditions from how they would under ordinary circumstances. Hence, a major consideration in assessing performance in contrived situations is whether that performance represents behavior under noncontrived conditions. In most studies, the relation between performances under contrived versus naturalistic conditions is assumed rather than demonstrated.

Natural Environment Versus Laboratory (or Clinic) Settings

A related dimension that distinguishes observations is the *setting* or *where* the assessment is conducted. Observations can be obtained in the natural environment or in the laboratory or special clinical setting. The setting in which the observations are actually conducted can be distinguished from whether or not the observations are contrived. For example, one study on a college campus focused on getting people to come to complete stops as their cars pulled up to stop signs (Austin, Hackett, Gravina, & Lebbon, 2006). This was a naturalistic *setting*—a real intersection, with real people driving in real cars. The *task* or *activity* was naturalistic as well; whether the individual stopped at the intersection was the activity and was not contrived. Observers sat inside a parked car where they could see and code the stop. Here is a case where the setting and activity were natural. Similarly, in the abduction lure study noted previously, the activity was contrived (staged interactions with each child) but the settings were naturalistic (at home and at school).

Ideally, direct observations are made in the natural setting in which clients normally function. Such observations may be especially likely to reflect performance that the client has identified as problematic. Naturalistic settings might include the community, at work, in the classroom, in the institution, or in some other settings in which people ordinarily function. Occasionally observations are made in the homes of persons who are seen in psychological treatment. For example, to evaluate children with conduct problems (e.g., oppositional, disruptive, and aggressive behavior), observers may assess family interaction directly in the home. The home is obviously a natural setting, but the activities are not completely natural. Restrictions may be placed on the family, such as having them remain in one or a few rooms and not spend time on the phone or watch television to help standardize the conditions of assessment. The assessment is in a naturalistic setting even though the actual circumstances of assessment are slightly contrived, that is, structured in such a way that the situation probably departs from ordinary living conditions.

Assessment of family interaction among children with conduct problems has also taken place in clinic settings in addition to the natural environment. Parents and their children are presented with tasks and games in a playroom setting, where they interact. Both the activities (games with new, special toys, or commands and requests made by the parents) and the setting (a clinic room) faintly resemble the home. Interactions during the tasks are recorded to evaluate how the parents and child respond to one another. Interestingly, the examples of children with conduct problems convey differences in whether the assessment was conducted in naturalistic (home) or clinic settings. However, in both situations, the assessment conditions were contrived in varying degrees because arrangements were made by the investigator that were likely to influence interactions and because assessment conditions helped to ensure that the desired observations would occur.

Assessment in natural settings raises obvious problems and obstacles, such as the cost required for conducting observations and reliability checks and ensuring and maintaining some standardization of the assessment conditions so that the relevant behaviors can be observed. Clinic and laboratory settings have been relied on heavily because of the convenience and standardization of assessment conditions they afford. In the vast majority of clinic observations, contrived situations are used. Tasks can be used that foster interactions that approximate those that might be seen at home yet that allow evaluation of the specific behaviors of interest (e.g., child compliance). When clients come to the clinic, it is difficult to observe direct samples of performance that are not under somewhat structured, simulated, or contrived conditions.

Overall, efforts are made in applied programs to standardize the situation in some way to permit observations and to ensure that the desired behavior occurs. Equally, efforts often are made to approximate natural situations. Real-life situations are used, but something about them will be contrived to allow the observations to be made.

Obtrusive Versus Unobtrusive Assessment

Another facet of assessment that can vary is whether participants are aware of the assessment. If clients are aware of the measurement process and that their behavior is being assessed, the observations are said to be *obtrusive*. Obtrusive only means that clients are aware of assessment. The obtrusiveness of an assessment procedure may be a matter of degree, so that subjects may be generally aware of assessment, aware that they are being observed but unsure of the target behaviors, and so on. The potential issue with obtrusive assessment is that it may be *reactive*, that is, that the assessment procedure may influence subject performance and provide data that do not represent how they would respond if they were unaware of the assessment. Awareness of the assessment process does not necessarily mean clients will perform differently, that is, obtrusiveness does not mean reactivity, but reactivity is possible. Unobtrusive assessment (when clients are not aware that any assessment is going on) of course is not likely to be reactive.[3]

Observations of overt performance may vary in the extent to which they are conducted under obtrusive or unobtrusive conditions. In many investigations that utilize direct observations, performance is assessed under obtrusive conditions. For example, observation of behavior problem children in the home or the clinic is conducted in situations in which families are aware that they are being observed. Similarly, clients who are seen for treatment of anxiety-based problems usually are fully aware that their behavior is assessed when avoidance behavior is evaluated under contrived conditions. Does this lead to reactivity, or differences in performance? This is not well studied.

Assessment in single-case research has an advantage in relation to reactivity of assessment. Ongoing, usually daily assessment means that clients are likely to become accustomed to the assessment procedures. I have been in scores of classrooms with two or more observers and the first day or two students look or turn around to see the observers. As the students are ignored (to avoid fostering interactions with observers), interest in the observers tends to drop out. The extended observations over weeks or months become rather mundane and uninteresting to the students.

Consider an example in a very different context. One study focused on the performance of collegiate rugby players on a team in the United Kingdom (Mellalieu, Hanton, & O'Brien, 2006). Five collegiate players were included in the project; the goal was to increase selected behaviors (e.g., number of tackles, number of times a player stole possession of the ball from an opposing player). Participants were aware of the assessments because individual behavioral goals were identified and later feedback was provided in relation to these goals. However, the assessments were obtained from videotapes over the course of 20 rugby games. This was obtrusive assessment—was

---

[3] One has to hedge a bit here about the relation of reactivity and unobtrusive measurement in light of psychological research findings on awareness and behavior change. It is possible that subjects will not be able to verbalize that they are aware of something, such as observers, but still be influenced by it. Many influences in the environment fall below our threshold of saying we recognize them, but they still exert influence on our behavior (Hassin, Uleman, & Bargh, 2005). For example, exposing people to the national flag subliminally (i.e., too briefly for them to be aware the flag was shown) changes their immediate political views, intentions, and vote (Hassin, Ferguson, Shidlovski, & Gross, 2007). Stated another way, it is now clear that something can be reactive even if it is not obtrusive, that is, recognized in consciousness.

it reactive? That is, did the players change in light of knowing the behaviors were observed? Any reactive effect is likely to be short lived. In general, whether obtrusive observation in single-case research leads to reactive effects has not been well studied. The likely reactivity is minimal because of the extended observation period of repeated assessment. Participants are likely to accommodate to the novelty of the situation and see observers as part of what becomes routine.

Occasionally, observations are conducted under *un*obtrusive assessment conditions. I mentioned one example already in which stopping at intersections was observed directly (Austin et al., 2006). Individuals who drove through the intersection presumably did not notice observers sitting in a nearby car and performed as they normally would. In another study, the goal was to encourage people at a supermarket to donate food to a food bank (Farrimond & Leland, 2006). A food bank bin was located near the main exit door of the supermarket. The measure to evaluate the program was the number of items donated and their monetary value. The food bank bin had been in place in the store for 9 years, so nothing was introduced to make the situation contrived. This was likely to be an unobtrusive assessment, a regular food drive in a regular market.

Unobtrusive behavioral observations raise an obstacle. Participation in research usually must be disclosed to the subjects or clients. Informed consent forms, statements about privacy, and other legal requirements to protect subject rights are standard research requirements. As full a disclosure to subjects as possible means that they are likely to be aware of the assessments. Occasionally, informed consent and disclosure might not be required if identity of the participants cannot be discerned and information about individuals cannot be connected to them. The broader point is merely to be aware of the assessment procedures. If all procedures used in a given project are obtrusive, perhaps they can be varied in the likelihood or degree of conspicuousness and hence in the reactivity they might generate.

Human Observers Versus Automated Recording

Another dimension that distinguishes how observations are obtained pertains to the data collection method. In most applied single-case research, human observers assess behavior. Observers watch the client(s) and record behavior according to one of the assessment strategies described earlier. Observers are commonly used to record behavior in the home, classroom, psychiatric hospital, laboratory, community, and clinical settings. Observers may include special persons introduced into the setting or others who are already present (e.g., teachers in class, spouses or parents in the home).

In contrast, observations can be gathered through the use of apparatuses or automated devices. Behavior is recorded through an apparatus that detects when the response has occurred, for how long it has occurred, or other features of performance.[4] With automated recording, humans are involved in assessment only to the extent that the apparatus needs to be calibrated or that persons must read and transcribe the

---

[4] Automatic recording here refers to apparatuses that register the responses of the client. Apparatuses that aid human observers are often used, such as wrist counters, event recorders, stop watches, and audio- and videotape recorders. These devices serve as useful aids in recording behavior, but they are still based on having human observers assess performance.

numerical values from the device, if these data are not automatically printed and summarized or added to a database.

A major area of research in which automated measures are used routinely is biofeedback. In this case, psychophysiological recording equipment is required to assess ongoing physiological responses. I mentioned an example previously in which muscle tension was directly assessed. Direct observation by human observers could not assess the tension by merely observing or assess the tension with the precision needed. Similarly, many other responses of interest are undetectable from merely looking at the client (e.g., brain wave activity, blood pressure, cardiac arrhythmias, and skin temperature). Some physiological signs might be monitored by observers (e.g., pulse rate by external pressure, heart rate by stethoscope), but psychophysiological assessment provides a more sensitive, accurate, and reliable recording system.

Automated assessment in single-case research has not been restricted to psychophysiological assessment. A variety of measures has been used to assess responses of applied interest, such as levels of noise from university dormitories (decibel meters) or speeding of cars (by radar). With such measures, human observers can be completely removed from assessment. In other instances, human observers have a minimal role. The apparatus registers the response in a quantitative fashion, which can be simply copied by an observer, if the data cannot be automatically be transferred to the computer. The observer merely transcribes the information from one source (the apparatus) to another (data sheets), a function that often is not difficult to program automatically but may be easier to achieve with human observers.

The use of automated records has the obvious advantage of reducing or eliminating errors of measurement that would otherwise be introduced by the presence of observers, a topic addressed in the next chapter. Humans must subjectively decide whether a response has begun, is completed, or has occurred at all. Limitations of the "apparatus" of human observers (e.g., the scanning capability of the eyes), subjective judgment in reaching decisions about the response, and the assessment of complex behaviors with unclear boundary conditions may increase the inaccuracies and inconsistencies of human observers. Automated apparatuses overcome many of the observational problems introduced by human observers. For example, hyperactivity of children is of keen interest in intervention studies. Many different methods have been used (e.g., direct observations, teacher report) to assess hyperactivity. Automated recording is available too. For example, one method evaluates the number of movements made by a subject. A counting unit is worn on the belt of the subject. The unit records movement detected by a set of mercury switches. The total number of times a mercury switch is opened is counted and automatically recorded. A threshold can be added for feedback (biofeedback) so that when the rate of movement exceeds some criterion, an audible signal can be provided (www.freepatentsonline.com/4112926.html).

Automated devices can be used to sample behavior in everyday situations and for extended periods. For example, in one investigation, there was interest in sampling behaviors performed throughout the day and examining the behaviors (laughing, singing, and socializing) as a measure of mood (Hasler, Mehl, Bootzin, & Vizire, 2008). Subjects wore a device (Electronically Activated Recorder) that was roughly the size of a cell phone clipped to their belts. The apparatus included a tie-clip microphone that could pick up their voice but also sounds in the environment. Approximately five times every hour the device automatically made 30-second recordings to pick up sounds from the environment. From these recordings, coders later evaluated three categories of behaviors of interest as well as sleep onset and waking up (by the absence and presence of sounds at night and in the morning). These direct observations of behavior were obtained throughout the entire day.

Apparatuses that automatically record responses overcome significant problems that can emerge with human observers. In addition, automated recordings often allow assessment of behavior for relatively long periods of time. Once the device is in place, it can record for extended periods (e.g., entire school day, all night during sleep). The expense of human observers often prohibits such extended assessment. Another advantage may relate to the impact of the assessment procedure on the responses. The presence of human observers may be obtrusive and influence the responses that are assessed. Automatic recording apparatuses often quickly become part of the physical environment and, depending on the apparatus, may less readily convey that behavior is being monitored.

To be sure, automated recordings introduce their own problems. For example, equipment can and often does fail, or it may lose its accuracy if not periodically checked and calibrated. Also, equipment is often expensive and less flexible in terms of the range of behaviors that can be observed or the range of situations that can be assessed. Some measures may not permit evaluation of performance and functioning in the natural environment or require a special setup that can only be conducted in a laboratory. On the other hand, advances in assessment and technology are astounding. An obvious advance is in the portability of apparatus. They are diminishing in size, obtrusiveness, and ability to run with little power use. Another advantage is the range of domains that can be measured. Biological functions and processes are where some of the advances are especially salient. It seems not much of a speculative leap to suggest that domains such as body temperature, biological rhythms, and hormone and neurotransmitter processes will correlate or serve as meaningful operational definitions of social, emotional, cognitive, and behavioral aspects of everyday functioning.

No measure can be expected to address all issues and considerations. I have already noted in the previous chapter that multiple measures are to be encouraged when possible because any measure or method of assessment has limitations. Automated devices have a special virtue that overcomes limitations of human observers and are recommended when possible.

General Comments

The conditions under which behavioral observations are obtained may vary markedly. The dimensions I have discussed do not exhaust all of the possibilities. Moreover, for purposes of presentation, three of the conditions of assessment were discussed as either naturalistic *or* contrived, in natural *or* laboratory settings, and as obtrusive *or* unobtrusive. It is important to reiterate that these characteristics vary along continua. For example, many laboratory or clinic situations may approximate or very much attempt to approximate a natural setting. As an illustration, the alcohol consumption of individuals hospitalized for alcoholic abuse is often measured by observing individuals as they drink in a simulated bar in the hospital. The bar is in a clinic setting but looks exactly like an ordinary bar. The conditions closely resemble the physical environment in which drinking often takes place. The range of conditions under which behavioral observations can be obtained provides many options for the investigator. When the strategies for assessment (e.g., frequency, interval observations) are added, the diversity of observational practices is even more impressive. ·

SUMMARY AND CONCLUSIONS

Typically, single-case research focuses on direct observations of overt performance. Direct observations were emphasized because they are used frequently and are not well covered in most assessment books that focus on traditional methods of psychological assessment. Important to reiterate is that single-case designs do not require assessment of overt behavior. Any assessment method that provides ongoing data over time can be used. As for direct observations, or any other modality of assessment, reliability and validity issues are pertinent.

When direct observations are used, different strategies of assessment are available, including *frequency counts, discrete categorization, number of clients who perform the behavior, interval recording, duration,* and *latency.* Other strategies include response measures specific to the particular responses, psychophysiological recording, and self-report. Depending on the precise focus, measures other than direct observation may be essential.

Apart from the strategies of assessment, observations can be obtained under a variety of conditions. The conditions may vary according to whether behavior is observed under *natural* or *contrived tasks and activities,* in *natural* or *laboratory settings,* by *obtrusive* or *unobtrusive means,* and whether behavior is recorded by *human observers* or by an *automated apparatus.* The different conditions of assessment vary in the advantages and limitations they provide, including the extent to which performance in the assessment situation reflects performance in other situations, whether the measures of performance are comparable over time and across persons, and the convenience and cost of assessing performance.

This chapter focused on various methods of assessment. I noted that direct observations of overt behavior constitute the most frequently used method. The next chapter discusses requirements for ensuring the quality of the observational methods and the consistency with which the information is obtained. Consistency of measurement is a bridge to later discussions of data evaluation. Evaluating interventions is aided markedly by ensuring that the assessment procedures are administered reliably.

CHAPTER 5

Ensuring the Quality of Measurement

CHAPTER OUTLINE

When direct observations of behavior are obtained by human observers, the possibility exists that observers will not record behavior consistently. However well specified the responses are, observers may need to make judgments about whether a response occurred or may inadvertently overlook or misrecord behaviors that occur in the situation. Central to the collection of direct observational data is evaluation of agreement among observers. *Interobserver agreement*, also referred to as *reliability*, refers to the extent to which observers agree in their scoring of behavior.[1] This chapter discusses interobserver agreement, conditions of evaluating agreement, and quality of assessment procedures.

INTEROBSERVER AGREEMENT

Importance of Assessing Agreement

Agreement between different observers is assessed for three major reasons. First, assessment is useful only to the extent that it can be achieved with some consistency. Obviously, if frequency counts differ depending upon who is counting, it will be difficult to know the client's actual performance. The client may be scored as performing a response frequently on some days and infrequently on other days as a function of who scores the behavior rather than actual changes in client performance. Inconsistent measurement introduces variation into the data, which adds to the variation stemming from ordinary normal fluctuations in client performance I mentioned earlier. Agreement between observers ensures that one potential source of variation, namely, inconsistencies among observers, is minimal.

Second, assessing agreement minimizes, circumvents, or reveals the biases that any individual observer may have. If a single observer were used to record a behavior, any recorded change may be a result of a change in the observer's definition of the behavior over time rather than in the actual behavior of the client. Over time the observer might become lenient or stringent in applying the response definition. Alternatively, the observer might expect and perceive improvement based on the implementation of an intervention designed to alter behavior, even though no actual changes in behavior occur. Using more than one observer and checking interobserver agreement provide a partial check on the consistency with which response definitions are applied over time.

Finally, agreement between observers partially reflects whether the behavior is well defined. Interobserver agreement on the occurrences of behavior is one way to evaluate the extent to which the definition of behavior is sufficiently objective, clear, and complete—requirements for response definitions discussed in Chapter 3. Moreover, if observers readily agree on the occurrence of the response, it may be easier for persons who eventually carry out an intervention to agree on the occurrences and to apply the intervention consistently.

Agreement Versus Accuracy

Agreement between observers is assessed by having two or more persons observe the same client(s) at the same time. The observers work independently for the entire

---

[1] In applied research, "interobserver agreement" and "reliability" have been used interchangeably. For purposes of the present chapter, "interobserver agreement" is used primarily. "Reliability" as a term has an extensive history in assessment and has several different meanings. "Interobserver agreement" specifies the focus more precisely as the consistency between or among observers.

observation period, and the observations are compared when the session is over. A comparison of the observers' records reflects the consistency with which observers recorded the behavior of interest.

It is important to distinguish agreement between observers from accuracy of the observations. *Agreement* refers to evaluation of how well the data from separate observers correspond. High agreement means that observers correspond in the behaviors they score. Methods of quantifying the agreement are available, so that the extent to which observers do correspond in their observations can be carefully evaluated.

A major interest in assessing agreement is to evaluate whether observers are scoring behavior accurately. *Accuracy* refers to whether the observers' data reflect the client's actual performance. To measure the correspondence between how the client performs and observers' data, a standard or criterion is needed. Accuracy requires a firm standard that itself is reliable and valid. For example, accuracy is readily understandable in a situation in which two people score the answers that a student has made to a multiple-choice test. We can say that there really is a number that characterizes correct responses and this might even be obtained by automated scoring of the answer sheet (e.g., by a scanner). We can see if the observers agree with each other in scoring the test (interobserver agreement) and can tell if either observer had it right, that is, accurately scored the student's exam (accuracy).

Sometimes accuracy is evaluated by developing a reference point based on consensus that certain behaviors have or have not occurred. Accuracy may be evaluated by constructing a videotape in which certain behaviors are acted out and, hence, are known to be on the tape with a particular frequency, during particular intervals, or for a particular duration. Data that observers obtain from looking at the tape can be used to assess accuracy, since "true" performance is known. Alternatively, client behavior under naturalistic conditions (e.g., children in the classroom) may be videotaped. Several observers could score the tape repeatedly and decide what behaviors were present at any particular point in time. A new observer can rate the tape, and the data, when compared with the standard, reflect accuracy. When there is an agreement on a standard for how the client actually performed, a comparison of an observer's data with the standard reflects accuracy, that is, the correspondence of the observers' data to the "true" behavior.

Although investigators are interested in accuracy of observations, they usually must settle for interobserver agreement. In most settings, there are no clear criteria or permanent records of behavior to determine how the client really performed. Partially for practical reasons, the client's behavior cannot be videotaped or otherwise recorded each time a check on agreement is made. Use of equipment for automated recording without human observers circumvents this problem. However, for more commonly used procedures, human observers collect the data. Without a permanent record of the client's performance, it is difficult to determine how the client actually performed. In a check on agreement, two observers usually enter the situation and score behavior. The scores are compared, but neither score necessarily reflects how the client actually behaved. One wants performance of the client to be observed consistently (reliability) and to represent actual performance closely or well (validity) whether or not there is any index that could be used to verify exact performance.

In general, both interobserver agreement and accuracy involve comparing an observer's data with some other source. They differ in the extent to which the source of comparison can be entrusted to reflect the actual behavior of the client. Although accuracy and agreement are related, they need not go together. For example, an observer may record accurately (relative to a pre established standard) but show low interobserver agreement (with another observer whose observations are quite inaccurate). Conversely, an observer may show poor accuracy (in relation to the standard) but high interobserver agreement (with another observer who is inaccurate in a similar way). Hence, interobserver agreement is not a measure of accuracy. The general assumption is that if observers record the same behaviors, their data probably reflect what the client is doing. However, it is important to bear in mind that this is an assumption. Under special circumstances, discussed later in the chapter, the assumption may not be justified.

Conducting Checks on Agreement

Typically, an observer records the behavior of the client on a daily basis over the entire course of the investigation. Occasionally, another observer will also be used to check interobserver agreement. On such occasions, both observers will record the client's behavior. Obviously, it is important that the observers work independently, not look at each other's scoring sheets, and refrain from discussing their observations. The purpose of checking agreement is to determine how well observers agree when they record performance independently.

Checks on interobserver agreement are usually conducted on a regular basis throughout an investigation. If there are several different phases in the investigation, interobserver agreement usually is checked in each phase. It is possible that agreement varies over time as a function of changes in the client's behavior. The investigator is interested in having information on the consistency of observations over the course of the study. Hence, interobserver agreement is checked often and under each different condition or intervention that is in effect.

There are no precise rules for how often agreement should be checked. Several factors influence the decision. For example, with several observers or a relatively complex observational system, checks may need to be completed relatively often. Also, the extent to which observers in fact agree when agreement is checked may dictate the frequency of the checks. Initial checks on agreement may reveal that observers agree all or virtually all of the time. In such cases, agreement may need to be checked occasionally but not often. On the other hand, with other behaviors and observers, agreement may fluctuate greatly and checks will be required more often. As a general rule, agreement ought to be assessed within each phase of the investigation, preferably at least a few times within each phase. Yet checking on agreement is more complex than merely scheduling occasions in which two observers score behavior. How the checks on agreement are actually conducted may be as important as the frequency with which they are conducted, as will be evident later in the chapter.

METHODS OF ESTIMATING AGREEMENT

The methods available for estimating agreement partially depend on the assessment strategy (e.g., whether frequency or interval assessment is conducted). For any particular observational strategy, several different methods of estimating agreement are available. The major methods of computing reliability, their application to different observational formats, and considerations in their use are discussed next.

Frequency Ratio

Description. The frequency ratio is a method used to compute agreement when comparisons are made between the totals of two observers who independently record behaviors. The method is often used for frequency counts, but it can be applied to other assessment strategies as well (e.g., intervals of behavior, duration). Typically, the method is used when behavior can be freely performed and can theoretically take on any value. That is, there are no discrete trials or restricted set of opportunities for responding that can occur. For example, parents may count the number of times a child swears while at the dinner table. Theoretically, there is no limit to the frequency of the response (although laryngitis may set in if the response becomes too high). To assess agreement, both parents may independently keep a tally of the number of times a child says particular words. Agreement can be assessed by comparing the two totals that the parents have obtained at the end of dinner. To compute the frequency ratio, the following formula is used:

$$\text{Frequency Ratio} = \frac{\text{Smaller total}}{\text{Larger total}} \times 100$$

That is, the smaller total is divided by the larger total. The ratio usually is multiplied by 100 to form a percentage. In the preceding example, one parent may have observed 20 instances of swearing and the other may have observed 18 instances. The frequency ratio would be 18/20 or .9, which, when multiplied by 100, would make agreement 90%. The number reflects the finding that the totals obtained by each parent differ from each other by only 10% (or 100% agreement minus obtained agreement). For most uses, this ratio and this margin of difference would be fine as an indicator that behavior overall was observed consistently.

Problems and Considerations. Frequency ratios reflect agreement on the total number of behaviors scored by each observer. There is no way of determining within this method of agreement whether observers agreed on any particular instance of performance. It is even possible, although unlikely, that the observers may never agree on the occurrence of any particular behavior; they may see and record different instances of the behavior, even though their totals could be quite similar. In the preceding example, one parent observed 18 and the other observed 20 instances of swearing. It is possible that 38 (20 + 18) (or many more) instances occurred, and that the parents never scored the same instance of swearing. In practice, of course, large discrepancies between two observers scoring a discrete behavior such as swearing are unlikely. Nevertheless, the frequency ratio hides the fact that observers may not have actually agreed on the instances of behavior.

The absence of information on instances of behavior makes the agreement data from the frequency ratio somewhat ambiguous. The method, however, has still proved quite useful. If the totals of two observers are close (e.g., within a 10 to 20%

margin of error), then the method serves as a useful guideline for ensuring that they generally agree. The major problem with the frequency ratio rests not so much with the method but with the interpretation that may be inadvertently made. When a frequency ratio yields a percentage agreement of 90%, this does *not* mean that observers agreed 90% of the time or on 90% of the behaviors that occurred. The ratio merely reflects how close the totals fell to each other.

The frequency ratio of calculating agreement on totals for a given observation period is not restricted to frequency counts. The method can also be used to assess agreements on duration, interval assessment, and discrete categorization. In each case the ratio is computed for each session in which reliability is assessed by dividing the smaller total by the larger total. For example, a child's tantrums may be observed by a teacher and a teacher's aide using interval (or duration) assessment. After the session is completed, the total number of intervals (or amount of time in minutes) of tantrum behavior are compared and placed into the ratio and multiplied by 100. Although the frequency ratio can be extended to different response formats, it is usually restricted to frequency counts. More exact methods of computing agreement are available for other response formats to overcome the problem of knowing whether observers agreed on particular instances or samples of the behavior.

On balance, frequency ratios are easily computed and easily communicated to others. The problems I have identified are not necessarily reasons to avoid the ratios. In many cases, the problem may not be very likely because of the clarity of the behavior. The methodological goal of assessment is minimizing variability due to unreliability in the measurement procedures. High ratios mean high agreement on the total number of events for that observation period. That may be sufficient to describe performance and reflect change during an intervention phase, even if one or a few instances of the behavior (e.g., < 10%) were missed by one or the other observer.

Point-by-point Agreement Ratio

Description. An important method for computing reliability is to assess whether there is agreement on each instance of the observed behavior. The point-by-point agreement ratio is available for this purpose whenever there are discrete opportunities (e.g., number of trials, intervals, or correct answers) for the behavior to occur (occur/not occur, present/absent, appropriate/inappropriate). Whether observers agree is assessed at each opportunity for behavior to occur. For example, the discrete categorization method consists of several opportunities to record whether specific behaviors (e.g., room-cleaning behaviors) occur. For each of several behaviors, the observer can record whether the behavior was or was not performed (e.g., picking up one's clothing, making one's bed, putting food away). For a reliability check, two observers would record whether each of the behaviors was performed. The totals could be placed into a frequency ratio, as described previously. However, when one can identify each discrete behavior and whether observers agree on its occurrence, a finer-grained agreement measure can be used.

Because there were discrete response categories, a more exact method of computing agreement can be obtained. The scoring of the observers for each response can be compared directly to see whether both observers recorded a particular response as occurring. That is, if a checklist of behaviors had 10 different behaviors as possibly occurring or not, one could compare whether observers agreed on whether behavior 1 occurred or not, 2 occurred or not, and so on. Rather than looking at totals, agreement is evaluated on a response-by-response or point-by-point basis. The formula for computing point-by-point agreement consists of:

$$\text{Point-by-point agreement} = \frac{A}{A + D} \times 100$$

where

A = number of agreements from examining the data on a trial or opportunity-by-opportunity basis for the behavior to be scored

D = number of disagreements from examining the data on a trial or opportunity-by-opportunity basis for the behavior to be scored.

That is, agreements of the observers on the specific trials are divided by the number of agreements plus disagreements and multiplied by 100 to form a percentage. Agreements can be defined as instances in which both observers record the same thing. If both observers recorded the behavior as occurring, or they both scored the behavior as not occurring, an agreement would be scored. Disagreements are defined as instances in which one observer recorded the behavior as occurring and the other did not. The agreements and disagreements are tallied by comparing each behavior on a point-by-point basis.

A more concrete illustration of the computation of agreement by this method is provided using interval assessment, to which the point-by-point agreement ratio is applied most frequently. In interval assessment, two observers typically record and observe behavior for several intervals. In each interval (e.g., a 10-second period), observers record whether behavior (e.g., paying attention in class) occurred or not. Because each interval is recorded separately, point-by-point agreement can be evaluated. Agreement can be determined by comparing the intervals of both observers according to the formula just given.

In practice, agreements are usually defined as agreement between observers on occurrences of the behavior in interval assessment. The preceding formula is unchanged. However, agreements constitute only those intervals in which both observers marked the behavior as occurring. For example, assume observers recorded behavior for 50 10-second intervals and both observers agreed on the occurrence of the behavior in 20 intervals and disagreed in 5 intervals. Agreement (according to the point-by-point agreement formula) would be $20/(20 + 5) \times 100$, or 80%. Although observers recorded behavior for 50 intervals, all intervals were not used to calculate agreement. An interval is counted only if at least one observer recorded the occurrence of the behavior.

Excluding intervals in which neither observer records the behavior is based on the following reasoning. If these intervals were counted, they would be considered as agreements, since both observers "agree" that the response did not occur. Yet in observing behavior, many intervals may be marked without the occurrence of the behavior. If these were included as agreements, the estimate would be inflated beyond the level obtained when occurrences alone were counted as agreements. In the preceding example, behavior was not scored as occurring by either observer in 25 intervals.

By counting these as agreements, the point-by-point ratio would increase to 90%—that is, $45/(45+5) \times 100$, or 90%—rather than the 80% obtained originally. To avoid this increase, most investigators have restricted agreements to response occurrence.

Problems and Considerations. The advantage of the method is that it provides the opportunity to evaluate observer agreement for each response trial or observation interval and is more precise than the frequency ratio, which evaluates agreement on totals. Although the method is used most often for interval observation, it can be applied to other methods as well. For example, the formula can be used with frequency counts when there are discrete trials (e.g., number of correct arithmetic responses on a test) or discrete categories (e.g., number of chores), or a count of the number of people who perform a response. In any assessment format in which agreement can be evaluated on particular units or responses, the point-by-point ratio can be used.

Despite the greater precision of assessing exact agreement, many questions have been raised as to the method of computing agreement. For interval observations, investigators have questioned whether "agreements" in the formula should be restricted to intervals where both observers record an occurrence of the behavior or should also include intervals where both score a nonoccurrence. In one sense, both indicate that observers were in agreement for a particular interval. The issue is important because the estimate of reliability depends on the frequency of the client's behavior and whether occurrence and/or nonoccurrence agreements are counted. If the client performs the behavior relatively frequently or infrequently, observers are likely to have a high proportion of agreements on occurrences or nonoccurrences, respectively. Hence, the estimate of reliability may differ greatly depending on what is counted as an agreement between observers and how often behavior is scored as occurring. I return to this topic later in the chapter in the discussion of base rates.

Pearson Product-Moment Correlation

Description. The previous methods refer to procedures for estimating agreement on any particular occasion in which reliability is assessed. In each session or day in which agreement is assessed, the observers' data are entered into one of the formulas provided earlier. Typically, frequency or point-by-point agreement ratios are computed during each reliability check (that is, each day reliability is checked), and the mean level of agreement and range (low and high agreement levels) of the reliability checks over the course of the study or within different phases are reported.

One method of evaluating agreement over the entire course of an investigation is to compute a Pearson product-moment correlation (r). On each occasion in which interobserver agreement is assessed, a total for each observer is provided. This total may reflect the number of occurrences of the behavior or total intervals or duration. Essentially, each reliability occasion yields a pair of scores, one total from each observer. A correlation coefficient compares the totals across all occasions in which reliability was assessed. The correlation provides an estimate of agreement across all occasions in which reliability was checked rather than an estimate of agreement on any particular occasion.

The correlation can range from -1.00 through $+1.00$. A correlation of 0.00 means that the observers' scores are unrelated. That is, they tend not to go together at all. One observer may obtain a relatively high count of the behavior and the other observer's score may be high, low, or somewhere in between. A positive correlation between 0.00 to +1.00, particularly one in the high range (e.g., .80 or .90), means that the scores tend to go together. When one observer scores a high frequency of the behavior, the other one tends to do so as well, and when one scores a lower frequency of the behavior, so does the other one. If the correlation assumes a minus value (0.00 to –1.00) it means that observers tend to report scores that were in opposite directions: when one observer scored a higher frequency, the other invariably scored a lower frequency, and vice versa. (As a measure of agreement for observational data, correlations typically take on values between 0.00 and +1.00 rather than any negative values.)

Table 5.1 provides hypothetical data for 10 observation periods in which the frequency of a behavior was observed. Assume that the data were collected for 20 days and that on 10 of these days (every other day) two observers independently recorded behavior (even-numbered days). The pairs of scores from the reliability checks are listed. The correlation between these scores across all days is computed by a commonly used formula within the table. The *r* of .93 in the table means that the observers' scores are very much in the same direction—when one observer scores the behavior as occurring often or not often, the other does as well.

Problems and Considerations. The Pearson product-moment correlation assesses the extent to which observers covary in their scores. Covariation refers to the tendency of the scores (e.g., total frequencies or total agreements) to go together. If covariation is high, it means that both observers tended to obtain high scores on the same occasions and lower scores on other occasions. That is, their scores or totals tend to fluctuate in the same direction from occasion to occasion. The correlation says nothing about

Table 5.1 Scores for Two Observers to Compute Pearson Product-Moment Correlation

Days of Agreement Check	Observer 1 Totals = X	Observer 2 Totals = Y
2	25	29
4	12	20
6	19	17
8	30	31
10	33	33
12	18	20
14	26	28
16	15	20
18	10	11
20	17	19

Σ = sum
X = scores of Observer 1
Y = scores of Observer 2 $r = +.93$
XY = cross products of scores
N = number of checks

$$r = \frac{N\Sigma XY - \Sigma X\Sigma Y}{[N\Sigma X^2 - (\Sigma X)^2][N\Sigma Y^2 - (\Sigma Y)^2]}$$

whether the observers agree on the total amount of a behavior in any session. In fact, it is possible that one observer always scored behavior as occurring 20 (or any constant number) times more than the other observer for each session in which agreement was checked. If this amount of error were constant across all sessions, the correlation could still be perfect ($r = +1.00$). The correlation merely assesses the extent to which scores go together and not whether they are close to each other in absolute terms.

Because the correlation does not necessarily reflect exact agreement on total scores for a particular reliability session, it follows that it does not necessarily say anything about point-by-point agreement. The correlation relies on totals from the individual sessions, and so the observations of particular behaviors are lost. Thus, as a method of computing interobserver agreement, the Pearson product-moment correlation for the totals of each observer across sessions provides an inexact measure of agreement.

Another issue that arises in interpretation of the product-moment correlation pertains to the use of data across different phases. In single-case research, observations are usually obtained in the different phases of the design. In the simplest case, observations may be obtained before a particular intervention is in effect, followed by a period in which an intervention is applied to alter behavior. When the intervention is implemented, behavior is likely to increase or decrease, depending on the type of intervention and the purpose of the program. From the standpoint of a product-moment correlation, the change in frequency of behavior in the different phases may affect the estimate of agreement obtained by comparing observer totals. If behavior is high in the initial phase (e.g., hyperactive behaviors) and low during the intervention, the correlation of observer scores may be somewhat misleading. Both observers may tend to have high frequencies of behavior in the initial phase and low frequencies in the intervention phase. The tendency of the observers' scores to be high or low together is partially a function of the very different rates of behavior associated with the different phases. Agreement may be inflated in part because of the effects of the different rates between the phases. Agreement within each of the phases (initial baseline [pretreatment] phase *or* intervention phase) may not have been as high as the calculation of agreement between both phases. For the product-moment correlation, the possible artifact introduced by different rates of performance across phases can be remedied by calculating a correlation separately for each phase. The separate correlations can be averaged (by Fisher's z' transformation) to form an average (mean) correlation.[2]

General Comments

The previously discussed methods of computing agreement address different characteristics of the data. Selection of the method is determined in part by the observational strategy used and the unit of data. The unit of data refers to what the investigator uses as a measure to evaluate the client's performance on a day-to-day basis. The investigator may plot total frequency or total number of occurrences on a graphical display of the data in order to evaluate, demonstrate, or convey to others the impact of the

---

[2] The transformation is needed because r is not normally distributed and merely averaging their numbers misrepresents the mean. The transformation is readily obtained on the Web by typing "Table of Fishers z' transformation" in any search engine. There is one site available at the time of this writing: http://faculty.vassar.edu/lowry/tabs.html

intervention. In such a case, a frequency ratio or product-moment correlation may be selected to shed light on agreement on the totals. On the other hand, if a more refined and precise measure is obtained such as point-by-point agreement, then high agreement leads to the comforting conclusion that totals must also be closely approximated. Most investigators aim for point-by point agreement when possible because this is the most stringent measure of agreement. Even so, I would argue for an additional measure of agreement on the total to convey the consistency of measurement on the unit of data that is plotted and from which conclusions about the intervention will be drawn.

Even though agreement on totals for a given observation session is usually the primary interest, more analytic point-by-point agreement may be examined for several purposes. When point-by-point agreement is assessed, the investigator has greater information about how adequately several behaviors are defined and observed. Point-by-point agreement for different behaviors, rather than a frequency ratio for the composite total, provides information about exactly where any sources of disagreements emerge. Feedback to observers, further training, and refinement of particular definitions are likely to result from analysis of point-by-point agreement. Selection of the methods of computing agreement is also based on other considerations, including the frequency of behavior and the definition of agreements, two issues that now require greater elaboration.

BASE RATES AND CHANCE AGREEMENT

The methods of assessing agreement presented previously, especially the point-by-point agreement ratio, are the most commonly used methods in single-case research when direct observations are used. Usually, when the estimates of agreement are relatively high (e.g., 80% or $r = .80$), investigators assume that observers generally agree in their observations. However, investigators have been alert to the fact that a given estimate such as 80 or 90% does not mean the same thing under all circumstances. The level of agreement is in part a function of how frequently the behavior is scored as occurring.

If behavior is occurring with a relatively high frequency, observers are more likely to have high levels of agreement with the usual point-by-point ratio formula than if behavior is occurring with a relatively low frequency. The *base rate* of behavior, that is, the level of occurrence or number of intervals in which behavior is recorded as occurring, contributes to the estimated level of agreement.[3] The possible influence of high or low frequency of behavior on interobserver agreement applies to any observations in which point-by-point agreement is assessed. The interval method is used as an example because it is one of the most frequently used assessment methods.

A client may perform the response in most of the intervals in which he or she is observed. If two observers mark the behavior as occurring in many of the intervals, they are likely to agree merely because of the high rate of occurrence. When many occurrences are marked by both observers, high correspondence between observers is inevitable. To be more concrete, assume that the client performs the behavior in 90

---

[3] The base rate should not be confused with the baseline rate. The base rate refers to the proportion of intervals or relative frequency of the behavior. Baseline rate usually refers to the rate of performance when no intervention is in effect to alter the behavior.

of 100 intervals and that both observers coincidentally score the behavior as occurring in 90% of the intervals. Agreement between the observers is likely to be high simply because of the fact that a large proportion of intervals was marked as occurrences. That is, agreement will be high as a function of chance.

Chance in this context refers to the level of agreement that would be expected by *randomly* marking occurrences for a given number of intervals. Agreement would be high whether or not observers saw the same behavior as occurring in each interval. Even if both observers were blindfolded but marked a large number of intervals as occurrences, agreement might be high. Exactly how high chance agreement would be depends on what is counted as an agreement. In the point-by-point ratio, recall that reliability was computed by dividing agreements by agreements plus disagreements and multiplying by 100. An agreement usually means that both observers recorded the behavior as occurring. But if behavior is occurring at a high rate, reliability may be especially high on the basis of chance.

The actual formula for computing the *chance* level of agreement on occurrences is:

$$\text{Chance agreement on occurrences} = \frac{o_1 \text{ occurrences} \times o_2 \text{ occurrences}}{\text{total intervals}^2} \times 100$$

where

o_1 occurrences = the number of intervals in which Observer 1 scored the behavior as occurring

o_2 occurrences = the number of intervals in which Observer 2 scored the behavior as occurring,

total intervals^2 = all intervals of observation squared.

If the client performs the behavior frequently, o_1 and o_2 occurrences are likely to be high. In the preceding hypothetical example, both observers recorded 90 occurrences of the behavior. With such frequent recordings of occurrences, by just randomly marking this number of intervals, "chance" agreement would be high. In the preceding formula, chance would be 81% ($[90 \times 90/100^2] \times 100$). Merely because occurrence intervals are quite frequent, agreement would appear high. When investigators report agreement at this level, it may be important to know whether this level would have been expected anyway merely as a function of chance.

Perhaps the problem of high agreement based on chance could be avoided by only counting those intervals in which observers agreed on *non*occurrences as agreements. The intervals in which they agreed on occurrences could be omitted. If only the number of intervals when both observers agreed on behavior not occurring were counted as agreements, the chance level of agreement would be lower. In fact, chance agreement on nonoccurrences would be calculated by the following formula:

$$\text{Chance agreement on nonoccurrences} = \frac{o_1 \text{ nonoccurrences} \times o_2 \text{ nonoccurrences}}{\text{total intervals}^2} \times 100$$

In the previous example, both observers recorded nonoccurrences in 10 of the 100 intervals, making chance agreement on nonoccurrences 1% ($[10 \times 10]/100^2 \times 100$).[4]

---

[4] The level of agreement expected by chance is based on the proportion of intervals in which observers report the behavior as occurring or not occurring. Although chance agreement can be calculated

When agreements are defined as nonoccurrences that are scored at a low frequency, chance agreement is low. Hence, if the point-by-point ratio were computed and observers agreed 80% of the time on nonoccurrences, this would clearly mean they agreed well above the level expected by chance.

Defining agreements on the basis of nonoccurrences is not a general solution, because in many cases nonoccurrences may be relatively high (e.g., when the behavior rarely occurs). Moreover, as an intervention project proceeds, it is likely that in different phases occurrences will be relatively high and nonoccurrences will be relatively low and that this pattern will be reversed. The question for investigators that has received considerable attention is how to compute agreement between observers over the course of an experiment while taking into account the changing level of agreement that would be expected by chance. Several methods of addressing this question have been suggested.[5]

ALTERNATIVE METHODS OF HANDLING EXPECTED ("CHANCE") LEVELS OF AGREEMENT

Variations of Occurrence and Nonoccurrence Agreement

The problem of base rates occurs when the intervals that are counted as agreements in a reliability check are the ones scored at a high rate. Typically, agreements are defined as instances in which both observers record the behavior as occurring. If occurrences are scored relatively often, the expected level of agreement on the basis of chance is relatively high. One solution is to vary the definition of agreements in the point-by-point ratio to reduce the expected level of agreement based on "chance." Agreements on occurrences would be calculated only when the rate of behavior is low, that is, when relatively few intervals are scored as occurrences of the response. This is somewhat different from the usual way in which agreements on occurrences are counted even when occurrences are scored frequently. Hence, with low rates of occurrences, point-by-point agreement on occurrences provides a stringent measure of how observers agree without a high level expected by chance. Conversely, when the occurrences of behavior are relatively high, agreement can be computed on intervals in which both observers record the behavior as not occurring. With a high rate of occurrences, agreement on nonoccurrences is not likely to be inflated by chance.

Although the recommendation is sound, the solution is somewhat cumbersome. First, over time in a given investigation, it is likely that the rates of occurrence of response will change at different points so that high and low rates occur in different phases. The definition of agreement would also change at different times. The primary interest in assessing agreement is determining whether observers see the behavior as

---

[4] (Continued) by the formulas provided here, other sources provide probability functions in which chance agreement can be determined simply and directly (e.g., Ary, Covalt, & Suen, 1990; Hartmann, 1982).

[5] A series of articles on the topic of interobserver agreement and alternative methods of computing agreement based on estimates of chance appeared several years ago and remain applicable. See separate issues of the *Journal of Applied Behavior Analysis* (1977, Volume 10, pp. 97–150; and 1979, Volume 12, pp. 523–571).

occurring. Constantly changing the definition of agreements within a study handles the problem of chance agreement but does not provide a clear and direct measure of agreement on scoring the behavior.

Another problem with the proposed solution is that agreement estimates tend to fluctuate markedly when the intervals that define agreement are infrequent. For example, if 100 intervals are observed and behavior occurs in only 2 intervals, the recommendation would be to compute agreement on occurrence intervals. Assume that one observer records two occurrences, that the other records only one, and that they both agree on this one. Reliability will be based only on computing agreement for the two intervals, and will be 50% (agreements = 1, disagreements = 1, and overall reliability equals agreements divided by agreements plus disagreements). If the observer who provided the check on reliability scored 0, 1, or if both occurrences were in agreement with the primary observer, agreement would be 0, 50, or 100%, respectively. Thus, with a small number of intervals counted as agreements, reliability estimates fluctuate widely and are subject to misinterpretation in their own right. Perhaps the simplest solution is to report reliability separately for occurrence and nonoccurrence intervals throughout the investigation. This allows the reader or consumer of research to judge whether agreement is discrepant based on the ways in which it is computed and whether the rate of occurrences of the behavior, which presumably changes over different phases of the design, influences agreement.

Plotting Agreement Data

A major purpose of obtaining agreement estimates is to ensure that there is sufficient consistency in the measure so as to represent the effects of the intervention. Whether one way of computing agreement versus another misrepresents the data can be addressed by plotting the data separately for both the primary observer and the secondary observer. Usually, only the data for the primary observer are plotted. However, the data obtained from the secondary observer can also be plotted so that the similarity in the scores from the observers can be seen on the graphic display.

An interesting advantage of this recommendation is that one can determine whether the observers disagree to such an extent that the conclusions drawn from the data would differ because of the extent of the disagreement. For example, Figure 5.1 shows hypothetical data for baseline and intervention phases. The data for the primary observer are plotted for each day of observation (circles). The occasional reliability checks by a second observer are also plotted (squares). The data in the upper panel show that both observers were relatively close in their estimates of performance. If the data of the second observer were substituted for those of the first, the pattern of data showing superior performance during the intervention phase would not be altered.

In contrast, the lower panel shows marked discrepancies between the primary and secondary observer. The discrepancy is referred to as "marked" because of the impact that the differences would have on the conclusions reached about the changes in behavior. If the data of the second observer were used, it would not be clear that performance really improved during the intervention phase. The data for the second observer suggest that perhaps there was no change in performance over the two phases

INTEROBSERVER AGREEMENT

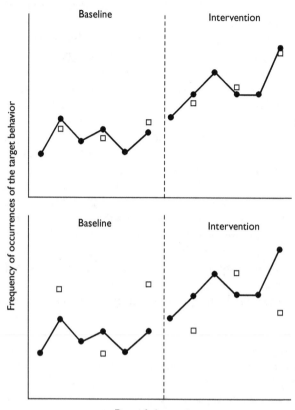

Figure 5.1. Hypothetical data showing observations from the primary observer (circles connected by lines) and the second observer, whose data are used to check agreement (squares). The *upper panel* shows close correspondence between observers; the conclusions about behavior change from baseline to intervention phases would not vary if the data from the second observer were substituted in place of the data from the primary observer. The *lower panel* shows marked discrepancies between observers; the conclusions about behavior change would be very different depending on which observer's data were used.

or, alternatively, that there is bias in the observations and that no clear conclusion can be reached.

In any case, plotting the data from both observers provides useful information about how closely the observers actually agreed in their totals for occurrences of the response. Independently of the numerical estimate of agreement, graphic display permits one to examine whether the scores from each observer would lead to different conclusions about the effects of an intervention, which is a very important reason for evaluating agreement in the first place. Plotting data from a second observer whose data are used to evaluate agreement provides an important source of information that could be hidden by agreement ratios that are potentially inflated by "chance."

Correlational Statistics

Another means of addressing the problem of chance agreement and the misleading interpretations that might result from high percentage agreement is to use correlational statistics. One correlational statistic that is commonly used is *kappa* (*k*) (Cohen, 1965). Kappa is especially suited for categorical data such as interval observation or discrete categorization when each response or interval is recorded as occurring or not. Kappa provides an estimate of agreement between observers that is corrected for chance. When observers agree at the same level one would expect on the basis of chance, $k = 0$. If agreement surpasses the expected chance level, k exceeds 0 and approaches a maximum of $+1.00$.[6]

Kappa is computed by the following formula:

$$k = \frac{P_o - P_c}{1 - P_c}$$

where

P_o = the proportion of agreements between observers on occurrences and nonoccurrences (or agreements on occurrences and nonoccurrences divided by the total number of agreements and disagreements).

P_c = the proportion of expected agreements on the basis of chance (is computed by multiplying the number of occurrences for Observer 1 times the number of occurrences for Observer 2 plus the number of nonoccurrences for Observer 1 times the number of nonoccurrences for Observer 2. The sum of these is divided by the total number of intervals squared).

For example, two observers may observe a child for 100 intervals. Observer 1 scores 80 intervals of occurrence of aggressive behavior and 20 intervals of nonoccurrence. Observer 2 scores 70 intervals of aggressive behavior and 30 intervals of nonoccurrence. Assume that observers agree on 70 of the occurrence intervals and on 20 nonoccurrence intervals and disagree on the remaining 10 intervals. Using the preceding formula, $P_o = .90$ and $P_c = .62$ with kappa = .74. Although there is no firm or universally agreed upon rule, generally kappa > .7 is viewed as acceptable agreement.

The advantage of kappa is that it corrects for chance based on the observed frequency of occurrence and nonoccurrence intervals. Other agreement measures are difficult to interpret because chance agreement may yield a high positive value (e.g., 80%) which gives the impression that high agreement has been obtained. For example, with the preceding data used in the computation of *k*, a point-by-point ratio agreement on occurrence and nonoccurrence intervals combined would yield 90% agreement. However, on the basis of chance alone, the percent agreement would be 62. Kappa provides a measure of agreement over and above chance.[7]

---

[6] Kappa values can be negative and move from 0.00 to -1.00 in the unlikely event that agreement between observers is less than the level expected by chance.

[7] Kappa is not the only correlational statistic that can estimate agreement on categorical data (see Hartmann, 1982). For example, another estimate very similar to kappa is phi (Φ), which also extends from -1.00 through +1.00 and yields 0.00 when agreement is at the chance level. The advantage of

General Comments

Several alternatives have been suggested to take into account chance or expected levels of agreement. A few of the solutions were highlighted here, which merely served to raise the issue and to convey major options. There is no clear consensus on which of the solutions adequately resolves the problem without introducing new complexities. And, in the applied literature, investigators have not uniformly adopted one particular way of handling the problem. At this point, there is consensus on the problem that chance agreement can obscure estimates of reliability. Further, there is general agreement that in reporting reliability, it is useful to consider one of the many different ways of conveying or incorporating chance agreement. Hence, as a general guideline, it is probably useful to compute and report agreement expected on the basis of chance or to compute agreement in alternative formats (e.g., separately for occurrences and nonoccurrences) to provide additional data that convey how observers actually concur in their observations.

As alternatives are considered for computing agreement and considering the impact of base rates and chance, it is important to keep in mind the primary goal. Reliability computation and assessment are not ends in their own right, but rather serve a critical methodological issue. Do the data reflect performance of the client, and will the data permit evaluation of the intervention? High levels of agreement optimize the extent to which these ends can be achieved. In any given demonstration, whether agreement is 70 or 80% depending on the method of computation may or may not make a difference. Impact of the intervention, for example, can be such that the difference in how reliability is computed is nugatory. This can be evident by plotting data of both primary and secondary observers to address the question directly: do different data sources appreciably alter the conclusions that would be reached about the client's behavior or the effect of the intervention?

There are many ways of measuring interrater agreement. They include measures I did not mention (e.g., intraclass correlation) and variations of others (e.g., kappa) I have not covered (see Broemeling, 2009; Shoukri, 2005). I have included those methods of evaluating agreement that are most commonly used. The goal was to convey specific practices and how and when they are used. In addition, the methods of evaluating interrater agreement served as a way of discussing critical issues that need to be considered (e.g., goals of assessing agreement to begin with, base rates, interpretation of agreement statistics). Understanding of these latter issues is critical. Agreement is not an end itself but a means to enhance interpretation of the data and this depends on understanding these other issues as well as how reliability information is obtained, as discussed next.

SOURCES OF ARTIFACT AND BIAS

Interpretation of agreement estimates depends on knowing several features about the circumstances in which agreement is assessed. Sources of bias that can obscure interpretation of interobserver agreement include reactivity of reliability assessment,

---

[7] (Continued) phi is that a conversion table has been provided to convey levels of phi based on obtained agreement on occurrences and nonoccurrences (Lewin & Wakefield, 1979). Thus, investigators can convert their usual data into phi equivalents without computational difficulties.

observer drift, observer expectancies and experimenter feedback, and complexity of the observations.[8]

Reactivity of Reliability Assessment

Interobserver agreement is usually checked periodically during an investigation. Typically, observers are aware that their observations are being checked, if for no other reason than another observer may be present on just those occasions and both observers must coordinate their recording to observe the same person at the same time. Because observers are aware that reliability is being checked, the situation is potentially reactive. *Reactivity* refers to changes that people make when their behavior is being monitored or evaluated. Awareness does not invariably lead to reactivity. Yet one must be alert to the possibility that there is an influence. Indeed, research has shown that observer awareness that reliability is being checked influences the observations they make. When observers are led to believe that agreement is being assessed on some occasions and not assessed on others, their agreement is higher, even though their agreement is checked on all occasions (see Kent & Foster, 1977, for a review). In fact, agreement was assessed even when they did not believe they were being checked. The general findings are consistent; observers show higher interobserver agreement when they are aware that reliability is being checked than when they are unaware.

It is not entirely clear why agreement is higher under conditions when observers are aware that reliability is being checked. When observers are aware of reliability checks, they may modify the behavioral definitions or codes slightly to concur with the other observer with whom their data are compared and observe differently. One study found that observers recorded much less disruptive student behavior in the classroom during occasions on which they thought agreement was being checked. The broader point is the more critical one: interpretation of estimates of agreement depends very much on the conditions of reliability assessment. Estimates obtained when observers are unaware of agreement checks tend to be lower than those obtained when they are aware of these checks.

Awareness of assessing agreement can be handled in different ways. As a general rule, the conditions of reliability assessment should be similar to the conditions in which data are ordinarily obtained. If observers ordinarily believe that their behaviors are not being monitored, these conditions should be maintained during reliability checks. In practice, it may be difficult to conduct agreement checks without observers being aware of the checks. Measuring interobserver agreement usually involves special arrangements that are not ordinarily in effect each day. For example, in most investigations two observers usually do not record the behavior of the same target subject at the same time unless agreement is being assessed. Hence, it may be difficult to conduct checks without alerting observers to this fact. An alternative might be to lead observers to believe that all their observations are being monitored over the course of the investigation. This latter

---

[8] Many of the sources of bias and artifact in conducting observations were evaluated in the 1970s and 1980s. Thus many "classic" (but also old) references constitute the primary literature. Key findings and recommendations of the early studies remain cogent and applicable. Original studies are only highlighted in this section; the reader is referred to reviews of the studies in these secondary sources (Hartmann, Barrios, & Wood, 2004; Kazdin, 1977a; Kent & Foster, 1977).

alternative would appear to be advantageous, given evidence that observers tend to be more accurate when they believe their agreement is being assessed.

Observer Drift

Observers usually receive extensive instruction and feedback regarding accuracy in applying the definitions for recording behavior. Training is designed to ensure that observers adhere to the definitions of behavior and record behavior at a consistent level of accuracy. Once mastery is achieved and estimates of agreement are consistently high, it is assumed that observers continue to apply the same definition of behavior over time. However, observers may "drift" from the original definition of behavior. *Observer drift* refers to the tendency of observers to change the manner in which they apply definitions of behavior over time.

The hazard of drift is that it is not easily detected. Interobserver agreement may remain high even though the observers are deviating from the original definitions of behavior. If observers consistently work together and communicate with each other, they may develop similar variations of the original definitions (Hawkins & Dobes, 1977). Thus, high levels of agreement can be maintained even if accuracy declines. Drift is detected by comparing interobserver agreement among a subgroup of observers who constantly work together with agreement across subgroups who have not worked with each other. Over time, subgroups of observers may modify and apply the definitions of behavior differently, which can only be detected by comparing data from observers who have not worked together.

If observers modify the definitions of behavior over time, the data from different phases may not be comparable. For example, if disruptive behaviors in the classroom or at home are observed, the data from different days in the study may not reflect precisely the same behaviors, due to observer drift. And, as already noted, the differences in the definitions of behavior may occur even though observers continue to show high interobserver agreement.

Observer drift can be controlled in a variety of ways. First, observers can undergo continuous training over the course of the investigation. Videotapes of the clients can be shown in periodic retraining sessions where the codes are discussed among all observers. Observers can meet as a group, rate behavior in the situation, and receive feedback regarding the accuracy of their observations, that is, their adherence to the original codes. The feedback can convey the extent to which observers correctly invoke the definitions for scoring behavior. Feedback for accuracy in applying the definitions helps reduce drift from the original behavioral codes.

Second, all observations of the client can be videotaped. Observers can score the tapes in random order at the end of the investigation. Drift would not differentially bias data in different phases because tapes are rated in random order. This alternative is somewhat impractical because of the time and expense of taping the client's behavior for several observation sessions. Moreover, the investigator needs the data on a day-to-day basis to make decisions regarding when to implement or withdraw the intervention, a characteristic of single-case designs that will become clearer in subsequent chapters. Yet taped samples of behavior from selected occasions could be compared with actual observations obtained by observers in the setting to assess whether drift has occurred over time.

Finally, drift might also be controlled by periodically bringing newly trained observers into the setting to assess interobserver agreement. Comparison of newly trained observers with observers who have continuously participated in the investigation can reveal whether the codes are applied differently over time. Presumably, new observers would adhere more closely to the original definitions than other observers who have had the opportunity to drift from the original definitions.

Observer Expectancies and Feedback

Another potential source of bias is the expectancies of observers regarding the client's behavior and the feedback observers receive from the experimenter in relation to that behavior. If observers are led to expect change (e.g., an increase or decrease in behavior), these expectancies do not usually bias observational data (see Kent & Foster, 1977). Yet expectancies can influence the observations when combined with feedback from the experimenter. Instructions to expect change combined with feedback for scoring reductions can lead to decreases in the disruptive behavior that the observers reported (O'Leary, Kent, & Kanowitz, 1975). In this study, observers were only rating a videotape of classroom behavior in which no changes in the disruptive behaviors occurred over time. Thus, the expectancies and feedback about the effects of treatment affected the data generated by the observers. Investigators probably rarely apply feedback to observers in this fashion, but the study is instructive to show the malleability of observer data to such external influences.

It is reassuring that research suggests that expectancies alone are not likely to influence behavioral observations. However, it may be crucial to control the feedback that observers obtain about the data and whether the investigator's expectations are confirmed. Obviously, any feedback provided to observers should be restricted to information about the accuracy of their observations, rather than information about changes in the client's behavior, in order to prevent or minimize drift.

Complexity of the Observations

In the situations discussed up to this point, the assumption has been made that observers score only one behavior at a time. Often observers record several behaviors within a given observational period. For example, with interval assessment, the observers may score several different behaviors during a particular interval. Research has shown that complexity of the observations influences agreement and accuracy of the observations.

Complexity has been investigated in different ways. For example, complexity can refer to the *number of different responses* that are scored in a given period. Observational codes that consist of several categories of responses are more complex than those with fewer categories. As might be expected, observers have been found to be more accurate and show higher agreement when there are fewer categories of behavior to score (see Kazdin, 1977a, for a review). Complexity can also refer to the *range of client behaviors that are performed*. Within a given scoring system, clients may perform many different behaviors over time. The greater the number of different behaviors that clients perform, the lower the interobserver agreement is likely to be. The precise reasons why complexity of observations and interobserver agreement are inversely related are not entirely clear. Presumably, with complex observational systems in which several behaviors must be scored, observers may have difficulty in making discriminations among all of the codes and definitions or are more likely to make errors. With much more information to process and code, errors in applying the codes and scoring would be expected to increase.

In training observers, the temptation is to provide relatively simplified conditions of assessment in order to ensure that observers understand each of the definitions and apply them consistently. When several codes, behaviors, or subjects are to be observed in the investigation, observers need to be trained to record behavior with the same level of complexity. High levels of interobserver agreement need to be established for the exact conditions under which observers will be required to perform.

ACCEPTABLE LEVELS OF AGREEMENT

The question for researchers invariably is, "When all is said and done, what is an acceptable level of agreement?" As the discussion conveys, the number by itself is not easily interpreted based on method of computation, chance and base rates, number and complexity of behaviors, and various sources of bias that may be present. The level of agreement that is acceptable is one that indicates to the researcher that the observers are sufficiently consistent in their recordings of behavior, that behaviors are adequately defined, and that the measure will be sensitive to changes in the client's performance over time. This general statement may be unsatisfying, but the goal of checking agreement is to address design requirements that require describing stable patterns of performance and identifying change when change occurs. If very small changes in behavior are likely to occur, an error in assessment (e.g., disagreement) could obscure the outcome. The small changes may be obscured by a little variability (error) in assessment. In contrast, if large changes are likely to occur, slightly more disagreement can be tolerated. The added variability in the observations would not obscure the marked changes in performance.

The magnitude of change is only one influence. The variability in performance of the client also is critical. For example, assume that the client's "real" behavior (free from any observer bias) shows relatively little variability over time. Also, assume that across baseline and intervention phases, dramatic changes in behavior occur. Under conditions of slight variability and marked changes, moderate inconsistencies in the data may not interfere with drawing conclusions about intervention effects. On the other hand, if the variability in the client's behavior is relatively large and the changes over time are not especially dramatic, a moderate amount of inconsistency among observers may hide the change. Hence, although high agreement between observers is always a goal, the level of agreement that is acceptable to detect systematic changes in the client's performance depends on the client's behavior and the effects of intervention.

Traditionally, agreement was regarded as acceptable if it met or surpassed .80, or 80%, computed by frequency or point-by-point agreement ratios. Of course, high levels of agreement may not necessarily be acceptable if the formula for computing agreement or the conditions for evaluating agreement introduce potential biases or artifacts. Conversely, lower levels of agreement may be quite useful and acceptable if the conditions under which they were obtained minimize sources of bias and artifact. Hence, it is not only the quantitative estimate that ought to be evaluated, but also how that estimate was obtained and under what conditions.

In light of the large number of considerations embedded in the estimate of inter-observer agreement, concrete guidelines that apply to all methods of computing agreement, conditions in which agreement is assessed, and patterns of data are difficult to provide. The traditional guideline of seeking agreement at or above .80 is a useful guideline, but attaining this criterion is not necessarily meaningful or acceptable, given other conditions that could contribute to this estimate. As a general recommendation, it is important not to lose sight of why one is measuring agreement in the first place, namely, to minimize error in the data and variability that might obscure drawing inferences about change. This consideration leads one to evaluate client variability and likelihood of being able to detect change rather than the possibly mindless focus on a number. As a more concrete recommendation, given the current status of views of agreement, I would encourage investigators to consider more than one method for estimating agreement and to specify carefully the conditions in which the checks on agreement are conducted. With added information, the investigator and those who read reports of applied research will be in a better position to evaluate the assessment procedures and whether and how the procedures influence the conclusions.

SUMMARY AND CONCLUSIONS

Reliability of assessment is critical in all scientific research and among all of the different methods (e.g., ratings, questionnaires, direct observations, automated) that are used in single-case research. Direct observation, the most frequently used method of assessment in single-case research, has its own challenges in both the computation of agreement and the conditions under which agreement is assessed.

A crucial component of direct observation of behavior is to ensure that observers score behavior consistently. Consistent assessment is essential to ensure that minimal variation is introduced into the data by observers and to check on the adequacy of the response definition(s). Interobserver agreement is assessed periodically by having two or more persons simultaneously but independently observe the client and record behavior. The resulting scores are compared to evaluate consistency of the observations.

Several commonly used methods to assess agreement consist of *frequency ratio*, *point-by-point agreement ratio*, and *Pearson product-moment correlation*. These methods provide different information, including, respectively, correspondence of observers on the total frequency of behavior for a given observational session, the exact agreement of observers on specific occurrences of the behavior within a session, or the covariation of observer data across several sessions.

A major issue in evaluating agreement data pertains to the *base rate* of the client's performance. As the frequency of behavior or occurrences increases, the level of agreement on these occurrences between observers increases as a function of chance. Thus, if behavior is recorded as relatively frequent, agreement between the observers is likely to be high. Without calculating the expected or chance level of agreement, investigators may believe that high observer agreement is a function of the well-defined behaviors and high levels of consistency between observers. Point-by-point agreement ratios as usually calculated do not consider the chance level of agreement and may be misleading. Hence, alternative methods of calculating agreement have been proposed, based on the relative frequency of occurrences or nonoccurrences of the response, graphic displays of the data from the observer who serves to check reliability, and computation of correlational measures (e.g., kappa, phi).

Several sources of bias and artifact have been identified that may influence the agreement data. These include *reactivity of assessment, observer drift, expectancies of the observers and feedback from the experimenter,* and *complexity of the observations.* In general, observers tend to agree more and to be more accurate when they are aware, rather than unaware, that their observations are being checked. The definitions that observers apply to behavior may depart ("drift") from the original definitions they held at the beginning of the investigation. Under some conditions, observers' expectancies of changes in the client's behavior and feedback indicating that the experimenter's expectancies are confirmed may bias the observations. Finally, accuracy of observations and interobserver agreement tend to decrease as a function of the complexity of the observational system (e.g., number of different categories to be observed and number of different behaviors clients perform within a given observational system).

It is important to keep in mind that the purpose of assessing agreement is to ensure that observers are consistent in their observations and that sufficient agreement exists to reflect change in the client's behavior over time. In conducting and reporting assessment of agreement, it may be advisable to consider more than one way to estimate and report agreement. Also, it is just as important to ensure that the conditions under which agreement is obtained circumvent or minimize the sources of bias and artifact. These sources are critical because they show that agreement can be high, but the data can very much misrepresent client behavior.

CHAPTER 6

Introduction to Single-Case Research and ABAB Designs

I mentioned that research design in general includes three interdependent components: assessment, experimental design, and data evaluation. Their interdependence derives from how they contribute to clarity of the conclusions and how each helps reduce, eliminate, or make implausible threats to validity. In the assessment chapters, I noted not only strategies for assessing outcomes but also features of assessment (e.g., inconsistencies, biases in conditions of assessment) that interfere with drawing conclusions about the intervention. Beginning with this chapter, we now discuss major design options of single-case research. Before discussing the first design option, some preliminary comments will be helpful to convey the goals of the designs and how these are shared with more familiar between-group research.

In both between-group and single-case designs the intervention is arranged in such a way as to make alternative threats to internal validity implausible. All experiments compare the effects of different conditions (independent variables) on performance (dependent variables). In traditional between-group experimentation, the comparison is made between groups of subjects who receive or who are exposed to different conditions. The "gold standard" for between-group research that evaluates interventions is the *randomized controlled trial* (RCT). Participants in the study are assigned randomly to one of two (or more) groups. In the simple case, there might be two groups: intervention and no intervention. The effect of the intervention is evaluated by comparing the performance of the different groups at the end of the study. In single-case research, inferences are usually made about the effects of the intervention by comparing different conditions presented to the same participant over time. Here too in the simple case performance of the participant may be compared under two conditions, intervention and no intervention. However, details of how single-case designs accomplish this comparison are novel and depart considerably from traditional between-group designs. The purpose of this chapter is to identify key characteristics of all single-case designs and how they contribute to the logic of drawing causal inferences. One family of single-case designs, referred to as ABAB designs, is also presented not only to convey the logic of single-case research but also to present options that can be used to evaluate intervention programs.

GENERAL REQUIREMENTS OF SINGLE-CASE DESIGNS

Continuous Assessment

The most fundamental design requirement of single-case experimentation is the reliance on repeated observations of performance over time. The client's performance is observed on several occasions, usually before the intervention is applied and continuously over the period while the intervention is in effect. Typically, observations are conducted on a daily basis or at least on multiple occasions each week. Continuous assessment is a basic requirement because single-case designs examine the effects of interventions on performance over time. Continuous assessment allows the investigator to examine the pattern and stability of performance before treatment is initiated. The pretreatment information over an extended period provides a picture of what performance is like without the intervention. When the intervention eventually is implemented, the observations are continued and the investigator can examine whether behavior changes coincide with administration of the intervention.

The role of continuous assessment in single-case research can be illustrated by examining a basic difference of between-group and single-case research. In both types of research, as already noted, the effects of a particular intervention on performance are examined. In the most basic case, the intervention is examined by comparing performance when the intervention is presented versus performance when it is withheld. In between-group research, the question is addressed by giving the intervention to some persons (treatment group) but not to others (no treatment group). One or two observations (e.g., pre- and post-treatment assessment) are obtained for several different persons. In single-case research, the effects of the intervention are examined by observing the influence of the intervention and no intervention on the performance of the same person(s). *Instead of one or two observations of several persons, several observations are obtained for one or a few persons.* Continuous assessment refers to those several observations that are needed to make the comparison of interest with the individual subject.

Baseline Assessment

Each of the single-case experimental designs usually begins with observing behavior for several days before the intervention is implemented. This initial period of observation, referred to as the *baseline phase*, provides information about the level of behavior before a special intervention begins. The baseline phase serves two critical functions. The first is referred to as *the descriptive function*. The data collected during the baseline phase describe the existing level of performance or the extent to which the client engages in the behavior or domain that is to be altered. The second is referred to as *the predictive function*. The baseline data serve as the basis for predicting the level of performance for the immediate future if the intervention is not provided. Of course, a description of present performance does not necessarily provide a statement of what performance would really be like in the future. Performance might change even without the intervention (e.g., from history or maturation, as two influences). The only way to be certain of future performance without the intervention would be to continue baseline observations without implementing the intervention. This cannot be done because the purpose is to implement and evaluate the intervention in order to improve the client's functioning in some way. What can be done is to observe baseline performance for several days to provide a sufficient or reasonable basis for making a prediction of future performance. The prediction is achieved by *projecting* or *extrapolating* a continuation of baseline performance into the future.

A hypothetical example can be used to illustrate how observations during the baseline phase are used to predict future performance and how this prediction is pivotal to drawing inferences about the effects of the intervention. Figure 6.1 illustrates a hypothetical case in which observations were collected on a child in a special education class and focused on frequency of shouting out complaints or comments to a teacher. As evident in the figure, observations during the baseline (pretreatment) phase were

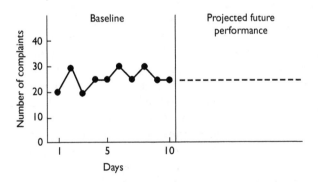

Figure 6.1. Hypothetical example of baseline observations of frequency of complaining. The data in baseline (solid line) are used to predict the likely rate of performance in the future (dashed line).

obtained for 10 days. The hypothetical baseline data suggest a reasonably consistent pattern of shouting out complaints each day in the classroom.

We do not really know what performance will be like on Days 11, 12, and so on—all those days after baseline that were not yet observed. Yet, the baseline level can be used to project the likely level of performance in the immediate future if conditions continue as they are. The projected (dashed) line suggests the approximate level of future performance. This projected level is essential for single-case experimentation because it serves as one criterion to evaluate whether the intervention leads to change. Presumably, if treatment is effective, performance will differ from the projected level of baseline. For example, if a program is designed to reduce shouting and is successful in doing so, the line (data points) for shouting out should be well below the projected line that represents the level of baseline. In any case, continuous assessment in the beginning of single-case experimental designs consists of observation of baseline or pretreatment performance. As the individual single-case designs are described later, the importance of initial baseline assessment will become especially clear.

Stability of Performance

Since baseline performance is used to predict how the client will behave in the future, it is important that the data are stable. A *stable rate* of performance is characterized by the absence of a trend (or slope) in the data and relatively little variability in performance. The notions of trend and variability raise separate issues, even though they both relate to stability.

Trend in the Data. A *trend*, also called *slope*, refers to the tendency for performance to decrease or increase systematically or consistently over time. One of three simple data patterns might be evident during baseline observations. First, baseline data may show no trend or slope. In this case, performance is best represented by a horizontal line indicating that it is not increasing or decreasing over time. As a hypothetical example, observations may be obtained on the disruptive and inappropriate classroom behaviors of a child who is identified because he is hyperactive (e.g., rarely in his seat, disrupts, handles the work of others while they are working, and blurts out comments during class). The upper panel of Figure 6.2 shows baseline performance with no trend. The absence of trend in baseline provides a relatively clear basis for evaluating subsequent intervention effects. Improvements in performance are likely to be reflected in a trend that departs from the horizontal line of baseline performance.

If behavior does show a trend during baseline, behavior would be increasing or decreasing over time. The trend during baseline may or may not present problems for evaluating intervention effects, depending on the direction of the trend in relation to the desired change in behavior. Performance may be changing in the direction *opposite* from that which treatment is designed to achieve. For example, our child with disruptive behavior may show an increase in the behavior during baseline observations. The middle panel of Figure 6.2 shows how baseline data might appear; over the period of observations the client's behavior is becoming worse, that is, more disruptive. Because the intervention will attempt to alter behavior in the opposite direction, that is, improve behavior, this initial trend is not likely to interfere with evaluating intervention effects.

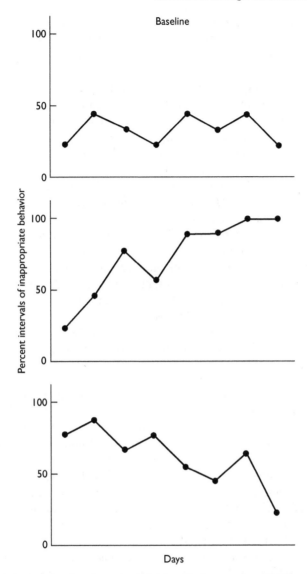

Figure 6.2. Hypothetical data for disruptive behavior of a hyperactive child. The *upper panel* shows a stable rate of performance with no systematic trend over time. The *middle panel* shows a systematic trend with behavior becoming worse over time. The *lower panel* shows a systematic trend with behavior becoming better over time. This latter pattern of data (lower panel) is the most likely one to interfere with evaluation of interventions, because the change is in the same direction as of change anticipated with treatment.

In contrast, the baseline trend may be in the *same direction* that the intervention is likely to produce. Essentially, the baseline phase may show improvements in behavior. For example, the behavior of the child may improve over the course of baseline as disruptive and inappropriate behaviors decrease, as shown in the lower panel of Figure 6.2. Because the intervention attempts to improve performance, it may be difficult to evaluate the effect of the subsequent intervention. The projected level of performance for baseline is toward improvement. A very strong intervention effect of treatment would be needed to show clearly that treatment surpassed this projected level from baseline.

If baseline is showing an improvement, one might raise the question of why an intervention should be provided at all. Yet even when behavior is improving during baseline, it may not be improving quickly enough. For example, a child with autism may show a gradual decrease in headbanging during baseline observations. The reduction may be so gradual that serious self-injury might be inflicted unless the behavior is treated quickly. At a broader level, such as a school or entire city, rates of vandalism and robbery, respectively, may be declining but still be too high or be declining too slowly to allow their courses to unfold. Hence, even though behavior is changing in the desired direction, additional changes may be needed.

Occasionally, a trend may exist in the data and still not interfere with evaluating treatments. Also, when trends do exist, several design options and data-evaluation procedures can help clarify the effects of the intervention (see Chapters 12 and 14 and the appendix at the end of the book). For present purposes, it is important to convey that the one feature of a stable baseline is little or no trend, and that the absence of trend provides a clear basis for evaluating intervention effects. Presumably, when the intervention is implemented, a trend toward improvement in behavior will be evident. This is readily detected with an initial baseline that does not already show a trend toward improvement.[1]

Variability in the Data. In addition to trend, stability of the data refers to the fluctuation or variability in the subject's performance over time. Excessive variability in the data during baseline or other phases can interfere with drawing conclusions about treatment. As a general rule, the greater the variability in the data, the more difficult it is to draw conclusions about the effects of the intervention.

Excessive variability is a relative notion. Whether the variability is excessive and interferes with drawing conclusions about the intervention depends on many factors, such as the initial level of behavior during the baseline phase and the magnitude of behavior change when the intervention is implemented. In the extreme case, baseline performance may fluctuate daily from extremely high to extremely low levels (e.g., 0 to 100%). Such a pattern of performance is illustrated in Figure 6.3 (upper panel), in which hypothetical baseline data are provided. With such extreme fluctuations in performance, it is difficult to predict any particular level of future performance.

Alternatively, baseline data may show relatively little variability. A typical example is represented in the hypothetical data in the lower panel of Figure 6.3. Performance fluctuates, but the extent of the fluctuation is small compared with the upper panel. With relatively slight fluctuations, the projected pattern of future performance is relatively clear and hence intervention effects will be less difficult to evaluate. Sometimes

---

[1] This section presents simple trends in the data (e.g., no slope, accelerating, decelerating slope) and is a useful point of departure. A more subtle point is that trends in the data can be more complex and not readily visible by just looking at a graph. The appendix at the end of the book conveys the complexities such trends can raise for data evaluation.

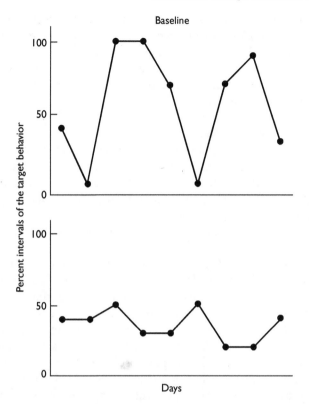

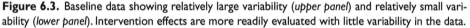

Figure 6.3. Baseline data showing relatively large variability (*upper panel*) and relatively small variability (*lower panel*). Intervention effects are more readily evaluated with little variability in the data.

there is no variability in performance during baseline because the behavior never occurs (or, less likely, it occurs every time). In many programs, the behavior one wishes to develop (e.g., exercising at home or at a gym, taking one's medication, practicing a musical instrument, initiating conversations with others in an assisted-living home) does not occur at all before the intervention. The baseline observations might show zero occurrences each day and of course no variability.

Ideally, baseline data will show little variability. Actually, this is not "ideally," but usually the case. Variability in the data can be due to variability in the performance of the individual but can also be due to error or variation in the observations (low reliability of the measure). This is one of the reasons why reliability of the observations is important to ensure, as detailed in the previous chapter. Occasionally relatively large variability may exist in the data. Several options are available to minimize the impact of such variability on drawing conclusions about intervention effects (see Chapter 14). However, the evaluation of intervention effects is greatly facilitated by relatively consistent performance during baseline.

ABAB DESIGNS: BASIC CHARACTERISTICS

In applied settings, there are many design options. Assessing performance continuously over time and obtaining stable rates of performance are pivotal to all of the designs.

Precisely how these features are essential for demonstrating intervention effects can be conveyed by discussing ABAB designs, which are the most basic experimental designs in single-case research. ABAB designs consist of a family of experimental arrangements in which observations of performance are made over time for a given client (or group of clients). Over the course of the investigation, changes are made in the experimental conditions to which the client is exposed.

Description and Underlying Rationale

The ABAB design examines the effects of an intervention by alternating the baseline condition (A phase), when no intervention is in effect, with the intervention condition (B phase). The A and B phases are repeated again to complete the four phases. The effects of the intervention are clear if performance improves during the first intervention phase, reverts to or approaches original baseline levels of performance when treatment is withdrawn, and improves when treatment is reinstated in the second intervention phase.[2]

The simple description of the ABAB design does not convey the underlying rationale that accounts for its experimental utility. The rationale is crucial to convey because it underlies all variations of the ABAB designs and indeed all single-case designs. The initial phase begins with baseline observations when behavior is observed under conditions before treatment is implemented. This phase is continued until the rate of the response appears to be stable or until it is evident that the response does not improve over time. As mentioned previously, baseline observations serve two purposes, namely, to describe the current level of behavior and to predict what behavior would be like in the future if no intervention were implemented. The description of behavior before treatment is obviously necessary to give the investigator an idea of the nature of the problem. From the standpoint of the design, the crucial feature of baseline is the prediction of behavior in the future. A stable rate of behavior is needed to project what behavior would probably be like in the immediate future. Figure 6.4 shows hypothetical data for an ABAB design. During baseline, the level of behavior is assessed (solid line), and this line is projected to predict the level of behavior into the future (dashed line). When a projection can be made with some degree of confidence, the intervention (B) phase is implemented.

---

[2] Another way to say this is: We begin by observation (first A phase) in which we collect data and do not at this point try to help the client; then we do something to make the client better in some way (improve behavior in the first B phase); take away the effective intervention to make the client worse (second A phase); and then put the intervention back in place to make the client better (second B phase). Return-to-baseline conditions is unacceptable if this means making the client worse. One can and ought to have the client's interest in mind in single-case research that is conducted in any applied setting. (In basic laboratory research, the goals are different; the client participates to help with some scientific question and any direct benefit usually is not an intended or expected outcome. Reversal of behavior in such contexts is not likely to be objectionable.) At this point in the discussion, it is important only to focus on the logic of the design. That logic will be needed to elaborate other designs and to grasp why single-case experiments are as rigorous as any other methodology.

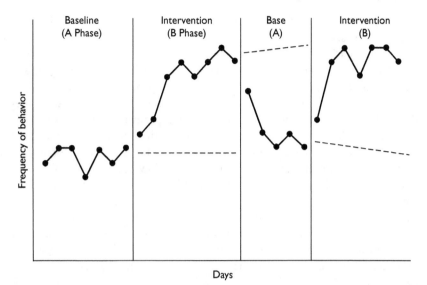

Figure 6.4. Hypothetical data for an ABAB design. The solid lines in each phase reflect the actual data. The dashed lines indicate the projection or predicted level of performance from the previous phase.

The intervention phase has similar purposes to the baseline phase, namely, to describe current performance and to predict performance in the future if conditions were unchanged. However, there is an added purpose of the intervention phase. In the baseline phase a prediction was made about future performance. In the intervention phase, the investigator can test whether performance during the intervention phase (phase B, solid line) actually departs from the projected level of baseline (phase B, dashed line). In effect, baseline observations were used to make a prediction about performance. During the first intervention phase, data can test the prediction. Do the data during the intervention phase depart from the projected level of baseline? If the answer is yes, this shows that there is a change in performance. In Figure 6.4, it is clear that performance changed during the first intervention phase. At this point in the design, it is not entirely clear that the intervention was responsible for change. Other factors, such as history and maturation, might be proposed to account for change and cannot be convincingly ruled out. I mentioned that a critical goal of research is making threats to validity implausible or as implausible as possible. Generally, just the first two (AB) phases would not do this very well. We need at least the second A phase (to have ABA) to carry out the three functions I have noted: describe, predict, and test the prediction.

In the third phase (the second A of ABA), the intervention is usually withdrawn and the conditions of baseline are restored. This second A phase has three purposes, as I just mentioned. The two purposes common to the other phases are included, namely, to describe current performance and to predict what performance would be like in the future if this phase were continued. A third purpose is similar to that of the intervention phase, namely, to test the prediction from a prior phase. Let us break this down a bit. One purpose of the intervention phase was to make a prediction of what performance would be like in the future if the conditions remain unchanged (see dashed line, second A phase). The second A phase tests to see whether this level of performance in fact occurred. By comparing the solid and dashed lines in the second A phase, it is clear that the predicted and obtained levels of performance differ. Thus, the change that occurs suggests that something altered performance from its projected course.

There is one final and unique purpose of the second A phase that is rarely discussed. The *first* A phase made a prediction of what performance would be like in the future (the dashed line in the first B phase). This was the first prediction in the design, and, like any prediction, it may be incorrect. The second A phase restores the conditions of baseline and can test the first prediction. If behavior had continued without an intervention, would it have continued at the same level as the original baseline or would it have changed markedly? The second A phase examines whether performance would have been at or near the level predicted originally. A comparison of the solid line of the second A phase with the dashed line of the first B phase, in Figure 6.4, shows that the lines really are no different. Thus, performance predicted by the original baseline phase was generally accurate. Performance would have remained at this level without the intervention.

In the final phase of the ABAB design, the intervention is reinstated again. This phase serves the same purposes as the previous phase, namely to describe performance, to test whether performance departs from the projected level of the previous phase, and to test whether performance is the same as predicted from the previous intervention phase. (If additional phases were added to the design, the purpose of the second B phase would of course be to predict future performance.)

In short, the logic of the ABAB design and its variations consists of making and testing predictions about performance under different conditions. Essentially, data in the separate phases provide information about present performance, predict the probable level of future performance, and test the extent to which predictions of performance from previous phases were accurate. By repeatedly altering experimental conditions in the design, there are several opportunities to compare phases and to test whether performance is altered by the intervention. If behavior changes when the intervention is introduced, reverts to or near baseline levels after the intervention is withdrawn, and again improves when treatment is reinstated, then the pattern of results suggests rather strongly that the intervention was responsible for change. Various threats to internal validity, outlined earlier, might have accounted for change in one of the phases. For example, coincidental changes in the behavior of others (e.g., parents, teachers, spouses, an annoying peer, bosses at work), external events (e.g., in the news, traffic ticket), or in the internal states of the individual (e.g., allergy reaction, change in medication, onset of a worsening cold) might be responsible for changing behavior. However, these events or potential influences or any particular threat or set of threats to validity are not very plausible in explaining the pattern of data across phases. The most plausible explanation is that the intervention and its withdrawal accounted for changes.

Illustrations

The ABAB design and its underlying rationale are nicely illustrated in an investigation that focused on TV watching of an 11-year-old Latina girl who was obese (height = 5'3"; weight 172 lbs [1.6 meters, 78.2 kg]) (Jason & Brackshaw, 1999). The 50th percentile (median) height and weight for a girl this age is approximately 4'6" and 80 lbs (1.4 meters, 36.3 kg). The family tried several different treatments that had not worked. The girl watched 6 hours of TV during the week and 10 on the weekend and often ate while watching TV. Needless to say, many factors contribute to obesity. Yet eating while watching TV among children is recognized as a key contributor. A program was devised in conjunction with the family in which exercise was used to earn TV time. TV watching was observed daily. The girl pedaled on a stationary bicycle connected to the TV. The TV could be programmed so that a predetermined amount of pedaling would be accumulated to provide a fixed amount of time on the TV. Riding and watching TV were not possible at the same time, but the girl could earn TV time.

Figure 6.5 shows that an ABAB design was used to evaluate the effects of the program beginning with baseline. During the intervention phase, TV viewing was contingent on exercising. Baseline (A phase) was reinstated, followed again by the intervention (B) phase. Approximately 2½ months later, a follow-up assessment was made without the bicycle attached to the TV, as shown in the figure. TV viewing had dropped from baseline, mean TV viewing of 4.4 hours per day during baseline to less than 1 hour per day at the end of the program. Also, the girl had lost 20 lbs (9.1 kg). A follow-up assessment 1 year later, not in the graph, indicated that TV viewing remained at the same level as it was at the end of treatment (about 1 hour) and that the weight loss had been maintained. From the standpoint of the design, the graph conveys rather clearly that TV watching changed markedly in responses to changes in the program.

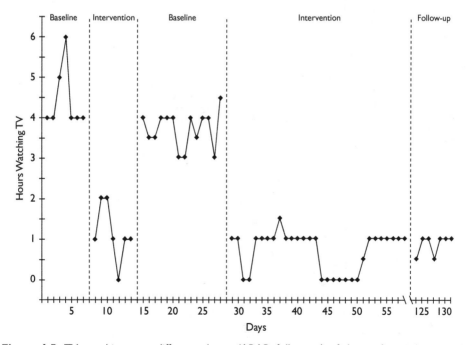

Figure 6.5. TV watching over different phases (ABAB, follow-up) of the study. *(Source: Jason & Brackshaw, 1999.)*

In this next example, the focus was on vocal stereotype among children diagnosed with autism spectrum disorder and who were referred because their vocalizations interfered with their participation in other special educational activities (Ahearn, Clark, MacDonald, & Chung, 2007). Vocal stereotype refers to vocalizations such as singing, babbling, repetitive grunts, squeals, and other phrases (e.g., "ee, ee, ee, ee") that are not related to contextual cues in the situation and appear to serve no communication function as part of interaction with others. Individual sessions were conducted, 5 minutes in duration, in which a child sat in the room with the teacher. Both stereotypic and appropriate vocalizations (e.g., "I want a tickle," "Could I have a chip?") that were functional and communicated content were recorded. Baseline (no intervention) was followed with an intervention phase that included response interruption and redirection. This consisted of immediately interrupting any vocal stereotype statement and redirecting the child to other vocalizations. The teacher would state the child's name and then ask a question that required an appropriate response (e.g., "What is your name?" "What color is your shirt?"). Any spontaneous appropriate verbal statement was praised (e.g., "Super job talking!"). Observations were obtained using interval assessment to score the presence or absence of the stereotypic and appropriate vocalizations. The response interruption and redirection was evaluated in an ABAB design. Figure 6.6 provides

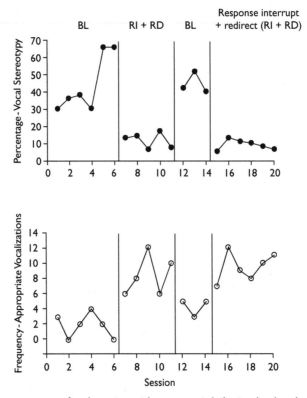

Figure 6.6. The percentage of each session with stereotypic behavior (top) and appropriate speech (bottom). *(Source: Ahearn et al., 2007.)*

data for one of the children, a 3-year-old boy named Mitch. The top graph shows vocal stereotypic sounds; the bottom graph shows appropriate vocalizations. As evident in both graphs, whenever the response interruption and redirection intervention was implemented there was a dramatic reduction in stereotypic statements and an increase in appropriate vocalizations.

The design reveals that the intervention was responsible for changes in verbal behavior. But the immediate response might be, "Why is this demonstration important if the gains in child behavior are lost immediately when there is a return-to-baseline condition?" Within this study and prior to the intervention, the investigators evaluated different ways in which child behavior might be altered and then tested the response interruption and redirection alternative that emerged from that in order to see if in fact it would control behavior. The demonstration confirmed that the intervention did have impact on behavior. Once this was identified, teachers of the children were trained to implement the intervention. Teachers reviewed videotapes of the session and were given instructions on how to implement the procedures. Assessments were conducted in the classroom periodically (probes) to see if the procedure was carried out there. The results, not graphed, indicated large reductions when in the natural environment with their teachers. That is, the treatments were immediately extended to situations where no further reversals were needed.

The illustrations convey how the ABAB designs achieve the goals of ruling out or making threats to validity implausible. The changes when the phase was shifted from no intervention (A) to intervention (B) and back and forth again make the intervention the most plausible explanation for what led to the change. If one invoked the logic of single-case designs (describe, predict, and test a prior prediction), then the interventions are very likely to be the reason for the change. There is no certainty in science from any single empirical test, but the preceding illustrations are strong demonstrations of intervention effects.

DESIGN VARIATIONS

ABAB designs vary as a function of several factors, including the procedures that are implemented to "reverse" behavior in the second A phase, the order of the phases, the number of phases, and the number of different interventions included in the design. Although the underlying rationale for all of the variations is the same, it is important to illustrate major design options.

"Reversal" Phase

A characteristic of the ABAB design is that the intervention is terminated or withdrawn during the second A or reversal phase in order to determine whether behavior change can be attributed to the intervention.[3] Withdrawing the intervention (e.g., reinforcement procedure, drug) and thereby returning to baseline conditions is the most frequently used variation to achieve this reversal of performance.

---

[3] The term "reversal" is used to note that pattern of behavior reverses or goes in the opposite direction from what was achieved during the intervention phase. The language is a little loose in noting that behavior "reverses."

Returning to baseline conditions during the second A phase is only one way to show a relation between performance and treatment. Another alternative is to continue the intervention in some way but in a way that will make it ineffective or less effective. For example, praise is a very effective intervention when administered immediately after behavior. The behavior that is praised is likely to increase over time. If praise for a specific behavior were given during the intervention (B phase), one could change how the praise is delivered during the second A or reversal phase. Praise could be given randomly based on whatever the child is doing or based on a certain amount of time that elapsed. The intervention (B) depends on praise following a specific behavior. Merely praising randomly or for just any behavior during the second A phase is likely to lead to a return of the behavior to baseline levels—the equivalent of removing the program. This strategy is selected to show that it is not the event (e.g., praise) per se that leads to behavior change but rather the relation between the event and the behavior.

A third variation of the reversal phase is to continue consequences but alter the behaviors that are associated with the consequences. For example, if the intervention consists of reinforcing (providing rewarding consequences for) a particular behavior, the reversal phase can consist of reinforcing all behaviors *except* the one that was reinforced during the intervention phase. The effect of this is to apply the intervention to foster return to baseline behaviors.

In many uses of single-case designs, consequences such as praise and tokens are not used. Consequently, applying these differently or less effectively in a return-to-baseline phase compared to how they were applied in an intervention phase may not be applicable. In these cases, suspension or withdrawal of the intervention would serve as the return-to-baseline or reversal phase. For example, stimulant medication is an effective (evidence-based) intervention for Attention-Deficit/Hyperactivity Disorder (hyperactivity) in children. If this were evaluated for a given child in an ABAB design, it would be reasonable to apply the medication in each B phase and no medication in the A phases. There might be a placebo in the second A phase if that were a plausible concern.

Order of the Phases

The ABAB version suggests that observing behavior under baseline conditions (A phase) is the first step in the design. Once the logic of the design is grasped, that is, how each phase describes, predicts, and tests an earlier prediction, the rigid ordering of the phases can be seen as somewhat arbitrary. In many circumstances, the design may begin with the intervention (or B) phase. The intervention may need to be implemented immediately because of the severity of the behavior (e.g., self-destructive behavior, endangering one's peers). In cases where clinical or educational considerations dictate immediate interventions, it may be unreasonable to insist on collecting baseline data. (Of course, return-to-baseline phases might not be possible either, a problem discussed later.)

Second, in many cases, baseline levels of performance are obvious because the behavior may never have occurred. For example, when behavior has never been performed (e.g., exercise for many of us, practicing a musical instrument, reading, eating healthful foods), the intervention may begin without baseline. When a behavior is fairly well known to be performed at a zero rate over an extended period, beginning with a baseline phase may serve no useful purpose. (One could always check with a few days of baseline if there were any doubt. Also, one might conduct assessment for a day or two to address or resolve any logistical or practical issues raised by the assessment procedures.) The design would still require a reversal of treatment conditions at some point.

In each of the previous cases, the design may begin with the intervention phase and continue as a BABA design. The logic of the design and the methodological functions of the alternating phases are unchanged. Drawing inferences about the impact of treatment depends on the pattern of results discussed earlier. For example, in one investigation a BABA design was used to evaluate the effects of token reinforcement delivered to two young men with mental retardation who engaged in little social interaction (Kazdin & Polster, 1973). The program, conducted in a sheltered workshop, consisted of providing tokens to each man when he conversed with another person, among the other 40 to 50 peers who were working there. Conversing was defined as a verbal exchange in which the client and peer made informative comments to each other (e.g., about news, television, sports) rather than just general greetings and replies (e.g., "Hi, how are you?" "Fine."). Because social behaviors were considered by staff to be consistently low during the periods before the program, staff wished to begin an intervention immediately. Hence, the reinforcement program was begun in the first phase and evaluated in a BABA design, as illustrated for one of the clients in Figure 6.7. Social interaction steadily increased in the first phase (reinforcement) and ceased almost completely when the program was withdrawn (reversal). When reinforcement was reinstated,

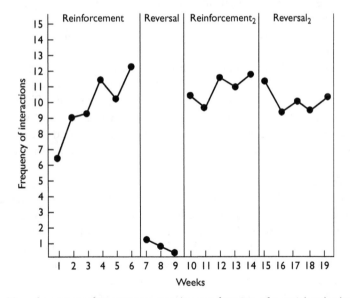

Figure 6.7. Mean frequency of interactions per day as a function of a social and token reinforcement program evaluated in a BABA design. The initial intervention phase (B) was followed by no-intervention or baseline (A), followed by B again. In the second B phase, the praise and tokens were given out less frequently in order to fade the program. When the program was completely eliminated (final phase A), behaviors were maintained.   *(Source: Kazdin & Polster, 1973.)*

social interaction was again high. The pattern of the first three phases suggested that the intervention was responsible for change. Hence, in the second reinforcement phase, the consequences were given less frequently (intermittently) to gradually remove the program. The goal of achieving change had been met, so the priority switched to trying to maintain behavior when the program was ultimately discontinued. Behavior tended to be maintained in the final reversal phase even though the program was withdrawn. The BAB part of the design clearly reflects the logic of the design (describe, predict, test a prior prediction).

Number of Phases

A basic dimension that distinguishes variations of the ABAB design is the number of phases. The ABAB design with four phases elaborated earlier has been a very commonly used version and also is very useful to convey the logic of the design and its ability to make very implausible threats to experimental validity. Several other options are available. As an absolute minimum, the design must include at least three phases, such as the ABA (baseline, intervention, baseline) or BAB (intervention, baseline, intervention). Four phases are clearly better. The basis for noting it is better refers to the importance of replicating the effects of the intervention within the study (Horner et al., 2005). The "describe, predict, and test" logic of the design begins in full bloom in the second phase of the ABAB version of the design. During the first intervention (B), there is a test to see if performance departs from what was predicted by baseline (A). Extending this, each of the last three phases of the ABAB design tests predictions made from extrapolations of the prior phase. In this way the effects of the intervention are replicated. That is, is there consistency in the impact of the intervention in each test? ABA without the ABAB does not do this nearly as well. In a three-phase version, we really do not see the replicated effect of the intervention in a final B phase.

More generally, a demonstration with two phases (AB) is not a true experiment and does not rule out the threats to validity. At the other extreme, several phases may be included as in an ABABAB design in which the intervention effect is repeatedly demonstrated. Confidence that the intervention exerted impact and was responsible for the effect increases as the number of AB phases increases in the design and the describe, predict, and test prediction sequence is replicated in a consistent fashion.

Number of Different Interventions

ABAB designs can vary in the number of different interventions they include. As usually discussed, the design consists of one intervention that is implemented in the two B phases (ABAB) in the investigation. Occasionally, investigators may include separate interventions (B and C phases) in the same design. Separate interventions may be needed in situations where the first one does not alter behavior or does not achieve a sufficient change for the desired result. In applied settings as in schools or clinics, the ability to see effects of the intervention and then to change or add a new intervention to improve the outcome is one of the strengths of single-case designs. Another reason for using two interventions in the same design is to evaluate the relative effectiveness. The interventions (B, C) may be administered at different points in the design as represented by ABCBCA or ABCABC designs.

An illustration of a design that evaluated two intervention plans was a study designed to reduce the problem behaviors of school students (Ingram, Lewis-Palmer, & Sugai, 2005). Two sixth-grade boys participated and were observed during their classrooms while science or math lessons were being taught. The boys were identified because of their problem behaviors (e.g., not engaging in the task, playing with related objects, staring away from the teacher). Two interventions were evaluated. The first is called *functional behavioral assessment* and is a procedure designed to identify precisely what is controlling behavior in terms of antecedents that trigger the behavior, consequences that might maintain behavior, and events that might exacerbate the behaviors). The information is obtained from systematically interviewing the teachers and the students. Two brief comments place this in context. There is a larger empirical literature on functional assessment that is an empirical way to identify what factors are controlling behavior; once these are identified they can be used for intervention (Austin & Carr, 2000). In addition, many schools are encouraging or mandating functional behavior assessments in light of evidence that interventions based on such assessments can be very effective.

In this study, the intervention derived from the functional assessment varied for each child and can only be highlighted here. For Carter, one of the boys, the assessment identified specific tasks likely to be associated with not being engaged, a specific condition (being tired) that appeared to exacerbate this, and consequences such as the ability to escape from the task and peer attention that were maintaining not being engaged. The function-based intervention for Carter included him self-assessing the extent to which he was on task (every 5 minutes), raising his hand and recruiting teacher help for difficult work, being allowed to take 10 minutes if he indicated he was tired (he never did), and earning positive consequences (e.g., 5 minutes of computer time) for his work if he remained on task. If he was not engaged in work, the teacher would redirect him by providing a prompt to restart his work. This individualized intervention has broad research behind it, but is it needed? A second intervention, referred to as nonfunction-based intervention, was still evidence-based but less intricate. At the beginning of the class for the nonfunction-based intervention, Carter was told he could earn tokens (points) for appropriate behavior (points could be exchanged for snacks, pencils). He monitored (self-assessed his behavior) but was not allowed breaks and anytime he was not working this was simply ignored rather than redirected. Problem behaviors were assessed once per day in a 10-minute period at a time when off-task behaviors had been identified as a problem.

Figure 6.8 shows the effects of the two interventions on problem behavior in an ABCBC design for one of the students. The results convey that the function-based intervention was consistently associated with sharp reductions in behavioral problems. Nonfunction-based intervention had little or no effect. At the very final phase the function-based intervention was modified slightly (to extend his self-assessment period to 10 rather than 5 minutes). The findings are clear. The intervention that considered more of the factors that prompted and sustained problem behavior had clear impact. From the standpoint of the design, it is clear that the "describe, test, and predict" elements of single-case designs were met and that the effects of the intervention were reproduced at different points in the design.

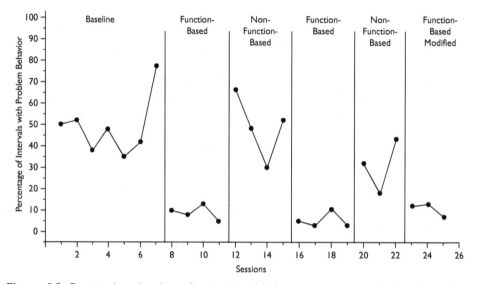

Figure 6.8. Function-based and non-function-based behavior interventions designed to reduce problem behavior in a sixth-grade boy. *(Source: Ingram et al., 2005.)*

General Comments

I have mentioned some of the dimensions on which ABAB designs vary. I noted that this is not a design but a family of designs. It is not possible to mention all of the possible variants—an infinite number based on the number of phases, interventions, ordering of phases, and types of reversal. Yet it is not critical to review all the variants even if the number were smaller. The most important point is to convey the logic of the design and to convey what each phase is trying to accomplish (e.g., describe, predict, and test). The specific design variation that the investigator selects is partially determined by purposes of the project, the results evident during the course of treatment (e.g., little or no behavior change with the first intervention), and the exigencies or constraints of the situation (e.g., limited time in which to complete the investigation). It is important to keep the overall central purpose in mind, namely, to make inferences that the intervention is the most if not only plausible explanation of the effect.

PROBLEMS AND LIMITATIONS

The defining characteristic of the ABAB designs and their variations consists of alternating phases in such a way that performance is expected to improve at some points and to return to or to approach baseline rates at other points. The need to show a "reversal" of behavior is pivotal if causal inferences are to be drawn about the impact of the intervention. Several problems arise with the designs as a result of this requirement.

Absence of a "Reversal" of Behavior

It is quite possible that behavior will not revert toward baseline levels once the intervention is withdrawn or altered. In such cases, it is not clear that the intervention was responsible for change. Threats to validity such as history and maturation now enter as possible explanations of why the change occurred. Extraneous factors associated with the intervention may have led to change. These factors (e.g., changes in home or school situation, illness or improvement from an illness, better sleep at night) may have coincidentally occurred when the intervention was implemented and remained in effect after the intervention was withdrawn.

There are sound reasons why an intervention may be responsible for change in a situation in which the behavior does not revert to or near baseline levels as needed by the design. First, the intervention may have led to change initially but behavior may have come under the control of other influences. For example, developing social interaction skills among a withdrawn child or reading in children might well be increased with an intervention. Yet, in a reversal phase, there may not be return of behavior to baseline levels. Social interaction brings about interactions with others and these may "trap" or lock in the behavior; the same for reading which can introduce a child to a world of adventure, suspense, travel, and more. Behaviors sometimes have their own consequences that sustain them. We want behaviors and other domains we train to be maintained and there are ways to program that (Kazdin, 2001), but sometimes it happens without special efforts. From the standpoint of the design, absence of a reversal makes the demonstration ambiguous. Second and related, some interventions focus on skills (e.g., reading, math, athletic, music, or dance skills). As skills develop with an intervention, they are not erased by a return to baseline. Performance (e.g., number of problems completed) might return to baseline if that is the measure, but if skill is the measure, it would not be erased by stopping a program.

Third, behaviors may not revert to baseline levels of performance because people who administered the program continue the intervention in some way. Many intervention programs evaluated in ABAB designs consist of altering the behavior of persons (parents, teachers, and staff) who will influence the client's target behavior. After behavior change in the client has been achieved, it may be difficult to convince behavior-change agents to alter their performance to approximate their behavior during the original baseline. It may not be a matter of convincing behavior-change agents; their behavior may be permanently altered in some fashion, even locked in by the consequences it had.

Finally, behavior may not revert to baseline levels if the change has been dramatic and permanent. It is readily conceivable that the intervention reduced or eliminated hitting, tantrums, or shouting. Yet, returning to baseline levels in an ABAB design does not bring the behavior back. From the standpoint of the client or student whose behavior has been changed, this is wonderful news—the behavior change has been nicely established and merely changing conditions does not bring the original problematic behavior back.

In each of the preceding instances, the intervention may be withdrawn and the behavior or domain of functioning does not return to baseline or near baseline levels. The intervention may have been responsible for change, but we cannot tell. There are options that one can invoke and draw on elements of other designs, but strictly speaking the design requires the data pattern we have discussed.

Undesirability of "Reversing" Behavior
Certainly a major issue in evaluating ABAB designs is whether reversal phases should be used at all. If behavior could be returned to baseline levels as part of the design, is

such a change ethical? Attempting to return behavior to baseline levels is tantamount to making the client worse. In many cases, it is obvious that a withdrawal of treatment is clearly not in the interest of the client; a reversal of behavior would be difficult if not impossible to defend ethically. For example, children with autism or developmental disabilities sometimes injure themselves severely by hitting their heads for extended periods of time. If a program decreased this behavior, it would be ethically unacceptable to show that head banging would return in a phase in which treatment were withdrawn. Extensive physical damage to the child might result. Even in situations where the behavior is not dangerous, it may be difficult to justify suspension of the program on ethical grounds. A phase in which treatment is withdrawn is essentially designed to make the person's behavior worse in some way. Whether behavior should be made worse and when such a goal would be justified are difficult issues to resolve.

Returning to baseline conditions also has implications for those responsible for the client. During the intervention, behavior-change agents (teachers, parents) may see and benefit from changes of their student or child. Suspending their improved intervention efforts attempts to erase gains they have made in their actions to improve the client. Thus, reintroducing the conditions of baseline raises the same concerns and questions as it does for the client.

Ethical considerations may be enough, but there are additional considerations. The client, those responsible for the client, and investigators (like this author) may not find the design acceptable in many circumstances. Single-case designs are often used in applied settings where the goal of helping people and having an important impact is central. Design issues need to be weighed against considerations that make designs acceptable to the various persons involved.

There is another side in favor of a return-to-baseline phase that is relevant to the client. There is value in knowing what is responsible for client change and knowing that it was the intervention rather than other influences (e.g., placebo effects, increased attention to the client, conducting observations that made the client temporarily behave differently). The client may require further intervention in the future; certainly there will be other clients who are likely to profit as well. Knowing that the intervention specifically led to change has great applied importance rather than serving as a mere academic exercise or effort to appease some god of research design who likes sacrifices. An example was provided previously (Ahearn et al., 2007) in which the ABAB design was used to identify an effective intervention for changing verbal behavior (stereotypy) of children with autistic spectrum disorder. Once identified, the teachers were trained to use the intervention, and further checks were done in the classroom to ensure that the intervention continued to be effective.

In the general case, the decision about whether to use an ABAB design with its return-to-baseline phase has multiple considerations. If in doubt about the desirability of such a phase, there are other designs that do not require a reversal phase. The goal to establish that the intervention was responsible for change can be achieved in many ways, as discussed in the next chapters. In fact, there are many options.

EVALUATION OF THE DESIGN

The ABAB design and its variations can provide convincing evidence that an intervention was responsible for change. Indeed, when the data pattern shows that performance changes consistently as the phases are altered, the evidence is dramatic. Nevertheless, there are limitations peculiar to ABAB designs, particularly when they are considered for use in applied and clinical settings.

In ABAB designs, the methodological and applied priorities of the investigator may compete. The investigator has an explicit hope that behavior will revert toward baseline levels when the intervention is withdrawn. Such a reversal is required to demonstrate an effect of the intervention. The educator, clinician, counselor, or parent, on the other hand, hopes that the behavior will be maintained after treatment is withdrawn. Indeed, the intended purpose of most interventions or treatments is to attain a permanent change even after the intervention is withdrawn. The interests in achieving a reversal and not achieving a reversal are obviously contradictory.

Of course, showing a reversal in behavior is not always a problem in applied settings. Reversal phases often are very brief, lasting only one or two sessions or days (e.g., Brooks, Todd, Tofflemoyer, & Horner, 2003; Wehby & Hollahan, 2000). Occasionally, especially when the intervention only has been implemented for a brief period, a brief reversal phase shows an immediate and dramatic return of behavior to baseline levels. The "describe, predict, and test a prior prediction" requirements of the design are readily met without keeping the non-intervention phase in place. However, short reversal phases are usually possible only when behavior shows rapid reversals, that is, becomes worse relatively quickly after the intervention is withdrawn. To have behaviors become worse even for short periods is usually undesirable. The goal of the treatment is to achieve changes that are maintained rather than quickly lost as soon as the intervention is withdrawn.

It is possible to include a reversal phase in the design to show that the intervention was responsible for change and still attempt to maintain behavior. After experimental control has been demonstrated in a return-to-baseline phase, procedures can be included to maintain performance after all treatment has been withdrawn. Thus, the design is ABABC where C adds special procedures that can maintain behavior. The ABAB part already established that the B was responsible for change. Now one adds procedures (e.g., gradually withdrawing the intervention) that have been established to maintain behavior. ABAB design and its variations are not necessarily incompatible with achieving maintenance of behavior.

Finally, in some circumstances the intervention can become permanent so that there is no need for a reversal in the usual way. For example, elimination of thumb sucking was the goal of a program for a 9-year-old boy (Watson, Meeks, Dufrene, & Lindsay, 2002). His thumb sucking was exacerbating an already existing dental problem. Several interventions (positive reinforcement for not thumb sucking, placing pepper sauce on the boy's thumb) had not worked. The boy sucked his thumb while holding a pillow (a transitional object like a stuffed animal). Occasionally, a behavior (e.g., thumb sucking) can be altered by changing another response (e.g., holding the pillow) with which it is highly associated. The intervention consisted of removal of the pillow. Figure 6.9 conveys an ABAB design. During baseline and return to baseline, the boy had the pillow available to hold and thumb sucking was relatively frequent. The data pattern clearly shows the impact of the intervention. In the final treatment phase, the pillow was no longer available and the behavior was eliminated. The effect was maintained 8 weeks later. The point of this example is to convey that maintaining

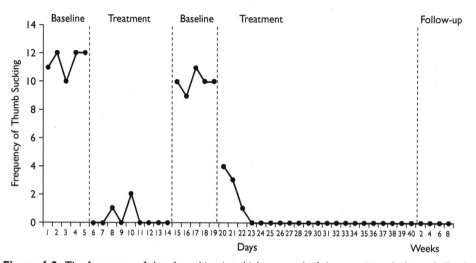

Figure 6.9. The frequency of thumb sucking in which removal of the transitional object (pillow) served as the intervention, as evaluated in an ABAB design. The final phase, referred to as follow-up, checked on the frequency of thumb sucking 8 weeks after the end of the intervention phase. *(Source: T. S. Watson et al., 2002.)*

behavior is not incompatible with an ABAB design. In this instance, the intervention became permanent. Sometimes experimental control can be demonstrated, followed by different ways of maintaining behavior, a topic discussed further in Chapter 10.

Despite the ways in which concerns about reversal phase can be combated, this does not change the demands of the design. The usual requirement of returning behavior to baseline levels or implementing a less effective intervention when a more effective one seems to be available raises potential problems for applied settings. Hence, in many situations, the investigator may wish to select one of the many other designs that do not require undoing the apparent benefits of treatment even if only for a short period.

SUMMARY AND CONCLUSIONS

The chapter began with a discussion of general requirements of single-case designs. We have discussed the requirements and logic of all single-case designs, not just the ABAB designs. These requirements of single-case designs included continuous assessment, evaluation of the client's behavior during baseline (no-intervention) and intervention phases, and achieving stable measures of performance. These assessment and data requirements are pivotal to the logic of single-case designs, that is, how the designs can be used to draw causal conclusions about intervention effects.

The underlying logic of single-case designs and that of more traditional between-group designs is the same, namely, to make and test predictions about performance. In single-case designs, data from the continuous assessment in different phases are used to *describe* current performance and *predict* what it would be like in the future without an intervention. Then the data during the intervention phase *test* that prediction. The most critical part of the chapter may be conveying that logic rather than focusing on any particular design. The logic conveys what the researcher is trying to accomplish by altering phases, and that logic serves as a useful guide in using a given design and making decisions about changing phases.

With ABAB designs, the effect of an intervention is demonstrated by alternating intervention and baseline conditions in separate phases over time. The designs may vary in the procedures that are used to cause behavior to return to or approach baseline levels. Withdrawing the intervention or altering the intervention in a way that critical ingredients are omitted is commonly used in this return-to-baseline phase. ABAB designs can vary in many ways including the order in which the baseline and intervention phases are presented, the number of phases, and the number of different interventions that are presented in the design. Given the different dimensions, an infinite number of ABAB design options is available. However, the underlying rationale and the manner in which intervention effects are demonstrated remain the same.

ABAB designs represent methodologically powerful experimental tools for demonstrating intervention effects. When the pattern of the data reveals shifts in performance as phases are altered, the evidence for intervention effects is very dramatic. For research in applied settings such as schools, the home, and business, the central feature of the designs may raise special problems. Specifically, the designs require that phases be alternated so that performance improves at some points and reverts toward baseline levels at other points. In some cases, a reversal of behavior does not occur, which creates problems in drawing inferences about the intervention. In other cases, it may be undesirable to withdraw or alter treatment, and serious ethical questions may be raised. When the requirements of the design compete with applied priorities, other designs may be more appropriate for demonstrating intervention effects.

CHAPTER 7

Multiple-Baseline Designs

With multiple-baseline designs, intervention effects are evaluated by a method quite different from that described for ABAB designs. The effects are demonstrated by introducing the intervention to different baselines (e.g., behaviors or persons) at different points in time. If each baseline changes when the intervention is introduced, the effects can be attributed to the intervention rather than to extraneous events. Once the intervention is implemented to alter a particular behavior, it need not be withdrawn. Thus, within the design, there is no need to return behavior to or near baseline levels of performance. Hence, multiple-baseline designs do not share the practical or ethical concerns raised in ABAB designs by temporarily withdrawing the intervention.

BASIC CHARACTERISTICS OF THE DESIGNS

Description and Underlying Rationale

In the multiple-baseline design, inferences are based on examining performance across several different baselines. The manner in which inferences are drawn is illustrated by discussing the *multiple-baseline design across behaviors*. This is a commonly used variation in which the different baselines refer to several different behaviors of a particular person or group of persons.

Baseline data are gathered on two or more behaviors. Consider a hypothetical example in which three separate behaviors are observed, as portrayed in Figure 7.1. The data gathered on each of the behaviors serve the purposes common to each single-case design. That is, the baseline data for each behavior describe the current level of performance and predict future performance. After performance is stable for all of the behaviors, the intervention is applied to the first behavior. Data continue to be gathered for each behavior. If the intervention is effective, one would expect changes in the behavior to which the intervention is applied. On the other hand, the behaviors that have yet to receive the intervention should remain at baseline levels. After all, no intervention was implemented to alter these behaviors. When the first behavior changes and the others remain at their baseline levels, this suggests that the intervention was responsible for the change. However, the data are not entirely clear at this point. It might well be that some historical or maturational event (threat to validity) coincidentally led to a change in the first behavior. So, after performance stabilizes across all behaviors, the intervention is applied to the second behavior. At this point both the first and second behavior are receiving the intervention, and data continue to be gathered for all behaviors. As evident in Figure 7.1, the second behavior in this hypothetical example also improved when the intervention was introduced. Finally, after continuing observation of all behaviors, the intervention is applied to the final behavior, and it too changed when the intervention was introduced.

The multiple-baseline design demonstrates the effect of an intervention by showing that behavior changes when and only when the intervention is applied. The pattern of data in Figure 7.1 argues strongly that the intervention, rather than some extraneous event, was responsible for change. Extraneous factors might have influenced performance. For example, it is possible that some event at home, school, or work coincided with the onset of the intervention and altered behavior. Yet one would not expect this extraneous influence to alter only one of the behaviors and at the exact point that the intervention was applied. A coincidence of this sort is possible, so the intervention is applied at different points in time to two or more behaviors. The pattern of results illustrates that whenever the intervention is applied, behavior changes. The repeated demonstration that behavior changes in response to staggered applications of the intervention usually makes the influence of extraneous factors implausible.

As in the ABAB designs, the multiple-baseline designs are based on testing of predictions. Each time the intervention is introduced, a test is made between the level of performance during the intervention and the projected level of the previous baseline. Essentially, each behavior is a "mini" AB experiment that tests a prediction of the projected baseline performance and whether performance continues at the same level after treatment is applied. Predicting and testing of predictions over time for a single baseline is similar for ABAB and multiple-baseline designs.

A unique feature of multiple-baseline designs is the testing of predictions across different behaviors. Essentially, the different behaviors in the design serve as control conditions to evaluate what changes can be expected without the application of treatment. At any point in which the intervention is applied to one behavior and not to

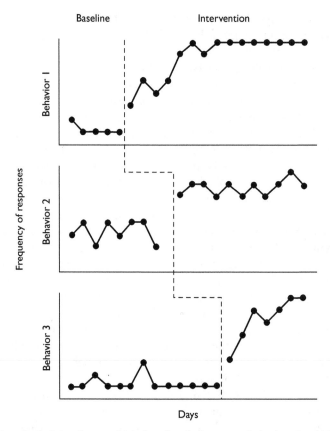

Figure 7.1. Hypothetical data for a multiple-baseline design across behaviors in which the intervention was introduced to three behaviors at different points in time.

remaining behaviors, a comparison exists between treatment and no-treatment conditions. The behavior that receives treatment should change, that is, show a clear departure from the level of performance predicted by baseline. Yet it is important to examine whether other baselines that have yet to receive treatment show any changes during the same period. The comparison of performance across the behaviors at the same points in time is critical to the multiple-baseline design. The baselines that do not receive treatment show the likely fluctuations of performance if no changes occur in the environment. When only the treated behavior changes, this suggests that normal fluctuations in performance would not account for the change. The repeated demonstration of changes in specific behaviors when the intervention is applied provides a convincing demonstration that the intervention was responsible for change.

An important question is, "How long does one wait after introducing the intervention to the first behavior before introducing the intervention to the second and third behavior—that is, what is the lapse in time?" There is no fixed answer in terms of days or observations. One waits for performance to be stable with little or no trend in the behaviors yet to receive the intervention. The hypothetical data in Figure 7.1 suggest that 4 days (please count the data points) after the intervention was introduced to Behavior 1, it was introduced to Behavior 2; then 4 days later to Behavior 3. There is no reason stemming from the logic of the design to keep the days or intervals constant before introducing the intervention to the next baseline. The critical feature is that the introduction of the intervention is staggered, not that there is any consistency in the amount of time before introducing the intervention to the next baseline. One waits for baselines to be stable. So if the intervention has been applied to the first baseline, one continues without implementing the intervention for the second and third baseline for a few days. Ideally, one will see the first behavior change and the others (still without the intervention) continue without showing a change. As these baselines are stable (no new trend or high variability), the intervention is extended to the second baseline. Number of days does not determine the decision; clarity of the pattern does.

Illustrations

Multiple-baseline designs across behaviors or domains of functioning have been used frequently. This first example focused on a business application, specifically a grocery store with 60 employees (Carter, Holmström, Simpanen, & Melin, 1988). The project was designed to reduce theft of items in the store, and it focused the intervention on employees. The domains of function or behaviors selected were stealing candy, personal hygiene products, and trinket jewelry. These products were selected on the basis of industry statistics about frequently stolen items but also confirmed by initial evaluation of thefts from the store's records. Each type of item included many different items (i.e., 10 types of candy, 6 hygiene items, 27 trinket jewelry items). Computerized scanning of items delivered to the store (inventory) and sold from the register could be readily monitored and checked by observers who tracked the inventory from this information. Items not accounted for by inventory or sales were considered thefts. The investigators were not interested in who did the stealing but merely in reducing or eliminating it. The intervention was introduced to employees who were informed about the project and its focus. The project began with observation across the three areas of stealing or domains of responding.

The intervention consisted of listing the items (e.g., all the candy types) and then posting a graph in the employee lunchroom of the number of thefts for the entire group of items (e.g., all candy items). When the intervention was introduced for candy theft, there was no mention of hygiene or jewelry items. After 2 weeks of the intervention, hygiene items were added. The products in this category were also listed and a graph was added to the candy graph to convey the amount of theft. After 1½ weeks the intervention was extended to the final baseline, theft of jewelry.

Figure 7.2 conveys the effect of the intervention across the three baselines. The effects are reasonably clear. When the items were identified and graphed for employees (intervention) there was a reduction in theft for each of the baselines. The daily rate of theft during baseline for candy, hygiene, and jewelry were means of 4.7, 1.6, and 2 items, respectively; these means fell to 1.2, and .8 and only 1 item for the whole 3-week intervention period. The pattern shows that the intervention was associated with the change and that change did not occur before the intervention was implemented. What we know from the demonstration is that the intervention led to reductions in theft. As the authors noted, it is likely that employee theft decreased. Only employees were

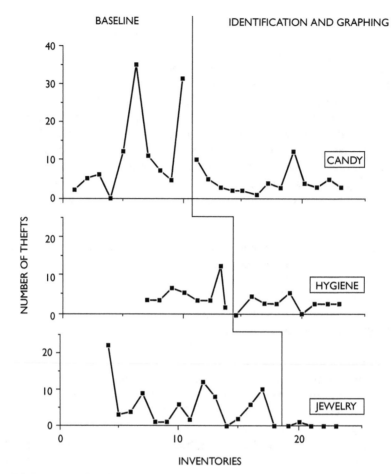

Figure 7.2. Number of thefts (biweekly) of candy items, hygiene items, and jewelry items. The intervention (identifying items and providing graphed information for the items as presented) was introduced at different points in time.   *(Source: Carter et al., 1988.)*

made aware of the intervention. On the other hand, customer theft may have declined, if employees were more vigilant in their monitoring of the customers. Reducing overall theft rather than identifying the source was the primary goal of the project.

In this next example, the focus was on teaching reading to a 6-year-old girl with multiple psychiatric diagnoses including hyperactivity and language disorders (Attention-Deficit/Hyperactivity Disorder, Receptive-Expressive Language Disorder) (McCollough, Weber, Derby, & McLaughlin, 2008). She was reading below grade level and made many errors while reading. Individual sessions were designed to teach reading by focusing on sounds and providing feedback and praise during the intervention phases for responses to cue cards with the words on them. The intervention was based on a method (referred to as Direct Instruction) and a commercially available book (*Teach Your Child to Read in 100 Easy Lessons*) that provided structured lessons on how to teach reading (Engelmann, Haddox, & Bruner, 1983). Across the lessons the student traverses several important steps (e.g., learning sounds, blends, and words, reading) to develop reading. The intervention was evaluated in a multiple-baseline design across different sets of words. Each set here can be viewed as different responses, that is, word groups that served as baselines. In each session, words from all sets were tested to assess the number of words from that set that were correctly read. The intervention was introduced to the first, second, and third set in a multiple-baseline design.

Figure 7.3 provides a graphical display of the number of words that were correctly pronounced. As evident in the figure, the effects of training were evident when the intervention (feedback, praise) was introduced for correct responding but not before. Two points are worth underscoring with this example. First, the first baseline in the figure (top) included only one session. Usually, one would want more than one data point for the baseline because of the logic of the design in which data from each phase is used to describe and predict performance. While it might have been useful to have another session or two, it is clear when all baseline phases (three sets of words) are considered that the criteria for the multiple-baseline design were met. The effects are fairly clear. The second point pertains to the goal of any reading program. While training the child to read specific words may be of interest, the goal is to develop reading, a broader skill that transfers to behaviors not included in training. In this case, each session also included words that were not specifically trained for each set. The untrained words showed a similar pattern. Thus, when sounds and other skills were trained within a given word set, reading other words in that set also improved.

The examples convey the utility of multiple-baseline designs in demonstrating the effect of an intervention. They also show the practical utility of the designs. One can intervene on a small scale (e.g., one baseline) to establish that the intervention is working or working sufficiently well. Then, as change is evident, the intervention can be extended more broadly.

DESIGN VARIATIONS

The underlying rationale of the design has been discussed by elaborating the multiple-baseline design across behaviors. The several baselines need not refer to different behaviors of a particular person or group of persons. Variations of the design include observations across different individuals or across different situations, settings, or time periods. In addition, multiple-baseline designs may vary along other dimensions, such as the number of baselines and the manner in which a particular intervention is applied to these baselines.

Multiple-baseline Design Across Individuals

In this variation of the design, baseline data are gathered for a particular behavior performed by two or more persons. The multiple baselines refer to the *number of persons* whose behaviors are observed. The design begins with observations of baseline performance of the same behavior for each person. After the behavior of each person has reached a stable rate, the intervention is applied to only one of them while baseline conditions are continued for the other(s). The behavior of the person exposed to the intervention would be expected to change; the behaviors of the others would be expected to continue at their baseline levels. When behaviors stabilize for all persons, the intervention is extended to another person. This procedure is

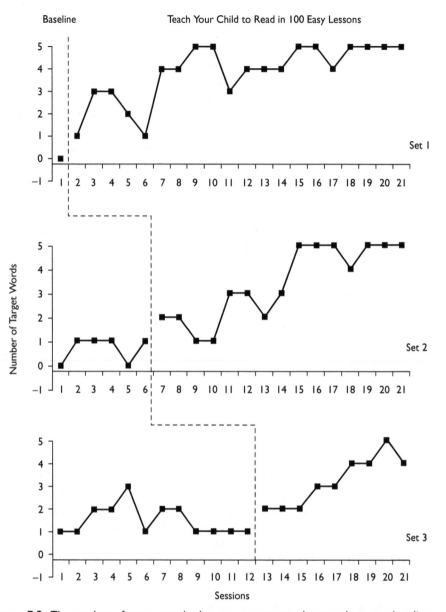

Figure 7.3. The number of target words that were pronounced correctly across baseline and intervention (*Teach Your Child*) phases. Three sets of words were delineated to serve as the baselines in the multiple-baseline design. The intervention was introduced to each in a staggered fashion and was effective in altering the baseline for which it was introduced.   (*Source: McCollough et al., 2008.*)

continued until all of the persons for whom baseline data were collected receive the intervention. The effect of the intervention is demonstrated when a change in each person's performance is obtained at the point when the intervention is introduced and not before.

In an application you might never anticipate, cocktail servers in a bar were trained to carry their serving trays correctly (Scherrer & Wilder, 2008). They had reported sore muscles and joints, and this appeared to be due in part to the way they carried their trays while serving drinks to customers. In consultation with an occupational therapist, appropriate carrying positions were identified (e.g., tray resting on finger tips, keeping the wrist straight, holding the tray next to the body, keeping shoulders down from the neck, not reaching across the table to unload drinks). Eight such specific behaviors were identified and considered to reflect a safer way of serving, that is, that might reduce risk of injury. The behaviors were included in a checklist to note correct (safe) and incorrect carrying and were recorded by observers who were in the bar 3 to 4 nights per week over the course of 8 weeks. Baseline observations were made of three cocktail servers (one male, two females), 21 to 24 years of age. Observation of each server was made for 15 minutes during which three separate checks (or serving opportunities) could be made to assess the percentage of correct behaviors.

An intervention consisted of a single training session outside of the time when the people were serving. The training included these components: explaining the correct positions to carry trays with drinks and serve them, a trainer modeling the correct positions, and having the cocktail server describe and then demonstrate the correct positions to the trainer. The server had to show mastery by demonstrating the techniques correctly four times. The training session took 45 minutes to 1 hour for each cocktail server. The training was done individually (separately) because a multiple-baseline design across individuals was used. Consequently, training was introduced at different points in time as each server was trained.

Figure 7.4 shows the evening observations during the shift at the bar in which the percentage of behaviors performed correctly was graphed. As evident in the figure, the training session was given to Sara first. Her behavior changed markedly, while there was no change in the behavior of Mike or Tanya, who had not yet had training. Training was introduced at different points to Mike and Tanya, and at each point there were marked increases in correct tray carrying. The pattern of results provides a strong demonstration that it was the intervention that led to change. Informal comments after the demonstration suggested that the effects were maintained and that the servers reported less soreness or greater ease in completing the tasks when they used the better tray-carrying procedures.

The multiple-baseline design across individuals is well suited to situations in which a single behavior or set of behaviors is to be changed among different persons and can be introduced to one or a few individuals at a time. The previous example was conducted in a bar! Any setting where there is a group or a few individuals (e.g., classroom, playground, athletic practice) and where the intervention can be introduced sequentially can accommodate the design. As with other variations of the design, no reversal or experimental conditions are required to demonstrate the effects of the intervention.

Multiple-baseline Design Across Situations, Settings, or Time

In this variation of the design, baseline data are gathered for a particular behavior performed by one or more persons. The multiple baselines refer to the *different situations, settings, or time periods* of the day in which observations are obtained. The design begins with observations of baseline performance in each of the situations.

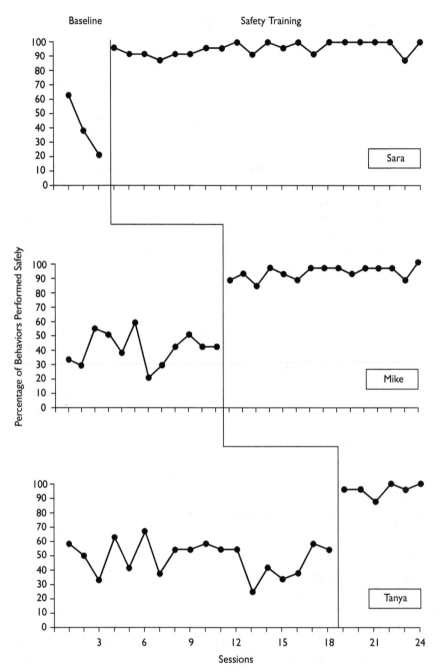

Figure 7.4. Percentage of behaviors performed safely among three cocktail servers during baseline and after the intervention (a single training session) introduced in a multiple-baseline design across individuals.   *(Source: Scherrer & Wilder, 2008.)*

After the behavior is stable in each situation, the intervention is applied to alter behavior in one of the situations while baseline conditions are continued for the others. Performance in the situation to which the intervention has been applied should show a change; performance in the other situations should not. When behavior stabilizes in all of the situations, the intervention is extended to performance in the other situations. This procedure is continued until performance in all of the situations for which baseline data were collected receive the intervention.

This illustration focused on the safety of health-care workers in the context of performing surgery (Cunningham & Austin, 2007). Health-care workers suffer many injuries as a function of working with hazardous procedures or materials. Some states have enacted laws to help protect workers from "sharps injuries" (e.g., being stuck with a needle) given the special risk of such injuries for employees (e.g., HIV/AIDS). This study focused on the exchange of instruments between the surgeon and scrub nurse. The goal was to increase the use of the "hands-free technique," which requires that a neutral zone be established between the surgeon and nurse. This neutral zone is a place where the instruments are put as the instruments are exchanged. In this way, the two people do not touch the instrument at the same time and the risk of sharps injuries is greatly reduced. This was a multiple-baseline design across settings: two settings were selected, namely, an operating room of an inpatient surgery unit and an operating room of an outpatient surgery unit of a hospital serving a nine-county region in a Midwestern state in the United States.

Observations were conducted during surgical procedures for 30 minutes, beginning at the time an opening incision was made in the patient. Observers were in the operating room, collected information, and recorded all exchanges as either hand-to-hand (unsafe) or neutral zone (safe, hands-free procedure). The percentage of these exchanges that were hands-free constituted the dependent measure. The intervention consisted of goal setting, task clarification, and feedback to use the safe-exchange procedure. At the beginning of the intervention phase, staff members were informed of the hospital policy, which included use of hands-free procedure, and the goal was set to increase the percentage of hands-free exchanges. Hospital policy aimed at 75%, but the rate was only at 32%. Modeling was used to convey the exact ways of making the exchanges, and feedback was provided to the staff regarding the weekly percentages and whether the goal was met. Also praise was provided for improvements at a weekly staff meeting.

Figure 7.5 shows that the intervention was introduced in a multiple-baseline design across two surgery settings. When the intervention was introduced to the inpatient operating room (top of figure), the percentage of safe exchanges (hands-free, using the neutral zone) increased sharply, so to speak. No changes were evident in the outpatient operating room, where the intervention had yet to be introduced. When the intervention was introduced there, improvements were evident as well. There was one day when the surgeon could not reach for the instrument in the neutral zone, as noted on the figure. Overall, the results convey that behavior changed when the intervention was introduced and not before. The design added a third phase in order to check to see if the behaviors were maintained. Approximately 5 months after the end of the intervention phase (the intervention had been suspended) both units were observed for a week. As evident in the figure, the effects of the intervention were maintained.

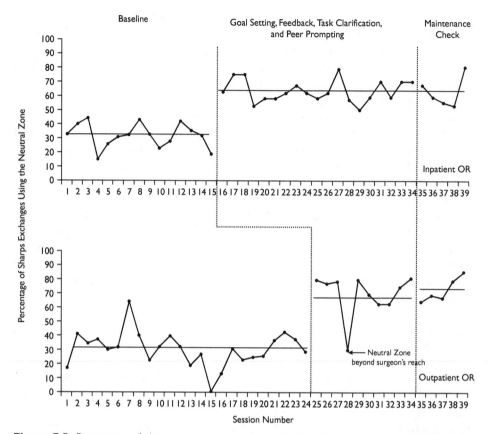

Figure 7.5. Percentage of sharp instruments exchanged using the neutral zone (hands-free safe procedure) across inpatient and outpatient operating rooms. The solid lines in each phase represent the mean (average) for that phase.   *(Source: T. R. Cunningham & Austin, 2007.)*

When a particular behavior needs to be altered in two or more situations (e.g., home, school), the multiple-baseline design across situations or settings is especially useful. The intervention is first implemented in one situation and, if effective, is extended gradually to other situations as well. The intervention is extended until all situations in which baseline data were gathered are included.

The design can be used even if there is only one situation, but separate periods can be designated. For example, if the goal is to change behavior in a particular setting, two (or more) time periods can be delineated such as in the morning and afternoon. The multiple-baseline design focuses on the same individual and same behavior but gathers (and graphs) data separately for these time periods. Thus, developing behavior of a child in an elementary school classroom might delineate two periods (e.g., before lunch and after lunch) and evaluate the intervention in a multiple-baseline across these two periods. These periods could provide data for the baselines.

Number of Baselines

A major dimension that distinguishes variations of the multiple-baseline design is the number of baselines (i.e., behaviors, persons, or situations). I included an example (surgery settings) with two baselines (please see Figure 7.5). Clearly in that example, two baselines served the purposes of enabling inferences to be drawn about the role of the intervention. With two baselines, the data pattern may need to be especially clear, indeed perfect, to make implausible other influences that may have caused the effect. Although two might meet the design criteria in principle, three baselines is the recommended minimum and often that number is exceeded. Other things being equal, demonstration that the intervention was responsible for change is clearer the larger the number of baselines that show the predicted pattern of performance. By "clearer" I mean the extent to which the change is likely to be attributed to the intervention rather than to extraneous influences and various threats to validity.

There is another, more practical reason to include more rather than fewer base-lines. It is always possible that one of the baselines may not change or change very much when the intervention is introduced. If only two baselines were included and one of them did not change, the results cannot easily be attributed to the intervention because the requisite pattern of data was not obtained. On the other hand, if several (e.g., five) baselines were included in the design and one of them did not change, the effects of the intervention may still be very clear. The remaining baselines may show that whenever the intervention was introduced, performance changed, with the one exception. The clear pattern of performance for most of the behaviors still strongly suggests that the intervention was responsible for change rather than the threats to internal validity. The problem of inconsistent effects of the intervention across different baselines is addressed later in the chapter. At this point it is important only to note that the inclusion of several baselines beyond the minimum of two or three may clarify the effects of the intervention. Occasionally, baseline data are obtained and intervention effects are evident across several (e.g., eight or nine) behaviors, persons, or situations.

The adequacy of the demonstration that the intervention was responsible for change is not merely a function of the number of baselines assessed. Other factors, such as the stability of the behaviors during the baseline phases and the magnitude and rapidity of change once the intervention is applied also determine the ease with which inferences can be drawn about the role of the intervention.

Partial Applications of Treatment

Multiple-baseline designs vary in the manner in which treatment is applied to the various baselines. For the variations discussed thus far, a particular intervention is applied to the different behaviors at different points in time. Several variations of the designs depart from this procedure. In some circumstances, the intervention may be applied to the first behavior (individuals or situations) and produce little or no change. It may not be useful to continue applying this intervention to other behaviors. The intervention may not achieve enough change in the first behavior to warrant further use. Hence, a second intervention may be applied following a sort of ABC design for the first behavior. If the second intervention (C) produces change, it is applied to other behaviors in the usual fashion of the multiple-baseline design. The design is different only in the fact that the first intervention was not applied to all of the behaviors, persons, or situations.

For example, a simple intervention was used to increase the frequency that drivers would stop at stop signs at three separate intersections in different parts of a city (in

Florida) (Van Houten & Retting, 2001). Over 700,000 accidents occur at stop signs, and 3,000 of these are fatal (1998 statistics). In this study two prompting procedures were used to increase full stops. Video cameras recorded stopping, and the videotapes were scored later by observers. A multiple-baseline design across three sites (intersections) was the design. The first intervention consisted of a sign posted under the stop sign that said in black letters on a white background, "LOOK BOTH WAYS." The second intervention consisted of animated eyes on a screen that scanned left and right once per second. The animated-eyes screen was placed in front of the stop sign and included a microwave sensor that detected approaching vehicles. Once a vehicle was detected, the eyes moved from side to side that is, looking both ways, for 6 seconds.

Figure 7.6 shows that the "look both ways" sign did not have much of an effect. This intervention was not implemented for the other intersections. Presumably, if it were very effective, this would be the intervention extended to other baselines. The animated-eyes intervention was presented, and that increased the percentage of drivers

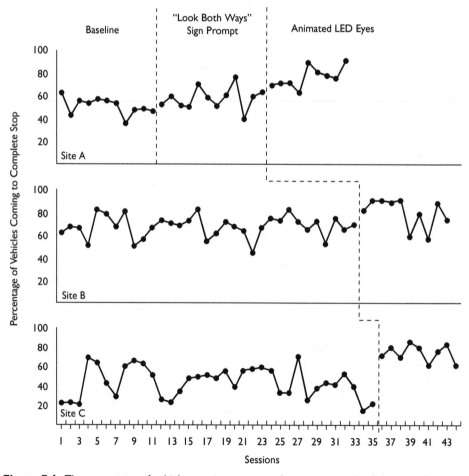

Figure 7.6. The percentage of vehicles coming to a complete stop at each of the sites (intersections) in a multiple-baseline design across sites. *(Source: Van Houten & Retting, 2001.)*

coming to a complete stop. As evident from the middle and lower panels, this latter intervention was extended to each of the other intersections and was associated with change. The example conveys a strength of single-case designs, namely, trying out an intervention, evaluating its impact in real time, and making a decision to try something else if further change is needed.

Another variation of the design that involves partial application of treatment is the case in which one (or more) of the baselines never receives treatment. Essentially, the final baseline (behavior, person, or situation) is observed over the course of the investigation and serves as a control for extraneous changes that might occur because of events (history) or changes in measurement. For example, a program was devised to alter the disruptive behavior of three African American students (ages 8 to 10) in a special education classroom comprised of eight students (Musser, Bray, Kehle, & Jenson, 2001). The three students met criteria for psychiatric disorders, namely, Oppositional Defiant Disorder (extremes of stubbornness, noncompliance) and Attention-Deficit/Hyperactivity Disorder (inattention, hyperactivity). The focus was on reducing disruptive behaviors in class (e.g., talking out, making noises, being out of one's seat, swearing and name calling). Daily baseline observations of disruptive behavior were made in class. The intervention included several components: posting classroom rules on the student's desk (e.g., sit in your seat unless you have permission to leave, raise your hand for permission to speak), special instructions/requests by the teacher (e.g., using the word "please" before a request was made of the student, standing close to the student), rewards for compliance and good behavior (e.g., praise, stickers exchangeable for prizes), and mild punishment (e.g., taking away a sticker).

Figure 7.7 shows that the program was introduced in a multiple-baseline design across the three students. Two other students in the same class and of the same age and ethnicity and also with diagnoses of disruptive behavior disorders were assessed over the course of the study but never received the intervention. As the figure shows, the intervention led to change for each of the three students at each point that the intervention was introduced and not before. The pattern strongly suggests that the intervention rather than any extraneous influences accounted for the change. This conclusion is further bolstered by the two control students who were observed over time in the same class. Essentially these students remained in the baseline phase over the course of the study and continued to perform at the same level over time. The two control baselines (students) are not needed but provide yet another way of showing that extraneous influences are not likely to explain the pattern of the data across all of the baselines students. This is a very clear demonstration aided by showing that with the intervention there was change and without the intervention (for each of the three students and for the two control students) there was no change. One point to mention in passing: In the follow-up (final) phase, the program was removed completely and behavior was maintained. That is, return to baseline did not lead to a loss of the gains.

General Comments

The preceding discussion highlights major variations of the multiple-baseline design. Perhaps the major source of diversity is whether the multiple baselines refer to the behaviors of a particular person, to different persons, or to performance in different situations.

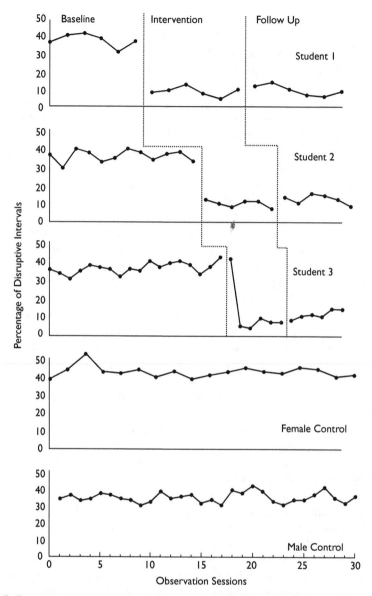

Figure 7.7. Disruptive behavior (percentage of intervals) of special education students. The intervention was introduced in a multiple-baseline design across three students. Two similar children (bottom two graphs) served as controls; their behavior was assessed over the course of the program but never received the intervention. In the final follow-up phase the program was completely withdrawn. *(Source: Musser et al., 2001.)*

There are many permutations of multiple-baseline designs that stem from considering contexts or settings. For example, government programs (e.g., money for implementing a special educational intervention, novel ideas for improving the proportion of children who obtain vaccinations) at the local or federal level might be introduced across schools, school districts, agencies, and states in a multiple-baseline fashion to evaluate their impact. Apart from contexts or settings, numerous other variations of multiple-baseline designs exist. The variations usually involve combinations of the dimensions discussed previously. Variations also occasionally involve components of ABAB designs; these will be addressed in Chapter 10, in which combined designs are discussed.

PROBLEMS AND LIMITATIONS

Several sources of ambiguity can arise in drawing inferences about intervention effects using multiple-baseline designs. Ambiguities can result from the interdependence of the behaviors, persons, or situations that serve as the baselines or from inconsistent effects of the intervention on the different baselines. Finally, both practical and methodological problems may arise when the intervention is withheld from one or more of the behaviors, persons, or situations for a protracted period of time.

Interdependence of the Baselines

The critical requirement for demonstrating unambiguous effects of the intervention in a multiple-baseline design is that each baseline (behavior, person, or situation) changes only when the intervention is introduced and not before. Sometimes the baselines may be interdependent, so that change in one of the baselines carries over to another baseline even though the intervention has not been extended to that latter baseline. This effect can interfere with drawing conclusions about the intervention in each version of the multiple-baseline design.

In the design *across behaviors*, changing the first behavior may be associated with changes in one of the other behaviors even though those behaviors have yet to be included in the intervention (e.g., Whalen, Schreibman, & Ingersoll, 2006). Common experience would suggest interdependence of behaviors. Some behaviors (e.g., communication, social interaction) may be pivotal to other activities and have ripple effects in changing other behaviors (cf. Koegel & Kern-Koegel, 2006; Rosales-Ruiz & Baer, 1997). In situations where generalization across responses occurs, the multiple-baseline design across behaviors may not show a clear relation between the intervention and behavior change.

In the multiple-baseline design *across individuals*, it is possible that altering the behavior of one person influences other persons who have yet to receive the intervention. In investigations in situations where one person can observe the performance of others, such as classmates at school or siblings at home, changes in the behavior of one person occasionally result in changes in other persons. For example, a program designed to reduce thumb sucking in a 9-year-old boy was very effective in eliminating the behavior (Watson et al., 2002). No intervention was provided to the boy's 5-year-old brother, whose behavior also changed and for whom thumb sucking was also eliminated. It could have been that the brother who received the intervention was a cue for the behavior or modeled the behavior. The interpretation is not clear, but the effects are. The intervention in this case spread to another person for whom no direct intervention was provided. Similarly, in the multiple-baseline design across *situations*, *settings*, or *time*, altering the behavior of the person in one situation may lead to generalization of performance across other situations. The specific effect of the intervention may not be clear.

In each of the preceding cases, if intervention effects extended beyond the specific baseline to which the intervention was applied, the results would be ambiguous. It is possible that extraneous events coincided with the application of the intervention and led to general changes in performance. Alternatively, it is possible that the intervention accounted for the changes in several behaviors, persons, or situations even though it was only applied to one. The problem is not that the intervention failed to produce the change; it may have. Rather, the problem lies in unambiguously inferring that the intervention was the causal agent.

Interdependence of the baselines is a potential problem in each of the multiple-baseline designs. However, three points provide a perspective on the threat of interdependence of the baselines. First, few demonstrations report the interdependence of baselines. Yes, it could be that it occurs all of the time but these papers do not get published. In my own experience, the interdependence rarely occurs. Second, when changes do occur prematurely for the baselines (behaviors, situations) that have yet to receive the intervention, this does not necessarily mean that the demonstration is ambiguous. The specific effect of the demonstration may be clear for a few but not all of the baselines. Third, single-case designs allow for design changes and improvisation during the demonstration. Thus, the investigator may introduce features of other designs, such as a return-to-baseline phase for one or more of the behaviors, to show that the intervention was responsible for change. I discuss combined designs later to convey this option.

Inconsistent Effects of the Intervention

Another potential problem of multiple-baseline designs is that the intervention may produce inconsistent effects on the behaviors, persons, or situations to which it is introduced. "Inconsistent effects" means that some behaviors are altered when the intervention is introduced and others are not. The inconsistent effects of an intervention in a multiple-baseline design raise obvious problems. In the most serious case, the design might include only two behaviors, the minimum (but not recommended) number of baselines required. The intervention is introduced to both behaviors at different points in time, but only one of these behaviors changes. The results are usually too ambiguous to meet the requirements of the design. Extraneous factors other than the intervention might well account for behavior changes, so the internal validity of the investigation has not been achieved. This concern is one reason why three baselines is a recommended minimum for multiple-baseline designs and more can make the investigator merrier.

Alternatively, if several behaviors are included in the design and one or two do not change when the intervention is introduced, this may be an entirely different matter. The effects of the intervention may still be quite clear from the two, three, or more behaviors that did change when the intervention was introduced. The behaviors that did not change are exceptions. Of course, the fact that some behaviors changed and others did not raises questions about the generality or strength of the intervention. But the internal validity of the demonstration, namely, that the intervention was responsible for change, is not an issue. In short, the pattern of the data need not be perfect to permit the inference that the intervention was responsible for change. If several of the baselines show the intended effect, an exception may not necessarily interfere with drawing causal inferences about the role of the intervention. As I noted, experimental design is about making competing interpretations of the intervention effect implausible. An overall pattern in the data with an exception of one of the baselines may still leave the intervention as the most reasonable explanation of the results.

Prolonged Baselines

Multiple-baseline designs depend on withholding the intervention from each baseline (behavior, person, or situation) for a period of time. The intervention is applied to the first behavior while it is temporarily withheld from the second, third, and other behaviors. Eventually, of course, the intervention is extended to each of the baselines. If several behaviors (or persons, or situations) are included in the design, the possibility exists that several days or weeks might elapse before the final behavior receives treatment. Several issues arise when the intervention is withheld for extended periods.

Obviously, applied and ethical considerations may argue against withholding the intervention. If the intervention improves behavior when it is applied initially, perhaps it should be extended immediately to other behaviors. Withholding the intervention may be unethical, especially if there is a hint in the data from the initial baselines that the intervention influences behavior. Of course, the ethical issue here is not unique to multiple-baseline or single-case designs but can be raised in virtually any area of experimentation in which an intervention of unknown effectiveness is under evaluation or where a promising intervention is withheld. Whether it is ethical to withhold an intervention or treatment may depend on some assurances that the treatment is helpful and is responsible for change. These latter questions, of course, are the basis of using experimental designs to evaluate interventions in the first place.

Although some justification may exist for temporarily withholding interventions for purposes of evaluation, concerns increase when the period of withholding the intervention is protracted. If the final behaviors in the design will not receive the intervention for several days or weeks, this may be unacceptable in light of applied considerations. As discussed later, there are ways to use the multiple-baseline design so that the final behaviors receive the intervention with relatively little delay.

Aside from ethical and applied considerations, methodological problems may arise when baseline phases are prolonged for one or more of the behaviors. As noted earlier, the multiple-baseline design depends on showing that performance changes when and only when the intervention is introduced. When baseline phases are extended for a prolonged period, performance may sometimes improve slightly even before the intervention is applied. Several reasons may account for the improvement. First, the interdependence of the various behaviors that are included in the design may be responsible for changes in a behavior that has yet to receive the intervention. Indeed, as more and more behaviors receive the intervention in the design, the likelihood that other behaviors yet to receive treatment will show the indirect or generalized benefits of the treatment may increase.

Second, over an extended period, clients may have increased opportunities to develop the desired behaviors either through direct practice or the observation of others. For example, if persons are measured each day on their social behavior, play skills, or compliance to instructions, improvements may eventually appear in baseline phases for behaviors (or persons) that have yet to receive the intervention. The prolonged baseline assessment may provide some opportunities to improve performance through repeated practice or modeling to improve in performance.

Third, the social environment of the child may have changed in direct response to the individual's changes in one or more behaviors. Others in the environment may respond differently and that could affect a variety of the individual's behaviors, whether or not the intervention is introduced. Collateral changes are always possible but might be more likely with protracted baselines where the effects of indirect influence might increase over time. In any case, when some behaviors (or persons, or situations) show improvements before the intervention is introduced, the requirements of the multiple-baseline design may not be met.

The ethical, applied, and methodological problems that may result from prolonged baselines can usually be avoided. To begin with, multiple-baseline designs usually do not include a large number of behaviors (e.g., six or more), so that the delays in applying the intervention to the final behavior are not great. Even if several baselines are used, the problems of prolonged baselines can be avoided in a number of ways. First, when several behaviors are observed, few data points may be needed for the baseline phases for some of the behaviors. For example, if six behaviors are observed, baseline phases for the first few behaviors may last only one or a few days. Also, the delay or lag period between implementing treatment for one behavior and implementing the same treatment for the next behavior need not be very long. A lag of a few days may be all that is necessary, so that the total period of the baseline phase before the final behavior receives treatment may not be particularly long.

Also, when several behaviors are included in the multiple-baseline design, treatment can be introduced for two (or more) behaviors at the same point in time. The demonstration still takes advantage of the multiple-baseline design, but it does not require implementing the treatment for only one behavior at a time. For example, a hypothetical multiple-baseline design is presented in Figure 7.8 in which six behaviors are observed. In a multiple-baseline design, treatment might be applied to each of the behaviors, one at a time (see left panel of figure). It might take several days before the final behavior could be included in treatment. Alternatively, the treatment could be extended to each of the behaviors two at a time (see right panel of the figure). This variation of the design does not decrease the strength of the demonstration, because the intervention is still introduced at two (or more) different points in time. The obvious advantage is that the final behavior is treated much sooner in this version of the design than in the version in which each behavior is treated separately. In short, delays in applying the intervention to the final behavior (or person, or situation) can be reduced by applying the treatment to more than one behavior at a time.

Prolonged baselines raise assessment obstacles if one has to conduct daily assessment for several baselines for an extended period. It may be a burden or simply not feasible to observe all of the baselines daily. Two options have been used to handle observational challenges and still allow the design to proceed. First, instead of every day, observations could be made only occasionally for some of the baselines, especially if the baselines are stable. It is critical here to keep in mind not the design per se but the purpose of the design. For each baseline, we need a stable estimate to describe present performance and predict future performance. This can be accomplished in a feasible way that may involve only intermittent assessment. The periodic or intermittent

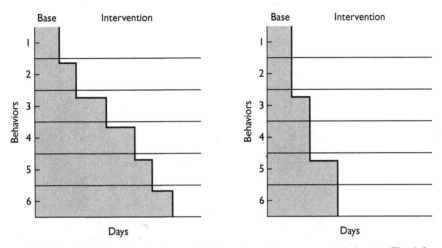

Figure 7.8. Hypothetical example of a multiple-baseline design across six behaviors. The *left panel* shows a design in which the intervention is introduced to each behavior, one at a time. The *right panel* shows a design in which the intervention is introduced to two behaviors at a time. The shaded area conveys the different durations of baseline phases in each version of the design. The illustration is a multiple-baseline across behaviors, but of course the same point applies if the baselines were across people or settings.

assessment of behavior when interventions are not in effect for that behavior is referred to as probes or *probe assessment*. Probes provide an estimate of what daily performance would be like. For example, hypothetical data are presented in Figure 7.9, which illustrates a multiple-baseline design across behaviors. Instead of assessing behavior every day, probes are illustrated in two of the baseline phases. The probes provide a sample of data and avoid the burden of daily assessment for an extended period. Certainly an advantage of probe assessment is the reduction in cost in terms of the time the observer must spend collecting baseline data. If probes are to be used to reduce the number of assessment occasions, the investigator needs to have an a priori presumption that performance is stable. The clearest instance of stability would be if behavior never occurs or reflects a complex skill that is not likely to change over time without special training.[1]

Another option is to begin assessments at different points. In this instance, there may be multiple baselines but observation does not begin at the same point for each one. For example, two baselines may be observed in the usual way, but additional baselines may be added. Those additions may be planned from the beginning but postponed because of the lack of resources for assessing all the baselines or they may be unplanned. As the intervention begins, it may become clear or advisable to add new behaviors or new situations. I have explained the logic of the design to help with these practical situations. The data within the phases of single-case designs are intended to

---

[1] Probes can be used for other purposes such as the assessment of maintenance or the transfer of behavior to other situations or settings (see Chapter 10).

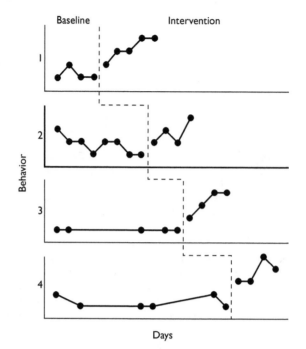

Figure 7.9. Hypothetical data for a multiple-baseline design across behaviors. Daily observations were conducted and are plotted for the first and second behaviors. Probes (intermittent assessment) were conducted for the baselines of the third and fourth behaviors.

serve the describe, predict, and test prediction functions. Thus, one can depart from rigid application of designs as long as the functions are served.

EVALUATION OF THE DESIGN

Multiple-baseline designs have a number of advantages that make them very useful in applied settings. To begin with, the designs do not depend on withdrawing treatment to show that behavior change is a function of the intervention. Hence, there is no need to reduce or temporarily suspend treatment effects for purposes of the design. This characteristic makes multiple-baseline designs a highly preferred alternative to ABAB designs and their variations.

Another feature of the designs makes them quite suited to practical considerations and demands of applied settings. The designs require applying the intervention to one behavior (person or situation) at a time. The *gradual* application of the intervention across the different behaviors has practical benefits. In many applied settings, parents, teachers, supervisors, institutional staff, or other change agents are responsible for applying the intervention. Considerable skill may be required to apply the intervention effectively. Implementing the intervention on a small scale (one behavior or individual) allows change agents to proceed gradually and extend the scope of the intervention (to other behaviors and individuals) only after having mastered the initial applications. In situations in which behavior-change agents are learning new skills in applying an intervention, the gradual application can be very useful.

A related advantage is that the application to only one behavior at a time permits a test of the effectiveness of the procedure. Before the intervention is applied widely, the preliminary effects on the first behavior can be examined. If treatment effects are not sufficiently strong, or if the procedure is not implemented correctly, it is useful to learn this early, before applying the procedure widely across all behaviors, persons, or situations of interest.

In specific variations of the multiple-baseline design, the gradual manner in which treatment is extended can also be useful for the clients (e.g., students, children, employees). For example, in the multiple-baseline design across behaviors or situations, the intervention is first applied to only one behavior or to behavior in only one situation. Gradually, other behaviors and situations are incorporated into the program. This follows a useful model of developing behaviors gradually (shaping) for the client, since early in the program changes are only required for one behavior or in one situation. As the client improves, increased demands are placed on performance.

In an era of increased emphasis on evidence-based interventions, many programs are under increased pressure to document the effects of their interventions. Classrooms; colleges; institutions for children, adolescents, and adults; communities; state and local agencies; and businesses have an endless stream of programs directed to wonderful causes but with no data on their behalf. Those who administer the program recognize that a randomized controlled trial or assigning some units (classes, wards, districts) to the intervention condition and withholding the intervention from other units is not possible. This has led to methodological helplessness, that is, the cognition that doing a careful evaluation of the program and its effects is not possible.

A multiple-baseline design is likely to be quite feasible. There is no need for a no-intervention control group (as in between-group study), nor to withhold some special program, nor to withhold it for very long (as in a multiple-baseline design). In settings where control groups are not possible, multiple-baseline design is a viable alternative. I would argue further that even if a control group were possible, multiple-baseline designs are likely to be preferred. In applied settings, we are interested in seeing individuals change and tinkering with our interventions to make sure this happens. Single-case designs allow for decision making in response to client performance (e.g., when to change phases, whether a new intervention ought to be tried). In contrast, in most between-group studies, the treatment regimen is fixed in duration. Overall, the manner in which treatment is implemented to meet the methodological requirements of the multiple-baseline design may be quite harmonious with practical considerations regarding how behavior change agents and clients perform. Gradual introduction of the intervention across baselines and no need for withdrawal of the intervention make methodological and client considerations quite compatible.

SUMMARY AND CONCLUSIONS

Multiple-baseline designs demonstrate the effects of an intervention by presenting the intervention to each of several different baselines at different points in time. A clear effect is evident if performance changes when and only when the intervention is applied. Several variations of the design exist, depending primarily on whether the *multiple-baseline data are collected across behaviors, persons, situations, settings, or time.* The designs may also vary as a function of the number of baselines and the manner in which treatment is applied. The designs require a minimum of two baselines, but three or more are strongly recommended to optimize clarity of the intervention effect. The strength of the demonstration that the intervention, rather than extraneous events, was responsible for change is a function of the number of behaviors to which treatment is applied, the stability of baseline performance for each of the behaviors, and the magnitude and rapidity of the changes in behavior once treatment is applied.

Sources of ambiguity may make it difficult to draw inferences about the effects of the intervention. First, problems may arise when different baselines are interdependent so that implementation of treatment for one behavior (or person, or situation) leads to changes in other behaviors (or persons, or situations) as well, even though these latter behaviors have not received treatment. Another problem may arise in the designs if the intervention appears to alter some behaviors but does not alter other behaviors when the intervention is applied. If several behaviors are included in the design, a failure of one of the behaviors to change may not raise a problem. The effects may still be quite clear from the several behaviors that did change when the intervention was introduced.

A final problem that may arise with multiple-baseline designs pertains to withholding treatment for a prolonged period while the investigator is waiting to apply the intervention to the final behavior, person, or situation. Practical and ethical considerations may create difficulties in withholding treatment for a protracted period. Also, it is possible that extended baselines will introduce ambiguity into the demonstration. In cases in which persons are retested on several occasions or have the opportunity to observe the desired behavior among other subjects before the intervention is applied to them, extended baseline assessment may lead to systematic improvements or decrements in behavior. Demonstration of the effects of the intervention on extended baselines may be difficult. Prolonged baselines can be avoided by utilizing short baseline phases or brief lags before applying treatment to the next baseline, and by implementing the intervention across two or more behaviors (or persons, or situations) simultaneously in the design. Thus, the intervention need not be withheld even for the final behaviors in the multiple-baseline design. Multiple-baseline designs are quite popular, in part, because they do not require reversals of performance. Also, the designs are consistent with many of the demands of applied settings in which the intervention is implemented on a small scale first before being extended widely.

Changing-Criterion Designs

With a changing-criterion design, the effect of the intervention is demonstrated by showing that behavior changes gradually over the course of the intervention phase. The behavior improves in increments or steps to match a criterion for performance that is specified as part of the intervention. For example, if praise or points are provided to a child for practicing a musical instrument, a criterion (e.g., amount of time spent practicing) is specified to the child as the requirement for earning the rewarding consequences. As the child's performance matches or meets that criterion with some consistency, the criterion is shifted to a new level (e.g., more minutes) to earn the consequences. The required level of performance in a changing-criterion design is altered repeatedly over the course of the intervention to improve performance over time. The effects of the intervention are shown when performance repeatedly changes to meet the criterion. Graphically, this appears as a step-like function in which performance matches the criterion, the criterion is shifted, and the performance matches the new criterion, and so on, until the desired level of performance is achieved.

Unlike the ABAB designs, the changing-criterion design does not require withdrawing or temporarily suspending the intervention to demonstrate the relation between the intervention and behavior. Unlike multiple-baseline designs, the design does not require multiple behaviors (settings, or situations) or require withholding the intervention temporarily so that it can be introduced sequentially across baselines. The changing-criterion design neither withdraws nor withholds treatment as part of the demonstration.

BASIC CHARACTERISTICS OF THE DESIGN

Description and Underlying Rationale

The changing-criterion design begins with a baseline phase in which continuous observations of a single behavior are made for one or more persons. After the baseline (or A) phase, the intervention (or B) phase is begun. The unique feature of a changing-criterion design is the use of several *subphases* (b_1, b_2, to b_n). I refer to them as subphases (little b) because they are all in the intervention phase; the number of these subphases can vary up to any number (n) within the intervention phase. During the intervention phase, a criterion is set for performance. For example, in programs based on the use of reinforcing consequences, the client is instructed that he or she will receive the consequences if a certain level of performance is achieved. If performance meets or surpasses the criterion, the consequence is provided. As performance meets that criterion, the criterion is made slightly more stringent. This continues in a few subphases in which the criterion is repeatedly changed.

As an illustration, a person may be interested in exercising more. Baseline may reveal that the person never exercises (i.e., zero minutes per day). The intervention phase may begin by setting a criterion such as 10 minutes of exercise per day. If the criterion is met or exceeded (10 or more minutes of exercise), the client may earn a reinforcing consequence (e.g., special privilege at home, money toward purchasing a desired item). Whether the criterion is met is determined each day. Only if performance meets or surpasses the criterion will the consequence be earned. If performance consistently meets the criterion for several days, the criterion is increased slightly (e.g., 20 minutes of exercise). As performance stabilizes at this new level, the criterion is again shifted upward to another level. The criterion continues to be altered in this manner until the desired level of performance (e.g., exercise) is met.

A hypothetical example of the changing-criterion design is illustrated in Figure 8.1, which shows a baseline phase that is followed by an intervention phase. Within the intervention phase, several subphases are delineated (by vertical dashed lines). In each subphase, a different criterion for performance is specified (dashed horizontal line within each subphase). As performance stabilizes and consistently meets the criterion, the criterion is made more stringent, and criterion changes are made repeatedly over the course of the design.

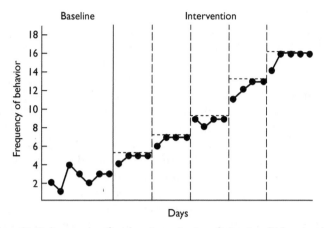

Figure 8.1. Hypothetical example of a changing-criterion design in which several subphases are presented during the intervention phase. The subphases differ in the criterion (dashed line) for performance that is required of the subject.

The underlying rationale of the changing-criterion resembles that of designs discussed previously. As in the ABAB and multiple-baseline designs, the baseline phase serves to describe current performance and to predict performance in the future. The intervention phases of these designs test that prediction to see if performance departs from what is expected, if baseline were to continue. Similarly, the subphases of the changing-criterion design also make and test predictions. In each subphase, a criterion or performance standard is set. If the intervention is responsible for change, performance would be expected to follow the shifts in the criterion from subphase to subphase. In contrast, if behavior fluctuates randomly (no systematic pattern) or tends to increase or decrease without following the criterion shifts, it is more likely or at least plausible to assume that extraneous factors rather than the intervention controlled behavior. In such instances, the intervention cannot be accorded a causal role in accounting for performance. On the other hand, if performance corresponds closely to the changes in the criterion, then the intervention can be considered to be responsible for the change.

Illustrations

An illustration of the design was provided in a program designed to develop reading in Craig, a 26-year-old European American man diagnosed with paranoid schizophrenia and living in a community-based treatment program (Skinner, Skinner, & Armstrong, 2000). The client had many symptoms including delusional thoughts, paranoid ideation, auditory hallucinations, and flat affect. The goal was to develop leisure reading as part of his activities. The client asked the staff to help improve his reading. He could read but did not sustain the task. For this project, Craig selected the reading material from a local library. The goal of the program was to increase the number of pages he would read out loud. This was accomplished by increasing the number of pages read over time. Number of pages read continuously was counted, that is, with no pause of more than 30 seconds. A delay due to asking about the meaning of a word or looking a word up in a dictionary was excluded from counting as a pause. Each day Craig continued reading where he left off on the previous day. There was only one session per day. Craig did not have to read and could say no or not have a session if he did not want one. A changing-criterion design was used for the demonstration.

During baseline, Craig or a staff member could initiate his reading. No special program was implemented to improve reading. During the intervention phase, Craig could earn a soft drink if he met the criterion for the number of pages read. Before the session, a staff member showed Craig the end point of the pages he needed to read in order to meet the criterion. The criterion increased by one page after Craig met the required number of pages on 3 days. Early in the program, the soft drink was given immediately after reading. Soon, he asked to walk to the store for this. Walking to the store, discussing the reading, and selecting the drink were considered good ways to integrate him more into the community. After 6 weeks of the program, Craig asked to end the program; he no longer wanted to read out loud. Seven weeks later, after expressing interest in a book someone else was reading, there was an unprompted and unplanned assessment, which is identified in the final phase as a maintenance probe (M).

Figure 8.2 shows that the number of pages read was low. During the intervention phase, number of pages read increased and showed a step-like function as the criterion (number of pages) was increased. Reading very closely followed the criterion shifts. During baseline, Craig elected to read only 40% of the time (2 of 5 days); during the intervention phase he elected to read on 76% of the days. Moreover, on those days, he met the criterion for reinforcement on 25 of 26 (96%) of the occasions. Reading was maintained 7 weeks after the program had ended. Although the out-loud reading program was discontinued, Craig continued to borrow books from the public library, kept a book on his night stand, and was observed reading silently. The program began with out-loud reading, Craig's initial preference, but silent reading appeared to continue after that particular program ended.

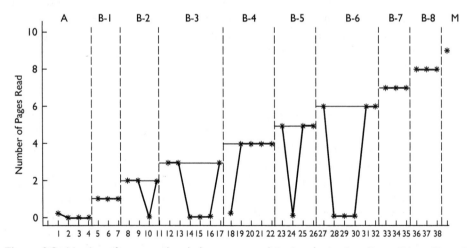

Figure 8.2. Number of pages read each day across conditions and criteria.   *(Source: Skinner, Skinner, & Armstrong, 2000.)*

As another illustration, a study focused on a 15-year-old girl named Amy with insulin-dependent diabetes. She had been instructed to check her blood sugar 6 to 12 times per day (Allen & Evans, 2001). Among the challenges is avoiding hypoglycemia (low blood sugar), which is extremely unpleasant and characterized by symptoms of dizziness, sweating, headaches, and impaired vision. This can also lead to seizures and loss of consciousness. Children and their parents often are hypervigilant to do anything to avoid low blood sugar including deliberately maintaining high blood glucose levels. The result of maintaining high levels can be poor metabolic control and increased health risk for complications (e.g., blindness, renal failure, nerve damage, and heart disease). Amy was checking her blood glucose levels 80 to 90 times per day (at a cost of about $600 per week) and was maintaining her blood glucose levels too high.

A blood glucose monitor was used that automatically recorded the number of checks (up to 100 checks) and then downloaded the information to a computer. The test included a finger prick, application of the blood to a reagent test strip, insertion of the strip into the monitor, and a display of glucose levels. An intervention was used to decrease the number of times blood glucose checks were made each day. Amy parent's gradually reduced access to the materials (test strips) that were needed for the test. A changing-criterion design was used in which fewer and fewer tests were allowed. If Amy met the criterion, she was allowed to earn a maximum of five additional tests (blood glucose checks). Access to the test materials was reduced gradually over time. The parents selected the criterion of how many tests (test strips) would be available in each subphase. As shown in Figure 8.3, the criterion first dropped by 20 checks and then by smaller increments. Over a 9-month period, Amy decreased her use of monitoring from over 80 to 12 times per day. Better metabolic control was also achieved; by the end of the 9 months, blood glucose levels were at or near the target levels (i.e., neither hypo- or hyper-glucose levels).

DESIGN VARIATIONS

Most applications of the changing-criterion design closely follow the basic design just illustrated. Features of the basic design can vary, including the number of changes that are made in the criterion, the duration of the subphases at each criterion, the amount or magnitude of change in the criterion at each step, magnitude of the changes in the criteria, and the directionality of the shifts in the criterion.

Subphases During the Intervention

There are critical decision points in using the design that make for variation. Three critical questions need to be answered: How many subphases are required? How long should each subphase be? And how large should the changes be from one criterion shift to the next? In traditional between-group research, questions like these (e.g., how long is the intervention provided?) are answered before the study begins; in single-case designs the questions are usually not answered ahead of time. In single-case designs both the intervention and the design have a flexibility that individualizes each to the client based on how the client is responding and whether the criteria are met (e.g., stable performance) in a given phase. Even so, some guidelines can be provided.

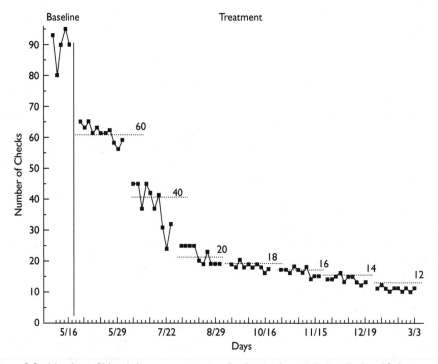

Figure 8.3. Number of blood glucose monitoring checks conducted during the last 10 days at each criterion level. Maximum test strips allotted at each level are indicated by dashed lines (the changing criteria) and corresponding numbers of checks. The number of checks above the criterion level reflect the number of additional test strips earned by Amy.   *(Source: Allen & Evans, 2001.)*

How Many Are Required? After baseline, the intervention in which the criterion is changed is implemented. Minimally, at least two changes in the criterion and therefore two subphases of B are needed. During the intervention one sets the criterion level, sees if performance comes to or near that level, looks for a stable or clear pattern at that first criterion level, and then makes at least one more shift in that criterion. Stated another way, this simple version of the design has a baseline phase (A) and an intervention phase (B) that has b_1 and b_2 as subphases. The design depends on showing that criterion shifts lead to performance shifts, and in principle two might be sufficient. In practice, and as illustrated by the examples in this chapter, many more criterion shifts (e.g., ranging from 3 up to 25) are used (e.g., Allen & Evans, 2001; Facon, Sahiri, & Riviere, 2008; McDougall, 2005). Although two are minimal, three or more are much more common and are recommended here.

How Long (Days, Sessions) Should the Subphases Be? A separate decision from how many criterion shifts is how long each shift should be, that is, how many days or sessions, before moving to the next criterion level. Each of these criterion shifts ought to be long enough to achieve at least one of two characteristics: stable responding and correspondence of behavior and the criterion. As to stable responding (little or no trend, minimal variability), the criterion shifts serve as subphases (e.g., b_1, b_2, ... b_n) in relation to how the design works. In the logic of single-case designs, data in a phase or subphase are intended to describe current performance, predict what performance would be like in the immediate future if conditions were not changed again, and test whether the new level of performance departs from a prior phase (or in this case a prior criterion level or subphase). Consequently, a criterion shift should be in place long enough to permit one to see stable performance that can be used for these purposes. As an exception, if the criterion shifts are large and performance of the client leaps to match these, the phases can be brief.

If behavior meets the new criterion quickly and shows low variability, the subphases can be relatively brief (two to five days or sessions). If behavior does not change quite so clearly when the criterion is shifted, the subphase may need to be longer. As is invariably the case in single-case designs, the duration of any phase or subphase varies in response to the client's performance. In this design, the subphases do not need to be of the same duration, but they do need to meet the larger goal of allowing the investigator to discern a pattern and to infer how likely it is that the pattern of behavior during one subphase and across a few subphases is due to the criteria shift and intervention.

How Large Should the Changes Be from One Criterion Shift to the Next? A concern in drawing inferences is that one should not be able to look at the graphical display and say, "There seems to be a gradual trend toward improvement while the intervention is in effect." This pattern might suggest that some other influence (history, maturation, responses of others in the setting that are not part of the intervention) rather than the specific intervention might account for the effect.

The design requires showing shifts in performance in response to shifts in the criterion. The larger the shifts (bigger the steps) required and the more immediate the shifts in client performance, the greater the clarity of the demonstration. That is, with larger criterion shifts and performance changes that match them, the intervention as the source of influence becomes the most plausible account of the results. I return to this later because there is a potential conflict in meeting the ideals of the design (several large criterion shifts) and developing behavior gradually (shaping) along some continuum (more time, more responses).

As a general rule, one would like to show a step-like function in performance during the intervention phase, with subphases moving client behavior in ways that are not smooth or consistent with some overall gradual change that could be readily due to some other event. For example, if one is increasing duration of performance on a task (completing homework, practicing a musical instrument, walking for a person whose medical regimen requires that as part of treatment for an injury or recovery), one would not change the criterion in the subphases by 1 or 2 minutes but would make larger jumps if possible (e.g., 10 or 15 minutes). More examples will better convey how this is accomplished.

Point or Range of Responses as the Criterion

In the usual version of the design, the criterion shifts are based on a specific point. For example, to earn some consequence, the first criterion may be set as smoking fewer than 15 cigarettes per day or reading for 20 or more minutes. These criteria (e.g., 15 and 20) are specific points. Each criterion is changed over the course of the intervention phase. A design variation is to use a range with an upper and lower criterion level rather than a single point (McDougall, 2005; McDougall, Hawkins, Brady, & Jenkins, 2006). Performance of the client must fall within the range that has been specified for the person to receive the reinforcer or whatever the intervention is. When the criterion is changed, that new criterion also is a range. For example, the range for minutes of studying might move from 10 to 20 in the first criterion subphase to 25 to 35 in the second criterion subphase. The criterion is met for any performance that falls within that range.

This version of the design, referred to as the *range-bound changing-criterion design*, is nicely illustrated by the innovator of the design (McDougall, 2005). The study focused on improving the exercise and cardiovascular functioning of an obese adult. A behavioral self-management program was used (self-monitoring, graphing, goal setting, all completed by the client) to increase minutes of running. After baseline, there were several subphases in which the client selected the average number of minutes to be run that week. This began with 20 minutes as an average for the first criterion. A range was selected as +10% of the average. The client was considered to have met the goal if the number of minutes fell within the band or range of 20 + 2 (or 10%). Figure 8.4 shows several phases of the design and the band of acceptable performance considered to meet the criterion. The bands (ranges) become wider because 10% becomes a larger number as the average number of minutes moves upward in the criterion shifts. As evident in the figure, the criterion shifts exerted control over behavior. Performance followed the step-like function one seeks in the changing-criterion design.

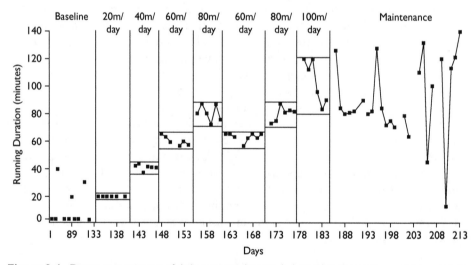

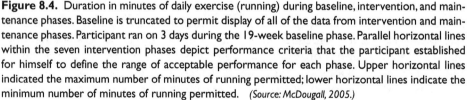

Figure 8.4. Duration in minutes of daily exercise (running) during baseline, intervention, and maintenance phases. Baseline is truncated to permit display of all of the data from intervention and maintenance phases. Participant ran on 3 days during the 19-week baseline phase. Parallel horizontal lines within the seven intervention phases depict performance criteria that the participant established for himself to define the range of acceptable performance for each phase. Upper horizontal lines indicated the maximum number of minutes of running permitted; lower horizontal lines indicate the minimum number of minutes of running permitted. *(Source: McDougall, 2005.)*

A few advantages of this design are worth underscoring. First, a range allows for greater flexibility in performance. In the example, the client did not want to run too much (and risk injury before being in better physical condition) but still wanted to be sure to run at least a minimum each day. The range was well suited to these competing interests. Related, human performance is variable from day to day, which is normal even if not completely understood. Allowing a range to serve as the criterion accommodates this characteristic better than aiming for an unvarying specific point as the criterion. The client's performance can fluctuate within a range and still meet the criterion for the intervention (e.g., reinforcer). The great flexibility of a range might make the intervention and overall program more acceptable to the client as well as to investigators contemplating use of the design.

Second, improved consistency in performance is a characteristic one often seeks in behavior. For example, having a child study or practice a skill each day for a relatively constant amount of time (e.g., 15 to 20 minutes) is much better for learning a topic or skill than practicing all in one session for 1 day a week with little or no practice at all on the other days. The range criterion requires improved performance but within a narrow range. Focusing on a range fosters consistency as well as an improved level of performance.

Third, the design allows one to quantify, for descriptive purposes, the proportion of days on which the client performed within the criterion. Across all subphases, there were many ranges as the criterion shifted. One can report the proportion of days in which performance fell within the range. There is no formal use of this information for drawing inferences, but the information provides a useful descriptive index. The higher the proportion of days falling within the criterion range, the greater the clarity of the results.

Directionality of Change

In the subphases of the design the criterion is usually made more stringent over the course of the intervention. For example, the criterion may be altered to decrease cigarette smoking or to increase the amount of time spent studying. The effects of the intervention are evaluated by examining a change in behavior in a particular direction over time, that is, in each case the performance is moving in the direction of improvement (fewer cigarettes smoked and more time studying) in a step-like fashion as behavior moves to each new step (criterion). The expected changes are unidirectional, that is, either an increase *or* a decrease in behavior.

Difficulties may arise in evaluating unidirectional changes over the course of the intervention phase in a changing-criterion design. Behavior may improve systematically as a function of extraneous factors rather than the intervention. It may be difficult to conclude that the intervention was responsible for change unless performance closely follows the criterion that is set in each subphase and unless there is a step-like pattern that suggests that the intervention and criterion shifts controlled behavior. The experimental control exerted by the intervention can be more readily detected by altering the criterion so that there are *bidirectional* changes in performance, that is, both increases and decreases in behavior.

In this variation of the design, the criterion is made increasingly more stringent in the usual fashion. However, during one of the subphases, the criterion is temporarily made slightly less stringent. For example, the criterion may be raised throughout the intervention phase. During one subphase, though, the criterion is lowered slightly to a previous criterion level. This subphase constitutes sort of a mini-reversal phase and draws on the same logic of the return-to-baseline phase of the ABAB design.

I refer to these as *mini-reversal phases* because the phase does not really return to baseline conditions or level of performance. We are still in the intervention phase, and something is in place to change behavior. However, the criterion is altered so that the direction of the expected change in behavior is opposite from the changes in the previous subphase. If the intervention is responsible for change, one would expect performance to follow the criterion rather than to continue to improve in the same way it was improving in the prior subphase. In the previous example of exercise (see Figure 8.4), there was a reversal phase in the design (see the 60 min-per-day average phase). This phase was not really needed insofar as the shifts in performance seemed to match the criterion shifts closely. Even so, the data pattern with the added bidirectional changes removes ambiguity about whether the intervention was responsible for change.

Another illustration of the use of a bidirectional change focused on an 11-year-old boy, George, with Separation Anxiety Disorder, a psychiatric disorder in which the child is very disturbed by separating from a parent or caregiver (Flood & Wilder, 2004). Difficulties in separating from parents (caregivers) at a young age are common and part of normal development. For some children, this may continue beyond early childhood and reflect more severe reactions that impair their daily functioning. These latter criteria, broadly speaking, influence whether the condition warrants treatment. George had intense emotional reactions and could not allow his mother to leave without displaying them.

Treatment was provided on an outpatient basis twice per week. Each of the sessions lasted up to 90 minutes. The intervention consisted of providing reinforcers for the absence of emotional behaviors and increases in the amount of time George could separate from his mother without these reactions. During baseline, George and his mother were in the treatment room, and the mother attempted to leave by saying she had something to do and would be back soon. Because George showed strong emotional reactions, she stayed. During the intervention sessions, the mother began in the room but left for varying periods. A duration was selected, in discussion with George about how much time he could remain apart from his mother. If George met this time and did not cry, whine, or show other emotional behavior, he could have access for 30 minutes to various toys and games or could receive a small piece of candy or a gift certificate that could be exchanged at a local toy store. If he did not meet the time, he would have a chance in the next session. While the mother was away (outside of the room or later off the premises) she would be called back (cell phone) if George had an emotional reaction to the separation. That ended the session.

Figure 8.5 shows a baseline phase and the intervention phases. More and more minutes free from emotional reactions were required to earn the reinforcer. Although the demonstration seemed clear—in fact, the criterion was matched for all but 1 day (Day 30)—a mini-reversal was introduced by decreasing the requirement to earn the reinforcer from 24 to 18 minutes. Behavior declined to the new criterion. In the final phase, the criterion was lowered on four occasions, and behavior fell to that level too. Throughout the study, performance matched the criterion. The demonstration is

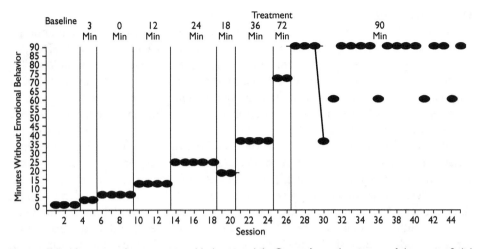

Figure 8.5. Minutes without emotional behavior while George's mother is out of the room. Solid lines in the data represent jointly established therapist and participant goals.   *(Source: Flood & Wilder, 2004.)*

particularly strong by showing changes in both directions, that is, bidirectional changes, as a function of the changing criteria.

In this example, there was little ambiguity about the effect of the intervention. In changing-criterion designs where behavior does not show this close correspondence, a bidirectional change may be particularly useful. When performance does not closely correspond to the criteria, the influence of the intervention may be difficult to detect. Adding a phase in which behavior changes in the opposite direction to follow a criterion reduces the ambiguity about the influence of treatment. Bidirectional changes are much less plausibly explained by extraneous factors (history, maturation) than are unidirectional changes.

The use of a mini-reversal phase in the design is helpful because of the bidirectional change it allows. The strength of this variation of the design is based on the underlying rationale of the ABAB designs. The mini-reversal usually does not raise all of the objections that characterize reversal phases of ABAB design. The mini-reversal does not consist of completely withdrawing treatment to achieve baseline performance. Rather, the intervention remains in effect, and the expected level of performance still represents an improvement over baseline. The amount of improvement is decreased slightly to show that behavior change depends on the criterion that is set. Of course, in a given case, the treatment goal may be to approach the terminal behavior as soon as possible. Examination of bidirectional changes or a mini-reversal might not be feasible. Yet, this is not usually a return to baseline but just a temporary lower level of performance. That lower level is still likely to be well above the baseline rates and still reflect improvement.[1]

---

[1] As implied in the discussion, a mini-reversal could be the second A phase in an ABAB design. Rather than withdrawing the intervention to return to baseline, the intervention might be modified to foster a slight change in the target behavior.

Other Variations

Another variation of the design is more esoteric in its applicability and is mentioned briefly. In this variation, referred to as the *distributed-criterion design* (McDougall, 2006), the application is for occasions in which multiple behaviors are of interest. The key feature of this variation is that multiple baselines, rather than just one baseline for a single target behavior, are incorporated into the changing-criterion design. These multiple behaviors are interrelated so that performance of one of the behaviors is known in some way to be related to the others.

Baseline data are gathered on two or more behaviors very much like a multiple-baseline design, where each is graphed separately. In the intervention phase, a separate criterion is specified for each of the baselines. All of the separate behaviors that are observed cannot respond or improve to the same extent, because of the relation among the behaviors. That is, if one performs the first behavior (e.g., studying arithmetic) for several minutes one might not be able to do the same for the second (and third) behavior (e.g., studying English, history). There is only so much study time that might be available. In this variation, the criterion (e.g., amount of time studying) is distributed or allocated across the interdependent behaviors. The effect of the intervention is demonstrated in two ways: by showing that behavior matches a criterion and by showing that two (or more) behaviors change as the criterion shift is made for one of the behaviors.

An example of the design, perhaps appreciated by readers of the book, focused on a professional who wanted to increase research productivity, defined as time devoted to working on three manuscripts for journal publication (McDougall, 2006). The tasks included analyzing data, making charts, and writing/editing the manuscript. The intervention was self-management (e.g., self-monitoring, goal setting, graphing of performance). A total time per day to be allocated across all of the tasks was decided at the outset to be a mean (average) of 3 hours per day. This feature is what made the behaviors, working on three separate manuscripts, interdependent. Thus, if one worked on one manuscript for all 3 hours, no more time would be available to work on the others. The design is called *distributed* changing-criterion design because the criterion (how much time to focus on each task) was spread (distributed) among the three tasks.

Time spent working on the three manuscripts was graphed, and a criterion was specified for working on each manuscript. In the first phase, 3 hours (180 minutes) were allocated as the criterion for the first manuscript with no hours or minutes for the second and third manuscripts. Once progress was made on the first manuscript, the criterion was changed to 2 hours, 1 hour, and no time for Manuscripts A, B, and C, respectively. Progress consisted of the manuscript being nearly complete, waiting for feedback from others, or submitting it to a journal for publication. Once one manuscript was nearly complete or finished, attention (time) could be allocated to the other manuscripts.

Figure 8.6 conveys the three criteria for Manuscripts A, B, and C, respectively, at the top of each phase after baseline. Thus, the criterion (180, 0, 0 minutes) means that the criterion was 3 hours (180 minutes) for the time devoted to Manuscript A and no time to each of the other manuscripts. One can see from this description and the graphical display that this is a combination of features of changing-criterion and multiple-baseline designs. Each baseline (time for Manuscript A, B, and C) changed when the criterion shift was made for that manuscript. The very stable baselines, the large changes

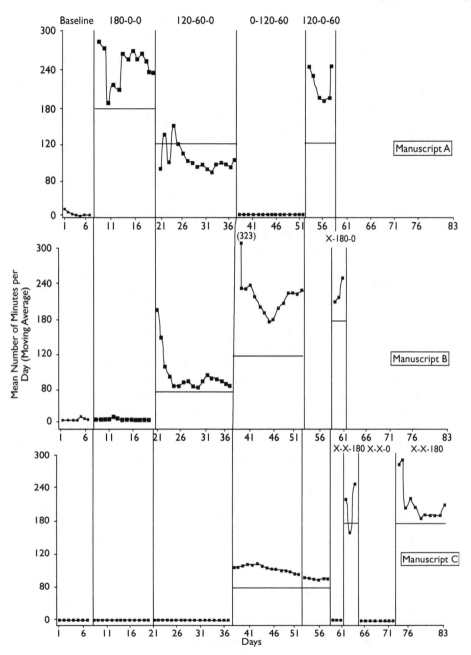

Figure 8.6. Moving average for research productivity (mean number of minutes expended daily) within baseline and intervention phases for Manuscripts A, B, and C. Horizontal lines indicate within-phase productivity criteria (i.e., minimum number of minutes to be expended on a manuscript) that the participant set. Labels for intervention phases are noted as numbered sequences (e.g., 120–60–0). The first number in the sequence indicates the within-phase criterion in minutes that the participant established for Manuscript A; the second and third numbers for Manuscripts B and C, respectively. "X" indicates that a criterion was no longer pertinent because work on the manuscript was completed.   *(Source: McDougall, 2006.)*

when the criterion was shifted, and the changes associated with each manuscript when and only when the criterion was changed all make this demonstration very strong.

The distributed-changing-criterion design is applicable to those instances in which time, effort, or some other dimension cannot be applied in an unlimited fashion to all the behaviors or goals of the program and when engaging in one behavior would affect how much time or effort could be placed into engaging in another. In this case, one "distributes" the time or effort across all of the behavior. The effects of the intervention are shown by performance matching the criterion for each of the baselines and matching the criterion among baselines as the time or effort criterion changes. In most instances, there is no need to focus on separate behaviors that are interrelated in the fashion noted in this example. If there are multiple tasks that are interdependent and cannot all be improved at the same time, this design variation would be quite suitable. A multiple-baseline design might accomplish the same end. However, a broader point is worth conveying as well. Single-case designs need not be rigid, and elements from different designs can readily be combined to strengthen inferences about the effects of the intervention.

General Comments
Changing-criterion designs can vary along several dimensions, such as the number of times the criterion is changed, the duration of the phases in which the criterion is altered, the magnitude of the criterion change, whether the criterion is specified as a point or range, and whether there are unidirectional or bidirectional changes in the criterion. In each of these variations, the logic of the design remains the same. One looks for the step-like pattern that reflects shifts in client performance as a function of shifts in the criterion that are related to the intervention (e.g., receiving some consequence). These steps can provide a dramatic illustration of the impact of the intervention as performance closely approximated each criterion shift. The design provides optimal clarity when bidirectional changes are sought. This variation borrows features of the ABAB design by utilizing a mini-reversal phase. Overall improvements or the impact of extraneous events cannot plausibly explain a step-like function and explain changes in different directions as the criterion is made increasingly stringent and then for a brief subphase less stringent. The strength of this latter variation has led some investigators to include a bidirectional phase even when the results might be clear from the step-like function moving in one rather than two directions over the course of the intervention phase.

PROBLEMS AND LIMITATIONS
The unique feature of the changing-criterion design is the intervention phase in which performance is expected to change in response to different criteria. Ambiguity may arise in drawing inferences about the intervention if performance does not follow or correspond to the shifts of the criterion. There are different ways in which this ambiguity can be manifested.

Gradual Improvement Not Clearly Connected to Shifts in the Criterion
There may be an overall improvement in behavior that is due to some general influence (e.g., the client finally starting some intervention to work on a problem, novelty effects). Perhaps it is not the specific intervention per se, but participating in any program or

structured activity that led to the change. For example, in the context of psychotherapy, expectations that the client will improve on the part of the therapist or the client may lead to improvement in a way that is analogous to a placebo effect in medicine. It is not the specific treatment per se but some general influence that causes the improvement. Alternatively, a new measurement procedure or introducing a new behavior-change agent may alter the motivation or performance of a client. That is not really the effect of the specific intervention but a more general influence on performance that causes the change. In such cases, one looks for a pattern in which performance improves overall and is not clearly changing in a step-like function in response to the criterion changes. In terms of threats to validity, the influence of history and maturation, as two examples, might account for a gradual change over time. This is the reason we want to see a step-like function on the graph that charts performance in response to the changing criteria. The greater the clarity of that step-like pattern, the more plausible it is that the intervention was responsible for change.

An investigator usually wants to see performance clearly change in response to criterion changes. Consider an early use of a changing-criterion design in an innovative program that reduced the cigarette smoking of a 24-year-old male (Friedman & Axelrod, 1973). During baseline, the client observed his own rate of cigarette smoking with a wrist counter. (His fiancé also independently counted smoking to assess reliability.) During the intervention phase, the client was instructed to set a criterion level of smoking each day that he thought he could follow. When he was able to smoke only the number of cigarettes specified by the self-imposed criterion, he was instructed to lower the criterion further.

The results are presented in Figure 8.7, in which the reduction and eventual termination of smoking are evident. In the intervention phase, several different criterion levels

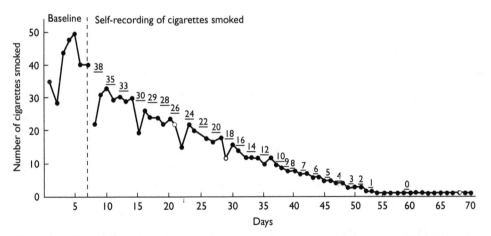

Figure 8.7. The number of cigarettes smoked each day during each of two experimental conditions. Baseline—the client kept a record of the number of cigarettes smoked during a 7-day period. Self-recording of cigarettes smoked—the client recorded the number of cigarettes smoked daily and attempted not to smoke more than at criterion level. The client set the original criterion and lowered the criteria at his own discretion. (The horizontal lines represent the criteria.) *(Source: Friedman & Axelrod, 1973.)*

(short horizontal lines with the criterion number as superscript) were used. Twenty-five different criterion levels were included in the intervention phase. Although it is quite obvious that smoking decreased, performance did not clearly follow the criteria that were set. One could argue that there is an overall pattern of decreased smoking—clearly something important and desirable. The criterion levels were not really followed closely until Day 40 (criterion set at eight), after which close correspondence is evident. Yet the overall pattern of performance (getting better and better) and the very small changes in the criterion make the inferences about the intervention open for dispute. The results might have been much clearer if a given criterion level were in effect for a longer period of time and if the criterion shifts were slightly larger to see if that level really influenced performance. Of course we ought not to lose sight of a large change on an important problem, but we have less clarity about the basis for the change.

Rapid Changes in Performance

Gradual change in performance that cannot be separated from the impact of criterion shifts is one problem in drawing inferences about the impact of the intervention. The other is when behavior changes rapidly and often exceeds the criterion. For example, consider a hypothetical program that is designed to reduce the daily calorie consumption of an overweight adult male. Baseline reveals that this person has been consuming 4,000 to 5,000 calories daily. (Recommended calories per day vary but typically are approximately 2,000 for an adult female and 2,500 for an adult male.) You have developed an intervention (e.g., spouse-controlled points chart with little non-food treats and privileges as backup reinforcers) and a changing-criterion design; you intend to make shifts in the criterion in the usual way to eventually get closer to 2,500 calories. Your first criterion, as the intervention phase begins, sets calories at 3,800 or below—any calorie day below that earns points tracked by the spouse (as well as lavish praise). You begin the program, and improvements immediately exceed the initial criterion set for calorie intake. The person earns the points because calories fell below the criterion. Yet, let us say that each of the days shows that the person was below 2,800 calories—well below the criterion of 3,800 calories. One might well shift to a new criterion, say, 2,500 calories per day and there just continues to be a rapid reduction, say, to 2,200 each day.

Rapid and large changes create two problems for the design. First, the changes make unclear that there is correspondence between the criterion and the change. Second, the changes make it difficult to demonstrate change with a higher or more stringent criterion. That is, the person's performance already reaches new heights and provides data points that may well spill over to a higher level (more stringent) criterion than was intended. There may be little room to show further changes in the criterion and few remaining opportunities to show that performance matches the criterion as that criterion is changed.

The changing-criterion design is especially well suited to situations in which behavior is to be altered gradually toward a terminal goal. This is the underlying rationale behind starting out with a relatively easy criterion and progressing over several different criterion levels. The rationale is sound. However, even though a criterion may only require small changes in behavior (e.g., calorie consumption, minutes of studying), it is possible that performance changes rapidly and greatly exceeds that criterion. In such cases, it may be difficult to evaluate intervention effects.

The effects of rapid changes in behavior that exceed criterion performance can be seen in a program designed to alter the fear in an 8-year-old boy named Rich. He met criteria for Autistic Disorder and was hospitalized at a facility for children with developmental disabilities (Ricciardi, Luiselli, & Camare, 2006).[2] Rich showed a very intense fear of animated figures (e.g., electronic animated toys that blinked, lighted, such as a dancing Elmo' doll, blinking holiday decorations). When seeing these stimuli, he would scream, try to escape, and hit anyone blocking his escape. He also met psychiatric diagnostic criteria for a phobia, which denotes persistent, excessive, and unreasonable fear and a strong response (e.g., in children, crying, tantrums, or clinging) in anticipation of exposure to the feared event or object. Several medications were tried and did not improve this behavior. An intervention program was used based on graduated exposure to fear or anxiety-provoking stimuli, one of the most well-established evidence-based treatments for avoidance and phobias. The intervention provided access to preferred toys if he remained in proximity to the feared objects. The toys were placed at varying distances over the course of the intervention, and the distance in meters (marked in units on the floor) was the criterion that constantly changed in a changing-criterion design. Proximity of the toys to the feared objects changed and gradually exposed him more closely to the materials over the course of the sessions. Rich could leave the session any time he wanted. Intervals (each 15 seconds) were observed to assess how long he remained at the specified distance criteria during baseline and intervention phases.

Figure 8.8 shows criteria during subphases of the intervention phase (horizontal dashed line) where the criterion of meters away from the feared object was assessed (5 meters, 4 meters, etc.). Performance clearly changed from baseline. Rich tolerated exposure to the feared objects. Other measures during treatment (not graphed) showed he could approach and touch the objects when asked to do so. At discharge from the hospital, Rich's mother was encouraged to take him to stores with objects like the ones he feared. She did, and she reported that he tolerated these experiences well.

Clinically, the results are excellent. Access to the preferred objects was associated with improvements, but it is not clear that the intervention was responsible for change given the requirements of the design and their stringent application. The behavior did not follow the criterion shifts at all. There is no step-like function because of the rapid changes in behavior. In short, the rapid shift in performance and departure from criterion levels make the role of the intervention somewhat unclear.

In practice, one might expect that criterion levels will often be surpassed. If the behavior is not easy for the client to monitor or does not have discrete cut points (e.g., number of steps in a complex task with discrete units, such as getting dressed, might be easier to track than minutes of the overall activity), it may be difficult for him or her to perform the behavior at the exact point that the criterion is met. The response

---

[2] Autistic Disorder is a formally recognized psychiatric disorder that emerges in early childhood and includes significant impairment in social interactions (e.g., avoids contacts with others, lacks interest in others), communication (e.g., stereotyped or repetitive use of language, inability to initiate or sustain a conversation), and repetitive and stereotyped patterns of behavior (e.g., repetitive routines and rituals). It has been referred to as a pervasive developmental disorder to convey the scope of impact it can have on functioning. However, there are varying degrees and it is part of a spectrum that reflects a range and severity of impairment.

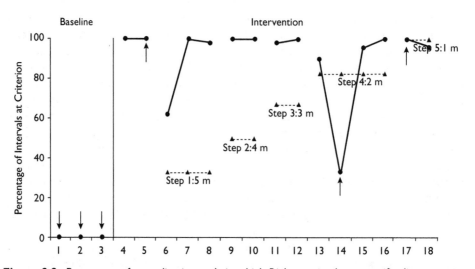

Figure 8.8. Percentage of recording intervals in which Rich remained at a specific distance criterion during baseline and intervention sessions. The distance criteria are depicted by the triangle data path; arrows indicated sessions in which he left the room.   *(Source: Ricciardi, Luiselli, & Camare, 2006.)*

pattern that tends to exceed the criterion level slightly will guarantee earning of the consequence. To the extent that the criterion is consistently exceeded, ambiguity in drawing inferences about the intervention may result. One could select a range as the criterion, as discussed previously. In this case, the client would earn the consequence if performance fell within the range rather than above or below it. However, in school, clinic, or other applied settings, we do not want to put any ceiling on good performance (e.g., you only earn this if your math scores fall between 70% and 80% correct, but not higher!). Again, a mini-reversal can reduce ambiguity on the few occasions it is likely to arise.

Correspondence of the Criterion and Behavior

The strength of the demonstration depends on showing a close correspondence between the criterion and behavior over the course of the intervention phase. In some of the examples in this chapter behavior fell exactly at the criterion levels or range on virtually all occasions of the intervention phase. In such instances, there is little ambiguity regarding the impact of the intervention. Typically, behavior will not fall exactly at the criterion level. When correspondence is not exact, it may be difficult to evaluate whether the intervention accounts for the change. Correspondence is a matter of degree, and ability to attribute the changes to the intervention is as well.

Consider an example of a changing-criterion design to evaluate a feeding program in a 3-year-old boy, Sam, who was born prematurely and had several medical conditions (e.g., lung disease, esophageal reflux) (Luiselli, 2000). He also refused to eat and required tube feeding through a pump activated through waking and sleeping hours.

He rejected all food. The intervention focused on developing self-feeding, a behavior divided into several steps for teaching and data evaluation (e.g., grasping a spoon, scooping up food, placing the spoon in his mouth, swallowing). Baby food was used as the meal, as suggested by the primary-care physician. Number of bites of food was used as the target behavior during the meal; a changing-criterion design was used to specify the number of bites Sam would have to eat to earn reinforcers at the end of the meal (access to toys for 30 minutes). If he did not meet the criterion he was merely told he would have the opportunity at the next meal. The meals began with one of Sam's parents reminding him of how many bites were required to earn the reinforcer, placing a card next to his bowl showing the number of bites that was the criterion during that time, and praising taking the bites of food.

Figure 8.9 shows the number of bites per meal over several days. The horizontal line specifies the criterion, and the data points show days above (higher than) or below (lower than) that criterion. If one looks at the baseline (no feeding) and the one-bite criterion phase it is clear that something happened when treatment began. It is also clear that over the course of treatment there was great change. Most would agree that the intervention was responsible for change, but many days are above or below the criterion, and the precise role of the intervention might be questioned. Did the behavior follow the criterion shifts? Clearly in some subphases the criterion was matched. The data are striking in the subphase, in which eight bites was the criterion and every day met that criterion.

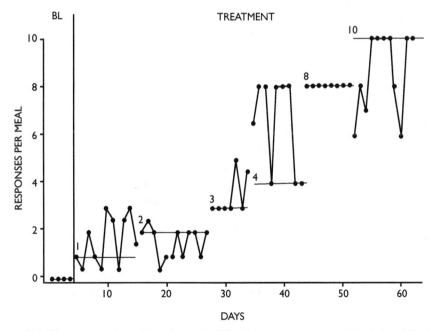

Figure 8.9. The average (mean) number of self-feeding responses recorded during daily lunch and supper meals. Horizontal dashed lines preceded by numbers indicate the imposed self-feeding response criterion during meals. *(Source: Luiselli, 2000.)*

Currently, no clearly accepted measure is available to evaluate the extent to which the criterion level and behavior correspond. Hence, a potential problem in changing-criterion designs is deciding when the criterion and performance correspond closely enough to allow the inference that treatment was responsible for change.[3] More is discussed on evaluating change in the data analysis chapter (and appendix) in relation to all of the single-case designs.

In some cases in which correspondence is not close between performance and the criterion for each phase, authors refer to the fact that average (mean) levels of performance across subphases show a stepwise relationship. Even though actual performance does not follow the criterion closely, in fact, the mean rate of performance within each subphase may change with each change in the criterion. Alternatively, investigators may note that performance fell at or near the criterion in each subphase on all or most of the occasions, and they may provide the proportion of instances. Hence, even though performance levels did not fall exactly at the criterion level, it is clear that the criterion was associated with a shift or new level of performance. As of yet, consistent procedures for evaluating correspondence between behavior and the criterion have not been adopted.

The ambiguities that arise when the criterion and performance levels do not closely correspond are largely resolved by examining bidirectional rather than unidirectional changes in the intervention phase. When bidirectional changes are made, the criterion may be more stringent and less stringent at different points during the intervention phase. It is easier to evaluate the impact of the intervention when looking for changes in different directions (decrease followed by an increase in performance) than when looking for a point-by-point correspondence between the criterion and performance. The bidirectional changes draw on the logic of single-case designs more generally, where one describes, predicts, and tests predictions of likely performance, as elaborated in the presentation of ABAB designs. Showing bidirectional changes makes implausible that extraneous factors could explain the pattern of results. Hence, when ambiguity exists in any particular case about the correspondence between the changing criterion and behavior, a mini-reversal over one of the subphases of the design can be very useful.

Magnitude of Criterion Shifts

The previous comments note that too gradual a change, too rapid a change, and too large a change can raise problems in drawing inferences in the design. What is the Goldilocks (just right) level? That is not quite the right question. The issue is showing a step-like function so that the investigator and those who consider the demonstration

---

[3] One suggestion to evaluate the correspondence between performance and the criterion over the course of the intervention phase might be to compute a Pearson product-moment correlation. The criterion level and actual performance would be paired each day to calculate a correlation. Unfortunately, a product-moment correlation may provide little or no information about the extent to which the criterion is matched. Actual performance may *never* match the changing criterion during the intervention phase and the correlation could still be perfect ($r = 1.00$). The correlation could result from the fact that the differences between the criterion and performance were constant and always in the same direction. The product-moment correlation provides information about the extent to which the two data points (criterion and actual performance) covary over assessment occasions but not whether one matches the other in absolute value.

are persuaded that it was the intervention that provides the best explanation of the pattern in the data.

In designing the study, perhaps the most important design consideration is the magnitude of the criterion shift that is made over the subphases when the intervention is in effect. The basic design specifies that the criterion is changed at several different points. Yet no clear guidelines are inherent in the design that convey how much the criterion should be changed at any given point. The particular clinical problem or focus and the client's performance determine the amount of change made in the criterion over the course of the intervention phase. The client's ability to meet initial criterion levels and relatively small shifts in the criterion may signal the investigator that larger shifts (i.e., more stringent criteria) might be attempted. Alternatively, failure of the client to meet the constantly changing criteria may suggest that smaller changes might be required.

Even deciding the criterion that should be set at the inception of the intervention phase may pose questions. For example, if decreasing the consumption of cigarettes is the target focus, the intervention phase may begin by setting the criterion slightly below baseline levels. The lowest or near-lowest baseline data point might serve as the first criterion for the intervention phase. Alternatively, the investigator might specify that a 10 or 15% reduction of the mean baseline level would be the first criterion. In either case, it is important to set a criterion that the client can meet. The appropriate place to begin, that is, the initial criterion, may need to be negotiated with the client.

As performance meets the criterion, the client may need to be consulted again to decide the next criterion level. At each step, the client may be consulted to help decide the criterion level that represents the next subphase of the design. In many cases, of course, the client may not be able to negotiate the procedures and changes in the criterion (e.g., children and adolescents with severe developmental disabilities; elderly with severe cognitive impairment).

With or without the aid of the client, the investigator decides the steps or changes in the criterion. Three general guidelines can be provided. First, the investigator usually should proceed gradually in changing the criterion to maximize the likelihood that the client can meet each criterion. Abrupt and large shifts in the criterion may mean that relatively stringent performance demands are placed on the client. The client may be less likely to meet stringent criterion levels than more graduated criterion levels. Thus, the magnitude of the change in the criterion should be relatively modest to maximize the likelihood that the client can successfully meet that level.

Second, the investigator should change the criteria over the course of the intervention phase so that correspondence between the criteria and behavior can be detected. The change in each criterion must be large enough so that one can discern that performance changes when the criterion is altered. The investigator may make very small changes in the criterion. However, if variability in performance is relatively large, it may be difficult to discern that the performance followed the criterion. Hence, there is a general relationship between the variability in the client's performance and the amount of change in the criterion that may need to be made. The more variability in day-to-day performance during the intervention phase, the greater the change needed in the criterion from subphase to subphase to reflect change.

The relationship between variability in performance and the changes in the criteria necessary to reflect change is illustrated in two hypothetical changing-criterion designs displayed in Figure 8.10. The upper panel shows that subject variability is relatively high during the intervention phase, and it is relatively difficult to detect that the performance follows the changing criterion. The lower panel shows that subject variability is relatively small during the intervention phase and follows the criterion closely. In fact, for the lower panel, smaller changes in the criteria probably would have been adequate and the correspondence between performance and criteria would have been clear. In contrast, the upper panel shows that much larger shifts in the criterion would be needed to demonstrate unambiguously that performance changed systematically.

It is important to bear in mind that changes in the criterion need not be in equal steps over the course of the intervention. And there is no virtue in consistency in single-case designs. So a 10% increase in the criterion need not be a guiding principle—just the opposite. As I have noted, the strength of the single-case designs is making decisions in response to the data. Unequal steps up or down (bidirectional) are fine.

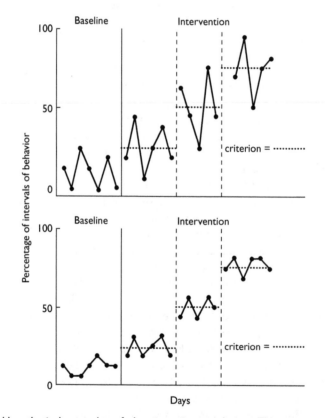

Figure 8.10. Hypothetical examples of changing-criterion designs. The *upper panel* shows data with relatively high variability (fluctuations). The *lower panel* shows relatively low variability. Greater variability makes it more difficult to show that performance matches or is influenced by the changing criterion. In both of these graphs, the mean level of performance increased with each subphase during the intervention phase. The influence of the criterion is clearer in the lower panel because the data points hover more closely to the criterion in each subphase.

It is important to never lose site of the goal, namely, to rule out the likelihood that extraneous influences (e.g., history, maturation, novelty) could explain the data pattern. We do not need equal steps in criterion changes to accomplish the goal. If anything, one might argue that the goal is better achieved by not changing in equal-size steps. For example, in the beginning or first two subphases of the intervention phase, smaller changes in the criterion may be needed to maximize opportunities for the client's success. As progress is made, the client may be able to make larger steps in reducing or increasing the behavior. Correspondence of client behavior and the criteria that vary by large steps can strengthen the demonstration because few other interpretations (e.g., history, maturation) are likely to compete with the intervention in plausibly explaining the results.

General Comments

Ambiguities that arise in the changing-criterion design usually pertain to the correspondence between the multiple criteria (across subphases) and behavior. Some of the potential problems of the lack of correspondence can be anticipated and possibly circumvented by the investigator as a function of how and when the criteria are changed. The purpose of changing the criterion from the standpoint of the design is to provide several subphases during the intervention phase. In each subphase, it is important to be able to assess the extent to which performance meets the criterion. Across all subphases, it is crucial to be able to evaluate the extent to which the criteria have been followed in general. These specific and overall judgments can be facilitated by keeping individual subphases in effect until performance stabilizes. Also, the magnitude of the criterion shifts should be made so that the association between performance and the criterion can be detected. The criterion should be changed so that performance at the new criterion level will clearly depart from performance of the previous criterion level. Finally, a change in the intervention phase to a previous criterion level will often be very helpful in determining the relation between the intervention and behavior change.

EVALUATION OF THE DESIGN

The changing-criterion design has several features that make it useful in applied settings as well as methodologically sound. The design does not require withdrawing treatment, as in the ABAB design. The multiple problems related to reverting behavior to baseline levels are avoided. (The mini-reversals are not a return-to-baseline conditions but a return to slightly lower levels of improvement.) Also, the design does not require withholding treatment from some of the different behaviors, persons, or situations in need of the intervention, as is the case with variations of the multiple-baseline design. A convincing demonstration of the effect of the intervention is provided if the level of performance in the intervention phase matches the criterion as that criterion is changed.

The most salient practical advantage of the design is the gradual approximation of the final level of the desired performance. Repeatedly changing the criterion means that the goal of the program is approached gradually. A large number of behaviors in education and treatment may be approached in this gradual fashion (e.g., amount of reading, time studying, time without disruptive behavior). Increased demands are placed on the client (i.e., more stringent criteria) only after the client has shown mastery of performance at an easier level.[4]

There is a potential conflict between developing behavior gradually and meeting the requirements of the changing-criterion design. In developing behavior, progress or the requirements may be small in response to how the client is doing. The design usually requires changes in the criterion in steps that are large enough to show that performance clearly corresponds to the criterion level and continues to do so as the criterion is altered. In fact, in principle, if large changes are made (the steps are large) and correspondence of performance matches these large steps, the design is maximally persuasive as an experimental demonstration. So the potential conflict is changing the criterion gradually enough to constitute sound training, that is, encouraging approximations of behavior, and changing the criterion in steps that allow the investigator to see and show that performance really does change in response to the changing criterion. One way to resolve this is to begin with small shifts in the criterion for the purposes of training, as needed. However, along the way, include one phase that lowers rather than increases the criterion slightly to show a mini-reversal.

There are many excellent features of the changing-criterion design. Even so, the design has been used much less often than have other designs. One can only speculate as to why. First, the guidelines for using the design, such as where to set criteria, when to change, and how to decide whether there is correspondence of the criterion and performance, are slightly less clear than guidelines for using other designs. Second and related, developing behavior gradually does not have clear guidelines and has an "art" feature. One moves the client's behavior forward progressively, but how much progress and at what increments of steps? Here is a case where the design connects with substantive issues about behavior change more generally, that is, how to develop performance gradually and to reach a criterion. The design is quite useful because of the shaping feature and flexibility in changing the criteria for performance. With mini-reversals (that are not a complete return to baseline levels) the designs can reflect unequivocal control over behavior and make implausible the influence of extraneous events in explaining the results.

SUMMARY AND CONCLUSIONS

The changing-criterion design demonstrates the effect of an intervention by showing that performance changes at several different points during the intervention phase as the criterion is altered. A clear effect is evident if performance closely follows the changing criterion. In most uses of the design, the criterion for performance is made

---

[4] A behavior-change technique referred to as *shaping* is important to mention. Shaping consists of providing reinforcers (e.g., praise, approval, feedback, points) for successive approximations of a final response. One identifies a final goal response (e.g., completing 45 minutes of homework or music practice, cleaning all toys from the floor of one's room, eating < 3,000 calories per day, exercising 5 days a week, going to bed at a specific time earlier than the current bedtime, reading a book on methodology each week). Also, a reinforcer is identified (e.g., praise, graphed feedback, point system with backup rewards). Shaping begins by providing the reinforcer for a small change in the goal response (e.g., 10 minutes of homework if baseline showed 0 minutes). As behavior changes and is consistent, the criterion is increased. This is an effective technique to alter behavior and is consistent with the methodological requirements of changing-criterion designs.

increasingly more stringent over the course of the intervention phase. Hence, behavior continues to change in the same direction. In one variation of the design, the criterion may be made slightly less stringent at some point in the intervention phase to determine whether the direction of performance changes. The use of a *mini-reversal phase* to show that behavior increases and decreases depending on the criterion can clarify the demonstration when close correspondence between performance and the criterion level is not achieved.

An important issue in evaluating the changing-criterion design is deciding when correspondence between the criterion and performance has been achieved. Unless there is a close point-by-point correspondence between the criterion level and performance, it may be difficult to infer that the intervention was responsible for change. Typically, investigators have inferred a causal relationship if performance follows a step-like function so that changes in the criterion are followed by changes in performance, even if performance does not exactly meet the criterion level.

Drawing inferences may be especially difficult if performance changes rapidly and in a leap beyond the criterion as soon as the intervention is implemented. The design depends on showing gradual changes in performance as the terminal goal is approached. If performance greatly exceeds the criterion level, the intervention may still be responsible for change. Yet because the underlying rationale of the design depends on showing a close relationship between performance and criterion levels, conclusions about the impact of treatment will be difficult to infer.

Certainly a noteworthy feature of the design is that it is based on gradual changes in behavior. The design is consistent with developing performance gradually; few performance requirements are made initially, and these requirements are gradually increased as the client masters earlier criterion levels. In many educational and clinical situations, the investigator may wish to change client performance gradually. For behaviors involving complex skills or where improvements require relatively large departures from how the client usually behaves, gradual approximations may be especially useful. Hence, the changing-criterion design may be well suited to a variety of problems, clients, and settings.

Multiple-Treatment Designs

The designs discussed in previous chapters usually restrict themselves to the evaluation of a single intervention or treatment. In applied settings such as the classroom, home, or health-care setting, the investigator often is interested in comparing and testing two or more interventions, identifying which one is more or most effective, and applying that to optimize change in the client. Difficulties arise when the investigator is interested in comparing two or more interventions within the same subject. If two or more treatments are applied to the same subject in ABAB or multiple-baseline designs, they are given in separate phases so that one comes before the other at some point in the design. The *sequence* in which the interventions appear partially restricts the conclusions that can be reached about the relative effects of two or more treatments. In an ABCABC design, for example, the effects of C may be better (or worse) because it followed B. The effects of the two interventions (B and C) may be very different if they were each administered by themselves without one being preceded by the other. Also, evaluating multiple interventions in a design such as ABAB or multiple-baseline takes time (many days) as each intervention (B, C) requires several days or more to show stable levels to meet the describe, predict, and test functions over time. Multiple-treatment designs allow the comparison of two or more treatments that are usually within the same intervention phase. This chapter presents characteristics of the designs and highlights some of their many variations.[1]

BASIC CHARACTERISTICS OF THE DESIGNS

Many variants of multi-treatment designs have been used. They share some overall characteristics regarding the manner in which separate treatments are compared. In each of the designs, a single behavior of one or more persons is observed to obtain baseline data. After baseline, the intervention phase is implemented, in which the behavior is subjected to two or more interventions. These interventions are implemented in the same intervention phase. Both are *not* in effect at the same time. For example, two procedures such as praise and reprimands might be compared to determine their separate effects on disruptive behavior in an elementary school classroom. Both interventions would not be implemented at the same moment. The interventions have to be administered separately in some way so their separate impact can be evaluated and compared. In a manner of speaking, the interventions must "take turns" in terms of when they are applied. The variations of multiple-treatment designs depend primarily on the precise manner in which the different interventions are scheduled so they can be evaluated.

MAJOR DESIGN VARIATIONS

Multi-element Design

Description and Underlying Rationale. The multi-element design consists of implementation of two or more interventions in the same phase. The unique and defining feature of the multi-element design is that the separate interventions are associated or consistently paired with distinct stimulus conditions. The major purpose of the design is to show that the client performs differently under the different treatment

---

[1] Many terms have been used to represent multiple-treatment designs, and these could occupy their own chapter. The terminology reflects variations in how multiple treatments are compared. Some of the inconsistencies in terminology stem from how the designs were first used (e.g., basic research on reinforcement schedules) and efforts to craft new variations of how to compare treatments. The critical issue for this book is understanding how the design variations can be used in applied settings and what the critical components are to draw influences about the impact of the interventions. The key feature of the designs in this chapter is the use of more than one intervention in a way that allows relatively rapid comparison of their impact.

conditions, as reflected in differences in performance associated with the different stimulus conditions.

The multi-element design has been used extensively in laboratory research with non-human animals in which the effects of different reinforcement schedules have been examined. That use helped establish "multiple-schedule design" as another term. Different reinforcement schedules were administered at different times during an intervention phase. Each schedule is associated with a distinct stimulus (e.g., a light that is on or off). After the stimulus has been associated with its respective intervention, a clear discrimination is evident in performance. When one stimulus is presented, one pattern of performance is obtained. When the other stimulus is presented, a different pattern of performance is obtained. The difference in performance among the stimulus conditions is a function of the different interventions associated with each stimulus. The design is used to demonstrate that the client or organism can discriminate in response to the different stimulus conditions. The multi-element term reflects in part the broad use of this design beyond examining schedules of reinforcement.

The underlying rationale unique to this design pertains to the differences in responding that are evident under the different stimulus conditions. If the client makes a discrimination in performance between the different stimulus conditions and their respective interventions, the data should show clear differences in performance. On any given day, the different stimulus conditions and their respective interventions are implemented. Performance may vary markedly depending on the precise condition in effect at that time. If the stimulus conditions and interventions do not differentially influence performance, one would expect an unsystematic pattern across the different intervention conditions, and performance will not differ. Similarly, if extraneous events (and threats to validity) rather than the treatment conditions were influencing performance, one might see a general improvement or decrement over time. Improvements due to extraneous events would be likely to appear under each of the different stimulus conditions. When performance does differ across the stimulus conditions, this is plausibly explained by the differential effectiveness of the interventions.

Illustration.   The design emphasizes the control that certain stimulus conditions exert after being paired with various interventions. An excellent example of the design is from a study that focused on compliance of two 4-year-old children; the children were occasionally noncompliant (Wilder, Atwell, & Wine, 2006). The study focused on implementation of the intervention, that is, how faithfully implementation was carried out or, stated another way, whether the intervention was delivered as it was intended. The extent to which the intervention is delivered as intended is referred to as *treatment integrity* or *treatment fidelity*. This is a critical topic in any area of intervention research (e.g., educational programs, surgery, medication, cognitive behavioral techniques, rehabilitation) and is discussed in single-case and between-group designs (see McIntyre, Gresham, DiGennaro, & Reed, 2007; Perepletchikova & Kazdin, 2005). In education and clinical psychology, for example, developing effective (evidence-based) interventions is only part of the challenge. Once they are developed, getting individuals (teachers, therapists) to implement them at all or to implement them correctly is a challenge. In any case, an effective treatment is not likely to be very effective if it is not implemented carefully.

This study focused on the issue by measuring compliance with instructions administered by an adult in three different situations or contexts: in a small room, in the classroom, and on the playground. To obtain compliance, the intervention consisted of asking the child to perform one of three instructions (e.g., give me the snack item, put the toy away, and come here). If the child did this within 10 seconds, this was counted as compliance; if not, this was counted as noncompliance. Praise was provided for immediate compliance during the intervention phase. In addition, if the child did not comply immediately, the trainer went through a sequence of steps to promote compliance. These steps included making eye contact with the child, stating the child's name, repeating the instruction, modeling correct performance, and guiding the child to perform the activity.

The purpose of the study was to compare three variations of carrying out this procedure that reflect treatment integrity, that is, how faithfully the procedures were executed by the trainer, namely, 100%, 50%, or 0% of the time. In the 100% condition, the trainer followed the procedure each time the child did not comply, that is, the praise and prompting were implemented as intended. In the 50% level, the trainer did the procedure as specified on only half of the opportunities. On the other half of the trials (instruction opportunities), the therapist did not do any aspect of the procedure. In the 0% level, the procedure was never done.

A multi-element design requires different interventions. I have described these (100%, 50%, and 0%) and noted that the interventions have to be consistently associated with a particular stimulus condition. In this case, the instructions were the stimulus conditions. A particular instruction (e.g., pick up a toy) was always associated with one of the interventions (e.g., 100%) and the other interventions (50%, 0%) with one of the other instructions. There were two children, so which instruction was associated with which intervention was varied. In short, interventions were associated with specific conditions (in this case specific instructions) to see if the three interventions made any difference. If they did make a difference, one would expect to see different patterns of responding on the part of the child.

Figure 9.1 presents the compliance data for two children. During baseline, no intervention was provided and the separate lines reflect the different instructions. That is, for all three instructions, there was no intervention during baseline. During the intervention phase the three levels of integrity were compared. When the intervention was implemented 100% of the time, compliance was very high; 50% of the time, above baseline but not as high as 100%; 0% of the time, essentially a continuation of baseline, and no real change occurred in child behavior. All of the changes can be seen in relation to the respective instructions with which each one was associated.

The design clearly conveys different intervention effects associated with the instructions. In passing, it is useful to punctuate the significance of the demonstration in two contexts. First, the use of behavioral techniques (e.g., use of antecedents, behaviors, and consequences) to change behavior is very effective in diverse contexts (home, school) and constitute an evidence-based treatment for oppositional behavior among children. This demonstration underscores the importance of treatment

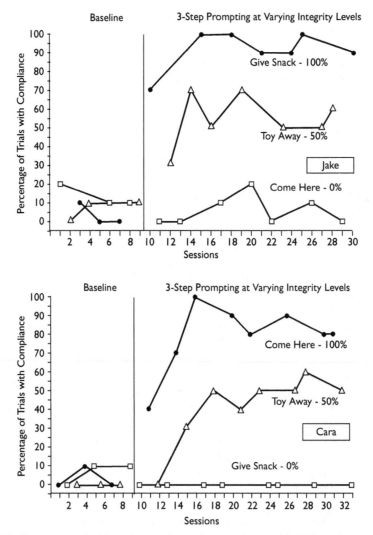

Figure 9.1. Percentage of trials with compliance for two 4-year-old children. A prompting procedure was used to foster compliance, if the child did not comply with the instruction immediately. The prompting procedure (accompanied by praise whenever compliance occurred) was done exactly the same way. During the intervention phase, three levels of implementing the procedures were compared: the trainer implemented the intervention 100%, 50%, or 0% of the time. These levels of carrying out the procedure were associated with specific instructions.   (Source: Wilder et al., 2006.)

integrity; the techniques convey what to do (e.g., reinforce and prompt) but no less important is the how, that is, whether the procedures are faithfully rendered. Second, noncompliance in children is often talked about as if it is "in" the child. It is true that some individuals are more oppositional than others. Yet, this study helps to convey that contexts and interventions of others can greatly influence compliance and noncompliance as well.

Alternating-treatments or Simultaneous-treatment Design

Description and Underlying Rationale. In the multi-element design, separate interventions are applied under different stimulus conditions. Typically, each intervention is associated (paired) with a particular stimulus (e.g., adult, time period, or "instruction" in the previous example) to show that performance varies systematically as a function of the stimulus that is presented. Usually the multi-element design is reserved for instances in which the interventions are purposely paired with particular stimuli. In this way intervention effects are seen when performance varies as a function of that stimulus or context.

As noted earlier, in applied research the usual priority is to evaluate the relative impact of two or more treatments free from the influence of any particular stimulus condition or context. That is, we want to find out what intervention (e.g., to develop reading) is the more or most effective, and we are not interested in showing that this is associated with some unique stimuli (e.g., a teacher, class period). Multiple treatments can be readily compared in single-case research without associating the treatments with a particular stimulus or context. In fact, the goal is to evaluate the impact of treatments in a way to be sure they are not merely tied to, connected with, or confounded by a particular condition.

When different treatment conditions are varied or alternated across different stimulus conditions (e.g., times of the day, teachers, or settings), the design can be distinguished from a multi-element design. The treatments are administered across different stimulus conditions, but the interventions are balanced (equally distributed) across these conditions. At the end of the intervention phase, one can examine the effects of the interventions in a way that is not confounded by or uniquely associated with a particular stimulus condition or context. Stated another away, in a multi-element design the interventions are purposely connected to a particular stimulus or context; in an alternating-treatments design, the interventions are purposely balanced across and disconnected with a particular stimulus.

The underlying rationale of the design is similar to that of the multi-element design. After baseline observations, two or more interventions are implemented in the same phase to alter a particular behavior. The distinguishing feature is that the different interventions are distributed or varied across stimulus conditions in such a way that the influence of these interventions can be separated from the influence associated with the different stimulus conditions. The different names of the design reflect how to best represent what is actually done. The different interventions are *alternated* during the intervention phases, explaining why some have chosen to refer to this as an *alternating conditions* or *alternating-treatments design* (Barlow & Hayes, 1979; Ulman & Sulzer-Azaroff, 1975). The different conditions are administered in the same phase, usually on the same day, and thus the design has also been referred to as a *simultaneous-treatment* or *concurrent schedule design* (Hersen & Barlow, 1976; Kazdin & Hartmann, 1978).[2]

---

[2] None of the terms for this design quite accurately describes its unique features. "Alternating-treatments" design incorrectly suggests that the interventions must be active interventions. Yet, "no treatment" or continuation of baseline can be used as one of the conditions that is alternated so there is only one treatment. The word "treatment" too is odd. Many if not most applications of the design have been in education where nothing is being "treated" (e.g., in any medical or

The design usually begins with baseline observation of the target response. The observations are obtained daily under two or more conditions, such as two times per day (e.g., morning or afternoon) or in two different locations (e.g., classroom and playground). During the baseline phase, the target behavior is observed daily under each of the conditions or settings. After baseline observations, the intervention phase is begun. In the usual case, two different interventions are compared. Both interventions are implemented each day. However, the interventions are administered under the different stimulus conditions (e.g., times of the day, situations or settings). The interventions are administered an equal number of times across each of the conditions of administration so that, unlike the multi-element design, the interventions are not uniquely associated with a particular stimulus. The intervention phase is continued until the response stabilizes under the separate interventions.

The crucial feature of the design is the unique intervention phase in which separate interventions are administered concurrently. Hence, it is worthwhile to detail how the interventions are varied during this phase. Consider as a hypothetical example a design in which two interventions (I_1 and I_2) are to be compared. The interventions are to be implemented daily but across two separate time periods (T_1 and T_2) or sessions during the day. The interventions are balanced across the time periods. *Balancing* refers to the fact that each intervention is administered under each of the conditions an equal number of times. On any given day the interventions are administered under separate conditions, but both are administered.

Table 9.1 illustrates different ways in which the interventions might be administered on a daily basis. As evident from Table 9.1A, each intervention is administered each day, and the time period in which a particular intervention is in effect is alternated daily. In Table 9.1A, the alternating pattern is accomplished by simply having one intervention administered first on one day, second on the next, and then just switching the order every day for the rest of the intervention phase. At the end of the intervention phase, each intervention was first (and second) an equal number of times or close to that (if the intervention phase were an odd rather than even number of days).

Table 9.1B shows that the alternating pattern could be randomly determined, with the restriction that throughout the intervention phase each intervention appears equally often in the first and second time period. This randomly ordered procedure can be determined by a table of random numbers in which one might search for an order of numbers and pull out numbers 1 and 2 from a long list of numbers to determine the order of presenting Interventions 1 and 2. (Of course, in true randomness, it is possible

---

[2] (Continued) psychological sense). Also, alternating treatments is sufficiently broad to encompass multi-element designs in which treatments are alternated. "Simultaneous-treatment" design incorrectly implies that the interventions are implemented simultaneously. If this were true, the effectiveness of the separate interventions could not be independently evaluated. They are usually administered concurrently. "Concurrent schedule" design implies that the interventions are restricted to reinforcement schedules, from basic and applied research within the behavior analysis. As noted in a prior chapter, many of the designs grew out of behavior analysis but now have novel applications where such topics as reinforcement schedules are not a focus. For present purposes, the term "alternating-treatments design" is used because it has been adopted by the majority of investigators reporting the design.

Table 9.1 The Administration of Two Interventions (I_1 and I_2) Balanced Across Two Time Periods (T_1 and T_2)

A. Alternating order every other day during the intervention phase

	Days						
Time periods	1	2	3	4	5	6	...n
T_1	I_1	I_2	I_1	I_2	I_1	I_2	
T_2	I_2	I_1	I_2	I_1	I_2	I_1	

B. Alternating in a random order during the intervention phase

	Days						
Time periods	1	2	3	4	5	6	...n
T_1	I_1	I_2	I_2	I_1	I_2	I_1	
T_2	I_2	I_1	I_1	I_2	I_1	I_2	

Note. The table conveys two different ways in which the Interventions (I) can be paired with and balanced across the different Time (T) periods; *n* relects an unspecified number of days, as determined by the investigator.

that a string of 1s would be in the table.) Consequently, one selects pairs of numbers with the restriction that a 1 and a 2 have to be in each pair. That way, at the end of the intervention phase each intervention appears equally often, although the order was random.

The table refers to the schedule of administering the different interventions during the first intervention phase. If one of the interventions is more effective than the other(s), the design usually concludes with a final phase in which that intervention is administered across all conditions. That is, the more (or most) effective intervention is applied across all time periods or situations included in the design.

A hypothetical example of the data plotted from a simple version of the alternating-treatments design is illustrated in Figure 9.2. In the example, observations were made daily for two time periods. The data for baseline are plotted in baseline separately for these periods. During the intervention phase, two separate interventions were implemented and were balanced across the time periods. In this phase, data are plotted according to the interventions so that the differential effects of the interventions can be seen. Because Intervention 1 was more effective than Intervention 2, it was implemented across both time periods in the final phase. This last phase provides an opportunity to see if behavior improves in the periods in which the less effective intervention had been administered. Hence, in this last phase, data are plotted according to the different time periods as they were balanced across the interventions, even though both receive the more effective procedure. As evident in the figure, performance improved in those time periods that previously had been associated with the less effective intervention.

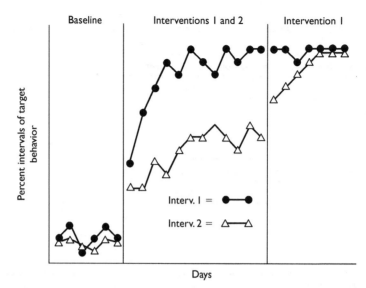

Figure 9.2. Hypothetical example of an alternating-treatments design. In baseline, the observations are plotted across the two different time periods. In the first intervention phase, both interventions are administered and balanced across the time periods. The data are plotted according to the different interventions. In the final phase, the more effective intervention (Intervention 1) was implemented across both time periods.

As an example, an alternating-treatments design was used to evaluate the classroom behavior of two boys with developmental disabilities who attended a special educational classroom (Kazdin & Geesey, 1977). Both boys were identified because of their disruptive behaviors. The goal was to increase attentive behavior in class. Each day baseline data were gathered at two time periods in the morning when separate academic tasks were assigned by the teacher. After the baseline phase, the intervention was implemented, which consisted of two variations of providing reinforcement. A token system was administered in which each child could earn marks (the tokens) on a card placed on his desk. The two variations of the program consisted of the manner in which the reinforcers would be dispensed. The programs differed according to whether the tokens could be exchanged for rewards that only the child would receive (self-exchange) or whether they could be exchanged for rewards for the child and the entire class (class-exchange). Thus, the child could earn for himself or for everyone. The expectation was that earning for many indviduals might be more effective because that exchange method mobilizes peer support (and possible pressure) for desirable behavior. Tokens were earned during the two observation periods each day. Different-colored cards were used to record the tokens in each period to separate the self- and the class-reward programs. When a predetermined number of tokens was earned on a card, the child selected from a lottery jar to determine which of the available rewards he would receive. This reward was given to the child or to everyone in class depending on which card had earned the reinforcers. Each program was implemented daily in one of the two observation periods. The programs were alternated daily so that one appeared during the first period on one day and during the second period on the next, and so on.

Figure 9.3 provides the results for Max, a 7-year-old boy. The data are plotted in two ways to show the overall effect of the program (upper panel) and the different effects of the separate interventions (lower panel). The upper portion of the figure shows that attentive behavior improved during the first and second observation periods with data combined (the two morning academic lessons). The lower portion illustrates the design but requires explanation. In baseline, the figure shows the two observation periods each day in which there was no intervention. Clearly the two periods did not vary. Nor would they be expected to, because the condition (no intervention) was the same. In the first intervention phase, data are plotted according to whether the self-exchange or class-exchange was in effect. The results indicated that Max was more attentive when he was working for rewards for the entire class rather than just for himself. Hence, in the third and final phase, the class-exchange period was implemented daily across both time periods. He no longer earned for himself alone, since this proved to be the less effective intervention. In the final phase, attentive behavior was consistently high across

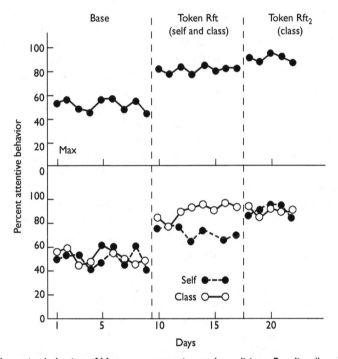

Figure 9.3. Attentive behavior of Max across experimental conditions. Baseline (base)—no experimental intervention. Token reinforcement (token rft)—implementation of the token program where tokens earned could purchase rewards for himself (self) or the entire class (class). Second phase of token reinforcement (token rft₂)—implementation of the class exchange intervention across both time periods. The *upper panel* presents the overall data collapsed across time periods and interventions. The *lower panel* presents the data according to the time periods across which the interventions were balanced, although the interventions were presented only in the last two phases. *(Source: Kazdin & Geesey, 1977.)*

both time periods. This last phase suggests further that the class-exchange method was indeed the more effective intervention, because it raised the level of performance for the time periods previously devoted to self-exchange.

Occasionally, continuation of baseline serves as one of the "interventions" or "treatments" during the intervention phase (e.g., Hughes & Carter, 2002; Pluck, Ghafari, Glynn, & McNaughton, 1984). An example of an alternating-treatments design in which baseline constituted one of the alternating conditions was used to evaluate an intervention designed to reduce the frequency of stereotyped repetitive movements among hospitalized children with developmental and intellectual disabilities (Ollendick, Shapiro, & Barrett, 1981). Three children, ages 7 to 8, exhibited stereotypic behaviors such as repetitive hand gestures and hair twirling. Observations of the children were made in a classroom setting while each child performed various visual-motor tasks (e.g., puzzles). Behavior was observed each day for three sessions, after which the intervention phase was implemented. During the intervention phase, three conditions were compared, including two active interventions and a continuation of baseline. One intervention consisted of physically restraining the child's hands on the table for 30 seconds so he or she could not perform the repetitive behaviors (physical restraint). The second intervention consisted of physically guiding the child to engage in the appropriate use of the task materials (positive practice). Instead of merely restraining the child, this procedure was designed to develop appropriate alternative behaviors the children could perform with their hands. The final condition during the intervention phase was a continuation of baseline. Physical restraint, positive practice, and continuation of baseline were implemented each day across the three different time periods.

Figure 9.4 shows the results for one child who engaged in hand-posturing gestures. As evident from the first intervention phase, both physical restraint and positive practice led to reductions in performance; the practice procedure was more effective. The extent of the reduction is especially clear in light of the continuation of baseline as a third condition during the intervention phase. When baseline (no-treatment) conditions were in effect during the intervention phase, performance remained at the approximate level of the original baseline phase. In the final phase, positive practice was applied to all of the time periods each day. Practice proved to be the more effective of the two interventions in the previous phase and was implemented in the final phase across all time periods. Thus, the strength of this intervention is especially clear from the design.

Continuation of baseline in the intervention phase allows direct assessment of what performance is like without treatment. Of course, including baseline as another condition in the intervention phase introduces a new complexity to the design. As discussed later in the chapter, increasing the number of conditions compared in the intervention phase raises potential problems. Yet if performance during the initial baseline phase is unstable or shows a trend that the investigator believes may interfere with the evaluation of the interventions, it may be especially useful to continue baseline as one of the conditions in the design.

Versions without Initial Baseline. Alternating-treatments designs are often used without an initial baseline phase, and this version warrants comment and illustration. In many programs, the goal is to identify quickly what among multiple alternatives is

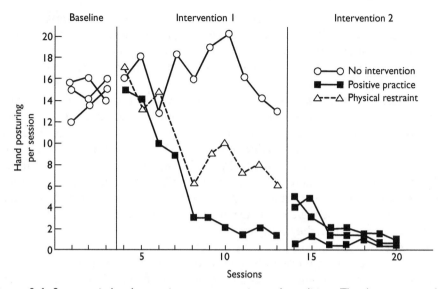

Figure 9.4. Stereotypic hand posturing across experimental conditions. The three separate lines in each phase represent three separate time periods in each session. Only in the initial intervention phase were the three separate conditions in effect, balanced across the time periods. In the second intervention phase, positive practice was in effect for all three periods.   *(Source: Ollendick, Shapiro, & Barrett, 1981.)*

effective and to do so in a rapidly changing design. A common version is used to identify what controls self-stimulatory or self-destructive behavior among individuals with developmental disabilities. Often individual one-to-one sessions are used in which 5 or 10 minutes will be provided for each of three or more interventions. The interventions might be how the investigator responds to the behavior (e.g., attend, ignore, make some demand to work on a task). The goal is to identify what might be controlling the problem behavior and to do so very quickly. Remarkable successes have been achieved in showing that one or more of such conditions, varied quickly in a brief period, have an impact on reducing the problem behavior.[3] There might be little or no baseline and the conditions are just compared to see if one emerges as markedly influencing

---

[3] A very important area of work in behavioral research (applied behavior analysis) is referred to as *functional analysis*, a topic beyond the scope of the present book. Briefly, functional analysis is an effort to understand what factors are controlling behavior. Through careful assessment in advance and then through direct empirical tests, the investigator hypothesizes what influences might be operating. These are then tested empirically. For example, in a one-to-one situation with a child who hits himself, an investigator sitting across from the child might alternate three interventions: attending to the child when he hits himself (to see if that is controlling the behavior), turning away from the child, giving the child a task or making a demand. These interventions might be provided all on the same day and all within a laboratory session. Very quickly one can determine which one is associated with a reduction of self-hitting and that information can now form the basis of an intervention that is not conducted in a one-to-one laboratory session. For further details of functional analysis, see other sources (e.g., Cooper et al., 2007; Iwata, Kahng, Wallace, & Lindberg, 2000).

performance. Essentially, the paradigm is to test hypotheses about what might be controlling behavior. The intervention that emerges might well serve as the basis for developing an intervention that can be evaluated in an additional or other design.

There are many occasions in which the absence of an initial baseline raises special issues and ambiguities. For example, in one program, the goal was to identify if positive teacher affect (e.g., smiling, showing a very positive vocal tone, and showing enthusiasm) influenced the affect of the children (e.g., smiling, laughing) as well as their correct task performance on classroom work (Park, Singer, & Gibson, 2005). Four children, ages 6 to 11 and with various disabilities (e.g., Down's syndrome, cerebral palsy) participated. Each was brought individually to a room during recess, seated in front of a table, and given a task. There were two "conditions": one with teacher positive affect and the other with neutral affect (e.g., flat voice tone, expressionless face, low enthusiasm). Children were videotaped and the tapes were scored for affect; correct responses were scored from the task they completed.

Figure 9.5 provides the results for the four children and shows that teacher positive affect was associated with more positive affect of the children. As noted in the graph, there was no baseline, and the interventions showed a difference. Not graphed, three of these four students also showed a slightly higher percentage of correct responses on their assignments in the positive-affect condition. What can we conclude? We can conclude that one treatment was more effective than the other, which was the main goal of the demonstration. However, the absence of baseline raises an ambiguity. It is possible that baseline was even higher (more positive affect of the children) than the performance achieved with these two conditions. More likely, it is possible that the neutral was really not neutral but actually negative and made the children less happy than usual. After all, the neutral condition included presentation that is probably more negative than most people interacting with children. It may be that the baseline and positive affect were not really different, and that the neutral condition made the child look worse (less positive affect). I am not saying this is accurate. I am merely saying that the interpretation I provide cannot be addressed by the design. Is the concern just some esoteric methodological nuance? Not really. Other alternating-treatments designs have shown that when the interventions have different effects, one intervention might make children worse (e.g., Washington, Deitz, White, & Schwartz, 2002). The effects of the interventions are aided greatly by collection of initial baseline data to allow evaluation.

A compromise to provide some baseline data is to use the alternating-treatments design where one of the conditions is baseline. In this version, there is no initial baseline phase. Rather the intervention and baseline conditions begin in one phase. An example of this was reported with a 9-year-old girl referred for off-task and disruptive behavior and failure to complete her work (McCurdy, Skinner, Grantham, Watson, & Hindman, 2001). Each day in-seat mathematics assignments were provided to her from a workbook. The two conditions included regular, unaltered workbook assignments (control or baseline assignments) and the experimental condition in which some additional and easier problems were interspersed with the usual set of problems. The rationale is derived from prior work noting that completion of tasks successfully may augment the rewarding value of the assignment and increase the likelihood of engaging in the assignments and paying attention. The two conditions were alternated across days in the classroom.

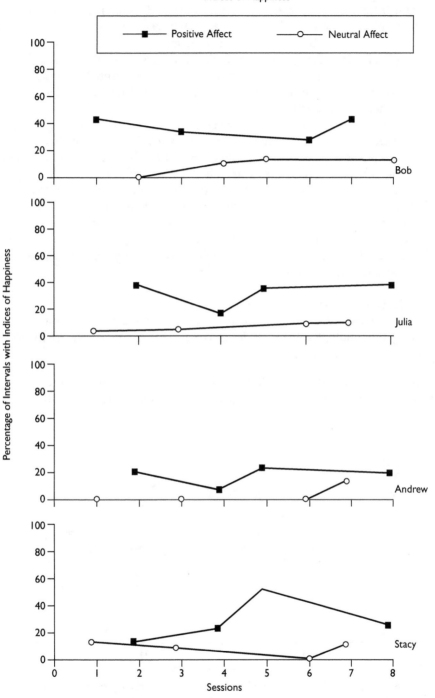

Figure 9.5. Student's level of happiness (percent of intervals) under two conditions in an alternating-treatments design. The conditions were positive affect and neutral affect on the part of the teacher. *(Source: S. Park, Singer, & Gibson, 2005.)*

Figure 9.6 shows the effects of the experimental condition. Performance was higher for the experimental sessions than for control (baseline) sessions even though no baseline phase was provided. The differences between the two conditions seemed to attenuate over time, an effect that could not be detected without some baseline (before or during the intervention phase). In principle it is possible that "real" baseline (with no intervention or alternating conditions) would be different from the control sessions. However, the inclusion of baseline as one of the conditions helps one judge the magnitude of the impact of the experimental condition.

The different variations of the alternating-treatments designs are given special attention here in part because of their different uses and strengths. The strongest demonstration is one that begins with a baseline phase. This allows application of the logic of the design (describe, predict, test) and allows for the ability to judge the magnitude of the intervention effect. That is, did the interventions help or harm relative to baseline? On the other hand, in an area of behavioral research (functional analysis), there is often interest in isolating very quickly which among multiple interventions is controlling behavior in a laboratory session. An extensive baseline phase is not used here. The goal is to identify one intervention that might be controlling behavior and to extend that to everyday settings to serve as the intervention.

Other Multiple-treatment Design Options
The multi-element and alternating-treatments designs discussed already are the more commonly used multiple-treatment designs. A few other options are briefly noted to convey flexibility in the designs.

Simultaneous Availability of All Conditions. As noted previously, in the usual alternating-treatments or simultaneous-treatment design, the interventions are scheduled

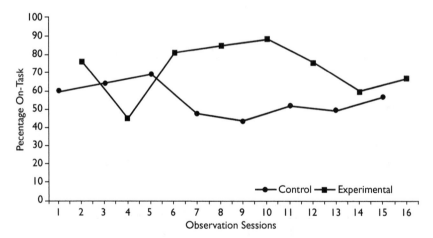

Figure 9.6. Percentage of intervals of on task behavior in an alternating-treatments design in which experimental and control (no intervention) conditions were compared. The student worked on mathematics assignments. The experimental assignments interspersed some easy problems to make the task more rewarding. *(Source: McCurdy et al., 2001.)*

at different periods each day. The pattern of performance in effect during each of the different interventions is used as a basis to infer the effectiveness of the different interventions. Almost always, the interventions are scheduled at entirely different times during the day. It is possible to make each intervention available at the same time. The different interventions are available but are in some way selected by the client.

A historically early and very clear demonstration of this variation compared the effects of three procedures (praise and attention, verbal admonishment, and ignoring) on reducing the bragging of a 9-year-old hospitalized boy (Browning, 1967). One of the boy's problem behaviors was extensive bragging that consisted of untrue and grandiose stories about himself. After baseline observations, the staff implemented the procedures just mentioned in an alternating-treatments design. The different treatments were balanced across three groups of staff members (two persons in each group). Each week, the staff members associated with a particular intervention were rotated so that all the staff eventually administered each of the interventions.

The unique feature of the design is that during the day, all of the staff were available to the child. The specific consequence the child received for bragging depended on the staff members with whom he was in contact. The boy had access to and could seek out the staff members of his choosing. And the staff provided the different consequences to the child according to the interventions to which they had been assigned for that week. The measure of treatment effects was the frequency and duration of bragging directed at the various staff members. The results indicated that bragging incidents tended to diminish in duration in the presence of staff members who ignored the behavior relative to those who administered the attention or admonishment.

This design variation is slightly different from the previous ones because all treatments were available simultaneously. The intervention that was implemented was determined by the child, who approached particular staff members. This variation of the design is useful for measuring a client's preference for a particular intervention. The client can seek those staff members who perform a particular intervention. Since all staff members are equally available, the extent to which those who administer a particular intervention are sought out may be of interest in its own right.

The variation of the design in which all interventions are actually available at the same time and the client selects the persons with whom he or she interacts has been rarely used. This design has features of multi-element designs because the interventions are associated with particular conditions. Methodologically, this variation is best suited to measure preferences for a particular condition, which is somewhat different from the usual question of interest, namely, the effectiveness of different conditions.

Randomization Design. Multiple-treatment designs for single subjects alternate the interventions or conditions in various ways during the intervention phase. The designs discussed previously resemble a randomization design (Edgington, 1996), which refers to a way of presenting the different treatments. The design developed largely through concern with the requirements for statistical evaluation of alternative treatments rather than from the mainstream of single-case experimental research.[4]

The randomization design, as applied to one subject or a group of subjects, refers to presentation of alternative interventions in a random order. For example, baseline (A) and treatment (B) conditions could be presented to subjects on a daily basis in the following order: ABBABABAAB. Each day a different condition is presented, usually with the restriction that each is presented an equal number of times. Because the condition administered on any particular day is randomly determined, the results are amenable to several statistical tests (Edgington, 1996; Edgington & Onghena, 2007; Todman & Dugard, 2001).

Features of the randomization design are included in versions of an alternating-treatments design. For example, in the intervention phase of an alternating-treatments design, two or more interventions must be balanced across stimulus conditions (e.g., time periods). When the order in which the treatments are applied is determined randomly (see Table 9.1B), the phase meets the requirements of a randomization design. Essentially, a randomization design consists of one way of ordering the treatments in the intervention phase of a multiple-treatment design.

Technically, the design can be used without an initial baseline if two or more treatments (B, C) or baseline and one or more conditions are compared during the intervention phase. It is almost always better to have a baseline phase to strengthen the basis of the describe, predict, and test functions of the various phases in any single-case design. However, in a multiple-treatment design "baseline" (no intervention) can be one of the conditions that is varied and presented in a randomized order if a randomization design is used. This is discussed further a bit later in the chapter, under "Additional Design Variations."

Randomization designs have not been reported very frequently in applied work, although excellent examples are available (e.g., Washington et al., 2002). The methodological issue of concern when comparing interventions in the same phase is to ensure that one can separate the intervention effects from any conditions with which they might be associated. Hence investigators are concerned with balancing interventions across the conditions (e.g., time periods; settings) so inferences can be drawn about the interventions, unconfounded by other factors. Randomization is useful in deciding how to order presentation of conditions if there is some reason that bias could enter into pairing of conditions with the intervention and in other situations if randomization is just as convenient given applied situations and the demands of administering interventions. For example, it might make a difference in implementing a program if interventions were alternated in ways that were more predictable than randomization but still not biased (e.g., so treatment A is not always in the morning and B always in the afternoon).

---

[4] It is useful to distinguish randomization *design* from randomization *tests*, although they are related. *Design* refers to the arrangement of the experimental conditions, in this case the order in which they are presented to the client. *Tests* refer to the statistical techniques that are used to analyze the data. A randomization design does not have to be analyzed statistically, and if the data are analyzed statistically the tests need not be randomization tests. This chapter focuses on design; statistical tests are discussed later (Appendix) (see also Edgington & Onghena, 2007; Todman & Dugard, 2001).

As I noted, randomization designs are used infrequently for reasons one can only surmise. A plausible view is the difficulties randomization thrusts on the logic of the design and the practical issues about implementation. The logic of the designs depends on describe, predict, and test functions of the data patterns. These are aided by having stable rates of performance to see trends and likely patterns that will characterize the future. A constantly changing back-and-forth intervention might well show patterns, but this requires intervention conditions that can shift daily or the equivalent (as dictated by random order) and highly responsive clients who can show quite different effects as soon as the intervention is implemented. The describe, predict, and test logic can be readily invoked, but the data have to be unusually favorable to see the immediate flipping of performance. The practical challenges of randomization are another issue that may have restricted use of the design. In most applied settings (e.g., schools, special education classrooms) one cannot easily flip the intervention randomly at least on a daily basis. The demands of randomization make planning and implementing interventions more complex than they might otherwise be. Integrity of the individual interventions and responsiveness of the client to change—always important in any intervention study—are slightly more demanding when daily shifts might be needed because of randomization. Does it sound as if I am "against" randomization? It is not a matter of for or against. Randomization is a tool that may be quite useful in single-case designs and can contribute to ruling out threats to validity—the reasons we are discussing and using designs in the first place.

In this chapter, randomization was discussed primarily as a way of arranging interventions in multiple-treatment designs. There are broader roles of randomization in single-case research beyond these specific designs. First, randomization of conditions facilitates the application of special statistical techniques that can be used to evaluate interventions in single-case designs (Todman & Dugard, 2001). Second, randomization has been discussed in a broader context of single-case research and as a method to infuse many different types of designs (Kratochwill & Levin, in press). We will return to randomization in these other contexts later in the book.

Combining Components. Many of the designs I have presented in this and previous chapters convey clear, well-delineated examples of the designs (e.g., ABAB, multiple-baseline). In learning the designs, clear examples are very helpful so one can present the fundamentals without too many distractions. Researchers who work within the single-case approach often combine designs and pull together components (e.g., randomization). The result is often an excellent demonstration, but it is not clear what the design was or how to classify it. Invariably in such cases, the designs are hybrids and combinations. I shall convey combined designs more fully in the next chapter. However, it is useful here to illustrate how several features discussed in this chapter can be combined.

This study was conducted on a large college campus and was designed to see if prompts and feedback could increase the proportion of drivers who came to a complete stop at a stop sign (Austin et al., 2006). Drivers who came to two intersections (called Stop A and Stop B) were observed each morning by observers parked in a car adjacent to the intersections. Each driver approaching these separate stop signs was coded according to whether he or she stopped or did not stop. Stopped meant all visible tires were not rotating, a measure that was highly reliable. During the intervention phase a volunteer stood near Stop sign A with a large poster that read, "Please Stop—I care." This instruction, of course, was designed to promote stopping. If the driver stopped, the volunteer flashed the reverse side of the poster that said "Thank You for Stopping." This provided feedback and social reinforcement. The intervention was only associated with Stop sign A and never with Stop sign B. Stop signs A and B were at opposite sides of an intersection, and apparently the arrangement made it possible for only those drivers coming to the A Stop sign to see the poster and receive the instructions and praise, although drivers coming to A or B signs could see the volunteer standing.

The design began with baseline observations, and these were graphed separately for Stop signs A and B as the percentage of drivers who made complete stops. During the intervention phase, the poster (instructions and social reinforcement) was provided by a volunteer standing near the intersection of Stop sign A. Prompts and reinforcement were never provided by anyone at the intersection of Stop B. So, because the interventions are associated with one condition (Stop sign A) but not another (Stop sign B), this is a multi-element feature of the design.

There is more in the design—there were two alternating conditions during the intervention phase. One condition was the volunteer present and with the poster, as already mentioned. The other condition during intervention was continuation of baseline. Some days during the intervention phase there was no volunteer at all. That is, during the intervention phase some days had the volunteer present (the intervention), and other days had no volunteer present (so conditions at the interaction were just like baseline). Intervention and continuation of baseline days were randomly ordered. Thus, randomization of the two conditions during the intervention phase was another component in the design.

Figure 9.7 nicely conveys the design and results. The top and bottom portions of the figure show that during baseline (solid line with filled dark circles) only a small percentage of drivers stopped at either Stop sign A (upper portion) or B (bottom portion). The solid line with dark circles shows baseline during the "true" baseline phase, and then during the randomly determined baseline days throughout the study. The line with the open circles shows the effect of the intervention (top figure). During the intervention phase, when the volunteer flashed the poster (sign visible days), the percentage of drivers who stopped really increased—this could not have been any historical event or other such influence because some of the days, which were randomly determined, did not have the volunteer present and performance remained at baseline levels. The top figure alone provides a strong demonstration. Stop sign B never had the intervention but the data were plotted to determine whether the volunteer was visible versus more baseline days. For reasons that are not clear, seeing the volunteer in the distance was associated with a slight increase in percentage of drivers who stopped. It is possible that the volunteer was mistaken for a pedestrian and that fostered increased stopping or that some individuals at Stop sign B had previously experienced the intersection at Stop sign A.

Overall, the design combines multiple features of different designs (multi-element, alternating-treatments design, randomization). The multi-element component is based on separate stimulus conditions (Stop signs A and B) associated with different interventions (instructions/praise vs. none). The alternating-treatments feature stems from varying two conditions (intervention and baseline) during the intervention phase. And

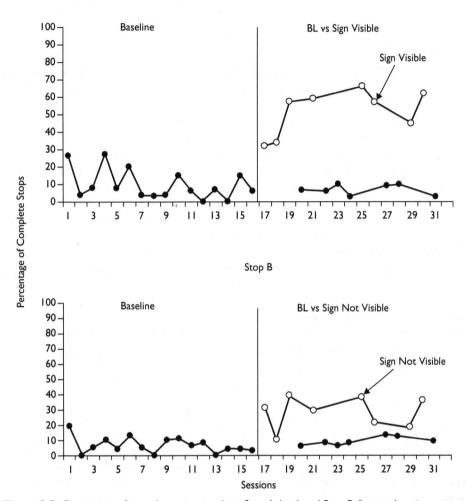

Figure 9.7. Percentage of complete stops made at Stop A (top) and Stop B (bottom).   *(Source: Austin et al., 2006.)*

randomization refers to how the two conditions were varied daily. As to the results, the graph (top portion) conveys the clear impact of the intervention. There is some ambiguity as to why drivers at Stop sign B improved (continued baseline). Inclusion of this condition was very helpful. It was important to show that the intervention was better than no intervention, and the continuation of baseline helps establish that.

ADDITIONAL DESIGN VARIATIONS

Conditions Included in the Design

The primary purpose of employing a multiple-treatment design is to evaluate the relative effectiveness of two or more interventions and to do so relatively quickly. Thus, variations discussed up to this point have emphasized the comparison of interventions, that is, viable treatments or methods designed to alter behavior. Not all of the conditions compared in the intervention phase need to be active treatments. In some variations, one of the conditions included in the intervention phase is a continuation of baseline conditions, that is, no intervention. The previous example of the combined components included baseline as one of the interventions, but it is worth underscoring the use more explicitly and without combinations of many other elegant procedures included in that example.

As you will recall regarding single-case designs more generally, one purpose of the initial baseline is to project (predict) what performance would be like in the future if no treatment were implemented. In a multiple-treatment design, it is possible to implement one or more interventions *and* to continue baseline conditions, all in the same phase. In addition to projecting what baseline would be like in the future, it is possible to assess baseline levels of performance concurrently with the intervention(s). If performance changes under those time periods in which the interventions are in effect but remains at the original baseline level during the periods in which baseline conditions are continued, this provides a dramatic and persuasive demonstration that behavior changes resulted from the intervention. Because the baseline conditions are continued in the intervention phase, the investigator has a direct measure of performance without the intervention. Any extraneous influences that might be confounded with the onset of the intervention phase should affect the baseline conditions that have been continued. By continuing baseline in the intervention phase, greater assurances are provided that the intervention accounts for change. Moreover, the investigator can judge the magnitude of the changes due to the intervention by directly comparing performance during the intervention phase under baseline and intervention conditions that are assessed concurrently.

In general, in a multi-treatment design, we usually think of comparing two or more treatments. However, one variation is to compare two conditions concurrently: one that is an intervention and the other that is a continuation of baseline. This makes multi-treatment designs useful even when the investigator is interested in only one intervention. For example, if a teacher or school administrator has an idea how to generate enthusiasm and involvement especially well on classroom assignments, that method could be the intervention and then it could be put in an alternating-treatments design in which it was implemented once each day in the morning or afternoon. When the special intervention is not implemented that day, the other period is teaching as usual (baseline).

The continuation of baseline during an intervention phase (as one of the conditions) has yet another use. If performance during the initial baseline phase is unstable or shows a trend that the investigator believes may interfere with the evaluation of the interventions, it may be especially useful to continue baseline as one of the conditions in the design. This provides a direct test of whether the intervention has an impact on the pattern of behavior. Rather than predict what performance would be like if baseline continued, we have a direct record.

Final Phase of the Design
The alternating-treatments design is defined by a baseline phase followed by an intervention phase in which two or more interventions are presented. The designs often

include a third and final phase that contributes to the strength of the demonstration. If one of the two conditions is shown to be more effective than the other during the intervention phase, it is often implemented on all occasions and under all stimulus conditions in the final phase of the design. When the final phase of the alternating-treatments design consists of applying the more (or most) effective intervention across all of the stimulus conditions, the design bears some resemblance to a multiple-baseline design.

Essentially, the design includes two intervention phases, one in which two (or more) interventions are compared and one in which the more (most) effective one is applied. The "multiple baselines" do not refer to different behaviors or settings but rather to the different time periods each day in which the observations are obtained. The more (most) effective intervention is applied to one time period (or balanced across time periods or situations) during the first intervention phase. In the second intervention phase, the more (most) effective intervention is extended to all of the time periods. Thus, the more (most) effective intervention is introduced to the time periods at different points in the design (first intervention phase, then second intervention phase).

Of course, the design is not exactly like a multiple-baseline design because the more (or most) effective intervention is introduced to time periods that may not have continued under baseline conditions. Rather, less effective interventions have been applied to these time periods during the first intervention phase. On the other hand, when the alternating-treatments design compares one intervention with a continuation of baseline, then the two intervention phases correspond closely to a multiple-baseline design. The intervention is introduced to one of the daily time periods in the first intervention phase while the other time period continues in baseline conditions. In the second intervention phase, the intervention is extended to all time periods in exactly the manner of a multiple-baseline design.

I mention the final phase and relations of different designs not just to confuse the reader. There will be other opportunities for that. Rather, it is important to convey the elements or components (phases, options) of single-case designs. It is tempting to ask or even demand, "What design is *that*?" when the design cannot be easily classified. The design per se and its classification are not really so critical. Rather, the logic of single-case designs (describe, predict, test) and the goal of experiments (ruling out threats to validity) are critical. The logic and goals need to be satisfied, and these trump all other considerations. The many different elements or components provide valuable tools for improvising single-case designs to handle different situations and also for adding or altering later phases in a design if needed to clarify the demonstration.

General Comments

Multiple-treatment designs can vary along more dimensions than the conditions that are implemented in the first and second intervention phases, as discussed previously. For example, designs differ in the number of interventions or conditions that are compared and the number of conditions or contexts across which the interventions are balanced. However important as these dimensions are, they do not alter basic features of the designs.

The designs are not as commonly used as ABAB and multiple-baseline designs. When they are used, the demonstrations tend to be experimentally strong. The main reason is that as often as not investigators include a feature in the design that draws on some other design. For example, the design only requires the baseline and intervention phase. The different interventions during the intervention phase provide the data points to see if performance under each intervention departs from baseline and from data points from the other intervention. The describe, predict, and test features of the different phases of single-case designs are accommodated within the two phases. Investigators often include a third phase that further strengthens the demonstration. I mentioned the multiple-baseline feature of adding a third phase in which the more (or most) effective intervention is introduced across all conditions.

In addition, a third or final phase of the design may consist of withdrawing all of the treatments. Thus, a reversal phase is included, and the logic of the design follows that of ABAB designs discussed earlier. Of course, an attractive feature of the multiple-treatment designs is the ability to demonstrate an experimental effect without withdrawing treatment. I mention the use of a reversal phase here not to advocate that addition specifically but rather to convey variations that are used occasionally to strengthen further the conclusions that can be drawn about the impact of the intervention. The full range of variations of the designs becomes clearer as we turn to the problems that may emerge in multiple-treatment designs and how these problems can be addressed.

PROBLEMS AND CONSIDERATIONS

Among single-case experimental designs, those in which multiple treatments are compared are relatively complex. Hence, several considerations are raised by their use in terms of the types of interventions and behaviors suitable for the designs, the extent to which interventions can be delineated by the clients, the number of interventions and conditions (time periods, settings), and the possibility that multiple-treatment interference may influence the results.

Omitting the Initial Baseline

Two or more interventions are compared during the intervention phase. Occasionally, a variation is used in which the investigator begins the two interventions (e.g., alternating-treatments design) without a baseline (e.g., Reinhartsen, Garfinkle, & Wolery, 2002; Wacker et al., 1990). If one intervention greatly exceeds the effect of the other, the absence of baseline is not so much of an issue. The goal is to see if one intervention is more effective than another, and this can be accomplished without an initial baseline. However, if the two interventions are not different in their effects, there is an important question that cannot be addressed. Were both interventions effective (i.e., better than baseline) or was neither effective (e.g., no different from baseline)? Also, I mentioned before that it is possible that the intervention that looks better may be no different from baseline but looks good because the other intervention made things worse (Washington et al., 2002). It is even possible that both interventions made behavior worse than baseline. This is not merely an intellectual possibility; interventions occasionally make people worse (e.g., Dodge, Dishion, & Lansford, 2006; Feldman, Caplinger, & Wodarski, 1983).

For example, in one project, two interventions were compared with the goal of increasing physical activity of four elementary school students (Grissom, Ward,

Martin, & Leenders, 2005). Students wore a small device (accelerometers) every day to assess level of activity; the goal was to increase activity, and this measure automatically recorded the information that was downloaded to a computer at the end of the lesson. Two interventions were: (1) wearing a heart-rate monitor that provided an audible prompt when student activity increased beyond a specific level and (2) not wearing a monitor and not receiving feedback. The alternating-treatments design showed these interventions to be no different from each other in their effect. This is not surprising; among all of the interventions psychology has to offer, feedback all by itself is not one of the stronger interventions in terms of magnitude of effect and number of individuals usually affected. However, we cannot judge a critical question—did both interventions improve activity beyond baseline? It would have been good to have the pre-intervention (baseline) phase to have the descriptive and predictive features of baseline. This might have been a brief or extended period of wearing the accelerometers several days before any intervention began—it could be that the heart rate device raised both conditions during the intervention phase and in fact made a difference.

A baseline is not always feasible and is not always needed. Even in an ABAB design, one can begin with the intervention and make this a BAB or BABA design. Yet, in multiple-treatment designs, the absence of differences between the two treatments can introduce ambiguity that would not otherwise be present with even a very brief baseline. As a general rule for single-case designs, begin with a baseline phase if ever possible. In the case of this example, even two data points in baseline may not be completely sufficient to describe and predict performance, but they still would have been an excellent addition.

Type of Intervention and Behaviors
Multiple-treatment designs depend on showing changes for a given behavior across daily sessions or time periods. If two (or more) interventions are alternated on a given day, behavior must be able to shift rapidly to demonstrate differential effects of the interventions. The need for behavior to change rapidly dictates both the types of interventions and the behaviors that can be studied in multiple-treatment designs.

Interventions suitable for multiple-treatment designs may need to show rapid effects initially and to have little or no carryover effects when terminated. Consider the initial requirement of rapid start-up effects. Because two (or more) interventions are usually implemented on the same day, it is important that the intervention not take too long within a given session to begin to show its effects. For example, if each intervention is administered in one of two 1-hour time periods each day, relatively little time exists to show a change in behavior before the intervention is terminated for that day. Not all treatments may produce effects relatively quickly. This problem is obvious in some forms of medication used to treat clinical problems in adults and children (e.g., depression), in which days or weeks may be required before therapeutic effects can be observed. However, the problem is likely to be as evident with psychosocial and educational influences (e.g., instructions and praise vs. a group program, teaching strategies or special educational materials that build skills) that would be compared (e.g., in a classroom). The moment or first few time periods that one intervention is in place does not necessarily lead to an immediate impact on the behavior of the students. The impact of each intervention may only emerge slowly. In addition, the differential impact of the interventions (on the assumption that there is one) may also take time to emerge.

In many behavioral programs in which intervention effects are based on reinforcement and punishment, the effects of the intervention have been evident within a relatively short period. If several opportunities (occurrences of the behavior) exist to apply the consequences within a given time period, intervention effects may be relatively rapid. Yet many interventions based on consequences (e.g., extinction where consequences are not provided) may not show rapidly changing effects. Also, many other interventions (e.g., academic skill building, cognitive therapy for a clinical disorder, modeling, and peer tutoring) are studied in single-case designs, and changes are expected to accrue slowly. Rapid shifts in performance as a function of changing treatments may be difficult to demonstrate. The slow "start-up" time for intervention effects depends on the intervention as well as the behavior or domain of interest.

When treatments are alternated within a single day, as is often the case in multiple-treatment designs, there is an initial start-up time necessary for treatment to demonstrate an effect. This is not invariably a problem. However, investigators might ask themselves in advance, "Is it reasonable to expect the different interventions to show their effects and any differential effects within the time periods each is provided?" The answer is influenced by many considerations. Prominent among these is the two interventions that are compared. In general, the greater the contrast in the interventions (e.g., stark procedural differences) and the stronger the expected differences in impact, the less likely that the brevity of the time period will make a difference. As a clear case, if the two conditions compared are intervention versus baseline in the same phase, as mentioned previously, the discrimination and differences between the conditions are more likely to be evident. Any time two (or more interventions) are compared, each may need time to have impact and to show differential impact. The clients are exposed to the balancing of interventions across different conditions (e.g., time periods) and that can make discriminating between the different interventions slightly more complex. In contrast, in a multi-element design, each intervention is paired with a particular stimulus or context, which can help clients discriminate between the interventions.

Another requirement is that interventions must have little or no carryover effects after they are terminated. If the effects of the first intervention linger after it is no longer presented, the intervention that follows would be confounded by the previous one. For example, it might be difficult to compare medication and behavioral procedures in an alternating-treatments design. It might be impossible to administer both treatments on the same day (e.g., morning and afternoon periods) because of the carryover that most medications have. The lingering effects of the medication might influence the effectiveness of the other intervention. One could evaluate whether the other intervention (and medication) is more or less effective when it was preceded by or when it followed medication.

Pharmacological interventions are not the only ones that can have carryover effects. Interventions based on environmental changes and interpersonal interaction also may have carryover effects and thus may obscure evaluation of the separate effects of the interventions, a point to which I return later in the discussion of multiple-treatment interference. In any case, if two or more interventions are to be compared, it is important to be able to terminate each of the interventions quickly with little or no lingering effect that will blur and mix their impact. If interventions cannot be removed quickly, they will be difficult to compare with each other in an alternating-treatments design.

Apart from the interventions, the behaviors or outcomes of interest studied in multiple-treatment designs must be susceptible to rapid changes. Behaviors that depend upon improvements over an extended period may not be able to shift rapidly in response to session-by-session changes in the intervention. For example, it would be difficult to evaluate two or more interventions for reducing weight of persons who are obese. Changes in the measure (weight in kilograms or pounds) would not vary to a significant degree unless an effective treatment was continued without interruption over an extended period. Constantly alternating the interventions on a daily basis might not affect weight at all. On the other hand, alternative measures (e.g., calories consumed at different times during the day) may well permit use of the design.

Aside from being able to change rapidly, the frequency of the behavior may also be a determinant of the extent to which interventions can show changes in multiple-treatment designs. For example, if the purpose of the interventions is to decrease the occurrence of low-frequency behaviors (e.g., severe aggressive acts), it may be difficult to show a differential effect of the interventions. Too few opportunities may exist for the intervention to be applied in any particular session. Indeed, the behavior may not even occur in some of the sessions. Thus, even though a session may be devoted to a particular intervention, that intervention may not actually be applied. Such a session cannot be fairly represented as one in which this particular intervention was employed.

High frequency of occurrences of the behavior also may present problems for reflecting differences among interventions. If there is an upper limit to the number of responses because of a limited set of discrete opportunities for the behavior to occur, it may be difficult to show differential improvements. For example, a child may receive two different programs to improve academic performance. Each day, the child receives a worksheet with 20 problems at two different times as the basis for assessing change. During each time period, there are only 20 opportunities for correct responding. If baseline performance is 50% correct (10 problems completed), this means that the differences between treatments can only be detected, on the average, in response to the 10 other problems. If each intervention is moderately effective, there is likely to be a *ceiling (or floor) effect*, that is, absence of differences because of the restricted upper (or lower) limit to the measure. Perhaps the interventions would have differed in effectiveness if the measure were not restricted to a limited number of response opportunities.

The restricted range as a problem when multiple interventions are compared is illustrated in a study designed to decrease absenteeism among employees working at a human service organization (Luiselli et al., 2009). The employees included approximately 60 (number varied over time) teachers and child-care staff members in a private school serving individuals with autism and related developmental disabilities. The measure was the percentage of staff absent each day independent of the reason for the absence. The investigators wished to compare three interventions in what might be referred to as ABCD evaluation, beginning with baseline (A). The interventions included: B—providing an informational brochure to convey information and then to preview a lottery in which attendance increased the possibility of earning a monetary bonus; C—the actual lottery in which this was implemented; and D—the lottery plus public posting of graphs that charted daily and weekly absences.

Figure 9.8 shows that absenteeism during baseline was increasing, a direction opposite from the goal of the program. The first intervention (brochure) led to a marked drop in absenteeism. The second (lottery) and third (lottery + public posting) were implemented, but it is very difficult to evaluate if these latter interventions made any difference. The brochure reduced absenteeism so strongly that there may have been a floor effect, that is, not much room on the measure to show the effects of any other intervention. In the brochure phase, absenteeism was close to 3.6% of the staff. This may be near or at a genuine limit as people are absent for legitimate reasons (e.g., illness, child holidays that require a parent to stay home). When multiple interventions are compared, it is important to be sure that the measure allows for differentiation among the interventions if the interventions are differentially effective. This cannot be known in advance, but providing multiple interventions to the same subjects is a situation in which this is more likely to be a problem than when providing different interventions to different groups of subjects (between-group design).

In general, differential effectiveness of the intervention is likely to depend on several opportunities for the behavior to occur. If two or more active interventions are compared that are likely to change behavior, the differences in their effects on performance are relatively smaller than those evident if one intervention is simply compared to a continuation of baseline. In order for the design to be sensitive to relatively less marked differences between or among interventions, the frequency of the behavior must be such that differences could be shown. If the goal is to improve some behavior, low frequency of behavior may present problems if it means that there are few

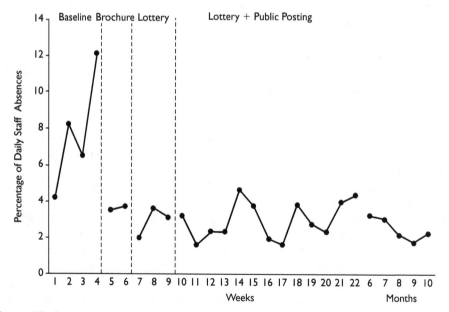

Figure 9.8. Percentage of daily staff absences each week across multiple treatments. *(Source: Luiselli et al., 2009.)*

opportunities to apply the procedures being compared. High frequency of behavior may be a problem if the range of responses is restricted by an upper limit that impedes demonstration of differences among effective interventions designed to increase that behavior.

Discriminability of the Interventions

When multiple interventions are administered to one client in the same phase, the client must be able to make at least two sorts of discriminations. First, the client must be able to discriminate whether those who administer the interventions or time periods are associated with a particular intervention. In the multi-element design, this discrimination may not be very difficult because the interventions are constantly associated with a particular stimulus. In the alternating-treatments design, the client must be able to discern that the specific interventions constantly vary across the different stimulus conditions. In the beginning of the intervention phase, the client may inadvertently associate a particular intervention with a particular stimulus condition (e.g., time period, staff member, or setting). If the interventions are to show different effects on performance, it will be important for the client to respond to the interventions that are in effect independently of who administers them. Second, the client must be able to distinguish the separate interventions. Since the design is aimed at showing that the interventions can produce different effects, the client must be able to tell which intervention is in effect at any particular time. Discriminating the different interventions may depend on the procedures themselves.

The ease of making a discrimination, of course, depends on the *similarity of the interventions* or *procedures* that are compared. If two very different procedures are compared, the clients are more likely to be able to discriminate which intervention is in effect than if subtle variations of the same procedure are compared. For example, if the investigation compared the effects of 5 versus 15 minutes of isolation as a punishment technique, it might be difficult for the client to discriminate which intervention was in effect. Although the interventions might produce different effects if they were administered to separate groups of subjects or to the same subject in different phases over time, they may not produce a difference or produce smaller differences when alternated daily, in part because the client cannot discriminate consistently which one is in effect at any particular point in time.

The discriminability of the different interventions may depend on the *frequency* with which each intervention is actually invoked, as alluded to earlier. The more frequently the intervention is applied during a given time period, the more likely the client will be able to tell which intervention is in effect. If in a given time interval the intervention is applied rarely, the procedures are not likely to show a difference across the observation periods. In some special circumstances where the goal of treatment is to reduce the frequency of behavior, the number of times the intervention is applied may decrease over time, as behavior improves and the problem occurs less often. As behavior decreases in frequency, the different treatments will be applied less often, and the client may be less able to tell which treatment is in effect. For example, if reprimands and isolation are compared as two procedures to decrease behavior, each procedure might show some effect within the first few days of treatment. As the behaviors decrease in frequency, so will the opportunities to administer the interventions. The client may have increased difficulty in determining at any point which of the different interventions is in effect.

To ensure that clients can discriminate which intervention is in effect at any particular point in time, investigators can provide daily instructions before each of the treatments that is administered in an alternating-treatments design. The instructions tell the client explicitly which condition will be in effect at a particular point in time. As a general guideline, instructions might be very valuable to enhance the discrimination of the different treatments, especially if there are several different treatments, if the balancing of treatments across conditions is complex, or if the interventions are only in effect for brief periods during the day.[5]

Number of Interventions and Stimulus Conditions

A central feature of the alternating-treatments design is balancing the conditions of administration with the separate interventions so that the intervention effects can be evaluated separately from the effects of the conditions. Theoretically, any number of different interventions can be compared during the intervention phase. In practice, only a few interventions usually can be compared. The problem is that as the number of interventions increases, so does the number of sessions or days needed to balance interventions across the conditions of administration. If several interventions are compared, an extraordinarily large number of days would be required to balance the interventions across all of the conditions. As a general rule, two or three interventions or conditions are optimal for avoiding the complexities of balancing the interventions across the conditions of administration. Indeed, most multiple-treatment designs have compared two or three interventions.

The difficulty of balancing interventions also depends on the number of stimulus conditions included in the design. In the usual variation, the two interventions are varied across two levels (e.g., morning or afternoon) of one stimulus dimension (e.g., time periods). In some variations, the interventions may be varied across two stimulus dimensions (e.g., time periods and staff members). Thus, two interventions (I_1 and I_2) might be balanced across two time periods (T_1 and T_2) and two staff members (S_1 and S_2). The interventions must be paired equally often across all time period and staff combinations (T_1S_1, T_1S_2, T_2S_1, T_2S_2) during the intervention phase. As the number of dimensions or stimulus conditions increases, longer periods are needed to ensure that balancing is complete. The number of interventions and stimulus conditions included in the design may be limited by practical constraints or the duration of the intervention phase. In general, most alternating-treatments designs balance the interventions across two levels of a particular dimension (e.g., time periods). Some variations have included more levels of a particular dimension (e.g., three time periods) or two or more separate

---

[5] Interestingly, if instructions precede each intervention to convey to the clients exactly which procedure is in effect, the distinction between multi-element and alternating-treatments designs becomes blurred. In effect, the instructions become stimuli that are consistently associated with particular interventions. However, the blurred distinction need not become an issue. In the alternating-treatments design, an attempt is made to balance the interventions across diverse stimulus conditions (with the exception of instructions), and in the multi-element design the balance is not usually attempted. Indeed, in the latter design, the purpose is to show that particular stimuli come to exert control over behavior because of their constant association with particular treatments.

dimensions (e.g., time periods and staff) (e.g., Ollendick et al., 1981). From a practical standpoint, the investigation can be simplified by balancing interventions across only two levels of one dimension.

Multiple-treatment Interference

In any design in which two or more treatments (interventions) are provided to the same subject, multiple-treatment interference may limit the conclusions that can be drawn (Hains & Baer, 1989; Kazdin, 2003). As noted previously, multiple-treatment interference refers to the effect of one treatment being influenced by the effects of the other. The concept can be illustrated by the simple case in which participants receive two interventions with one right after the other. For example, training in behavioral management skills was provided to parents of children with developmental disabilities to reduce inappropriate parenting behaviors (giving ambiguous commands, unwittingly reinforcing inappropriate child behavior, physical aggression) (Phaneuf & McIntyre, 2007). Parents received group treatment (Intervention 1) for several sessions. This was followed by adding individual video feedback for parent behavior (Intervention 2). The results indicated that inappropriate parenting behaviors were lower with the combined (second intervention) than with the first intervention. Does this mean the second intervention is generally more effective? It is possible that the effects are due to beginning with the group intervention alone; the results may not apply if Intervention 2 were introduced first. The effects of Intervention 2 may be quite different depending on whether it followed the prior intervention or was provided without that prior intervention. In short, when there is treatment preceded or followed by another, the effects of the latter treatment may be in part a function of what preceded it, that is, multiple-treatment interference.

Multiple-treatment interference may result from many different arrangements of administering treatments. For example, if two treatments are examined in an ABAB design (e.g., ABCBC), multiple-treatment interference may result from the sequence in which the treatments are administered. The effects of the different interventions (B, C) may be due to the sequence in which they appeared. It is not possible to evaluate and draw conclusions about the effects of C alone, because it was preceded by B, which may have influenced all subsequent performance.

Occasionally, investigators include a reversal phase in ABAB designs with multiple treatments (e.g., ABAC), with the belief that recovery of baseline levels of performance removes the possibility of multiple-treatment interference. However, intervening reversal phases (e.g., ABACABAC) do not alter the possible influence of sequence effects. Even though baseline levels of performance are recovered, it is still possible that the effects of C are influenced in part by the previous history of Condition B. Behavior may be more (or less) easily altered by the second intervention because of the intervention that preceded it. An intervening reversal (or A) phase does not eliminate that possibility.

Multiple-treatment interference is a methodological issue, but an example from everyday life is useful to convey how sequence effects or embedding one intervention in another can make a difference in practical ways. In making requests of children, there are some requests a given child is unlikely to comply with. These are individual for each child and are readily measured. Examples of these requests might be asking him or her to do a chore, to get ready for school, or to stop doing this or that. One can show that for a given child the likelihood of complying is low for a given set of requests. These are called *low-probability requests* because they are very unlikely to get compliance. One can get much better compliance with these low-probability requests by preceding them by asking the child to do things he or she will more readily do. Immediately preceding a low-probability request (please go pick up your toys, work on your math homework while I am out of the classroom) with a small number of *high-probability requests* (e.g., please give me a high five, clap your hands, put your name on your homework sheet, read the first math problem) increases the likelihood that the low-probability request will be completed. Stated another way to make it more relevant to the present discussion, low-probability requests (by definition) do not yield very much compliance. However, compliance with these requests can be greatly increased by preceding them with some high-probability requests. The sequence of high- then low-probability requests makes the latter requests much more likely, an example that conveys how juxtaposing different interventions or conditions can alter the impact of one of them. Developing compliance and using high-probability requests is an intervention strategy to develop and shape compliance (e.g., Humm, Blampied, & Liberty, 2005; Wehby & Hollahan, 2000). This is a strategic use of multiple-treatment interference.

In multi-element and alternating-treatments designs, multiple-treatment interference refers to the possibility that the effect of any intervention may be influenced by the other intervention(s) to which it is juxtaposed. Here the influence is not the sequence of B appearing before C. On any given day, both B and C might be provided. Multiple-treatment interference refers to the possibility that the effects obtained for a given intervention may differ from what they would be if the intervention were administered by itself in a separate phase without the juxtaposition of other treatments. As an example, one alternating-treatments design compared the effects of token reinforcement and response cost (fines or loss of tokens) on attentive behavior of children (ages 9 to 12 and with developmental disabilities) (Shapiro, Kazdin, & McGonigle, 1982). In the design, token reinforcement, response cost, and continuation of baseline were implemented at different points. Token reinforcement was more effective (and showed less variability in its impact) when compared to a continuation of baseline during the same intervention phase than when it was compared to response cost.

More generally, two or more interventions might be administered in a multi-element or alternating-treatments design. The methodological point: the effects of each intervention might be "interfered with" (altered) by the presentation of the other either before or during the other intervention. Stated more generally, the results of a particular intervention in a multiple-treatment design may be determined in part by the other intervention(s) to which it is compared.

It is possible that juxtaposing two interventions will dilute their unique effects. Neither may be in place sufficiently long to exert its unique influence, if one exists. Alternatively, the uniqueness could be lost because two similar variants are put next to each other. In alternating-treatments designs, there are examples in the interventions that are compared and that produce few or no differences within subjects or were not consistent among subjects (e.g., in teaching reading, using symbols for communication for individuals with communication disorders) (Ardoin, McCall, & Klubnik, 2007; Hetzroni, Quist, & Lloyd, 2002). It is possible that the interventions in fact are equally effective, but it is also possible that using similar methods in the same phase in an alternating fashion made them less distinct in impact than they would have been if given to separate subjects or provided sequentially (ABCABC) in the design.

It is important to be aware of multiple-treatment interference as a methodological issue because it may affect the conclusions reached about the effects of treatment for a specific client but also affect generality of the findings to others. The issue applies if two or more interventions are alternated in some way, as in the case of multiple-treatment designs presented in this chapter, or in other designs in which two interventions are presented in sequence over time (e.g., ABCAC). In this latter case, for example, investigators are wont to note that Intervention C (e.g., in an ABCAC design) may be more effective than B in their discussion of the results and then state that Intervention C ought to be used more generally. All this might be true, but the intervention was not "really" C but rather C-preceded-by-B. Conclusions about the effect of C alone require a different and further study.

In general, researchers using single-case designs have not given much attention to multiple-treatment interference, and perhaps understandably so (but see Hains & Baer, 1989). The designs are most often used in applied settings with clients in need of change in an important area of functioning (e.g., self-injury of a child with developmental disability, greatly disruptive behavior in a special education class). In such instances, the investigator is interested in identifying an effective intervention and one that has palpable and immediate impact. This might lead to plans for an ABAB or multiple-baseline design but Intervention B is not as effective as needed. Consequently, a second intervention (C) is introduced. It is quite possible that the second intervention produces an effect due in part to the other condition with which it is compared (multiple-treatment design) or the intervention that preceded it (ABCBC design), but the priority of evaluating this possibility has been overshadowed by the applied goal of the program.

It is important to at least mention rather than elaborate that applied goals are usually served by the best science, i.e., when we have an understanding of how interventions work. In the present discussion, we want to know whether an intervention is truly effective (or more or less effective) based on whether it is connected to some other condition or whether it can be provided by itself. A given application might give priority to helping one child, one classroom, or one group, but our other goal is to extend findings to help many. The best investment in that goal is to understand what interventions work, whether their effects depend on special conditions or other variables, and how the interventions can be administered to help the many who might profit from their application. Knowing whether multiple-treatment interference makes a difference is quite relevant to this broader applied goal.

EVALUATION OF THE DESIGNS

Multiple-treatment designs have several advantages that make them especially useful for applied research. To begin with, the designs do not depend on a reversal of conditions, as do the ABAB designs. Hence, problems of behavior failing to reverse or the undesirability of reversing behavior are avoided. Similarly, the designs do not depend on temporarily withholding treatment, as is the case in multiple-baseline designs in which the intervention is applied to one behavior (or person, or situation) at a time, while the remaining behaviors can continue in extended baseline phases. In multiple-treatment designs, the interventions are applied and continued throughout the investigation. The strength of the demonstration depends on showing that treatments produce differential effects across the time periods or situations in which performance is observed.

A second advantage of the design is particularly noteworthy. Most of the single-case experimental designs depend heavily on obtaining baseline data that are relatively stable and show no trend in the therapeutic direction. A stable baseline with no trend is the ideal pattern in virtually all circumstances. If baseline data show improvements, special difficulties can arise in evaluating the impact of subsequent interventions. In multiple-treatment designs, interventions can be implemented and evaluated even when baseline data show initial trends. The designs rely on comparing performance associated with the alternating conditions. The differences can still be detected when superimposed on any existing trend in the data.

A third main advantage of the design is that it can compare different treatments for a given individual within a relatively short period. If two or more interventions were compared in an ABAB or multiple-baseline design, the interventions must follow one another in separate phases. Providing each intervention in a separate phase could greatly extend the duration of the investigation. In multiple-treatment designs, the interventions can be compared in the same phase, so that within a relatively short period one can assess if two or more interventions have different impact. The phase in which both interventions are compared need not necessarily be longer than intervention phases of other single-case designs. Yet only one intervention phase is needed in the alternating-treatments design to compare separate interventions. In classroom and institutional settings, when time is at a premium, the need to identify the more or most effective intervention relatively quickly among available alternatives can be extremely important.

Of course, in discussing the comparison of two or more treatments in a single-case design, the topic of multiple-treatment interference cannot be ignored. When two or more treatments are compared in sequence, as in an ABAB design, the possibility exists that the effects of one intervention are partially attributable to the sequence in which it appeared. In a multiple-treatment design, these specific sequence effects are not a problem, because separate phases with different interventions do not follow each other. However, multiple-treatment interference may take another form. As discussed earlier, the effects of one treatment may be due in part to the other condition to which it is juxtaposed. Hence, in all of the single-case experimental designs in which two or more treatments are given to the same subject, multiple-treatment interference remains an issue, even though it may take different forms. The advantage of the multiple-treatment designs is not in the elimination of multiple-treatment interference. Rather, the advantage stems from the efficiency in comparing different treatments in a single phase. As soon as one intervention emerges as more effective than another, it can be implemented across all time periods or settings.

There is yet another advantage of multiple-treatment designs that has not been addressed. In the alternating-treatments design, the interventions are balanced across various stimulus conditions (e.g., time periods, staff members, or settings). The data are usually plotted according to the interventions so that one can determine which among the alternatives is the more effective. It is possible to plot the data in another way to examine the impact of the stimulus conditions on client behavior. For example, if the interventions are balanced across two teachers or staff members or two time periods (e.g., morning and afternoon classes), then the data can be plotted to examine if client behavior varies as a function of teachers (or time periods). In many situations, it may be valuable to identify whether some staff members are having greater effects on client performance than others independently of the particular intervention they are administering. Because the staff members are balanced across the interventions, the separate effects of the staff and interventions can be plotted. If the data are plotted according to the staff members who administer the interventions in the different periods each day, one can identify those who might warrant additional training, assistance, or emulation

SUMMARY AND CONCLUSIONS

Multiple-treatment designs are used to compare the effectiveness of two or more interventions or conditions that are administered to the same subject or group of subjects. The designs demonstrate an effect of the interventions by presenting each of them in a single intervention phase after an initial baseline phase. The manner in which the separate interventions are administered during the intervention phase serves as the basis for distinguishing various multiple-treatment designs.

In the *multi-element design*, two or more interventions are usually administered in the intervention phase. Each intervention is consistently associated with a particular stimulus or context (e.g., a teacher or staff member, setting, or time). The purpose of the design is to demonstrate that a particular stimulus, because of its consistent association with one of the interventions, exerts control over performance. The differential effectiveness of the intervention is evident if performance is superior under the stimulus condition or context with which a particular intervention has been connected.

In the *alternating-treatments design* (also referred to as *simultaneous-treatment design*), two or more interventions or conditions are also administered in the same intervention phase. Each of the interventions is balanced across the various stimulus conditions (e.g., teacher or staff member, setting, or time) so that the effects of the interventions can be separated from these conditions of administration. When one of the interventions emerges as the more (or most) effective during the intervention phase, a final phase is usually included in the design in which that intervention is implemented across all stimulus conditions or occasions. Alternating-treatments designs usually evaluate two or more interventions. However, the interventions can be compared with no treatment or a continuation of baseline conditions.

Several considerations are relevant for evaluating whether a multiple-treatment design will be appropriate in any given situation. First, because the designs depend on showing rapid changes in performance for a given behavior in response to interventions that may change on the same day, special restrictions may be placed on the types of interventions and behaviors that can be included. Second, because multiple treatments are often administered in close proximity (e.g., on the same day), it is important to ensure that the interventions will be discriminable to the clients so that they know when each is in effect. Related, the interventions must be applied and experienced by the client, perhaps even frequently, because each is in place so that behavior can respond differently to the different interventions. Third, the number of interventions and stimulus conditions employed in the investigation may have practical limits. The requirements for balancing the interventions across stimulus conditions become more demanding as the number of interventions and stimulus conditions increase.

Finally, a major issue of designs in which two or more conditions are provided to the same subjects is *multiple-treatment interference.* Multiple-treatment designs avoid sequence effects, that is, following one intervention by another in separate phases (i.e., sequence effects), which is a potential problem when two or more treatments are evaluated in ABAB designs. However, multiple-treatment designs juxtapose the different treatments in a way that still influences the inferences that can be drawn about the treatment. The possibility remains that the effect of a particular intervention may result in part from the particular intervention to which it is contrasted. The extent to which multiple-treatment interference influences the results of the designs described in this chapter has not been well studied.

Multiple-treatment designs have several advantages. The intervention need not be withdrawn or withheld from the clients as part of the methodological requirements of the design. Also, the effects of different treatments can be compared relatively quickly (i.e., in a single phase), so that the more (or most) effective intervention can be applied. Also, because the designs depend on differential effects of varied conditions on behavior, trends during the initial baseline phase need not impede initiating the interventions. Finally, when the interventions are balanced across stimulus conditions (e.g., staff, teacher, and classrooms) the separate effects of the interventions and these conditions can be examined. In general, the designs are often well suited to the demands of clinical, educational, and rehabilitation settings. Where there are viable treatments to be explored, an interest in identifying which might be more or most effective, and a need to avoid withdrawal or reversal phases, the designs can be extremely useful.

CHAPTER 10

Additional Design Options

Variations of the designs discussed to this point constitute the majority of evaluation strategies used in single-case research. Several other options are available that represent novel variations on single-case designs, special design features to address questions about the maintenance or generalization of behavior, and combinations of single-case and between-group design strategies. The total population of design variations would be impossible to convey. Moreover, it might not even be useful. The variations derive from understanding how the designs work—what I have referred to as the logic of single-case designs and how they rule out or make implausible various threats to validity. Even so, this chapter conveys some of the available variations because of their special uses and their bridges to traditional between-group designs. The chapter discusses several design options, the rationales for their use, and the benefits of different strategies for applied research.

COMBINED DESIGNS

Description and Underlying Rationale

Although the designs discussed in previous chapters are most often used in their "pure" forms, features from two or more designs are frequently combined. I provided some examples in variations of other designs, but it is important to illustrate and discuss these more explicitly. Combined designs are those that include features from two or more designs within the same investigation. The purpose of using combined designs is to increase the strength of the experimental demonstration. The clarity of the results can be enhanced by showing that the intervention effects meet the requirements of more than one design. For example, an intervention may be evaluated in a multiple-baseline design across individuals. The intervention is introduced to subjects at different points in time and shows the expected pattern of results. The investigator may include a reversal phase for one or more of the subjects to show that behavior reverts to or near the original baseline level. Demonstration of the impact of the intervention may be especially persuasive, because requirements of multiple-baseline and ABAB designs were met.

The use of combined designs would seem to be an example of methodological overkill. That is, the design may include more features than necessary for clearly demonstrating an experimental effect. Yet combined designs are not merely used for experimental elegance. Rather, the designs often address genuine problems that are anticipated or actually emerge within an investigation.

The investigator may anticipate a problem that could compete with drawing valid inferences about intervention effects. For example, the investigator may select a multiple-baseline design (e.g., across behaviors) and may believe that altering one of the baselines might well influence other baselines. A combined design may be selected. If baselines are likely to be interdependent, which the investigator may have good reason to suspect, he or she may want to plan some other feature in the design to reduce ambiguities if requirements of the multiple-baseline design were not met. A reversal phase might be planned in the event that the effects of the intervention across the multiple baselines are not clear. Perhaps the reversal phase would not be used but would be kept as an option in case the effects from the multiple-baseline portion of the design are unclear. And if it were used, it would be possible to apply it to only one of the baselines.

Alternatively, in the discussion of changing-criterion designs, I mentioned that performance must match the changing criterion rather closely to provide a clear demonstration. Many investigators add a mini-reversal to show bidirectional changes in performance during the intervention phase. This combination gains the strength of features of both changing-criterion and ABAB designs, and it nicely overcomes the less-than-perfect correspondence of performance and criteria across subphases.

Combined designs do not necessarily result from plans that the investigator makes in advance of the investigation. Unexpected ambiguities often emerge over the course of the investigation. Ambiguity refers to the possibility that the extraneous events rather than the intervention may have led to change. Perhaps the extraneous events cannot be so easily ruled out in light of the data pattern. The investigator decides whether a feature from some other design might be added to clarify the demonstration. Combined designs often reflect the fact that the investigator is reacting to the data by invoking elements of different designs to resolve the ambiguity of the demonstration. The ability of single-case designs to respond to the data is a methodological strength of the approach. This ability is a strength from an applied perspective as well. Clients (students, patients, and children) are likely to benefit if changes in the intervention can be made based on emerging data.

Variations

Combined designs incorporate features from different designs. Perhaps the most commonly used combined design integrates features of ABAB and multiple-baseline designs. An excellent and still timely example of combining features of an ABAB design and a multiple-baseline design across behaviors was reported in an investigation designed to help an 82-year-old man who had suffered a massive heart attack (Dapcich-Miura & Hovell, 1979). After leaving the hospital, the patient was instructed to increase his physical activity, to eat foods high in potassium (e.g., orange juice and bananas), and to take medication.[1] A reinforcement program was implemented in which he received tokens (poker chips) each time he walked around the block, drank juice, and took his medication. The tokens could be saved and exchanged for selecting the dinner menu at home or for going out to a restaurant of his choice.

The results, illustrated in Figure 10.1, show that the reinforcement program was gradually extended to each of the behaviors over time in the usual multiple-baseline design. Also, baseline conditions were temporarily reinstated to follow an ABAB design. The results are quite clear. The data met the experimental criteria for each of the designs. With such clear effects of the multiple-baseline portion of the design, one might wonder why a reversal phase was implemented at all. Actually, the investigators were interested in evaluating whether the behaviors would be maintained without the intervention. Temporarily withdrawing the intervention resulted in immediate losses of the desired behaviors. There are procedures that can be used to maintain behavior (Kazdin, 2001); the reversal phase suggests that something is needed to accomplish that.

In another illustration, features of an ABAB design and multiple-baseline design were used to evaluate treatment for interventions for high school students with moderate mental retardation (IQs ranging from 40 to 53) (Hughes, Alberto, & Fredrick, 2006). The students worked in various settings (e.g., book warehouse, nursing home, YMCA) where they were assigned to complete the activities (e.g., emptying boxes, cleaning). Each student was identified because of problem behaviors (e.g., not starting work immediately, being off task or talking on multiple occasions within an observational session, asking questions repeatedly unrelated to one's work, not complying with requests, and others), which were individualized for each student. The intervention consisted of providing verbal instructions (prompts) to work (e.g., "It's time to start your work.") along with praise (e.g., "You are doing a good job." "Nice work—keep it up."). The effect of the intervention was tested in brief sessions before the intervention

---

[1] A diet high in potassium was encouraged because the patient's medication probably included diuretics (medications that increase the flow of urine). With such medication, potassium is often lost from the body and has to be consumed in extra quantities.

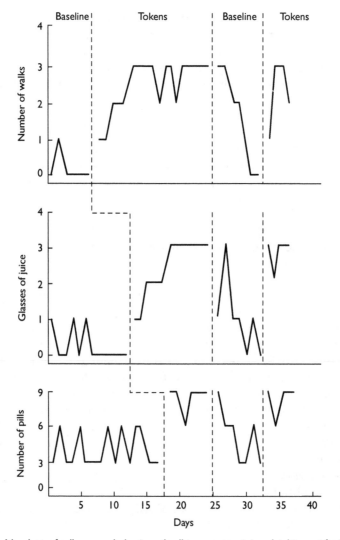

Figure 10.1. Number of adherence behaviors (walking, orange juice drinking, and pill taking) per day under baseline and token reinforcement conditions.   *(Source: Dapcich-Miura & Hovel, 1979.)*

phase was implemented more fully. That brief demonstration conveyed that prompts and praise definitely improved behavior, so these were implemented in the daily work regimen. The prompts and praise were prerecorded on a tape that each student was instructed to listen to while they were working. Each received a tape player; the statements on the tape were personalized with the name of each person and included a set of prompts or praise every 2 minutes. Data were gathered in the work setting for 20 minutes to evaluate the effects of the prompting procedure on reducing problem behavior. Sessions were conducted across two time periods (AM and PM) that served as a basis for the multiple-baseline part of the design.

Figure 10.2 shows the effects of the taped prompts to pay attention on problem behaviors. The intervention was introduced in the morning (AM) and afternoon (PM) time periods in a multiple-baseline design. As evident, the prompting procedure led to change when it was introduced to the first baseline (AM). No change was evident in the second baseline (with missing sessions of observation) until the intervention was introduced. Thus, the requirements of a multiple-baseline demonstration were met. In addition, there was a return-to-baseline (Baseline 2) and then a reintroduction of the intervention (Attention Prompts 2). The first four phases in the AM and the PM form an ABAB design. The final follow-up phase included the Attention Prompts phase again, 2 weeks later. The results of the demonstration are very clear. Problematic behaviors were reduced by the prompting and praise procedures. The next task, not the goal of this study, would be to see if the behaviors can be maintained without the intervention.

When ABAB and multiple-baseline designs are combined, there is no need to extend the reversal or return-to-baseline phase across all of the behaviors, persons, or situations. One example is the case of an intervention that focused on four institutionalized individuals (ages 9 to 21) with developmental disabilities (Favell, McGimsey, & Jones, 1980). The individuals ate their food rapidly, which is not merely socially unacceptable but can raise health problems (e.g., vomiting or aspiration). To develop slower eating, the investigators provided praise and a bite of a favorite food to residents who paused between bites. Verbal instructions and physical guidance (physical prompts) were used initially by stating "wait" and by manually guiding the persons to wait. These prompts were removed and praise was given less frequently as eating rates became stable.

A multiple-baseline design across two individuals illustrates the effects of the intervention, as shown in Figure 10.3. A reversal phase was used with the first person, which further demonstrated the effects of the intervention. The design is interesting to note because the reversal phase was only employed for one of the baselines (people). Because multiple-baseline designs are often selected to circumvent use of return-to-baseline phases, the partial application of a reversal phase in a combined design may be more useful than the withdrawal of the intervention across all of the behaviors, persons, or situations.

Although features of ABAB and multiple-baseline designs are commonly combined, other design combinations have been used as well. In the usual case, reversal phases are added to other designs, as noted in the chapters on the changing-criterion and multiple-treatment designs. Yet, other variations are easily found. A combined alternating-treatments and multiple-baseline design was illustrated in a report of a child with severe developmental disability and who engaged in self-injurious behavior (Wacker et al., 1990). The primary question was whether making requests of the child would influence the amount of self-injurious behavior. In the active demands or request of the child, the child was asked specifically to participate in an activity; in the passive demand condition, the child was not asked but was allowed to engage in activities on his own. The two demand conditions were the "treatments" in an alternating-treatments design and were administered at different times each session. No baseline was included, in part because demanding conditions were already in place and hence there might be no "true" baseline without some demand condition already going on. The example begins with a comparison of two interventions without baselines.

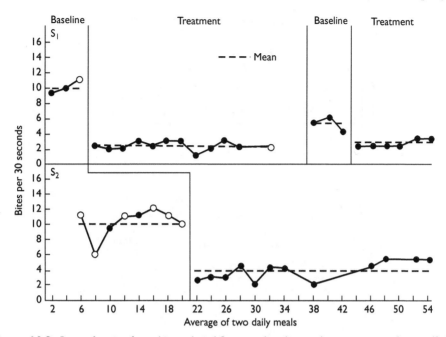

Figure 10.3. Rate of eating for subjects I and 2 across baseline and treatment conditions. (Solid data points represent data from two daily meals; open data points represent data from a single meal.)   *(Source: Favell, McGimsey, & Jones, 1980.)*

Figure 10.4 shows that self-injurious behavior was higher in the passive than in the active condition in each of the four contexts. In an alternating-treatments design, the more or most effective intervention is often implemented in the final phase. The figure shows that the active demand condition was introduced in the final phase and in the fashion of a multiple-baseline design across different activities. Self-injury remained low once active demands were used for all observation periods, and this is evident across each of the baselines as the active-only demands phase was introduced. This is a strong demonstration of an intervention effect without any baseline.

Problems and Considerations
The use of combined designs can greatly enhance the clarity of intervention effects in single-case designs. Features of different designs complement each other, so that the weaknesses of any particular design are not likely to interfere with drawing valid inferences. For example, it would not be a problem if behavior does not perfectly match a criterion or range of criteria in a changing-criterion design if that design also includes components of a multiple-baseline or ABAB design; nor would it be a problem if each behavior did not show a change when and only when the intervention was introduced in a multiple-baseline design if intervention effects were clearly shown through the use of a return-to-baseline phase. Thus, within a single demonstration, combined designs provide different opportunities for showing that the intervention is responsible for the change.

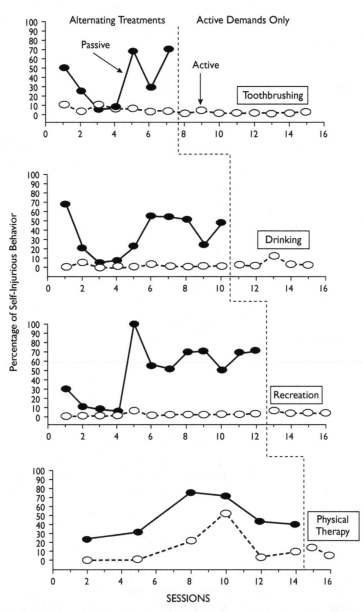

Figure 10.4. Self-injurious behavior in a design that combines alternating-treatments and multiple-baseline features. Passive and active demands were made of the child to evaluate their impact on self-injury (phase 2); active demands were associated with lower self-injury and were provided for all observation periods in the second phase. This second phase was introduced in a multiple-baseline fashion across different types of activities and contexts. Self-injury remained at the low rate achieved during the period in which active demands was compared to passive demands. *(Source: Wacker et al., 1990.)*

Most combined designs consist of adding a reversal or return-to-baseline phase to another type of design. A reversal phase can clarify the conclusions that are drawn from multiple-baseline, changing-criterion, and multiple-treatment designs. Interestingly, when the basic design is an ABAB design, components from other designs are often difficult to add to form a combined design if they are not planned in advance. In an ABAB design, components of multiple-baseline or multiple-treatment designs may be difficult to include, because special features ordinarily included in other designs (e.g., different baselines or observation periods) are required. On the other hand, it may be possible to use changing criteria during the intervention phase of an ABAB design to help demonstrate control over behavior.

The advantages of combined designs bear some costs. The problems or concerns from each of the constituent designs can emerge. For example, in a commonly used combined ABAB and multiple-baseline design, the investigator has to contend with the disadvantages of reversal phases (from an ABAB design) and with the possibility of extended baseline phases for behaviors that are the last to receive the intervention (from a multiple-baseline design). These potential problems do not interfere with drawing inferences about the intervention, because in one way or another a causal relationship can be demonstrated. However, practical considerations may introduce difficulties in meeting criteria for both of the designs. Indeed, such considerations often dictate the selection of one design (e.g., multiple baseline) over another (e.g., ABAB). Given the range of options available within a particular type of design and the combinations of different designs, it is not possible to state flatly what disadvantages or advantages will emerge in a combined design.

In combining designs, I have mentioned combinations of ABAB with other designs. In Chapter 6, where ABAB designs were first introduced, I noted that one reason the design may not be appropriate in many clinical, educational, and institutional settings is precisely because of the reversal phase and suspending the benefits of treatment for purposes of the design. There is an option that has not received sufficient attention in combined designs, namely, the use of the mini-reversal phase, as I called them in discussion of changing-criterion designs. In these latter designs, the criterion for performance is made increasingly more stringent, in keeping with the core feature of the designs. Investigators occasionally make a mini-reversal in which the intervention is not withdrawn, but rather for a brief period the criterion is made less stringent. This is a reversal that allows demonstration of a change in direction of performance as the criterion is made more *and* less stringent across subphases of the changing-criterion design.

Mini-reversal phases have two distinct advantages. First, they are reversal phases and accomplish the purposes of such phases as they are used in ABAB designs (i.e., describe, predict, and test prior predictions) in keeping with the logic of single-case designs. Second, the reversal is not complete in the sense of a return or hoped for return-to-baseline levels of performance. In fact, the change in criterion in a mini-reversal still has performance at a level of improvement well above baseline levels. Thus one does not withdraw treatment or eliminate the gains by a complete suspension of the intervention. The mini-reversals of changing-criterion designs might be the first choice of investigators seeking to draw on the logic and benefits of an ABAB design in using a combined design.

DESIGN ADDITIONS TO EXAMINE TRANSFER OF
TRAINING AND RESPONSE MAINTENANCE

The discussions of designs in previous chapters have focused primarily on techniques to evaluate whether an intervention was responsible for change. Typically, the effects of an intervention are replicated in some way in the design to demonstrate that the intervention rather than extraneous factors produced the results. Early in the development of effective behavior-change techniques (e.g., in the 1960s), the priority obviously was on showing that change could be obtained in several areas pertinent to work in clinics, schools (e.g., in education and special education), hospitals (medical and psychiatric), institutions for various populations (e.g., individuals with developmental disability, pervasive developmental disorders), the community (e.g., use of energy in the home, wearing seat belts while driving), and many others (Kazdin, 2001). The priority has not changed. It is still the case that most programs in the schools, rehabilitation settings, and juvenile and adult justice systems are not evaluated empirically and not evidence based. Thus, we still need evaluations to show that much of what we are doing leads to change and does not harm.

That said, for many interventions evidence has accumulated that changes can be achieved with children, adolescents, and adults in the diverse settings in which they function (e.g., at home, at school, work, and in the community) (e.g., Austin & Carr, 2000; Cooper et al., 2007). As the ability to change behavior became well documented, priority shifted to the obvious next questions: If behavior can be changed, can we get those changes to extend to other situations and settings (referred to as *transfer of training*), and can we get the behaviors to continue over time even after the intervention has been withdrawn (referred to as *response maintenance*)? There are procedures to accomplish both in terms of techniques for developing change (see Cooper et al., 2007; Kazdin, 2001). The investigation of transfer of training and response maintenance can be facilitated by several design options, including the use of probe techniques and withdrawal of treatment, as discussed next.

Probes

Probes were introduced and illustrated earlier (Chapter 3) and were defined as the assessment of behavior on selected occasions, usually when no intervention is in place to alter or influence that behavior. Probes are commonly used to determine whether a behavior not focused on directly has changed over the course of the investigation. For example, a successful program may have helped a very shy and withdrawn child interact in the classroom under the careful control of a program implemented by the teacher, but do the changes carry over to the playground? Probe assessments can help answer the question. Because the intervention is not in effect during the periods or situations in which the probes are assessed, the data from probe assessment address the generality of behavior across responses and situations.

Consider probes as a design addition that can be applied to any of the single-case designs. We use this tool if we want to evaluate the spread of effects of our intervention, usually to other situations, but this could also include other behaviors of the same individual. Probes could also be used to evaluate change over time by conducting an assessment occasionally at separate points over the course of follow-up, although this is less often their use.

I mentioned in the discussion of multiple-baseline designs that occasionally the intervention might be applied to one behavior (individual or situation) and that the change might spread to other behaviors even before the intervention is applied to them. In a multiple-baseline design across two or more situations, the clarity of the demonstration depends on showing that change occurred when and only when the intervention was introduced and not before. The generality of change can be an obstacle in versions of the design. In most situations, we want transfer of the behavior to other situations. We change behavior in one classroom, but we also want the changes to transfer or extend to other classrooms as needed; we train a child to say "thank you" when a relative provides a birthday gift, but we want "thank yous" to extend well beyond those occasions and beyond relatives. Probes can be used to sample behavior outside of the situation in which an intervention is applied to see if there is generality of the behavior.

Probes have been used to evaluate different aspects of generality. Typically, the investigator trains a particular response and examines whether the response occurs under slightly different conditions from those included in training or at different times. The use of probes was nicely illustrated in a study designed to increase bicycle helmet use among middle school students (Van Houten, Van Houten, & Malenfant, 2007). Approximately 70% of children age 5 to 14 ride bicycles. Annually, several hundred children are killed, and over 40,000 are injured by bicycle accidents. Head injuries are the chief cause of hospital admissions and death. Bicycle helmet wearing reduces the risk of death and injury by over 85%.

In this study, the goal was to increase helmet use among children who commuted by bike to school. Adult and peer observers were trained to observe helmet use daily, including whether the helmet was worn and worn correctly (e.g., buckled snugly, buckled in the correct place). As students left school, observers recorded the students who were wearing helmets and this was converted to a percentage of riders. After baseline, the intervention consisted of having an assembly where instructions about the use of helmets was provided, goal setting by the group (what percentage should they aim for), and posting the percentage of correct helmet use each week in the school cafeteria and school entrance. Also, students were told that if they met their goal, there would be a party (with pizza, ice cream, and small prizes).

The intervention was evaluated in a multiple-baseline design across three schools, and the results are presented in Figure 10.5. Probes were used to evaluate the extent to which helmet use was carried out at locations other than the school where the primary program and observations had been conducted. Locations were selected approximately one-half mile from the school where most students needed to pass on their way home. This was referred to as the distance probe (because it was some distance from the school). In addition, generalization probes were included to see if helmet use extended to the ride *to* school. (Recall that the program was based on whether students wore helmets on their way home.) The multiple-baseline data suggest that the intervention was responsible for change. Perhaps the third school is slightly ambiguous because there appeared to be a slight trend toward improvement at the end of baseline. Even so, the overall pattern supports the effects of the intervention. Both the distance probes (diamonds in the figure) and the generalization probes for the morning period (triangles) indicated that behavior during the probe assessment was consistent with

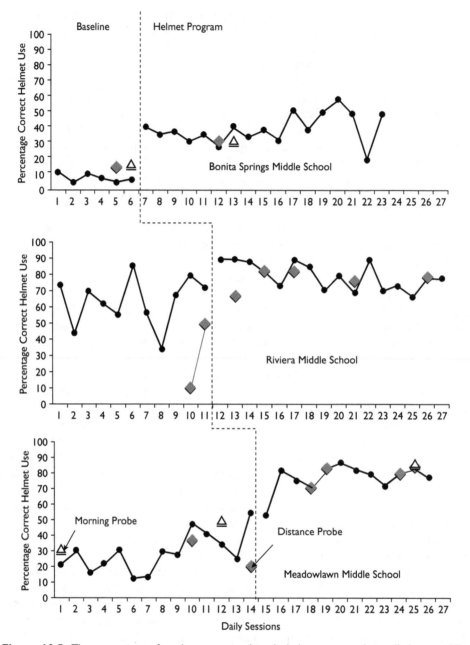

Figure 10.5. The percentage of students wearing bicycle helmets correctly at all three middle schools. The last 4 days of the helmet program at Riviera were after the party, as was the last day of the helmet program at Meadowlawn. Gray diamonds show the percentage of helmet use during the distance probes taken after school. Open triangles show the percentage of helmet use during the morning probes.   *(Source: Van Houten et al., 2007.)*

the behavior during the time the children left school. Helmet use when leaving school was very similar to helmet use farther away from school and in coming to school even though neither of these was specifically included in the program.

The use of probes represents a relatively economical way of evaluating the generality of responses across a variety of conditions. The use is economical, because assessment is conducted only on some occasions rather than on a continuous (e.g., daily) basis. An important feature of probe assessment is that it provides a preview of what can be expected beyond the conditions of training. Often training is conducted in one setting (e.g., classroom) with the hope that it will carry over to other settings (e.g., playground, home). Probes can provide assessment of performance across settings and yield information on the extent to which generalization occurs. If generalization does occur, this should be evident in probe assessment. If generalization does not occur, the investigator can then implement procedures designed to promote generality and can evaluate their effects through changes on the probe assessment.

Graduated Withdrawal of the Intervention

Evaluating whether behavior change *transfers* to other settings and conditions is nicely handled by probe designs. Of equal interest is evaluating whether behavior is maintained after the program is terminated. A component that can be added to the design is a graduated withdrawal of the intervention to evaluate maintenance of behavior.

The study or interest of maintaining behavior after withdrawing treatment seems to conflict with a core design we have discussed, namely, the ABAB design. We expect (and methodologists long for) return-to-baseline levels of behavior once the intervention (B) is withdrawn and there is a return-to-baseline (second A) phase. Of course, for the sake of the client and for all clients to whom our interventions might be applied, we want behavior to be maintained. When we change performance in the classroom with a temporary intervention for a child or the class as a whole we want the effects to continue after removing the intervention. As mentioned earlier, we might train a child to say "thank you" by praising this early in life. We certainly want "thank you" to continue (be maintained) long after our intervention has ended, and long after the child is out of the home.

In many programs, the intervention is withdrawn abruptly, either during an ABAB design or after the investigation is terminated. As might be expected, under such circumstances behaviors often revert to or near baseline levels. The rapidity of the return of behavior to baseline levels may in part be a function of the manner in which the intervention is withdrawn. Short intervention periods (e.g., a few days) and abruptly returning to baseline conditions would be expected to lead to abrupt loss of behavioral gains. Under these circumstances, the behaviors have not been allowed to occur often, to move toward actions that are routine, or possibly maintained by the everyday environment. Clearly we want intervention effects to be maintained. Graduated withdrawal of the intervention can be added to the design to assess whether responses are maintained. As with probes, this is an element that can be added to any design. After the intervention effects have been demonstrated unambiguously, withdrawal procedures can be added to evaluate response maintenance (see Rusch & Kazdin, 1981).

As an illustration, in one program eight children (ages 6 to 8) were identified and referred to a special classroom for their oppositional, aggressive, and antisocial behavior (Ducharme, Folino, & DeRosie, 2008). An intervention referred to as "error-less acquiescence training" was used to develop social skills. The authors developed acquiescence in the children (e.g., flexibility in responding to peers, sharing, taking turns, going along with someone else's ideas, letting others go first, and others) with the notion that this would be a keystone skill, that is, a behavior that when developed would be associated with a broad range of other desirable behaviors not specifically developed. Training consisted of gradually introducing conditions associated with the problem behavior, moving to increasingly challenging situations, and providing reinforcement for managing these situations. Training was conducted within the classroom in a special area where a skill was taught. The eight children were taught in two groups of four. Observers recorded prosocial and antisocial behaviors, cleaning up (putting away toys), and acquiescing. Observations were made in the classroom, and training was introduced in a multiple-baseline design across the two groups of children.

The intervention phase consisted of developing acquiescence and then gradually withdrawing the intervention procedures. During the intervention phase, training was conducted (Phase 1) in which there was discussion of the skill, incorrect and correct modeling of the skill (with discussion), and role playing. The skills were part of acquiescence and included behaviors mentioned previously (e.g., sharing, taking turns). Children had the opportunity to play as part of the session and received prompts, feedback, and praise for use of the skills. The intervention was gradually withdrawn. In Phase 2, the amount of instruction was reduced; the discussion and modeling of the incorrect skills was dropped and modeling of the correct behavior was decreased over this phase. Role playing was the only training component that remained. Yet, during the play activity part of the sessions, prompts and other components of Phase 1 continued. In Phase 3, all instructional components including role playing were dropped, and other features such as prompts, feedback, and reinforcement during play were dropped. The final phase of the study essentially was a return to baseline.

Figure 10.6 presents the data for changes in the frequency of antisocial behavior. As the figure shows, the intervention was introduced in a multiple-baseline design across the children (two groups). The effects are clear in showing that the antisocial behaviors decreased when the intervention was introduced and not before. (Data are not presented here for developing acquiescence behaviors, prosocial behaviors, and cleaning up, which also showed this pattern.) Withdrawal of the intervention during the phases of the intervention phase was complete in the final phase, namely a return to baseline. For all but one or two of the children, antisocial behavior was maintained at the low level achieved during treatment.

This is an excellent demonstration insofar as the design established that the intervention led to change (multiple-baseline design). The investigators wanted to develop and maintain the behaviors, so the intervention was gradually withdrawn. The return-to-baseline phase did not show a reversal. One was not needed for the design. Rather this was a test of how to maintain the behavior. When an ABAB design is used, there is a need to show a reversal. In such designs, the second B phase is one in which the intervention is faded or gradually withdrawn. For example, exposure and reinforcement were used to overcome a needle phobia of an 18-year-old adolescent diagnosed with Type 2 diabetes, autism, and mental retardation (Shabani & Fisher, 2006). The person had not allowed others to draw the blood necessary for the monitoring of insulin,

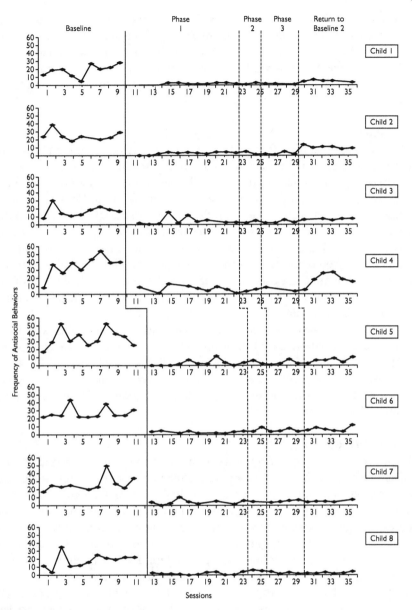

Figure 10.6. Frequency of antisocial behaviors across baseline, intervention, and return-to-baseline phases. The intervention was evaluated in a multiple-baseline design across children (divided into two groups). The intervention implemented in Phase 1 was then gradually faded or withdrawn.   *(Source: Ducharme et al., 2008.)*

for a period of more than 2 years. In an ABAB design, the intervention was shown to reduce his avoidance in the testing procedure. Strong effects were demonstrated in the ABA portion of the design. Then a lengthy second B phase was used to fade the procedure. As the intervention was gradually withdrawn the behavior was maintained at high levels. A 2-month follow-up indicated that blood could be drawn at home with no problems.

General Comments

Generalization of intervention effects across situations and maintenance of these effects over time reflect important substantive issues in any area of intervention research. I highlight design opportunities to study these. Probes and withdrawal of interventions seem to depart from critical design features I have emphasized. Continuous assessment is essential in single-case designs. Probes represent strategic use of noncontinuous assessment to answer questions about generalization of effects across situations as well as behaviors. Similarly, withdrawal of interventions has been discussed as a reversal phase where one expects a return of behavior to baseline levels. Yet, return-to-baseline phases sometimes are used to evaluate maintenance. Gradually withdrawing an intervention is a strategy that allows for a return to baseline with the expectation that behavior will be maintained.

As with other designs and other features, probes and withdrawal phases are tools to add to single-case evaluation. Each is an element that can be incorporated into specific designs. However, neither is a substitute for the requirements of a design. The investigator demonstrates change and the effects of the intervention in the usual way. These other components are superimposed on that demonstration to address questions of generalization or maintenance.

BETWEEN-GROUP DESIGNS

Traditionally, research in psychology, education, medicine, counseling, and other scientific disciplines in which interventions are evaluated focuses on comparing different groups. This is research in the tradition of quantitative research in which there is null hypothesis testing and statistical evaluation of the data. I refer to the studies as traditional between-group designs here to emphasize that major comparisons are made between or among groups receiving different interventions or intervention and control conditions. I use "between-group" because "group design" alone might not convey the point. Many "single-case" studies use groups of individuals (e.g., an entire classroom or community) in which case the group is combined and counted as a "single case." (One has to forego terminological purity to even enter the door to methodology. Between-group research—must it be about just two groups? When there are three groups, should that not be "among-group research"?)

In the simplest between-group study, one group receives an intervention and another group does not. Participants are assigned to groups randomly. When interventions are compared and evaluated (e.g., educational program, psychotherapy, chemotherapy), this basic design is referred to as a randomized controlled trial (RCT), as mentioned earlier in the book. The random assignment of participants to conditions increases the likelihood that the groups are equivalent on potentially critical variables that may relate to outcome as well as on the measures that are to be used to evaluate the intervention. Differences at the end of the study are more likely to be due to intervention effects than to pre-existing characteristics of the groups. Traditional between-group designs, their variations, and unique methodological features and problems have been described in numerous sources (e.g., Kazdin, 2003; Rosenthal & Rosnow, 2007; Shadish, Cook, & Campbell, 2002) and are not elaborated here. I mention between-group studies because they are often used in combination with single-case designs. Hence it is useful to discuss the contribution of between-group methodology to single-case designs.

Utility of Between-group Designs in Relation to Intervention Research

Between-group designs often provide important information that is not easily obtained or is not obtained in the same way as it is in single-case designs. Between-group methodology provides alternative ways to gather information of applied interest and provides an important way to replicate findings obtained from research using the subjects as their own controls.

Between-group research is well suited to several types of questions in relation to interventions (e.g., treatment, educational, rehabilitation, school-based prevention programs). Table 10.1 highlights these briefly, and each is discussed here. First, between-group comparisons are especially useful when the investigator is interested in *comparing two or more treatments*. Difficulties occasionally arise in comparing different treatments with the same subject. Difficulties are obvious if the investigator is interested in comparing interventions with theoretically discrepant or conflicting rationales (e.g., family therapy, individual therapy). One treatment would appear to contradict or undermine the rationale of the other treatment, and the credibility of the second treatment would be in question. Even if two treatments are applied that appear to be consistent, their juxtaposition in different phases for the same subject may be difficult. As already discussed, when two or more treatments are given to the same subjects, multiple-treatment interference is a methodological risk, that is, the effects of one treatment may be influenced by other treatment(s). Multiple-treatment interference is a concern if treatments are implemented in different phases (e.g., as in variations of ABCABC designs) or are implemented in the same phase (e.g., as in multiple-treatment designs). Comparison of treatments between groups provides an evaluation of each intervention without the possible influence of the other.

Table 10.1 Key Contributions of Between-Group Research

Between-group designs have special strengths in evaluating interventions. Group studies are particularly well suited for:

- Comparing the effects of two or more interventions;
- Identifying the magnitude of change relative to no intervention;
- Examining the prevalence or incidence of a particular condition or disorder;
- Evaluating the change and course of functioning over extended time periods;
- Evaluating correlates (concurrent features), risk factors (correlates that predict), and protective factors (correlates that attenuate or moderate the influence of risk factors);
- Testing the feasibility and generality of implementing interventions across multi-sites;
- Evaluating moderators and factors that may interact (statistically) with an intervention; and
- Evaluating mediators and mechanisms, that is, processes that may account for or explain how changes come about.

See text for terminology embedded within this list.

A second contribution of between-group methodology to applied research is to provide information about the *magnitude of change* between groups that do and do not receive the intervention. Often the investigator is not only interested in demonstrating that change has occurred but is also interested in measuring the magnitude of change in relation to persons who have yet to receive the intervention. Magnitude is often evaluated in research in terms of effect size, a measure of impact of the intervention in standard deviation units in which intervention and non-intervention groups are compared.[2] Also, one can estimate magnitude by noting and comparing the percentage of individuals in each group that meet some predetermined and meaningful criterion. For example, in psychological and medical research, two such measures might be percentage of treated individuals, relative to controls, who were free from all symptoms of panic disorder by the end of treatment or years later or who survived for 5 years without any recurrence of cancer, respectively. Essentially, a no-treatment group provides an estimate of these outcomes that occur without intervention, and that is a very much needed baseline comparison against which the performance of the intervention group is evaluated.

A third contribution is to *identify the rates of dysfunction* or other characteristics in the population. For example, studies that are designed to assess prevalence rates (how many people have a particular condition such as a disease or psychiatric disorder) and incidence rates (how many new cases with the condition emerge in a given period) are often large-scale group studies. Group studies and large-scale studies that sample broadly to represent diverse types of individuals are needed. From that information, analyses can identify subgroups as especially likely or unlikely to develop a condition.

A fourth contribution of between-group research is to study *changes over extended period of time* (e.g., decades). Longitudinal studies often delineate groups (e.g., at risk or not at risk for some adverse mental or physical health outcome in adulthood; or those with and without preacademic skills before they enter school) and follow them for decades to identify and understand factors over the course of development that may predict the outcome or avoidance of the outcome.

A fifth contribution is *elaborating features associated (correlated) with a disorder or condition of interest*. This is accomplished concurrently by examining what characteristics go together in a large population. For example, children who have difficulties with math and reading have what other characteristics (e.g., in other academic subjects, in social behavior, in family characteristics)? In addition, the characteristics can be studied prospectively in a sample to identify early characteristics (e.g., in the home, neighborhood, prenatally) that correlate with some later outcome of interest (e.g., psychiatric disorder, genius, achievement). Early predictors of later outcomes are called "risk factors" (even when the outcomes are positive). Also, a group known to be at risk for

---

[2] *Effect size* (ES) refers to the magnitude of the difference between two (or more) conditions or groups and is expressed in standard deviation units. For the case in which there are two groups in the study, effect size equals the differences between means, divided by the standard deviation:

$$ES = \frac{m_1 - m_2}{s}$$

where m_1 and m_2 are the sample means for two groups or conditions (e.g., intervention and control groups), and s equals the pooled standard deviation for these groups.

some outcome (e.g., because of exposure to cigarette smoking in utero or to violence in childhood) is often studied to identify who does not later show the expected outcome. These correlates are called "protective factors" (even though they are not known to really have a direct role in protecting). Concurrent or prospective characteristics (e.g., risk and protective factors) studied in a large group or population are all correlates or associated features; they can lead to a deeper understanding of important pathways to or processes toward an outcome.

A variation of correlational research is worth highlighting in passing. This work focuses on naturalistic interventions that are not under the control of the experimenter. Between-group comparisons are exceedingly important to address questions about differences between or among groups that are distinguished on the basis of circumstances out of the experimenter's control. Such research can address such important applied questions as: Does the consumption of cigarettes, alcohol, or coffee contribute to certain diseases? Do some family characteristics predispose children to psychiatric disorders? Does television viewing have an impact on children? These are correlational longitudinal studies that require one or more groups of individuals.

A sixth use of between-group methodology for applied research arises when multisite studies are used to evaluate *generality of findings across settings*. With large-scale investigations, several settings and locations may be employed to evaluate a particular intervention or to compare competing interventions. Because of the magnitude of the project (e.g., several schools, cities, hospitals), some of the central characteristics of single-case methodology may not be feasible. For example, in large-scale applications across schools, resources may not permit such luxuries as continuous assessment on a daily basis over time. By virtue of costs of assessment, observers, and travel to and from schools, assessment may be made at a few points in time (e.g., pretreatment, posttreatment, and follow-up). In such cases, between-group research may be the more feasible strategy because it requires fewer resources for assessment.

A seventh contribution of between-group research is to *examine moderators* or moderating variables. *Moderators* are those variables that may interact with the intervention to produce an outcome. A moderator is any variable that influences the magnitude or direction of the relation between the intervention and the outcome. For example, if the intervention is more effective with younger rather than older children or with males rather than females, then age and sex, respectively, would be moderators. Moderators are also discussed as statistical interactions in which the effect of one variable (e.g., treatment) depends on the level or characteristic of another variable (e.g., ethnicity). Group studies can evaluate these interactions in ways that are not readily available in single-case research. For example, being physically abused as a child does not greatly increase the likelihood of engaging in criminal or antisocial behavior (e.g., aggression, stealing) as an adult. However, if one is physically abused and also has a subtle genetic characteristic (polymorphism) that affects a receptor of a brain neurotransmitter, the likelihood of criminal and antisocial behavior in adulthood is greatly increased (Caspi et al., 2002; Kim-Cohen et al., 2006).[3] That is, the effects of

---

[3] The genetic characteristic (polymorphism) relates to the enzyme monoamine oxidase A (MAO-A) which metabolizes serotonin. Other human (e.g., natural mutations) and non-human animal research (e.g., genetic studies) has shown this enzyme to be implicated in aggressive behavior. In

child abuse on later antisocial behavior are moderated by a genetic characteristic. This research requires between-group designs to identify individuals with and without out the various combinations of the characteristics of interest.

Studying the separate and combined effects of two or more interventions is another example of moderator research. The investigator may be interested in studying two or more variables simultaneously. For example, the investigator may wish to examine the effects of feedback and reinforcement alone and in combination. Two levels of feedback (feedback vs. no feedback) and two levels of reinforcement (contingent praise vs. no praise) may be combined to produce four different combinations of the variables. Four groups are included in the design; each group receives one of the four different combinations. Between-group research is required to study such combinations. In single-case research it is difficult to explore interactions of the interventions with other variables to ask questions about generality of intervention effects, that is, the extent to which intervention effects extend across other variables.

A final contribution of between-group intervention research is the study of *mediators and mechanisms* of change (Kazdin, 2007). In our research and applications, we begin with the idea that the intervention will be effective but also have an underlying view as to why it will exert impact; we have a "small theory," as this is sometimes called (Lipsey, 1996). That theory of what might be going on influences what we are to measure. That is, we can test our small theory rather than just assume why the intervention works by including measures of the processes we consider to be responsible for change. The focus on mediators and mechanisms of change directly reflect this interest. *Mediator* refers to an intervening process that may explain why the effect occurred. Showing that some intervening process (e.g., changes in cognitions) is correlated with therapeutic change and that therapeutic change is not likely to occur without these changes would be an example of a mediator. Establishing a mediator is based on statistical relation between some intervening process and some outcome. A mediator does not necessarily explain precisely how some outcome comes about. *Mechanism* refers to a specific process that shows more precisely how the change comes about. A mechanism reflects a deeper level of knowledge by showing not only that change depends on the presence of an intervening process but also how that process unfolds to produce an outcome. Between-group research has been quite useful in studying mediators and mechanisms.

It is useful to highlight several of the strengths of between-group research. At the same time, the danger is to imply or foster the belief that one design strategy can answer a particular question and the other design strategy cannot. This might be true in a

---

[3] (Continued) the initial demonstration, Caspi et al. (2002) found that abused children with a genetic polymorphism related to the metabolism of serotonin have much higher rates of antisocial behaviors than those without this polymorphism. Among boys with the genetic characteristic and maltreatment, 85% developed some form of antisocial behavior (diagnosis of Conduct Disorder, personality assessment of aggression, symptoms of adult personality disorder, or court conviction of violent crime) by the age of 26. Individuals with the combined allele and maltreatment constituted only 12% of the sample but accounted for 44% of the cohort's violent convictions. Further research has replicated and extended the finding by noting that parent neglect as well as abuse in conjunction with the polymorphism increases risk for conduct problems and violence (Foley et al., 2004; Jaffee et al., 2005).

given instance, but the contributions of different designs are more nuanced. Consider an important case in point.

There has been increased interest in understanding mediators and mechanisms of change, as highlighted above as a contribution of between-group research. To understand mediators, usually a group study is done in which there is pretreatment measure (e.g., anxiety among patients referred for that), some measure in the middle of treatment (e.g., thought processes that might be considered by the investigator to be responsible for, i.e., mediate, therapeutic change), and posttreatment measures. Stated generally, the goal of the study is to see if changes in the thought processes might be the basis of improvements at the end of treatment. A variety of statistical tests are applied in an effort to see if patients improve (in anxiety) only if they show these cognitive changes (thought processes). Between-group studies are the standard way of conducting research on mediators (see Kazdin, 2007). The statistical tests used in such research require a group (e.g., the treatment group in a treatment group and no-treatment group study) to evaluate the statistical relation of cognitive processes and changes in anxiety. It is near impossible to identify single-case experiments in applied settings that have studied mediators.

Consider for a moment the following. Single-case designs cannot only study mediators, but bring unique and needed advantages. In group research, mediators (thought processes in the above example) are measured at a fixed and predetermined point in time or let us say even two points in time. So if there are 15 sessions of therapy the investigator may measure thought processes somewhere in the middle (e.g., session 8) or end (e.g., session 15) or perhaps at two places during treatment (e.g., session 5 and 20). The point of "when" does not matter for this discussion. Here is an enormous problem that group investigations of mediators encounter. The mediator of change for each person might well be changes in thought process. However, when that change occurs might be different for each individual. Your change in the putatively critical thought processes might be at session 5, mine at session 11. Your change might be rapid if we saw a graph of thought processes assessed continuously over time (e.g., each session). My changes might be gradual and slow. In short, in proposing a mediator of change investigators do not really believe that change in the mediator can be assessed at only one or two points and accurately capture each subject. The weakness of group studies in evaluating mediators is assuming there is a fixed point that is appropriate to assess the mediator. In fact, single-case designs can come to the rescue.

We need ongoing assessment of each subject to see the relation of the mediator to outcome. A mediator may show little or no relation to some outcome in a between-group study merely because the mediator was not assessed at the optimum point for each subject in the study. An assumption in the study is that a particular point adequately sampled the change in the mediator for all subjects. This assumption is almost certainly false. Mediators could be readily studied in single-case designs that allowed examination of the relation of the mediator-outcome for each subject and then that combined the data if some larger purpose would be served. Glossing over individual differences as if they did not exist can actually hamper identifying of mediators of change.

I use the point about mediators not to advocate, or not only to advocate, for the use of single-case designs in this context. Rather I wish to note that between-group research can evaluate many critical questions but these are not all unique to that research strategy. The mediator example might be a strong illustration of the point because mediators are rarely studied in single-case designs but would draw on one of the strengths of the designs, namely, continuous and ongoing assessment.

Illustrations of Between-group Designs

It is useful to illustrate between-group designs with a few key studies to convey several of the contributions they make. First, comparing different treatment or treatment and control conditions is often more feasible in a between-group study. Consider an example of interventions for cigarette smoking, an obviously significant health problem. All sorts of interventions have been tried and evaluated. One opportunity that exists for intervention is to have physicians advise their patients who smoke to stop smoking. What if physicians just told their patients to stop smoking? This seems very naïve as an intervention. We know fairly well that instructions, requests, understanding, insight, knowledge, and other interventions like this are generally very weak. By weak I mean they affect few people, produce variable effects, and are not among the more effective ways of changing behavior. All that said, it would be useful to know if comments from physicians to stop smoking would make a difference.

In the United States, the average physician visit is 12 to 15 minutes in duration. In controlled trials, patients who are cigarette smokers have been assigned randomly to receive or not receive an intervention that merely consists of statements to stop smoking from the physician or nurse. Two examples of these statements used in research are: (1) "I think it is important for you to quit tobacco use now," and (2) "As your clinician I want you to know that quitting tobacco is the most important thing you can do to protect your health." Comments like these have a small but reliable effect in leading to abstinence. Individuals who receive the message have a 2.5% greater abstinence rate than those assigned to no intervention. Although very brief comments (1 minute) are sufficient to achieve an effect, there is a dose–response relation. That is, the more time and advice lead to slightly greater abstinence rates (Fiore et al., 2000; Rice & Stead, 2008; Stead, Bergson, & Lancaster, 2008).

No doubt the intervention might be tested in single-case designs (e.g., multiple-baseline across doctors, clinics, and perhaps patients within a setting). However, the between-group study is well suited to the question because a large number of people are required to obtain an estimate of abstinence rates. Also, the key question requires a control group that gives the base rate of abstinence without any special physician intervention. The question of interest was nicely addressed between groups. Several between-group studies have replicated the effects of brief comments, and such comments have now become standard physical exam practice among physicians.

The advantage of between-group studies can be seen where there is interest in large-scale, multi-site evaluations of an intervention. Among the questions are the relative effectiveness of separate and combined interventions and the shorter- and longer-term effects of such interventions. For example, the largest study for treatments of child hyperactivity is the NIMH Multimodal Treatment Study of Children with Attention-Deficit/Hyperactivity Disorder (MTA Study). In seven sites, 579 children (ages 7 to 9) were included in a 14-month regimen of treatment (MTA Cooperative Group, 1999a, 1999b; Swanson et al., 2002). All children met diagnostic criteria for ADHD, the diagnostic category that includes excessive activity and impulsiveness in contemporary psychiatric diagnosis. The standard treatment is stimulant medication, which has been well studied and shown to decrease hyperactivity while the child is on medication. Behavioral management treatment has not been as effective. In this study, treatment conditions were compared that included: (1) medication management; (2) behavioral treatment involving parents, school, and child programs; (3) medication and behavioral treatment combined; and (4) treatment as usual in the community. Treatment as usual in the community consisted mostly of medication (for two-thirds of children) but did not include the careful management and titration of medication as did the medication management condition.

Among the key findings, participants in both the medication and the combined treatment showed greater improvement than those in the behavioral-treatment-only or treatment-as-usual groups. On core symptoms of ADHD, medication and combined treatments were no different. There was some superiority of the combined treatment in relation to non-ADHD symptoms and prosocial functioning (e.g., internalizing symptoms, prosocial skill at school, parent–child relations), but these were not strong. The pattern of results was similar up to 2 years later, after treatment had been terminated. This study illustrates several advantages of a between-group design including comparison of different treatment conditions (without the concern of multiple-treatment interference) and evaluation of treatment on a large scale and across many sites. Also, because of the large sample, subsequent reports could examine child characteristics (moderators) that might influence responsiveness to treatment.

A final example conveys the utility of between-group research in testing mechanisms of action in the context of intervention research. Background for this work stems from years of careful non-human animal research on mechanisms of learning and extinction of fear responses. Briefly, elimination of fear appears to depend on a particular receptor in the brain (N-methyl-D-aspartate in the amygdala) (see Davis, Myers, Chhatwal, & Ressler, 2006). Non-human animal research has shown that chemically blocking the receptor interferes with extinction and that making the receptor work better enhances the extinction process. The laboratory research has moved to psychotherapy trials for the treatment of anxiety. Exposure therapy, based on an extinction model, is one of the most well-studied treatments for anxiety. There are variations of the treatment, but the essential ingredient is repeated or extended contact with the anxiety-provoking stimuli. Such exposure leads to extinction, that is, the stimuli no longer evokes an anxiety reaction. Drawing on laboratory findings, investigators have evaluated whether manipulating the mechanism that influences extinction can be used to enhance the benefits of exposure-based treatment. Controlled trials have compared two forms of exposure therapy: the regular version of the therapy and that same version with use of a medication (D-cycloserine) that activates the receptor mentioned previously. Activation of the receptor would be expected to augment extinction of anxiety and improve the effectiveness of treatment. As expected, the enhanced exposure treatment is more effective, and this finding has now been replicated with samples seen for different types of anxiety including acrophobia (fear of heights), obsessive-compulsive disorder, and social anxiety (e.g., Hofmann et al., 2006; Kushner et al., 2007; Ressler et al., 2004; Wilhelm et al., 2008). These studies have been completed between-groups in RCTs in which some individuals received the enhanced intervention and others did not or they received exposure therapy with a placebo (to control for taking a medication and any expectancy that might invoke).

These illustrations highlight the very special contributions of between-group research, which has dimensions that cannot be readily addressed in single-case designs. More generally, between-group and single-case designs have their unique strengths but also share in the questions they can address. Design features from these different traditions are occasionally combined.

Illustrations of Single-case and Between-group Designs Combined

Between-group and single-case designs reflect different methodological approaches, but they occasionally are combined. There are many reasons to combine the designs. One would be to overcome the possibility of multiple-treatment interference when more than one intervention is provided for the same people. Between-group studies provide interventions to separate sets of individuals. Another reason is that between-group studies usually require many subjects (for statistical power) and sometimes not nearly enough subjects are available to detect a difference between conditions (e.g., see Kazdin & Bass, 1989). Single-case designs with continuous assessment (many assessments, few subjects) can be used here. Yet, combined designs can do more. Consider some examples of combined between-group and single-case designs.

An example of a combined between-group and single-case design focused on 10 individuals (ages 6 to 36) who were diagnosed with Tourette's syndrome (Azrin & Peterson, 1990). The disorder, considered to be neurologically based, consists of multiple motor and vocal tics such as head, neck, and hand twitching; eye rolling; shouting of profane words; grunting; repetitive coughing or throat clearing; or other utterances. The tics, which begin in childhood, usually are quite conspicuous. In this program, features of a between-group design and multiple-baseline design were combined. The 10 cases were assigned either to receive treatment or to wait for a 3-month period (waiting-list control group). The assignments were made on a random basis. Tics were assessed daily with recordings at home and periodically with videotapes of each person at the clinic. The treatment consisted of habit reversal, which includes several different behavior therapy treatments, such as being made more aware of the behavior, self-monitoring, relaxation training, and practicing a response that competes with the tic (i.e., is incompatible with the tic, such as contracting the muscles in a different way, or breathing in a way that prevents making certain sounds). Also, family members praised improved performance at home. Many of the components have been used as separate interventions for various problems.

The results are shown in Figure 10.7, which graphs the number of tics per hour at home and at the clinic for the treatment group and the waiting-list control group. The baseline phase for the waiting-list group is longer because of the wait period before treatment was given to them. Hence, the continuous observations over baseline and treatment also meet criteria for a multiple-baseline design (across groups). The results indicate that the intervention clearly showed marked impact on tics. This is important because Tourette's syndrome has not been effectively treated with various psychotherapies or pharmacological treatments. The demonstration is persuasive in large part because of the combination of multiple-baseline and group-design strategies. Would either design alone have been persuasive? Probably the multiple-baseline portion is clear, but in group research 10 cases is not enough to assign to even one group, let alone two. To detect differences between groups usually requires larger sample sizes

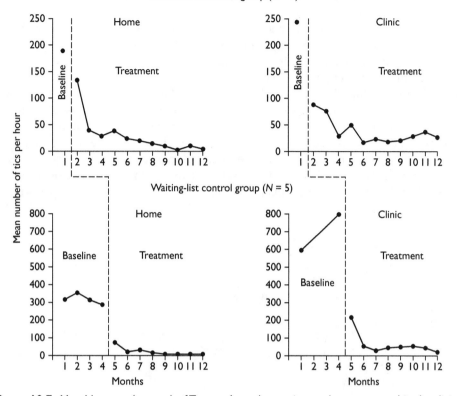

Figure 10.7. Monthly mean (average) of Tourette's syndrome tics per hour measured in the clinic and home settings for subjects in the immediate treatment (upper panel) and waiting-list (lower panel) groups. The data illustrate the combined multiple-baseline design across two groups: one group that received treatment immediately and one group that waited for the initial period.   *(Source: Azrin & Peterson, 1990.)*

(statistical power again). However, in this combined study, the group data provide very useful information about the likely changes over time without an intervention during the waiting period.

Another combined design evaluated a parenting program to prevent child abuse (Peterson et al., 2002). Women who had young children, who used physical discipline, and who were high in anger toward their children (self-report scale) participated. They were assigned randomly to receive either the 16-week program (that taught parent-management skills and anger control) or no treatment. Women in both groups completed daily diaries that included answering open-ended questions about what their children did and how they responded. No specific questions were asked about harsh punishment (slapping, pushing, screaming) or about whether the child's disruptive behavior was ignored or followed with time out from reinforcement, two of the many parenting skills that were trained. Observers coded the diaries to assess frequency of harsh punishment and use of better strategies (ignoring or time out). Eighty-one women (approximately 65% European American, 28% African American, and 7% other minorities) completed the study.

Figure 10.8 shows the continuous data on parent harsh discipline over the weeks of the study. Quite clearly, physical punishment declined in the group that received the training, as demonstrated in a between-group part of the design. Figure 10.9 adds to the information by showing the impact of training a parent in the use of time out. In this latter figure, baseline observations of the frequency of using time out were quite similar for intervention and nonintervention groups. At the point that training was introduced (vertical line) in this procedure for the intervention group, frequency of using time out increased. This single-case feature of the design closely resembles a multiple-baseline design across groups in which the intervention is introduced to one group (to one baseline) but not to the other. The results show that change in the use of time out occurred when the intervention was introduced and not before. In a complete multiple-baseline

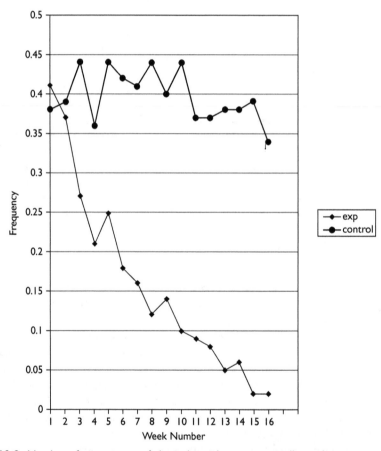

Figure 10.8. Number of occurrences of physical punishment reportedly used as a strategy of discipline by the mothers each day for the experimental (intervention) group (bottom line in the graph) and nonintervention control group (top line). The observations were made daily. However, the graph shows the mean for each week over the 16 weeks.   *(Source: Peterson et al., 2002.)*

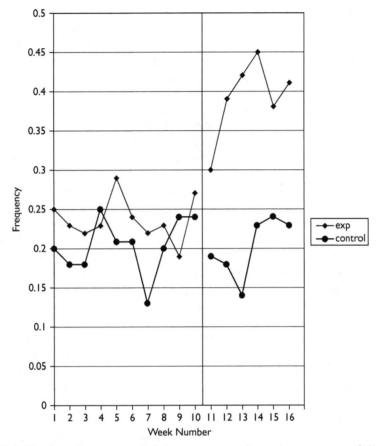

Figure 10.9. Number of occurrences of time out reportedly used as a strategy of discipline by the mothers each day for the experimental (intervention) and control groups. The vertical line indicates the point in which time out was trained as a parenting skill for the intervention group. At that point there is an increase in the use of time out for that group but not for the control group. The observations were made daily. However, the graph shows the mean for each week over the 16 weeks. *(Source: Peterson et al., 2002.)*

design, the intervention would have been introduced to the second group (baseline). Even without that, the effects are clear. The demonstration also resembles a multiple-treatment design. After baseline two conditions were evaluated (training in time out vs. no training). The figure shows that the two "treatments" (intervention, no-intervention) vary in their impact. Overall, elements of single-case design convey rather clearly that the intervention led to change. The continuous data allow one to see the progress over the course of training (Figure 10.8), which is not otherwise evident in the usual between-group design where only a pretest and posttest are used.

General Comments
Historically, between-group designs are often criticized by proponents of single-case research. Conversely, advocates of between-group research rarely acknowledge that

single-case research can make a contribution to science. Both positions are difficult to defend, are unnecessary, and ignore why we do research and what research design accomplishes. First, often alternative design methodologies are differentially suited to different research questions. Between-group designs appear to be particularly appropriate for larger scale investigations, for comparative studies, and for the evaluation of moderators. Single-case designs are especially useful in demonstrating the impact of interventions on individuals and in making decisions to improve intervention effects while the intervention is in place. Single-case designs also permit the experimental study of rare phenomena. Accumulating cases with unique or low-frequency problems so that they can be studied in between-group research is not feasible.

Second, on the many occasions in which both methodologies might address similar or identical questions (e.g., Does this intervention have any effect?), the yield may be different. In our own training and teaching of students, we have not conveyed in our presentation of research design and methodology more generally that the findings one obtains can vary as a function of assessment methods (of the same construct) as well as a function of the design. So, for example, we know that studying the phenomenon in longitudinal designs (group studies with the same cases studied over time) can yield findings that differ from those obtained in cross-sectional designs (group studies with different cases studied at a single point in time but with different participants representing the different age groups). If one is interested in characteristics of individuals at ages 5, 15, and 25, this could be studied by sampling three groups of people at these different ages (cross-sectional study) or by sampling a large group of 5-year-old children and measuring them at different ages (at age 5, 15, and 25) over time. Findings from such studies are often different, in part because the three different groups (cohorts) in the first study are exposed to many different influences (e.g., in the culture, in health care) and those influences are not the same when one group (5-year-olds) is followed over time. There are many other reasons but this conveys the point, namely, that different methods can have different yields—and often do (e.g., Aldwin & Gilmer, 2004; Chassin, Presson, Sherman, Montello, & McGrew, 1986). We want between-group designs and single-case designs *because* of the different facets of a phenomenon they may reveal. It is very informative when there are consistencies among findings that are studied with different methods. Also, when there are inconsistencies, this raises important questions about why. Answers to the why questions greatly enhance our understanding of phenomena.

There are unique virtues of each of the design strategies. Without drawing on different methodologies, one loses entire pockets of research. For example, virtually every school district, school, or classroom in the United States has some "program" designed to help students read, write, do better in some way, and prevent some problem (e.g., suicide, unprotected sex, the use of drugs). In almost every case, the program is not evaluated, not really known or shown to work, and cannot be evaluated if one has to wait for a between-group study and an RCT. However, many of these programs (within one classroom, one school) could be more easily evaluated in a design that did not require groups, larger numbers, and random assignment. A multiple-baseline across behaviors, children, or class periods is merely one set of viable options. Similarly, in the context of psychotherapy, most treatments used in practice are not evidence-based treatments, that is, shown from research to be effective, a topic warranting a separate book. Even if they were, we do not know in any given case whether a patient receiving such a treatment were to benefit. Single-case methods (e.g., ongoing assessment, probes) and designs can improve the quality of patient care and demonstration of change, which is not possible with the usual group research.

Overall, the issue of research is not a question of the superiority of one type of design over another. Different methodologies are means of addressing the overall goal, namely, understanding the influence of the variety of variables that affect functioning. Alternative design and data-evaluation strategies are not in competition but rather address particular questions in service of the overall goal.

SUMMARY AND CONCLUSIONS

Although single-case designs are usually implemented in the manner described in previous chapters, elements from different designs are frequently combined. *Combined designs* can increase the strength of the experimental demonstration. The use of combined designs may be planned in advance or decided on the basis of the emerging data. If the conditions of a particular design fail to be met or are not met convincingly, components from other designs may be introduced to improve the clarity of the demonstration. A common example might be a multiple-baseline design, where there is a little ambiguity about whether each behavior changed when and only when the intervention was introduced or in a changing-criterion design where there was a general improvement in behavior that sort of met the criterion changes but did not do so very persuasively. In each case, a mini-reversal in one of the baselines in a multiple-baseline design or a bidirectional criterion shift in a changing-criterion design could be improvised to clarify the demonstration.

Apart from combined designs, special features may be added to existing designs to evaluate whether or the extent to which intervention effects generalize or extend to responses, situations, and settings that are not included in training. *Probes* were discussed as a valuable tool to explore generality across responses and settings. With probes, assessment is conducted for responses other than those included in training or for the target response in settings where training has not taken place. Assessment can provide information about the extent to which training effects extend to other areas of performance. *Graduated withdrawal of the intervention* was also discussed as a way of evaluating maintenance of the intervention effects. The intervention is gradually withdrawn to see if behavior continues to be performed (maintained). Withdrawal can be graduated in many ways and may include reducing the components of the intervention or how it is implemented to resemble the conditions of everyday life. The goal is to remove the intervention completely while the behavior remains at the level achieved during the intervention phase.

Finally, the contribution of *between-group designs* to questions of applied research was discussed. Between-group designs are especially useful in comparing two or more treatments; identifying the magnitude of change relative to no treatment; examining the prevalence or incidence of a particular condition or disorder; evaluating the change and course of functioning over extended time periods; evaluating correlates, risk factors, and protective factors in relation to a characteristic or outcome of interest; testing the feasibility and generality of implementing interventions across multiple sites;

evaluating moderators and factors that may interact (statistically) with an intervention; and evaluating mediators and mechanisms that may account for or explain how changes come about. Between-group designs were discussed because they are often used in conjunction with single-case designs.

In general, the present chapter discussed some of the complexities in combining design strategies and adding elements from different methodologies to address applied questions. The combinations of various design strategies convey the diverse alternatives available in single-case research beyond the individual design variations discussed in previous chapters.

Quasi-Single-Case Experimental Designs

The previous chapters described single-case experimental designs. These are *true experiments*, which consist of investigations that permit maximum control over the independent variable or manipulation of interest. This control permits one to rule out or make very implausible threats to internal validity and to make causal statements about the impact of the intervention. The term "true experiment" has been defined by leading methodologists (and my mentors!) as an arrangement in which randomization is central (Campbell & Stanley, 1963; Cook & Campbell, 1979). Randomization is possible in both between-group and single-case research, as I have noted previously and will revisit. Randomization has a well-deserved respect in distributing possibly confounding variables across groups or conditions so they are less likely to bias results and let those threats to validity run freely and get into all sorts of trouble. Even with randomization, groups or conditions are not necessarily equivalent before the intervention or after if there is a loss of subjects (e.g., Hsu, 1989; Kazdin, 2003). Randomization in any design is never a guarantee that valid inferences can be drawn.

For the present chapter, if not more broadly, it is useful to consider all design arrangements on a continuum. I refer to this as a *continuum of confidence* in which the confidence reflects the extent to which one can be assured that the intervention was responsible for change. On the left side of the continuum, we can place the anecdotal case study in which skepticism, disbelief, and low confidence in the conclusions are generally well earned. On the right side of the continuum is an arrangement that allows a strong inference that the intervention was the reason that change occurred and that all or most of the threats to validity are not at all plausible in explaining the findings. In considering experiments of any kind, the emphasis must be on strength of the allowable conclusions rather than on any specific procedure that comprises the design. Randomization can contribute greatly to the right side of the continuum and has deservedly special status, as I have noted.

A true experiment is a study in which the arrangement is such that ambiguity of the finding is absolutely minimal. Most often randomization helps enormously, but it is not essential. Consider an ABABABAB design where the ideal pattern in the data and the describe, predict, and test functions of all the phases are met). There might not be randomization but the allowable inference about the intervention (B) is unusually strong and the best one can hope for in one study. (The salvation of science is replication and our confidence in a finding stems largely from multiple instances that it can be obtained.) As we see later, randomization can be part of many single-case designs (Kratochwill & Levin, in press) beyond my coverage of the procedure in the discussion of multiple-treatment designs. In any case, true experiments in the present context refer to demonstrations that permit the strongest possible inferences that empirical studies allow. In single-case research, true experiments refer to arrangements in which the investigator is able to control assessment occasions (e.g., over time, across subjects) and implementation and withdrawal of the intervention to meet the requirements of the design. The level of control is evident in presenting or withdrawing the intervention over time (e.g., ABAB designs) or across behaviors or participants (e.g., multiple-baseline designs) and so on for each of the other designs.

Quasi-experiments refer to those designs in which the conditions of true experiments are approximated (Campbell & Stanley, 1963).[1] Some facet of the study such as presentation, withdrawal, or alteration of the intervention is not readily under the control of the investigator. For example, an investigator may be asked to implement a reading program for students placed in a special education class. The investigator may be able to obtain a pretest assessment of reading levels of the students (one data point at pretreatment) but have no resources for continuous daily assessment of reading over time. Also, design features that make the arrangement a true experiment (withdrawal of the intervention as in an ABAB design or sequential implementation of the intervention in a multiple-baseline fashion) may not be feasible because of some practical or ethical consideration. The luxuries of a true experiment (whether between-group or single-case) are not possible. What can one do? A great deal. Quasi-experiments can provide very strong bases for drawing inferences; these designs, their logic, use, and application serve as the basis of the present chapter.

BACKGROUND

Why We Need Quasi-experiments
An initial question might be proposed: Why do we even need quasi-experimental designs, especially if we know from the outset that we will not be able to draw strong causal inferences? Consider extremes of methodological practices as two ends of a continuum. On one end, say the right side of the continuum, we have true experiments in all their pristine elegance with careful assessment, and careful control over the intervention and its presentation and withdrawal. On the left side of the continuum, we have the anecdotal case study, a narrative description of what happened (in therapy for an individual, in the classroom for a teacher, or with a diet for a person). The assessment is not systematic or replicable, and the intervention was not well-described, controlled, or presented in a way that would permit demonstration of change. It is rare that inferences can be drawn from such case studies. Quasi-experiments serve as a useful way of conceptualizing the middle ground of the continuum. These include all of the arrangements that might be developed or used to draw inferences.

As to why we need them, consider the following. The intervention world is filled with "programs." These are extremely well-intended interventions to help people in relation to physical health, mental health, education, rehabilitation, summer camp for children with all sorts of goals, the elderly, and so on. In the United States, for example,

---

[1] True experiments and quasi-experiments do not exhaust the ways in which experiments are classified. Observational studies refer to several designs in which the investigator selects groups or conditions and makes comparisons (e.g., between individuals with depression vs. those without depression or between individuals with early educational disadvantage who later graduate vs. do not graduate college). In these studies, groups are selected who received some intervention not under control of the investigator. Observational studies have generated enormous advances in generating and testing hypotheses in key areas we often take for granted (e.g., risk factors for cancer, effects of cigarette smoking, impact of divorce on children) (see Kazdin, 2001). These designs are not discussed because the focus of the book and chapter is on intervention research where the investigator manipulates some condition. Sometimes the investigator can control how that intervention is provided and to whom (true experiments) or can only approximate control of these conditions (quasi-experiments).

there is an endless array of federal, state, county, and city programs. These are interventions designed for groups with important and special needs, which might include children with disability or in poverty, partners who are abused or in need of assistance, homeless persons, and support groups of all sorts. There is nothing in my comment that impugns programs per se or these foci in particular. I love programs (and whenever I go to a baseball game, I buy one). We are fortunate to be in a society where resources and genuine efforts are deployed to help.

All of that said, it is rare that programs include the means to evaluate their impact and to provide information that would justify continuation of the program. Many programs (e.g., delivering meals to those without food) have immediate goals that may not require intricate outcome assessment—delivery of the program itself is viewed as improving life. Many other programs are designed to have broader impact (e.g., abuse prevention, parent–teacher meetings in the schools, wilderness programs for youth with delinquent behavior, special education, late-night basketball to control juvenile mischief and crime) but are rarely evaluated. The options for evaluation (true experiments) are recognized as too costly and not feasible; agencies that fund the program rarely fund evaluation of the effects of the program. Consequently, most programs are not evaluated at all. There are anecdotal reports about all the good the programs seem to be accomplishing. Yet, we know that programs sometimes are not effective and that sometimes programs actually harm (i.e., are known to make people worse as demonstrated in true experiments). For example, group programs and therapies that place children with aggressive and other antisocial behaviors together as part of treatment have made the children worse (see Dishion, McCord, & Poulin, 1999; Dodge et al., 2006; Feldman et al., 1983), as I have mentioned previously. Placing such children in groups, even if these groups are designed for treatment purposes, can foster further bonding to deviant peers, which in turn, increases subsequent deviant behavior. This is important to know.[2]

The prospect of well-intended programs not working or making people worse in some way is not restricted to a particular problem domain or sample. For example, programs have been designed to foster abstinence among teenagers with the goal of preventing pregnancy, sexually transmitted diseases, and risky sexual behavior early in life. These programs involve a curriculum and conclude with individuals taking a virginity pledge, that is, pledging abstinence from sexual intercourse. At one point in the United States, 13% of adolescents had taken the pledge (Bearman & Bruckner, 2005). Do the programs work, that is, do they have the intended effects? We would want to know not only because of the importance of the consequences (e.g., sexually transmitted diseases, teen pregnancy) but also to determine whether the money allocated to such programs ($204 million in 2008) is the best use of the funds for that goal.

---

[2] Group treatment of youths with antisocial behavior does not invariably lead to those individuals becoming worse. A selective review of the evidence shows this is not automatic at all and when it does occur not all relevant measures may reflect deterioration of performance (Weiss et al., 2005). Also, some group treatments designed for youth with disruptive, even if not delinquent behaviors, are well established as effective (Lochman, 2010). The point here is merely to recognize that deleterious effects of treatment can occur and have documented instances in controlled studies (e.g., Feldman et al., 1983, still an excellent example).

One cannot do an RCT very easily, but one can look at those who pledge and those who do not and match them on all sorts of variables that make competing rival hypotheses implausible.

In one such exemplary study, the groups were selected and matched on 112 variables (e.g., sex, ethnicity, religion, vocabulary, and many more) (Rosenbaum, 2009). Five years after the pledge, the results indicated that pledgers and nonpledgers did not differ in level of premarital sex, sexually transmitted diseases, anal or oral sex, age of first having sex, or number of sexual partners. Pledgers used birth control and condoms *less* often than nonpledgers in the past year or when they had their last sex. In short, the intervention does not look like it was effective, and if anything it may have decreased taking precautions during sex. As an ancillary but not irrelevant finding, 5 years after taking the virginity pledge, 82% of the pledgers denied having ever pledged. The findings are disappointing, but the evaluation is critical. Other interventions are needed to obtain the goals of pledging; the next $200+ million we spend should pursue other alternatives. We want our programs to be effective; the only thing worse than failing would be continuing the illusion that the programs are working.

There are many other examples that could be cited to convey the importance of evaluation. In so many instances, assigning individuals to different conditions (pledging vs. no pledging) is not possible. It is reassuring methodologically to know that it is not necessary all of the time. Important answers to important questions can come from understanding how to increase the interpretability of findings.

Evaluation is not a luxury; it is related to quality intervention (education, medicine, psychotherapy). Indeed, there is a dangerous irresponsibility in not evaluating our interventions (e.g., harming our clientele, using resources, money and professional time that could be better spent). We want evaluation to ensure that programs are having their intended effects and, if they are, to determine whether we can make the effects better. Some form of evaluation is needed. Quasi-experiments might well be an option. If you were trained in traditional between-group methodology, then you are likely to be skeptical of the scientific contributions of single-case experiments. Now I am asking for more. Single-case experiments that are not the best controlled, that is, not true experiments. Bear with me. As in the preceding example, we want to draw inferences even when conditions do not allow for true experiments.

Methodology as Problem Solving

Prior chapters presented major single-case experimental designs and their variations. As a general rule, when one uses a true-experimental design, whether single-case or between-group designs, one is assured that many threats to validity are well handled, addressed, and made implausible. A true-experimental design does not guarantee that key threats to internal validity are addressed or ruled out. For example, in a group study (RCT), participants are randomly assigned to treatment and control conditions and complete measures before and after the study. Random assignment does not guarantee that the groups are equivalent before treatment begins. Even with random assignment, groups could be different from each other on critical characteristics, and that difference could readily explain why at the end of the study treatment was better (or worse, or no different from the control condition at the end of the study) (see Kazdin, 2001). Even so, true experiments are likely to address the threats, and we use them with that in mind. Actually, we do not use them very often "with that in mind." We use design practices in a rote way because they are so strong as a basis for drawing inferences. Indeed, after years of investigation, many researchers might not be able to specify the threats we are using the designs to rule out. That is probably fine. I refer to this here as "rote methodology" to convey that we select designs and strategies of true experiments automatically. This is not to demean or judge the designs or the process of their use but rather to make a point about quasi-experimental designs.

Quasi-experimental designs cannot be done by rote. Strategies are pieced together to address likely threats to validity. Methodology at its best is problem solving, a cognitive strategy designed to address circumstances that are less than ideal and to devise solutions to achieve the goal. From a methodological standpoint, the goal is to draw well-based conclusions about the impact of the intervention by ruling out or making threats to validity implausible. Quasi-experiments can do this well but one must keep in mind what one is trying to accomplish and then improvise in a way that true experiments do not require.

The skill of the investigator is required because he or she is placed in situations in which all of the ideal conditions (of true experiments) are not available, but the goal (drawing valid inferences) is the same. Consider this situation for a moment: one morning someone comes to your home or apartment and says right now you are going to be transported to a lush tropical island. You are told that your goal is to survive (feed, clothe, and protect yourself) for 2 weeks, after which you will be brought back home. You are told that all you can take with you is what you are wearing. (Hearing that, you quickly dress with a few more clothes to sneak by with an extra shirt, jacket, and socks.) Hours later (first-class flight, four movies, five rich meals, eight crying infants) you land on the island. You are told that you will be staying at a five-star hotel and that you have unlimited access to all of the facilities (beach, pool, several restaurants, room service, gift shops, etc.); you may use the credit card handed to you, but there probably will be no need for it. As you walk down the stairs of the airplane to the tarmac, you can see lush and beautiful palms swaying gently from the ocean breeze and are relieved. This scenario is equivalent to the control of a true experiment. Consider the same scenario in which you are transported and given the same goal, namely to survive (feed, clothe, and protect yourself for 2 weeks). On your flight over, you are in the middle seat, between two people who just realized they went to high-school together and are trashing peers and teachers from the old days. You finally land on the make-shift runway, and you are told the island is all nature—no hotels, no roads, no gift shop, no restaurants, and so on. As you leave the plane you look at the palms and they are really sweaty—not the trees, your hands. Your goal is to survive—the goal has not changed. But, you have to scrap together all of your skills, knowledge, ingenuity, and talent to survive. Welcome to the world of quasi-experiments—the methodology reality show. If you are new to them, we can call them queasy experiments.

Our goal is to draw valid inferences and rule out or make implausible threats to validity. True experiments do that—but one can arrange situations to do that fairly well in quasi-experiments. It is a matter of thinking and problem solving—we are on the lush island—but now rather than survive, we must evaluate a program or intervention of some kind. Does the intervention have an effect, make any difference, or help anyone? The question is what can be done on the part of the investigator to improve the quality of the inferences that can be drawn? Stated another way, what can the investigator do to help make competing interpretations of the results implausible?

Consider a between-group study that is a quasi-experiment. There were not quite perfect controls, and people were not assigned randomly to groups. This is a study that focused on the impact of secondhand smoke, which is known to have adverse cardiovascular effects including heart disease. Eliminating smoking in indoor spaces is the best way to protect nonsmokers. Some cities have instituted smoke-free ordinances—do they make a difference? The best way to test this would be to randomly select cities in the country and then randomly assign a subset of these to be smoke free and others not to be smoke free. This RCT is not going to happen for a host of reasons. What can one do? A quasi-experiment with the idea of making implausible the threats to validity is a good answer.

In one such quasi-experiment (referred to as The Pueblo Heart Study) with several reports, the question has been examined by selecting and comparing three cities (Centers for Disease Control, 2009). Pueblo, Colorado, had a smoke-free ordinance and was compared to two nearby cities over a 3-year period. The two nearby cities did not have smoke-free ordinances and served as comparison cities. The results: In Pueblo, with implementation of its smoke-free ordinance, hospitalization rates for acute myocardial infarction (heart attacks) markedly decreased from before to after the ordinance was implemented. No changes in hospitalization rates were evident in the two comparison cities. Does this finding establish and prove that secondhand smoking leads to increased heart attacks? No, but no one study does that. Also, we would want to know more about the comparability of the three cities and their hospitals, demographic composition of the cities, and more. Furthermore, was it reduced secondary smoking or more people just quitting smoking, which also results from a ban? All these and more are good questions, but one should not lose sight of the strength of the evaluation. The findings suggest that bans do make a difference. Of course, it must be replicated. It has been. The findings hold. Threats to validity (e.g., history, maturation, testing) are not very plausible as an explanation of the findings. Still we need to learn more about what facets of smoking changed and what their specific impact was.

There are many situations in which we believe we are helping or we have an idea that we think will make an important difference in society. The challenge is to add evaluation to that. If the most rigorous research can be done, yes always, we seize that opportunity. But the other side is the problem. When the most rigorous study cannot be done, this is not the time to go by our anecdotal experience. Many threats to validity can be made implausible to help draw valid inferences. This is methodology at its best (using ingenuity to improve the inferences that can be drawn), not methodology at its easiest (random assignment and careful control).

WHAT TO DO TO IMPROVE THE QUALITY OF INFERENCES

We begin with a situation in which a true experiment cannot be used and take the challenge as follows: What can be added or utilized from what we know about research methodology in general and single-case designs in particular to improve the information and quality of inferences that can be drawn? The default position (no systematic evaluation) is the anecdotal case study with its full bloom of ambiguity. We must do better to draw inferences. We have a "case" that may involve an individual, a classroom, a business, or some program for children or adolescents in a school or community setting or for victims of domestic violence in a women's shelter. Our goal is to draw inferences about the impact of an intervention. The enemy, as it were, is ambiguity and all of those threats to validity that usually make the anecdotal case study a poor basis for drawing inferences about interventions. There are several things we can do and information we can bring to bear that greatly increase the extent to which threats to validity are ruled out or made implausible (Kazdin, 1981; Sechrest et al., 1996). To evaluate a program and improve inferences, these are key steps, even if they cannot all be followed.

Collect Systematic Data

As a point of departure for quasi-experiments, we begin with systematic assessment information. We could use self-report inventories, ratings by other persons, and direct measures of overt behavior. All systematic measures have their own problems and limitations (e.g., reactivity, response biases) but still they provide a stronger basis for determining whether change has occurred after an intervention than anecdotal narrative reports. If more standardized information is available, at least the investigator (educator, therapist, and teacher) has a better basis for claiming that change has been achieved. The data do not allow one to infer the basis for the change. Yet, systematic assessment and the resulting data serve as a prerequisite, because they provide information that change has in fact occurred.

Assess Behavior (or Program Outcomes) on Multiple Occasions

Another dimension that can distinguish single-case demonstrations is the number and timing of the assessment occasions. Major options consist of collecting information on a one- or two-shot basis (e.g., posttreatment only or pre- and posttreatment) or continuously over time (e.g., every day, a few times per week, or right before each intervention session). When information is collected on one or two occasions (pre, post), threats to internal validity associated with assessment (e.g., testing, instrumentation, statistical regression) can be especially difficult to rule out. With continuous assessment over time, these threats are much less plausible, especially if continuous assessment begins before treatment (baseline) and continues over the course of treatment (intervention phase). Continuous assessment allows one to examine the pattern of the data and whether the pattern appears to have been altered at the point in which the intervention was introduced. That is, "the describe, predict, and test" aspects of single-case designs begin to come into play by having at least the first two (AB) phases of a true experiment. If a single-case demonstration includes continuous assessment on several occasions over time, often the threats to internal validity related to assessment can be ruled out.

Consider Past and Future Projections of Performance

Inferences about the impact of an intervention can be aided by information about performance in the past and likely performance in the near future. In single-case experiments, baseline observations provide this information, and shifts from baseline to intervention phases provide further information. Without the luxury of baseline observations, we can sometimes bring to bear information that is a rough but still helpful approximation. For some behaviors or problems, there may be an extended history that is fairly reliable even without rigorous baseline assessment. This might be true if there has been no occurrence of the behavior (e.g., exercise) or if the characteristic is likely to have been stable, based in the previous weeks or months (e.g., weight of an obese person). A history of stable performance inferred in this way is not as perfect as continuous days of observation, but it may be close. To the extent that there is such a history, one can assume that the behavior or characteristic would continue unless some special event (e.g., treatment) altered its course. Consequently, if performance changes when treatment is applied, the likelihood that treatment caused the change is increased. Thus, the history of the problem may influence the plausibility that extraneous events or other processes (history, maturation), other than treatment, could plausibly account for the change.

Apart from the history of the problem, projections about the likely performance in the future or the likely course and outcome are relevant as well. For example, the problem may be one that would not improve without intervention (e.g., terminal illness, reading deficit). Knowing the likely outcome strengthens the inferences that can be drawn about the impact of an intervention that alters this course. The client's improvement controverts the expected prediction of the course of the problem and bolsters the likelihood that the intervention led to change.

The course of clinical problems is important to know because the present level of the problem by itself can be deceiving or incomplete information. A given presenting problem may look the same (e.g., same degree of severity), but projection of the immediate future may depend on knowing a bit about the past. For example, rates of recovery from an episode of depression in adults are very high within the first few weeks or months. However, the probability of recovery diminishes as the episode becomes longer (Patten, 2006). Thus, if a quasi-experiment shows a reduction in depression associated with the onset of treatment, the demonstration may be more or less persuasive based on information about the duration of the episode (past) and therefore the likelihood that it would have changed in the future.

Consider the Type of Effect Associated with Treatment

Demonstrations vary in terms of the type of effects or changes that are evident as treatment is applied. The immediacy and magnitude of change contribute to the inferences that can be drawn about the role of treatment. Usually, the more immediate the change after the onset of the intervention, the stronger a case can be made that the intervention, rather than other events, was responsible for change. A historical event (something in the news, event in the individual's personal life) might occur coincidentally with the onset of the intervention, and might explain the pattern, but usually that is not very likely. On the other hand, gradual changes or changes that begin after the intervention may raise greater ambiguity. Many maturational changes and changes over time are gradual, and we look for an intervention to show a pattern not likely to be confused with such changes.

Aside from the immediacy of change, the magnitude of the change is important as well. When marked changes in performance are achieved, this suggests that only a special event, probably the intervention, could be responsible. Of course, the magnitude and immediacy of change, when combined, increase the confidence one can place in according the intervention a causal role. Rapid and dramatic changes provide a strong basis for attributing the effects to the intervention. Gradual and relatively small changes might more easily be discounted by random fluctuations of performance, normal cycles of behavior, or developmental changes. (The criteria for inferring change are discussed further in Chapter 12 on data evaluation.)

Use Multiple and Heterogeneous Participants

The number of clients included in a quasi-experiment can influence the confidence that can be placed in any inferences drawn about the intervention. Demonstrations with two or more cases, rather than with one case, provide a stronger basis for inferring the effects of the intervention. Essentially, each case can be viewed as a replication of the original effect that seemed to result from intervening. If two or more cases improve it is unlikely that any particular extraneous event (history) or internal process (maturation) could be responsible for change. Historical events and maturation probably varied among the cases, and the common experience, namely, the intervention, may be the most plausible reason for the changes.

The heterogeneity of the cases or diversity of the types of persons may also contribute to inferences about the cause of change. If change is demonstrated among several clients who differ in subject and demographic variables (e.g., age, ethnicity, gender, social class, clinical problems), the inferences that can be made about the intervention are stronger than if this diversity does not exist. With a heterogeneous set of clients, the likelihood is diminished that they share history or maturational influences. They do share exposure to the intervention and thus the intervention becomes the most plausible explanation of the results.

In methodology when more and more diverse participants are discussed, the underlying concern is usually external validity, that is, the extent to which the results generalize. The common concern is how one can generalize to others with only one subject, a topic taken up in a later chapter. Here we are using more than one subject and diverse subjects to address internal validity, that is, the likelihood that the intervention rather than extraneous events could explain the change. With more and more diverse subjects, the same threat to validity (e.g., same history, same maturational rate) is not very plausible.

General Comments

The characteristics I have mentioned can be used to strengthen the inferences drawn from situations where experimental control is not possible, that is, quasi-experiments. Depending on how the different characteristics are addressed within a particular demonstration, it is quite possible that the inferences closely approximate those that could be obtained from a true single-case experiment. Not all of the dimensions are under the control of the investigator (e.g., immediacy and strength of intervention effects). On the other hand, critical features upon which conclusions depend, such as the use of replicable measures and assessment on multiple occasions, can be controlled in the situation and can greatly enhance the demonstration.

ILLUSTRATIONS OF QUASI-EXPERIMENTAL DESIGNS

Selected Variations and How They Address Threats to Validity

It is useful to consider a few of the examples of quasi-experiments with the single case that vary on the characteristics mentioned previously. These convey how the quality of the inferences that are drawn can vary and what the investigator can do to strengthen the demonstration. Table 11.1 illustrates a few types of single-case demonstration studies that differ on some of the dimensions mentioned previously. Also, the extent to which each type of case rules out the specific threats to internal validity is presented. For each type of case the collection of data was included because, as noted earlier, the absence of objective or quantifiable data usually precludes drawing conclusions about whether change occurred.

Study 1: With Pre- and Post-assessment. Use of pre- and posttreatment assessment for the individual increases the informational yield well beyond unsystematic anecdotal reports. Table 11.1 illustrates a single-case (column noted as Study 1) with pre- and post-assessment but without other characteristics that would help rule out threats to internal validity. Improved assessment permits comments about whether change has occurred. This is not trivial. The goal of intervention programs in the context of education, rehabilitation, medicine, psychotherapy, and counseling is to effect some change (e.g., in affect, behavior, and/or cognition, academic performance). A basic requirement is to put into place a system in which change can be assessed systematically and routinely. Increasingly, accountability for delivery of services (e.g., education, health care) has focused on improved outcome assessment. Out of concern for the people we serve

Table 11.1 Selected Types of Hypothetical Cases and the Threats to Internal Validity They Address

Type of N = 1 study	Study 1 Pre- & postassessment	Study 2 Repeated assessment & marked changes	Study 3 Multiple cases, continuous assessment, stable performance
Characteristics of case present (yes) or absent/not specified (no)			
Objective data	yes	yes	yes
Continuous assessment	no	yes	yes
Stability of problem	no	no	yes
Immediate and marked effects	no	yes	no
Multiple cases	no	no	yes
Major threats to internal validity ruled out (+) or not ruled out (−)			
History	−	?	+
Maturation	−	?	+
Testing	−	+	+
Instrumentation	−	+	+
Statistical regression	−	+	+

Note: In the table, a "+" indicates that the threat to internal validity is probably controlled, a "−" indicates that the threat remains a problem, and a "?" indicates that the threat may remain uncontrolled. In preparation of the table, selected threats were omitted because they arise primarily in the comparison of different groups in experiments. They are not usually a problem for a case study, which, of course, does not rely on group comparisons.

and with enormous expenditures of funds, we should always ask, "Is there any impact at all?" Systematic assessment is a good first step because many programs may not be producing change or change of a magnitude that makes a difference.

Assessment alone is valuable for identifying change, but determining the basis of the change is another matter. Ruling out various threats to internal validity and concluding that treatment led to change depend on other dimensions (listed in the table) than the assessment procedures alone. It is quite possible that events occurring in time (history), processes of change within the individual (maturation), repeated exposure to assessment (testing), changes in the scoring criteria (instrumentation), or reversion of the score to the mean (regression) rather than treatment led to change. In short, threats to internal validity are not ruled out in this situation, so the basis for change remains a matter of surmise.

Study 2: With Repeated Assessment and Marked Changes.   If the single-case demonstration includes assessment on multiple occasions before and after treatment and the changes associated with the intervention are relatively marked, the inferences that can be drawn about treatment are vastly improved. Table 11.1 illustrates the characteristics of such a case, along with the extent to which specific threats to internal validity are addressed. The fact that continuous assessment is included is important in ruling out the specific threats to internal validity related to assessment. Also, changes coincide with the onset of treatment. This pattern of change is not likely to result from exposure to repeated testing or changes in the instrument. When continuous assessment is used, any changes due to testing or instrumentation would be evident before treatment began. Similarly, regression to the mean from one data point to another, a potential problem with assessment conducted at only two points in time, is eliminated. Repeated observation over time shows a pattern in the data. Extreme scores may be a problem for any particular assessment occasion in relation to the immediately prior occasion. However, these changes cannot account for the pattern of performance for an extended period.

Aside from continuous assessment, this illustration includes relatively marked treatment effects, that is, changes that are relatively immediate and large. These types of changes produced in treatment help reduce the possibility that history and maturation explain the results. Maturation in particular may be relatively implausible because maturational changes are not likely to be abrupt and large. Nevertheless, a "?" was placed in the table because maturation cannot be ruled out completely. In this case example, information on the stability of the problem in the past and future was not included. Hence, it is not known whether the clinical problem might ordinarily change on its own and whether maturational influences are plausible. Some problems that are episodic (e.g., depression) in nature conceivably could show marked changes that have little to do with treatment. With immediate and large changes in behavior, history and maturation may be ruled out too, although these are likely to depend on other dimensions in the table that specifically were omitted from this case.

Study 3: With Multiple Cases, Continuous Assessment, and Stability Information.
Several cases rather than only one may be studied. The cases may be treated one at a time and accumulated into a final summary statement of treatment effects or may be

treated as a single group at the same time. In this illustration, assessment information is available on repeated occasions before and during treatment. Also, the stability of the problem is known in this example. Stability refers to the dimension of past–future projections and denotes that other research suggests that the problem does not usually change over time. When the problem is known to be highly stable or to follow a particular course without treatment, the investigator has an implicit prediction of the effects of no treatment. The results can be compared with this predicted level of performance.

As is evident in Table 11.1, several threats to internal validity are addressed by a single-case demonstration meeting the specified characteristics. History and maturation are not likely to interfere with drawing conclusions about the causal role of treatment because several different cases are included. All cases are not likely to have a single historical event or maturational process in common that could account for the results. Knowledge about the stability of the problem in the future also helps to rule out the influence of history and maturation. If the problem is known to be stable over time, this means that ordinary historical events and maturational processes do not provide a strong enough influence in their own right. Because of the use of multiple subjects and the knowledge about the stability of the problem, history and maturation probably are implausible explanations of change in behavior.

The threats to internal validity related to testing are handled largely by continuous assessment over time. Repeated testing, changes in the instrument, and reversion of scores toward the mean may influence performance from one occasion to another. Yet problems associated with testing are not likely to influence the pattern of data over a large number of occasions. Also, information about the stability of the problem helps to further make changes due to testing implausible. The fact that the problem is known to be stable means that it probably would not change merely as a function of repeated assessment.

In general, a single-case demonstration of the type illustrated in this example provides a strong basis for drawing valid inferences about the impact of treatment. The manner in which the multiple-case report is designed does not constitute an experiment, as usually conceived, because each case represents an uncontrolled demonstration. However, characteristics of the type of case study can rule out specific threats to internal validity in a manner approaching that of true experiments.

Examples of Quasi-experiments

A few illustrations convey more concretely the continuum of confidence one might place in the notion that the intervention was responsible for change. Each illustration qualifies as a quasi-experiment because it captures features of true experiments and varies in the extent to which specific threats can be made implausible.

Pre–post Assessment. In single-case research, assessment usually is continuous, that is, repeated observations for the participant or group within phases (baseline) and more than one phase. And, as the reader knows all too well now, the multiple data points permit one to apply the logic of single-case designs (describe, predict, test). In between-group research, there is usually pre- and posttreatment assessment, and the strength of the demonstration stems from comparing an intervention group with a control (e.g., no treatment) group. Occasionally, researchers report evaluation of a single group with just pre- and postassessment. Although assessment can document that change occurred, this is usually a weak basis on which to draw any inferences about the intervention.

As an example, a treatment study was reported that focused on treating panic disorder among adults (Milrod et al., 2001). Twenty-one adults participated (ages 18 to 50; 66% female; 76% European American, 19% African American, and 4% Asian American) who experienced panic disorder. Key symptoms include a period of intense fear or discomfort that may include pounding heart, sweating, trembling or shaking, shortness of breath, feeling of choking, fear of losing control, chest pain, and others. Apart from the importance of alleviating the disorder itself, individuals with panic disorder report poor physical health and have higher rates of substance and alcohol abuse, and suicide. Also individuals with panic disorder use health-care services more frequently than patients with any other psychiatric diagnosis. All individuals received psychodynamic psychotherapy for 24 sessions, delivered two times per week. Before starting therapy several pretreatment measures were taken (related to panic, anxiety, and depression); at the end of treatment, the measures were completed again.

At the end of treatment, the group (17 of 21 individuals completed treatment) showed a statistically significant improvement including reduced anxiety, depression, panic, and other domains on several self-report scales. The benefit of the assessment is that we know that the patients changed. The difficulty in drawing inferences is that several threats to internal validity are not ruled out by the design. It is possible that patients improved just because of taking the test on separate occasions (testing) and that they came into the study at an extreme point and showed changes at posttreatment as a result (statistical regression), or that they just got better over time after they came to treatment independently of receiving sessions (history and maturation). Patients often show great changes when assessed on two occasions before treatment begins. The act of coming to treatment (history) alone may promote improvement.

The investigators referred to this as pilot work and an open study and recognized that the design did not permit inferences about the intervention.[3] I cite the example here because one group (or one subject) with pre- and postassessment is only a step up from an anecdotal case study, but inferences about the intervention really cannot be drawn. It is a step in the sense that change is demonstrated, usually by a measure that has some validity to it, as distinguished from the narrative, unsystematic anecdotes. Even so, continuous assessment would strengthen the same demonstration because seeing a pattern of data over time would rule out testing, regression, maturation, and

---

[3] An *open study* (also called open label study) in medicine refers to a study in which a medication is used but there is no attempt to hide what the drug is from those who administer it. Usually in controlled trials, those who administer and even receive the medication may be "blinded," that is, not informed whether they are receiving the drug or the placebo. This procedure reduces bias associated with knowing who received what and possibly influencing their reactions, behaviors, or outcomes. However, the term is often used for an uncontrolled study in which there is one group and there is pre- and postassessment.

history as causes and we might be able to draw on some aspect of the describe, predict, test features that such assessment allows.

Continuous Assessment Helps to Evaluate Change. More assessment points help rule out some of the threats related to testing. Repeated testing and regression are effects likely to be evident when there are just two occasions of assessment (pre, post), and one cannot tell if these effects or the intervention led to change. Continuous assessment helps a little more than just pre–post assessment.

For example, treatment was applied to decrease the weight of an obese 55-year-old woman (180 lb. [81.8 kg], 5'5" [1.65 meters]) (Martin & Sachs, 1973). The woman had been advised to lose weight, a recommendation of some urgency in light of her recent heart attack. The woman was treated as an outpatient. The treatment consisted of developing a contract or agreement with the therapist based on adherence to a variety of rules and recommendations that would alter her eating habits. Several rules were developed pertaining to rewarding herself for resisting tempting foods, self-recording what was eaten after meals and snacks, weighing herself frequently each day, chewing foods slowly, and others. The patient had been weighed before treatment, and therapy began with weekly assessment for a 4½-week period.

The results of the program, which appear in Figure 11.1, indicate that the woman's initial weight of 180 lb. was followed by a gradual decline in weight over the next few weeks before treatment was terminated. For present purposes, what can be said about the impact of treatment? Actually, statements about the effects of the treatment in accounting for the changes would be tentative at best. The stability of her pretreatment weight is unclear. The first data point indicated that the woman weighed 180 lb.

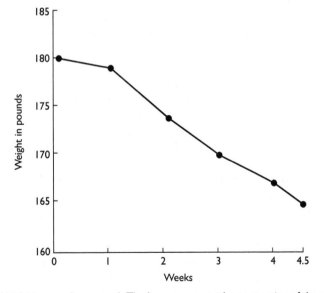

Figure 11.1. Weight in pounds per week. The line represents the connecting of the weights, respectively, on Days 0, 7, 14, 21, 28, and 31 of the weight loss program.   *(Source: Martin & Sachs, 1973.)*

before treatment. Perhaps this weight would have declined over the next few weeks even without a special weight-reduction program. The absence of clear information regarding the stability of the woman's weight before treatment makes evaluation of her subsequent loss rather difficult. The fact that the decline is gradual and modest, albeit understandable given the expected course of weight reduction, introduces further ambiguity. The weight loss is clear, but it would be difficult to argue strongly that the historical events, maturational processes, or repeated assessment could not have led to the same results.

Continuous Assessment Over Baseline and Intervention Phases Help Further. The next illustration provides a slightly more persuasive demonstration that treatment may have led to the results. This case included a 45-year-old female with low back pain traced to degeneration of several disks in her spine (as demonstrated by magnetic resonance imaging, or MRI) (Vlaeyen, de Jong, Onghena, Kerckhoffs-Hansen, & Kole-Snijders, 2002). Injections, medications, and physical therapy produced little improvement in her pain. As background to this, fear of physical movement among individuals experiencing pain fosters avoiding activities, which in turn predicts future disability. Fear of further pain is a significant problem among many such patients and promotes a downward course in their pain, disability, and mood. The study evaluated the effects of exposure therapy, an evidence-based treatment for anxiety and fear. Exposure therapy consisted of practice activities and movements with a physical therapist. The activities were graded according to how much fear they evoked; the exposure sessions began with the less fearful actions. Several measures were used to assess pain. Prior to coming to treatment, the patient filled out and mailed forms about pain experience to the researcher. Other measures of the patient included viewing photos of movements and rating fear and concern over harm the activity would produce. The exposure treatment was evaluated in an AB design. After 1 week of baseline, the intervention consisted of fifteen 90-minute sessions over a 5-week period. The results are plotted in Figure 11.2 for two separate measures (fear of movement and pain intensity).

The results suggest that the intervention may have been responsible for change. The inference is aided by continuous assessment over time before and during the intervention phase and the pattern of the data. Baseline showed high levels of fear and pain intensity and suggests that no change was likely to occur with continued observations alone. When the intervention was introduced, pain fear and intensity declined and continued to show a marked reduction by the end of the intervention phase.

A few features of the demonstration may detract from the confidence one might place in according treatment a causal role. The gradual decline evident in the figure might also have resulted from other influences than the treatment, including some event not in the report that may have occurred with the onset of treatment (history) or boredom with continuing the assessment procedure (maturation). As it turns out, another case was included in the report and showed similar effects, which makes these threats less likely for this report. Also, the fact that the patient was responsible for providing the ratings, even though these were standard measures, raises concerns about whether accuracy of scoring changed over time (instrumentation), rather than actual

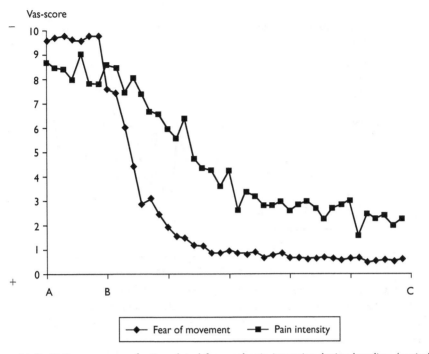

Figure 11.2. Daily measures of pain related fear and pain intensity during baseline (period of A to B, see bottom of the graph) and exposure treatment (B to C). The series or line of data points marked by diamonds and squares represent ratings of fear of movement and pain intensity, respectively. The Visual Analogue Scale (VAS) was used to obtain these ratings. *(Source: Vlaeyen et al., 2002.)*

fear. Yet the data can be taken as presented without undue methodological skepticism. As such, the intervention appears to have led to change, but the quasi-experimental nature of the design and the pattern of results make it difficult to rule out threats to internal validity with great confidence.

Continuous Assessment and Marked Changes. In the next illustration, the effects of the intervention appeared even clearer than in the previous example. In this report, a female adult with agoraphobia and panic attacks participated in outpatient treatment to overcome her fear of leaving home and her self-imposed restriction to her home (O'Donohue, Plaud, & Hecker, 1992). The patient kept a record of her activities and the time devoted to them. Also, at the beginning of treatment, activities that might be reinforcing were identified. The intervention consisted of instructing her to engage in rewarding activities (e.g., time with her pet, reading, entertaining visitors) only when outside of the home. Examples included walking down the street, socializing with neighbors, and watching TV at a neighbor's home.

The effects of the procedure in increasing time out of the home are illustrated in Figure 11.3. The baseline period indicated a consistent pattern of no time spent outside of the home. When the intervention began, time outside the home sharply increased and remained high at 2- and 18-month follow-up assessments. Acquaintances and

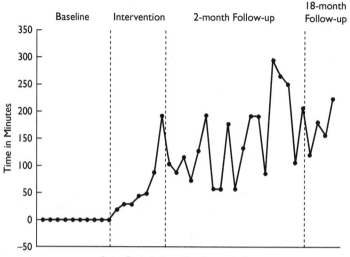

Figure 11.3. Total time an adult patient with agoraphobia and panic spent in activities outside of the home over baseline, intervention, and two follow-up assessment periods. *(Source: O'Donohue et al., 1992.)*

relatives, who reported on specific activities in which the patient had engaged, corroborated these changes. The stable and very clear baseline and the marked changes with onset of the intervention suggest that history, maturation, or other threats could not readily account for the results. Within the limits of quasi-experimental designs, the results are relatively clear.

Continuous Assessment, Marked Changes, and Multiple Subjects. Among the previous examples, the likelihood that the intervention accounted for change was increasingly plausible in light of characteristics of the report. In this final illustration, the effects of the intervention are extremely clear, although clearly not from a true experiment. The purpose of this report was to investigate a novel method of treating bedwetting (enuresis) among children (Azrin, Hontos, & Besalel-Azrin, 1979). Forty-four children, ranging in age from 3 to 15 years, were included. Their families collected data on the number of nighttime bedwetting accidents for 7 days before treatment. After baseline, the training procedure was implemented: the child was required to practice getting up from bed at night, remaking the bed after he or she wet the bed, and changing clothes. Other procedures were included as well, such as waking the child early at night in the beginning of training and developing increased bladder capacity by reinforcing increases in urine volume. The parents and children practiced some of the procedures in the training session, but the intervention was essentially carried out at home when the child wet his or her bed.

The effects of training are illustrated in Figure 11.4, which shows bedwetting during the pretraining (baseline) and training periods. The demonstration is a quasi-experimental design with several of the conditions discussed previously included

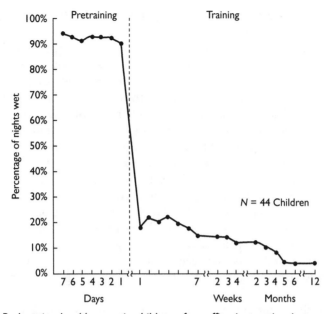

Figure 11.4. Bedwetting by 44 enuretic children after office instruction in an operant learning method. Each data point designates the percentage of nights on which bedwetting occurred. The data prior to the dotted line are for a 7-day period prior to training. The data are presented daily for the first week, weekly for the first month, and monthly for the first 6 months and for the 12th month. *(Source: Azrin et al., 1979.)*

to make threats to internal validity implausible. The data suggest that the problem was relatively stable for the group as a whole during the baseline period. Also, the changes in performance at the onset of treatment were immediate and marked. Finally, several subjects were included who probably were not very homogeneous because their ages encompassed young children through teenagers. In light of these characteristics of the demonstration, it is not very plausible that the changes could be accounted for by history, maturation, repeated assessment, changes in the assessment procedures, or statistical regression.

Other Variations and Illustrations. It is in the very nature of quasi-experimental designs that they will not fall into neat categories. My prior comments focus on dimensions or features that can strengthen the inferences that are drawn. However, there are many variants in which judgments have to be made about whether threats to validity are plausible and whether the logic of the single-case designs is met. Consider brief examples to convey the point.

This initial example focused on alcohol consumption and binge drinking among college students (Fournier, Ehrhart, Glindemann, & Geller, 2004). Surveys suggest that most students (80 to 90%) consume alcoholic beverages. Excessive drinking or binge drinking is associated with many problems that colleges seek to control, including sexual assault, unplanned and unsafe sex, property damage, violence, auto accidents, and poor academic performance. This program was conducted in a university setting and encompassed 356 college students (ages 19 to 24) who participated while attending one of four consecutive parties hosted by the same fraternity on campus. Blood alcohol concentration (BAC) was the dependent measure and was assessed with a hand-held breathalyzer. Students were evaluated for BAC at the end of each party. The four parties were divided into two parties of baseline (no intervention, or A phase) and two parties with the intervention (or B phase). The design was AABB, clearly placing this within the realm of a quasi-experiment. This arrangement is like an extended AB design. Baseline parties included the assessment. Intervention parties included providing fliers to each person noting that individuals with BAC levels below .05 would be entered into a $100 cash raffle. (The legal limit of intoxication in Virginia, the state in which this was conducted, is .08, and the study selected a level below that.) The flier also included information on how to maintain low intoxication (e.g., consume water between alcoholic beverages, snack on food) and a chart (referred to as nomogram) that showed how to calculate BAC from body weight, number of drinks consumed, and how long one as been drinking, with separate charts for males and females (because of differences in metabolizing alcohol). At the end of the two intervention parties, there was a drawing, and cash was provided to the winner.

Figure 11.5 shows three measures to evaluate the program across baseline and intervention parties. Each side of the graph measures something slightly different, including the percentage of individuals who met the goal (left side) and the mean blood alcohol concentrations. Consider the dashed line with triangles. It is clear that the mean BAC was lower during the two intervention parties than during the two baseline parties. The other lines in the graph also convey that the percentage of individuals who fell under the criterion for the raffle (.05) as well as the legal limit (.08) increased during the intervention phase. The changes from AA to BB were statistically significant in a number of tests (for each of the measures in the figure). Of course, statistical significance is about whether there is change and not about whether the change was caused by the intervention, which is about the design. What can we conclude? Are there plausible threats to validity that might explain the pattern of data?

Selection is a threat to validity here and is usually only mentioned in the context of group designs. In this case, it is possible that the participants in the baseline (AA) parties were different in systematic ways from those in the intervention (BB) parties. Perhaps, people who really liked to drink stopped going to the parties or left very soon after arriving. Those remaining to be tested could be less likely to drink or drink very much even without an intervention. The authors note that the mix of party goers (e.g., age, sex, and proportion of fraternity and nonfraternity members) did not vary among the parties, and that partially speaks to the concern. History could be a threat too. It is possible that between AA and BB phases something happened on campus. It is not quite fair to raise this vacuously without having some idea of an event, but still it is worth noting. An ABAB design rules out history in most cases because history (maturation and other threats) does not reverse behavior in a back-and-forth fashion. With an AABB design, a historical event could explain the data. Overall and in my view, it remains parsimonious to interpret the demonstration as showing that the intervention

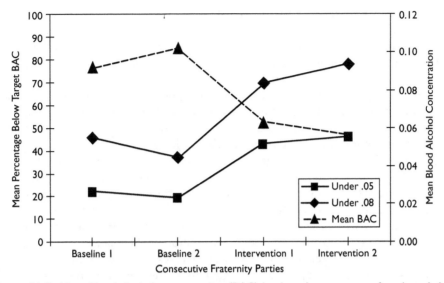

Figure 11.5. Mean blood alcohol concentration (BAC) levels and percentages of students below BACs at the four fraternity parties in an AABB quasi-experimental design. *(Source: Fournier et al., 2004.)*

led to change. For each line in the graph, the two baseline points do not overlap with the two intervention points.

A final example focused on the treatment of Posttraumatic Stress Disorder (PTSD) among earthquake survivors. PTSD is a severe anxiety reaction precipitated by a traumatic event including natural disasters (e.g., earthquake, flood), combat or military exposure, terrorist attacks, sexual or physical assault, child sexual or physical abuse, and accidents (e.g., automobile). Severe anxiety continues long after the event as the individual relives the event, dreams about it, and can have the full anxiety reaction when exposed to any reminder of the event.

Effective and brief treatment (one to four sessions) of earthquake survivors with PTSD has been developed and carefully evaluated in RCTs (e.g., Basoglu, Salcioglu, & Livanou, 2007; Basoglu, Salcioglu, Livanou, Kalender, & Acar, 2005). The treatment encourages individuals to expose themselves to fear-evoking cues to develop a sense of control and to develop cognitive strategies to cope with avoidance and anxiety. In this report, a highly structured self-help manual was provided to see if the benefits of the treatment could be obtained by individuals themselves when provided after an initial therapist contact (Basoglu, Salcioglu, & Livanou, 2009). Quasi-single-case evaluations were made of a self-help manual. The manual (51 pages) discussed PTSD and depression, self-assessment, how to conduct self-exposure sessions, how to cope with avoidance of anxiety, and other components. The treatment was a 9-week program, all administered individually by the clients themselves. Outcome evaluation was based on several clinician-administered and self-administered measures. This report included eight adults (mean age of 40) who survived the 1999 earthquake in Turkey and suffered PTSD. (The intervention was conducted in 2003–2004, so the symptoms continued long after the initial trauma.) To illustrate the results, I have sampled one of the measures (the Clinician-Administered PTSD Scale) that is a standard measure in this area of work.

This was a quasi-experiment that might be simply referred to as an AB design. However, it is a little more complex. In baseline, there were two assessments (4 weeks apart). Then the self-help manual was provided for the 9 weeks of treatment. No assessments were conducted during the treatment, but immediately after, there was a posttreatment assessment. Follow-up assessments were then conducted at 1, 3, and 6 months. Figure 11.6 provides the data for the eight cases. The measure is one of PTSD symptoms, so improvement would be reflected in decreases in anxiety. Two questions are before us: Was there any change from baseline to posttreatment? And what is the likelihood that the intervention accounted for change? Looking at the data from eight cases, we can see that, with the exception of Case 6, the change from baseline to post-treatment assessment is consistent. Patients improved. It helps to have two rather than one assessment occasions in baseline to give us a better idea of trend and stability (and to rule out regression to the mean as an explanation of the change from baseline to posttreatment). We can see that in baseline some cases improved from the first to the second assessment (Cases 2, 5, 7, 8). Repeated assessment on measures often leads to slight improvements. However, for these cases, the data at post- and follow-up assessments still suggest a change through visual examination of the data, that is, not like the data in baseline. This was bolstered by statistical evaluation that showed that change from Baseline 1 to Baseline 2 for all the cases combined was not statistically significant. However, changes from baseline to posttreatment and to the follow-up assessments were statistically significant.

This is a quasi-experiment; if conceived as an ABAB design, this is "missing" two phases. However, the design has multiple-baseline features in which the intervention was implemented across different people. The implementation was not at the same time, in all likelihood, so no clear historical event could explain the pattern of change after the intervention. Maturational events, too, are not a likely explanation; the clients were all different ages, and the symptoms were still strong long after the earthquake. Both of these points make maturation not very plausible as an explanation of the change in symptoms. Also, the interpretation of the intervention is facilitated by other information, namely, the authors had developed versions of this treatment and tested them carefully in other contexts. The present demonstration is a valuable extension by testing the manual with individual cases. We know that individuals can administer treatment themselves, which is a critical finding because the scope of national disasters (e.g., earthquakes, tsunamis, hurricanes) does not permit individual therapy administered by mental health professionals to be provided to the survivors who suffer trauma.

General Comments. I have emphasized the goals of research design (to make various threats to validity implausible) and the logic of single-case designs (e.g., describe, predict, test the prediction) for reasons that are particularly salient for this chapter. Experimental design practices serve the preceding goals and are not ends in themselves. Thus, one evaluates quasi-experiments (and true experiments) in terms of how well they make implausible competing interpretations of the findings. Many quasi-experiments illustrated previously make a very strong case. It is not always the case

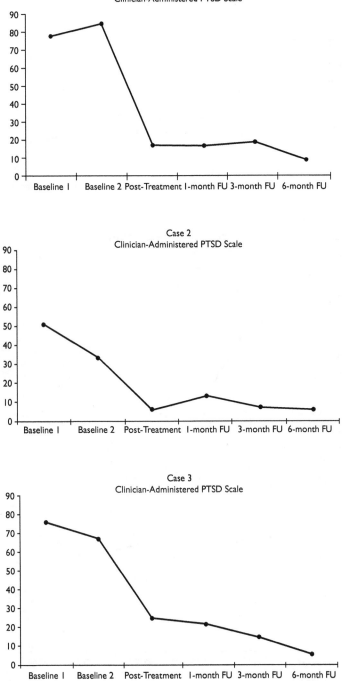

Figure 11.6. Clinician-administered measure of PTSD symptoms for each of eight cases. The design included two assessments during baseline, one assessment immediately after the self-administered treatment, and three assessments over the course of follow-up.   *(Source: Basoglu et al., 2009.)*

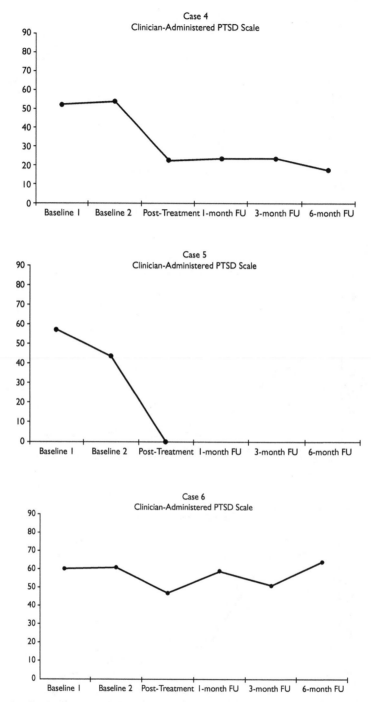

Figure 11.6. *Continued*

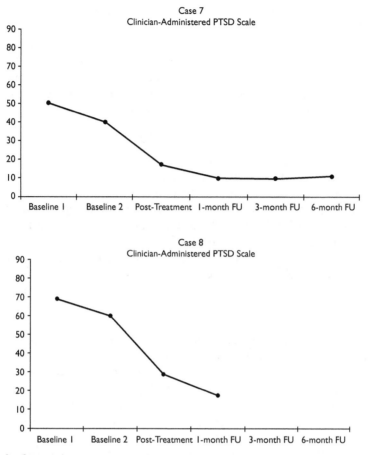

Figure 11.6. *Continued*

that a true experiment or even an RCT automatically makes a strong case because of the design. When there is loss of subjects in some groups or diffusion of the intervention, whether the study is an ABAB design or RCT does not automatically correct the problems. Understanding what competes with drawing inferences is important in all designs. Quasi-experimental designs merely make the importance of this understanding more salient.

If one focuses on practices rather than the goals of research, there can be a methodological helplessness that emerges. For example, a teacher or superintendent has a creative intervention idea for a classroom or school. How to evaluate this? If one believes only a controlled study can be used with randomized assignment, most likely the program will never be evaluated. The goals of research are to see if the novel intervention makes a difference when other influences are controlled. In any given case, the arrangement of approximations or quasi-experiments (single-case or between-group) can reduce the plausibility of threats to validity in ways that approach true experiments. I discussed and illustrated key dimensions that can greatly strengthen inferences that can be drawn about intervention effects.

Design features from single-case experiments are not mere methodological niceties. When integrated with applied work in educational, clinic, and other settings, they can also improve the quality of care (Horner et al., 2005; Kazdin, 2008b). Continuous assessment, for example, provides feedback about whether the program is having its intended effect. This is basic. At the very least, programs ought to have an assessment component. Quasi-experiments go beyond assessment, of course, and focus further on drawing inferences about what caused the change and when change occurred.

PERSPECTIVE ON QUASI-EXPERIMENTS

In seeking answers to critical questions, we want to begin with true experiments when possible. In applied settings, often such experiments are not possible. Constraints on the situation (e.g., limitations of withholding the math or reading program from some classes but not others) and clinical issues (e.g., the patient ought to have the intervention immediately) are some of the impediments. We ought to be consoled by the knowledge that most of the sciences (e.g., geology, anthropology, meteorology, astronomy, epidemiology, zoology) do not rely on true experiments for critical findings and yet have made enormous advances. This is worth mentioning to begin with the premise that much can be learned in a cumulative and rigorous way without being able to control the situation experimentally.

For those sciences and disciplines involved in intervention research (e.g., medicine, education, psychology, counseling, social work) research training focuses on true experiments. The RCT is endlessly referred to as the "gold standard," but it has been the only standard included in training. Understandably, with that training, many of us are bothered by less well-controlled studies, which is why I sometimes refer to the designs of this chapter as *queasy-experimental designs*. No matter what the designs are called, quasi or queasy, very strong inferences can be drawn from them. However, the designs often require greater ingenuity in selecting controls or analyzing the data to make various threats to validity implausible.

The ingenuity requires thought about the specific situation and what might be done to combat this or that threat to validity that is especially problematic. We begin by adding assessment and then consider what might help us show that it was the intervention rather than extraneous influences that account for the change. Facets of single-case designs might be brought to bear. Perhaps assessment on multiple occasions will help us draw on the describe, predict, and test feature of single-case experiments, perhaps we can infer what performance in the past and future would be like without the luxury of baseline observations, or perhaps we can show a similar intervention effect in two individuals (two AB designs with a brief baseline and intervention phase, but not staggered in a multiple-baseline fashion).

SUMMARY AND CONCLUSIONS

It is useful to consider the present chapter in relation to a continuum of rigor and clarity of research methods. I mentioned a continuum that has uncontrolled anecdotal case study on the left side and true experiments on the right side. There is general agreement that the anecdotal case study is not an acceptable basis for drawing inferences in science. The absence of systematic assessment and any effort to control the situation makes the anecdotal case study a resort where all the threats to validity frolic and join together. With true experiments, these threats are reined in, controlled, made implausible, or completely ruled out. All the threats are kept in their cages where they cannot get out and harm our ability to draw inferences. The vast territory in the middle of the continuum—quasi-experiments—was the focus of this chapter. With quasi-experiments, there are threats running around here and there and we shepherd them to places where we can keep an eye on them and make them more or less implausible. Quasi-experimental arrangements can vastly improve on the anecdotal case study and provide a strong basis of knowledge even though these arrangements are not true experiments.

In schools, clinics, rehabilitation facilities, and other applied settings, the conditions for using true single-case experiments cannot always be met. Nevertheless, selected features of the designs can be used to form *quasi-single-case experiments*. The use of key features such as assessment over time and consideration of some of the criteria for data evaluation can strengthen the inferences that can be draw about intervention effects. In this chapter, several types of single-case demonstrations were presented that included critical components or approximations of true experiments. These components included drawing on information about the nature of change, the abruptness of change, and the likely course without treatment that can be used to make threats to internal validity implausible.

Unlike prior chapters, quasi-experiments are not formally recognized designs (e.g., as in ABAB or multiple-baseline designs). Quasi experiments are defined by those situations in which the investigator does not have control over critical facets of the arrangement of the intervention. The challenge is drawing on components of design to help improve the quality of our inferences. A range of situations was presented to show how information can be brought to bear in which change probably could be attributed to the intervention. Examples were presented that began with systematic assessment and that showed change over the course of intervention. The demonstrations vary in what can be brought to bear to draw inferences. In each case the use of systematic assessment alone was valuable. Systematic assessment at least provides the basis for inferring that change occurred, and this is a critical step in evaluating all programs whether at the level of states, schools, or individuals.

Data Evaluation

Previous chapters have discussed fundamental issues about assessment and experimental design for single-case research. I mentioned that the third component of methodology after assessment and design is data evaluation. The three components work in concert to permit one to draw inferences about the intervention. Assuming that the behavior (or domain of interest) has been adequately assessed and that the intervention was evaluated in an appropriate experimental design, one important matter remains: evaluating the data. Data evaluation consists of describing and making inferences about the changes. These inferences are not about what caused the change—that facet has much to do with the experimental design and whether the conditions were arranged to allow for that conclusion. Data evaluation focuses on whether the change is likely to be reliable and not likely to be due to chance fluctuations in performance.

In applied investigations where single-case designs are used, separate criteria are invoked to evaluate the data (Risley, 1970). The *experimental criterion* refers to whether the changes in behavior or the domain of interest is reliable. The *applied criterion* refers to whether the changes are important, that is, whether they make a difference that has applied significance. It is possible that reliable effects (experimental criterion) would be produced but that these effects would not have made an important change in the clients' lives (applied criterion). At first blush, these criteria might not seem to be unique to single-case research. In between-group studies we do not merely want to show that one intervention (e.g., method of teaching reading or math; form of psychotherapy) is better than another statistically (statistical significance). We want to show that the intervention also makes a difference that is of applied importance. Experimental and applied criteria are nicely intertwined in single-case research as a way to evaluate change; both are addressed in this chapter.

The primary method of data evaluation for single-case research is based on visual inspection. The chapter presents the underlying rationale, key criteria, and critical issues. Researchers trained in traditional between-group methods (i.e., all of us!) are more on home turf with statistical methods of data evaluation. Statistical tests are used in single-case research but not routinely. Statistical analyses of single-case data are still not common, but there are important advances that cast visual inspection and statistical tests in a new light. The appendix at the end of the book elaborates statistical analyses for the single case and considerations that influence both visual inspection and statistical tests. (If you like drama, intrigue, and methodological twists and turns, the appendix is a must, and the written version is much better than the movie.)

Evaluation of the data through visual inspection depends heavily on graphing of the data. In single-case research graphing is not only or merely a descriptive tool, it is part of the inferential process. Were reliable effects demonstrated by the intervention? Data are displayed graphically and evaluated. This chapter covers the methods and rationale of data evaluation in single-case designs, and the next chapter highlights commonly used methods of graphing to aid data evaluation.

VISUAL INSPECTION

The experimental criterion refers to a comparison of performance during the intervention with what performance would be like if the intervention had not been implemented. The purpose of the experimental criterion is to decide whether a veridical or reliable change has been demonstrated as well as whether that change can be attributed to the intervention. In traditional between-group research, the experimental criterion is met primarily by comparing performance between or among groups and examining the differences statistically. Groups receive different conditions (e.g., treatment vs. no treatment), and statistical tests are used to evaluate whether performance after treatment is sufficiently different to attain conventional levels of statistical significance ($p < .05$, .01).

In single-case research, the experimental criterion is met by examining the effects of the intervention at different points over time. The effects of the intervention are replicated (reproduced) at different points so that a judgment can be made based on the overall pattern of data. The manner in which intervention effects are replicated depends on the specific design. The underlying rationale of each design, outlined in previous chapters, conveys the ways in which baseline performance is used to predict future performance, and subsequent applications of the intervention test whether the predicted level is violated. For example, in the ABAB design the intervention effect is replicated over time for a single subject or group of subjects. The effect of the intervention is clear when systematic changes in behavior occur during each phase in which the intervention is presented or withdrawn. Similarly, in a multiple-baseline design, the intervention effect is replicated across the dimension for which multiple-baseline data have been gathered. The experimental criterion is met by determining whether performance shifts at each point that the intervention is introduced.

The manner in which a decision is reached about whether the data pattern reflects a systematic intervention effect is referred to as *visual inspection*. Visual inspection refers to reaching a judgment about the reliability or consistency of intervention effects by visually examining the graphed data. Visual examination of the data would seem to be subject to a tremendous amount of bias and subjectivity. If data evaluation is based on visually examining the pattern of the data, intervention effects (like beauty) might be in the eyes of the beholder.[1] To be sure, several problems can emerge with visual inspection, and these are highlighted in this chapter and detailed further in the appendix. However, it is important to convey the underlying rationale of visual inspection, how the method is carried out, and its strengths and weakness.

Description and Underlying Rationale

Visual inspection can be used in part because of the sorts of intervention effects that are sought in applied research. The underlying rationale is to encourage investigators to focus on interventions that produce potent effects and effects that would be obvious from merely inspecting the data (Baer, 1977; Michael, 1974; Sidman, 1960). Weak results are not regarded as meeting the stringent criteria of visual inspection. Hence, visual inspection is intended to serve as a filter or screening device to allow only clear and potent interventions to be interpreted as producing reliable effects. In contrast, in traditional between-group research, statistical evaluation is used to decide whether the effects (differences between groups) are reliable. Statistical evaluation is often more sensitive than visual inspection in detecting intervention effects. Intervention effects

---

[1] As the reader may well know, the expression that "beauty is in the eye of the beholder," is not quite accurate. Actually, research shows that there is considerable agreement in what beauty is, and who is beautiful, although there are individual taste preferences as well (e.g., Honekopp, 2006).

may be statistically significant even if they are relatively weak. The same effect might not be detected by visual inspection. Traditionally, the insensitivity of visual inspection for detecting weak effects has been viewed as an advantage rather than a disadvantage because it encourages investigators to look for potent interventions or to develop weak interventions to the point that large effects are produced (Parsonson & Baer, 1978, 1992).

Statistical evaluation and visual inspection are not fundamentally different with respect to their underlying rationale (Baer, 1977). Both methods of data evaluation attempt to avoid committing what have been referred to in statistics as Type I and Type II errors:

- Type I error refers to concluding that the intervention (or variable) produced an effect when, in fact, the results could be due to chance.
- Type II error refers to concluding that the intervention did *not* produce an effect when, in fact, it did.

Researchers typically give higher priority to avoiding a Type I error, concluding that a variable has an effect when the findings may have occurred by chance. In statistical analyses the probability of committing a Type I error can be specified by the level of confidence of the statistical test or α (e.g., $p \leq .05$). Specifically, one can say that if the investigation were carried out 100 times (or actually an infinite number of times) 5 (or 5%) of these would show a statistically significant result by "chance."

With visual inspection, the probability of a Type I error is not known. Hence, to avoid chance effects, the investigator looks for highly consistent effects that can be readily seen. By minimizing the probability of a Type I error, the probability of a Type II error is increased. Investigators relying on visual inspection are more likely than are those relying on statistical analyses to commit more Type II errors, that is, discarding or discounting effects that may be real but are not clear. Thus, reliance on visual inspection will overlook or discount many reliable but weak effects.

Criteria for Visual Inspection
Several situations arise in applied research in which intervention effects are likely to be so dramatic that one can easily see (from visual inspection) the change. For example, the behavior of interest (e.g., reading, exercising) may never be present. This can be stated by characterizing the data; the mean (e.g., number of times, number of minutes) and the standard deviation are zero. In such circumstances, even a minor increase in the target behavior during the intervention phase would be easily detected. Similarly, when the behavior of interest occurs very frequently during the baseline phase (e.g., reports of hallucinations, aggressive acts, cigarette smoking) and stops completely during the intervention phase, the magnitude of change usually permits clear judgments based on visual inspection. In short, in cases in which behavior is at the opposite extremes of the assessment range before and during treatment, the ease of invoking visual inspection can be readily understood. Indeed, the changes are self-evident and there is almost no need to make explicit the criteria for visual inspection. In any type of research, whether single-case or between-group, very dramatic changes might be so stark that there is no question that something important, reliable, and veridical took place. This type of change has been referred to as "slam bang" effects (Gilbert, Light, & Mosteller, 1975).

Table 12.1 Visual Inspection Criteria to Evaluate Data from Single-Case Experiments

Characteristics Related to Magnitude of the Change

1. Changes in Means across Phases—shifts in the average rate of performance on the continuous measure as phases (e.g., A,B) are changed.
2. Changes in Level across Phases—shift or discontinuity of performance (a leap, jump) from the end of one phase (e.g., A) to the very beginning of the next phase (e.g., B) and back again as the phase shifts again.

Characteristics Related to the Rate of Change

3. Changes in Trend or Slope—the trend line that characterizes the data within each phase (e.g., A,B) and that reflects a change from the trend line from a prior or subsequent phase.
4. Latency of the Change—the amount of time or the period between the onset of a condition (e.g., B or intervention) and the changes in performance. A short latency (immediate) change in the conditions (A,B) contributes to inferring that the condition was responsible for that change.

Overall Pattern

5. Nonoverlapping Data across Phases—this is a combined criterion involving some or all of the above criteria. The effects are unusually clear because the numerical data points on the graph in one phase (e.g., tantrums that lasted between 20 and 40 minutes on all the days of baseline) do not overlap (share any same numerical values) with the days during the intervention phases (e.g., tantrums lasted from 1 to 5 minutes).

Note: Visual inspection usually consists of invoking the first four criteria. The nonoverlapping-data criterion is equivalent to the "slam bang" effect mentioned in the text. From a data-evaluation perspective this effect is immediately evident from a graphic display of the data and would be readily acknowledged by all or most individuals perusing the data. The four other criteria are a matter of degree and the investigator must examine each one as well as the overall pattern they reflect.

In most situations, the data do not show a change from one extreme of the assessment scale to the other, and the criteria for making judgments by visual inspection need to be considered deliberately. Table 12.1 provides the criteria for visual inspection for easy reference but each criterion is elaborated next.

Visual inspection primarily depends on four characteristics of the data that are related to the magnitude and the rate of the changes across phases. The two characteristics related to magnitude are changes in *mean* and *level*. The two characteristics related to rate are changes in *trend* and *latency* of the change. It is important to examine each of these characteristics separately, even though in any applied set of data they act in concert.

Changes in means across phases refer to shifts in the *average* rate, level, or number on the measure. Consistent changes in means across phases can serve as a basis for deciding whether the data pattern meets the requirements of the design. A hypothetical example showing changes in means across the intervention phase is illustrated in an ABAB design in Figure 12.1. As evident in the figure, performance on the average (horizontal dashed line in each phase) changed in response to the different baseline and intervention phases. Visual inspection of this pattern suggests that the intervention was associated with changes as reflected on this particular criterion.

Changes in level are a little less familiar and refer to the *shift or discontinuity of performance from the end of one phase to the beginning of the next phase*. A change in level is independent of the change in mean. When one asks about what happened immediately after the intervention was implemented or withdrawn, the question is about the level of performance. Figure 12.2 shows change in level across phases in ABAB design. The figure shows that whenever the phase was altered, behavior assumed a new rate and shifted up or down rather quickly. The arrows in the figure show a space from the last day of one phase and the first day of the next phase.

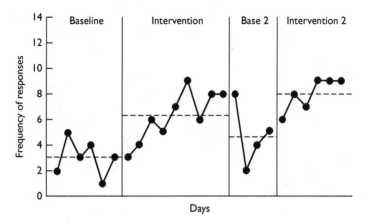

Figure 12.1. Hypothetical example of performance in an ABAB design with means in each phase represented with dashed lines.

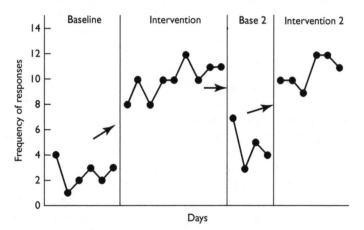

Figure 12.2. Hypothetical example of performance in an ABAB design. The arrows point to the changes in level or discontinuities associated with a change from one phase to another.

It so happens that a change in level in this latter example would also be accompanied by a change in mean across the phases. However, level and mean changes do not necessarily go together. It is possible but not usually the case that a rapid change in level occurs but that the mean remains the same across phases or that the mean changes but no abrupt shift in level has occurred.

Changes in trend are of obvious importance in applying visual inspection. Trend or slope refers to the tendency for the data to show systematic increases or decreases over time. Altering phases within the design may show that the direction of behavior changes as the intervention is applied or withdrawn. Figure 12.3 illustrates a hypothetical example in which trends have changed over the course of the phase in an ABAB design. Discussing the figure with this criterion in mind, we might say there was no trend (horizontal line or zero slope) in baseline, an accelerating slope during the

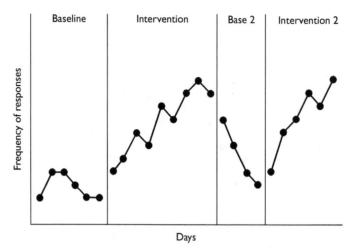

Figure 12.3. Hypothetical example of performance in an ABAB design with changes in trend across phases. Baseline shows a relatively stable or possibly decreasing trend. When the intervention is introduced, an accelerating trend is evident. This trend is reversed when the intervention is withdrawn (Base 2) and is reinstated when the intervention is reintroduced.

intervention phase, a decelerating slope during the return to baseline, and an accelerating slope again in the second intervention phase. The effects are dramatic as if to suggest that behavior is turned off and on based on what occurred during the phases. The slopes moving in different directions fit well with the logic of single-case designs I mentioned previously (describe, predict, and test). A marked change in slope conveys that something happened that is reliable and changed the predicted pattern (slope) of performance from each prior phase.

Finally, the *latency of the change* that occurs when phases are altered is an important characteristic of the data for invoking visual inspection. Latency refers to the period between the onset or termination of one condition (e.g., intervention, return to baseline) and changes in performance. The more closely in time that the change occurs after the experimental conditions have been altered, the clearer the intervention effect. There is a commonsense feature of this. If I tell my child to clean her room, and she does this immediately, the chances are my request was the intervention responsible for change. If I tell my child to clean her room, and she does this a month later, my request could have been responsible but the delay very much suggests that something else was involved.

A hypothetical example is provided in Figure 12.4, showing only the first two phases of separate ABAB designs. In the top panel, implementation of the intervention after baseline was associated with a rapid change in performance. In the bottom panel, the intervention did not immediately lead to change. The time between the onset of the intervention and behavior change was longer than in the top panel, and it is slightly less clear that the intervention may have led to the change. As a general rule, the shorter the period between the onset of the intervention and behavior change, the easier it is to infer that the intervention led to change.

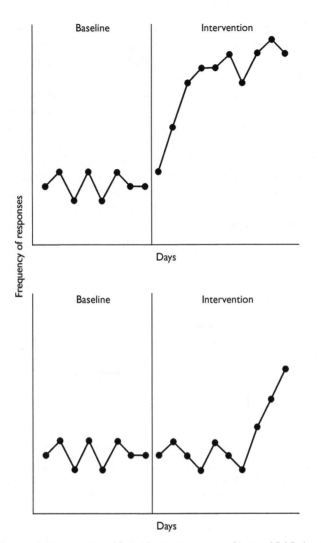

Figure 12.4. Hypothetical examples of first AB phases as part of larger ABAB designs. *Upper panel* shows that when the intervention was introduced, behavior changed rapidly. *Lower panel* shows that when the intervention was introduced, behavior change was delayed. The changes in both upper and lower panels are reasonably clear. Yet as a general rule, as the latency between the onset of the intervention and behavior change increases, questions are more likely to arise about whether the intervention or extraneous factors accounted for change.

The importance of the latency of the change after the onset of the intervention depends on the type of intervention and domain of functioning. For example, one would not expect rapid changes in applying a diet or exercise regimen to treat obesity. Weight reduction usually reflects gradual changes after interventions begin. In contrast, stimulant medication is the primary treatment used to control hyperactivity among children diagnosed with Attention-Deficit/Hyperactivity Disorder. The medication usually produces rapid effects and one can see changes on the day the medication is provided (one often sees a return to baseline levels on the same day, as the stimulant is metabolized). More generally, drawing inferences about the intervention also includes considerations about how the intervention is likely to work (e.g., rapidly, gradually) and how that expectation fits the data pattern.

Visual inspection is conducted by judging the extent of changes in means, levels, and trends, and the latency of change evident across phases and whether the changes are consistent with the requirements of the particular design. The individual components are important but one looks at the gestalt too, that is, the parts all together and the whole they provide. Figure 12.5 illustrates some hypothetical patterns for AB phases only to convey some of the combinations of the criteria and how they may or may not go together. The figure conveys permutations of the four criteria. This is only a small set of the range of possibilities because each criterion is a matter of degree and there will be more phases (e.g., ABAB rather than just AB or more opportunities to evaluate phase changes as in a multiple-baseline design). Even so, with the relatively simple

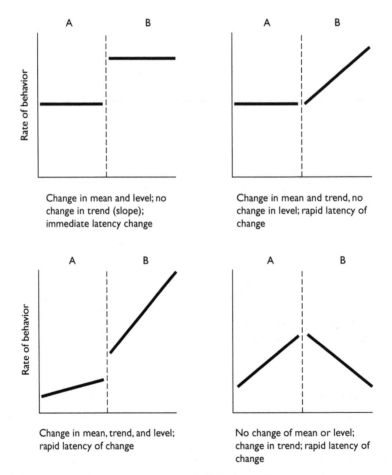

Change in mean and level; no change in trend (slope); immediate latency change

Change in mean and trend, no change in level; rapid latency of change

Change in mean, trend, and level; rapid latency of change

No change of mean or level; change in trend; rapid latency of change

Figure 12.5. Examples of data patterns over two (AB) phases illustrating changes in means, levels, trends, and latency.

graphs, one can begin to see potential complexities and how it might not be quite so easy to apply the criteria. I have crafted the graphs to convey in each case that something happened during the B phase, but sometimes the slope remained the same (top left); sometimes the means remained the same (bottom right) and so on. Shortly we will look at some real examples that better represent full designs (not just AB phases).

The ease of applying the criteria and examining the data pattern as a whole depend on background characteristics I mentioned when describing the logic of single-case designs. Whether a particular effect will be considered reliable through visual inspection depends on the variability of performance, trends within a particular phase, and whether the phases provide clear estimates for the describe, predict, and test functions of the design. Data that present minimal variability, show consistent patterns over relatively extended phases, and show that the changes in means, levels, or trends are replicable across phases for a given subject or across several subjects are more easily interpreted than data in which one or more of these characteristics are not obtained.

Changes in means, levels, and trends, and latencies of change across phases may go together, thereby making visual inspection easy to invoke. For example, data across phases may not overlap. *Nonoverlapping data* refers to the finding that the values of the data points during the baseline phase do not approach any of the values of the data points attained during the intervention phase. For example, if one looks at Figure 12.5, the two graphs on the left show that not one data point in baseline (A) was the same as or within the range of data points during the intervention (B). Those were hypothetical graphs and omitted the normal day-to-day variability in performance. Nonoverlapping data where that variability is evident, that is, in real data, are even more impressive. In short, if there are changes in the means, levels, trends, and latencies across phases and the data do not overlap, there is little quibble about whether the changes are reliable and meet the experimental criteria. The challenges come when data are not perfect, and these challenges are evident whether visual inspection or statistical analyses are used (please see the appendix for a more extended discussion of these challenges).

Illustrations

A few illustrations are helpful to convey application of the criteria in situations one is likely to encounter, that is, an imperfect world in which the participants have not read this chapter and are not doing what we would like to see (e.g., nonoverlapping data across phases). Visual inspection does not require perfection. Here are some examples.

In this example, the focus was on children undergoing restorative dental treatment (O'Callaghan, Allen, Powell, & Salama, 2006). It is common for young children to be disruptive and difficult to manage during their dental care, with estimates of 20 to 25% of all children showing disruptive behavior during such work. This not only makes administration of the activities of cleaning and scraping of one's teeth difficult, but actually can expose children to injury as they suddenly move about during invasive procedures. Allowing brief breaks or periods of escape from the procedures can reduce the difficult-to-manage behaviors. This program included five children (ages 4 to 7 years, three girls, two boys) with disruptive behavior and in need of at least three visits for tooth preparation and restoration. Each visit lasted 45 to 90 minutes. The intervention consisted of giving breaks to the child based on a fixed-time schedule. A small apparatus was attached to the dentist's waist band to signal when these breaks would occur. A video camera in the room recorded all sessions. Child behavior, including bodily movements, complaining, moaning, gagging, and crying, was recorded in intervals (of 15 seconds). The goal was to reduce the disruptive behaviors.

A multiple-baseline design was used across subjects with baseline (measured in minutes) across all of the visits combined. The intervention consisted of introducing brief periods in which there was a 10-second pause or break in the procedure. At first the breaks were frequent (every 15 seconds), but then they extended to every 1 minute. The procedure for giving breaks was explained to the child and initially practiced. Also, each break was cued by the dentist as, "It's break time."

Figure 12.6 displays the results across children. Disruptive behavior decreased for all children during the intervention period. However, as one looks at the data (graph) for each child, it is clear that all four criteria for visual inspection are *not* met in each graph. Across all five children the means change from baseline to intervention. As for changes in level (discontinuity at point of intervention for each child), possibly two (Elaine and George) show this effect. As for changes in trend, perhaps all but one (George) show a different slope from baseline through intervention phases. Finally, as for latency of the change, the change was immediate for all but two children (Melissa and Kevin). Clearly, the criteria differentially apply to the children. This might be analogous to between-group research that shows significant differences among or between groups on some measures but not on others. (Between-group studies do not usually examine the effects that were evident with some individuals but not others.) How do we interpret this? If one looks at the overall graph, it is reasonably safe to conclude that the intervention probably accounts for the change. Each child's behavior changed as the intervention was introduced and not before.

Consider another example where invoking the criteria is a little more difficult. In this example, the goal was to change the behavior of individuals who took orders in the drive-through window of fast-food restaurants (Wiesman, 2006). The goal was to get the order takers to ask customers to "upsize" their orders. Upsizing (sometimes called "supersizing") or up-selling is a common practice in many businesses (sales of computer hardware and software; travel, hotels) where customers who are buying are encouraged to buy a little more of what they are getting or something closely related. A familiar example occurs at movie theaters. If we order a small (12 oz., or 340.19 grams) size soft drink, usually we are immediately informed that for 25 cents more we can have 32 oz. (907.18 g)—and a catheter. This study in the fast-food restaurant wanted the order takers to ask customers to upsize their orders as they communicated through speakers and headsets, in keeping with fast-food restaurant procedures. The upsizing was asking individuals to order a combination meal (sandwich, fries, and beverage) that involved larger portions of what they ordered at an additional price. Two different fast-food restaurants were studied: one on an interstate highway and another in a small college town. They were affiliated with the same national food chain but were 11 miles apart. Observations were made by observers who were near enough to hear the conversation of the customer and order taker and record yes or no if upsizing was offered. A multiple-baseline design across the two settings was used to evaluate an intervention. The intervention consisted of praise by managers as they saw the behavior of the order takers throughout the shift, weekly

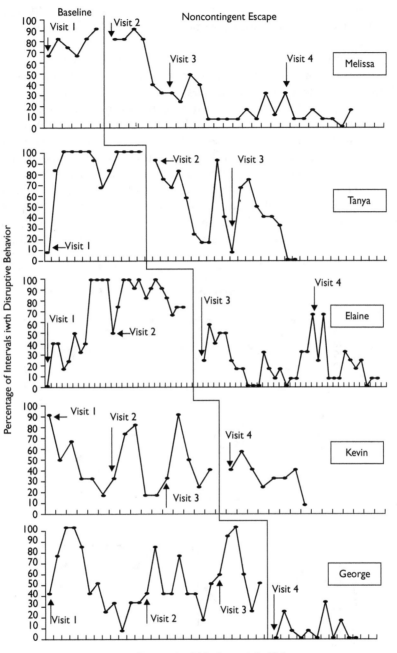

Figure 12.6. Percentage of (15-second) intervals containing disruptive behavior for each child across visits.   *(Source: O'Callaghan et al., 2006.)*

praise for keeping the upsizing requests of customers above 80% (of the opportunities), and graphed feedback. The purpose here is to discuss the data that are presented in Figure 12.7.

Was the intervention effective, and were the changes likely to be due to the intervention? Probably most would agree but perhaps express a minute reservation. During the intervention phase two changes are clear. The mean increased over baseline, and the variability (up and down range of the data points) decreased. In addition, changes in level (when the intervention was introduced) were also evident. Slope changed as well, at least in the top graph. However, the top graph shows a clear trend toward improvement without the intervention, and that introduces a slight ambiguity. The second graph shows no trend or a slight trend toward decrements in the desired behavior. Overall I would say that the intervention accounts for the change in light of the demonstration. Experimental control might have been helped by one more setting. As I noted in the chapter on multiple-baseline designs, two baselines are an absolute minimum but requires a perfectly clear data pattern. A third baseline can make a difference in

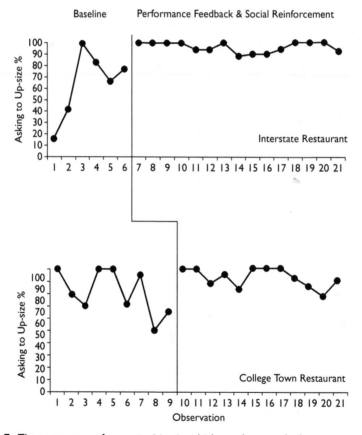

Figure 12.7. The percentage of opportunities in which employees asked customers to upsize a meal during baseline and intervention phases in a multiple-baseline design across two drive-through restaurants.   *(Source: Wiesman, 2006.)*

case one of the baselines is not quite so clear, and that is largely why three baselines is a recommended minimum.

Other points are important to note about the demonstration. First, employee behavior (asking to upsize) was evident in baseline at a high rate (e.g., mean of 65% in baseline for the top graph). This increased to 96%. There was a clear change in mean, and the change made a difference to the business. Although exact profit gains could not be estimated, thousands of combination (upsized) meals were sold, and a profit of $.25 was made each time. Over time, every month, this could make a huge profit difference. Seemingly small changes, perhaps like those graphed, can be large when impact accumulates over time and across many people (customers).

These two examples can be placed in the context of other examples in this and prior chapters. Because the designs may have many phases (ABAB, ABCABC) or baselines (multiple-baselines), there are many opportunities to invoke the criteria. Invoking the criteria for visual inspection requires judgments about the pattern of data in the entire design and not merely changes across one or two phases. Unambiguous effects require that the criteria mentioned previously be met throughout the design, that is, across the different phase shifts. To the extent that the criteria are not consistently met, conclusions about the reliability of intervention effects become tentative. For example, changes in an ABAB design may show non-overlapping data points for the first AB phases but no clear differences across the second AB phases. The absence of a consistent pattern of data that meets the criteria mentioned previously limits the conclusions that can be drawn.

Problems and Considerations

Lack of Concrete Decision-making Rules. The use of visual inspection as the primary basis for evaluating data in single-case designs has raised major concerns. First, there are no concrete decision rules for determining whether a particular demonstration shows or fails to show a reliable effect. The process of visual inspection would seem to permit, if not actively foster, subjectivity and inconsistency in the evaluation of intervention effects. The situation can be contrasted with statistical analyses as used in between-group research. Groups are compared and cutoff points (e.g., $p < .05$) are invoked to decide whether or not an effect was reliable or whether an effect is small, medium, or large (e.g., effect size). Statistical significance gives a binary decision-making tool (significant or not), although we investigators squeeze subjectivity in by using phrases with no real legitimacy in null hypothesis testing, as reflected in such desperate terms as "approached significance," "was almost statistically significant," or "showed a trend toward significance." Apart from these, statistical indices have their own degree of inherent arbitrary factors, problems, and objections.[2] Yet, decision making based on statistical significance seems

---

[2] Researchers trained in the tradition of quantitative research (between-group designs, statistical analyses, null hypothesis testing) often object to the subjectivity of visual inspection. Occasionally, there is an extreme view that visual inspection is purely in the eye of the beholder, but there are explicit criteria as I have noted. As important, perhaps, statistical analyses are not free from subjectivity, that is, views about what to do that have pivotal consequences for drawing conclusions. Many statistical tests (e.g., factor analysis, regression, cluster analyses, time-series analysis, path analyses)

more straightforward than decision making based on visual inspection. Two or more investigators applying a given statistical test to the data ought to reach the same conclusion about the impact of the intervention, that is, whether the difference was statistically significant or not.

There is an empirical question underlying the concern. Can different judges viewing single-case data graphed in the usual way reach similar decisions about whether there was an effect? It is one thing to say there are criteria, but quite another to see if they can be reliably invoked. In fact, several studies have shown that judges, even when they are experts in single-case research, often disagree about particular data patterns and whether the effects were reliable (e.g., DeProspero & Cohen, 1979; Franklin, Gorman, Beasley, & Allison, 1997; Jones, Weinrott, & Vaught, 1978; Normand & Bailey, 2006; Park, Marascuilo, & Gaylord-Ross, 1990). (The appendix elaborates the concern insofar as it has served as an impetus for statistical evaluation.) Thus the absence of clear decision rules that can be reliably invoked is a problem when the results are not crystal clear.

Efforts have been made to improve reliability in judging data by visual inspection by providing explicit training (e.g., lectures, instructions), by using visual aids in graphing the results (e.g., novel ways of presenting trend lines), and by specifying criteria in relation to those aids to make the process of visual inspection replicable and more explicit (Fisher, Kelley, & Lomas, 2003; Harbst, Ottenbacher, & Harris, 1991; Normand & Bailey, 2006; Skiba et al., 1989; Stewart, Carr, Brandt, & McHenry, 2007; Swoboda, Kratochwill, & Levin, 2009). These efforts have produced mixed results. Sometimes their impact still does not lead to high agreement; sometimes their effects are not maintained. At this point, no training regimen has emerged that redresses the unreliability in making judgments with visual inspection criteria.

Multiple Influences in Reaching a Decision.   One of the difficulties of visual inspection is that multiple factors contribute to judgments about the data. The range of factors and how they are integrated to reach a decision are not clear. The extent of agreement among judges using visual inspection is a complex function of changes in means, levels, and trends as well as the background variables, such as variability, stability, and replication of effects within or across subjects (DeProspero & Cohen, 1979; Matyas & Greenwood, 1990). All of these criteria, and perhaps others yet to be made explicit, are combined to reach a final judgment about the effects of the intervention. How to weight the different variables and criteria to make a decision could be very subjective.

---

[2] (Continued) include a number of decision points about various solutions, parameter estimates, and levels or criteria to continue or include variables in the analysis or model. These decisions are rarely made explicit in the data analyses. In many instances "default" criteria in the data-analytic programs do not convey that a critical choice has been made and that the basis of this choice can be readily challenged because there is no necessary objective reason that one choice is better than another. These are not minor facets of statistical analyses. For example, meta-analyses of psychotherapy are extremely popular, and those less familiar with the methods of conducting meta-analyses may view the analyses as straightforward. Yet conclusions about the effectiveness of psychotherapy can vary widely depending precisely on how the statistics for the meta-analyses (e.g., effect size) are computed (Matt, 1989; Matt & Navarro, 1997; Weisz, Weiss, Han, Granger, & Morton, 1995).

The decision is really a complex mental multiple regression equation where the set of variables all have some weight in leading to the decision. That is, even though we might not be using statistics to make the decision, there is a way in which the decision is fundamentally a statistical one. We as observers are weighing the variables differently and subjectively (subjective beta weights so to speak). In cases in which the effects of the intervention are not dramatic, it is not surprising that judges disagree.

There are special characteristics of single-case data that cannot be detected visually and considered suitably when invoking visual inspection. Two of these briefly are the fact that the data from one occasion to the next can be correlated. This phenomenon, referred to as *serial dependence* (detailed in the appendix), cannot be easily "seen" but requires statistical evaluation to detect.[3] However, data that are correlated in this way are associated with even less agreement when invoking visual inspection. In addition, trends in the data (e.g., baseline) are not all straight lines that are easily detected. Some trends can be picked up only through statistical evaluation of the data. Hidden trends can obscure or mislead when trying to determine if the intervention produced a reliable change. Interestingly, such trends can interfere with both visual inspection and statistical data-evaluation methods. (Please see the appendix for more lengthy discussions on these points.)

A pertinent side comment pertains to research on decision making outside of the context of visual inspection and data evaluation. We have learned that decision making and judgment are influenced by all sorts of factors of which we are unaware and cannot weigh explicitly. For example, influences in the environment (e.g., smells, sights, stimuli placed in the background) register insofar as they have direct influence on us, but do not register at a level of consciousness, that is, we cannot state that we noticed them, and we categorically state they had no influences on us when challenged (Bargh & Morsella, 2008). I mention this because advances in other areas of psychology have elaborated many nuances of decision making. In the context of the visual inspection, I doubt that smells in the air influence the decision as to whether the intervention altered a patient's depression when introduced in a multiple-baseline design. Yet, the absence of a starkly clear demonstration where the visual inspection criteria are met, allows for more influences to operate. For example, in one project, undergraduates (with no experience in single-case designs) were asked to judge changes in AB graphs (hypothetical data) (Spirrison & Mauney, 1994). There was a small correlation ($r = .3$) between whether they said there were changes and the extent to which they thought the intervention was acceptable (reasonable, appropriate). That is, characteristics or attributes of the intervention influenced judgments about the impact of that intervention. This is one demonstration to show that visual inspection unwittingly can reflect other factors than whether the criteria for visual inspection were met.

---

[3] When the subject has multiple data points, there can be significant serial dependence or autocorrelation, a property of the data in which the error terms from one data point to the next are correlated. That is, data are autocorrelated when performance of behavior on one day is influenced or correlated with performance on the next. This feature introduces an unobservable characteristic that can influence judgment from visual inspection and also influence the results of statistical evaluation. These and related matters are elaborated in the appendix.

The disagreement among judges using visual inspection has been used as an argument to favor statistical analysis of the data as a supplement to or replacement of visual inspection. The attractive feature of statistical analysis is that once the statistic is decided, the result that is achieved is usually consistent across investigators. And the final result (statistical significance) is not altered by the judgment of the investigator. Yet, statistics are not the arbiter of what is a "true" effect, and there are scores of statistical options that do not yield the same result (please see the appendix).

Search for Only Marked Effects. Another criticism levied against visual inspection is that it regards only those effects that are very marked as significant. Many interventions might prove to be consistent in the effects they produce but are relatively weak. Such effects might not be detected by visual inspection and would be overlooked. I mentioned that single-case designs began to flourish in behavioral research, and that there was an explicit interest in identifying only those interventions whose effects were unequivocal. Visual inspection was seen as a filter well suited to this goal (Baer, 1977). Interventions that pass the stringent criteria of visual inspection without equivocation are likely to be powerful and consistent.

With a perspective of time, some changes in intervention priorities, and extension of single-case designs to novel areas, the original rationale is more readily challenged. First, analyses of published single-case data reveal that many studies do not produce strong intervention effects. The effects are actually debatable as to whether such effects are present at all (Glass, 1997; Parker, Cryer, & Byrns, 2006). So the rationale of using visual inspection as a filter to detect only strong effects is an ideal not routinely met.

Second, judgments about whether there was a change are somewhat opposite from the notion of identifying marked effects. When judges make errors from visual inspection, they are more likely to say there is an effect when there is not one rather than fail to detect existent effects (Matyas & Greenwood, 1991; Normand & Bailey, 2006). That is, the search for marked effects is based on the view that unclear and iffy effects will not be identified. Actually, judges "detect" nonexistent effects, the opposite from the intended goals of visual inspection. This is the equivalence of Type I error, mentioned previously.

Third, looking for marked effects may confuse the experimental and applied criteria for evaluating data. As I noted, the experimental criterion focuses on the reliability of the finding and whether change can be explained by normal fluctuations, preexisting patterns in the data, and chance effects. For this criterion, the strength of the effect is not critical per se. The applied criterion refers to whether the impact is so large as to make a palpable difference. These criteria are related; an effect that meets the applied criterion by definition is likely to be so strong as to reflect a reliable change and meet the experimental criterion. The applied criterion (e.g., teaching reading to children who could not read; eliminating self-injury in an adolescent with a developmental disability) is a stringent bar. Even so, an intervention effect could be reliable and meet the experimental criterion without having genuine impact on the life of an individual. The concern that we only want to identify potent effects mixes these criteria a bit. We want to identify reliable effects (experimental criterion) and, as shown later, we can even meet an important applied criterion with very weak effects.

Overlooking weak but reliable effects can have unfortunate consequences. The possibility exists that interventions when first developed may have weak effects. It would be unfortunate if these interventions were prematurely discarded before they could be developed further. Interventions with reliable but weak effects might eventually achieve potent effects if investigators developed them further. Insofar as the stringent criteria of visual inspection discourage the pursuit of interventions that do not have potent effects, it may be a detriment to developing effective interventions.

General Comments. The concerns I have noted are the primary ones that are invoked when visual inspection is evaluated. A caveat ought to be mentioned about the disagreement or apparent unreliability of visual inspection. First, in fact the conditions of visual inspection often are met. Examples throughout this book are not randomly drawn from the literature, but their sheer number conveys that change can be detected and it is often quite clear that the change can be attributed to the intervention because the design requirements and data-evaluation criteria were met.

Second, many of the studies that evaluate visual inspection have raters evaluate changes across AB designs. The data are sometimes real or sometimes computer generated; the raters often, but not always, are students or individuals without training. Thus, the data criticizing visual inspection have their own problems. In single-case research in everyday settings, AB designs are not sufficient either for the design or for data evaluation. One looks for the "describe, predict, and test" logic of the design in multiple phases (ABAB design) or in other multiple replications of the effect (multiple-baseline designs). That is, we profit from the full design in making the judgments and not just two phases. Also, data from naïve raters not trained in or familiar with visual inspection are not quite direct tests of how visual inspection is applied. Again, not all studies of visual inspection rely on inexperienced raters and present AB designs. I mention these caveats not as a defense of visual inspection, but rather to convey that the research on visual inspection has its own issues and sources of ambiguity.

On balance, what conclusions might be reasonable to make? First, visual inspection requires that a particular pattern of data is present in baseline and across subsequent phases. These include little or no trend or trend in directions opposite from the trend expected in the following phase and slight variability. Also, the specific criteria, when met (e.g., change in means, level, etc.) readily allow application of visual inspection. Often the criteria are not met or are incompletely met and the effects are debatable.

Second, as the data pattern is less persuasive and moves away from little or no trend and less clear changes in mean, level, and so on, extraneous factors are more likely to enter into the judgment about whether there is a reliable effect. There are two extremes that are easily picked up by visual inspection: (1) something really large happened and all the criteria for visual inspection were met, including nonoverlapping data across phases; and (2) nothing at all happened and none of the criteria was met. In this latter case, the data just looked like one baseline even though several interventions were tried. The middle ground, but not all of the middle ground, could invite subjectivity. However, design and data evaluation act in concert, so if four of five behaviors in a multiple-baseline design across behaviors show changes in most of the visual inspection criteria, the "subjectivity" is likely to be reliable. Visual inspection ought not to be cast aside.

When single-case designs were coming into their own, it made sense perhaps to carve out an identity by showing how visual inspection was unique and accomplished things that were not achieved by statistical tests. Visual inspection and statistical evaluation, very much like single-case designs and traditional between-group designs, are tools for drawing inferences. There is no need to limit one's tools, and indeed there are several disadvantages in doing so. Few studies provide statistical evaluation and evaluation of the individual data via visual inspection. When they do, they convey the critical point: the methods have a slightly different yield and each provides information the other did not provide (e.g., Brossart, Meythaler, Parker, McNamara, & Elliot, 2008; Feather & Ronan, 2006; Molloy, 1990).

STATISTICAL EVALUATION

Visual inspection constitutes the criterion used most frequently to evaluate data from single-case experiments. The reason for this pertains to the historical development of the designs and the larger methodological approach of which they are a part, namely, the experimental analysis of behavior (Kazdin, 1978). Systematic investigation of the single subject began in laboratory research with non-human animals. The careful control afforded by laboratory conditions helped to meet major requirements of the designs, including minimal variability and stable rates of performance. Potent variables were examined (e.g., schedules of reinforcement) with effects that could be easily detected against the highly stable baseline levels. Indeed, one could readily see immediate changes in behavior (e.g., lever pressing) in response to shifts in conditions across phases. The lawfulness and regularity of behavior in relation to selected variables obviated the need for statistical tests.

As the single-case experimental approach was extended to human behavior, applications began to encompass a variety of populations, behaviors, and settings. The interest in investigating and identifying potent variables has not changed. Invariably, we want to identify interventions that exert impact and have clinically important outcomes. However, the complexity of the situations in which applied investigations are conducted occasionally has made evaluations of intervention effects more difficult. Control over and standardization of the assessment of behaviors, extraneous factors that can influence performance, and characteristics of the organisms (humans) themselves are reduced, compared with laboratory conditions. As evident in many of the examples throughout the book, interventions that draw on single-case designs are used in restaurants, at traffic intersections, in operating rooms where surgery is performed, and all sorts of other settings of everyday life. Hence, the potential sources of variation that may make interventions more difficult to evaluate are increased in applied research. In selected situations, the criteria for invoking visual inspection are not invariably or unequivocally met. Against that backdrop, statistical tests began to be used to compare data from different phases and to answer such questions as: Are the means from all baseline phases different from the means of all intervention phases in an ABAB design? Are the changes over time within an intervention phase statistically significant? The use of statistics was seen as an aid rather than an approach to replace visual inspection.

Reasons for Using Statistical Tests

When the data meet the criteria for visual inspection outlined earlier, there is little need to corroborate the results with statistical tests, except to comfort those not as familiar with the approach. In many situations, however, the ideal data patterns may not emerge, and statistical tests may provide important advantages. Consider a few of the circumstances in which statistical analyses may be especially useful.

Trend in the Data. Visual inspection depends on having stable baseline phases in which no trend in the direction of the expected change is evident. Evaluation of intervention effects is extremely difficult when baseline performance is systematically improving. In this case, the intervention still may be required to accelerate the rate of improvement. Rates of crime, HIV, motorcycle accidents, and cigarette smoking, for examples, all might be declining in a given city or county, but still will be high and warrant intervention. As a real example, heart attacks and death from heart disease are declining in the United States, although this is still the single greatest cause of death. In these examples, improvements in baseline are not a reason for doing nothing. An intervention might still be important to accelerate the process. Visual inspection criteria may be difficult to invoke with initial improvements already underway during baseline. As a more general statement, trend during baselines may interfere with applying visual inspection and drawing inferences. What we have learned is that complex patterns can form trends that are not detectable visually. Statistical analyses can examine whether a reliable change has occurred during the intervention phase over and above what would be expected by some trend, whether that trend could or could not be detected visually (please see the appendix). Hence, statistical analyses can provide information that may be difficult to obtain through visual inspection.

Increased Intrasubject Variability. Single-case designs have routinely been used in applied settings (e.g., psychiatric hospitals, institutions for persons with developmental disabilities, classrooms, day-care centers, juvenile detention centers, foster-care facilities). Rather amazingly, investigators in these settings have been able to control (experimentally) several features of the environment, including behavior of the staff and events occurring during the day other than the intervention, that may influence performance and implementation of the intervention. Careful control also reduces extra, unnecessary, and excess variability in the data that serves as a threat to data-evaluation validity. For example, in a classroom study, the investigator may carefully monitor the intervention so that it is implemented with little or no variation over time. Also, teacher interactions with the children may be carefully monitored and controlled. Students may receive the same or similar tasks while the observations are in effect. Because extraneous factors are held relatively constant for purposes of experimental control, variability in subject performance can be held to a minimum. As noted earlier, visual inspection is more easily applied to single-case data when variability is small.

Now that interventions and single-case designs have been extended to everyday life settings (e.g., business, restaurants, etc.), control over the environment and potential influences on behavior are reduced, and variability in subject performance may be relatively large. With larger variability, visual inspection may be more difficult to apply than in well-controlled settings. Statistical evaluation may be of greater use in examining whether reliable changes have been obtained. Statistical evaluation is not necessarily "better" in any way, but rather provides a tool that might reduce ambiguity about the reliability of the effect.

Investigation of New Research Areas.   Applied research has stressed the importance of investigating interventions that produce marked effects on behavior. In many instances, especially in new areas of research, intervention effects may be relatively weak. The investigator working in a new area is likely to be unfamiliar with the intervention and the conditions that maximize its efficacy. As the investigator learns more about the intervention, he or she can change the procedure to improve its efficacy. Also, an intervention may appear weak when applied to everyone but strong as we learn for whom that intervention is especially well suited.

In the initial stages of research, it may be important to identify promising interventions that warrant further scrutiny. Visual inspection may be too stringent a criterion and lead to rejection or discounting of interventions that produce reliable but weak effects. Such interventions should not be abandoned because they do not achieve large changes initially. These interventions may be developed further through subsequent research and eventually produce large effects that could be detected through visual inspection. Even if such interventions would not eventually produce strong effects in their own right, they may be important because they can enhance or contribute to the effectiveness of other procedures. Hence, statistical analyses may serve a useful purpose in detecting reliable but weaker influences that could prove to be quite valuable.

Small Changes May Be Important.   The rationale underlying visual inspection has been the search for large changes in the performance of individual subjects. Over the years, single-case designs and the interventions typically evaluated by these designs have been extended to a wide range of problems. In the process, a public-health perspective has assumed increased significance. That perspective reflects concern for the public at large—large numbers of people—and what can be done for them. From a public-health perspective, little things (intervention effects) can mean a lot. For selected problems, it is not always the case that the value of the intervention effect can be determined on the basis of the magnitude of change in an individual person's performance. Small changes in the behavior of individual subjects or in the behaviors of large groups of subjects often are very important.

Consider three related situations in which small changes are important. First, small changes can be especially important when the effort and costs of delivering treatment are low and treatment can be administered on a large scale. Previously (Chapter 10), I mentioned an example of a brief intervention conducted during a physical examination and designed to reduce cigarette smoking among patients. Physician visits are relatively brief (median = 12 to 15 minutes) in the United States. Scores of controlled trials have shown that physician (or nurse) advice during the visit can have reliable but small impact on smoking. The physician says something like the following to patients who are cigarette smokers: "I think it is important for you to quit tobacco use now," or "As your clinician, I want you to know that quitting tobacco is the most important thing you can do to protect your health." The outcome effects are small but consistent (e.g., Fiore et al., 2000; Rice & Stead, 2008; Stead, Bergson, & Lancaster, 2008). The comments led to approximately a 2.5% increment in abstinence rates of smoking compared to no intervention. Internal medicine practice guidelines now recommend that physicians include in their visit specific advice to stop smoking. We know from psychological research that advice, feedback, recommendations, raising awareness, and so on are not among the strong interventions. Even so, a reliable effect that is low in cost and can be administered on a large scale can have enormous benefits. The benefits are for the individuals who stopped smoking, for their families (secondary and tertiary smoking are now known to have deleterious health effects), and for society at large (the cost burden of smoking). Graphing of cigarette smoking (e.g., proportion of individuals who become abstinent during baseline and after the physician-advice intervention) might not satisify visual inspection criteria. The effect is weak and small, but important.

Second and related to the that, in many social contexts a small change is significant because of the focus and its qualitative rather than quantitative features. For example, a small and perhaps even minute reduction in violent crimes (e.g., murder, rape) in a community would be important. An intervention program (e.g., a special police patrol program, improved lighting and video survelleince) may produce only small quantitative changes (e.g., five fewer murders per year). When graphed against the larger baseline background (e.g., 100 murders per year) perhaps visual inspection would not be able to detect the small changes. Loss of life and the trauma to victims and their families are significant if reliably reduced in any amount. In many areas of public life (e.g., a terrorist attack, death of police and fire-fighters, loss of mother or child at child-birth, and train, plane, and other vehicle accidents), the value stems from having any impact. Loss of a life makes a difference, and a "weak" intervention that "only" saves a few lives is hugely important.

Third, small changes in the behavior of individuals can accumulate to produce large effects. Depending on what is graphed (individual behavior or outcomes accumulated across many individuals) visual inspection might or might not be up to the task of detecting an effect. For example, an intervention designed to reduce energy consumption (e.g., use of one's personal car, use of energy-saving appliances) may show relatively weak effects on the behavior of individual subjects—just a little bit of energy saved. The results may not be dramatic by visual inspection criteria. As a dramatic illustration, use of one energy-efficient (fluorescent) light bulb in each of approximately 110 million households in the United States would have the impact of reducing greenhouse gasses equivalent to taking 1.3 million cars off the road (Fishman, 2006; www.energystar. gov). In short, small changes, when accrued over a large number of individuals, can be important because of the larger changes these would signal for an entire group. To the extent that statistical analyses can contribute to data evaluation in these circumstances, they provide an important contribution.

In general, there are many circumstances in which we may want to be able to detect intervention effects that may be small at the level of individual behavior or indeed relatively small at the larger level of the group. Small but reliable changes may be very noteworthy given the significance of the focus, ease of delivery of the intervention, and the larger impact these changes have across many people. Visual inspection may not detect small changes that are reliable. Statistical analyses may help determine whether the intervention had a reliable, even though undramatic effect on behavior.

Replicability in Data Evaluation. Perhaps the most general argument that might favor the use of statistical tests pertains to what we are trying to do in science. We have invented the scientific method that is designed to reduce subjectivity and bias as much as possible. We develop assessments and validate our instruments, we use control groups and conditions, we keep experimenters naïve with respect to intervention conditions, and we have in mind that the threats to validity are stalking us and our findings like hungry ants at a picnic. The goal is not some methodological elegance for its own sake, but to understand our world in such a way that the findings are replicable by others and do not depend on opinion and subjectivity. These are aspirations. Humans and perhaps consequently visual inspection and statistics are infused with subjectivity, but we try to control or limit the impact of that subjectivity on our science.

The goal of producing replicable findings raises two points about visual inspection. First, we need data-analytic tools whenever possible that lead to consistency in reaching conclusions. Visual inspection and statistical analysis sometimes do this and sometimes do not. However, for visual inspection, especially with less than very clear data patterns, it is difficult to convey what the exact rules are. That is one reason that interjudge agreement on visual inspection data is not high. Second, in the early years of elaborating single-case designs visual inspection was pitted against statistical analyses. There are many reasons to use statistical tests, as I have elaborated previously. But another one has to do with replication. We can be more confident of a finding by showing that the finding is obtained under different conditions. Some of the conditions include: when we use a different measure of the same construct (e.g., self-report and direct observation), different designs (single-case and between-group), and data-analytic techniques (e.g., visual inspection, statistics; statistical significance and clinical significance). Now that single-case designs have diffused into many areas of work and across many disciplines, more and more investigators report the use of both visual inspection and statistical techniques to examine their data (e.g., Cox, Cox, & Cox, 2000; Levesque et al., 2004; Quesnel, Savard, Simard, Ivers, & Morin, 2003; Savard et al., 1998). The added information can be helpful. In many cases, the different methods confirm that the intervention was effective. In some cases, the different methods confirm that not much has happened, that is, little or no effect of the intervention (e.g., Pasiali, 2004).

It is still the case that visual inspection is the primary criterion to evaluate single-case data. There are many statistical tests that can and have been applied to single-case data. I highlight these, provide examples, and convey further issues about statistical evaluation and visual inspection in the appendix at the end of the book. Reserving that discussion for later allows me to provide details here about the practices more frequently used in single-case data evaluation.

EVALUATION OF THE APPLIED OR CLINICAL
SIGNIFICANCE OF THE CHANGE

Visual inspection and statistical data evaluation methods address the experimental criterion for evaluating change, that is, whether the changes in performance are reliable and beyond what might be considered chance fluctuations. As noted earlier, an applied criterion is also invoked to evaluate the intervention. This criterion refers to the applied significance of the changes in behavior or whether the intervention makes a genuine difference in the everyday functioning of the client. By "genuine difference" I refer to one in which the client and others would see a change that positively affects the individual's life.

In many instances, the criterion for deciding whether a clinically significant change has been achieved may be obvious. Perhaps the clearest instances are when a maladaptive, deviant, or personally harmful behavior is occurring frequently (baseline) and the intervention completely eliminates the behavior or when a positive behavior (reading) never occurs and is at a high rate after the intervention. As an example of the former, an intervention may eliminate head banging of a child with autism or a developmental disability. If the baseline was a mean of 100 instances of head banging per hour, and the behavior was eliminated, most would agree that this was an important and clinically significant change. If the intervention reduced the rate from 100 to 75 or 50 instances per hour, the change may be reliable (by visual inspection or statistical evaluation) but it is probably not clinically important. Self-injurious behavior is maladaptive and potentially dangerous if it occurs at all. Thus, without a virtual or complete elimination of self-injurious behavior, the clinical value of the treatment may be challenged. Similarly, for many other behaviors (e.g., use of illicit substances, driving while intoxicated, experiencing panic in social situations, or reading methodology articles during family Thanksgiving reunions) the complete elimination would make it reasonable to infer that the impact was important.

An intervention program will not invariably make such dramatic changes (e.g., from a lot of problem behavior to none or from no occurrences of a positive behavior to a high rate of that behavior). Even when change is dramatic in relation to the criteria for visual inspection (e.g., changes in mean, level, latency, etc.) this does not mean that the change is important or makes a difference. Other criteria must be invoked.

Two broad and related strategies have been used. *Social validation* and *clinical significance* have emerged from single-case and between-group methodologies, respectively. Each presents multiple options for evaluating the changes following intervention effects, and these are highlighted in Table 12.2. I have added a third category called *social impact* when the goal is on broader outcomes than individual client performance. I highlight and illustrate the different methods next.

Social Validation

Social validation refers generally to consideration of social criteria for evaluating the focus of treatment, the procedures that are used, and the effects that these treatments have on performance (Schwartz & Baer, 1991; Wolf, 1978). For present purposes, the feature of the effects or impact of treatment is especially relevant to this discussion. As noted in the table, there are two methods of social validation used to evaluate the impact of the intervention: social comparison and subjective evaluation.

Social Comparison. With the social comparison method, the behavior of the client before and after treatment is compared with the behavior of nondeviant ("normal") peers who are functioning well in the community or context in which they are evaluated. The question asked by this comparison is whether the client's behavior after treatment is distinguishable from the behavior of his or her peers who are functioning adequately in the environment. Presumably, if the client's behavior warrants intervention, that

Table 12.2 Means of Evaluating the Applied or Clinical Significance of Change in Intervention Studies

Type of Measure	Defined	Criteria
A. Social Validation		
1. Social Comparison Method	Client's performance is evaluated in relation to the performance of a normative sample before and after treatment.	At the end of treatment, client functioning falls within the range of a normative sample.
2. Subjective Evaluation	Impressions of the client or those who interact with the client that treatment change makes a perceptible difference.	Ratings at the end of treatment to indicate that current functioning is better or that the original problem is minimal or not evident.
B. Clinical Significance		
1. Normative Comparison	Same as Social Comparison Method.	Same as Social Comparison Method.
2. Departure from a Dysfunctional Level of Functioning	Individual makes a large change on a measure. The change departs from the pretreatment mean.	A large change (e.g., two or more standard deviations) from the pretreatment mean. This degree of change would be a clear departure from dysfunctional levels. Can be departure from another sample or set of untreated individuals or from one's original score on the measure.
3. No Longer Meeting Criteria for a Psychiatric Diagnosis	Before treatment the individual met formal criteria for a psychiatric diagnosis (e.g., Major Depression, Panic Disorder, Conduct Disorder) but no longer does after the intervention.	Reassessment after the intervention is applied, showing that using the same measure and criteria, individuals no longer meet diagnostic criteria for the disorder that was treated.
C. Social Impact	Change on a measure that is recognized or considered to be critically important in everyday life; usually not a psychological scale or measure devised for the purposes of research.	Change reflected on such measures as arrest, truancy, hospitalization, disease, and death.

behavior should initially deviate from normative levels of performance. If treatment produces a clinically important change, at least with many clinical problems, the client's behavior should be brought within normative levels.

The essential feature of social comparison is to identify the client's peers, that is, persons who are similar to the client in such variables as age, gender, ethnicity, and socioeconomic class, but who are functioning adequately or well and whose behaviors do not warrant intervention. Presumably, a clinically important change would be evident if the intervention brought the clients to within the level of their peers whose behaviors are considered to be adequate.

The critical feature is obtaining information that can be used as a benchmark. For example, a program focused on training appropriate eating behaviors among individuals with developmental disabilities who seldom used utensils, constantly spilled food on themselves, stole food from others, and ate food previously spilled on the floor (O'Brien & Azrin, 1972). A behavioral intervention (using prompts, praise, and food reinforcement for appropriate eating) was used to develop appropriate eating behaviors. Although training increased appropriate eating behaviors, one can still ask whether the improvements really were important and whether behavior approached the eating skills of persons who are regarded as functioning well or normally in everyday life. To address these questions, the investigators compared the group that received training with the eating habits of 12 customers in a local restaurant. These customers were watched by observers, who recorded their eating behavior, using the same measure of inappropriate eating. This represents a benchmark of people who have not been identified as having deficits in their eating behaviors. The mean of this group is represented by the dashed line in Figure 12.8. As evident in the figure, after training, the level of inappropriate mealtime behaviors among the persons with developmental disabilities was even lower than the rate of inappropriate eating by customers in the restaurant. These results suggest that the magnitude of changes achieved with training brought behavior to acceptable levels of persons functioning in everyday life.

Consider as another example a program designed to develop helping behaviors among four children (5 to 6 years of age) in a private school and with a diagnosis of autism (Reeve et al., 2007). The goal was to teach a social behavior (helping in the classroom). This was selected because, among social behaviors, helping acts tend to lead to more prolonged interactions. Prior to the program the children engaged in no helping behaviors. The intervention, which consisted of training in each of several activities (e.g., modeling, instructions, and guidance), led to changes in helping behavior. The intervention was evaluated in a multiple-baseline design across children. The effects

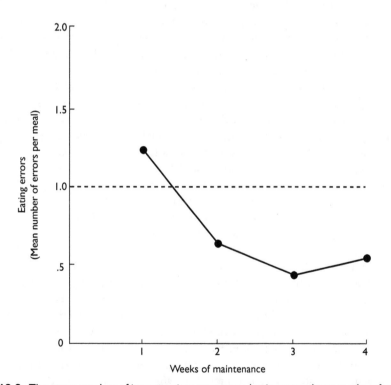

Figure 12.8. The mean number of inappropriate responses (eating errors) per meal performed by the training group of individuals with developmental disabilities. The dashed horizontal line represents the mean number of these same responses performed by 12 customers in a restaurant under ordinary eating conditions (normative sample).   *(Source: O'Brien & Azrin, 1972.)*

were very clear, in part because baseline was consistently at a rate of zero (no helping) for all the children. To evaluate the changes further, the investigators videotaped the helping behaviors of the four children toward the end of their training and then obtained videotapes of other, typically developing children asked to engage in the same behaviors. The question to be addressed is whether the level of helping achieved with training the children with autism placed them near or closer to the helping behavior of children not identified as showing impairment. A total of 80 videotapes were made; college students rated the tapes in random order; the instances of helping were similar for the two groups.

In the preceding examples, social comparison is intended to further inform what the changes mean. Do the social comparison data convey that the changes were important? That is difficult to answer and may involve other considerations, such as how the clients or others viewed the changes and whether the changes carry over to other settings and are maintained over time. Yet the examples convey how social comparison data provide a very useful benchmark for evaluating intervention effects and placing changes in an important social context of how other people are behaving. The challenge is obtaining a suitable sample for comparison purposes, a topic to which I return later in the chapter.

Subjective Evaluation. With the subjective evaluation method, the client's behavior is evaluated by persons who are likely to have contact with him or her in everyday life and who evaluate whether distinct improvements in performance can be seen. The question addressed by this method is whether behavior changes have led to qualitative or clearly perceptible differences in how the client is viewed by others.

Subjective evaluation as a means of validating the effects of treatment usually consists of global evaluations of behavior. The behaviors that have been altered are observed by persons who interact with the client or who are in a special position (e.g., through expertise) to judge those behaviors. Global evaluations are made to provide an overall appraisal of the client's performance after treatment. It is possible that systematic changes in behavior are demonstrated, but that persons in everyday life cannot see a "real" difference in performance. If the client has made an important change, this should be obvious to persons who are in a position to judge the client. Hence, judgments by persons in everyday contact with the client add a crucial dimension for evaluating the applied or clinical significance of the change.

An excellent example is the case of Steven, a college student who sought treatment to eliminate two muscle tics (uncontrolled movements) (Wright & Miltenberger, 1987). The example conveys the complementary role of objective information and subjective evaluation to establish not only that there was a change, but also that the change is one others can see as making a difference. Steven's tics involved head movements and excessive eyebrow raising. Individual treatment sessions were conducted in which he was trained to monitor and identify when the tics occurred and in general to be more aware of their occurrence. In addition, he self-monitored tics throughout the day. Assessment sessions were conducted in which Steven read at the clinic or college library and observers recorded the tics. Self-monitoring and awareness training procedures were evaluated in a multiple-baseline design in which each tic declined in frequency as treatment was applied.

Was the reduction important or did it make a difference either to Steven or to others? At the end of treatment Steven's responses to a questionnaire indicated that he no longer was distressed by the tics and that he felt they were no longer very noticeable to others. In addition, four observers rated randomly selected videotapes of Steven without knowing which tapes came from before or after treatment. Observers rated the tics from the posttreatment tapes as not at all distracting, normal to very normal in appearance, and small to very small in magnitude. In contrast, they had rated tics on the pretreatment tapes as much more severe on these dimensions. Observers were then informed which were the posttreatment tapes and asked to report how satisfied they would be if they had achieved the same results as Steven had. All observers reported that they would have been satisfied with the treatment results. The subjective evaluations from Steven and independent observers help attest to the importance of the changes, that is, they made a difference to the client and to others.

Subjective evaluation usually refers to global evaluations by individuals in contact with the client, but as evident in the example of Steven, the client's evaluations can be sought as well to evaluate whether the difference obtained with the intervention makes a genuine difference in his or her perception. Self-evaluation as a means for social validation has been used much less frequently than has been evaluation by others, for at least two reasons. First, interventions evaluated with single-case designs often focus on populations with severe disability or impairment (e.g., children with developmental disabilities, severe intellectual impairment, autism) or on community behaviors and settings (e.g., seat-belt use among drivers and their passengers). Self-evaluation in these cases is not feasible.

Second, self-evaluations often reflect overall satisfaction with an intervention and may not relate well to actual changes in behaviors or problems for which the intervention was provided. Of course, subjective evaluation often is a critical focus. How one feels about one's own mood (e.g., depression), one's relationship (e.g., feelings about one's partner or spouse), environmental events (e.g., sources of stress), and physical and mental condition (e.g., overall health, happiness) are important facets of life. In some situations, self-report provides critical data that have no substitute. For example, in one program, an adolescent was treated for muscle tension that impaired her functioning and caused her severe pain (Warnes & Allen, 2005). The program was evaluated by an automated psychophysiological measure (electromyography). Yet, daily self-report on pain also was assessed. Getting better on an objective measure of muscle tension is no substitute for asking individuals if they are feeling better. Both measures showed the effects of the program. As studies like these show, assessement of overt behavior and subjective evaluation need not compete, but provide important complementary information.

It is important to underscore the role of subjective evaluation in another context. When single-case designs emerged in applied settings, as I have noted, overt behavior was the primary and often the exclusive measure to reflect the effects of an intervention. This has changed over the years as outcomes reflect other aspects of functioning (e.g., depression, anxiety, cognitions) where nonovert behavioral measures are used. Subjective evaluation draws attention to the importance of other dimensions and is a check on the impact of what a study might show. For example, in one program, an intervention was designed to reduce the disruptive behavior of boys identified because of their behavioral problems (Reitman, Murphy, Hupp, & O'Callaghan, 2004). The intervention was very effective in altering child behavior, with impressive graphs, in keeping with many other examples I have provided. Subjective evaluation was added at the end of the program to determine whether the teachers noticed a difference. Improvement was not noted by teachers on standardized teacher ratings. This is an instructive finding. Were the changes potent enough? Were the operational definitions targeting the problems relevant? Were the teachers merely biased or oblivious to the changes? Subjective evaluation is an important supplement to convey how the intervention effects are perceived and are affecting others.

Clinical Significance

Social validation grew out of single-case research. A related development grew out of psychotherapy research and the tradition of between-group designs. Psychotherapy research has a long history—treatments are evaluated in relation to changing clinical problems such as depression, anxiety, panic disorder, and many other problems. Data are evaluated by comparing means of groups that receive various conditions. At the end of a study, one treatment may be more effective than another, and patients may have improved. "More effective" and "improved" are statistical concepts even though they sound like clinical concepts, that is, that something has made a real difference. "More effective" only means that groups were different on statistical tests; "improved" only means that change from pre- to posttreatment was statistically significant for the group. These both reflect the experimental criterion that evaluates the reliability of the finding. Neither concept necessarily reflects an applied criterion, namely, whether the change makes any real difference in the lives of individuals. Clinical significance has been introduced as a criterion to supplement statistical evaluation in the same way social validation was introduced to supplement visual inspection.

The concept of clinical significance in group research is not new or unique to psychotherapy or to psychology. The concept has been recognized and is easily conveyed in medical research. For example, in cancer treatment studies, one treatment might be considered better than another because it extends life (survival after the treatment). With a measure such as "survival," it is easy to mix experimental and applied criteria of change. As a measure, survival sounds and is important. However, "better" in this context refers to statistical significance (experimental criterion). The difference may be in 5 days, 5 weeks, or 5 months more of survival. Is that difference important (applied criterion)? Perhaps this is for the patient to judge. Perhaps the judgment for us or for the patient depends on further information such as the quality of life during that additional survival time. If that extra survival time is of poor quality (greater pain, immobility, comatose, or with side effects) that may contribute to the evaluation. Concerns about quality of life in such treatment studies reflect interest in elaborating the importance of the treatment effects in ways that are relevant to patients and that complement survival data.

Although the ideas underlying clinical significance are not new, the topic arose formally in the context of psychotherapy research and the tradition of between-group research. Three indices have been used to evaluate whether change on key measures make a difference, that is, are clinically significant. These measures were highlighted in Table 12.2.

Falling within a Normative Range.   The first index relates to the use of normative sample. The question asked by this method is, "to what extent do patients or clients after completing treatment (or some other intervention) fall within the normative range of performance?" Prior to treatment, the clients presumably would depart considerably from their well-functioning peers on the measures and in the domain that led to their selection (e.g., anxiety, depression, social withdrawal). Demonstrating that after treatment these same persons were indistinguishable from or within the range of a normative, well-functioning sample on the measures of interest would be a reasonable definition of a clinically important change (Kazdin, 1977b; Kendall & Grove, 1988). This is the same as the social comparison method mentioned in the context of social validation. I remention the index here because it has been used more often in between-group research than in single-case research. Use of this index of clinical significance is facilitated by using outcome measures that have extensive normative data on patients by age and sex. Hence one can easily compare the results for a treated sample with that normative base. Single-case designs often use measures of overt behavior; between-group designs more often use self- and other-report scales. These latter scales are more easily standardized by administering the measures to thousands of individuals who may vary by age, ethnicity, socioeconomic standing, nationality, and other such factors. Large databases of samples of individuals functioning in the community have been used frequently in between-group research to evaluate the clinical significance of change.

As a rather typical example, one of our own studies evaluated treatments for children ages 7 to 13 referred for aggressive and antisocial behavior (Kazdin, Siegel, & Bass, 1992). The effectiveness of three conditions was examined including problem-solving skills training (PSST), parent management training (PMT), and PSST+PMT combined. PSST is a cognitively based procedure in which children are trained to approach interpersonal situations in ways that help them identify and carry out prosocial solutions. PMT is a procedure designed to change parent–child interactions in the home in concrete ways that promote prosocial child behavior. Two outcome measures are plotted for the three groups at pretreatment, posttreatment, and a 1-year follow-up (see Figure 12.9). The measures were the parent- and teacher-completed versions of the Child Behavior Checklist (Achenbach, 1991), which assess a wide range of emotional and behavioral problems. Extensive normative data (of nonreferred, community children) available for boys and girls within the age group have indicated that the 90th percentile score on overall (total) symptoms is the score that best distinguishes clinic from community (normative) samples of children. As shown in Figure 12.9, scores at this percentile from community youths were used to define the upper limit of the "normal range" of emotional and behavioral problems. Clinically significant change was defined as whether children's scores fell below this cutoff, that is, within the normative range. The figure shows that children's scores were well above this range before treatment on the parent (left panel) and teacher (right panel) measures. Each group approached or fell within the "normal" range at posttreatment, although the combined treatment was superior in this regard.

The results in the figure provide group means (average performance of each group). One also can compute how many individuals fall within the normative range at the end of treatment. In the present example, for the parent-based measure referred to in the figure, results at posttreatment indicated that 33%, 39%, and 64%

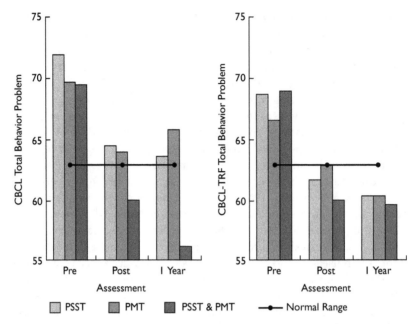

Figure 12.9. Mean scores (T scores) for Problem-Solving Skills Training (PSST), Parent Management Training (PMT), and both combined (PSST + PMT) for the total behavior problem scales of the parent-completed Child Behavior Checklist (CBCL, *left panel*) and the teacher-completed Child Behavior Checklist—Teacher Report Form (TRF-CBCL *right panel*). The horizontal line reflects the upper limit of the nonclinical ("normal") range of children of the same age and sex. Scores below this line fall within the normal range.   *(Source: Kazdin, Siegel, & Bass, 1992.)*

of youths from PSST, PMT, and combined treatment, respectively, achieved scores that fell within the normative range. These percentages are different (statistically significant) and suggest the superiority of the combined treatment on the percentage of youths returned to "normative" levels of functioning. The results underscore the importance of evaluating clinical significance. In this study, even with statistically significant changes within groups and differences between groups, most youths who received treatment continued to fall outside of the normative range of their nonclinically referred peers.

Departure from Dysfunctional Behavior. Another method to define clinical significance uses a dysfunctional level for comparison. In clinical work, patients are selected because of their dysfunction in the area of focus. Perhaps they were recruited for extreme scores on measures of depression. At the end of treatment, if a clinically important change is made, scores of the clients ought to depart markedly from their original scores. The departure of course ought to be in the direction of improvement (e.g., reduced symptoms). There is no logical justification for deciding how much of a change or reduction in symptoms is needed, and different criteria have been suggested and used (Jacobson & Revenstorf, 1988; Jacobson, Roberts, Berns, & McGlinchey, 1999). One variant denotes intervention effects as clinically significant when there is a departure of two standard deviations from the mean of the pretreatment performance (i.e., so-called dysfunctional sample). Thus, at posttreatment, individuals whose scores depart at least two standard deviations from the mean of the dysfunctional group (e.g., untreated cases from a no-treatment control group) would be regarded as having changed in an important way.

Why a criterion of two standard deviations? First, if the individual is two standard deviations away from the mean of the original group, this suggests that he or she is not represented by that mean and distribution from which that sample was drawn; indeed, two standard deviations above (or below) the mean reflects the 98th (or 2nd) percentile. Second and related, two standard deviations approximates the criterion used for statistical significance when groups are compared (e.g., 1.96 standard deviations for a two-tailed t test that compares groups for the $p < .05$ level of significance).

As an illustration, a study for the treatment of depression among adults compared two variations of problem-solving strategies (Nezu & Perri, 1989). To evaluate the clinical significance of change, the investigators examined the proportion of cases in each group whose score on measures of depression fell two or more standard deviations below (i.e., less depressed) the mean of the untreated sample. For example, on one measure (the Beck Depression Inventory), 85.7% of the cases that received the full problem-solving condition achieved this level of change. In contrast, 50% of the cases that received the abbreviated problem-solving condition achieved this level of change. The more effective treatment led to a clinically significant change for the large majority of the cases, and clearly one treatment was better than the other in this regard. The comparisons add important information about the impact of treatment.

For many measures used to evaluate treatment or other interventions, normative data that could serve as a criterion for evaluating clinical significance are not available. That is, we cannot tell whether at the end of treatment cases fall within a normative range. However, one can still evaluate how much change the individual made and whether that change is so large as to reflect a score that is quite different from the mean of a dysfunctional level (pretreatment) or sample (no-treatment group). Of course, if normative data are available, one can evaluate the clinical significance of change by assessing whether the client's behavior returns to normative levels and also departs from dysfunctional levels.

No Longer Meeting Diagnostic Criteria. Occasionally, clinical significance is evaluated by evaluating whether the diagnostic status of the individual has changed with treatment. In many treatment studies, individuals are recruited and screened on the basis of whether they meet criteria for a psychiatric diagnosis (e.g., Major Depression, Posttraumatic Stress Disorder). Those with a diagnosis are included in the study and assigned to various treatment and control conditions. Clinical significance has been defined by evaluating whether the individual, at the end of treatment, continues to meet criteria for the original (or other) diagnoses. Presumably, if treatment has achieved a sufficient change the individual no longer meets criteria for the diagnosis. Sometimes this is referred to as showing that the individual has recovered.

For example, in one study, adolescents who met standard psychiatric diagnostic criteria for clinical depression were assigned to one of three groups: adolescent treatment, adolescent and parent treatment, or a wait-list condition (Lewinsohn, Clarke,

Hops, & Andrews, 1990). At the end of treatment, 57% and 52% of the cases in the two treatment groups, respectively, and 95% of the cases in the control group continued to meet diagnostic criteria for depression. A smaller proportion of cases in the treatment groups continued to meet diagnostic criteria for the disorder.

There is something appealing about showing that after treatment the individual no longer meets diagnostic criteria for the disorder that was treated. It suggests that the condition (problem, disorder) is gone or "cured." Yet, many clinical problems that have formal psychiatric diagnoses (e.g., Depression, Autism, Attention-Deficit/Hyperactivity Disorder, Generalized Anxiety Disorder) are on a continuum (sometimes referred to as a spectrum). So no longer meeting the diagnostic criteria for a disorder is not a cure. (As we occasionally tell our students, only hams are "cured.") Not meeting the criteria for the diagnosis of a disorder (e.g., depression) can be achieved by showing a change in only one or two symptoms.

Social Impact Measures

Single-case research often focuses on important social problems or on individual behaviors (e.g., use of seat belts, driving safely, keeping poisonous household cleaners out of the reach of children) that if altered on a large scale could have important personal as well as social consequences (e.g., injury and death). For example, prevention programs often focus on infants or young children from socioeconomically disadvantaged homes who are at risk for later mental and physical health problems (Mrazek & Haggerty, 1994). Occasionally follow-up data are obtained 10 to 20 years later. Social impact measures such as higher rates of school attendance, high-school graduation, and employment, and lower rates of arrest and reliance on public assistance are evident among those who received an early intervention, compared to nonintervention controls. These measures and outcomes are clearly significant to society as well as to the individuals who benefit directly.

In health care and education, cost is often of interest and used as a basis for deciding social impact. Presumably an intervention has significant social impact if it can reduce monetary costs. One cost question both for evaluating large-scale social interventions as well as individual treatment is the benefits that derive from the costs. Cost-benefit analysis is designed to evaluate the monetary costs of an intervention with the benefits that are obtained. The benefits must also be measured in monetary terms. Evidence that clients return to work, miss fewer days of work, have fewer car accidents, or stay out of hospitals or prisons are examples of benefits that can be translated into monetary terms. Of course, many important outcomes (e.g., personal happiness, family harmony) are not readily translated to monetary gains.

Cost-effectiveness analysis does not require placing a monetary value on the benefits and can be more readily used for evaluating treatment. Cost-effectiveness analysis examines the costs of treatment relative to a particular outcome. The analysis permits comparison of different treatment techniques if the treatment benefits are designed to be the same (e.g., reduction of drinking, increase in family harmony). For example, one study compared two variations of parent training for parents of kindergarten children with behavior problems (Cunningham, Bremner, & Boyle, 1995). One variation consisted of individual treatment provided at a clinical service; the other consisted of group-based treatment conducted in the community (at community centers or schools). Both treatments were better than a wait-list control condition. On several outcome measures, the community-based treatment was more effective. Even if the treatments were equally effective, the monetary costs (e.g., start-up costs, travel time of families, costs of the therapist/trainer in providing treatment) of individual treatment were approximately six times greater per family than the group treatment. Also, the community-based treatment is much more likely to have impact on individuals and society at large because it can be disseminated more broadly than individual therapy.

Within psychotherapy research, costs, cost-benefit, and cost-effectiveness measures are infrequently used, with notable exceptions (e.g., Cunningham et al., 1995; Simon et al., 2001). Cost is deceptively simple as a measure, which is one of the reasons why the measure is infrequently used in intervention studies. The complexities include the fact that cost is not merely the price of a few items on a list. What is included in cost estimates, how to place a price on them, and how to evaluate the costs of not providing treatment hint at a few of the challenges.

The interest in cost often stems from evaluating cost of treatment in relation to the alternatives. So, for example, one could or could not treat alcoholism among workers at a major company. Both of these have costs. Treating alcoholism has the costs of providing services. Yet, not treating alcoholism has costs as well, because alcoholism leads to many missed days at work, reduced worker productivity, and increased illness and injury. Hence the cost of treatment is not the issue but rather the cost of treatment versus no treatment, both of which may be expensive. A common statement that better reflects this is the notion that the cost of education in society is very high, but not that high when compared to the cost of ignorance. Similarly, the costs of treating some problems (e.g., depression, substance use, conduct disorder) are enormous but must be weighed against the cost of not providing treatment. For example, the annual cost of anxiety disorders in the United States is estimated at $42.3 billion (or $1,542 per sufferer) (Greenberg et al., 1999). Psychotherapy can reduce costs by reducing work impairment and lost days at work (see Gabbard, Lazar, Hornberger, & Spiegel, 1997).

Measures of social impact are infrequently used in single-case research, but they are in keeping with the goal of extending the evaluation to measures that are of applied significance. The measures are relevant when the goal is beyond individual behavior or interventions on a small scale. In some cases, the focus of a study awaits to be extended on a larger scale. For example, a demonstration project mentioned previously showed that safe driving (stopping at a stop sign) could be improved at one intersection on a college campus (Austin et al., 2006). Other measures (e.g., fewer accidents, reduced injuries and death) either within the demonstration or from a large-scale extension would be excellent indices of social impact.

Problems and Considerations

Measures of applied significance (social validity and clinical significance) have taken on increased importance over the years in many disciplines such as education, counseling, psychology, and health care. We have learned that our interventions can lead to statistically significant change on all sorts of measures, and that they can produce seemingly impressive results on a small scale and on well-validated measures (e.g., direct observations, various psychological scales). A key question asked by consumers (e.g., legislators, mental health agencies, insurance companies) is whether any of the work makes a real difference. Measures of social validity and clinical significance in varying degrees are designed to address this legitimate interest. Although social validity, clinical significance, and social impact measures are important, each raises critical issues pertaining to interpretation of the data. Let me highlight a few of the issues in relation to social validity.

Social Comparison and Return to Normative Levels. One criterion (for social validity and clinical significance) was showing that at the end of the interventions individuals fell within the normative range of performance of the behavior. Defining a normative sample is not quite so easy. To begin with, among adults (18 years of age and older) in the United States functioning "normally" in the community (i.e., a normative sample), approximately 1 in 4 (25%) meet criteria for a diagnosable psychiatric disorder (National Institute of Mental Health, 2008). Approximately one half of the individuals in that 25% meet criteria for two or more psychiatric disorders. Again, these statistics are based on individuals in everyday life, walking the streets, coming to classes, teaching classes, and writing methodology books—well maybe not the latter, but you get the point. A sample of people from everyday life includes individuals with significant social, emotional, and behavioral problems. Normative functioning also varies as a function of several sample characteristics. Age, sex, identity, ethnicity, and culture are some of the features. So any comparison ought to match on key factors, but what are the key factors and how many ought to be included?

Second, to whom should individuals with severe developmental disability, chronic psychiatric impairment, or extensive prison records be compared in evaluating treatment or rehabilitation programs? Developing normative levels of performance might be an unrealistic ideal in treatment, if that level is based on individuals functioning well in the community. Defining and identifying a normative population raises additional problems. Presumably, forming a normative group ought to take such moderators into account.

Third, even if a normative group can be identified, exactly what range of their behaviors would be defined as within the normative level? Among individuals whose behaviors are not identified as problematic there will be a range of acceptable behaviors. Defining the upper and lower limits of that range (e.g., $\pm$ one standard deviation) is somewhat arbitrary unless data show that scores above or below a particular cutoff have different short- or long-term consequences on other measures of interest (e.g., hospitalization, showing another disorder).

Fourth, for many measures of interest, bringing individuals into the normative range is a questionable goal. Consider, for example, reading skills of elementary school children. A clinically significant change might well be to move children with reading dysfunction so that they fall within the normative range. However, perhaps the normative range itself should be questioned as a goal. The reading of most children might be accelerated from current normative levels. Thus, a normative criterion itself needs to be considered. More extreme would be bringing youth who abuse drugs and alcohol to the level of their peers. For some groups, the peer group itself might be engaging in a level of deviant behavior that is potentially maladaptive.

Finally, it is quite possible that performance falls within the normative range or departs markedly from a deviant group but does not reflect how the individual is functioning in everyday life. Paper-and-pencil measures, questionnaires, interviews, and other frequently used measures may not reflect adaptive functioning for a given individual. Even for measures with high levels of established validity, performance of a given individual does not mean that he or she is happy, doing well, or adjusting in different spheres of life. There is a difference in what is shown on a psychological measure and what is evident in everyday life so that falling into the normative range on such measures does not really have a clear meaning (Blanton & Jaccard, 2006; Kazdin, 2006).

Subjective Evaluation. The subjective evaluation method as a means of examining the clinical importance of intervention effects also raises critical issues. First, global rating scales usually serve as the basis for obtaining subjective evaluations. Such scales are more readily susceptible to biases on the part of raters than are questionnaires and interviews or direct observations in which the items are more concrete and anchored to clearer descriptors. Because subjective evaluations are global rather than concrete, they are likely to be highly variable (e.g., have different meanings and interpretations) among those who respond. Also, subjective evaluations, whether completed by the clients or others in contact with the clients, are likely to be fairly nonspecific in their ability to differentiate among different treatments.

Second, the fact that the client or persons associated with a client notice a difference in behavior as a function of the client's treatment does not mean that the client in fact has changed or has changed very much. Persons in contact with the client may perceive a small change and report this in their ratings. But this does not necessarily mean that treatment has alleviated the problem for which treatment was sought or brings the client within normative levels of functioning.

In general, one must treat subjective evaluations cautiously; it is possible that subjective evaluations will reflect change when other measures of change do not. Subjective evaluations might be especially limited as the sole or primary outcome measure for most clinical dysfunctions. For example, clients might really believe they are doing much better (subjective evaluation) but continue to have the dependence or addiction (e.g., alcohol) or impairment that they experienced at the beginning of treatment. It is quite possible that one feels better about something without having changed at all. This concern raises caution about interpretation but does not condemn subjective evaluation.

Subjective ratings provide important information. It really does make a difference how people feel and think (e.g., about themselves, their lives, their marriages, their partners). When all is said and done, whether treatment makes people experience life as better is no less central as an outcome criterion than performance on the best available psychological measure. Subjective evaluation is designed to supplement other measures and to address these broader issues.

General Comments. I have highlighted concerns with measures of social validation. There are parallel issues in relation to individual indices of clinical significance and social impact measures that are lengthy discussions beyond the present scope (see Kazdin, 2001). The unifying issue of the concerns pertains to assessment validity: How does one know that the index genuinely reflects client functioning in everyday life? The usual way of measuring validity is showing that scores on a measure correlate with performance elsewhere, but this does not address the matter (see Blanton & Jaccard, 2006). Does the measure selected for social validation, clinical significance, or social impact clearly reflect a difference that is important in the lives of the clients? How does one know? For some of the measures, such as subjective evaluation, perceiving that there is a difference defines an important change. For other measures, very little assessment work has been completed to show that huge changes on a measure or being closer to a normative sample and further away from a dysfunctional sample has palpably improved the client's everyday functioning (see Kazdin, 2006).

There is no single way to measure applied or clinical significance of intervention effects. Despite the problems I have outlined, it is important to include one or more measures when possible. Measures other than those highlighted previously might be devised to evaluate clinical significance. It is not difficult to conceive of other ways to operationalize clinical significance. For example, in psychotherapy research, measures of symptoms are usually used to evaluate clinical significance. Yet, one might assess other constructs such as quality of life, impairment, or participation in life (e.g., activities, relationships). The investigator involved in intervention research ought to attend to the question, "Did the treatment make a genuine difference in the lives of the recipients?" and ought to select one or more measures to provide an answer.

Among the dilemmas is that we are not always looking for large change. A small change often can be sufficient or just enough to make a difference. If treatment makes people a little better (e.g., a little less depressed or anxious, a little more confident, or they drink or smoke less), this may be enough to have them enter parts of life (e.g., social events, relationships, work, new hobbies) that they would not otherwise do. It is easy to conceive of instances in which a small effect of therapy could have just enough impact to affect people's lives in important and palpable ways. As an example, making a dysfunctional marriage a little better may have an important impact on the couple and the individual spouses (e.g., deciding to remain married) even though on a measure of marital bliss, the couple still falls outside the normative range or has not changed two or so standard deviations.

Notwithstanding these considerations, the researcher is encouraged to include one or more measures of social validity or clinical significance in any intervention study. The purpose of the addition is to move beyond establishing reliability of the intervention effect (e.g., through visual inspection or statistical analyses) and to show that the impact makes a difference. Measures of social validity, clinical significance, or social impact address a critical question, and in applied work, arguably the most critical question: Do our interventions make a difference in ways that the public cares about? This might be answered in all sorts of ways, but some attempt should be made that goes beyond showing reliable effects through visual inspection and statistical tests.

SUMMARY AND CONCLUSIONS

Data from single-case experiments are evaluated according to experimental and applied criteria. The *experimental criterion* refers to judgments about whether behavior change has occurred and is a reliable effect, that is, one that is not likely to be due to fluctuations in behavior. The *applied criterion* refers to whether the effects of the intervention are important or make a genuine difference.

In single-case experiments, visual inspection usually is used to evaluate whether the experimental criterion has been met. Data from the experiment are graphed and judgments are made about whether change has occurred and whether the data pattern meets the requirements of the design. Several characteristics of the data contribute to judging whether behavior has changed and whether that change can be attributed to the intervention. *Changes in the mean* (average) performance across phases, *changes in the level* of performance (shift at the point that the phase is changed), *changes in trend* (differences in the direction and rate of change or slope across phases), and *latency of change* (rapidity of change at the point that the intervention is introduced or withdrawn) all contribute to judging whether a reliable effect has occurred. Invoking these criteria is greatly facilitated by stable baselines and minimal day-to-day variability, which allow the changes in the data to be detected.

The primary basis for using visual inspection is that it serves as a filter that may allow only especially potent interventions to be agreed on as significant. Yet objections have been raised about the use of visual inspection in situations where intervention effects are not spectacular. Judges occasionally disagree about whether reliable effects were obtained. Also, the decision rules for inferring that a change has been demonstrated are not always explicit or consistently invoked for visual inspection.

Statistical analyses occasionally are used as an alternative way of analyzing the data, although they continue to serve as an ancillary way of evaluating intervention in single-case research. Statistical tests may be especially useful when several of the desired characteristics of the data required for visual inspection are not met. For example, when baselines are unstable and show a systematic trend in a therapeutic direction, selected statistical analyses can more readily evaluate intervention effects than visual inspection. The search for reliable albeit weak intervention effects is especially difficult with visual inspection. These interventions may be important to detect, especially in the early stages of research before the intervention is well understood and developed. Finally, there are several situations in which detecting small changes may be important and statistical analyses may be especially useful here.

Data evaluation via visual inspection or statistical analyses is designed to identify the reliability of the effect and whether a change has occurred that could not be attributed to chance. There also is interest in the applied criterion, that is, whether behavior changes are clinically significant. Examining the importance of intervention effects entails *social validation*, that is, considering social criteria for evaluating treatment outcomes. Two methods of social validation are relevant for evaluating intervention effects. The *social comparison method* considers whether the intervention has brought the client's behavior to the level of his or her peers who are functioning adequately in everyday life. The *subjective evaluation method* consists of having persons who interact with the client or who are in a special position (e.g., through expertise) to judge whether the changes evident in treatment reflect a noticeable difference in everyday life.

In group research, *clinical significance* has emerged as a parallel focus, namely, to evaluate the importance of change. Social comparison has been one of the methods. Other methods include identifying whether the degree of change for individuals is so large (e.g., two standard deviations away from the pretreatment mean) as to depart markedly from dysfunctional behavior and whether individuals at the end of the treatment no longer meet criteria for psychiatric diagnosis.

Social impact measures were also mentioned as a way of identifying whether the intervention procedure made an important difference. These measures focus on important social problems or on the large-scale impact of an intervention beyond changing the behavior of one or more individuals. Measures of impact might reflect safety, health, energy use, cost, rates of arrest or hospitalization, and other such indices that are of broader social interest.

Measures of social validity, clinical significance, and social impact, as any set of measures, raise their own interpretive challenges. Nevertheless they address an important issue in applied work, namely, what genuine impact has the intervention had to show that it makes a difference to the individual, to those with whom he or she is in contact, and to society at large? The measures I have outlined or others that might be generated with similar goals provide important information often neglected in applied work.

CHAPTER 13

Graphic Display of Data for Visual Inspection

Chapter 12 provided a discussion of visual inspection, its underlying rationale, and how it is invoked in single-case experimental research. Several characteristics of the data are crucial for reaching this decision, including the changes in means, levels, and trends across phases and the rapidity of the changes when experimental conditions (phases) are changed. In all research, whether single-case or between-group, graphical display of the data can be a useful aid in conveying at a glance what a flood of numbers and mind-numbing tables might obscure. In single-case research graphical display assumes even greater importance.

Visual inspection requires that the data be graphically displayed so that various characteristics of the data and criteria for data evaluation can be examined. Thus, it is important to keep the criteria for visual inspection in mind when one plots the data or uses aids to enhance or facilitate application of the criteria. Graphing of data in research, design, mathematics, marketing, and many other disciplines is a topic of significance in its own right with scores of options for data presentation (e.g., Henry, 1995;

Kosslyn, 2006; Tufte, 2001; Wilkinson, Wills, Rope, Norton, & Dubbs, 2005). Single-case research relies on a small number of the options. This chapter discusses major options for displaying the data graphically to help the investigator apply the criteria of visual inspection to single-case data.[1] Commonly used graphs and descriptive aids that can be added to simple graphs to facilitate interpretation of the results are discussed and illustrated.

BASIC TYPES OF GRAPHS

Data from single-case research can be displayed in several different types of graphs. In each type, the data are plotted so that the dependent measure is on the *ordinate* (vertical or y-axis) and the data are plotted over time, represented by the *abscissa* (horizontal or x-axis). Typical ordinate values include such labels as frequency of responses, percentage of intervals, number of correct responses, and so on. Typical abscissa values or labels include sessions, days, weeks, or months.

As noted in Figure 13.1, four quadrants of the graph can be identified in the general case. The quadrants vary as a function of whether the values are negative or positive on each axis. In single-case research, almost all graphs would fit into the top right quadrant (marked by bold lines) where the y-axis (ordinate) and x-axis (abscissa) values are *positive*. The values for the ordinate range from zero to some higher positive number. For example, single-case research focuses on many areas (e.g., number of obsessive thoughts, arithmetic problems completed, years of survival, or amount of energy conserved in the home) where the goal is to increase or decrease the occurrence of some behavior or domain of functioning. Negative numbers or response values are usually not possible. Similarly, the focus is usually on performance over time from Day 1 to some point in the future. Hence, the x-axis usually is not a negative number, which would go back into history.

A variety of types of graphs can be used to present single-case data. For present purposes, three major types of graphs are discussed and illustrated. Emphasis is placed on the use of the graphs in relation to the criteria for invoking visual inspection.

Simple Line Graph

The most commonly used method of plotting data in single-case research consists of noting the day-by-day (or session-by-session) performance of the subject over time. The data for the subject are plotted each day in a noncumulative fashion. The score for that day can take on any value of the dependent measure and may be higher or lower than values obtained on previous occasions. Data points within each phase are connected to produce a line. This method of plotting the data is represented in virtually all of the examples of graphs in previous chapters. However, it is useful to illustrate briefly this type of figure in the general case to examine its characteristics more closely.

---

[1] The chapter provides an overview of the main types of graphs in single-case designs and is about how to construct or prepare graphs or to utilize readily available software and database management programs to do that. Several other helpful resources are available for these facets of graphing in relation to single-case research (Barton et al., 2007; Carr & Burkholder, 1998; Moran & Hirschbine, 2002; Riley-Tillman & Burns, 2009).

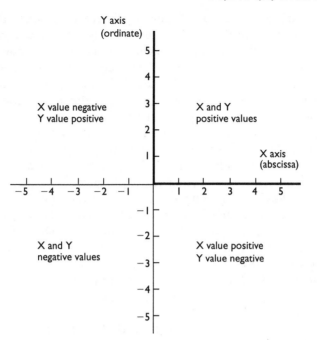

Figure 13.1. X and Y axes for graphic display of data. Bold lines indicate the quadrant used in the majority of graphs in single-case research.

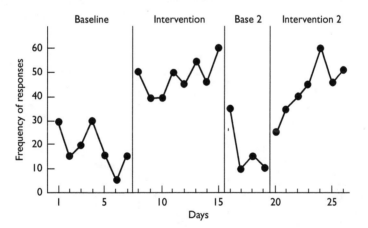

Figure 13.2. Hypothetical example of ABAB design as plotted on a simple line graph in which frequency of responses is the ordinate and days is the abscissa.

Figure 13.2 provides a hypothetical example in which data are plotted in a simple line graph. The crucial feature to note is that the data on different days can show an increase or decrease over time. That is, the data points on a given day can be higher or lower than the data points of other days. The actual score that the subject receives for a given day is plotted as such. Hence, performance on a particular occasion is easily discerned from the graph. For example, on Day 10 of Figure 13.2, the reader can easily discern that the target response occurred 40 times and on the next day the frequency increased to 50 responses. Hence, the daily level of performance and the pattern of how well or poorly the subject is doing in relation to the dependent values are easily detected.

The obvious advantage of the simple line graph is that one can immediately determine how the subject is performing at a glance. The simple line graph represents a relatively nontechnical format for presenting the session-by-session data. Much of single-case research is conducted in applied settings where the need exists to communicate the results of the intervention to parents, teachers, employees, nurses, and others who are unfamiliar with alternative data presentation techniques. The simple line graph provides a format that is relatively easy to grasp.

An important feature of the simple line graph, even for the better trained eye, is that it facilitates the evaluation of various characteristics of the data as they relate to visual inspection. Changes in mean, level, slope, and the rapidity of changes in performance are especially easy to examine in simple line graphs. And, as discussed later in this chapter, several descriptive aids can be added to simple line graphs to facilitate decisions about mean, level, and trend changes over time.

Cumulative Graph

The cumulative graph consists of noting the level of performance of the subject over time in an additive fashion. The score the subject receives on one occasion is added to the value of the scores plotted on previous occasions. The score obtained for the subject on a given day may assume any value of the dependent measure. Yet the value of the score that is plotted is *the accumulated total* for all previous days. Consider as a hypothetical example data plotted in Figure 13.3, the same data that were plotted in

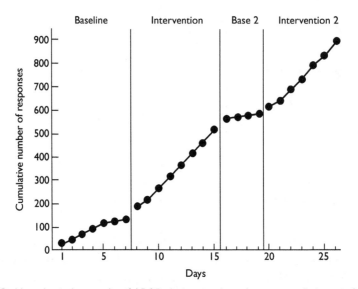

Figure 13.3. Hypothetical example of ABAB design as plotted on a cumulative graph. Each data point consists of the data for that day plus the total for all previous days.

Figure 13.2. On the first day, the subject obtained a score of 30. On the next day the subject received a score of 15. The 15 is not plotted as such. Rather, it is added to the 30 so that the cumulative graph shows a 45 for Day 2. The graph continues in this fashion so that all data are plotted in relation to all previous data.

As an example, one investigation was designed to help fiction writers increase their writing productivity (Porritt et al., 2006). The first 10 individuals from an Internet group of writers (approximately 4,000) who volunteered participated in an Internet-based program. To be included they also had to indicate that they were working on a manuscript and were dissatisfied with their productivity. Participants mailed in via the Internet a copy of their manuscripts each day. Words of the manuscript were automatically counted (by software, Microsoft Word®) each day and served as the outcome measure of intervention effects. (Also, the content was judged to ensure the new material was relevant and related to the story so they could not be meaningless additions.) All communication including the intervention was completed via the Web including a Web page for the group and individual Web pages for each participant. The intervention included providing individual goals for writing, graphic display of the number of words written, public acknowledgment (email that went to all participants), personalized emails to give feedback, special recognition in email if the person met his or her goals for that week, and points earned for their writing that could be used to obtain critiques of one's manuscript from another writer. The 10 participants were divided into two groups, and the intervention package was evaluated in a multiple-baseline design across groups.

Figure 13.4 presents the impact of the intervention on the cumulative number of words written. The intervention was introduced to two groups at different points in time. In the figure the solid line in the intervention phase represents the predicted level of performance from baseline. This is a useful addition to illustrate the logic of the design, but also because many people are unfamiliar with cumulative graphs. Little or no change in word productivity would be represented by a low slope or no slope (horizontal line). More and a lot of change would be reflected in a steeper slope because each day's words add to the previous days—more words, steeper slope. The figure conveys very clearly that baseline was not moving very steeply, as illustrated by baseline data and the extrapolation of what would be likely to happen if baseline were continued. During the intervention there was a clear change on the cumulative words as the angle of the slope became steeper and departed from the projected line of baseline. Writing productivity increased during the intervention phase. The graph is clear once one accommodates to the notion of accumulated data.

In an educational application, a multiple-treatment design was used to evaluate two procedures to develop mastery of words among adults (ages 20 to 48) with developmental disabilities and who worked in a day vocational program (Worsdell et al., 2005). Most were involved in continuing education and were selected for their need for improving in sight word reading. Individual sessions were conducted in which words were presented (based on assessment of the person's reading level). The number of words mastered consisted of words read without mistakes. During the intervention two ways of correcting errors were compared across multiple and varying word lists. Briefly, when an error was made, the individual was asked to repeat the word once. The trainer said, "No, the word is…. Say…." This was called the Single-Repetition (SR)

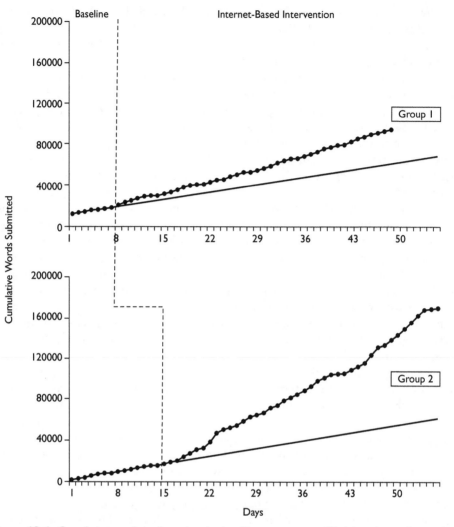

Figure 13.4. Cumulative number of words submitted by two groups of fiction writers who participated in the Internet-based intervention. The solid line represents the trend extrapolated from the rate of change during the baseline.   *(Source: Porritt et al., 2006.)*

condition. The other condition provided multiple opportunities to repeat the word. After an error, the correction was made and the client was asked to repeat the word five times, a procedure referred to as the Multiple-Repetition (MR) condition. Once a word was mastered, it was pulled from the list and new words were added. Figure 13.5 shows the multiple-baseline design across six clients included in the demonstration. It is clear from the graph that changes occurred when the intervention was introduced, with especially conspicuous slope changes, meeting the criteria of the multiple-baseline design. Also, the comparison of MR and SR sessions conveys that the MR condition was better in leading to word mastery. The cumulative graph is quite useful. We would

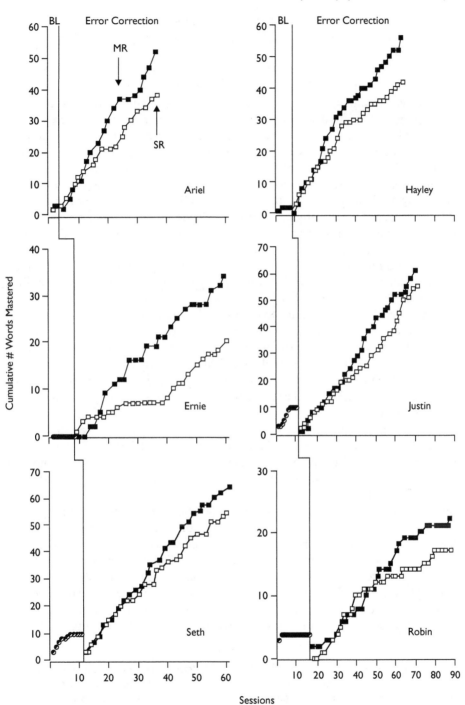

Figure 13.5. The cumulative number of words mastered during baseline (no correction of errors) and during the intervention in which two interventions were compared: single-response repetition (SR) and multiple-response repetition (MR). This is a combined multiple-baseline and multi-treatment design.   *(Source: Worsdell et al., 2005.)*

like to know which method has led to mastery of more words. The sheer number of words a person masters is meaningful, and the cumulative graph is clear in showing the different totals overall.

Historically, the use of cumulative graphs in single-case research can be traced primarily to non-human animal laboratory research in the experimental analysis of behavior (see Kazdin, 1978). The frequency of responses was often plotted as a function of time (rate) and accumulated over the course of the experiment. Data were recorded automatically on a *cumulative record,* an apparatus that records accumulated response rates. The cumulative record was a convenient way to plot large numbers of responses over time. The focus of much of the research was on the rate of responding rather than on absolute numbers of responses on discrete occasions such as days or sessions (Skinner, 1938). A simple line graph is not as useful to study rate over time, because the time periods of the investigation are not divided into discrete sessions (e.g., days). The experimenter might study changes in rate over the course of varying time periods rather than discrete sessions.[2]

In applied research, cumulative graphs are used only occasionally, but examples can be readily found (e.g., Mueller, Moore, Doggett, & Tingstrom, 2000; Sundberg, Endicott, & Eigenheer, 2000). Part of the reason is that they are not as familiar or as easily interpreted as are noncumulative graphs. The cumulative graph does not quickly convey the level of performance on a given day for the subject. For example, a teacher may wish to know how many arithmetic problems or what percentage of problems a child answered correctly on a particular day. This is not easy to cull from a cumulative graph. The absolute number of responses on a given day may be important to detect and communicate quickly to others. Noncumulative graphs are likely to be more helpful in this regard.

The move away from cumulative graphs also is associated with an expanded range of dependent measures. Cumulative graphs have been used in basic laboratory research to study rate of responding. The parameter of time (frequency/time) was very important to consider in evaluating the effects of the independent variable. In applied research, responses per minute or per session usually are not as crucial as the total number of responses alone. For example, an intervention may be directed toward reducing violent acts in a special school for violent youth. Although the rate of aggressive responses over time and the changes in rate may be of interest, the primary interest usually is simply in the total number of these responses for a given day. The analysis of moment-to-moment changes, often of great interest in basic laboratory research, usually is of less interest in applied research. Even so, cumulative graphs ought not to be ruled out. There are many measures, especially in relation to social impact, in which the accumulation of multiple responses and the cumulative impact are of concern. For example, cumulative

---

[2] A cumulative graph was especially useful in detecting patterns of responding and immediate changes over time. For example, in much early work in operant conditioning, schedules of reinforcement were studied in which variations in presenting reinforcing consequences served as the independent variable. Schedule effects can be easily detected in a cumulative graph in which the rate of response changes in response to alterations of reinforcement schedules. The increases in rate are reflected in changes of the slope of the cumulative record; absence of responding is reflected in a horizontal line (see Ferster & Skinner, 1957).

injuries and death from accidents, cumulative energy saved, and cumulative donations to philanthropic causes are all of interest because in the end it is the total accumulation we care about. Even at the individual level, cumulative responses often are of interest as individuals set goals (e.g., cumulative miles of jogging for an exercise buff or pages written for an author).

Bar Graph

A bar graph provides a simple and relatively clear way of presenting data.[3] The graph presents the data in vertical or occasionally horizontal columns (bars) to represent performance under different conditions. Each bar or column represents the *mean* or average level *of performance* for a separate phase. For example, the mean of all of the data points for baseline would be plotted as a single column; the mean for the intervention and for subsequent phases would be obtained and presented separately in the same fashion. Figure 13.6 illustrates a hypothetical ABAB design in which the data are presented in a simple line graph (upper panel); the same data are presented as a bar graph (lower panel).

Bar graphs are occasionally used to present data in single-case research. In a previous figure (13.5), data were presented in a cumulative graph to show the effects of two different procedures to correct reading errors. That figure showed the accumulated words mastered on a session-by-session basis. The same data are replotted in Figure 13.7 in a bar graph. The information is not redundant with the cumulative graphs. From the bar graph, we see the means for the two procedures that were used and whether they made a difference and if so how much.

The advantage of bar graphs is that they present the results in one of the easiest formats to interpret. Day-to-day performance within a given phase is averaged, and that average (mean) is reflected in the height of the bar. From the standpoint of data evaluation, the graph presents only one of the characteristics used for visual inspection (changes in means). Fluctuations in performance, trends, and information about duration of the phases are usually omitted. The advantage in simplifying the format for presenting the data has a price. The interpretation of data from single-case experiments very much depends on seeing several characteristics (e.g., changes in level, mean, trend). Insofar as bar graphs exclude portions of the original data, less information is presented to the naive reader from which well-based conclusions can be reached.

---

[3] In single-case research, "bar graph" and "histogram" occasionally are used interchangeably, although in other contexts they are readily distinguished (http://education.mit.edu/starlogo/graphing/graphing.html#Histogram, http://www.ncsu.edu/labwrite/res/gh/gh-bargraph.html). Both refer to displays in which the data are represented by columns (usually vertical, but occasionally horizontal). Histogram is a type of bar graph, often plotting the frequency of different values in a population (e.g., how many people in the country are ages 1–10, 11–20). Each bar represents the number of people in each age group. The text will use bar graph as the more general term. In single-case research, the use of such graphs is primarily in the context of presenting means (averages) of the data. For example, the results of an ABAB design could be presented so that each bar represents the mean of each phase on the measure of interest (e.g., items answered correctly). Alternatively, sometimes bars are used to present the means for asssessments administerd once or twice (e.g., pre- and postassessment for several subjects).

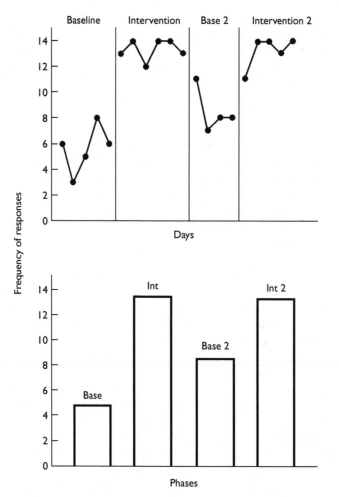

Figure 13.6. Hypothetical example of an ABAB design in which the data are represented in a simple line graph *(upper panel)* and a bar graph *(lower panel)*.

The features of the data not revealed by a bar graph may contribute to misinterpretations about the pattern of change over time. For example, trends in baseline and/or intervention phases may not be represented in bar graphs, which could have implications for the conclusions that are reached. Hypothetical data are plotted in Figure 13.8 to show the sorts of problems that can arise. In the upper left panel, a continuous improvement is shown over baseline and intervention phases in the simple line graph. Clearly the upper left shows that something is going on, that is, that there is a strong trend toward improvement that began in baseline and that there is no reason to think the intervention made any difference. Remember, we use the baseline in the upper left graph to predict what performance would be like in the future if baseline were to continue. The data in the intervention phase are perfectly in keeping with the baseline projection, and we could not conclude there is any intervention effect. Replotting the same data in a bar graph, shown in the upper right panel, suggests that

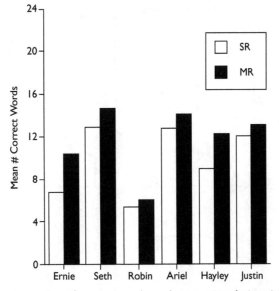

Figure 13.7. The mean number of correct words read per session during: single-response repetition (SR) and multiple-response repetition (MR) methods of correcting errors (see also Figure 13.5). This is a combined multiple-baseline and multi-treatment design.   *(Source: Worsdell et al., 2005.)*

the intervention had a large effect. The bar graph plots the means. The differences in means are merely a product of the overall trend, but the trend requires a simple line graph to detect.

In the lower panel, another set of data is plotted, this time showing that behavior was increasing during baseline (e.g., became worse) and changing in its trend with the intervention. The simple line graph suggests that the intervention reversed the direction of change. Yet the bar graph shows that the averages from the phases are virtually identical. Consider the lower right and left panels and how they might be misused. Suppose the measure were crime rate in a city and were plotted over a year. The left lower panel graph shows that things were getting worse in baseline but better during the intervention. The intervention might be the policy and practices of a new mayor who claimed that she would reduce crime. When running for re-election, her aides plot the data on the left lower panel, which immediately conveys that crime was increasing before she took office and that during her year the trend was completely reversed. However, her opponent running for office might plot the data differently with the bar graph on the lower right. It is clear from looking at the bar graph that the mean crime rate has not changed at all. The incumbent mayor could say, "Look what I did for the city" (and point to the left lower panel), and the challenger running for office could say, "Yes, I am looking and there was no change overall" (and point to the lower right panel). Both graphs are perfectly accurate, but they differ in how much information they reveal and how they display the information. Nothing in the bar graph is inaccurate, but here is a case where incomplete data are critical (and politically mischievous). (The methodologically informed contender running for office would emphasize the

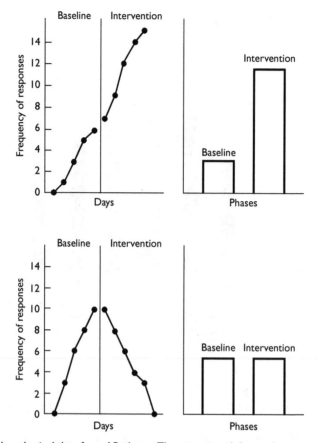

Figure 13.8. Hypothetical data from AB phases. The *upper panel* shows the same data plotted in a simple line graph (left) and replotted as a bar graph (right). The bar graph suggests large changes in behavior, but the simple line graph suggests the changes were due to a trend beginning in baseline and continuing during the intervention phase. The *lower panel* provides an example in which the intervention was associated with a marked change as shown in the simple line graph (left), but the bar graph (right) suggests no change from baseline to intervention phases.

AB design, as a quasi-experiment, and how other hypotheses [threats to validity] could account for all of the effects. He would lose the election but have the admiration of all methodologists.)

Bar graphs are also useful for simplifying data. The audience for one's results may dictate the use of a bar graph because of this simplifying feature. We do not teach most researchers about changes in variability and stability of baselines and criteria for visual inspection, let alone informing the public about any of this. When presenting information to the public, loss of many of the details (trends, shift in level) has a virtue we seek, namely, conveying a message that is at once accurate but as free from nuances as possible. In short, bar graphs have a use both in research as well as in communicating information broadly. In this chapter, I am emphasizing the importance of graphing continuous data so that one can apply criteria of visual inspection. In this context, bar graphs are usually a helpful complement to data plotted in ways that provide the day-to-day performance. Occasionally investigators present the data in the usual simple line graph to show the day-to-day performance (e.g., in a multiple-baseline design) but then summarize the effects by presenting a bar graph that just conveys means. For example, in a project that provided treatment of posttraumatic stress symptoms in children, cognitive behavior therapy was introduced in a multiple-baseline design across four children (Feather & Ronan, 2006). Single-case data were plotted in the usual multiple-baseline design fashion to show the impact of the intervention. In the study there were assessments over three follow-up periods (3-, 6-, and 12-month follow-up). The authors also summarized the results nicely by providing a bar graph that gave mean symptoms scores of all four children in baseline, intervention phases, and follow-up. The presentation of the data in different ways as in this example can reflect the best of all possible worlds because the detailed, continuous assessment for the multiple-baseline designs conveys the needed information for visual inspection; the summary bar graph simplifies the presentation to consumers who are interested in a summary/bottom-line statement.

GRAPHS ARE NOT NEUTRAL

A misunderstanding about data presentation and analyses is the supercynical view that data and statistics lie. It is true that data can misrepresent, as illustrated in the hypothetical example of crime rates plotted as a simple line graph or bar graph—that lead to conclusions that crime rate has improved or has not changed. More generally, data from any individual study are incomplete and only represent partial information. Apart from issues related to graphing, any single study may not represent findings that would apply to varied samples (e.g., different ethnic or cultural groups), different measures of the target focus, and different settings to which the intervention might be applied. Protections in science about misrepresentation include replication of findings and their extension to new populations, measures, and circumstances. In any given study, one cannot evaluate all domains that might be relevant. Also, when one does have extensive data, an investigator is rarely allowed to present all of the data (e.g., each client's performance, each day, etc.) although more and more publication outlets, investigators, and funding agencies wish to make all data available for reanalysis. So we begin with the notion that all of the data are rarely presented. Add to that pressures (e.g., our own, sponsors of the research) that can influence data presentation as well and there is more than merely omission caused by the mass amount of information. As we are called on to summarize the data, we want to provide the reader with maximum information to convey how we drew inferences and what the data show. It is possible to distort by leaving out information. In single-case research, the graph should make available all of the data that permit evaluation of the criteria for visual inspection, at the very least.

Another consideration in presenting the data pertains to the audience. If one is presenting the information to other researchers, the complexities of the data in their full bloom might be presented. This might include data to permit visual inspection and statistical analyses (for the researchers) but summary descriptive statistics (for the consumer). For example, one study focused on oppositional, aggressive, and antisocial behaviors of eight children (ages 6 to 8) who were referred to a special classroom because of their problem behavior (Ducharme et al., 2008). An intervention was introduced to train them to interact differently with others. The intervention was introduced in a multiple-baseline design across children and was shown to be responsible for change. (Although unnecessary for the present discussion, the reader may wish to see the original multiple-baseline graph, Figure 10.6 in Chapter 10.) For the consumer of the research (parents, teachers, school administrators), it would be helpful to have a bottom line. Did the intervention help anyone? Did antisocial behavior decrease? The investigators assessed play in naturally occurring sessions before and after treatment and plotted these data in a bar graph for each child, as shown in Figure 13.9. The data are very straightforward; the intervention made a difference. We do not need to

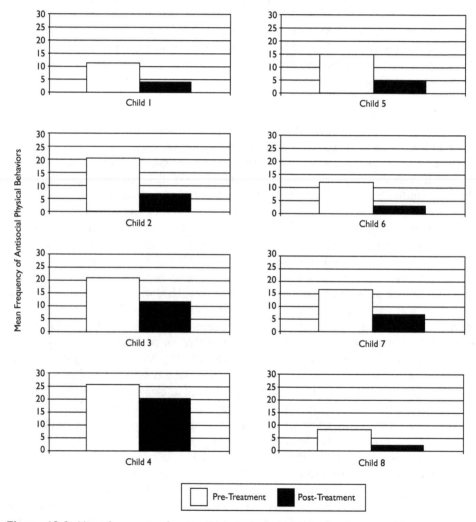

Figure 13.9. Mean frequency of antisocial behaviors during pretreatment and posttreatment (generalization sessions in a classroom without intervention). The impact of the intervention was demonstrated separately in a multiple-baseline design across children. *(Source: Ducharme et al., 2008.)*

be concerned about whether the intervention led to change or whether omission of so much information (level, trends) distorts the data. All of these concerns were addressed in the simple line graph. The bar graph as a supplement to other information can be extremely useful and can add clarity.

In presenting data, the goal is to provide all the information feasible to allow the reader to make an evaluation. In the case of graphing and visual inspection, this means allowing the reader to apply the criteria or to see how the investigator applied the criteria. In addition, the goal may be to communicate the major findings. These different goals may require different presentations of the same data.

DESCRIPTIVE AIDS FOR VISUAL INSPECTION

As noted earlier, inferences based on visual inspection rely on several characteristics of single-case data. In the usual case, simple line graphs are used to represent the data over time and across phases. The ease of inferring reliable intervention effects depends among other things on evaluating changes in the mean, level, and trend across phases, and the rapidity of changes when conditions are altered. Several aids are available that can permit the investigator to present more information on the simple line graph to address these characteristics and also to communicate the results more completely and clearly.

Changes in Means

The easiest source of information to add to a simple line graph that can facilitate visual inspection is the plotting of means. The data are presented in the usual way so that day-to-day performance is displayed. The mean for each phase is plotted as a horizontal line within the phase. Plotting these means as horizontal lines or in an equivalent way for each phase readily permits the reader to compare the overall effects of the different conditions, that is, provides a summary statement.

For example, a multiple-baseline design was used to evaluate a program designed to teach reading to three elementary school students (7 years of age) diagnosed with learning disabilities (Gilbert, Williams, & McLaughlin, 1996). Training included discussion of vocabulary, teaching of phonetic rules (sounds), and practice. Students read into a recorder for 4 minutes; the number of correct words read per minute was assessed from that. Figure 13.10 shows the effects of the program. Within each phase for each child, the horizontal line reflects the mean (average) correct words per minute. This is a very simple but helpful addition.

Another example provides a demonstration with effects that are much less clear than the previous example. In this demonstration, feedback was used to improve the performance of boys (9 to 10 years old) who participated in a football team and league (Komaki & Barnett, 1977). The goal was to improve execution of the plays by selected members of the team (backfield and center). A checklist of players' behaviors was scored after each play to measure if each player did what he was supposed to. During the feedback phase, the coach pointed out what was done correctly and incorrectly after each play. The feedback from the coach was introduced in a multiple-baseline design across various plays. Figure 13.11 shows that performance tended to improve at each point at which the intervention was introduced. The means are represented in each phase by the horizontal dotted lines. In this example, the means are especially useful because intervention effects are not very strong. Changes in level or trend are not apparent from

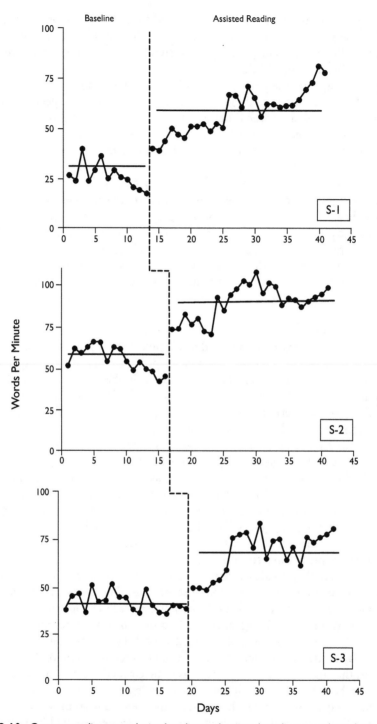

Figure 13.10. Correct reading rates during baseline and assisted reading as evaluated in a multiple-baseline design across subjects. The horizontal line in each phase represents the mean. *(Source: Gilbert, Williams, & McLaughlin, 1996.)*

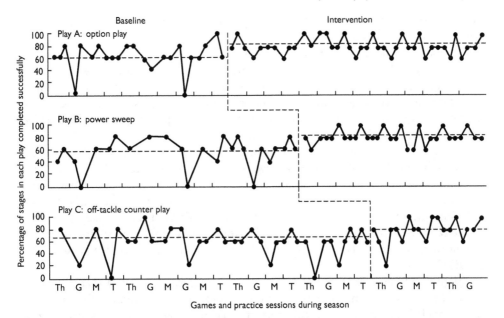

Figure 13.11. Percentage of stages successfully completed for Plays A, B, and C during football practice (M = Monday, T = Tuesday, Th = Thursday) and game (G) situations. Each data point refers to the execution of a single play.   *(Source: Komaki & Barnett, 1977.)*

baseline to intervention phases. Also, rapid effects associated with implementation of the intervention are not evident either. The plot of means shows a weak but seemingly consistent effect across the baselines. Without the means, it might be much less clear that any change occurred at all.

The plotting of means represents an easy tool for conveying slightly more information in simple line graphs than would otherwise be available. Essentially, plotting of means combines the advantages of simple line graphs and bar graphs. The advantage of plotting means in a simple line graph rather than using a bar graph is that the day-to-day performance can be taken into account when interpreting the means.

Plot a Measure of Variability

Variability of the data is critical for evaluating change whether in means or trends. Although variability per se is not explicitly one of the criteria for visual inspection, I mention this here in relation to aids for graphing. When researchers who use single-case designs report the results, means are usually mentioned among phases, even if they are not plotted graphically. In contrast, mention or illustration of a measure of variability about those means is rarely included. However, the meaning of means, so to speak, derives in part from their departure from each other across phases. Departure is not merely a difference in absolute numerical terms. For example, if the mean of baseline is 20 and the mean of the intervention phase is 24, how do we interpret that? If all the data in baseline were identical scores of 20 and all the data in the intervention phase were scores of 24, those would be hugely different (and nonoverlapping). More likely than not there are fluctuations day to day and hence it might be useful to add a descriptive aid to look at where means lie in relation to each other in light of that fluctuation, that is, a measure of variability.

A research practice that spans single-case and between-group research that is useful in this regard is to plot a measure of variability. In single-case designs, different options have been used such as plus and minus one standard deviation above the mean or occasionally the range (highest and lowest score). One measure that is useful and common across many areas of research is to use error bars that reflect the *standard error of the mean* of that phase.[4]

Consider an example to illustrate how this is done and what we gain. Table 13.1 provides hypothetical data for the first two phases (AB) of an ABAB design. The baseline phase was 7 days, followed immediately by the intervention phase of 8 days. From these data, we can compute measures of variability that will be used in our graphs of the data. First we compute the means and standard deviations in each phase, as provided in the table. Second, from the standard deviation, we compute the standard error of the mean, by the formula provided. Error bars consist of the mean plus or minus one standard error.

Figure 13.12 presents the data from both AB phases. The mean for each phase is represented by a horizontal line (in the upper panel) or by the height of the bar (in the lower panel). The results convey that performance increased in the intervention phase. In the lower panel (bar graph) I have added error bars that convey one standard error above and below the mean. The height of each bar reflects that one standard error in terms of the range of scores. This range is relatively narrow and adds useful information about fluctuation. We can see that the mean of one phase is not close to the range (one standard error above or below the mean) of the other phase. We cannot tell from the bar graph if the individual data points overlap very much from baseline to intervention phase (although we can see that they do not from the line graph above that). The narrow error bars suggest that data points within a phase are in close proximity of each other, that is, variability is not that large.

How does this help us in any way? First, the range helps standardize our evaluations of variability. Data can vary, and visual inspection alone cannot capture that variability in a precise or standard way. Indeed, the *appearance* of variability in a graph

---

[4] The standard error of the mean refers to the estimate of the *standard deviation of a sampling distribution of means*. The mean in any study (or the mean of the phase in the hypothetical example) is an estimate of the true mean in the population. Consider for a moment that we conduct the study in the hypothetical example many different times and assess performance under the conditions (e.g., baseline). Let us say we do this an infinite number of times. Each time we do, the 6 days of baseline draws from this larger pool of all the performances under baseline. In each study or on each occasion that we sampled 6 days of baseline, we would get a mean. These means form a sampling distribution of means, that is, each mean is a data point. The overall mean or the mean of these means would provide the "real" or population mean (μ). But not all the means that were sampled would be the same; they would vary a bit. The standard error of the mean is the standard deviation of the sampling distribution of the means and reflects how much sample means may be expected to depart from the population mean. In a single study we conduct, the standard error of the mean helps us to estimate, with some level of confidence, the likelihood that the population mean will fall within the range we present.

Table 13.1 Hypothetical Data for AB (Baseline, Intervention) Phases in Which Percent or Frequency of Some Behavior Is Occurring. (Numbers in the Columns Are the Data for Days of Baseline and the Intervention)

	Baseline	Intervention
	16	16
	12	18
	13	19
	17	20
	14	18
	13	21
	14	21
		20
N days of observation	7	8
Mean score for the phase	14.14	19.13
Standard Deviation (s)	1.77	1.73
Standard Error (se)	.67	.61

Standard deviation (s) =

$$s = \sqrt{\frac{\sum_{i=1}^{N}(x_i - \bar{x})^2}{N-1}}$$

where x with a bar above it is the value of the mean,

N is the sample size, and

x_i represents each data value from i = 1 (the first) to i = N (the last). The Σ symbol indicates that you must add up the sum

Standard Error = sd

$$SE_{\bar{x}} = \frac{s}{\sqrt{n}}$$

where s is the sample standard deviation

n is the size (number of items) of the sample.

can be quite different depending on the range of the ordinate of the graph. If the scores range from 25 to 45, the scores will look like there is less variability if they are plotted on a graph that can range from 0 to 200, as compared with a graph that can range from 20 to 50. Error bars provide an objective and readily interpretable metric.

Second, for many readers there might be comfort in the use of error bars because they bridge visual inspection and statistical analyses. The reader trained in quantitative methods can immediately recognize that error bars are similar to *confidence intervals* that are used as part of statistical analyses to convey the likelihood that the true mean falls within a particular range.[5]

---

[5] Confidence intervals (CIs) provide a range of values within which the true mean is likely to lie. Even though this is a range, it also includes the information that one obtains from a statistical test of significance, because z values used for significance testing (e.g., z score of 1.96 for p = .05, or 2.58 for p = .01) are used to form the upper and lower CI. The formula for computing CIs is:

CIs = m $\pm z_\alpha s_m$

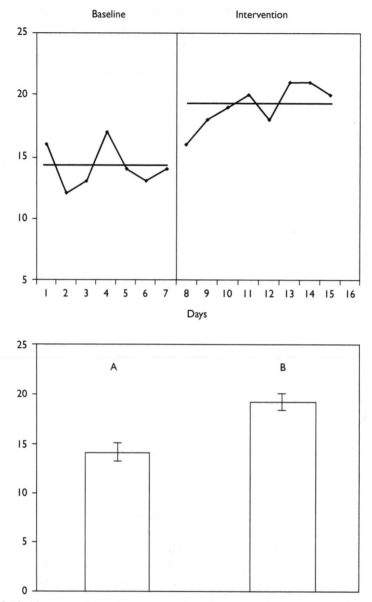

Figure 13.12. Hypothetical data from AB phases that are plotted as a line graph (*upper panel*) or bar graph (*lower panel*). Horizontal lines in the line graph represent the means; the bars in the bar graph represent means. The vertical lines above and below the means represent the error bars plus and minus one standard error around the mean.

---

[5] (Continued) where

m = the mean score (e.g., for a given phase in a single case design);

z_a = the z score value (two-tailed) under the normal curve, depending on the confidence level (e.g., z = 1.96 and 2.58 for p = .05 and p = .01, respectively); and

Presentation of the Data to Clarify Patterns

The previously discussed indices provide measures of variability (e.g., standard deviation, standard error, confidence interval) that provide a standardized way of communicating fluctuation within phases. There is another issue that can emerge in the data and in relation to graphing. There may be excessive variability in the data. There is no standard definition for "excessive variability." To convey the concept, consider the data within phase to reflect scores that vary day to day and range from the lowest to the highest (e.g., 0 to 100% of the time) possible scores on the measure or at least to approximate use of the full range of available scores. For example, baseline performance might fluctuate from 10 to 90% of the intervals of some observed behavior, even though no effort was made to intervene. Invariably, the investigator wants to understand the sources of variability and control them if possible, a topic to which we return in the next chapter. However, there is a graphing option that is occasionally used to present the data when excessive variability cannot be controlled or no attempt has been made to control it. The graphing solution does not reduce variability per se but rather the *appearance* of variability in the data.

The appearance of day-to-day variability can be reduced by plotting the data in *blocks of time* rather than on a daily basis. For example, if data are collected every day, they need not be plotted on a daily basis. Data can be aggregated over consecutive days (blocks), and the average of each block can be plotted. By representing two or more days with a single averaged data point, the data appear more stable. Figure 13.13 presents hypothetical data in one phase that show day-to-day performance that is highly variable (upper panel). The same data appear in the middle panel in which the averages for 2-day blocks are plotted. The fluctuation in performance is greatly reduced in the middle panel, giving the appearance of much more stable data. Finally, in the bottom panel the data are aggregated into 5-day blocks. That is, performances for 5 consecutive days are averaged into a single data point, which is plotted. The appearance of variability is reduced even further.

In single-case research, consecutive data points can be aggregated in the fashion illustrated in the figure. In general, the larger the number of days included in a block, the lower the variability that will appear in the graph. Of course, once the size of the block is decided (e.g., 2 or 3 days) all data throughout the investigation ought to be plotted in this fashion so the data are treated in this transformed (averaged) way in a consistent fashion. It is important to note that the aggregating and averaging procedure only affects the appearance of variability in the data. When the appearance is altered,

---

[5] (Continued)

s_m = the standard error of measurement, i.e., the estimate of the standard deviation of a sampling distribution of means or the standard deviation divided by the square root of N ($s_m = s/\sqrt{N}$).

As the formula notes, to obtain these values, one multiplies the standard error of the mean (as used in computing error bars) by z value (e.g., 1.96) and adds this to the mean for the upper limit of the interval and subtracts that same value from the mean for the lower limit of the interval. This is exactly the procedure used to compute error bars. The error bars were 1 standard error above and below the mean; with CIs we are using 1.96 (or 2.58) standard errors above and below the mean. These latter numbers are used because they reflect the $p = .05$ (or $p = .01$) thresholds when statistical tests (e.g., t or F) are used to define statistical significance.

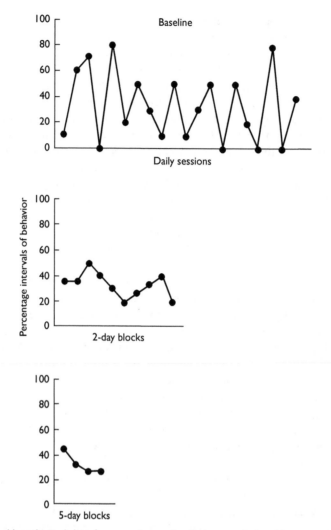

Figure 13.13. Hypothetical data for one phase of a single-case design. ***Upper panel*** shows data plotted on a daily basis. ***Middle panel*** shows the same data plotted in 2-day blocks. ***Lower panel*** shows the same data plotted in 5-day blocks. Together the figures show that the appearance of variability can be reduced by plotting data into blocks.

changes in means, levels, and trends across phases may be easier to detect than when the original data are examined.

A few cautions are worth noting. First, aggregating data points into blocks reduces the number of data points in the graph for each of the phases. If 10 days of baseline are observed but plotted in blocks of 5 days, then only two data points (number of days/ block size or 10/5 = 2) will appear in baseline. Unless the data are quite stable, these few data points may not serve as a sufficient basis for predicting performance in subsequent phases. (But if the data were "quite stable" there might be no need to place them into 5-day blocks and average them.) Although blocking the data in the fashion described reduces the number of data points, the resulting data are usually markedly more stable than the daily data. Thus, what one loses in number of points is compensated for by the stability of the data points based on averages obtained from aggregated days.

Second and related, aggregating days into blocks will reduce the number of data points and could undermine the key purposes of collecting continuous data. For example, one study reduced the frequent aggression of a male in a psychiatric hospital (Bisconer, Green, Mallon-Czajka, & Johnson, 2006). The patient met criteria for multiple psychiatric diagnoses, including many symptoms of psychoses. An intervention program provided praise and tangible rewards each day by psychiatric nurses on the ward for periods of appropriate and nonaggressive behavior. Figure 13.14 shows the results. Baseline lasted for 3 months, the data were averaged over a 3-month block. That means only the first data point in the graph (#1) was baseline. By averaging in 3-month blocks we only have that data point. One data point is not a good basis for the main reason we conduct assessment in a phase (describe, predict, and test). That is, from this one point we really cannot see if there any trends, we cannot really get a good picture to invoke the data-evaluation criteria. Was the program effective? We can say that there was a change in aggression toward oneself and others. Here is a case where the data are available but the averaging of them introduced ambiguity. It would be fine to plot baseline on a month-by-month basis (with three data points) and a couple of months of intervention in a similar way, and then to switch to 3-month blocks if one wished. Averaging led to one data point for baseline and leaves unclear key characteristics of the data.

Third, the actual data plotted in blocks can distort daily performance. Plotting data on a daily basis rather than in blocks is not inherently superior or more veridical. However, variability in the data evident in daily observations may represent a meaningful, important, or interesting characteristic of performance. Averaging hides this variability, which, in a particular situation, may obfuscate important information in its

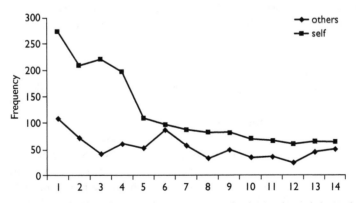

Figure 13.14. Number of physically aggressive actions on the hospital ward during baseline (first data point) and over the course of treatment. Each data point (1–14) represents the average score of daily aggression averaged over a 3-month block. One baseline data point represents 3 months of observations averaged.   *(Source: Bisconer et al., 2006.)*

own right. For example, a hyperactive child in a classroom situation may show marked differences in how he or she performs from day to day. On some days the child may show very high levels of activity and inappropriate behavior, while on other days his or her behavior may be no different from that of peers functioning well in class. The variability in behavior may be important or important to alter. The overall activity of the child but also the marked inconsistency (variability) over days represents characteristics that may have implications for designing treatments. For example, there might be influences that could be identified on the days of normative rather than hyperactive behavior, and these influences might be harnessed to help the child.

Changes in Level

Another source of information on which visual inspection often relies is changes in level across phases, that is, the discontinuity or shift in the data at each point that the experimental condition is changed (e.g., change from A to B or from B to A phases). Typically this change refers to the difference in the last day of one phase and the first day of the next. No special technique is needed to describe this change. (One technique to describe the changes in level in ratio form has been devised as part of the split-middle technique of estimating trends and is mentioned in the next section.)

Of course, the investigator may be interested in going beyond merely *describing* changes in level. The issue is not whether there is simply a shift in performance from the last day of one phase to the first day of the next. Performance normally varies on a daily basis, so it is unlikely that performance will be at the same level two days in a row (unless the behavior never occurs). When conditions are changed, the major interest is whether the change in level is beyond what would be expected from ordinary fluctuations in performance. That is, is the shift in performance large enough to depart from what would be expected given the usual variability in performance?

The *evaluation* of the change in level is different from the description of the change. First, the measure of variability discussed previously can provide useful information. One can determine if performance is within or outside of the plotted range of variability from the prior phase. There are no fixed decision-making guidelines, but viewing the shift in relation to normal variability (e.g., plus or minus one or two standard deviations) is helpful in making the judgment about a change in level when that change is not obvious.

Changes in Trend

Inferring a change of trend does not have to rely on merely looking at the data within a phase. That is unsystematic to say the least because of the task, namely, looking at the data points and imagining what line (vector) best represents the angle of the slope. Again, when trends are clear, flat (zero slope) in baseline, or sharply accelerating line and decelerating lines across phases, one may need no clear aid. However, there are options, some of which are easily implemented to plot the trend within each phase. The trend line computed in some standardized fashion is a much more defensible procedure for addressing the logic of the designs (describe, predict, test). Trend lines allow one to see the extent to which trends have changed across phases.

A fairly easy visual aid is to use a spreadsheet that allows one to move from a database where the numbers are entered for each phase to a graph (e.g., Carr & Burkholder,

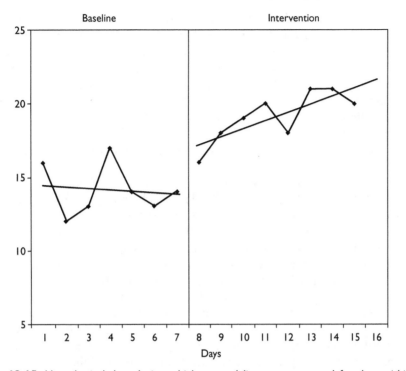

Figure 13.15. Hypothetical data during which a trend line was computed for data within two phases (A, B). In this example, the data were entered in Microsoft Excel™; a line graph was selected as the option to chart the data, and then compute trend line was added to give the linear slope that best represented the data within each phase.

1998). For example, if one has an ABAB design, the daily number is entered for whatever behavior or measure (e.g., percent of intervals or frequency). The data are then plotted in a simple line graph. Within the database program, one can shade (click on, mark, highlight) the data within the phase and click on compute trend line or regression line. Figure 13.15 presents hypothetical data for the first two phases of an ABAB design. A trend line was computed separately for each phase that easily allows the investigator and reader to see changes in trend. There are many options, but the simplest is a linear (least squares) regression that is readily available in database programs. A linear regression line is fit to a series of data points as those plotted in Figure 13.15. A regression line is drawn through the individual data points that comes as close as possible to the points. A separate line is drawn for the data in baseline and intervention phases for each phase of the design. As noted in the figure, the trend within each phase can be readily seen and the trends across phases can be compared.[6]

---

[6] In the appendix at the end of the book, problems with linear regression will be raised. Briefly, a characteristic of single-case data (called serial dependence) is that data points and their error terms from one day to the next can be correlated (called autocorrelation). This characteristic has rather significant implications for visual inspection and statistical evaluation of single-case data.

An example to show what a trend line can add is provided in a study that focused on three women (28, 43, and 44 years old, ethnicity not noted) (Billette, Guay, & Marchand, 2008). How much they were disturbed by their symptoms was one of the measures and was rated from 0 (not at all) to 100 (extremely). The treatment was cognitive behavior therapy (CBT) with 22 to 27 individually administered sessions, each lasting from 60 to 90 minutes. The treatment included many components (e.g., psychoeducation about trauma and sexual assault, anxiety management techniques, cognitive restructuring, and others beyond the scope of the illustration). A few sessions were provided to the spouse to increase support and involve the husband more in the treatment.

Figure 13.16 conveys the results for the measure I mentioned. The first phase was baseline, the second phase was CBT. The graph conveys that the intervention was introduced in a multiple-baseline design across the three women. After the last person was treated, there was a 3-month follow-up assessment for all individuals. The individual day-to-day data should fluctuate. Not shown in the figure, the means changed for each participant. For example, the means for baseline, intervention, and follow-up phases for Participant 1 were 54.5, 19.6, and 9.5, respectively. A regression slope (trend line) was used as a visual aid to characterize the trends within each phase for each participant. The lines help visually with the presentation because of the marked day-to-day variability. We see that slope during the intervention phase was different from the slope in baseline. The slopes at follow-up are not too informative, largely because the symptoms were clearly low. The trend lines are very helpful. Also, by the nature of the intervention (multiple sessions) one would expect a gradual change over time rather than an abrupt change when some incentive is altered on a more malleable problem.

There are many techniques to evaluate trends in the data. For example, one technique to describe trends in single-case research is the split-middle technique (White, 1972, 1974). This technique permits examination of the trend within each phase and allows comparison of trends across phases. The method has been developed in the context of assessing rate of behavior (frequency/time). Another approach is to use time-series analyses, a statistical data-evaluation method to incorporate trends in the data in deciding whether there is any change across phases (Box, Jenkins, & Reinsel, 1994) (see appendix for discussion and illustration). In the case of graphing data in single-case research, trend within each phase is infrequently plotted and no one method has dominated the few instances in which such information is provided.

Rapidity of Change
Another criterion for invoking inspection discussed earlier refers to the latency between the change in experimental conditions and a change in performance. Relatively rapid changes in performance after the intervention is applied or withdrawn contribute to the decision, based on visual inspection, that the intervention probably led to the change.

---

[6] (Continued) Linear regression can ignore complex relations within the data and assume that those relations are not present.

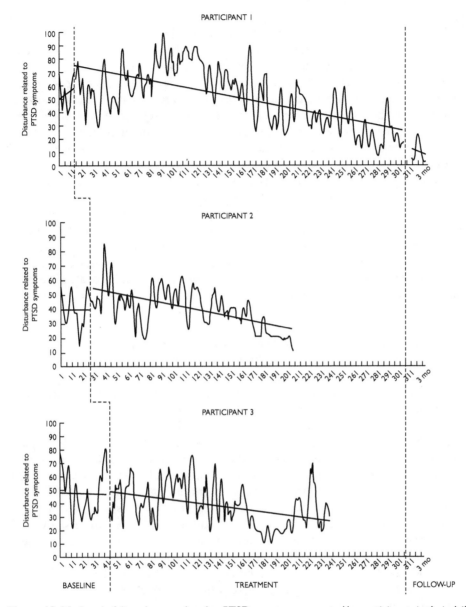

Figure 13.16. Level of disturbance related to PTSD symptoms reported by participants in their daily self-monitoring at baseline, during treatment, and at follow-up. The intervention (cognitive behavior therapy sessions) was introduced in a multiple-baseline design across the three women.   *(Source: Billette, Guay, & Marchand, 2008.)*

One of the difficulties in specifying rapidity of change as a descriptive characteristic of the data pertains to defining a change. Behavior usually changes from one day to the next. But this fluctuation represents ordinary variability. At what point can the change be confidently identified as a departure from this ordinary variability?

When experimental conditions are altered, it may be difficult to define objectively the point or points at which changes in performance are evident. Without an agreed upon criterion, the points that define change may be quite subjective. A plot of variability of performance provides a guideline. One can see at the point of intervention if the amount of change exceeds the variability range for baseline data. That is, one can look at the error bar of variability above and below the mean of baseline to see if the first few days of the intervention phase are outside of that range. Again, there are no objective criteria to make the decision by visual inspection.

Rapidity of change is a difficult notion to specify because it is a joint function of changes in level and slope. A marked change in level and in slope usually reflects a rapid change. For example, baseline may show a stable rate and no trend. The onset of the intervention may show a shift in level of 50 percentage points and a steep accelerating trend indicating that the change has occurred quickly and the rate of behavior change from day to day is marked.

General Comments

There is no standard practice or rule about what aids to provide in presenting data. Indeed, sometimes practices in single-case as well as between-group designs are dictated by publication (e.g., journal) policies rather than by methodological principles. However, it is useful to consider the overall goal, namely, to foster and facilitate comprehension of the results by the audience. So the question for the investigator is what information can be provided to the audience(s) to enhance that goal. An investigator is part of the audience and would want to know as many facets as available to understand nuances within a given subject and among many subjects. Other consumers (one's peers, lay consumers) are likely to be less interested in nuances. One guide is to consider what will aid application of the criteria for visual inspection? What will aid deciding whether the changes were reliable (e.g., by visual inspection or statistical criteria)? There are often different audiences to consider (other researchers, teachers), and different decisions might be made about what to present to each one. People in everyday life do not talk about the criteria for visual inspection very much (although you should have been at last year's Methodologist's New Year's Eve bash in which this discussion got very heated). People in everyday life want to know, did the intervention work; did performance improve?

Additional information can err on the side of too much or information that is not needed. For example, in one of the examples (Figure 13.10), means were plotted across phases. No harm was done, but the results were so clear, perhaps they were not needed there. In the next example (Figure 13.11), plotting the means was helpful because the changes and visual inspection criteria were not so clear. In short, consider the goal to aid application of the data-evaluation criteria. More generally, what will help the consumer of the evaluation understand the results—and of course that may vary by who the consumers are. I have highlighted some of the basic aids that can enhance inspection of the day-to-day data points.

SUMMARY AND CONCLUSIONS

This chapter has discussed basic options for graphing data to facilitate application of visual inspection. *Simple line graphs*, *cumulative graphs*, and *bar graphs* were discussed briefly. Virtually all of the graphs in single-case research derive from these three types or their combinations. Among the available options and combinations, the simple line graph is the most commonly reported.

As noted in the earlier discussion of data evaluation (Chapter 12), visual inspection is more than simply looking at plotted data and arbitrarily deciding whether the data reflect a reliable effect. Several characteristics of the data should be examined, including changes in means, levels, and trends, and the rapidity of changes. Selected descriptive aids are available that can be incorporated into simple graphing procedures to facilitate examination of some of these data characteristics. The chapter has discussed *plotting means*, *computing ratios to express changes in level*, and *plotting trends* as some of the aids to facilitate visual inspection.

This chapter and the prior one elaborate data-evaluation methods. The statistical aids in this chapter included those that describe the data. Statistical evaluation of course goes beyond description. Significance testing is used to draw inferences about the reliability (experimental criterion) of an effect or change. Statistical analyses are covered in the appendix.

CHAPTER 14

Evaluation of Single-Case Designs: Challenges, Limitations, and Directions

Previous chapters have discussed issues and potential problems associated with specific single-case designs. This chapter discusses these more general issues, concerns, and limitations that transcend individual designs including trend and variability in the data, duration of phases, and when to shift phases. Other issues that are covered include the range of research questions that single-case designs can and cannot address, generality of results from the designs, and replication of effects. Although this chapter and the next emphasize issues in relation to single-case research, some of these can be addressed better when placed in the context of between-group research.

COMMON METHODOLOGICAL PROBLEMS AND OBSTACLES

Traditionally, research designs are preplanned so that most of the details about who receives the intervention and often the duration (or dose) of the intervention are decided before the subjects participate in the study. In single-case designs, many crucial decisions about the design are made only as the data are collected. Examples include deciding how long a baseline phase should be and when to present or withdraw the intervention. Inferences about the intervention depend on the data pattern within and across phases. The pattern of the data determines the decisions made within the design.

Each single-case design usually begins with a baseline phase followed by the intervention phase. The intervention is evaluated by comparing performance across phases. For these comparisons to be made easily, the investigator has to be sure that the changes from one phase to another are likely to be due to the intervention rather than to a continuation of an existing trend or to chance fluctuations (high or low points) in the data. A fundamental design issue is deciding *when to change phases* so as to maximize the clarity of data interpretation.

There are no widely agreed upon rules for altering phases. However, there is general agreement that the point at which the conditions are changed in the design is extremely important because subsequent evaluation of intervention effects depends on how clear the changes are across phases. The usual rule of thumb is to alter conditions (phases) only when the data are stable. As noted earlier, stability refers to the absence of trend and relatively small variability in performance. Trends and excessive variability during any of the phases, particularly during baseline, can interfere with evaluating intervention effects. Although both trend and variability were discussed earlier, it is important to build on that earlier discussion and address problems that may arise and various solutions that can facilitate drawing inferences about intervention effects.

Trends in the Data

As noted earlier, drawing inferences about intervention effects is greatly facilitated when baseline levels show no trend (slope) or a trend in the direction opposite from that predicted by the intervention. A problem may emerge, at least from the standpoint of the design, when baseline data show a trend in the same direction as expected to result from the intervention. Changes in level and trend are more difficult to detect during the intervention phase if performance is already improving during baseline.

It may be possible to continue baseline for a little longer to see if the data pattern will stabilize and whether a seeming trend (e.g., increase in the behavior 2 days in a row) really is a trend. Of course, in many applied settings, there are external pressures to begin the intervention as soon as possible, and more baseline days are a luxury. It is one matter for an investigator to understand what baseline is trying to accomplish, one purpose of this book, but quite another to convey the message and evoke sympathy from a client or a client's family experiencing a need for an intervention or from an administrator whose programs, funding, and future are on the line to intervene now. Also, the problem (e.g., drinking alcohol in a college dormitory, dangerous behavior in a classroom) may require immediate intervention. Behavior may require intervention even though some improvements are occurring. If prolonged baselines cannot be invoked to wait for stable data, other options are available.

First, the intervention can be implemented even though there is a trend toward improved performance during baseline. If an ABAB design, or in this case a BABA design, is possible in light of ethical or practical issues, the A phase can consist of an active intervention that is designed not to return to baseline but to actively change the direction of the behavior and the trend. The design begins with an intervention (B) and then during the A phase some intervention is used to change the direction of the behavior *opposite* from that of the direction of the intervention phase. For example, in a pioneering application of behavioral techniques, staff on a ward of a psychiatric hospital unwittingly provided attention (social reinforcement) for "irrational talk" of a patient with psychoses (Ayllon & Haughton, 1964). The patient would comment on delusions or make other statements that had no clear external referents. The staff, trying to be helpful, comforting, and sympathetic, would provide attention to the patient. The investigators raised the question, could staff attention actually influence such statements, or were the statements merely uncontrollable expressions of the psychiatric disorder?

After baseline observations of patient comments, the intervention phase began in which attention from the staff was used to reinforce rational comments. Whenever the patient spoke more normally, the staff provided immediate attention. Any irrational comments were ignored. A reversal phase was introduced. The investigators could have merely withdrawn all attention during the reversal phase. Instead, during the reversal phase attention was provided for all comments that were *not* rational, that is, behavior other than the focus during the intervention phase. During the reversal phase, reinforcement was given for all behavior except the original one that was targeted (referred to as differential reinforcement of other behavior). This has the advantage of quickly reversing the direction (trend) of performance, as it did in this example. Hence, across an ABAB design, for example, the effects of the intervention on behavior are likely to be readily apparent. In general, other procedures that will alter the direction of performance can help reduce ambiguities caused by initial baseline performance that shows a trend in a therapeutic direction. Of course, this design option may be methodologically sound but clinically untenable because it includes specific provisions for making the client's behavior worse.

A second alternative for reducing the ambiguity that initial trends in the data may present is to select design options in which such a trend in a therapeutic direction will have little or no impact on drawing conclusions about intervention effects. For example, a multiple-baseline design is usually not impeded by initial trends in baseline. It is unlikely that all of the baselines (behaviors, persons, or behaviors in different situations) will show a trend in a therapeutic direction. The intervention can be invoked for those behaviors that are relatively stable while baseline conditions are continued for other behaviors in which trends appear. If the need exists to intervene for the behaviors that do show an initial trend, this too is unlikely to interfere with drawing inferences about intervention effects. Conclusions about intervention effects are reached on the basis of the pattern of data across all of the behaviors or baselines in the multiple-baseline design. Ambiguity of the changes across one or two of the baselines may not necessarily impede drawing an overall conclusion, depending on the number of baselines, the magnitude of intervention effects, and how other criteria for visual inspection are met.

Similarly, drawing inferences about intervention effects is usually not threatened by an initial baseline trend in a therapeutic direction in an alternating-treatments design. In this design, conclusions are reached on the basis of the effects of different conditions usually implemented in the same phase. The differential effects of alternative interventions can be detected even though there may be an overall trend in the data. The main question is whether differences between or among the alternative interventions occur, and this need not be interfered with by an overall trend in the data. If one of the conditions included in an intervention phase of an alternating-treatments design is a continuation of baseline, the investigator can directly assess whether the interventions surpass performance obtained concurrently under the continued baseline conditions. A trend need not impede conclusions about the intervention that is evaluated in a changing-criterion design. This design depends on evaluating whether the performance matches a changing criterion in a step-like fashion. Even if performance improves during baseline, control exerted by the intervention can still be evaluated by comparing the criterion level with performance throughout the design, and if necessary by using bidirectional changes in the criteria, as discussed in an earlier chapter.

Another option for handling initial trend in baseline is to utilize statistical techniques to evaluate the effects of the intervention relative to baseline performance. Techniques that describe and plot initial baseline trends such as computing trend lines, as discussed in the previous chapter on graphing, can help visually examine whether an initial trend in baseline is similar to trends during the intervention phase(s). In addition, statistical techniques (e.g., time-series analysis) can assess whether the intervention has made reliable changes over and above what would be expected from a continuation of initial trend. This is a more sophisticated solution that solves a variety of problems, including identifying trends that visual inspection cannot detect (please see the appendix).

In general, an initial trend during baseline may not necessarily interfere with drawing inferences about the intervention. Various design options and data-evaluation techniques can be used to reduce or eliminate ambiguity about intervention effects. It is crucial for the investigator to have in mind one of the alternatives for reducing ambiguity if an initial trend is evident in baseline. Without taking explicit steps in altering the design or applying special data-evaluation techniques, trend in a therapeutic direction during baseline or return-to-baseline phases may compete with obtaining clear effects.

Variability

Evaluation of intervention effects is facilitated by having relatively little variability in the data in a given phase and across all phases. The larger the daily fluctuations, the larger the behavior change required to demonstrate an effect. Large fluctuations in the data do not always make evaluation of the intervention difficult. For example, sometimes baseline performance may show large fluctuations about (around) the mean value. When the intervention is implemented, not only may the mean performance change, but variability may become markedly less as well. Hence, the intervention effect is very clear, because both change in means and a reduction in variability occurred. The difficulties arise primarily when baseline and intervention conditions both show relatively large fluctuations in performance. In the previous chapter I discussed a graphing option about reducing the appearance of excessive variability by blocking the data into groups of sessions and plotting the mean of each block. The present discussion addresses the more fundamental task of understanding and controlling or reducing excessive variability.

Variability in the data is a property of ordinary behavior in virtually all settings. Presumably variability is due to all sorts of factors that affect our functioning. Where there is excessive variability that may interfere with drawing inferences or obtaining a clear pattern in the data, we then try to identify some of these factors. Excessive variability in the data indicates absence of experimental control over the behavior and lack of understanding of the factors that contribute to performance (Sidman, 1960).

When baseline performance appears highly variable, several factors may be identified that contribute to variability. First, the client may be performing relatively consistently, that is, shows little variability in performance, although this is not accurately reflected in the data. One factor that might hide consistency is the manner in which observations are conducted. Observers may introduce variability in performance to the extent that they score inconsistently or depart (drift) from the original definitions of behavior. Careful checks on interobserver agreement and periodic retraining sessions may help reduce observer deviations from the intended procedures.

Second, the conditions under which observations are obtained may contribute to and increase variability in performance. Excessive variability may suggest that greater standardization is needed over the conditions in which the observations are obtained. Client performance may vary as a function of the persons present in the situation, the time of day in which observations are obtained, and events preceding the observation period or events anticipated after the observation period. These other influences are "interventions" that may vary daily (e.g., another child in class who is very disruptive, regular assignments on some fixed days of the week that generate or control variability in performance, activities on some days that precede or follow recess). Normally, such factors that naturally vary from day to day can be ignored and baseline observations may still show relatively low variability. On the other hand, when variability is excessive, the investigator may wish to identify or attempt to identify features of the setting that can be standardized further.

Standardization amounts to making the day-to-day situation more homogeneous, which is likely to decrease factors that influence variability. An occasional objection to this recommendation is that we want to see behavior under "realistic" circumstances and so the variability and the natural environment ought not to be altered or managed. This concern is questionable in all sorts of contexts (e.g., training a musician to play a piece, teaching a pilot to learn how to fly, and developing skills in an athlete). In each context, performance and practice under controlled conditions are part of the early learning process. Our goal is to foster the desired behaviors in the natural environment, but that goal does not require introducing all of the conditions (e.g., for a musician— the audience, the pressure, the full musical piece rather than sections) early in observations and training. The initial goal is to assess behavior and then see if we can change it. Extending the newly acquired behavior to other situations where more factors are allowed to vary can follow the initial demonstration (see Kazdin, 2001). If variability is excessive, look to see if the environment includes some influences that might be contributing. Obviously, some factors that vary on a daily basis (e.g., client's diet, weather) may be less easily controlled than others (e.g., presence of peers in the same room, use of the same or similar activities while the client is being observed).

For whatever reason, behavior may simply be quite variable even after the just-mentioned procedures have been explored. Indeed, the goal of an intervention program may be to alter the variability of the client's performance (i.e., make performance more consistent by reinforcing behavior within a range as discussed in the chapter on changing-criterion designs), rather than or in addition to changing the mean rate. Variability may remain relatively large, and the need to intervene cannot be postponed to identify contributory sources. In such cases, the investigator may use aids such as plotting data into blocks, graphing mean performance in each of the phases, and adding trend lines within phases to help clarify the pattern and facilitate data evaluation, as mentioned in the previous chapter.

Whether the variability will interfere with evaluation of the intervention effects is determined in part by the type of changes produced by the intervention and the sensitivity of the measure to reflecting such changes (e.g., no ceiling or floor effects). Marked changes in performance may be very clear because of simultaneous changes in the mean, level, and trend across phases and fast latency of change. So the extent to which variability interferes with drawing inferences is a function of the magnitude and type of change produced by the intervention. The main point is that with relatively large variability, stronger intervention effects are needed to infer that a systematic change has occurred.

Duration of the Phases

An important issue in single-case research is deciding how long the phases will be over the course of the design. The duration of the phases usually is not specified in advance of the investigation. The reason is that the investigator examines the data and determines whether the information is sufficiently clear to make predictions about performance. The presence or suggestion of trends or excessive variability during the baseline phase or tentative, weak, or delayed treatment effects during the intervention phase may require more prolonged phases.

A common methodological problem is altering phases before a clear pattern emerges. For example, most of the data may indicate a clear pattern for the baseline phase. Yet, after a few days of relatively stable baseline performance, one or two data points may be higher or lower than all of the previous data. The questions that immediately arise are whether a trend is emerging in baseline, whether one of the threats to validity (e.g., history) could explain the data, or whether the data points are merely part of random (unsystematic) variability. It is prudent to continue the condition without shifting phases. If one or two more days of data reveal that there is no trend, the intervention can be implemented as planned. The few "extra" data points provide increased confidence that there was no emerging trend and can greatly facilitate subsequent evaluation of the intervention.

Occasionally, an investigator may obtain an extreme data point during baseline in the opposite direction of the change anticipated with the intervention. This extreme point may be interpreted as suggesting that if there is any trend, it is in the opposite direction of intervention effects. Investigators may shift phases when an extreme point is noted in the previous phase in the direction opposite from the predicted effects of the phase. Yet an extreme score in one direction is likely to be followed by a score that reverts in the direction of the mean, a characteristic known as *statistical regression* (see Chapter 2).

It is important to be alert to the possibility of regression. If one single extreme score occurs, it may be unwise to shift phases. Such a shift might capitalize on regression. This immediate "improvement" in performance might be interpreted to be the result of shifting from one condition to another (change in level) when in fact it might be accounted for by regression. As data continue to be collected in the new phase, the investigator could, of course, see if the intervention is having an effect on behavior. Yet, if changes in level or means are examined across phases, shifting phases at points of extreme scores could systematically bias the conclusions.

In general, phases in single-case experimental designs ought to be continued until data patterns are relatively clear. This does not always mean that phases are long. For example, in some cases, return-to-baseline or reversal phases in ABAB designs may be very brief, such as only 1 or 2 days or sessions (e.g., Kodak, Grow, & Northrup, 2004; Stricker, Miltenberger, Garlinghouse, Deaver, & Anderson, 2001). The brevity of each phase is determined in part by the clarity of the data within that phase and in relation to adjacent phases.

Suggesting a requisite number of data points is useful as a practical guideline. As a minimum, 3 to 5 days is probably useful as a general rule. However, it is much more important to convey the rationale underlying the recommendation, namely, to provide a clear basis for predicting and testing predictions about performance. A simple rule has many problems. For one, it is likely that some phases require longer durations than others. For example, it is usually important to have the initial baseline of a slightly longer duration than return-to-baseline phases in ABAB designs. The initial baseline of any design provides the first information about trends and variability in the data and serves uniquely as an important point of reference for all subsequent phases. Consequently, this is not a phase to be rushed.

All that said, it is always important to bear in mind the goals of any methodological practice rather than rigid practices. Thus, it is not only conceivable that there will be brief baseline phases, but there are examples where they make sense. For example, in a program designed to teach bicycle riding to a 9-year-old boy with Asperger's syndrome, data were collected on various steps that entailed bicycle riding (Cameron, Shapiro, & Ainsleigh, 2005). The initial baseline phase consisted of one session that confirmed that the child could not ride a bicycle (and his score was zero). Also, the child reacted with an extreme emotional response to the task in baseline. The data showed a clear pattern of developing bike riding in a changing-criterion design, and the one-session baseline was quite fine. Yes, two data points are much better than one (because from two one can see initial variability) and three is much better than two (to help infer a trend), but when behavior is at zero and that confirms the view of all parties (e.g., parents or teachers saying that "the child cannot do this, has never done this, and never will unless you do something pretty soon"), one day is fine. More commonly, multiple-baseline designs are likely to have short baseline phases (e.g., one or a few sessions) because the strength of a demonstration does not depend on any single phase and the short baseline of one subject (or behavior or setting) on which data are collected will have longer baselines for the subjects yet to receive the intervention. More generally, rules about the duration of experimental phases in single-case research are difficult to specify and when specified are often difficult to justify without great qualification.

Aside from the duration of individual phases, investigators occasionally ask whether phases in a study ought to be of equal or approximately equal duration within a given investigation (e.g., each phase 10 days). Hopefully, the reader at this point will answer with an unequivocal "no." The rationale for posing phases of equal duration is sound, so before justifying "no" the reasons are important to acknowledge. First, posing phases of equal duration occasionally is based on the view that in a given period of time (e.g., a week or month), maturational or cyclical influences may lead to a certain pattern of performance. For example, if the setting (e.g., classroom, business activities at a company) has a fixed routine for each day or each week, perhaps one would want to be sure that each phase included the full routine so that extraneous events may be roughly constant or equal in each phase and do not bias the data in one phase. Essentially, the investigator may want to be sure that conditions (the routines) are relatively constant across baseline and intervention phases. This is reasonable.

Second, the investigator may be planning on the use of statistical analyses to evaluate the results. Statistical analyses often are more powerful (able to detect differences where there are differences) when there are several observations and an equal number of observations. Thus, this would be a reason to plan on phases of equal duration. Finally, communicating the program to others is facilitated by satisfying the legitimate query, how long will the baseline and treatment phases last? Everyone's anxiety is allayed when one can give a clear answer the way one usually can in a pre-arranged and planned between-group study.

Although phases of equal or nearly equal duration might be convenient for all of the preceding reasons, try to resist whenever possible. The reason is fundamental and pertains to the logic of single-case designs. We are interested in obtaining data that help with the describe, predict, and test prediction features of the design. An equal number of days in each phase is not elegant or prized and could even interfere. Phases of equal duration do not necessarily strengthen the design. In fact, if duration is given primacy as a consideration, ambiguity may be introduced by altering or waiting to alter conditions merely because a criterion number of days has or has not elapsed.

Typically, the duration of the phases is determined by judgment on the part of the investigator based on his or her view that a clear data pattern is evident. Of course, practical considerations often operate as well (e.g., end of the school year) that place constraints on durations of the phases. From the standpoint of the design, the pattern of the data should dictate decisions to alter the phases. That pattern is judged by how it may serve our overall goal of obtaining data in the phases that adequately describe performance, predict performance in the immediate future if conditions were not to change, and test the prediction of a previous phase.

Criteria for Shifting Phases

Currently, no agreed-upon objective decision rules exist for altering phases. The duration of phases depends on having stable data. Typically, stability of performance in a particular phase can be defined by two characteristics of the data, namely, trend and variability. A criterion or decision rule for shifting phases usually needs to take into account these parameters. One criterion is to define stability of the data in a given phase in terms of a number of consecutive sessions or days that fall within a prespecified range of the mean such as plus or minus 1 or 1½ standard deviations around the mean. The method can ensure that data do not show a systematic increase or decrease over time (trend) and fall within a particular range (variability). When the specified criteria are met, the phase is terminated and the next condition can be presented. An obvious obstacle is that one has to accumulate some observations within a phase to have a reasonable estimate of the standard deviation. With only a few observations in the first few days of a phase, both the mean and the standard deviation may be changing markedly.

Another criterion might be requiring that so many days in a row fall within a particular range. For example, in one investigation of an ABAB design, a change from one phase to the other was made if 3 consecutive days of data were obtained that did not depart more than 10 percent from the mean of all previous days of that phase (Wilson, Robertson, Herlong, & Haynes, 1979). To obtain the mean within a given phase, a cumulative average was continually obtained. That is, each successive day was added to all previous days of that phase to obtain a new mean. When 3 consecutive days fell within 10% of that mean, the phase was changed. One could specify 2 days of 20%; there are no rules or guidelines here. The advantage is making the decision criteria explicit. That is always of value in science.

Specification of criteria for deciding when to alter conditions (phases) is fine. If criteria are specified in advance, alteration of conditions is less likely to take advantage of chance fluctuations in the data. In general, specifiable criteria will reduce the subjectivity of decision making within the design. As important, most investigators are trained in the between-group designs where design decisions are made in advance. Decisions made in advance seem more immune to bias than those made on the fly during the study. Specifying criteria for shifting phases is designed to combat that potential bias. However, specification of criteria in advance has its risks. A few shifts in performance during a given phase may cause the criteria not to be met. Behavior often oscillates, that is, goes back and forth between particular values. It may be difficult in advance of the baseline data to determine for a given subject what that range of oscillation or fluctuation will be. Waiting for the subject's performance to fall within a prespecified range may cause the investigator to "spend a lifetime" on the same study (Sidman, 1960, p. 260).

Problems may arise when multiple subjects are used. For example, in a multiple-baseline design across subjects (or behaviors, or situations), the data from different baselines may be quite different, and a single criterion for deciding when to change phases may not be easily met. Moreover, waiting for all the methodological stars to align (little variability, no trend, and no last-minute possibilities of a trend just starting to emerge) will raise practical obstacles and delayed interventions that are not feasible in most applied settings. We do not need the stars to align to draw valid inferences.

The purpose of specifying criteria is to have an objective definition of stability before shifting phases. But it is the stability of the data rather than meeting any particular prespecified criterion that is important. Stability is required to predict performance in subsequent phases. The prediction serves as a basis for detecting departures from this prediction from one phase to the next. It is conceivable that a criterion for shifting phases may not be met even though a reasonably clear pattern is evident that could serve as an adequate basis for predicting future performance. Stated more simply, specification of a criterion is a means toward an end, that is, defining stability, and not an end in itself. Data points may fall close to but not exactly within the criterion for shifting phases and progress through the investigation may be delayed. In the general case, and perhaps for applied settings in particular, it may be important to specify two or more criteria or rules for shifting phases within a given design so that if the data meet one of the criteria, the phase can be altered. A more flexible criterion or set of criteria may reduce the likelihood that a few data points could continually delay shifting of the phases. (You will know when you have not done this well if you say something like, "I think only one more year of baseline ought to do it.")

The previous comments are not intended to argue against use of objective criteria for defining stability in the data or for changing phases. Most investigators using single-case designs have not invoked specific criteria for shifting phases or for duration of the phases. It is not clear if the benefits of having objective criteria are compensated for by delaying shifts in phases or meeting the describe, predict, and test functions of data within each phase. As a general strategy, it might be advisable to specify criteria that are flexible and leave open the possibility of abandoning them if the logic of the design is jeopardized by a data pattern that somehow interferes with invoking the criteria.

GENERAL ISSUES AND LIMITATIONS

The methodological issues discussed herein refer to considerations that arise while conducting individual single-case experiments. The methodology of single-case research and its limitations can be examined from a more general perspective. The present discussion addresses major issues and limitations that apply to single-case experimental research.

Range of Intervention Outcome Questions

Single-case designs have been used in applied research primarily to evaluate the effectiveness of a variety of interventions. Typically, the interventions are designed to ameliorate a particular problem or to improve performance in the context of educational, clinical, community, and other applied settings. The focus is on the impact of the intervention on functioning of the individual or group. This type of research focuses on outcomes and is often called *outcome research*.

Several different types of outcome questions can be delineated in applied research. The questions vary in terms of what they ask about a particular intervention (e.g., special education, psychotherapy) and the impact that the intervention has on behavior or other domains of functioning (e.g., academic performance, symptoms of anxiety). The

Table 14.1 Strategies to Develop and Identify Effective Interventions

Intervention Strategy	Question Asked
Intervention Package Strategy	Does the intervention produce or lead to change?
Dismantling Strategy	What components are necessary, sufficient, and facilitative for change?
Parametric Strategy	What changes can be made in the specific treatment to increase its effectiveness?
Constructive Strategy	What components or other interventions can be added to enhance outcome?
Comparative Outcome Strategy	Which intervention is the more or most effective for a given problem and population?
Intervention-Moderator Strategy	Upon what subject, trainer, setting, context, or other characteristics does the effectiveness of the intervention depend?
Intervention-Mediator/Mechanism Strategy	What processes, mediators, or mechanisms explain how intervention effects are produced, i.e., why the change occurred?

Note: Intervention includes any program (treatment, educational, preventive, psychosocial, and medical) that is designed to produce change.

different questions are addressed by various *intervention evaluation strategies*. Major strategies are listed briefly in Table 14.1. As is evident in the table, the strategies raise questions about the outcome of a particular intervention and the manner in which the intervention influences behavior change. Between-group and single-case designs vary in how and in some cases how well they address these questions. The strengths and limitations of single-case designs can be conveyed by elaborating these questions.

Evaluating Intervention Packages. Most single-case research fits into the *intervention package strategy* in which a particular intervention (program, treatment) is compared with no intervention (baseline). The intervention package usually has multiple ingredients or components. For example, behavioral interventions often include instructions, modeling, feedback, and direct reinforcement to alter behavior. For purposes of evaluation, the intervention package is examined as a whole. The basic question is whether the intervention achieves change and does so reliably. The vast majority of examples of designs throughout the book illustrate the intervention package strategy.

In general, single-case research designs are highly suited to evaluating intervention packages and their effects on performance. This is a critical strength. The health care, educational, and service worlds are dominated by interventions with foci such as dieting, academic functioning, parenting, psychotherapy, care of the elderly, and prevention of this or that physical or psychological malady. Also, various agencies (family services, educational), organizations, and professionals have a program that promises to have an effect. For example, there is an endless stream of wilderness programs designed to provide interventions for children and adolescents with various forms of social, emotional, behavioral, and psychiatric problems (see http://www.wildernessprograms.org/Programs.html). What is lacking is rigorous (or even not so rigorous) evaluation to identify if any of these actually help people.

There are many reasons there are no evaluations, but one of them is that we have learned that our options are limited. By our training, most individuals have learned that what is needed is a randomized controlled clinical trial, that is, a between-group study. In a classroom, school, school district, and state, where there are many "programs," evaluation does not seem feasible and is too costly. The options look like a large-scale controlled group study or no evaluation.

Single-case designs are very well suited to the intervention package question and can address this question without objectionable no-treatment control groups often required in between-group research. Multiple groups are not needed. Moreover, the collection of continuous data allows one to see if there is change emerging and alter the intervention as needed if it is not. In a between-group evaluation of a program, one does not know the outcome until it is over and cannot do much about mediocre effects. For programs in real-world settings, we want to have feedback (data) to see if we are on the right track or if a new, different, or modified intervention is needed. For example, consider an intervention (B) designed to help students participate in science fairs available in the school. An intervention might be evaluated in multiple-baseline design across classrooms or grade levels. We may learn quickly that B is not very effective so we move to intervention C and use that across all of the baselines (classrooms) that have yet to receive the intervention. Implementation on a small or circumscribed scale also is an advantage of single-case designs.

Evaluating Intervention Components. Let me group three strategies here because they share strengths and limitations. The dismantling, parametric, and constructive strategies listed in Table 14.1 are similar to each other in that they attempt to analyze aspects of interventions that contribute to change. In its own way, each strategy examines what can be done to make the intervention more effective. Variations of the intervention are presented to the same subject to examine their relative impact.

The *dismantling strategy* attempts to compare the full intervention package with another condition, such as the package minus selected ingredients. An example in a between-group study would be evaluating an intervention package that consisted of a special curriculum for elementary school children, weekly testing of the children on what they have learned, and feedback to teachers for child performance. The dismantling strategy might test the entire package (provided to one group) versus the package minus the feedback to teachers (provided to another group).

The *parametric strategy* attempts to compare variations of the same intervention in which one particular dimension is altered to determine if it influences outcome. An example might be to evaluate an intervention of exercise three times a week on health (e.g., as reflected on heart rate, blood pressure, and mood). The parametric strategy would compare variations (e.g., three times vs. six times per week).

With the *constructive strategy*, a given intervention package is evaluated that usually is already known to be effective. The question is whether adding something new to that intervention such as another intervention makes a difference. For example, colorectal cancer is the third most common cancer and the second most frequent cause of cancer-related deaths in the United States. Two approved drugs for treatment operate somewhat differently in how they attack the cells, so it was reasonable to do a controlled trial comparing one of the drugs (Avastin) by itself and with the addition of the other approved drug (Avastin and Erbitux). The combined treatment made the cancer worse and produced more side effects as well (Mayer, 2009). More is not always better, but sometimes it is, and constructive strategy is the way to find out.

Single-case designs can ask the questions of all three strategies. Comparing different interventions or variations of an intervention were discussed and illustrated in Chapter 9 on multiple-treatment designs. Yet, from a methodological standpoint, a problem is multiple-treatment interference. That is, if two or more variations of treatment (or components) are presented to the same subject, one cannot really make a judgment about which treatment is more or less effective because the order or prior variation of treatment might well influence the impact of a subsequent treatment. For example, in a constructive strategy the investigator wishes to know if feedback, praise, and punishment (three interventions) are better in combination. She begins with a phase of feedback, then in a second phase adds praise, then in the final phase adds punishment. Any effects or lack of effects might be due to this special history or ordering of the interventions (e.g., which intervention was introduced first and second, and their gradual introduction). In a between-group study, separate groups would receive the various combinations and provide a demonstration free from the possibility of multiple-treatment interference. With a single case, there is no unambiguous way to evaluate interventions given in consecutive phases because of the intervention x sequence confound, that is the effects of the intervention may interact with (i.e., the x term) where it was placed in the design.

An apparent solution to the problem would be to administer two or more intervention conditions in a different order to different subjects. A minimum of two subjects would be needed (if two interventions were compared) so that each subject could receive the alternative interventions but in a different order. For example, there might be ABCBC and ACBCB phases provided for two or more subjects. If both (or all) subjects respond to the interventions consistently no matter what order in which they appeared (e.g., C was always much better than B), the effects of the sequence in which the interventions appeared (and multiple-treatment interference) can be ruled out as a significant influence. If presentation of the different conditions in different order yields inconsistent effects, then considerable ambiguity is introduced. If two subjects respond differently as a function of the order in which they received the interventions, the investigator cannot determine whether it was the sequence that each person received or characteristics of that particular person. The possible interaction (differential effects) of intervention and sequence needs to be evaluated among several subjects to ensure that a particular treatment-sequence combination is not unique to (i.e., does not interact with) characteristics of a particular subject. Simply altering the sequence among a few subjects does not necessarily avoid the sequence problem unless there is a way in the final analyses to separate the effects of interventions, sequences, subjects, and their interactions. In this discussion, I have assumed that there are two interventions (B, C) and that the investigator changes their order for two or more subjects. If there are more than two interventions, then it is difficult in single-case research to balance (alternate) the different conditions to include all the possible orders (each following and preceding the other) to draw inferences that are not confounded by order effects.

These methodological considerations should be tempered by considerations that lead researchers to add interventions in single-case research, that is, why they use a constructive strategy. More than one intervention or variation may be needed to achieve the desired changes. If the intervention produces mediocre effects and the participant gets only a little better with the intervention, what does the investigator do next? The answer is to tinker with the intervention a bit, which might consist of adding a new component (constructive strategy), adding more of some facet of the treatment (parametric strategy), or less likely removing some component that seems to be interfering with the effects of the intervention (dismantling). In applied work, researchers give higher priority to having impact than to the risk of misinterpreting the data because of multiple-treatment interference.

Multiple-treatment interference remains a threat to validity in any situation in which more than one intervention is presented to the same subject. Yet, the threat sounds esoteric and of little concern in relation to the practical challenge facing the investigator and setting. To alter the performance of the individual, the priority ought to be to place concerns about multiple-treatment interference in the back seat. Yet, we ought not to ignore the threat to validity. We want an intervention that also can be extended to many individuals, and to do that we need to know whether this intervention works by itself or requires some other component that is provided with or before the intervention.

In applied settings the critical challenge is to develop interventions that have immediate impact. Worrying about multiple-treatment interference in this context is a much lower priority. Thus, single-case designs are quite useful in developing effective interventions because these component-based strategies are needed to maximize impact. Yes, they leave open the possibility that the effects would not be evident if multiple-treatment interference were controlled (e.g., as in a between-group design). I hasten to add that multiple-treatment interference reflects the possibility that the order of the interventions or what preceded the intervention may make a difference. The fact that it could make a difference does not mean that it invariably does.

Comparing Different Interventions. The problem of evaluating variations of interventions as part of the dismantling, parametric, and constructive strategies extends to the *comparative strategy* as well. The comparative strategy examines the relative effectiveness of two or more different interventions. In most single-case experimental designs, comparisons of different interventions are obfuscated by the multiple-treatment interference effects noted earlier. I mention the comparative strategy separately, although the strategy and its concerns could be absorbed in the previous section. I do so because researchers often are keenly interested in the question, "Which intervention is better or best?" I also do so because single-case research has designs specifically devoted to comparing different treatments.

The multi-element and alternating-treatments designs attempt to provide an alternative in which two or more interventions or intervention variations can be compared in the same phase but under different or constantly changing stimulus conditions. These designs can resolve the sequence effects associated with presenting different conditions in consecutive phases. However, it is possible that the results are influenced by multiple-treatment interference, that is, the effects of introducing more than one treatment, as discussed in the chapter on these designs. Interventions, when juxtaposed to other interventions, may have different effects from those that would be obtained if they were administered to entirely different subjects.

Overall, evaluating different interventions introduces ambiguity for single-case research. The possible influence of administering one intervention on all subsequent interventions exists for ABAB, multiple-baseline, and changing-criterion designs. Similarly, the possibility that juxtaposing two or more interventions influences the effects that either treatment exerts is a potential problem for multiple-treatment designs. This ambiguity has not deterred researchers from raising questions that fit into the dismantling, parametric, constructive, or comparative strategies. Single-case designs are often used in applied settings where there is a practical issue of critical concern and there are views about what is the better or best strategy among those available. So, for example, to foster improved reading, better completion of homework, and higher achievement among students in a special education class, two viable intervention options may be worth testing. One could do a between-group randomized controlled trial—actually, that is a problem, as I have noted before. One cannot usually do one of these because of feasibility and cost. Alternatively, one could test the simpler, less costly intervention first in a single-case design and then add the more complex, possibly more costly intervention if the first one does not achieve the goals.

Multiple-treatment interference means that the results may only apply to other individuals who receive the two (or more) treatments juxtaposed in the way the design presented them (e.g., alternating treatments). This is a lower priority concern than the applied task (which treatment will stop inmates from stabbing each other, how do I get special education students to read, how can we get my relatives to stop throwing food during holiday meals). Give me the more or most effective intervention any day; once I have that, I will worry about testing for multiple-treatment interference.

Studying Variables that Influence the Impact of the Intervention. The *intervention-moderator strategy* asks questions about characteristics of the clients or other factors that influence the effectiveness of the intervention. A *moderator* is a variable that influences the relation of two (or more) variables of interest. That is, the relation between the intervention and performance or outcome varies as a function of some other characteristic. If an intervention is more effective for boys than for girls, child sex is called a moderator—it somehow relates to the effects of treatment. Moderators often are characteristics of people (e.g., age, sex, cultural background), but they can refer to any characteristic of the setting or context (e.g., classroom, class size) or even features of the intervention (e.g., duration of the program, who administers it such as parents vs. therapists) that have an influence on outcome.

Moderators are quite important, because there is a fairly safe statement to make about treatment (e.g., medical, psychological), education, rehabilitation, and other areas where interventions are designed to help. The statement, "An intervention, however effective, is not likely to work with everyone," is important to bear in mind. As familiar examples, aspirin (for headache), chemotherapy (for a given cancer), and insulin monitoring and injections (for diabetes) do not work for everyone. Granted, some interventions work for a higher proportion of people than others. But the scientific task is not to just leave it at the fact that the treatment did not work for everyone. The task is to find out for whom it did not work and why. The study of moderators is the beginning.

In everyday life, normal parenting raises the issue of moderators. If a parent or family has two or more children, at some point they go through the moderator amazement phase. We raised our children identically—same house, opportunities, foibles of our child rearing, and so on—so why are the children so different? For methodologically informed parents, the question actually goes like this: My child-rearing intervention was roughly the same for these children, but the outcomes (in kindness to me at holidays) are very different, so what might be the moderating variable(s)?[1]

As a research example, menopausal women have routinely been given estrogen, which is depleted during menopause. Depletion of the hormone contributes to many of the symptoms that emerge (e.g., hot flashes, flushes, night sweats and/or cold flashes, clammy feeling, irregular heartbeat, irritability, mood swings, sudden tears, difficulty sleeping, anxiety, feelings of dread, difficulty concentrating). Warnings emerged from the research when it was initially presented, noting that women who received estrogen replacement therapy were at higher risk for heart attacks. Further analyses of the data indicated that the relation between treatment and outcome was moderated by age. For women ages 50 to 59, risk of heart attack was reduced when compared to women ages 70 to 79, where the risk increased (Manson et al., 2007). Understanding the moderator and how it works can improve treatment and can direct individuals who are likely not to profit from the treatment or to experience untoward other effects to some other intervention.

More generally, one can see moderators emerge in intervention research. A common situation from research—one gives the same treatment or educational regimen to 50 individuals and, let us say, 30 respond really well, 10 respond pretty well, and 10 do not seem to change at all. A researcher does not just shrug her shoulders and say, "Okay, most of the news is good." Rather, the researcher invariably wants to understand why there were different responses and for whom treatment is likely to be effective. Ultimately, understanding can improve treatments for those who did not change at all or very much.

---

[1] Although there are obvious similarities in how parents raise their two or more children, there are critical differences as well. Siblings (e.g., ages 3 and 6) in the same home are under the influence of somewhat different factors including the biological health of the parents when they were conceived and born, child-rearing practices, often slight differences in socioeconomic status of the family, and the impact of the presence of a sibling in the home when the second (but not the first) child was born, among other factors. If for a moment you are skeptical that such sibling differences exist, permit me to mention my flash-photo theory. In most homes, photos of a first child are much more extensive than photos of a second child. Milestones for the first child (e.g., breathing, crawling, walking) are treated like the big bang that may have originated the universe. Indeed, for a couple without a child, the first child is a big bang. The second child is a slightly smaller bang in many ways in many homes, and this differential response is evident in the photo record of early childhood. That differential photo record might reflect larger issues related to child–parent contact in the environment that are not necessarily good or bad (e.g., parents are more relaxed, busier with two children) but make the environments of siblings different. Even if the home life and parenting were identical, the different biological make-up of the siblings might make them differentially sensitive to the same influences (e.g., hugging, shouting, instruction, lessons, peers, etc.). In short, siblings do not really grow up in the same environment because the physical and social environments actually are a bit different and the siblings vary in how any given influence has impact on them (e.g., Bouchard, Lykken, McGue, Segal, & Tellegen, 1990; Dunn & Plomin, 1990; Plomin, McClearn, McGuffin, & DeFries, 2000).

Moderators are of great interest in intervention research. Among the most salient areas is the role of ethnicity and culture. For example, in the context of evidence-based psychotherapies, most of the research has been based on European Caucasian samples. Even so, many of the findings, when evaluated empirically, show similar effects with (generalize to) other ethnic and cultural groups (e.g., African American, Latin American) (e.g., Miranda et al., 2005). However, ethnicity and culture make a difference, that is, moderate outcome effects. For example, psychotherapy for adults sometimes is more effective when treatment is provided in the native languages of the clients and is specifically designed for minority groups (Griner & Smith, 2006). The important role of ethnicity and culture in delivering and providing treatment services is beyond the role of this chapter (see Kazdin, 2008a). Yet, the issue conveys that moderators are not minor afterthoughts. There are different paths toward making treatment more effective. One is developing more potent interventions. Another is to do better triage, that is, direct people to those treatments from which they are likely to profit. This latter strategy requires understanding moderators.

The intervention-moderator strategy addresses whether the intervention is more or less effective as a function of some other variable, usually client characteristics. The usual way that between-group research approaches this question is through large-scale studies with data analyses (e.g., factorial designs, multi-way analyses of variance, and multiple regression analyses) that examine whether the effectiveness of treatment interacts with (is moderated by) the types of clients, where clients are grouped according to such variables as age, ethnicity, diagnosis, socioeconomic status, severity of behavior, or other dimensions that appear to be relevant to treatment.

Single-case research usually does not address questions of the characteristics of the client that may interact with treatment effects. If a few subjects are studied and respond differently, the investigator has no systematic way of determining whether treatment was more or less effective as a function of the treatment or the particular characteristics of the subjects. For example, in one study, four adolescents (ages 13 and 14) with developmental and intellectual disabilities were exposed to interventions to develop their word repertoire (e.g., defining words) (Riesen, McDonnell, Johnson, Polychronis, & Jameson, 2003). The individuals varied in psychiatric and physical disabilities; all had IQs at or below 70, one criterion included in defining intellectual disability (or mental retardation). They were functioning in a classroom where two interventions were evaluated. Briefly, the interventions consisted of different ways of presenting and fading instructions to help them learn and recite the definitions. Each adolescent was exposed to the two treatments in an alternating-treatments design. One intervention was better for two of the cases; the other intervention was better for the other two cases. The small sample does not permit analyses of these cases that might shed light on why they responded differently or the characteristics that correlate with responding to one treatment rather than another.

Many other examples evaluated in single-case designs can be cited where one intervention was more effective with some cases and the other intervention was more effective for others; where individuals responded differently or not at all to a given intervention; and where a few or most participants showed the predicted pattern of performance but one or some small number did not (e.g., Ardoin et al., 2007; Park et al., 2005). The results are not surprising and support the broad conclusion we have learned from psychology, namely, that there are individual differences. The issue for single-case designs is that when there are individual differences, we have no easy way of testing or evaluating what factor may have moderated the outcome. Were some individuals (e.g., those who responded) older, smarter, taller, less seriously impaired, etc.? Investigators are wont to speculate, but a data-based interpretation is not possible with few subjects. Between-group research is able to explore possible moderators (and their combinations) because of the sample sizes or test a priori hypotheses about who will respond to the different treatments.

In general, testing and evaluating moderators is a weakness of single-case research. This has not hampered the research. Interventions selected for study often have been very potent, and have had generality across many subjects (and species). Even so, moderation is a critical question inherent in all interventions, medical, psychological, educational, parental, and so on, because not everyone responds to even our best treatments. Understanding who does not respond can be a precursor to understanding why. Understanding why is often a precursor to being able to do something about it.

Studying Mediators and Mechanisms: Largely Unexplored. The *intervention-mediator/mechanism strategy*, the last one listed in Table 14.1, addresses the question pertaining to the reasons why changes come about, the mechanism of change, and the specific process through which the intervention works. Mediators, mechanisms, moderators, and causes are difficult to keep straight and are occasionally defined inconsistently in professional writings. As a point of reference, Table 14.2 summarizes key concepts that are interrelated to facilitate the discussion. I group "mediator" and "mechanism" together here in part because the distinction is not critical to the point I wish to make in this discussion, that is, how single-case and between-group research can address processes that explain how change comes about.

Single-case and between-group experimental designs can show a causal relation between an intervention and outcome. A causal relation does not establish how or why the effect occurred, that is, specific reason or underlying process. Cause can be readily distinguished from mechanism of action. Consider cigarette smoking and

---

Table 14.2 Key Terms and Concepts

Cause: A variable or intervention that leads to and is responsible for the outcome or change.

Mediator: An intervening variable that may account (statistically) for the relation between the independent and dependent variable. Something that mediates change may not necessarily explain the processes of how change came about. Also, the mediator could be a proxy for one or more other variables or be a general construct that is not necessarily intended to explain the mechanisms of change. A mediator may be a guide that points to possible mechanisms but is not necessarily a mechanism.

Mechanism: The basis for the effect, that is, the processes or events that are responsible for the change; the reasons why change occurred or how change came about.

Moderator: A characteristic that influences the direction or magnitude of the relation between an independent and dependent variable. For example, if the relation between variable x and y is different for males and females, sex is a moderator of the relation. Moderators are related to mediators and mechanisms because they suggest that different processes might be involved (e.g., for males or females).

Several sources can be consulted for further discussion of these concepts (e.g., Campbell & Stanley, 1963; Kazdin, 2007; Kraemer, Stice, Kazdin, Offord, & Kupfer, 2001; Kraemer, Wilson, Fairburn, & Agras, 2002).

lung cancer to help convey the distinction of cause and mechanism. Spanning decades, cross-sectional and longitudinal studies, research with humans, and experiments with non-human animals have established a causal role between cigarette smoking and lung cancer. (The causal role means that smoking can cause cancer; it does not mean that smoking is the only cause or that smoking invariably leads to cancer.) Establishing a causal relation does not automatically explain the mechanisms, that is, the process(es) through which lung cancer comes about. What is it specifically about cigarette smoking that leads to cancer, and what are the steps along the way? The mechanism has been uncovered by describing what happens in a sequence from smoking to mutation of cells into cancer (Denissenko, Pao, Tang, & Pfeifer, 1996). A chemical (benzo[a]pyrene) found in cigarette smoke induces genetic mutation at specific regions of the gene's DNA that is identical to the damage evident in lung cancer cells. This finding is considered to convey precisely how cigarette smoking leads to cancer at the molecular level.

A mechanism of action need not be biological. For example, for major depression among adults, cognitive therapy is the most well-established and researched form of psychotherapy (Hollon & Beck, 2004). Randomized controlled trials have shown repeatedly that the treatment is effective (i.e., causes change), but why is it effective and how does it work, that is, what mediates the effects, and what is the mechanism of change? Changes in specific cognitive processes during treatment have been proposed to account for the change. Group studies have challenged this interpretation because we know now that the benefits of treatment occur (i.e., treatment works) even without changes in the supposed cognitive processes (see Kazdin, 2007). In short, that the treatment works is clear; how the treatment works is not so clear.

Single-case research in applied settings is concerned primarily with identifying causes of change, especially intervention packages that make a difference. In this research, there has been less interest in understanding the mechanisms in the sense of processes that explain how the change comes about. However, many interventions used in single-case designs are based on learning (e.g., reinforcement, practice, acquisition, and extinction), and basic human and non-human animal research has examined molecular and neurological changes that these interventions cause (e.g., Brembs, Lorenzetti, Reyes, Baxter, & Byrne, 2002; Pagnoni, Zink, Montague, & Berns, 2002). Much of this work is based on the intensive study of individuals (e.g., in neuroimaging studies of a few individuals). It is not as if single-case designs with one or a few individuals cannot evaluate mechanisms. Indeed, as I noted previously (Chapter 10), there are ways in which the study of mechanisms may actually require the study of the single case and adoption of essential features (e.g., continuous assessment) of the methodology. However, the study of mechanisms has not been the priority of single-case research in applied settings.

The study of mediators has received increased attention in intervention research. Mediators are not the same as mechanisms but can be an important starting point to identify key constructs that might begin to explain how the changes come about. Mechanisms would be the more concrete and specific level of analysis that shows precisely how those constructs operate (Table 14.2). The study of mediators is accomplished by hypothesizing what that mediator is, assessing the mediator while the intervention is in place, assessing outcome or changes in the domain of interest (e.g., symptoms, problem behaviors), and establishing a connection between change in the mediator and change in the outcome. Although this can be achieved with the single-case and multiple-single cases, between-group has given this focus much more attention. This is due in part to the increased attention to the topic of mediation in the context of group research and advances in statistical techniques designed to evaluate and test for mediation (e.g., Baron & Kenny, 1986; Kenny, Kashy, & Bolger, 1998; Kraemer, Kiernan, Essex, & Kupfer, 2008; MacKinnon, 2008).

General Comments. A discussion of single-case research in relation to the range of intervention questions that are usually of interest is helpful at a broader level than merely noting strengths and weaknesses or threats to validity here and there. Any research design is merely a tool for the investigator to answer a question or to test or generate a hypothesis. Sometimes one reads the literature in an area and is impressed by how one design is slavishly adhered to in an almost rote way without considering options, some of which would be easier, others of which would be better in relation to the purpose the investigators have set for themselves. The intervention strategies help sensitize us as investigators to what we are trying to accomplish and how designs, single-case, between-group, and variations within them are or are not suited optimally to their purpose.

I stated before that in the intervention world (education, rehabilitation, therapy, counseling, health care, prevention) there is an endless array of programs designed to help people. No matter what the focus, intervention, or profession behind them, three key characteristics are surprisingly common:

1. The interventions are well intended.
2. They are unevaluated (no systematic assessment).
3. They have absolutely no evidence (research) indicating that they actually help.

Interventions in most contexts (local schools, state prisons, day-hospital treatment programs for individuals with mental illness) cannot easily be evaluated in a between-group study because of limited resources, feasibility, and time constraints. Single-case designs have their own constraints but could be much more feasibly used to evaluate programs in applied settings. The intervention package strategy alone would be a strong justification for insuring that single-case research were part of the graduate training curriculum for anyone trying to change behavior of anyone else (e.g., teachers, therapists, counselors, social workers, military generals, physicians).

Generality of the Findings

Single-Case Research. A major objection levied against single-case research is that the results may not be generalizable to persons other than those included in the study. After all, if we are studying just a few cases (e.g., one subject in an ABAB design or three subjects in a multiple-baseline design across subjects), how do we know the results apply to anyone else in the world? This objection raises several important issues. To begin with, single-case research grew out of an experimental philosophy that attempts to discover laws of individual performance (Kazdin, 1978). There is a methodological heritage of examining variables that affect performance of individuals rather than groups of persons. So the interest was in understanding individuals, and single-case research was based on the assumptions that lawful relations would not be idiosyncratic. Hence, the ultimate goal, even of single-case research, is to discover generalizable relations. There is nothing special here about the principle involved. Astronomy is quite concerned about studying individual planets, galaxies, and comets; Egyptologists are eager to find and elaborate individual tombs and pyramids; geneticists are keen to elaborate individual families as a way to reveal disease patterns, and so on for most of the sciences. Study of the individual often reveals generalizable and unique information, and understanding requires an elaboration of both.

I mentioned earlier in the book the distinction between single-case designs (as a methodology) and behavior analysis (as an experimental and applied substantive area where learning-based interventions are usually used to alter behavior). They overlap because those engaged in behavior analysis rely on single-case designs. Yet the distinction is important here. The development of behavior analysis in laboratory or applied contexts focused on identifying interventions that led to marked changes within the individual and variables that generalized across many individuals. Indeed, early experimental work (on schedules of reinforcement) demonstrated how changes in behavior generalized (were very similar) across species (e.g., humans, pigeons, rats, and monkeys) (Kazdin, 1978). Thus, generality was not an issue.

In applied work, the interventions (e.g., variations of reinforcement) have had very robust effects. Investigators who use single-case designs have emphasized the need to seek interventions that produce dramatic changes in performance. Interventions that produce dramatic effects are likely to be more generalizable across individuals than are effects that meet the relatively weaker criterion of statistical significance. Indeed, in any particular between-group investigation, the possibility remains that a statistically significant difference was obtained on the basis of chance. The results may not generalize to other attempts to replicate the study, not to mention to different sorts of subjects.

Single-case designs (as a methodology) do not inherently produce more or less generalizable effects. Findings obtained in single-case demonstrations appear to be highly generalizable because of the types of interventions that are commonly investigated. Over the years of reporting single-case designs, we have not learned and there is no evidence to my knowledge to support the view that findings from single-case research are more or less generalizable than findings from other research. This does not allay the natural reaction to wonder if a change in one subject represents a change in 100 subjects.

The problem of single-case research is not that the results lack generality among subjects. Rather, the problem is that there are difficulties largely inherent in the methodology for assessing the dimensions that may dictate generality of the results. In the prior discussion of the intervention-moderator strategy, I noted that single-case designs cannot easily address intervention × subject interactions, that is, whether treatments are differentially effective as a function of certain subject characteristics. This differential effectiveness comment pertains to generality because the moderator conveys for whom the intervention was or was not effective, that is, the characteristics of persons across which the effects generalize.

Between-Group Research. The generality of findings from single-case research is often discussed in relation to between-group research. Between-group research uses larger numbers of subjects than single-case research. Surely that must produce more generalizable findings. Actually, between-group research does not necessarily yield generalizable findings or more generalizable findings than single-case research for at least four reasons.

First, we as researchers are often comforted by the fact that group research includes many individuals. Unfortunately, the way the results are analyzed (usually a comparison of means among groups), we have no idea about how many individuals in the group showed a change or a change of any importance (applied significance). Results are evaluated on the basis of average *group* performance. For example, if a group of 20 patients who received treatment show greater change than 20 patients who did not receive treatment, little information is available about the generality of the results. We do not know by this group analysis alone how many persons in the treatment group were affected or affected in an important way (e.g., made a large change). Also, it is quite possible that a very small change among many individuals could lead to a significant effect, favoring treatment even though no one really changed in any palpable way. In short, we do not know how many changed or changed in a way that makes a difference, and the extent to which the mean for the group represents individual members of the group. Ambiguity about the generality of findings from between-group research is not inherent in this research approach. However, investigators rarely look at the individual subject data as well as the group data to make inferences about the generality of effects among subjects within a given treatment condition. Certainly, if the individual data were examined in between-group research, a great deal more might be said about the generality of the findings than what can be said in most instances now.

Second and related, as researchers we are encouraged (and for some funding agencies required) to include individuals of different ethnicities and cultures in our groups. This has unwittingly fostered the view that any finding might be more generalizable if a diverse set of participants is included. This is not an informed view. Merely including more diverse subjects alone does not establish, test, or demonstrate generality. Typically, there are insufficient numbers of various groups in the study to test generality, that is, whether diversity, ethnicity, or identity act as moderators of the intervention. So merely including a diverse sample in a group study does not by that fact alone mean the results will be more generalizable across subject characteristics. The generality could be tested within a study: Does each group respond similarly? If they do, we have shed light on the generality of findings among the different groups. But the tests are rarely requested (by the funding agencies) or reported by investigators. In short, merely including a more diverse sample does not automatically make the results more generalizable.

Third, subjects in between-group research are rarely sampled in such a way that they are random across a large population. Between-group research uses random *assignment* of subjects to groups but not random *selection* of the sample from the population (e.g., all college students, people from different parts of the country). Random assignment is not especially pertinent to generality of effects, although random selection is. There are exceptions in studies where random samples are drawn from a given country. For example, epidemiological studies sample randomly from individuals throughout communities (e.g., in studying disease, eating patterns, psychiatric diagnoses) with the goal in mind to represent the population. Sometimes studies sample many geographical locations, even though these are not chosen randomly. Multi-site intervention studies purposely carry out the study in several locations (e.g., a few regions of the country). Rarely do psychological and educational studies use random selection of cases or selection from diverse locations. Thus, the generality of group research too is in question.

Finally, between-group research often uses careful inclusion and exclusion criteria for selection of subjects. For example, if one wishes to test an intervention for clinical depression, not everyone who is depressed is allowed to participate. Depression occurs in childhood, adolescence, and adulthood. The group is likely to be restricted in age (e.g., let us say we just select adults 20 to 45 years of age). Many people who are depressed have other psychiatric disorders, and that makes depressed adults very different from each other (e.g., let us say we select those who only have major depression without other psychiatric disorders). We want subjects who can come to treatment for the 10 sessions we are planning (e.g., so we only take those who have transportation and who are not so depressed that they cannot leave their homes or need to be hospitalized). Some depressed patients are suicidal; it is likely we want to exclude those too and refer them to immediate care. This example could continue to show that between-group studies often screen who participates. Indeed it is very wise to do so because the broader the range of sample characteristics, the greater the variability in the study. Variability in the sample can make it much more difficult to demonstrate an effect of the intervention (Kazdin, 2003). In general, between-group research in schools, clinics, and other settings and for the purposes of education, treatment, and prevention often selects samples with extreme care and excludes many individuals purposely. This practice, while methodologically prudent for providing a strong test of intervention effects, is not the path of producing generalizable findings. This is not a criticism of between-group research but rather of the unexamined view that group studies produce findings that are generalizable or more generalizable than findings from another research tradition (e.g., single-case or qualitative research).

The redemption from this situation is that the generality of the findings in between-group research is readily albeit infrequently evaluated by the intervention-moderator strategy, as outlined previously. The performance of subgroups of persons within the study is not examined to assess whether intervention(s) are differentially effective as a function of some subject variable. Within single-case demonstrations with one or a few subjects, by definition, there is no immediate possibility to assess characteristics (moderators) that help explain the generality of effects, that is, for whom the effect did and did not occur. Hence, between-group research certainly can shed more light on the generality of the results than can single-case research. A factorial design (or other analysis such as multiple regression) examining intervention × subject interactions can provide information about the suitability of treatment for various subject populations. Also, with a large number of subjects in an intervention group, the investigator using a between-group study can comment on the percentage of subjects who show the pattern of change represented by the group mean. However, because subjects in any study are not selected randomly from a population, the percentage cannot be used as an estimate of the likely percentage of people to whom the findings would apply in the population.

Replication

Replication refers to repetition of the effect of an intervention and emerges as a critical concept in two ways. The first is related to the logic of single-case designs and the describe, predict, and test functions of collecting data in separate phases (e.g., ABAB), across separate baselines (e.g., variation of multiple-baseline designs), and so on with other designs. The impact of the intervention is repeatedly tested within a given demonstration, which is another way of saying the effect is replicated (Horner et al., 2005). In this sense replication is central to the designs and clarity of the demonstration.

The second aspect of replication pertains to evaluating generality of the intervention effect across subjects or conditions and serves as the basis of the present discussion. In relation to generality of a finding, replication is a critical ingredient for all research. Replication can examine the extent to which results obtained in one study extend (can be generalized) across a variety of settings, behaviors, measures, investigators, and other variables that conceivably could influence outcome. Direct or exact replication and systematic or approximate replication provide a useful way to convey critical points (Sidman, 1960). *Direct replication* refers to an attempt to repeat an experiment exactly as it was conducted originally. Ideally, the conditions and procedures (e.g., setting, measures, intervention, design) across the replication and original experiment are identical. *Systematic replication* refers to repetition of the experiment by systematically allowing features to vary. The conditions and procedures of the replication are deliberately designed only to approximate those of the original experiment.

It is useful to consider direct and systematic replication as on opposite ends of a continuum. A replication that is at the direct end of the spectrum would follow the original procedures as closely as possible. This is the easiest to do for the researcher who conducted the original investigation, since he or she has complete access to all of the procedures, the population from which the original sample was drawn, and nuances of the laboratory procedures (e.g., tasks for experimenters and subjects, all instructions, and data collection and reliability procedures) that optimize similarity with the original study. An exact replication is not possible, even by the original investigator, since repetition of the experiment involves new subjects tested at a different point in time and by different experimenters, all of which conceivably could lead to different results. Thus, all replications necessarily allow some factors to vary; the issue is the extent to which the replication study departs from the original investigation.

Direct and systematic replications add to knowledge in different ways. Replications that closely approximate the conditions of the original experiment increase one's confidence that the original finding is reliable and not likely to have resulted from chance, particular artifact, or be unique to a particular moment in time. Replications that deviate from the original conditions suggest that the findings hold across a wider range of conditions. Essentially, the greater the divergence of the replication from the conditions of the original experiment, the greater the generality of the finding.

If the results of direct and systematic replication research show that the intervention affects behaviors or other domains in new subjects across different conditions, the generality of the results has been demonstrated. The extent of the generality of the findings, of course, is a function of the characteristics of the subjects (e.g., age, ethnicity), applied or clinical focus, settings, and other conditions included in the replication studies. In any particular systematic replication study, it is useful to vary only one or a few of the dimensions along which the study could depart from the original experiment. If the results of a replication attempt differ from the original experiment, it is desirable to have a limited number of differences between the experiments so the possible reason(s) for the discrepancy of the results might be more easily identified. If there are multiple differences between the original experiment and replication experiments, discrepancies in results might be due to a host of factors not easily discerned without extensive further experimentation.

A limitation of single-case research occurs in replication attempts in which the results are inconsistent across subjects. For example, the effects of the intervention may be evaluated across several subjects in direct replication attempts. The results may be inconsistent or mixed, that is, some subjects may have shown clear changes and others may not. In fact, it is likely that replication attempts, whether direct or systematic replications, will yield inconsistent results because one would not expect all persons to respond in the same way. We have learned from intervention studies that not all persons respond to treatment even when these treatments are well known, well studied, and effective (e.g., aspirin for headache, chemotherapy for cancer, exposure therapy for anxiety, reading of methodology books for depression). Invariably there are always some individuals who do not respond and a finding does not usually generalize to everyone, whether in single-case or between-group research.

The problem with inconsistent effects is understanding *for whom* and *why* the results did not generalize across subjects. Herein rests the potential limitation of single-case research. When replication attempts reveal that some subjects did not respond, the investigator has to speculate on the reasons for lack of generality. There is no systematic or formal way within the investigation or even in a series of single-case investigations to identify the basis for the lack of generality. This is the problem already elaborated and illustrated in the previous discussion of evaluating moderators of intervention effects. Between-group designs, with their larger number of subjects, permit analyses to evaluate characteristics that may delineate who responds well or poorly. In such designs, one can form subgroups or place individuals on a dimension with regard to some characteristic (e.g., how severe, how smart, how socially skilled) and evaluate the impact of that variable. In this way, between-group studies can identify the characteristics of individuals to whom the intervention effects do and do not apply. The effects of treatment apparently do not generalize to everyone—once the variables are identified, one can begin to test more specific hypotheses about why.

Single-case designs could evaluate generality and replication more systematically. In principle, investigators, educators, and clinicians who collect data on cases seen at different settings could catalogue or code subject (or other) variables (e.g., age, severity of dysfunction) as well as behavior changes. The information, when accumulated across several cases and investigators, would form a data bank that could be analyzed for moderating variables. In the context of psychotherapy, there are rare examples where systematic data have been collected on individual clients seen in treatment (e.g., Clement, 2008). The accumulated data were used to describe treatment effects for subgroups as well as for individuals and to identify moderators of treatment outcome. This same concept on a larger scale and across many investigators might be able to address generality of effects.

General Comments

There are many questions to which single-case designs are well suited. The intervention package question perhaps is the one of most universal concern and that alone would give the designs a special place in research methodology and in training of researchers. The vast majority of programs for groups in everyday life (e.g., in education, medicine, law enforcement) cannot be subjected to an RCT for a variety of reasons (e.g., cost, needed sample sizes, availability of control conditions). Similarly, interventions designed for individuals (e.g., psychotherapy, special education, remedial or rehabilitation programs targeted to one person at a time) cannot be evaluated in group designs. The choice has been an RCT or no systematic evaluation (e.g., anecdotal case study). This is unfortunate because of the loss of time and money (in tinkering with programs that may not do very much) and even more so because of subjecting us to potentially wasteful and ineffective interventions. We (our children, our relatives) are all subjects in a set of unevaluated well-intentioned, anecdotal case studies. Single-case methods, either experiments or quasi-experiments, provide an alternative to anecdotal claims that the program seems to be working or was a good idea at the time! In relation to evaluation of intervention packages, single-case methods are very strong and often are more viable as options than are between-group studies.

Generality of the findings from single-case research often emerges as a concern—understandably so if only one or two cases are included in a study. Generality is a problem that is not overcome in group research, despite our comfort with the fact that with more people involved any effect must be more generalizable. Rarely are group studies evaluated in ways that allow us to know anything about how any individual responded and how many individuals (what proportion) responded and to what extent. The evaluation of moderators, not easily accomplished by single-case research, is one way to examine generality of findings, that is, for whom the effect does or does not apply or apply in varying degrees. Another way to evaluate generality of a finding, important in all research, is whether the results can be repeated in subsequent tests.

Replication is the key in science to address reliability of findings but also to evaluate generality across conditions (subjects, investigators). We want to identify those interventions that are robust across many different conditions. When interventions are not robust across conditions we want to know the restrictions and the moderating variables. Many studies and many different methods of study are needed. After decades of research and decades of concerns, in fact there is no clear evidence that findings from single-case and between-group experiments and quasi-experiments are any more or less generalizable across individuals and new conditions.

DIRECTIONS AND OPPORTUNITIES ON THE HORIZON

It is likely that the use of single-case designs will continue to expand to new settings, populations, and specialty areas or disciplines. The need for evaluation in many different settings and renewed social interest and pressure to identify "what works" alone would increase the demand for such designs. At the same time, single-case designs are not usually included in training of researchers. Aspects of training in the quantitative tradition may even interfere with drawing on single-case methods. For example, as I have mentioned previously the RCT is referred to as the "gold standard" for intervention research. After a while that view seems to have evolved to a more tacit and extreme version, namely, that it is the only standard and that anything else is "fool's gold." There are hazards in relying on, yet worshipping, any single method or approach to research design, a topic for the next chapter. Even so, is there a better way to integrate single-case methodology into the mainstream? Two opportunities are highlighted here.

Randomization: Motherhood and Apple Pie of Methodology

There is no question that among methodologists randomization arguably is the most valued concept. Indeed, the concept and use of randomization pervade our lives well beyond our research. (I myself use randomization for such things as determining whom to invite to a party at my home, selecting people from the phone book to whom I send season's greetings cards each December, and deciding the order of my meals, breakfast, lunch, and dinner on a given day.) Integration of single-case research into mainstream thinking and training might be enhanced by drawing on randomization a bit more.

Randomization is not routinely part of single-case designs or in fact used very much at all. The exception I noted was in one context, namely, how to order the way in which treatments are presented to subjects in multiple-treatment designs. Even that use is somewhat rare and represents only one way of presenting multiple treatments to the same subjects. That said, randomization may have a larger place in single-case research, improve features of the designs, and improve how the designs are viewed and accepted by investigators trained in the between-group (quantitative) research tradition.

Single-case designs compare different conditions, usually baseline and some intervention (A, B phases). Randomization could be integrated in such designs in many ways. In fact, randomization has been advocated for single-case research for over four decades (e.g., Edgington, 1969; Edgington & Onghena, 2007; Kratochwill & Levin, in press; Onghena, 1994). In the most recent reference, Kratochwill and Levin (in press) note many different ways in which randomization can be used. In between-group research, randomization usually means how subjects are assigned to conditions. In single-case research, randomization might be used to influence other facets of the study such as deciding the order of delivering the intervention or condition. For example, for each day (or week) which condition (e.g., A, B, or A,B,C) is to be administered could be determined randomly. Also, the point in time that an intervention is implemented or begins after a period of several days of baselines can be randomly determined. In a multiple-baseline design, both the when and to whom (which baseline is selected if there are multiple baselines across individuals) can also be randomly decided.

Randomization does not require that the condition presented to the subjects change every day (e.g., ABBAAABBABBAA). Blocks of days could be assigned randomly. For example, consider a 3-day block, which would mean 3 days in a row of a particular condition. Block 1 might be baseline; Block 2 could be the intervention with each block consisting of 3 days of that condition. The blocks could be assigned randomly multiple times, as determined from a random numbers table. The result might look like this: Blocks 112122, i.e., 6 blocks each with 3 days. A more familiar way to represent this would be an AABABB design. Each block includes 3 days (but blocks could be any number of days) of the condition so some of the practical issues and obstacles of changing conditions daily are circumvented. Also, randomization could be restricted so that each block appeared equally often.

Why consider randomization as a feature of single-case designs? First, randomization strengthens the conclusions. The goal of research design is to reduce or eliminate the plausibility that influences other than the intervention could account for the change. Those influences are threats to validity; they can be made implausible in single-case research even without using randomization. However, randomization strengthens the case.

Second and related, randomization might well augment the credibility and adoption of single-case designs. I mentioned before that in some classic writings on methodology, randomization is a defining feature of a true experiment (e.g., Campbell & Stanley, 1963; Cook & Campbell, 1979). Randomization helps make implausible threats to validity. The view of this book is that single-case designs are true experiments. For example, in experimental and applied single-case research, one can see variations of an ABAB design such as ABABABAB, i.e., many phases in which the criteria of the methodology (describe, predict, test) are obviously met. If behavior can be turned on and off, so to speak, demonstrating a causal relation and ruling out threats to validity reflect extraordinary clarity. Indeed, such clarity, in my mind, arguably exceeds the clarity of an RCT that shows some statistically significant differences between groups. Even so, it is the case that adding randomization to single-case research would not only be genuinely helpful in addressing threats to validity but might be the spoon full of sugar that makes single-case medicine go down.

Finally, randomization of how conditions are assigned or when interventions are introduced increases the range of statistical tests that can be applied to single-case research. Several statistical tests for single-case designs are not straightforward and research has identified many ambiguities surrounding their use and yield (please see the appendix). Randomization opens a range of options for statistical evaluation, including a number of tests that are more familiar and better studied than those still being developed in single-case research (e.g., Edgington & Onghena, 2007; Onghena, 1994; Todman & Dugard, 2001).

I would not expect randomization to be adopted extensively in single-case research. The ability to shift interventions within subjects is not so easy to do in applied settings (schools, hospitals). Moreover, shifting randomly or quickly could influence the impact of the intervention (e.g., diluting intervention effects if there is any obstacle in subjects being able to discriminate what condition is in effect). Also, flexibility within the design has been a core part of single-case research for making decisions about when to shift phases. All that said, randomization could be used more in single-case research, and there would be the advantages to that (see Kratochwill & Levin, in press). The main advantage might be more widespread acceptance of the designs and that in turn might lead to better and more frequent evaluation in many settings in which programs are used without any empirical basis as to their impact.

Integration of Research Findings

Research proliferates in so many areas and it is difficult to keep up and integrate many studies on a given topic. Decades ago, one could read or write a review of the literature in which one sifted through all the available studies and drew conclusions about the knowledge, limitations, and so on. These were called qualitative reviews and still dominate many journals that publish reviews. A clear breakthrough was the addition of reviews that were quantitative, especially those based on meta-analysis. (There were other options such as box score counting of studies and whether individual studies supported one claim versus another.)

Meta-analyses have been adopted as a set of procedures that permit one to look at a body of research and to combine studies. The studies can be combined by translating the results of each individual investigation to a common metric referred to as effect size (please see the appendix for a further discussion). If 2, 10, or 100 studies can be identified on a given topic and if they use slightly or completely different measures of outcome, the measures can be still be converted to effect size. Once converted, results from the studies can be combined. The reviewer now can draw conclusions about the findings from many studies, quantify the strength of the findings, and even ask and answer questions that were not asked in the individual studies themselves (e.g., Do self-report measures yield different results from those obtained by direct observation? Does random assignment make a difference in the results?).

Single-case research has been largely excluded from the process of integrating many studies quantitatively. The reason is that there is no clear way to translate the results of single-case designs into a common metric such as effect size. Scores of ways of measuring effect size have been proposed. Indeed, over 40 different ways of calculating effect size have been identified for single-case research (Swaminathan et al., 2008). Obviously this prompts one to ask, "What is the problem here?" As I have noted in the discussion of data evaluation (Chapter 12, appendix) single-case data have special characteristics because of collection observations of the same subject over time (serial dependence). Also, the designs have such features as sometimes relatively short phases and many occasions in which the effects of the intervention are replicated (e.g., changes across phases in an ABAB design or across subjects, behaviors, and settings in a multiple-baseline design). The net effect of these and other considerations means that effect size and its computation and interpretation are not at all straightforward. Based on several comparisons and studies (see appendix) there is no method of effect size that has emerged for widespread use for single-case research. Several issues need to be addressed and resolved. Researchers are working on the topic and one can hope that further developments will yield acceptable alternatives.

The integration of single-case research is critically important. Bodies of research are being neglected. As importantly, occasionally the methodology used to study a phenomenon influences the conclusions. We would want to know that by including in any quantitative review studies that rely on different methods, where a method means assessments, experimental designs, and data analyses. As with randomization, use of effect size measures ultimately will facilitate acceptance and integration of single-case studies.

SUMMARY AND CONCLUSIONS

In single-case designs, several problems may emerge that compete with drawing clear conclusions about the effects of the intervention. Major problems common to each of the designs include ambiguity introduced by trends and variability in the data, particularly during the baseline phases. *Baseline trends* toward improved performance may be handled in various ways, including continuing observations for protracted periods, using procedures to reverse the direction of the trend (e.g., brief period of actively fostering the opposite behavior that was the focus of the intervention phase), selecting designs that do not depend on the absence of trends in baseline, or using statistical techniques that take into account initial trends.

Excessive variability in performance may obscure intervention effects. The appearance of variability can be improved by blocking consecutive data points and plotting averages (means for that block of days) rather than plotting day-to-day performance. Of course, it is desirable, even if not always feasible, to search for possible contributors to variability, such as characteristics of the assessment procedures (e.g., low interobserver agreement) or the situation (e.g., variation among the environmental stimuli, activities, and people present in the setting).

A major issue for single-case research is deciding the *duration of phases*, an issue that encompasses problems related to trend and variability. It is difficult to identify rigid rules about the minimum number of data points necessary within a phase because the clarity and utility of a set of observations is a function of the data pattern in adjacent phases. Occasionally, objective criteria have been specified for deciding when to shift phases. Such criteria have the advantage of reducing the subjectivity that can enter into the decisions about shifting phases. However, single-case designs depend on making decisions about what the data show and how well they describe, predict, and test predictions about performance. These criteria require making decisions based on the data and not on preset criteria. Compromises are possible by allowing flexible rules for changing phases.

Another issue is the range of questions about intervention effects that can be addressed easily by single-case research. Among the many intervention outcome questions that serve as a basis for research, single-case designs are well suited to the *intervention package strategy*, that is, investigation of the effects of an overall intervention and comparison of that intervention with no treatment (baseline). *Dismantling, parametric, constructive,* and *comparative intervention strategies* raise potential problems because they require more than one intervention given to the same subject. The prospect and effects of multiple-treatment interference may lead to ambiguity about the relative merits of different interventions or variations of the same intervention. *Intervention-moderator* and *intervention-mediator/mechanism strategies* focus on characteristics that interact with the intervention or explain precisely for whom and why the intervention achieved changes. These strategies are evaluated in between-group research. Single-case studies cannot identify moderators as readily as can between-group research. Both single-case and between-group designs can identify mediators. Yet, as I noted previously, interest as well as advances in statistical techniques have fostered such work almost exclusively in between-group studies.

The *generality of results* from single-case research is also an issue. Concerns often have been voiced about the fact that only one or two subjects are studied at a time. This immediately raises the question about the extent to which findings extend to other persons or to a larger group. Actually, there is no evidence that findings from single-case research are any less generalizable than findings from between-group research. In fact, because of the type of interventions studied in single-case research, the case is sometimes made that the results may be more generalizable than those obtained in between-group research. While that is arguable, it conveys that generalizability is not automatically better as a function of methodology, that is, single case or between group. There is nothing inherent in the designs, including the use of one subject that makes the results less generalizable. The generality of findings from group research is often assumed because the research includes many people. This assumption is easily challenged based on how group studies analyze data. Such studies rarely look at the extent to which individuals changed or are represented by mean changes for the overall group. Also, how subjects are selected for inclusion (e.g., nonrandom selection, further exclusion and inclusion criteria) in between-group research can further limit the generality of the findings.

The area in which generality is a problem for single-case research is the investigation of the variables or subject characteristics that contribute to generality, i.e., moderators. In single-case research, it is difficult to evaluate interactions between treatments and subject characteristics. Statistical analyses especially well suited to group research (e.g., factorial designs, multiple regression analyses) are more appropriate for such questions and address the generality or external validity of the results directly. For all research, generality is better assured through replication of the effects of the intervention across subjects, situations, areas of functioning (e.g., academic performance, clinical problems), and other dimensions of interest. Direct and systematic replication were discussed to illustrate the ways in which this can be accomplished.

Finally, the chapter discussed randomization and quantitative integration of multiple studies (meta-analyses and effect size). These are two topics central to research in the quantitative tradition. They can also play a role in single-case research. Advantages for integrating these concepts, procedures, and practices were discussed.

Summing Up: Single-Case Research in Perspective

The individual subject has been used throughout history as the basis for drawing inferences both in basic and applied research, as highlighted in the introductory chapter of the book. Development of single-case designs as a distinct method of experimentation has emerged relatively recently. The various designs discussed in previous chapters provide alternative ways of ruling out or making implausible threats to validity. They constitute true experiments and reflect a methodology squarely in the realm of science.

This final chapter provides a perspective that clarifies essential features of the designs that permit their broad applicability. Also, it is important to consider the designs in the contexts of other approaches to research. Different methodologies include different levels and types of analysis of a given phenomenon. Single-case is one design tradition and can be viewed in the context of others (quantitative between-group research, qualitative research). The perspectives convey why any single methodology or tradition is inherently limiting and how valuable it would be to take advantage of all the methods to address the many crucial questions and challenges before us.

CHARACTERISTICS OF SINGLE-CASE RESEARCH

Single-case designs have been intertwined with a substantive focus and specific area of investigation within psychology. That focus is the experimental and applied analysis of behavior, which includes the methodology of single-case experiments as well as a conceptual and research focus that emphasizes operant conditioning. The designs have been extended to many areas of work and to many disciplines including education, clinical psychology, psychiatry, medicine, business and industry, counseling, social work, law enforcement and corrections, among others. The common feature of these many areas is the interest in developing interventions that make a difference to some facet of human functioning. The scope of the interventions has expanded greatly and well beyond the conceptual and research focus from which single-case designs emerged.

Despite the extension of the methodology to diverse disciplines and areas of research, the tendency exists to regard single-case designs as restricted to focusing on behavior analysis and operant conditioning in laboratory and applied settings. This is a completely understandable view because of the pairing of methods (single case) and substance (operant conditioning) in thousands of studies over a period spanning decades. Excellent work in basic and applied areas continues with these methods and substances paired.[1] However, the pairing may hamper extension of single-case designs in the many contexts in which they could be used. It is useful to discuss the essential and defining features of single-case designs and to distinguish those from characteristics with which the designs are often associated.

Essential Features of the Designs

By essential features of the designs, I refer to the defining ingredients. Two characteristics are defining features of single-case designs. First, the designs require *continuous assessment* over time. Measures are administered on multiple occasions within separate phases. Continuous assessment is used as a basis for drawing inferences about intervention effects. Patterns of performance can be detected by obtaining several data points under different conditions. I mentioned at the outset of the book that a useful way of differentiating between single-case and between-group methods is to remember that single-case designs usually assess few subjects on many occasions and between-group research usually assesses many subjects on few occasions. There are exceptions and combinations that make this only a useful mnemonic rather than a rule.

---

[1] Prominent journals that publish research in these are the *Journal of the Experimental Analysis of Behavior* and the *Journal of Applied Behavior Analysis*; and the professional organizations in which proponents of single-case research are especially active include Division 25 of the American Psychological Association and the Society for the Advancement of Behavior Analysis.

Second, *intervention effects are replicated within the same subject* over time.[2] Subjects serve as their own controls, and comparisons of the subject's performances are made as different conditions are implemented over time. Of course, the designs differ in the precise way in which intervention effects are replicated, but each design takes advantage of continuous assessment over time and evaluation of the subject's behavior under different conditions. The replication or within-subject study of the intervention addresses the logic and requirements of the design, namely, to describe, predict, and test predictions across phases.

These two characteristics are the basics and serve to convey how the designs rule out threats to validity, demonstrate causal relations, and build a knowledge base. There are many specific designs and design combinations in which these characteristics are structured. However, the essential components of the methodology are small in number.

Associated but Non-essential Features of the Designs

Several other characteristics often are associated with single-case designs but do not necessarily constitute defining characteristics. These are important to mention briefly to dispel misconceptions about the designs and their applicability.

Focus on One or a Few Subjects. Perhaps a characteristic that would seem to be central to the designs is the *focus on one or a few subjects*. After all, the designs are often referred to as "small-N research," "N-of-one research," or "single-case designs," as in the present text. Certainly it is true that the designs have developed to study the behavior of individual subjects intensively over time. However, investigation of one or a few subjects is not an essential or necessary feature of the methodology. The designs refer to particular types of experimental arrangements.

The number of subjects included in the design is somewhat arbitrary. So-called single-case research can use a group of subjects (e.g., in a community, in a state or province) in any design (e.g., ABAB) in which the entire group is treated as a subject or in which the number of subjects who engage in the behavior (e.g., recycle, use seat belts, pay their bills on time) is the outcome measure of interest. Also, one can use several different groups in one of the designs (e.g., multiple-baseline design across classrooms, schools, families, or communities). Single-case designs have evaluated interventions in which multiple schools, classrooms, and students participate and in which the actual or potential subjects included hundreds, thousands, or even more than a million subjects (e.g., Cox et al., 2000; Fournier et al., 2004; McSweeney, 1978; Parsons, Schepis, Reid, McCarn, & Green, 1987; Schnelle et al., 1978). In some studies, the number of subjects is not even known, as for example when monitoring compliance with a law (stopping at a stop sign) over a several-day period in which instances of an event (stopping) are counted without knowing how many different subjects or repeat subjects are included. In short, although single-case research can be and usually

---

[2] An exception to the replication of intervention effects within the same subject is the multiple-baseline design across subjects. In this instance, subjects serve as their own control, in the sense that each subject represents a separate AB design, and the replication of intervention effects is across subjects.

has been employed with one or a few subjects, this is not a necessary characteristic of the designs.

Focus on Overt Behavior. Another characteristic of single-case research has been the evaluation of the impact of interventions on *overt behavior*. The data for single-case research often consist of direct observations of performance. The association of single-case research with assessment of overt behavior is easily understandable from a historical standpoint. Single-case research grew out of the research on the *behavior* of organisms (e.g., B. F. Skinner, 1938). Behavior was defined in experimental research as overt performance on such measures as frequency or rate of responding (e.g., number of times a lever was pressed). The lawfulness of relations with different experimental manipulations and the similarities among different species (humans and non-humans) was easily seen in this laboratory paradigm.

As single-case designs were extended in applied settings (e.g., schools, hospitals, nursing homes) assessment of overt behavior has continued to be associated with the methodology. Yet single-case research designs are not necessarily restricted to overt performance. The methodology does require continuous assessment, and measures that can be obtained to meet this requirement can be employed. Other measures than overt performance can be found in single-case investigations. For example, self-report and psychophysiological measures have been included in single-case research (e.g., Glenn & Dallery, 2007; Twohig et al., 2007; Warnes & Allen, 2005). Also, how one feels about oneself, one's mood, one's ability to be in control of one's life, and similar non-behaviors are no less important in life and can be evaluated in single-case designs. It was once thought that self-report measures might not be useful or valid when continuously administered over time. That has long been dispelled by very well-developed measures completed by clients or therapists (e.g., Lambert et al., 1996). Also, self-report measures obtained by asking clients very specific questions about what happened in a confined period (e.g., past 24 hours) have been of demonstrated value in many studies (e.g., Chamberlain & Reid, 1987; Peterson et al., 2002). In any case, the assessment of overt behavior is not a necessary characteristic of single-case research. The designs require observations over time but not one method of assessment (e.g., direct observations) in particular.

Use of Visual Inspection. Another characteristic of research that would seem to be pivotal to single-case designs is the evaluation of data through *visual inspection* rather than statistical analyses. A major purpose of continuous measurement over time is to allow the investigator to *see* changes in the data as a function of stable patterns of performance within different conditions. Certainly as the designs started to enjoy more frequent use in applied settings, proponents made a strong case for visual inspection as a crucial characteristic of the methodology (Baer, 1977). That case was based on filtering out weak interventions to ensure something with potent effects would be readily apparent. No doubt many proponents would see visual inspection as being in the "essential" features category. However, there is no necessary connection between single-case research and visual inspection of the data.

Single-case designs refer to the manner in which the experimental situation is arranged to evaluate intervention effects and to rule out threats to validity. There is no fixed or necessary relationship between how the situation is arranged (the experimental design) and how the resulting information is evaluated (data analysis). Statistical analyses have been applied to single-case investigations. Although visual inspection continues to be the primary method of data evaluation for single-case research, this is not a necessary connection.

Psychological or Behavioral Interventions. A final characteristic is that single-case designs are used to investigate interventions derived from psychology and specifically learning (operant conditioning). As I mentioned, operant conditioning and single-case designs developed together, and the substantive content of the former was inextricably bound with the evaluative techniques of the latter. This connection has continued as noted in the journals identified previously (please see footnote 1). Even so there is no necessary connection between single-case designs and operant conditioning techniques.

A number of different types of interventions derived from clinical psychology, medicine, pharmacology, social psychology, and other areas not central to or derived from operant conditioning have been included in single-case research, as illustrated in examples in prior chapters. It is important to emphasize the breadth of applicability because the designs are relevant to virtually all situations in which the goal is to alter some facet of functioning. For example, there is keen interest in promoting sustainable environmental practices to mitigate and adapt to climate change. Interventions draw from so many areas, with direct attempts to alter the public's perception of risk from global warming, to educate and provide instruction, to alter attitudes, to influence by drawing on economics and decision making, and to implement social policy changes (Kazdin, 2009). The area is rich in interventions ripe for empirical evaluation, and where single-case designs would be quite useful. The designs can be used with interventions drawn from other disciplines with little or no knowledge of operant conditioning.

General Comments

Many arguments about the utility and limitations of single-case designs focus on features not central to the designs. For example, objections focus on nonstatistical data evaluation, the use of only one or two subjects, and restricting the evaluation to overt behavior. These features are part of single-case methodology, but they are not essential features. The designs can be used without them. I am not in any way advocating that these nonessential features be abandoned. Just the opposite. Our knowledge base is greatly enhanced by drawing on a broader array of research methods than we currently use. The essential *and* nonessential features of single-case designs can greatly expand our approaches, the domains of what we study (individual functioning), and the situations in which we can introduce evaluation. I mention the features as not essential because those trained in between-group research can easily identify one of the nonessential features and cast aside the entire methodology as not useful, rigorous, or indeed scientific. For example, the "failure" of single-case designs to use statistics routinely to decide whether the effect of an intervention is reliable sounds like scientific heresy and all by itself could taint the methodology for some. However, the use of single-case designs does not require automatic adoption of the visual inspection rather than statistical analyses or the other facets I have noted here as nonessential. I would encourage adoption of the package of essential and nonessential components but not if these held back researchers from exploring the methodology.

Another source of objection of single-case research has been the association of the methodology with a conceptual focus and area of work. Within psychology, operant conditioning (conceptual domain) and the analysis of behavior (approach to evaluation including single-case methods) have elaborated and continue to elaborate a range of influences on behavior in humans and non-human animals. Operant conditioning underscored the role of environmental influences (e.g., stimuli, consequences) on functioning. One of the phrases to capture portions of the model noted that our behavior is selected by the consequences it has on the environment. The position never was that "only the environment and consequences are important and nothing else." However, it was easy to isolate operant conditioning as it moved to explain human behavior, culture, government and law, and more domains from the standpoint of the model (e.g., Skinner, 1953a). Operant conditioning, years ago, was labeled "radical behaviorism" because of its heavy focus on environmental antecedents and consequences as key influences on behavior. Little or no attention or emphasis was accorded other influence such as cognitive processes (e.g., thoughts, beliefs, attributions, perceptions), emotions (e.g., mood, affect), characteristics of the individuals (e.g., personality, temperament), and biological underpinnings (e.g., brain and now genetic). One could quibble at the margins about exceptions, but these were exceptions and definitely perceived as exceptions. While operant conditioning in both basic and applied domains flourished, it also became isolated in part because of the model and view from the outside that operant conditioning too strongly rejected these other areas of functioning. In more recent years these other influences have been accorded much more attention and integration including, for example, cognition and neuroscience (e.g., Timberlake, Schaal, & Steinmetz, 2005; White, McCarthy, & Fantino, 1989). Even so, early minimization of cognition, emotion, individual differences, and biological underpinnings led to isolation and lack of integration of the many contributions of operant conditioning into much of mainstream psychology. The net effect is that rejection of a "radical" approach to human functioning has also diminished appreciation of a methodology that has no necessary connection to any particular conceptual view. It would be unfortunate if investigators eschewed a methodology with potentially broad utility because of historical antipathy over a particular theoretical position that need not necessarily be embraced. (It is for another book to lament the rejection of a theoretical position because of its prior characterization as unusually narrow. That theoretical position has generated very effective intervention approaches that are rarely taught.)

SPECIAL STRENGTHS OF SINGLE-CASE DESIGNS

Evaluation

I have mentioned that our world is filled with programs and interventions designed to help people. Special education schools, classrooms, and teachers, for example, develop innovative interventions or variations all of the time to have impact on students. In schools (elementary through university), interventions are aimed at improving academic performance and participation in some activities (e.g., engaging in sports and volunteer activities) and reducing participation in others (e.g., eating unhealthful foods, abusing alcohol, harassing and assaulting others). In hospitals, interventions are aimed at reducing medical errors and increasing safety practices to reduce the spread of illness while patients are in the hospital. In business, interventions are designed to improve health (via exercise programs), productivity, safety, and morale. Indeed, in virtually all institutional settings key facets of the day-to-day involve interventions with a goal in mind. In everyday life, interventions are directed to improve compliance with the laws (e.g., speed limit, use of safety belts) and our support of broad social goals (e.g., not littering, behaving in ways that promote a sustainable environment). Invariably new interventions (programs, plans, efforts, initiatives) are designed to improve the goals in these and other contexts. Do any of these interventions have any impact, and is that impact in the intended direction or does it make people worse? These questions cannot be answered suitably by anecdotal reports of what the program developer or consumers believe. One really needs systematic data.

Evaluating such programs in between-group studies with pre- and post-intervention testing, random assignment of individuals to conditions (e.g., including a no-intervention control group), and other features of traditional group comparison studies (e.g., invoking exclusion and inclusion recruitment criteria, using large samples) usually is not possible. Single-case designs, including quasi-single-case designs, provide viable alternatives. Continuous data collected over A and B phases (e.g., AB design) can be collected across different students, hospital units, and departments within an organization. Of course, if the implementation of the intervention (B) is staggered so each individual, unit, or section does not receive the intervention at the same time, this becomes a multiple-baseline design. A key feature of the designs, many observations but few subjects, can be very helpful in evaluating impact, that is, whether there is a change and whether the intervention is likely to account for that change. Most settings have a group already in place that can serve as the subject, that is, the group can be evaluated as if it were an individual. What is plotted as the data is the performance of the group as a whole (e.g., percentage of children in the school who complete their homework, number of families or homes that recycle). In short, single-case designs permit a broader range of opportunities to evaluate what we do.

Ongoing Feedback While the Intervention Is Applied

In single-case research, the continuous feedback from the data and the fluid decision making while the program is in play have distinct advantages. In between-group research, the intervention is preplanned and administered in keeping with that plan. The impact of treatment is evaluated at the end when the full treatment has been delivered (posttest assessment). This makes sense for research but not for people receiving the intervention. Single-case designs allow for evaluation of impact *while* the intervention is in place. We can evaluate whether the intervention is achieving change and whether the change is at the level we desire or need. Decisions can be made *during* the intervention to improve outcome. The continuous assessment during the intervention phase makes the designs quite user friendly to the investigator (teacher, doctor, or other person responsible for the intervention) and the client (person or group intended to benefit). If something is not working or not working sufficiently well, the investigator can make the change and continue to evaluate whether change comes about right away without waiting to see mediocre or no impact at posttest.

For example, in one project the goal was to train six boys and girls (6 to 7 years of age) to not play with handguns (Miltenberger et al., 2004). A real but disabled handgun was used; assessments were completed at home and at school while the child was left alone with the gun. Assessments were videotaped and later scored for the extent to which each child engaged in the appropriate behaviors on a 0-to-3-point scale in which 0 = touching the gun and 3 = not touching the gun, leaving the room, and telling an adult about the gun. In a multiple-baseline design across children, a behavioral skills training program was used that provided instructions, modeling, rehearsal, and feedback, all conducted in a simulated training situation rather than at home or at school. A few sessions of this were very effective in altering the behavior of three of the six children; the effects of training carried over to home or school.

Figure 15.1 shows the data for the three children who responded positively (Nigel, Brigitte, and Ned) in a multiple-baseline fashion in which change occurred when the intervention was introduced but not before. The data also show that when this training was introduced, three other children did not respond. A second intervention was added in which more intensive practice and rehearsal training were added and conducted in the school setting (in the situation or in situ training). The figure shows that two of the remaining three children (Ricky, Tina) responded well to this enhanced intervention. To alter the behavior of Jake, a third condition was provided, namely, an incentive. He could receive a treat for rehearsing the correct behaviors. Jake too achieved the criterion of engaging in the appropriate behaviors. A final 5-month follow-up assessment showed that the appropriate behaviors were maintained in the home, where the assessment was then conducted.

In many ways, this demonstration illustrates a very special strength of single-case designs. Interventions were implemented and evaluated. Decisions were made based on the data. New interventions were added to achieve the desired outcome. Pre–post data from a between-group study might have shown that the first intervention (behavioral skills program) worked (statistically significant difference if compared to a no-intervention control condition). Yet we see that the intervention would have left a significant proportion of people stranded, that is, with no change in the desired outcome.

Apart from the information provided, single-case designs allow for the gradual or small-scale implementation of the intervention. With one or a few cases, one can implement the intervention and see in a preliminary way whether this is having an effect. This allows the investigator to modify the intervention on a small scale if needed before applying the intervention to the entire class, school, or other larger scale setting. The investigator is posing and answering a set of questions: "Does the effect of the intervention look promising? If so, let us continue and extend the intervention to others. Alternatively, should the intervention be altered or changed completely?" If there is a strong intervention effect in the small-scale application with one or a few subjects, this does not necessarily mean that the effect will extend across all subjects or baselines. But the point here is that first starting out on a modest scale, across one phase for one or two individuals (ABAB) or across one baseline (in a multiple-baseline across individuals, situations, responses) helps the investigator preview the impact of treatment as well as master implementation and some of the practical issues that may relate to its effectiveness.

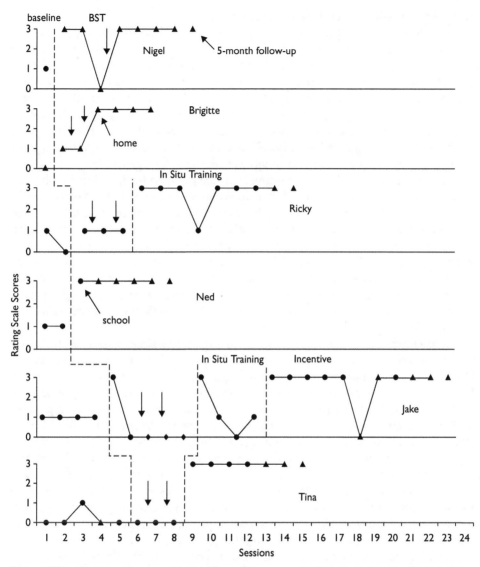

Figure 15.1. Rating scale scores (derived from videotapes of child behavior) in a multiple-baseline design across six children. Behavioral skills training (BST) was implemented and effective for three of the children (Nigel, Brigitte, Ned). In situation (in situ) training was introduced and effective for two of the three children (Ricky, Tina) who had not responded to BST. Finally, an incentive was added and was effective in altering the behavior of the child (Jake) who had not responded to the previous interventions. For all children, a 5-month follow-up assessment in the home showed that the behaviors were maintained.   *(Source: Miltenberger et al., 2004.)*

Tests of Generality: Extending Interventions

In the previous chapter I mentioned moderators, those variables that influence the effectiveness of an intervention. Actually, they can influence the direction of the effect (e.g., some people get better or worse) or the magnitude of the direction (e.g., some get a little better, some a lot better). Between-group research evaluates moderators well because subgroups (by ethnicity, by sex or identity, by severity or duration of some characteristic) can be identified in the data analysis and one can analyze whether the subgroups respond differently. Moderators refer to variables that affect generality of a result: Do the results generalize across all subjects, conditions, contexts, and situations? There is an important way in which single-case designs study generality.

First, the generalizability of a finding from the group to the individual is always a question. Between-group research, for example, focuses on means rather than on individuals. We may know that a treatment is better overall, but will the finding be true or generalize to any particular individual? For example, an evidence-based intervention developed in special education might well be good for a particular group. Now there is interest in helping a child in a very different context. No matter how well established an intervention, there is never a guarantee that it will work with any particular individual. Continuous evaluation and use of a single-case experimental or quasi-designs permit evaluation as the intervention is administered to individuals and tests generality of a finding from the group to the individual.

Second, whether a finding is from between-group or single-case designs, it may have been restricted to a particular group of people (e.g., of a certain age, ethnicity). One can do large-scale studies with different groups. Actually, that is not very feasible. For example, evidence-based psychotherapies rarely have been tested with the diverse ethnic groups in the United States.[3] As I have shown elsewhere, it would be impossible to do the necessary between-group studies to test the available treatments with each ethnic group and across a range of clinical problems (Kazdin, 2008a). Alternatively, one can begin to apply the intervention to other novel groups not included in the original demonstrations, whether group or single-case, to see if the effects are similar. Single-case designs would be one viable means to accomplish this with small-scale extensions to test the generality of findings. Consider the use of single-case designs to test generality as probes. These were assessments to test for generality within a study. We want to see how findings from research extend to other groups.

Third, generalizability across conditions is very important. Whether focusing on the individual or the group, often one wants to know whether a change achieved in some setting (e.g., home or military base) extends to other places (e.g., school, music lesson, or battlefield). The use of probes as part of assessment when such questions arise is another strength of the designs. Probes, or occasional and intermittent assessments, can complement the continuous data and provide information about whether changes extend to other settings and contexts or whether some other intervention might be needed in those settings.

---

[3] In North America (Canada, Mexico, United States), there are hundreds of ethnic and cultural groups and, of course, hundreds more elsewhere in the world (www.infoplease.com/ipa/A0855617. html).

Analyzing moderator effects is difficult in single-case research, as noted before. However, extending the intervention to other samples and conditions and testing whether the effects continue to be evident are readily achieved by single-case designs. Indeed, the gradual extension of an intervention across samples (e.g., one or a few individuals) is a very feasible way to proceed. Single-case tests of generality are not instead of, better than, or replacements for other tests that might be completed in group studies. Rather, single-case designs increase our options and the range of contexts in which generality can be evaluated.

We Care About Individuals

The special strengths mentioned previously address methodological and substantive issues about what we can know (e.g., effects of a program) and how we can test generality to others. I would like to add to the special strengths one that is laced with empathy, concern for others, and the priorities of our daily lives. I noted how single-case designs can evaluate groups (e.g., in classrooms or schools, the community at large), but let us return to the focus on the individual. A unique strength of single-case designs is providing a way to evaluate change and impact of interventions on a particular person. This is very important, as many of us have experienced or will experience in life. For many questions that guide our everyday life, we care very much about the individual. It is interesting to us personally and intellectually to ask about the group data. For example, we hear about a new treatment (e.g., for obesity, diabetes, blood pressure, or hair loss). Does it work? Is a change in the treatment associated with real change or is it another one of those bait-and-switch television ads that says "clinical evidence shows" (that does not mean randomized controlled trials) where we see two models, one cast as "before" and one cast as "after" receiving/taking the intervention?

I note the obvious, namely, that we owe so many advances in clinical work (e.g., psychological and medical science) to between-group research methods to help underscore the point about individuals. In our daily lives it is about individuals—ourselves, our loved ones, and about friends, and not about group data. As an illustration, my annual physical exam could easily turn into a methodological brawl. (I take heavy medication and have my impersonal trainer with me in the waiting room to help me restrain myself.) Once in the room with my physician but toward the end of my 9-minute appointment, we have an exchange that is pretty much like this:

MY PHYSICIAN: "You probably ought to have that medical test in about 5 years, just to make sure you don't have…[reader—insert your favorite serious disorder—my physician rotates several variations of cancers, heart disease, diabetes]."

ME: "That sounds *serious*; maybe I should have the test now."

MY P: "Actually the data (he means group) show that you probably do not need that medical test because the rate of that problem is pretty low at your age right now and for most people does not pick up for a few more years."

ME: "Just speaking generally, is it possible that I am one of the cases in the group that gets that disease on the early side?"

MY P: "Yes, of course, but not very likely."

ME: "I would really like the test, because what happened to the big group might not be what happens to me. Also, the test doesn't hurt (I am a medical coward) and the information could help with one of my personal priorities (staying alive)."

MY P: "Uh—you are probably fine without it, but in 3 or 4 years it would be pretty important. Well, I see that my next appointment is here—God willing, let's continue this discussion at your next physical."

Although not quite relevant, the astute reader will note how I refrained from challenging the group data. I held back on, "Were the findings replicated, what ethnic and cultural groups were included, were there any moderators, were the findings based on one- or two-tailed statistical tests, what precisely was the miss rate, that is, not identifying people my age whose problem was not detected and happen to die," and so on. (Actually, I have not really restrained myself—each of these questions in various combinations with the others has been asked at least twice—I vary the order with the hope of reducing multiple-question interference.)

To return to the point: I (and I expect you) respect the group data—some of my best friends even collect the stuff—but these data do not tell me whether I will be one of those cases and a person who would have profited from taking the medical test a little early. Single-case designs cannot solve my problem, and my physician is a superbly well-trained between-group guy. However, my story conveys the point. Critical questions—life and death questions—are often, if not almost always, about individuals. Consider a better example to convey the point.

Cancers that spread (metastatic cancers) have a poor prognosis. Understandably, people with such cancers experience depression, stress, anxiety, and related problems that impair quality of life, life satisfaction, and compliance with cancer treatment. Any intervention that could help manage depression and ease their course would be remarkable. In this example, cognitive behavior therapy was provided to women (ages 42 to 66) with breast cancer (one also had ovarian cancer as well) with metastases to at least one other site (e.g., liver, bone, lung, brain) (Levesque et al., 2004). The goal was to reduce depression and to develop an optimistic but realistic attitude toward their situation, as opposed to negative thinking (e.g., only about death) or overly positive thinking (e.g., hoping to be cured). Eight individual weekly sessions and three booster sessions of treatment were provided. Many measures were administered to assess depression, suicidality, anxiety, and quality of life. Two measures of depression are presented here. Figure 15.2 presents the group data on a clinician-completed measure of depression (The Structured Interview Guide for the Hamilton Depression Rating Scale) obtained from an interview of approximately 2 hours. The clinician was "blind" (naïve) to the procedures and goals of the study. Each bar in the graph represents the mean for the cases before, during, and after treatment and then again at two follow-up assessments. The group data convey rather clearly that there was a change on a clinician rating measure of depression over the course of treatment.

If I were one of the patients or a relative of one of the patients, I would not be very interested in the group data. We want to know about any intervention effects for the individual. Quality clinical care depends on that. Figure 15.3 presents the individual

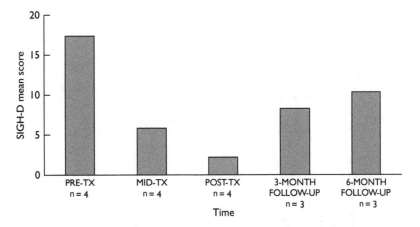

Figure 15.2. Mean depression scores from clinician interviews (The Structured Interview Guide for the Hamilton Depression Rating Scale; SIGH-D) for the group (N = 4, who completed treatment) at pre-, mid-, and post-treatment and two follow-up periods. Follow-up indicated depression higher than during treatment but still well below baseline.   *(Source: Levesque et al., 2004.)*

data for another standardized measure of depression (Hospital Anxiety and Depression Scale) that is specifically designed to assess depression among patients with physical illness (e.g., by removing somatic items that could be confused with manifestations of the physical illness). The figure shows four participants who completed treatment (Participant 3 had to be withdrawn for medical complications). Treatment was staggered in the multiple-baseline fashion. The focus is beyond the criteria for visual inspection. We see that individual data show the effects of the intervention and follow-up assessments. After the intervention, depression for some cases had decreased to the lowest points possible. This is important to know and important as a basis to see if the patients who did not respond so well require further attention.

We very much need single-case methods, experiments, and quasi-experiments to provide systematic information about the effects of interventions on individuals. Clinical judgment is not up to the task of providing the data we need in order to help, a point to which I return. Group studies, so essential in identifying and evaluating interventions, by themselves do not provide the proper tool to help us evaluate individuals in an ongoing way, to chart the effects of our interventions, and to help decide whether we ought to continue what we are doing or try something different. Single-case designs have as their strength the ability to do all of these.

MULTIPLE APPROACHES ARE ESSENTIAL
FOR UNDERSTANDING

Single-case designs and their contribution can be showcased better by placing them in two broad contexts. These include the different levels of analyses of social research and the different methodologies including between-group and qualitative research.

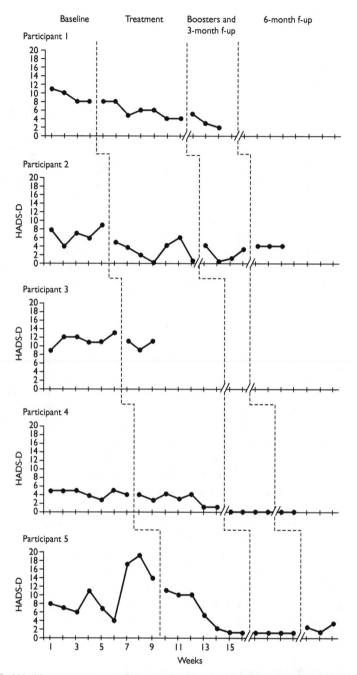

Figure 15.3. Weekly scores on a patient-completed measure of depression (Hospital Anxiety and Depression Scale; HADS-D for the depression items). After baseline, the treatment phase included weekly cognitive behavior therapy sessions; further sessions were provided during the booster period 3 months later; follow-up included no intervention. (Participant 3 had to withdraw due to medical complications.)   *(Source: Levesque et al., 2004.)*

Levels of Analysis

By levels of analysis I refer to the scale of investigation. For example, in learning research, one can focus on individual neurons or molecular changes in the brain. At another extreme, one can study learning by asking individuals to recall material they have read. Both levels of analysis focus on learning, but of course they are considerably different in their focus.

Extend the notion of levels and one can see the need for and role of different methodologies. In relation research on human and non-human animal functioning, many questions are of interest at the level of the *individual subject* or *case*. Single-case designs can answer questions about what is effective and whether change has come about for one or more individuals. This is very critical. For example, in the context of psychotherapy, several evidence-based treatments have emerged. These are psychosocial interventions that have been strongly supported in empirical research. Exposure therapy for anxiety, cognitive therapy for depression, and parent management training for conduct problems in children are three of many examples (see Nathan & Gorman, 2007; Weisz & Kazdin, 2010). In clinical practice with individual patients, assume that an evidence-based treatment is used. Will the treatment help a particular patient? We cannot really know because effective treatments do not always work, whether in medicine or psychology. Can we just ask the therapist about his or her opinion of whether it worked? We could, but research is not kind about the credibility of the information we are likely to obtain. Cognitive processes and perception lead us to misjudge often. In fact, therapists often are simply inaccurate in their evaluations of the impact of their treatments on patients (Love, Koob, & Hill, 2007). It would be helpful to have a methodology that can evaluate if changes occur with individual patients. The quality of clinical care could be greatly improved (Borckardt et al., 2008; Kazdin, 2008b). Single-case experiments and quasi-experiments provide such a methodology and could contribute enormously to the delivery of services. Their unique contribution is to provide the means to evaluate interventions for the individual client.

Second, many research questions we care about can be and actually must be addressed at the level of groups. In between-group research, one group is compared with one or more other groups. The unique contribution of between-group research is to examine the separate and combined effects of different variables (e.g., characteristics of the subjects that may moderate treatment). Large sample sizes and delineation of subgroups (by a categorical variable) or a range of some characteristic (by a dimensional variable) requires a group study. Also, I mentioned that evaluations of interventions (e.g., parametric, dismantling, comparative) are well suited to group studies because they can test treatment variations without multiple-treatment interference.

Many questions we have that are not part of intervention studies also require a group-level focus. For examples, we want to know about factors that contribute to problems, successes, and outcomes that occur when we do not intervene. Among children who are physically or sexually abused or who experience mental or physical health problems, what are the characteristics of those who turned out problem-free? What can be done in early childhood that decreases the likelihood that teenagers will engage in high-risk behaviors (e.g., driving while intoxicated, unprotected sex, cigarette smoking)? What is the relation of physical health (e.g., onset of colds, days lost from work due to health) and mental health (e.g., stress, adjustment)? Each of these questions requires the study of groups. Also, we want an estimate of the strength of relations among variables (e.g., correlation), and this requires groups.

Third, many questions we care about are beyond groups of individuals and actually refer to groups of studies. For example, questions about the effectiveness of interventions (e.g., in education, psychology, and medicine) are routinely addressed by examining and combining many different between-group studies. *Meta-analysis* is an approach to research that draws on individual studies (rather than subjects) as the unit of analysis, characterizes and combines studies, and draws conclusions based on this combined literature.[4] The questions focus on drawing from a body of literature (multiple studies) to see what new conclusions can be drawn, some of which could not be asked or were not asked by any of the individual studies included in the meta-analysis.

Each of the preceding levels of analysis for research focuses on important issues. It is difficult to argue convincingly in favor of one level of analysis to the exclusion of the others. And there would be no point. Uncovering the secrets of nature and developing strategies to address critical problems would profit from using the widest range of tools we have available. Assessments, experimental designs, and data-analytic strategies associated with the different levels of analyses extend our range.

Multiple Methodologies

A different way to place single-case designs in context is to mention three research traditions. First and most familiar is between-group research, which dominates training of students and researchers in the social and biological sciences. As the reader is well familiar, this involves groups, null hypotheses testing, and statistical tests, and is referred to as *quantitative research*. Second, in need of no elaboration at the end of the book, is *single-case research*. This type of research (groups not essential, no null hypothesis testing in the same way, and no need for statistical tests) is rarely included in training in the social or biological sciences and departs from research in the quantitative tradition.

Third is *qualitative research*, which consists of systematic, replicable, and rigorous ways of studying individuals and human experience much more intensively than either between-group or single-case research. In terms of a methodology, qualitative research often considers a small number of subjects, evaluates their experience in rich details, often with lengthy narrative descriptions, and may or may not use special software and statistical techniques to evaluate the content.[5] Qualitative methods, well beyond the scope of this chapter, convey yet another methodological approach to study phenomena. These methods look at phenomena in ways that reveal many facets of human experience that the between-group quantitative tradition has been partially designed to circumvent—in-depth evaluation, subjective views, and how individuals represent (perceive, feel) and react to their situations and contexts. For example, qualitative research can look at the experience of those who go through treatment and thematic

---

[4] For the reader unfamiliar with meta-analysis, many excellent sources are available and can be consulted (Cooper, Hedges, & Valentine, 2009; Hunter & Schmidt, 2004).

[5] It is important to note that the term "qualitative" is occasionally and mistakenly used to mean an unsystematic case or anecdotes. Qualitative methods meet the desiderata of science; the methods are systematic, replicable, and cumulative (see Berg, 2001; Denzin & Lincoln, 2005).

ways in which their lives and the lives of their partners are influenced. As the reader well knows, qualitative research methods are rarely covered in training in the social sciences.

The vast majority of research in the social sciences falls within the quantitative between-group tradition. If the work is intervention research (treatment, prevention, services), randomized controlled trials are recognized as the epitome of this tradition. Typically, RCTs include pre- and posttreatment assessment, multiple measures, rigorous control over the administration of treatment, and holding constant or controlling as much as possible to maximize the likelihood of identifying an effect if one truly exists (Kazdin, 2003). Quantitative research, and RCTs as its poster child, account for enormous gains in so many areas in medicine, education, counseling, psychology, rehabilitation, and more. The development of evidence-based interventions in education and psychotherapy are two prominent examples where great strides have been made.

The dominance and close-to-exclusive reliance on the quantitative tradition constrains our knowledge. The perspective and yield from a study are very much influenced by the methods we use. The level of analysis (individual, group, groups of studies), the types of measures that are used, the number of occasions on which they are administered (e.g., self-report at pre and post; behavioral measures continuously assessed over time; in-depth narratives), and other features either essential to or correlated with different methodologies reveal different facets of a phenomenon. Multiple methodologies and perspectives are essential without implying that one is better than the other. For example, the argument that tests of statistical significance are "better" than visual inspection criteria is difficult to make. Both means of evaluating the data include subjectivity and some arbitrariness but in different ways. Both should be treated cautiously and not worshipped (see appendix at the end of the book). And both have humorous features as we investigators squirm when the criteria are not quite met but we want them to be. A familiar example is from quantitative research where statistical tests are used to decide whether there is a difference or the intervention had an effect. In many articles, one can easily find such comments as, "My findings 'approached significance' or were 'almost statistically significant' or there was a 'trend toward significance.'" None of these terms is legitimate within the quantitative tradition of null hypothesis testing and the rules adopted for statistical significance.

The importance of multiple ways of examining phenomena is conveyed better by looking at other areas of science. As an illustration, most readers are familiar with the Hubble Space Telescope and its remarkable yield of information about space. The Hubble has been one of four orbiting observatories that look at space in a different light (visible, infrared, gamma rays, and X rays) (www.stsci.edu/science/goods). Each yields unique information and complements information provided by the others. Pointing the observatories to the same object or point in space yields entirely different pictures because of what is being assessed. Research methodology too can influence the yield; phenomena can vary as a function of the methodological lens through which they are viewed. For example, we have known for decades that even within the quantitative between-group tradition, findings for a given phenomenon can vary as a function of the type of design (e.g., cross-sectional vs. longitudinal; between vs. within subjects) (e.g., Chassin et al., 1986; Grice & Hunter, 1964). The findings are all real and veridical but convey different facets of the topic. Our view of the cosmos has grown enormously by expanding the ways in which we can look at it. Methodological ecumenicism that recognizes and utilizes quantitative, single-case, and qualitative traditions would have the same benefit.

CLOSING COMMENTS

If you are a researcher already, you will have seen me describe several features of single-case designs that clash with your (and my!) training. I have emphasized what we are trying to accomplish by doing research to allow evaluation of single-case methods more generally. We do studies to draw inferences and understand phenomena better than ordinary casual observations allow. The problems that emerge and compete with drawing clear conclusions are well codified as various sources of bias and artifact. The threats to validity highlighted early in the book reflect major sources of bias and artifact that can mislead us. The goals of research are to combat all the sources of ambiguity we can and to design a project that will permit valid (clear, verifiable, replicable) inferences.

Between-group designs, single-case designs, and qualitative research designs all can rule out various sources of artifact and bias. In their most rigorous forms, they can demonstrate causal relations. It is unfortunate that our training has usually limited our exposure, so we cannot readily draw from each of them. In the case of single-case designs, among the unfortunate consequences is that we live in a world of well-intentioned interventions that are rarely evaluated. Single-case designs, even if used in this one context, would permit more programs to examine whether or not we are helping when we think we are. But there is more to single-case designs than program evaluation. The designs greatly increase the armamentarium of the researcher interested in science, whether basic or applied.

Consider single-case designs in your work. Try one with an intervention that you believe is working well. The feedback that the data provide on a continuous basis is an excellent way to evaluate an intervention but also to make decisions as to whether the desired effects are obtained while the intervention is still in process and can be changed. This book was designed to elaborate single-case methodology and to describe design options, their utility, and their limitations. I hope you will explore this methodology to complement other design and evaluation methods you are using.

Statistical Analyses for Single-Case Designs: Issues and Illustrations

Data evaluation focuses on drawing inferences about whether the change is reliable and not likely to be due to chance fluctuations in the data. The experimental design determines largely whether the intervention can be identified as responsible for change, but the data-evaluation method handles the burden of making the decision about the change itself. Visual inspection has been and continues to be the dominant method of data evaluation of single-case designs, as discussed previously (Chapter 12). Indeed, estimates have placed the reliance on visual inspection as characterizing approximately 90% of studies from 1978 to 2003, with no clear changes over time (see Parker & Hagan-Burke, 2007b). That said, there has been increased interest over the same span of years in the use of statistical tests and advances in the tests themselves.

This appendix has four goals. First, the context for carrying out statistical tests in single-case data is discussed. This context includes but goes well beyond concerns about visual inspection. Research on visual inspection and how it is applied and the elaboration of novel statistical analyses for single-case research are parallel lines of research in the past few decades. Each is important to highlight because of the central issues and dilemmas it raises for data evaluation in single-case research.

Second, the appendix clarifies what is special about single-case data that dictates the use of but also provides challenges for statistical evaluation. Characteristics of the data and specific statistical tests for data evaluation of the single case include surprises. The statistical tests used in single-case research are different from the usual tests that have been taught in graduate training and in the between-group research tradition. In those instances in which the tests are familiar (e.g., t and F), there are some novel considerations and issues that emerge. Statistical analysis is more than some "new" tests. The data and the designs present challenges for statistical evaluation that are important to cover.

Third, the appendix enumerates statistical tests for the single-case and provides an illustration of one of the more prominently used tests. In the first edition of the book, several available tests were presented and illustrated. These included conventional t and F tests, time-series analysis, randomization tests, a test of ranks, and split-middle technique. Since that writing, many more tests and variations of some of these have been developed. No one test has captured the hearts or method sections of those who use statistical tests. Also, quite recent work has begun to evaluate available tests more analytically by comparing the strengths, varied results, and requirements of different tests. In light of the scope of advances, this appendix can only illustrate and highlight statistical evaluation and its yield. There are now many resources that detail individual statistical techniques and the relative merits of various options.[1]

Finally, perhaps the most central goal and possible contribution of this appendix is to convey the status and dilemma of data evaluation in single-case designs. There are weighty considerations, including clear strengths and limitations, of visual inspection and statistical evaluation. Considerations are presented to guide the researcher on the decision to use one or both types of analyses.

BACKGROUND AND CONTEXT

Visual Inspection: Application and Applicability

It is true to state that visual inspection remains the primary method of evaluating single-case designs, but in the past two or three decades many influences have placed this method under further scrutiny. The scrutiny has focused concretely on the applicability of the method but also the rationale for its use. First, several studies have shown that visual inspection criteria can be difficult to invoke reliably (e.g., Franklin et al., 1997; Matyas & Greenwood, 1990; Park et al., 1990). In the idealized data pattern or close approximations of that, all the criteria for visual inspection (e.g., mean, slope, level, latency criteria) are met; baselines (e.g., B phases in an ABAB design, or initial baselines in a multiple-baseline design) are stable (e.g., little variability, no trend), and the data points from phase to phase (e.g., ABAB) do not overlap. This pattern is not the one that raises concern; judges can identify large effects (Knapp, 1983; Matyas &

---

[1] Books are available that discuss statistical tests for single-case designs (e.g., Edgington & Onghena, 2007; Franklin, Allison, & Gorman, 1997; Satake, Maxwell, & Jagaroo, 2008). Several articles that present different tests or that compare multiple tests are referred to throughout this appendix.

Greenwood, 1990). Once one begins to depart from the ideal data pattern, inconsistency emerges when two or more judges are asked to evaluate the impact of the intervention. The unreliability of judging the data has been replicated among raters or evaluators with little or no experience with single-case designs (e.g., undergraduates), as well as among individuals in training and expert judges with direct experience with the designs (see Brossart, Parker, Olson, & Mahadevan, 2006; Harbst et al., 1991; Park et al., 1990). Can one train the judges and surmount the unreliability of judging the data? Training can help but does not eliminate the problem (e.g., Fisher et al., 2003; Harbst et al., 1991; Skiba et al., 1989) for reasons noted later. In any case, over time with a small but accumulating literature, there is increased recognition that making judgments about the data using visual inspection criteria can be unreliable.

Second, a key rationale for the use of visual inspection has undergone challenge as well. The method of data evaluation for applied research is based in part on the view that only large effects ought to be considered as reliable (Parsonson & Baer, 1978, 1992). Early in the development and use of the designs in applied settings this filtering aspect of visual inspection was viewed as a strength. The goal was to use single-case designs as part of the development of a technology of behavior change. Iffy, weak, and other such effects were not of interest or to be counted. This is easily understood when between-group research is used as a comparison. In between-group research, the goal is to show statistically significant differences between groups. But such differences can be obtained with minor changes on the measures or outcomes. Indeed, statistical significance is largely a function of sample size. That is, groups in any study will invariably differ to some extent; the larger the sample size, the more likely that difference will reach statistical significance.

Single-case research began with the notion that detecting a difference should be a "real" difference—one that meets an experimental criterion for reliability (a genuine difference not due to some trend or chance fluctuation) and applied criterion (some practical, educational, or therapeutic goal is achieved). The rationale is easily defensible in principle. In practice, the situation is rather different. Empirical analyses of publications of single-case research designs have shown that many intervention effects (e.g., over 25% in one study) in fact are small and debatable, if not completely illusory (Glass, 1997; Parker et al., 2006). The specific percentage is not critical and is subject to debate. Yet, the broader point may not be, namely, the rationale for using visual inspection and the advantage of filtering out weak effects are not how the criteria are used in many instances.

Third, the rationale of searching for large effects has another concern that has become clearer in the past decades. Small effects or changes can be very important for many reasons (Kazdin, 2001). Arguably, we want to know about reliable changes, whether they pass some stringent standard or not. Small effects might lead to a better understanding, and better understanding is a five-lane, freshly paved and painted highway to more effective interventions that *can* produce large effects. In addition, large intervention effects can actually be hidden in the data and appear as a small effect. If there is a moderator variable operating (e.g., ethnicity, age), the overall effect might look weak, because within that effect are strong and weak effects or even effects that are in the opposite direction for subgroups. If a single-case demonstration obtains a weak effect, that might not be a universal finding; for another group and in another context, the effect might well be large. Early filtering or exclusion of weak but reliable effects is unnecessary and potentially harmful to science and technology.[2] Finally on this point, we very much want weak interventions in our armamentarium, especially if they are low-cost and can be widely applied. Application of weak treatments (e.g., antismoking campaigns, TV ads to reduce child abuse) on a large scale can have important effects (Kazdin, 2008a).

Fourth, there are features of single-case data that elude visual detection but can greatly influence judgments about the data. One of these is referred to as *serial dependence* and refers to the fact that data from one occasion to the next (Day 1, Day 2) from the continuous observations over time may correlate with each other. I elaborate this more fully later because of its relevance to statistical evaluation. I mention this here to note that whether the data are serially dependent cannot always be "seen" by just looking at the graph. However, serial dependence can influence judgments about the effects of the intervention (Jones et al., 1978; Matyas & Greenwood, 1990).

A related feature of single-case data is the possibility of a slight trend that obscures evaluation of subsequent phases. Baseline trend is the more likely culprit. Again in the idealized pattern of single-case data (e.g., sharp changes in trend from phase to phase), the issue does not emerge. However, from published research we have learned that a high percentage of studies have a trend toward improvement in baseline (Parker et al., 2006). The trend may not be easily observable visually because it is not simply a straight line. There may be perturbations, random influences, and cycles that suggest to an observer (visual inspection) that there is no systematic trend. However, a trend can be quantified (modeled) and shown to characterize the data. In short, we have learned that there are characteristics of single-case data, patterns of many findings of single-case studies, and constraints on perception and visualization of what happened across phases that limit visual inspection. In many cases, visualization and invoking the criteria for visual inspection may not be up to the task of deciding whether the intervention effect was reliable.

These considerations I have highlighted convey challenges to visual inspection. Evaluation of the data is not merely a matter of holding the graphed data in one hand and a list of the criteria for visual inspection in another and drawing conclusions by clapping both hands together. Lack of stark intervention effects and nuances of the data (serial dependence) that are difficult to integrate visually occur and degrade reliability of invoking visual inspection. Visualization and graphing of data include a variety

---

[2] The importance of small effects is easy to illustrate. For example, in searching for fuels that will replace fossil fuel, sunlight has been thought to hold unrealized promise. The ability to convert sunlight to electricity has been a very small effect—reliable but small. That is, there was only 15% efficiency; in other words, turning sunlight into energy is hardly worth it, given the cost it takes to produce. However, that this conversion of sunlight to energy could be accomplished on any scale was important as a test of principle in looking for options for energy alternatives to fossil fuel. More recently, as the very small effect was studied more, improvements were made that now make conversion a large effect (approximately 40% efficiency). That is, there is the ability to convert sunlight to electricity on a scale of efficiency that is quite different from the early demonstrations. It would have harmed progress to use a filter for data evaluation that only would have identified large effects both for basic research and application.

of options that have not been explored in single-case research. Some of the options include ways to present the data based on nonlinear smoothing of the data, providing transformations, and methods to detect cyclical patterns, noise, and outliers among the data points (e.g., Clarke, Fokoue, & Zhang, 2009; Cleveland, 1993, 1994; Velleman, 1980). Many of the options have mathematical underpinnings that might have made Euclid change careers. However, there are user-friendly software graphing packages that allow exploration of many different ways to graph the data and to understand and reveal underlying properties (e.g., www.datadesk.com, www.wavemetrics.com). The options for presentation of data are beyond the scope of this discussion. I mention them because visual inspection in single-case research has yet to exploit the graphing and transformation options that might well provide more reliable ways of evaluating the data.

The ongoing research on visual inspection within single-case designs has not reduced reliance on this method of data evaluation. From issues related to unreliability of visual inspection, many researchers have concluded that some alternatives are needed. One not pursued that I have mentioned previously are the many options for graphing, modeling, and presenting data. The option that has been pursued is the use of statistical tests for the single case.

Statistical Analyses

Concerns about applying visual inspection criteria reliably are not the sole impetus for turning more to statistical analyses. Other developments have set the stage for increased use of statistics. First, single-case designs have expanded beyond the boundaries of behavioral research, and that has led to some changes directly related to use of statistical tests. The designs were restricted to one or two journals and disciplines in the late 1960s when the field (applied behavior analysis) that made these designs prominent emerged. Currently, many journals publish single-case research reflecting a range of disciplines (education, school psychology, clinical psychology, rehabilitation, occupational therapy, recreational therapy, internal medicine, psychiatry, social work, and more). Expansion of the methodology to new areas of work has led to expansion of other aspects of the methodology as well.

I mentioned that it is useful to consider research methodology as comprised of three broad components: assessment, experimental design, and data evaluation. Traditionally, these were very tightly intertwined. Single-case methodology included assessment meaning direct observation of behavior, experimental design meaning single-case designs, of course, and data evaluation meaning visual inspection. Yet, the extension of the designs to other areas has led to expansion of assessments in terms of format (e.g., not just behavioral measures but also self-report, clinician ratings) and domains of assessment (e.g., cognitive processes, experience of anxiety), as I illustrated in earlier chapters. The expansion includes a willingness to consider using statistical tests and slight discomfort with the somewhat ambiguous decision-making guidelines for using visual inspection. Also, for some researchers, the utility of single-case designs stems in part from not having to adopt behavioral assessment (which may not be the goal) or visual inspection (which violates the training of most researchers).

Second, changes within statistical evaluation in between-group research have had implications for evaluation of visual inspection. From the very inception of the development of tests of statistical significance in between-group research, there has been concern about the limitations. Statistical significance is dependent on sample size, gives a binary decision, and does not say anything about the magnitude or strength of the effect. One can readily conclude there is no effect (not statistically significant) when in fact there is (called Type II error). Spanning decades but exerting influence more recently has been the view that statistical significance should be supplemented by, if not replaced with, some measure of the magnitude of effect (Kirk, 1996). How large an effect is can be distinguished from whether the effect was statistically significant. Effect size has been the measure of magnitude of effect frequently advocated and does not suffer the same problems as does statistical significance. Many journals that publish mostly between-group intervention research encourage or require that the results include measures of effect size.[3]

A related development has been the proliferation of meta-analysis. Meta-analysis is a way of reviewing and integrating empirical studies on a given topic by translating the results of these studies (e.g., changes on outcome measures, differences among groups) to a common metric (effect size). This allows the reviewer (meta-analyst) to draw conclusions about the findings in a given area and to quantify the strength of effects. In addition, one can ask questions about the data from many studies combined that were not addressed in any of the individual studies included in the meta-analysis. Thus novel findings can emerge from a meta-analysis. Between-group researchers engaged in intervention research are encouraged or required to provide effect size information, depending on the journal and discipline. Even when researchers do not provide that information, often effect sizes can be obtained from other statistics that are in the original article (e.g., means, standard deviations for various measures). This information is used for meta-analyses.

Contrast the situation with single-case designs and the use of visual inspection. Visual inspection from one study to the next does not provide a systematic way of integrating and combining many studies or of asking new questions based on a large integrated database. Without some formal, replicable way of combining studies, much of the single-case work is neglected or viewed as difficult to integrate. Over the years, many researchers have proposed effect size measures for single-case designs (e.g., Busse, Kratochwill, & Elliott, 1995; Kromrey & Foster-Johnson, 1996; White et al., 1989). In fact, a recent review noted that over 40 different approaches for measuring effect size have been proposed for single-case research (Swaminathan et al., 2008). None has been widely adopted and only recently have some of the alternatives been carefully evaluated and compared (e.g., Manolov & Solanas, 2008a; Parker & Brossart, 2003; Parker & Hagan-Burke, 2007b). In short, there is no recommended method of computing effect size in single-case designs that is readily available and ready for prime time. The absence of a clear and widely used way of computing effect size limits the ability to accumulate and combine findings from single-case studies and integrating findings

---

[3] Effect size can be measured in many ways. The advantages of using effect size and alternative ways effect size can be measured and computed are discussed in several resources (e.g., Kazdin, 2003; Kirk, 1996; Schmidt, 1996; Wilkinson and Task Force on Statistical Inference, 1999). The present discussion does not depend on the use of a specific index of effect size.

of single-case and between-group studies. This too is quite relevant background of the current interest in using statistical tests.

Finally, more and more studies use statistical tests to analyze single-case data, sometimes along with visual inspection (e.g., Bradshaw, 2003; Feather & Ronan, 2006; Levesque et al., 2004; Molloy, 1990; Quesnel, Savard, Simard, Ivers, & Morin, 2003). Also, many articles have emerged that present new statistical tests for the single case, reanalyze prior data from published studies, or present new data to illustrate the analyses. Some of these articles compare multiple single-case statistical tests (e.g., Brossart et al., 2006; Parker & Brossart, 2003; Parker & Hagan-Burke, 2007a, 2007b). While it remains the case that visual inspection dominates, statistical evaluation has been on the march.

Two summary points ought to be emphasized in relation to the use of statistical tests. First, such tests represent an alternative to or a complementary method of evaluating the results of a single-case experiment. Second, statistical evaluation can permit accumulation of knowledge from many different investigations, even if they do not all use the same statistical tests. Enormous gains have been made in between-group research by looking at large literatures and drawing quantitatively based conclusions. Combining studies that use visual inspection to reach conclusions and pose and answer new questions from such a data set have yet to emerge in single-case research. Findings from visual inspection risk continued neglect from a broad scientific community if they cannot be integrated in a way that effect size has permitted in between-group research. The solution is not merely applying currently used effect size estimates and applying them to single-case research. Characteristics of single-case assessments and data (e.g., ongoing assessments, influence of the number of data points, serial dependence, as discussed below) make the usual formula not directly applicable (see Shadish, Rindskopf, & Hedges, 2008).

Serial Dependence in Single-Case Data

The context for statistical analysis pertains to the nature of single-case data. Single-case data are based on continuous observations over time for the same subject. This results in a characteristic of the data that is different from one or two observations collected from many subjects as in between-group research. The difference has implications for what statistics can be applied and how they can be applied.

The beginning point for statistical evaluation in single-case research is recognition of the structural feature referred to as *serial dependence*. Serial dependence refers to the relation of the data points to each other in the series of continuous observations. The dependence reflects the fact that the residuals (error) in the data points are correlated (or can be) from one occasion to the next. The dependence is measured by evaluating whether the data are correlated over time. This can be accomplished in different ways. The usual method is correlating the data by pairing adjacent data points (Days 1 and 2, Days 2 and 3, Days 3 and 4, etc.) and computing a correlation coefficient. The correlation is referred to as *autocorrelation* and is a measure of serial dependence. Correlating Days 1 and 2, 2 and 3, and so on is only one way to compute the correlation. To understand the data and how serial dependence operates, one can compute the relation of data points with different amounts of time (called lags) between them. For example, one could have a 2-day lag and correlate Days 1 and 3, 2 and 4, 3 and 5, and so on. The point to make here is conveyed by just considering the adjacent points, but many different lags (1, 2, and 3 days, etc.) can give a complete picture of the series. The different lags can detect characteristics of the data such as cycles that may be repetitive but not encompassed merely by correlating adjacent data points (1-day lag).

What is the autocorrelation? Autocorrelation is a correlation and can range from −1.00 to +1.00. Trends in the data tend to indicate that there is autocorrelation, but I mentioned previously that not all trends in the data can be detected visually (Parker et al., 2006). Autocorrelation can be negative as well as positive. Autocorrelation that is statistically significant can be used to define whether there is serial dependence in the data.[4]

Serial dependence is important to know for two reasons. First, the presence of serial dependence precludes the straightforward application of statistical techniques with which we are most familiar. For example, conventional t and F tests make several assumptions that we learned in our early training (e.g., homogeneity of variances of the groups, normally distributed data, independence of the error terms). We also learned that the data analyses are "robust" (from the Latin *robustus* "strong and hardy" and derived further from the word for oak). Although few of us grasped what that meant, we knew that violating the assumptions was not a huge problem and that a little violation of a statistical assumption here or there would not lead to an arrest. Moreover, for some of the assumptions, there are tricks (e.g., data transformation) one can use if the assumption is violated. In other words, we learned quickly that there are assumptions but if they are violated that is not a problem. There is an exception to all of this, namely, the assumption that the error terms (residuals) of the observations are uncorrelated. Violation of this assumption *does* make a difference and precludes the appropriate use of conventional t and F tests. If the autocorrelation is positive, standard errors that are used as part of statistical tests (i.e., the error term or denominator for the statistic) become smaller than they ought to be, and the results (t or F test) will be larger or biased in a positive degree. That is, more Type I errors will be made (i.e., showing a statistically significant effect when there would not have been one). If the autocorrelation is negative, standard errors will be large, and the overall t or F will be smaller than it would have otherwise been. This will lead to more Type II errors (i.e., showing no significant effect when there actually was one).

Second and related, if serial dependence exists in the data, the analysis needs to take that into account. The dependence reflects some trend or pattern in the underlying data. It may not be a simple linear trend, but a trend perhaps jolted by random effects and only detected across different lags. A data-analytic technique is needed to

---

[4] The reliance on a statistically significant correlation to make a decision about serial dependence has its risks. The significance of a correlation is highly dependent on the number of observations (degrees of freedom). If few observations (e.g., baseline of 10 days) are available to compute autocorrelation, it is quite possible that the resulting correlation would not be statistically significant. Serial dependence might be evident in the series (if that series were continued), but the limited number of observations may make the obtained correlation fail to reach significance. Autocorrelation is calculated on the residuals, which is accomplished by some statistical tests. In this discussion, I am focusing on autocorrelation of the raw data rather than of the residuals. Autocorrelation of the raw data is very likely to reflect dependence in the residuals.

account for the dependence and to discern whether any intervention effect is evident over and above some overarching but possibly subtle pattern. As I noted previously, vision and visual inspection are not up to the task.

Although it would be useful to begin with clear rules, there are important caveats instead. Not all time-series data show autocorrelation. This is an empirical matter, and one needs to test this. A difficulty is that single-case designs often do not include a sufficiently long baseline phase to compute the correlations and understand the model underlying the data (Matyas & Greenwood, 1997). Continuous data (also called time-series data) in many other disciplines (e.g., climate change, economics, dendrology [study of trees]) actually do have huge data sets that allow for understanding the structure of the series. In single-case research one usually wants to draw on the baseline data for computing autocorrelations, because the intervention phase introduces a new influence that could change the pattern.

Some time ago, the extent to which single-case data are likely to show serial dependence was debated (see Matyas & Greenwood, 1991; Sideridis & Greenwood, 1997), although estimates have ranged from approximately 10% to 80% of single-case data sets in published studies. Such variability conveys that there are other issues here, such as how autocorrelation is computed and the length of phases included in the study that might influence the conclusions. The current verdict after several studies is that serial dependence is likely to be present and ought to be taken into account in evaluation of the data. To do that requires statistical techniques that are not straightforward, as highlighted shortly. What has been of special interest perhaps is that serial dependence influences both visual inspection and statistical evaluation of the data.

STATISTICAL TESTS FOR SINGLE-CASE RESEARCH

Visual inspection criteria alert us to the types of changes we would like to detect including changes in means (across phases), trends, change in level (discontinuity of performance from one phase to the next), and latency of change. Characteristics of single-case data (e.g., serial dependence) and the likelihood of brief phases (few data points) alert us to features that have to be accommodated. Identifying a single statistical test or family of statistical tests that can accommodate these criteria and characteristics satisfactorily has yet to occur. In between-group research, there has been dominance of *t*, *F*, and all the related least-squares statistical analysis tests that have brought uniformity—indeed complacency—to research studies. That does not seem to be likely in single-case research in the immediate future.

Sampling of the Many Tests

There has been an enormous expansion of statistical tests for the single case in the past few decades. Table A.1 lists several of the tests to convey the point. The tests vary in precisely what aspects of the data they evaluate (e.g., changes in means, trend), how or whether they handle serial dependence, and whether they can be applied without lengthy phases that provide sufficient data within each phase.

Recent work conveys the flux and advances in statistical tests for the single case. The strengths and limitations of many of the tests have only begun to be scrutinized. A literature has emerged in which the tests are evaluated by applying them across different conditions. Often hypothetical data are generated to permit the evaluation of how

Table A.1 Selected Statistical Tests Available for the Single-Case Designs

Name	Resources
Binomial Test	White & Haring, 1980
C Statistic	Jones, 2003; Satake et al., 2008; Tryon, 1982
Clinical Outcome Indices	Parker & Hagan-Burke, 2007a
Conventional t, F, & χ^2 tests	Virtually any statistics book on between-group research; Satake et al., 2008
Double Bootstrap Method	McKnight, McKean, & Huitema, 2000
Last Treatment Day Technique	White et al., 1989
Logistic Regression	Brossert et al., 2008
Mean Baseline Reduction/Increment (for decreases and increases in behavior, respectively)	Lundervold & Bourland, 1988
Mean-only/mean-plus Trend Models	Allison & Gorman, 1993; Center, Skiba, & Casey, 1985–1986; Faith, Allison, & Gorman, 1997
Percent Zero Score (or 100%) for decreases and increases in behavior, respectively	Scotti, Evans, Meyer, & Walker, 1991
Percentage of Nonoverlapping Data Points	Busk & Serlin, 1992; Ma, 2006; Mastropieri & Scruggs, 1985–86; Wolery et al., 2008
Randomization Tests	Edgington & Onghena, 2007; Lall & Levin, 2004; Levin & Wampold, 1999
R_n Test of Ranks	Revusky, 1967
Split-Middle Technique	Fisher, Kelley, & Lomas, 2003; White 1972, 1974
Time-Series Analyses	Borckardt et al., 2008; Box et al., 1994; Glass et al., 1975; Hartmann et al., 1980
Trend Analysis Effect Size	Faith et al., 1997; Gorsuch, 1983

Notes: The list is not intended to be comprehensive. Several listings in the table are not individual tests but rather tests with multiple variations. In cases where more than one citation is provided, multiple variations of that test can be found. Where possible, I have tried to give recent references or readily available references rather than necessarily identify the first source in which a particular analysis might have been identified or recommended. Some tests in the table may be familiar because they are used in group data and between-group research. Inclusion of such tests here means that they have been applied to individual subjects. In several articles, the yields from multiple tests and their sensitivity to detecting change are compared under different conditions (see Brossart et al., 2006; J. M. Campbell, 2004; Lall & Levin, 2004; Manolov & Solanas, 2008a; Parker & Brossart, 2003; Parker et al., 2005).

the statistic performs under multiple data patterns (strength of intervention effect) and with diverse characteristics of the data (serial dependence, long vs. short duration phases). When data are taken from published studies, sometimes only the AB phases are evaluated. Several studies compared multiple statistical tests for the same data set (e.g., Brossart et al., 2006; Campbell, 2004; Lall & Levin, 2004; Manolov & Solanas, 2008a; Parker & Brossart, 2003; Parker et al., 2005). For example, in one excellent evaluation of five different statistical tests applied to the same data, the authors concluded that the results of the different methods varied so much as to preclude clear guidelines (Brossart et al., 2006). Different statistical tests emphasize different characteristics of the data (e.g., means, trends, last data point in the phase) and vary in their susceptibility to autocorrelation. What is important to note is that no one method emerges as suitable under all of the conditions, given variations in the magnitude of intervention effects and of autocorrelation, duration of the phases, and different designs. This is an area of active research and perhaps from that some subset of analyses will emerge. However, clear guidelines for what tests to use and when to use them are not easy to draw from this literature at this time.

Progress has been made in the past few decades and more recently in clarifying the problems. Also, among what has been learned is not only that conventional t and F tests are subject to misinterpretation because of serial dependence, but also that other tests (randomization tests, rank tests, split-middle technique) can be influenced as well. In short, since the first writing of this book, research has elaborated characteristics of single-case data, has clarified the scope of the impact of serial dependence, and has begun to evaluate alternative data-analytic strategies to accomplish the goals of visual inspection but more reliably. The burgeoning literature has not helped in generating guidelines regarding what tests to use and when to use them. If anything, the literature points to caution in relying on any one of the methods currently available.

Time-Series Analysis: Illustration

Many of the available tests are still undergoing evaluation, and new variations are emerging. Consequently, I have referred the reader to other sources where details of the analyses and their variations are provided (please see Table A.1). As an exception, I am highlighting time-series analysis for several reasons. First, variations of time-series analysis have been used and continue to be used for single-case data over a period spanning decades (e.g., Borckardt et al., 2008; Levesque et al., 2004; McSweeney, 1978; Savard et al., 1998; Schnelle, Kirchner, McNees, & Lawler, 1975). Consequently, while many statistical tests for the single case are only now being proposed and evaluated, time-series analysis stands out with a literature that can be consulted by interested researchers. Second, the method has been used in other disciplines and hence is developed well beyond the special use of single-case research. Third, statistical package software (e.g., SPSS, SAS, Systat, Statistica, Stata) include time-series analyses; hence the method is readily available. Finally, time-series analysis directly addresses serial dependence in the data and accommodates its impact.

Description. Time-series analysis compares data over time for separate phases for an individual subject or group of subjects (see Box & Jenkins, 1976; Box et al., 1994; Glass, Willson, & Gottman, 1975; Hartmann et al., 1980; Jones, Vaught, & Weinrott, 1977). The analysis examines whether there is a statistically significant change in level and trend from one phase to the next. Thus, the change is from phase A to B. The analysis can be applied to single-case designs in which there is a change in conditions across phases. All the phases can be examined; not just the first two phases of a design. For example, in ABAB designs, separate comparisons can be made for each set of adjacent phases (e.g., A_1B_1, A_2B_2, B_1A_2). In multiple-baseline designs, baseline (A) and treatment (B) phases may be implemented across different responses, persons, or situations.

Consider an example that permits evaluation of the data via visual inspection as well as time-series analysis. This study focused on the effectiveness of a cognitive-behavioral treatment (CBT) for insomnia among women treated for nonmetastatic breast cancer (Quesnel et al., 2003). Sleep disturbances are one of many psychological problems associated with the impact of cancer and characterize 30 to 50% of the patients. Patients participated if they completed radiation or chemotherapy and met diagnostic criteria for Chronic Insomnia Disorder (by criteria of *the International Classification of Diseases* or the *Diagnostic and Statistical Manual of Mental Disorders*). Several measures were used involving multiple assessment methods including clinical interviews, self-report daily diary and questionnaires, and electrophysiology (polysomnography) of sleep evaluated in a sleep lab. The intervention consisted of CBT conducted in eight weekly group sessions, approximately 90 minutes each. CBT included several components (stimulus control for insomnia, coping strategies, restructuring of dysfunctional thoughts). At pretreatment, posttreatment, and each follow-up assessment an extensive battery of measures was completed. Electrophysiological measures of sleep were obtained at pretreatment, posttreatment, and the 6-month follow-up.

Figure A.1 charts one of the continuous measures that consisted of a daily sleep diary kept by patients. The measure was used to report several characteristics of sleep (e.g., use of alcohol or medication, bedtime hour, duration of awakenings, and others). As evident in the figure, CBT was introduced in a multiple-baseline design across participants. The results suggest through visual inspection that introduction of treatment was associated with decreases in total wake time, although the effects are less clear for Participants 6 and 7. One can see that gains for those who responded to treatment appeared to be maintained at the follow-up periods.

Time-series analyses evaluated the statistical significance of the change for each participant across AB (baseline, treatment) phases. The analysis was selected because it takes into account serial dependence, can detect reliable intervention effects even if the effects are small, and evaluates changes in level and slope. Table A.2 reproduces information that corresponds to the data graphed in Figure A.1. For present purposes, consider the final two columns that convey whether the changes in level or slope were statistically significant. For all eight participants, either level or slope changed significantly when treatment was introduced. The statistical analyses convey that there was a reliable treatment effect; the complexity of the effect (level for some, slope for others) provides information that would be difficult to discern from visual inspection. Several other analyses were completed (and not discussed here) that demonstrated reductions in depression and physical fatigue and improved cognitive functioning. Measured but not part of the intervention, patients who had used sleep medication during the study stopped on their own while receiving CBT. At posttreatment and again at the 6-month follow-up, electrophysiological measures in the sleep lab revealed significant decreases in time awake and increases in sleep efficiency (proportion of time sleeping out of time in bed).

Time-series analysis was very helpful in evaluating data in which there was considerable variability for some of the participants in both baseline and intervention phases. Also, possible trends in the data and autocorrelation were modeled and handled by the analysis. Any trends in baseline, whether or not they could be easily detected by visual inspection, were readily incorporated in evaluating changes from A to B phases. Perhaps one might argue that visual inspection would have been able to detect changes, perhaps for Participants 2, 3, and 5 where the effects are among the clearest. Even here some statistic is needed to handle the invisible autocorrelation and trends that are not

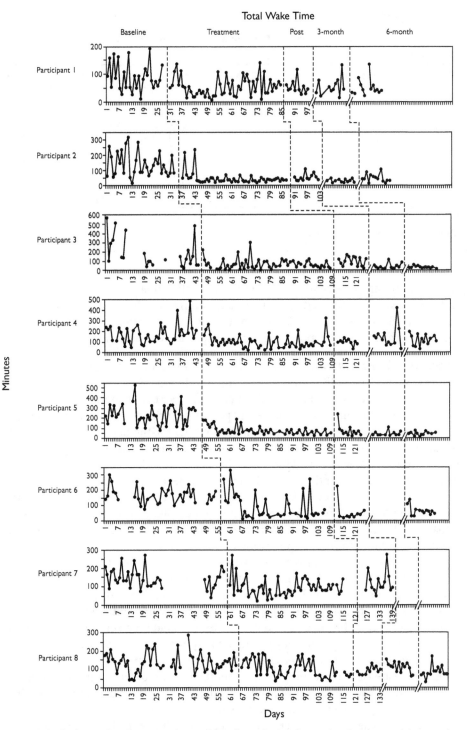

Figure A.1. Daily total wake time obtained by sleep diaries for each of eight participants who completed treatment. Missing data (e.g., baseline, Participant 7) reflects absence of the diary for those days. Treatment was cognitive-behavior therapy introduced in a multiple-baseline design across participants. *(Source: Quesnel et al., 2003.)*

Table A.2 Summary of the Results of Time-Series Analysis for One of the Measures (Total Wake Time) for Eight Participants

Variable and Participant	df	Outliers	R^2 (%)	Level (t test)	Slope (t test)
Total wake time					
I	85	4	42.6	−2.44*	0.30
2	92	5	73.6	−5.95**	0.23
3	87	5	77.2	−5.20**	1.34
4	112	3	59.2	1.48	−4.31**
5	114	2	73.0	−0.48	−7.44**
6	97	5	75.4	−0.23	−5.45**
7	100	2	42.9	−5.64**	1.17
8	114	1	40.5	1.35	−3.45**

*$p < .05.$ **$p < .01.$

(*Source:* Quesnel et al., 2003.)

simple ascending or descending straight lines. Baseline treatments need to be modeled in the analysis. By "modeled" I mean an algorithm is needed that best describes any pattern of data in baseline; this is required to determine whether intervention reflects a significant change. This is more than visual inspection can accomplish.

Important Considerations. The analysis makes some demands on the investigator that may dictate the utility of time-series analysis in any particular instance. To begin with, the design depends on having a sufficient number of data points. The data points are needed to determine the existence and pattern of serial dependence in the data and to derive the appropriate time-series analysis model for the data. The actual number of data points needed within each phase has been debated, and estimates have ranged from 20 to 100 (e.g., Box & Jenkins, 1970; Glass et al., 1975; Hartmann et al., 1980; Jones et al., 1977). Variations of time-series analysis have been used in which a smaller number of observations is required. For example, in one variation a minimum of 10 to 16 observations totaled across baseline and intervention phases (e.g., five to eight observations in each phase) is required (Borckardt et al., 2008). Consequently, shorter phase durations have not precluded application of the analysis.

In many single-case experiments, phases are relatively brief. For example, in an ABAB design, the second A phase may be relatively brief because of the problems associated with returning behavior to baseline levels. Similarly, in a multiple-baseline design, the initial baseline phases for some of the behaviors (individuals or situations) may be brief so that the intervention will not be withheld for a very long time. In these instances, too few data points may preclude the application of time-series analysis.

Second and related, time series is not a matter of plugging in numbers into a formula. There are steps performed on the data (by the computer program) that include model building, model estimation, and checking of the model against the data. Within these steps are contained such tasks as how to best describe the pattern of autocorrelation, what estimates of parameters are needed to maximize the fit of the model to the data, and once estimated how the model has contained, addressed, or removed autocorrelation. Once these are complete the analysis can test changes in level and slope that are associated with the intervention. Returning to a prior point, one reason many data points are recommended for the analysis is to execute these initial steps and provide a good estimate of the model and parameters that fit the data. From this very cursory description, one can see that there is much to understand about time-series analyses. Multiple models are available. Although software allows one to enter the data, it is important to understand the steps along the way to the final result and selection of the model. Results can vary as a function of accepting or not accepting default options within a program. Significance or lack of significance could easily be de-fault of the investigator if she or he is not informed.

Time-series analysis is especially useful when the idealized data requirements and criteria for visual inspection are not met. When there is a trend in the therapeutic direction in baseline, when variability is large, or when treatment effects are neither rapid nor marked, time-series analysis may be especially useful. Also, the analysis is especially useful when the investigator is interested in drawing conclusions about changes in either level or trend. As reviewed previously, considerable data suggest that trend is not easily detected by visual inspection once one moves beyond simple ascending or descending straight lines.

Time-series analysis represents an option, but I do not wish to imply it is a panacea for data evaluation for the single case. Among the cautions, time-series is not an analysis but rather a family of options and there lies the rub. There is no single way of doing the analysis that can be recommended as widely applicable across most designs or data sets. There are multiple options and decisions (e.g., how to model the data) and it is likely that these will yield different results. The availability of many examples already published can provide concrete illustrations of some of the options.

OBSTACLES TO USING STATISTICAL TESTS

Many Options, Few Guidelines

Several options are available for statistical analyses, and any investigator interested in an analysis has choices. It is important to note that although more analyses and more reports of statistical analyses of single-case research have become available, there is not a groundswell movement among those who use single-case designs to adopt any of them. It is not difficult to explain why. First, there are very few resources available that explain the statistics for the single case in a straightforward way and show how to apply them. Some of the analyses I have listed (Table A.1) have only one or two references showing how to use the analysis with single-case data. Yes there are exceptions for some of the tests where they are clearly described and illustrated. Randomization tests and time-series analysis, already mentioned, are two examples. For many other tests listed in the table, there are a few studies to provide guidance, even though without such guidance the procedures are not all that complex to apply. Even so, more resources are needed, especially when considered against the backdrop of what is available for other statistics more commonly used in between-group research. For between-group researchers popular statistical packages (e.g., SPSS, SAS) include multiple-statistical techniques for data evaluation, are constantly revised, and serve as one-stop shopping for many faculty members, postdocs, and graduate students doing empirical research. Software packages compete in their comprehensiveness of coverage and ease of use. In the case of single-case research, software is available to address specific tests, but there is nothing with the scope of coverage and ease of use that the more familiar statistical packages provide.

Second, single-case statistical tests and their application are not straightforward. There are many different tests and within a test (e.g., randomization, time-series analysis) many different versions. The options are daunting in part because what test is selected can make a huge difference. When different statistical tests are used to evaluate the same single-case data, quite different conclusions can be reached (e.g., Nourbakhsh & Ottenbacher, 1994; Parker & Brossart, 2003). Even if the "same" test is used but makes different assumptions or focuses on slightly different features of the data, the results can be quite different (e.g., Lall & Levin, 2004; Manolov & Solanas, 2008a, 2008b). Sometimes seeming nuances of the data set, such as the number of observations in a phase or the degree of autocorrelation, determine the extent to which there is likely to be bias (e.g., Type I error) in the conclusion and make a particular single-case statistic ill-advised or inappropriate (Sierra, Solanas, & Quera, 2005). Such issues are only now being elaborated, but for the person who seeks guidance in selecting a statistical test, I regret I cannot be more helpful.

One of the objections to visual inspection, noted in Chapter 12, was that the method is too subjective. Statistical tests, so the argument went, provide a more objective way of evaluating the data. There is a way in which this is definitely true. For the most part, once a statistical test is selected, the yield (decision rule about statistical significance) is more objective (e.g., automatic) than visual inspection. Yet, as the research highlighted in this appendix conveys, which statistical test is selected makes an enormous difference and can lead to varied and opposing conclusions about the impact of the intervention.

Related, matching specific tests to specific designs is not straightforward. Studies that have elaborated statistical analyses for the single-case commonly use AB phases as the paradigm to illustrate what the statistic does and how it works. Many graphs, sometimes hundreds, are generated by a computer to allow the systematic inclusion of various characteristics of the data. It is important to understand how various statistics operate, how autocorrelations of various magnitudes influence conclusions, and how different statistical tests compare with each other. However, in the trenches, we do single-case designs that are ABAB, changing-criterion, and multi-treatment designs; we have subphases (e.g., as we change the criterion repeatedly) or many different baselines (e.g., multiple-baseline across behaviors, individuals, and contexts); and we introduce another intervention (C) to see if we can have stronger impact than our first intervention (B). At this point in the emerging field of statistics for single-case designs, there are no clear guidelines to match designs and statistical tests. AB phase methods of data analysis do not automatically map on or transfer to the design applications that are used. For example, is a multiple-baseline design across three behaviors merely three AB designs with staggered applications of B? Do we evaluate each AB separately? That is not what the design intends to show. Also, the correlations in the data (autocorrelation) are not just within the data of one baseline. If this is a multiple-baseline across three (or more) behaviors (for the same individual) or one behavior for one individual in three (or more) settings, are all the baselines likely to bear some relation? Is there multiple autocorrelation—or perhaps we could draw from the coffee shops and ask, is there a "double autocorrelation grande with latte" we should worry about? As these questions emerge in relation to real data sets from single-case designs, one-eyed visual inspection in a very dark room while wearing a sleep mask is starting to look not so bad.

Finally, there are few training opportunities in single-case research methods, leaving aside the more esoteric topic of the statistics that might be used to analyze single-case data. Graduate training programs in education, psychology, counseling, school psychology, occupational and physical therapy, and other areas where such designs are applied are not likely even to mention single-case research designs, let alone actively teach a course in them. The challenge in preparing students for research careers is making sure they are skilled and fluent in quantitative, null hypothesis testing research methods, that is, the Esperanto of science. This means between-group designs and data-analytic techniques. Within the quantitative tradition, there is so much to teach. Ongoing advances (e.g., meditational analyses, growth curves, hierarchical linear modeling, structural equation modeling, instrumental variable techniques, propensity score matching, latent transition analysis) must constantly be added to the canon to prepare students competently. There is little time to train in other traditions (single-case experimental designs, qualitative research) given the scope of courses already required.

One of my prior arguments favoring the use of statistical tests was to identify reliable effects in single-case designs that did not meet the requirements of visual inspection. I argued that small but reliable effects could be important for all sorts of reasons. We know from research on visual inspection that judges often disagree when intervention effects are not very strong. Less clear is whether statistics for single-case designs can do appreciably better. Statistical analyses often raise issues such as power where sample size (e.g., number of observations) may be important and detecting a difference is a function of many factors beyond the impact of the intervention. How well will single-case statistical tests fare when trying to detect smaller effects that cannot be readily agreed on by visual inspection? Sufficient work is not available to answer this, but perhaps a preview can be seen from a few studies that indicate that some statistical tests will not be very useful or have sufficient statistical power unless effect sizes are very large (> 2.0) (e.g., Ferron & Sentovich, 2002; Manolov & Solanas, 2009).[5] That may be an exception or be restricted to all sorts of other conditions, but we are still in need of basic research that can result in practical advice to guide us.

Recommendations

Many years ago in evaluating statistical tests for single-case designs, I recommended the use of time-series analyses whenever possible (Kazdin, 1976, 1984). I have very much tried to resist the same recommendation this time because change in one's position at least conveys the illusion of progress in one's thinking. Also, in fact, since that time statistical tests for single-case designs have become an extraordinarily active area of research. I have mentioned many studies that compare alternative tests in evaluating

---

[5] An effect size of 2.0 would be considered to be very large. To place this in context, arbitrary but still commonly used guidelines note that small, medium, and large effect sizes correspond to .2, .5, and .8 (Cohen, 1988). Recall that in between-group research this is the difference between the intervention and control group as expressed in standard deviation units. As a benchmark, psychotherapy for adults when compared to no treatment produces an effect size of approximately .7, meaning that the distributions for these groups would have their means this far apart in standard deviation units.

real and simulated single-case data to understand and elaborate our options. At this time, at least from my readings, no statistical analysis has emerged clearly to recommend. Indeed, some of my earlier recommendations in the first edition of this book (e.g., rank tests, randomization tests) over the years have been shown to be influenced by serial dependence and hence raise more cautions. Time-series analysis is a very reasonable option that is better understood and used than are other analyses. Thus, one has a literature from which to draw and compare. Also, as evident in the illustration provided previously with cancer patients, the analysis can be used with real data, in real designs, with real clinical problems. There are other such applications that could be readily provided (e.g., Levesque et al., 2004; Savard et al., 1998). All that said, as I mentioned time-series analyses require multiple steps including estimation of models and parameters to fit the data and use of these to make the tests to evaluate change. A commitment in time is needed to understand what is going on under the hood as the computer spews out estimates and tables and whether the analysis is a good test in light of constraints of the data and the options within the analysis. Dare I say it, there is some visual inspection needed of the options to decide which among them is the most appropriate.

We know that when intervention effects from single-case data are not crystal clear, application of visual inspection criteria may not be reliable. We also know that single-case data are likely to be serially dependent and that this can misguide both visual inspection and statistical evaluation. In particular, trend is especially difficult to detect when evaluating visual inspection data unless there is a straight ascending or descending line formed by the data points. With these considerations in mind, it would be prudent to use more than one means of evaluating the data as the design permits, that is, both visual inspection and statistical analysis and perhaps time-series analysis if available as an option.

There is a compromise position I have not elaborated. Perhaps visual inspection will remain the primary method of evaluating single-case data but with statistical aids to facilitate their evaluation. The aids are not statistical tests that operate as an independent way to test the reliability of the finding. Rather, they may help apply visual inspection in a manner that is more reliable. For example, visual inspection is particularly weak in identifying complex trends and taking trends into account in evaluating the intervention (see Fisch, 2001). Perhaps we could provide techniques to aid visual inspection that plotted trends or used alternative ways of making visually hidden trends more apparent. Many different ways of computing and evaluating trends are available with the goal of aiding visual inspection. At this point, some applications have helped enhance the reliability of visual inspection (W. W. Fisher et al., 2003), but others have not (e.g., Borckardt, Murphy, Nash, & Shaw, 2004). Novel methods continue to be sought and might well bear fruit (e.g., Parker et al., 2006), but no firm recommendation is yet available to guide us to a compromise position. Visual aids have their own merit but cannot take the place of analyses that assess the reliability of the change.

CONCLUSIONS

The entire area of statistical evaluation for single-case designs has received increased attention in the past 10 years. The use of these statistical tests, discussion of the problems they raise, and suggestions for the development of alternative statistical techniques are likely to increase greatly in the future. We will need that work because little in the way of concrete recommendations can be provided.

The issue of major significance is suiting the statistic to the design. Statistical tests for any research may impose special requirements on the design in terms of how, when, to whom, and how long the intervention is to be applied. In basic laboratory research with non-human and human animals, the requirements of the designs can largely dictate how the experiment is arranged and conducted. In applied settings where many single-case designs are used, practical constraints (e.g., in the classroom) often make it difficult to implement various design requirements such as reversal phases or withholding treatment for an extended period on one of the several baselines. Some of the statistical tests mentioned in this appendix also make special design requirements such as including extended phases (time-series analysis) or randomly alternating treatment and no-treatment conditions (randomization tests). A decision must be made well in advance of a single-case investigation as to whether these and other requirements imposed by the design or by a statistical evaluation technique can be implemented.

The appendix raises multiple considerations for evaluating data in single-case research. A blind adoption of visual inspection or statistical analysis and too strong a preference for one instead of the other, in my opinion, is difficult to justify in light of current data. Each broad method has multiple strengths and weaknesses, and these vary under all sorts of other conditions. We would like simple rules to guide us and to teach our students. We have a couple, perhaps: (1) consider more than one means of evaluating the data, and (2) in relation to visual inspection and statistical analysis, do not take an "either/or" position. Either/or may work well in philosophy (Kirkegaard, 1843), but may not be wise in science.

REFERENCES

Achenbach, T. M. (1991). *Manual for the Child Behavior Checklist/4–18 and 1991 Profile.* Burlington: University of Vermont.

Achenbach, T. M. (2006). As others see us: Clinical and research implications of cross-informant correlations for psychopathology. *Current Directions in Psychological Science, 15,* 94–98.

Ahearn, W. H., Clark, K. M., MacDonald, R. P. F., & Chung, B. I. (2007). Assessing and treating vocal stereotypy in children with autism. *Journal of Applied Behavior Analysis, 40,* 263–275.

Aldwin, C. M., & Gilmer, D. F. (2004). *Health, illness and optimal aging: Biological and psychosocial perspectives.* Thousand Oaks, CA: Sage Publications.

Allen, K. D., & Evans, J. H. (2001). Exposure-based treatment to control excessive blood glucose monitoring. *Journal of Applied Behavior Analysis, 34,* 497–500.

Allison, D. B., & Gorman, B. S. (1993). Calculating effect sizes for meta-analysis: The case of the single case. *Behaviour Research Therapy, 31,* 621–631.

Allport, G. W. (1961). *Pattern and growth in personality.* New York: Holt, Rinehart & Winston.

American Psychiatric Association. (1994). *Diagnostic and statistical manual of mental disorders* (4th ed.). Washington, DC: American Psychiatric Association.

American Psychological Association. (2005). *Policy statement on evidence-based practice in psychology.* Washington, DC: American Psychological Association.

Ardoin, S. P., McCall, M., & Klubnik, C. (2007). Promoting generalization of oral reading fluency: Providing drill versus practice opportunities. *Journal of Behavioral Education, 16,* 55–70.

Ary, D., Covalt, W. C., & Suen, H. K. (1990). Graphic comparisons of interobserver agreement indices. *Journal of Psychopathology and Behavioral Assessment, 12,* 151–156.

Athens, E. S., Vollmer, T. R., & Pipkin, C. C. S. P. (2007). Shaping academic task engagement with percentile schedules. *Journal of Applied Behavior Analysis, 40,* 475–488.

Austin, J., & Carr, J. E. (Eds.). (2000). *Handbook of applied behavior analysis.* Reno, NV: Context Press.

Austin, J., Hackett, S., Gravina, N., & Lebbon, A. (2006). The effects of prompting and feedback on drivers' stopping at stop signs. *Journal of Applied Behavior Analysis, 39,* 117–121.

Ayllon, T. (1963). Intensive treatment of psychotic behavior by stimulus satiation and food reinforcement. *Behaviour Research and Therapy, 1,* 53–61.

Ayllon, T., & Haughton, E. (1964). Modification of symptomatic verbal behavior of mental patients. *Behaviour Research and Therapy, 2,* 87–97.

Ayllon, T., & Michael, J. (1959). The psychiatric nurse as a behavioral engineer. *Journal of the Experimental Analysis of Behavior, 2,* 323–334.

Ayllon, T., & Roberts, M. D. (1974). Eliminating discipline problems by strengthening academic performance. *Journal of Applied Behavior Analysis, 7,* 71–76.

Azrin, N. H., Hontos, P. T., & Besalel-Azrin, V. (1979). Elimination of enuresis without a conditioning apparatus: An extension by office instruction of the child and parents. *Behavior Therapy, 10,* 14–19.

Azrin, N. H., & Peterson, A. L. (1990). Treatment of Tourette's syndrome by habit reversal: A waiting-list control group. *Behavior Therapy, 21,* 305–318.

Baer, D. M. (1977). Perhaps it would be better not to know everything. *Journal of Applied Behavior Analysis, 10,* 167–172.

Baer, D. M., Wolf, M. M., & Risley, T. R. (1968). Some current dimensions of applied behavior analysis. *Journal of Applied Behavior Analysis, 1,* 91–97.

Baer, D. M., Wolf, M. M., & Risley, T. R. (1987). Some still-current dimensions of applied behavior analysis. *Journal of Applied Behavior Analysis, 20,* 313–328.

Bargh, J. A., & Morsella, E. (2008). The unconscious mind. *Perspectives on Psychological Science, 3,* 73–79.

Barlow, D. H., & Hayes, S. C. (1979). Alternating treatments design: One strategy for comparing the effects of two treatments in a single subject. *Journal of Applied Behavior Analysis, 12,* 199–210.

Baron, R. M., & Kenny, D. A. (1986). The moderator-mediator variable distinction in social psychological research: Conceptual, strategic, and statistical considerations. *Journal of Personality and Social Psychology, 51,* 1173–1182.

Barton, E. E., Reichow, B., & Wolery, M. (2007). Guidelines for graphing data with Microsoft PowerPoint™. *Journal of Early Intervention, 29,* 320–336.

Basoglu, M., Salcioglu, E., & Livanou, M. (2007). A randomized controlled study of single-session behavioural treatment of earthquake-related Post-traumatic stress Disorder using an earthquake simulator. *Psychological Medicine, 37,* 203–214.

Basoglu, M., Salcioglu, E., & Livanou, M. (2009). Single-case experimental studies of a self-help manual for traumatic stress in earthquake survivors. *Journal of Behavior Therapy and Experimental Psychiatry, 40,* 50–58.

Basoglu, M., Salcioglu, E., Livanou, M., Kalender, D., & Acar, G. (2005). Single-session behavioral treatment of earthquake-related Posttraumatic Stress Disorder: A randomized waiting list controlled trial. *Journal of Traumatic Stress, 18,* 1–11.

Battro, A. M. (2001). *Half a brain is enough: The story of Nico.* Cambridge, UK: Cambridge University Press.

Bearman, P. S., & Bruckner, H. (2005). After the promise: The STD consequences of adolescent virginity pledges. *Journal of Adolescent Health, 36,* 271–278.

Berg, B. L. (2001). *Qualitative research methods for the social sciences* (4th ed.). Needham Heights, MA: Allyn & Bacon.

Bijou, S. W. (1955). A systematic approach to an experimental analysis of young children. *Child Development, 26,* 161–168.

Bijou, S. W. (1957). Patterns of reinforcement and resistance to extinction in young children. *Child Development, 28,* 47–54.

Billette, V., Guay, S., & Marchand, A. (2008). Posttraumatic stress disorder and social support in female victims of sexual assault: The impact of spousal involvement on the efficacy of cognitive-behavioral therapy. *Behavior Modification, 32,* 876–896.

Bisconer, S. W., Green, M., Mallon-Czajka, J., & Johnson, J. S. (2006). Managing aggression in a psychiatric hospital using a behavioural plan: A case study. *Journal of Psychiatric and Mental Health Nursing, 13,* 515–521.

Bjorklund, D. F. (Ed.). (2000). *False-memory creation in children and adults: Theory, research, and implications.* Mahwah, NJ: Lawrence Erlbaum Associates.

Blanton, H., & Jaccard, J. (2006). Arbitrary metrics in psychology. *American Psychologist, 61,* 27–41.

Bolgar, H. (1965). The case study method. In B. B. Wolman (Ed.), *Handbook of clinical psychology.* New York: McGraw-Hill.

Borckardt, J. J., Murphy, M. D., Nash, M. R., & Shaw, D. (2004). An empirical examination of visual analysis procedures for clinical practice evaluation. *Journal of Social Service Research, 30,* 55–73.

Borckardt, J. J., Nash, M. R., Murphy, M. D., Moore, M., Shaw, D., & O'Neil, P. (2008). Clinical practice as natural laboratory for psychotherapy research: A guide to case-based time-series analysis. *American Psychologist, 63,* 77–95.

Boring, E. G. (1957). *A history of experimental psychology* (2nd ed). New York: Appleton-Century-Crofts.

Bouchard, T. J., Jr., Lykken, D. T., McGue, M., Segal, N. L., & Tellegen, A. (1990). Sources of human psychological differences: The Minnesota study of twins reared apart. *Science, 250,* 223–228.

Box, G. E. P., & Jenkins, G. M. (1970). *Time-series analysis: Forecasting and control.* San Francisco: Holden-Day.

Box, G. E. P., & Jenkins, G. (1976). *Time-series analysis: Forecasting and control* (Rev. ed.). San Francisco: Holden-Day.

Box, G. E. P., Jenkins, G. M., & Reinsel, G. C. (1994). *Time-series analysis: Forecasting and control* (3rd ed.). Englewood Cliffs, NJ: Prentice-Hall.

Bradshaw, W. (2003). Use of single-system research to evaluate the effectiveness of cognitive-behavioural treatment of schizophrenia. *British Journal of Social Work, 33,* 885–899.

Brainerd, C. J., & Reyna, V. F. (2005). *The science of false memory*. New York: Oxford University Press.

Brembs, B., Lorenzetti, F. D., Reyes, F. D., Baxter, D. A., & Byrne, J. H. (2002). Operant reward learning in *Aplysia*: Neuronal correlates and mechanisms. *Science, 296*, 1706–1709.

Breuer, J., & Freud, S. (1957). *Studies in hysteria*. New York: Basic Books.

Broemeling, L. D. (2009) *Bayesian methods for measures of agreement*. Boca Raton, FL: Chapman & Hall/Taylor & Francis.

Brooks, A., Todd, A. W., Tofflemoyer, S., & Horner, R. H. (2003). Use of functional assessment and a self-management system to increase academic engagement and work completion. *Journal of Positive Behavior Interventions, 5*, 144–152.

Brossart, D. F., Meythaler, J. M., Parker, R. I., McNamara, J., & Elliott, T. R. (2008). Advanced regression methods for single-case designs: Studying propranolol in the treatment for agitation associated with traumatic brain injury. *Journal of Rehabilitation Psychology, 53*, 357–369.

Brossart, D. F., Parker, R. I., Olson, E. A., & Mahadevan, L. (2006). The relationship between visual analysis and five statistical analyses in a simple AB single-case research design. *Behavior Modification, 30*, 531–563.

Browning, R. M. (1967). A same-subject design for simultaneous comparison of three reinforcement contingencies. *Behaviour Research and Therapy, 5*, 237–243.

Brunswik, E. (1955). Representative design and probabilistic theory in a functional psychology. *Psychological Review, 62*, 193–217.

Busk, P., & Serlin, R. (1992). Meta-analysis for single-participant research. In T. R. Kratochwill & J. R. Levin (Eds.), *Single-case research design and analysis: New directions for psychology and education*. Mahwah, NJ: Lawrence Erlbaum.

Busse, R. T., Kratochwill, T. R., & Elliott, S. N. (1995). Meta-analysis for single-case consultation outcomes: Applications to research and practice. *Journal of School Psychology, 33*, 269–285.

Calder, A. J., Keane, J., Manes, F., Antoun, N., & Young, A. W. (2000). Impaired recognition and experience of disgust following brain injury. *Nature Neuroscience, 3*, 1077–1078.

Cameron, M. J., Shapiro, R. L., & Ainsleigh, S. A. (2005). Bicycle riding: Pedaling made possible through positive behavioral interventions. *Journal of Positive Behavior Interventions, 7*, 153–158.

Campbell, D. T., & Stanley, J. C. (1963). Experimental and quasi-experimental designs for research and teaching. In N. L. Gage (Ed.), *Handbook of research on teaching*. Chicago: Rand McNally.

Campbell, J. M. (2004). Statistical comparison of four effect sizes for single-subject designs. *Behavior Modification, 28*, 234–246.

Carr, J. E., & Burkholder, E. O. (1998). Creating single-subject design graphs with Microsoft Excel™. *Journal of Applied Behavior Analysis, 31*, 245–251.

Carter, N., Holmström, A., Simpanen, M., & Melin, L. (1988). Theft reduction in a grocery store through product identification and graphing of losses for employees. *Journal of Applied Behavior Analysis, 21*, 385–389.

Caspi, A., McClay, J., Moffitt, T. E., Mill, J., Martin, J., Craig, I., Taylor, A., & Poulton, R. (2002). Role of genotype in the cycle of violence in maltreated children. *Science, 297*, 851–854.

Centers for Disease Control and Prevention. (2009). Reduced hospitalizations for acute myocardial infarction after implementation of a smoke-free ordinance—City of Pueblo, Colorado, 2002–2006. *Morbidity and Mortality Weekly Report, 57* (51), 1373–1377.

Center, B. A., Skiba, R. J., & Casey, A. (1985–1986). A methodology for the quantitative synthesis of intra-subject design research. *Journal of Special Education, 19*, 387–400.

Chaddock, R. E. (1925). *Principles and methods of statistics*. Boston: Houghton Mifflin.

Chamberlain, P., & Reid, J. B. (1987). Parent observation and report of child symptoms. *Behavioral Assessment, 9*, 97–109.

Chambless, D. L., & Ollendick, T. H. (2001). Empirically supported psychological interventions: Controversies and evidence. *Annual Review of Psychology, 52*, 685–716.

Chassan, J. B. (1967). *Research design in clinical psychology and psychiatry*. New York: Appleton-Century-Crofts.

Chassin, L., Presson, C. C., Sherman, S. J., Montello, D., & McGrew, J. (1986). Changes in peer and parent influence during adolescence: Longitudinal versus cross-sectional perspectives on smoking initiation. *Developmental Psychology, 22,* 327–334.

Clarke, B., Fokoue, E., & Zhang, H. H. (2009). *Principles and theory of data mining and machine learning.* New York: Springer.

Clayton, M., Helms, B., & Simpson, C. (2006). Active prompting to decrease cell phone use and increase seat belt use while driving. *Journal of Applied Behavior Analysis, 39,* 341–349.

Clement, P. W. (2007). Story of "Hope": Successful treatment of obsessive-compulsive disorder. *Pragmatic Case Studies in Psychotherapy, 3,* 1–36. (online at http://hdl.rutgers.edu/1782.1/pcsp_ journal)

Clement, P. W. (2008). Outcomes from 40 years of psychotherapy in a private practice. *American Journal of Psychotherapy, 62,* 215–239.

Cleveland, W. S. (1993). *Visualizing data.* Summit, NJ: Hobart Press.

Cleveland, W. S. (1994). *The elements of graphing data.* Summit, NJ: Hobart Press.

Cohen, J. (1965). Some statistical issues in psychological research. In B. B. Wolman (Ed.), *Handbook of clinical psychology.* New York: McGraw-Hill.

Cohen, J. (1988). *Statistical power analysis for the behavioral sciences* (2nd ed.). Hillsdale, NJ: Erlbaum.

Cook, T. D., & Campbell, D. T. (Eds.). (1979). *Quasi-experimentation: Design and analysis issues for field settings.* Chicago: Rand-McNally.

Cooper, H., Hedges, L. V., & Valentine, J. C. (Eds.). (2009). *The handbook of research synthesis and meta-analysis.* New York: Russell Sage Foundation.

Cooper, J. O., Heron, T. E., & Heward, W. L. (2007). *Applied behavior analysis* (2nd ed.). Upper Saddle River, NJ: Pearson Education.

Cox, B. S., Cox, A. B., & Cox, D. J. (2000). Motivating signage prompts safety belt use among drivers exiting senior communities. *Journal of Applied Behavior Analysis, 33,* 635–638.

Cunningham, C. E., Bremner, R., & Boyle, M. (1995). Large group community-based parenting programs for families of preschoolers at risk for disruptive behaviour disorders: Utilization, cost

effectiveness, and outcome. *Journal of Child Psychology and Psychiatry, 36,* 1141–1159.

Cunningham, T. R., & Austin, J. (2007). Using goal setting, task clarification, and feedback to increase the use of the hands-free technique by hospital operating room staff. *Journal of Applied Behavior Analysis, 40,* 673–677.

Dapcich-Miura, E., & Hovell, M. F. (1979). Contingency management of adherence to a complex medical regimen in an elderly heart patient. *Behavior Therapy, 10,* 193–201.

Davis, M., Myers, K. M., Chhatwal, J., & Ressler, K. J. (2006). Pharmacological treatments that facilitate extinction of fear: Relevance to psychotherapy. *NeuroRx, 3,* 82–96.

Dawes, R. M. (1994). *House of cards: Psychology and psychotherapy built on myth.* New York: Free Press.

De Los Reyes, A., & Kazdin, A. E. (2005). Informant discrepancies in the assessment of childhood psychopathology: A critical review, theoretical framework, and recommendations for further study. *Psychological Bulletin, 131,* 483–509.

DeMaster, B., Reid, J., & Twentyman, C. (1977). The effects of different amounts of feedback on observers' reliability. *Behavior Therapy, 8,* 317–329.

Denissenko, M. F., Pao, A., Tang, M., & Pfeifer, G. P. (1996). Preferential formation of benzo[a]pyrene adducts at lung cancer mutational hotspots in P53. *Science, 274,* 430–432.

Denzin, N. K., & Lincoln, Y. S. (Eds.). (2005). *The SAGE handbook of qualitative research* (3rd ed.). Thousand Oaks, CA: Sage.

DeProspero, A., & Cohen, S. (1979). Inconsistent visual analysis of intrasubject data. *Journal of Applied Behavior Analysis, 12,* 573–579.

DiGennaro, F. D., Martens, B. K., & Kleinmann, A. E. (2007). A comparison of performance feedback procedures on teachers' treatment implantation integrity and students' inappropriate behavior in special education classrooms. *Journal of Applied Behavior Analysis, 40,* 447–461.

Dishion, T. J., McCord, J., & Poulin, F. (1999). When interventions harm: Peer groups and problem behavior. *American Psychologist, 54,* 755–764.

Dittmer, C. G. (1926). *Introduction to social statistics.* Chicago: Shaw.

Dodge, K. A., Dishion, T. J., & Lansford, J. E. (Eds.). (2006). *Deviant peer influences in programs for youth: Problems and solutions.* New York: Guilford.

Doss, A. J., & Weisz, J. R. (2006). Syndrome co-occurrence and treatment outcomes in youth mental health clinics. *Journal of Consulting and Clinical Psychology, 74,* 416–425.

Drebing, C. E., Van Ormer, E. A., Krebs, C., Rosenheck, R., Rounsaville, B., Herz, L., & Penk, W. (2005). The impact of enhanced incentives for dually diagnosed veterans. *Journal of Applied Behavior Analysis, 38,* 359–372.

Ducharme, J. M., Folino, A., & DeRosie, J. (2008). Errorless acquiescence training: A potential "keystone" approach to building peer interaction skills in children with severe problem behavior. *Behavior Modification, 32,* 39–60.

Dukes, W. F. (1965). N = 1. *Psychological Bulletin, 64,* 74–79.

Dunn, J., & Plomin, R. (1990). *Separate lives: Why siblings are so different.* New York: Basic Books.

Edgington, E. S. (1969). *Statistical inference: The distribution free approach.* New York: McGraw Hill.

Edgington, E. S. (1996). Randomized single-subject experimental designs. *Behaviour Research and Therapy, 34,* 567–574.

Edgington, E. S., & Onghena, P. (2007). *Randomization tests* (4th ed.). Boca Raton, FL: Chapman & Hall/CRC.

Engleman, S., Haddox, P., & Bruner, E. (1983). *Teach your child to read in 100 easy lessons.* New York: Simon & Schuster.

Facon, B., Sahiri, S., & Rivière, V. (2008). A controlled single-case treatment of severe long-term selective mutism in a child with mental retardation. *Behavior Therapy, 39,* 313–321.

Faith, M. S., Gorman, B. G., & Allison, D. B. (1997). Meta-analytic evaluations of single-case designs. In D. B. Allison, B. Gorman, & R. Franklin (Eds.), *Methods for the design and analysis of single-case research.* Hillsdale, NJ: Lawrence Erlbaum.

Farrimond, S. J., & Leland, L. S., Jr. (2006). Increasing donations to supermarket food-bank bins using proximal prompts. *Journal of Applied Behavior Analysis, 39,* 249–251.

Favell, J. E., McGimsey, J. F., & Jones, M. L. (1980). Rapid eating in the retarded: Reduction by nonaversive procedures. *Behavior Modification, 4,* 481–492.

Feather, J. S., & Ronan, K. R. (2006). Trauma-focused cognitive-behavioural therapy for abused children with posttraumatic stress disorder. *New Zealand Journal of Psychology, 35,* 132–145.

Feehan, M., McGee, R., Stanton, W., & Silva, P. A. (1990). A 6-year follow-up of childhood enuresis: Prevalence in adolescence and consequences for mental health. *Journal of Paediatrics and Child Health, 26,* 75–79.

Feldman, R. A., Caplinger, T. E., & Wodarski, J. S. (1983). *The St. Louis conundrum: The effective treatment of antisocial youths.* Englewood Cliffs, NJ: Prentice-Hall.

Ferritor, D. E., Buckholdt, D., Hamblin, R. L., & Smith, L. (1972). The noneffects of contingent reinforcement for attending behavior on work accomplished. *Journal of Applied Behavior Analysis, 5,* 7–17.

Ferron, J., & Sentovich, C. (2002). Statistical power of randomization tests used with multiple-baseline designs. *Journal of Experimental Education, 70,* 165–178.

Ferster, C. B. (1961). Positive reinforcement and behavioral deficits in autistic children. *Child Development, 32,* 437–456.

Ferster, C. B., & Skinner, B. F. (1957). *Schedules of reinforcement.* New York: Appleton-Century-Crofts.

Fiore, M. C., Bailey, W. C., Cohen, S. J., Dorfman, S. F., Goldstein, H. G., Gritz, E. R., et al. (2000). *Treating tobacco use and dependence: Clinical practice guideline.* Rockville, MD: U.S. Department of Health and Human Services, Public Health Service.

Fisch, G. S. (2001). Evaluating data from behavioral analysis: Visual inspection or statistical models? *Behavioural Processes, 54,* 137–154.

Fisher, R. A. (1925). *Statistical methods for research workers.* Edinburgh, UK: Oliver & Boyd.

Fisher, W. W., Kelley, M. E., & Lomas, J. E. (2003). Visual aids and structured criteria for improving visual inspection and interpretation of single-case designs. *Journal of Applied Behavior Analysis, 36,* 387–406.

Fishman, C. (2006). How many light bulbs does it take to change the world? One. And you're looking at it. *Fast Company, 1008* (September), p. 74.

Flood, W. A., & Wilder, D. A. (2004). The use of differential reinforcement and fading to increase time away from a caregiver in a child with separation anxiety disorder. *Education and Treatment of Children, 27,* 1–8.

Foley, D., Wormley, B., Silberg, J., Maes, H., Hewitt, J., Eaves, L., & Riley, B. (2004). Childhood adversity, MAOA genotype, and risk for conduct disorder. *Archives of General Psychiatry, 61,* 738–744.

Foster, S. L., & Mash, E. J. (1999). Assessing social validity in clinical treatment research: Issues and procedures. *Journal of Consulting and Clinical Psychology, 67,* 308–319.

Fournier, A. K., Ehrhart, I. J., Glindemann, K. E., & Geller, E. S. (2004). Intervening to decrease alcohol abuse at university parties: Differential reinforcement of intoxication level. *Behavior Modification, 28,* 167–181.

Franklin, R. D., Allison, D. B., & Gorman, B. S. (Eds.). (1997). *Design and analysis of single-case research.* Mahwah, NJ: Lawrence Erlbaum Associates.

Franklin, R. D., Gorman, B. S., Beasley, T. M., & Allison, D. B. (1997). Graphical display and visual analysis. In R. D. Franklin, D. B. Allison, & B. S. Gorman (Eds.), *Design and analysis of single-case research.* Mahwah, NJ: Lawrence Erlbaum Associates.

Freedman, B. J., Rosenthal, L., Donahoe, C. P., Schlundt, D. G., & McFall, R. (1978). A social-behavioral analysis of skills deficits in delinquent and nondelinquent adolescent boys. *Journal of Consulting and Clinical Psychology, 46,* 1448–1462.

Freud, S. (1933). *New introductory lectures in psychoanalysis.* New York: Norton.

Friedman, J., & Axelrod, S. (1973). *The use of a changing-criterion procedure to reduce the frequency of smoking behavior.* Unpublished manuscript, Temple University.

Gabbard, G. O., Lazar, S. G., Hornberger, J., & Spiegel, D. (1997). The economic impact of psychotherapy: A review. *American Journal of Psychiatry, 154,* 147–155.

Garb, H. N. (2005). Clinical judgment and decision making. *Annual Review of Clinical Psychology, 1,* 67–89.

Gilbert, J. P., Light, R. J., & Mosteller, F. (1975). Assessing social interventions: An empirical base for policy. In C. A. Bennett & A. A. Lumsdaine (Eds.), *Evaluation and experiment: Some critical issues in assessing social programs.* New York: Academic Press.

Gilbert, L. M., Williams, R. L., & McLaughlin, T. F. (1996). Use of assisted reading to increase correct reading rates and decrease error rates of students with learning disabilities. *Journal of Applied Behavior Analysis, 29,* 255–257.

Gilovich, T., Griffin, D., & Kahneman, D. (2002). *Heuristics and biases: The psychology of intuitive judgment.* Cambridge, UK: Cambridge University Press.

Girolami, P. A., Boscoe, J. H., & Roscoe, N. (2007). Decreasing expulsions by a child with a feeding disorder: Using a brush to present and re-present food. *Journal of Applied Behavior Analysis, 40,* 749–753.

Glass, G. V. (1997). *Interrupted time series quasi-experiments: Complementary methods for research in education* (2nd ed.). Washington, DC: American Educational Research Association.

Glass, G. V., Willson, V. L., & Gottman, J. M. (1975). *Design and analysis of time-series experiments.* Boulder: Colorado Associated University Press.

Glenn, I. M., & Dallery, J. (2007). Effects of internet-based voucher reinforcement and a transdermal nicotine patch on cigarette smoking. *Journal of Applied Behavior Analysis, 40,* 1–13.

Goldiamond, I. (1962). The maintenance of ongoing fluent verbal behavior and stuttering. *Journal of Mathetics, 1,* 57–95.

Gore, A. (2006). *An inconvenient truth: The planetary emergency of global warming and what we can do about it.* New York: Rodale.

Gorsuch, R. L. (1983). Three methods for analyzing limited time-series (N of 1) data. *Behavioral Assessment, 5,* 141–154.

Greenberg, P. E., Sisitsky, T., Kessler, R. C., Finkelstein, S. N., Berndt, E. R., Davidson, J. R. T., Ballenger, J. C., & Fyer, A. J. (1999). The economic burden of anxiety disorders in the 1990s. *Journal of Clinical Psychiatry, 60,* 427–435.

Grice, C. R., & Hunter, J. J. (1964). Stimulus intensity effects depend upon the type of experimental design. *Psychological Review, 71,* 247–256.

Griner, D., & Smith, T. B. (2006). Culturally adapted mental health interventions: A meta-analytic review. *Psychotherapy: Theory, Research, Practice, Training, 43,* 531–548.

Grissom, T., Ward, P., Martin, B., & Leenders, N. Y. J. M. (2005). Physical activity in physical education. *Family Community Health, 28,* 125–129.

Gross, A., Miltenberger, R., Knudson, P., Bosch, A., & Breitwieser, C. B. (2007). Preliminary evaluation of a parent training program to prevent gun play. *Journal of Applied Behavior Analysis, 40,* 691–695.

Hains, A. H., & Baer, D. M. (1989). Interaction effects in multielement designs: Inevitable, desirable, and ignorable. *Journal of Applied Behavior Analysis, 22,* 57–69.

Hall, S. S., Maynes, N. P., & Reiss, A. L. (2009). Using percentile schedules to increase eye contact in children with Fragile X syndrome. *Journal of Applied Behavior Analysis, 42,* 171–176.

Hanley, G. P., Heal, N. A., Tiger, J. H., & Ingvarsson, E. T. (2007). Evaluation of a classwide teaching program for developing preschool life skills. *Journal of Applied Behavior Analysis, 40,* 277–300.

Harbst, K. B., Ottenbacher, K. J., & Harris, S. R. (1991). Interrater reliability of therapists' judgments of graphed data. *Physical Therapy, 71,* 107–115.

Harris, V. W., & Sherman, J. A. (1974). Homework assignments, consequences, and classroom performance in social studies and mathematics. *Journal of Applied Behavior Analysis, 7,* 505–519.

Hartmann, D. P. (1982). Assessing the dependability of observational data. In D. P. Hartmann (Ed.), *New directions for the methodology of behavioral sciences: Using observers to study behavior.* San Francisco: Jossey-Bass.

Hartmann, D. P., Barrios, B. A., & Wood, D. D. (2004). Principles of behavioral observation. In S. N. Haynes & E. M. Hieby (Eds.), *Comprehensive handbook of psychological assessment (Vol. 3, Behavioral assessment).* New York: John Wiley & Sons.

Hartmann, D. P., Gottman, J. M., Jones, R. R., Gardner, W., Kazdin, A. E., & Vaught, R. (1980). Interrupted time-series analysis and its application to behavioral data. *Journal of Applied Behavior Analysis, 13,* 543–559.

Hasler, B. P., Mehl, M. R., Bootzin, R. R., & Vazire, S. (2008). Preliminary evidence of diurnal rhythms in everyday behaviors associated with positive affect. *Journal of Research in Personality, 42,* 1537–1546.

Hassin, R. R., Ferguson, M. J., Shidlovski, D., & Gross, T. (2007). Subliminal exposure to national flags affects political thought and behavior. *Proceedings of the National Academy of Sciences, 104,* 19757–19761.

Hassin, R., Uleman, J., & Bargh, J. (Eds.). (2005). *The new unconscious.* New York: Oxford University Press.

Hawkins, R. P., & Dobes, R. W. (1977). Behavioral definitions in applied behavior analysis: Explicit or implicit. In B. C. Etzel, J. M. LeBlane, & D. M. Baer (Eds.), *New developments in behavioral research: Theory, methods, and applications. In honor of Sidney W. Bijou.* Hillsdale, NJ: Lawrence Erlbaum Associates.

Henry, G. T. (1995). *Graphing data: Techniques for display and analysis.* Thousand Oaks, CA: Sage Publications.

Hersen, M., & Barlow, D. H. (1976). *Single-case experimental designs: Strategies for studying behavior change.* New York: Pergamon.

Hetzroni, O. E., Quist, R. W., & Lloyd, L. L. (2002). Translucency and complexity: Effects on blissymbol learning using computer and teacher presentations. *Language, Speech, and Hearing Services in Schools, 33,* 291–303.

Himle, M. B., Chang, S., Woods, D. W., Pearlman, A., Buzzella, B., Bunaciu, L., & Piacentini, J. C. (2006). Establishing the feasibility of direct observation in the assessment of tics in children with chronic tic disorders. *Journal of Applied Behavior Analysis, 39,* 429–440.

Hofmann, S. G., Meuret, A. E., Smits, J. A., Simon, N. M., Pollack, M. H., Eisenmenger, K., Shiekh, M., & Otto, M. W. (2006). Augmentation of exposure therapy with D-cycloserine for social anxiety disorder. *Archives of General Psychiatry, 63,* 298–304.

Hollon, S. D., & Beck, A. T. (2004). Cognitive and cognitive behavioral therapies. In M. J. Lambert

(Ed.), *Bergin and Garfield's handbook of psychotherapy and behavior change* (5ᵗʰ ed.). New York: Wiley & Sons.

Honekopp, J. (2006). Once more: Is beauty in the eye of the beholder? Relative contributions of private and shared taste to judgments of facial attractiveness. *Journal of Experimental Psychology: Human Perception and Performance, 32*, 199–209.

Horner, R. H., Carr, E. G., Halle, J., McGee, G., Odom, S., & Wolery, M. (2005). The use of single-subject research to identify evidence-based practice in special education. *Exceptional Children, 71*, 165–179.

Hsu, L. M. (1989). Random sampling, randomization, and equivalence of contrasted groups in psychotherapy outcome research. *Journal of Consulting and Clinical Psychology, 57*, 131–137.

Hughes, C. A. O., & Carter, M. (2002). Toys and materials as setting events for the social interaction of preschool children with special needs. *Educational Psychology, 22*, 429–444.

Hughes, M. A., Alberto, P. A., & Fredrick, L. L. (2006). Self-operated auditory prompting systems as a function-based intervention in public community settings. *Journal of Positive Behavior Interventions, 8*, 230–243.

Humm, S. P., Blampied, N. M., & Liberty, K. A. (2005). Effects of parent-administered, home-based, high-probability request sequences on compliance by children with developmental disabilities. *Child and Family Behavior Therapy, 27*, 327–345.

Hunsley, J. (2007). Addressing key challenges in evidence-based practice in psychology. *Professional Psychology: Research and Practice, 38*, 113–121.

Hunter, J. E., & Schmidt, F. L. (2004). *Methods of meta-analysis: Correcting error and bias in research findings* (2ⁿᵈ ed.). Thousand Oaks, CA: Sage Publications

Ingram, K., Lewis-Palmer, T., & Sugai, G. (2005). Function-based intervention planning: Comparing the effectiveness of FBA function-based and non-function based intervention plans. *Journal of Positive Behavior Interventions, 7*, 224–236.

Institute of Medicine. (2001). *Crossing the quality chasm: A new health system for the 21st century.* Washington, DC: National Academy Press.

Iwata, B. A., Kahng, S. W., Wallace, M. D., & Lindberg, J. S. (2000). The functional analysis model of behavioral assessment. In J. Austin & J. E. Carr (Eds.), *Handbook of applied behavior analysis.* Reno, NV: Context Press.

Jacobson, N. S., & Revenstorf, D. (1988). Statistics for assessing the clinical significance of psychotherapy techniques: Issues, problems, and new developments. *Behavioral Assessment, 10*, 133–145.

Jacobson, N. S., Roberts, L. J., Berns, S. B., & McGlinchey, J. (1999). Methods for defining and determining the clinical significance of treatment effects in mental health research: Current status, new applications, and future directions. *Journal of Consulting and Clinical Psychology, 67*, 300–307.

Jaffee, S. R., Caspi, A., Moffitt, T. E., Dodge, K., Rutter, M., Taylor, A., & Tully, L. (2005). Nature × nurture: Genetic vulnerabilities interact with physical maltreatment to promote behavior problems. *Development and Psychopathology, 17*, 67–84.

Jason, L. A., & Brackshaw, E. (1999). Access to TV contingent on physical activity: Effects on reducing TV-viewing and body-weight. *Journal of Behavior Therapy and Experimental Psychiatry, 30*, 145–151.

Johnson, B. M., Miltenberger, R. G., Egemo-Helm, K., Jostad, C. M., Flessner, C., & Gatheridge, B. (2005). Evaluation of behavioral skills training for teaching abduction-prevention skills to young children. *Journal of Applied Behavior Analysis, 38*, 67–78.

Jones, M. C. (1924a). A laboratory study of fear: The case of Peter. *Pedagogical Seminary and Journal of Genetic Psychology, 31*, 308–315.

Jones, M. C. (1924b). The elimination of children's fears. *Journal of Experimental Psychology, 7*, 382–390.

Jones, R. R., Vaught, R. S., & Weinrott, M. (1977). Time-series analysis in operant research. *Journal of Applied Behavior Analysis, 10*, 151–166.

Jones, R. R., Weinrott, M. R., & Vaught, R. S. (1978). Effects of serial dependency on the agreement between visual and statistical inference. *Journal of Applied Behavior Analysis, 11*, 277–283.

Jones, W. P. (2003). Single-case time series with Bayesian analysis: A practitioner's guide. *Measurement and Education in Counseling and Development, 36*, 28–39.

Kazdin, A. E. (1976). Statistical analysis for single-case experimental designs. In M. Hersen & D. H. Barlow, *Single-case experimental designs: Strategies for studying behavior change.* Elmsford, NY: Pergamon.

Kazdin, A. E. (1977a). Artifact, bias, and complexity of assessment. The ABC's of reliability. *Journal of Applied Behavior Analysis, 10,* 141–150.

Kazdin, A. E. (1977b). Assessing the clinical or applied significance of behavior change through social validation. *Behavior Modification, 1,* 427–452.

Kazdin, A. E. (1977c). *The token economy: A review and evaluation.* New York: Plenum.

Kazdin, A. E. (1978). *History of behavior modification: Experimental foundations of contemporary research.* Baltimore: University Park Press.

Kazdin, A. E. (1981). Drawing valid inferences from case studies. *Journal of Consulting and Clinical Psychology, 49,* 183–192.

Kazdin, A. E. (1982). Symptom substitution, generalization, and response covariation: Implications for psychotherapy outcome. *Psychological Bulletin, 91,* 349–365.

Kazdin, A. E. (1984). Statistical analyses for single-case experimental designs. In D. H. Barlow & M. Hersen, *Single-case experimental designs: Strategies for studying behavior change* (2nd ed.). Elmsford, NY: Pergamon.

Kazdin, A. E. (1994). Informant variability in the assessment of childhood depression. In W. M. Reynolds & H. Johnston (Eds.), *Handbook of depression in children and adolescents.* New York: Plenum.

Kazdin, A. E. (2001). *Behavior modification in applied settings* (6th ed.). Long Grove, IL: Waveland Press.

Kazdin, A. E. (2003). *Research design in clinical psychology* (4th ed). Boston: Allyn & Bacon.

Kazdin, A. E. (2006). Arbitrary metrics: Implications for identifying evidence-based treatments. *American Psychologist, 61,* 42–49.

Kazdin, A. E. (2007). Mediators and mechanisms of change in psychotherapy research. *Annual Review of Clinical Psychology, 3,* 1–27.

Kazdin, A. E. (2008a). Evidence-based treatments and delivery of psychological services: Shifting our emphases to increase impact. *Psychological Services, 5,* 201–215.

Kazdin, A. E. (2008b). Evidence-based treatment and practice: New opportunities to bridge clinical research and practice, enhance the knowledge base, and improve patient care. *American Psychologist, 63,* 146–159.

Kazdin, A. E. (2009). Psychological science's contributions to a sustainable environment: Extending our reach to a grand challenge of society. *American Psychologist, 64,* 339–356.

Kazdin, A. E., & Bass, D. (1989). Power to detect differences between alternative treatments in comparative psychotherapy outcome research. *Journal of Consulting and Clinical Psychology, 57,* 138–147.

Kazdin, A. E., & Geesey, S. (1977). Simultaneous-treatment design comparisons of the effects of earning reinforcers for one's peers versus for oneself. *Behavior Therapy, 8,* 682–693.

Kazdin, A. E., & Hartmann, D. P. (1978). The simultaneous-treatment design. *Behavior Therapy, 9,* 912–922.

Kazdin, A. E., & Mascitelli, S. (1980). The opportunity to earn oneself off a token system as a reinforcer for attentive behavior. *Behavior Therapy, 11,* 68–78.

Kazdin, A. E., & Polster, R. (1973). Intermittent token reinforcement and response maintenance in extinction. *Behavior Therapy, 4,* 386–391.

Kazdin, A. E., Siegel, T., & Bass, D. (1992). Cognitive problem-solving skills training and parent management training in the treatment of antisocial behavior in children. *Journal of Consulting and Clinical Psychology, 60,* 733–747.

Kazdin, A. E., & Wassell, G. (2000). Therapeutic changes in children, parents, and families resulting from treatment of children with conduct problems. *Journal of the American Academy of Child and Adolescent Psychiatry, 39,* 414–420.

Kazdin, A. E., & Whitley, M. K. (2006). Comorbidity, case complexity, and effects of evidence-based treatment for children referred for disruptive behavior. *Journal of Consulting and Clinical Psychology, 74,* 455–467.

Kendall, P. C., & Grove, W. M. (1988). Normative comparisons in therapy outcome. *Behavioral Assessment, 10,* 147–158.

Kennedy, C. H. (2002). The maintenance of behavior change as an indicator of social validity. *Behavior Modification, 26,* 627–647.

Kenny, D. A., Kashy, D. A., & Bolger, N. (1998). Data analysis in social psychology. In D. Gilbert, S. T. Fiske, & G. Lindzey (Eds.), *Handbook of social psychology* (4ᵗʰ ed., Vol. 1).

Kent, R. N., & Foster, S. L. (1977). Direct observational procedures: Methodological issues in naturalistic settings. In A. R. Ciminero, K. S. Calhoun, & H. E. Adams (Eds.), *Handbook of behavioral assessment*. New York: Wiley.

Kierkegaard, S. (1843) *Either/or: A fragment of life.* Copenhagen: University Bookshop Reitzel. (Translated 1944, H. Milford, Oxford University Press)

Kim-Cohen, J., Caspi, A., Taylor, A., Williams, B., Newcombe, R., Craig, I. W., & Moffitt, T. E. (2006). MAOA, maltreatment, and gene–environment interaction predicting children's mental health: New evidence and a meta-analysis. *Molecular Psychiatry, 11,* 903–913.

Kirk, R. E. (1996). Practical significance: A concept whose time has come. *Educational and Psychological Measurement, 56,* 746–759.

Knapp, T. J. (1983). Behavior analysts' visual appraisal of behavior change in graphic display. *Behavioral Assessment, 5,* 155–164.

Kodak, T., Grow, L., & Northrup, J. (2004). Functional analysis and treatment of elopement for a child with Attention-Deficit-Hyperactivity Disorder. *Journal of Applied Behavior Analysis, 37,* 229–232.

Koegel, R. L., & Koegel, L. K. (2006). *Pivotal response treatments for autism: Communication, social, and academic development.* Baltimore: Brookes Publishing Company.

Komaki, J., & Barnett, F. T. (1977). A behavioral approach to coaching football: Improving the play execution of the offensive backfield on a youth football team. *Journal of Applied Behavior Analysis, 10,* 657–664.

Korchin, S. J. (1976). *Modern clinical psychology.* New York: Basic Books.

Kosslyn, S. M. (2006). *Graph design for the eye and mind.* New York: Oxford University Press.

Kraemer, H. C., Kiernan, M., Essex, M., & Kupfer, D. J. (2008). How and why criteria defining moderators and mediators differ between the Baron & Kenny and MacArthur approaches. *Health Psychology, 27* (Suppl.) S101–S108.

Kraemer, H. C., Stice, E., Kazdin, A. E., Offord, D. R., & Kupfer, D. J. (2001). How do risk factors work together? Mediators, moderators, independent, overlapping, and proxy-risk factors. *American Journal of Psychiatry, 158,* 848–856.

Kraemer, H. C., Wilson, G. T., Fairburn, C. G., & Agras, W. S. (2002). Mediators and moderators of treatment effects in randomized clinical trials. *Archives of General Psychiatry, 59,* 877–883.

Kratochwill, T. R. (2006). Evidence-based interventions and practices in school psychology: The scientific basis of the profession. In R. F. Subotnik & H. J. Walberg (Eds.), *The scientific basis of educational productivity.* Charlotte, NC: Information Age Publishing.

Kratochwill, T. R., Hoagwood, K. E., Frank, J. L., Levitt, J. M., Olin, S., Romanelli, L. H., & Saka, N. (2009). Evidence-based interventions and practices in school psychology: Challenges and opportunities. In T. B. Gutkin & C. R. Reynolds (Eds.), *The handbook of school psychology* (4th ed.). New York: John Wiley & Sons.

Kratochwill, T. R., & Levin, J. R. (in press). Enhancing the scientific credibility of single-case intervention research: Randomization to the rescue. *Psychological Methods.*

Kromrey, J. D., & Foster-Johnson, L. (1996). Determining the efficacy of intervention: The use of effect sizes for data analysis in single-subject research. *The Journal of Experimental Education, 65,* 73–93.

Kushner, M. G., Kim, S. W., Donahue, C., Thuras, P., Adson, D., Kotlyar, M., McCabe, J., Peterson, J., & Foa, E. B. (2007). D-cycloserine augmented exposure therapy for Obsessive-Compulsive Disorder. *Biological Psychiatry, 62,* 835–838.

Lall, V. F., & Levin, J. R. (2004). An empirical investigation of the statistical properties of generalized single-case randomization tests. *Journal of School Psychology, 42,* 61–86.

Lambert, M. J., Hansen, N. B., & Finch, A. E. (2001). Client-focused research: Using client outcome data to enhance treatment effects. *Journal of Consulting and Clinical Psychology, 69,* 159–172.

Lambert, M. J., Hansen, N. B., Umphress, V., Lunnen, K., Okiishi, J., Burlingame, G., Huefner, J. C., & Reisinger, C. W. (1996). *Administration and* scoring manual for the Outcome Questionnaire (OQ 45.2). Wilmington, DE: American Professional Credentialing Services.

Lambert, M. J., Vermeersch, D. A., Brown, G. S., & Burlingame, G. M. (2004). *Administration and scoring manual for the OQ-30.2*. Orem, UT: American Professional Credentialing Services.

Lambert, M. J., Whipple, J. L., Hawkins, E. J., Vermeersch, D. A., Nielsen, S. L., & Smart, D. W. (2003). Is it time for clinicians to routinely track patient outcome? A meta-analysis. *Clinical Psychology: Science and Practice, 10*, 288–301.

Levesque, M., Savard, J., Simard, S., Gauthier, J. G., & Ivers, H. (2004). Efficacy of cognitive therapy for depression among women with metastatic cancer: A single-case experimental study. *Journal of Behavior Therapy and Experimental Psychiatry, 35*, 287–305.

Levin, J. R., & Wampold, B. E. (1999). Generalized single-case randomization tests: Flexible analyses for a variety of situations. *School Psychology Quarterly, 14*, 59–93.

Lewin, L. M., & Wakefield, J. A., Jr. (1979). Percentage agreement and phi: A conversion table. *Journal of Applied Behavior Analysis, 12*, 299–301.

Lewinsohn, P. M., Clarke, G. N., Hops, H., & Andrews, J. (1990). Cognitive-behavioral treatment for depressed adolescents. *Behavior Therapy, 21*, 385–401.

Lindsley, O. R. (1956). Operant conditioning methods applied to research in chronic schizophrenia. *Psychiatric Research Reports, 5*, 118–139.

Lindsley, O. R. (1960). Characteristics of the behavior of chronic psychotics as revealed by free-operant conditioning methods. *Diseases of the Nervous System* (Monograph Supplement), *21*, 66–78.

Lipsey, M. W. (1996). Theory as method: Small theories of treatments. In L. Sechrest & A. G. Scott (Eds.), *New directions in program evaluation: Understanding causes and generalizing about them* (Serial No. 57). New York: Jossey-Bass.

Lochman, J. E. (2010). Anger control training for aggressive youth. In J. R. Weisz & A. E. Kazdin (Eds.), *Evidence-based psychotherapies for children and adolescents* (2nd ed.). New York: Guilford.

Love, S. M., Koob, J. J., & Hill, L. E. (2007). Meeting the challenges of evidence-based practice: Can mental health therapists evaluate their practice? *Brief Treatment and Crisis Intervention, 7*, 184–193.

Luiselli, J. K. (2000). Cueing, demand fading, and positive reinforcement to establish self-feeding and oral consumption in a child with chronic food refusal. *Behavior Modification, 24*, 348–358.

Luiselli, J. K., Reed, F. D. D., Christian, W. P., Markowski, A., Rue, H. C., St. Amand, C., & Ryan, C. J. (2009). Effects of an informational brochure, lottery-based financial incentive, and public posting on absenteeism of direct-care human service employees. *Behavior Modification, 33*, 175–181.

Lumley, V. A., Miltenberger, R. G., Long, E. S., Rapp, J. T., & Roberts, J. A. (1998). Evaluation of a sexual abuse prevention program for adults with mental retardation. *Journal of Applied Behavior Analysis, 31*, 91–101.

Lundervold, D., & Bourland, G. (1988). Quantitative analysis of treatment of aggression, self-injury, and property destruction. *Behavior Modification, 12*, 591–617.

Ma, H. (2006). An alternative method for quantitative synthesis of single-subject researches: Percentage of data points exceeding the median. *Behavior Modification, 30*, 598–617.

MacKinnon, D. P. (2008). *Introduction to statistical mediation analysis*. Mahwah, NJ: Erlbaum.

Macmillan, M. (2002). *An odd kind of fame: Stories of Phineas Gage*. Boston: MIT Press.

Manolov, R., & Solanas, A. (2008a). Comparing N = 1 effect size indices in presence of autocorrelation. *Behavior Modification, 32*, 860–875.

Manolov, R., & Solanas, A. (2008b). Randomization tests for ABAB designs: Comparing data-division-specific and common distributions. *Psicothema, 20*, 297–303.

Manolov, R., & Solanas, A. (2009). Problems of the randomization tests for AB designs. *Psicologica, 30*, 137–154.

Manson, J. E., Allison, M. A., Rossouw, J. E., Carr, J. J., Langer, R. D., Hsia J., et al. (2007). Estrogen therapy and coronary-artery calcification. *New England Journal of Medicine, 356*, 2591–2602.

Marholin, D. H., Steinman, W. M., McInnis, E. T., & Heads, T. B. (1975). The effect of a teacher's presence on the classroom behavior of conduct-problem children. *Journal of Abnormal Child Psychology, 3*, 11–25.

Martin, J. E., & Sachs, D. A. (1973). The effects of a self-control weight loss program on an obese woman. *Journal of Behavior Therapy and Experimental Psychiatry, 4*, 155–159.

Mastropieri, M. A., & Scruggs, T. E. (1985–86). Early intervention for socially withdrawn children. *The Journal of Special Education, 19*, 429–441.

Matt, G. E. (1989). Decision rules for selecting effect sizes in meta-analysis: A review and reanalysis of psychotherapy outcome studies. *Psychological Bulletin, 105*, 106–115.

Matt, G. E., & Navarro, A. M. (1997). What meta-analyses have and have not taught us about psychotherapy effects: A review and future directions. *Clinical Psychology Review, 17*, 1–32.

Matyas, T. A., & Greenwood, K. M. (1990). Visual analysis of single-case time series: Effects of variability, serial dependence, and magnitude of intervention effects. *Journal of Applied Behavior Analysis, 23*, 341–351.

Matyas, T. A., & Greenwood, K. M. (1991). Problems in the estimation of autocorrelation in brief time series and some implications for behavioral data. *Behavioral Assessment, 13*, 137–157.

Matyas, T. A., & Greenwood, K. M. (1997). Serial dependency in single-case time series. In R. D. Franklin, D. B. Allison, & B. S. Gorman (Eds.), *Design and analysis of single-case research.* Mahwah, NJ: Lawrence Erlbaum Associates.

Mayer, R. J. (2009). Targeted therapy for advanced colorectal cancer—More is not always better. *New England Journal of Medicine, 360*, 623–625.

McCollough, D., Weber, K., Derby, K. M., & McLaughlin, T. F. (2008). The effects of *Teach Your Child to Read in 100 Easy Lessons* on the acquisition and generalization of reading skills with a primary student with ADHD and PI. *Child and Family Behavior Therapy, 30*, 61–68.

McCurdy, M., Skinner, C. H., Grantham, K., Watson, T. S., & Hindman, P. M. (2001). Increasing on-task behavior in an elementary student during mathematics seatwork by interspersing additional brief problems. *School Psychology Review, 30*, 23–32.

McDougall, D. (2005). The range-bound changing criterion design. *Behavioral Interventions, 20*, 129–137.

McDougall, D. (2006). The distributed criterion design. *Journal of Behavioral Education, 15*, 237–247.

McDougall, D., Hawkins, J., Brady, M., & Jenkins, A. (2006). Recent innovations in the changing criterion design: Implications for research and practice in special education. *Journal of Special Education, 40*, 2–15.

McIntyre, L. L., Gresham, F. M., DiGennaro, F. D., & Reed, D. D. (2007). Treatment integrity of school-based interventions with children in the *Journal of Applied Behavior Analysis* 1991–2005. *Journal of Applied Behavior Analysis, 40*, 659–672.

McKnight, S., McKean, J. W., & Huitema, B. E. (2000). A double bootstrapping method to analyze linear models with autoregressive error terms. *Psychological Methods, 5*, 87–101.

McSweeney, A. J. (1978). Effects of response cost on the behavior of a million persons: Charging for directory assistance in Cincinnati. *Journal of Applied Behavior Analysis, 11*, 47–51.

Mellalieu, S. D., Hanton, S., & O'Brien, M. (2006). The effects of goal setting on rugby performance. *Journal of Applied Behavior Analysis, 39*, 257–261.

Michael, J. (1974). Statistical inference for individual organism research: Mixed blessing or curse? *Journal of Applied Behavior Analysis, 7*, 647–653.

Milrod, B., Busch, F., Leon, A. C., Aronson, A., Roiphe, J., Rudden, M., Singer, M., Shapiro, T., Goldman, H., Richter, D., & Shear, M. K. (2001). A pilot open trial of brief psychodynamic psychotherapy for panic disorder. *Journal of Psychotherapy Practice and Research, 10*, 239–245.

Miltenberger, R. G., Flessner, C., Gatheridge, B., Johnson, B., Satterlund, M., & Egemo, K. (2004). Evaluation of behavioral skills training to prevent gun play in children. *Journal of Applied Behavior Analysis, 37*, 513–516.

Miranda, J., Bernal, G., Lau, A. S., Kohn, L., Hwang, W. C., & LaFromboise, T. (2005). State of the science on psychosocial interventions for ethnic minorities. *Annual Review of Clinical Psychology, 1*, 113–143.

Molloy, G. N. (1990). An illustrative case for the value of individual analysis following a between-group experimental design. *Behaviour Change, 7,* 172–178.

Moore, K., Delaney, J. A., & Dixon, M. R. (2007). Using indices of happiness to examine the influence of environmental enhancements for nursing home residents with Alzheimer's disease. *Journal of Applied Behavior Analysis, 40,* 541–544.

Moran, D. J., & Hirschbine, B. (2002). Constructing single-subject reversal design graphs using Microsoft Excel˜: A comprehensive tutorial. *The Behavioral Analyst Today, 3,* 62–70.

Mrazek, P. J., & Haggerty, R. J. (Eds.). (1994). *Reducing risks for mental disorders: Frontiers of preventive intervention research.* Washington, DC: National Academy Press.

MTA Cooperative Group. (1999a). A 14-month randomized clinical trial of treatment strategies for attention-deficit/hyperactivity disorder. *Archives of General Psychiatry, 56,* 1073–1086.

MTA Cooperative Group. (1999b). Moderators and mediators of treatment response for children with attention-deficit/hyperactivity disorder. *Archives of General Psychiatry, 56,* 1088–1096.

Mueller, M. M., Moore, J., Doggett, R. A., & Tingstrom, D. (2000). The effectiveness of contingency specific and contingency nonspecific prompts in controlling bathroom graffiti. *Journal of Applied Behavior Analysis, 33,* 89–92.

Musser, E. H., Bray, M. A., Kehle, T. J., & Jenson, W. R. (2001). Reducing disruptive behaviors in students with serious emotional disturbance. *School Psychology Review, 30,* 294–304.

Nathan, P. E., & Gorman, J. M. (Eds.). (2007). *A guide to treatments that work.* New York: Oxford University Press.

National Institute of Mental Health. (2008). The numbers count: Mental disorders in America. http://www.nimh.nih.gov/health/publications/the-numbers-count-mental-disorders-in-america/index.shtml

Nezu, A. M., & Perri, M. G. (1989). Social problem-solving therapy for unipolar depression: An initial dismantling investigation. *Journal of Consulting and Clinical Psychology, 57,* 408–413.

Normand, M. P., & Bailey, J. S. (2006). The effects of celeration lines on visual data analysis. *Behavior Modification, 39,* 295–314.

Nourbakhsh, M. R., & Ottenbacher, K. J. (1994). The statistical analysis of single-subject data: A comparative examination. *Physical Therapy, 74,* 80–88.

Nutter, D., & Reid, D. H. (1978). Teaching retarded women a clothing selection skill using community norms. *Journal of Applied Behavior Analysis, 11,* 475–487.

O'Brien, F., & Azrin, N. H. (1972). Developing proper mealtime behaviors of the institutionalized retarded. *Journal of Applied Behavior Analysis, 5,* 389–399.

O'Callaghan, P. M., Allen, K. D., Powell, S., & Salama, F. (2006). The efficacy of noncontingent escape for decreasing children's disruptive behavior during restorative dental treatment. *Journal of Applied Behavior Analysis, 39,* 161–171.

O'Donohue, W., Plaud, J. J., & Hecker, J. E. (1992). The possible function of positive reinforcement in home-bound agoraphobia: A case study. *Journal of Behavior Therapy and Experimental Psychiatry, 23,* 303–312.

O'Leary, K. D., Kent, R. N., & Kanowitz, J. (1975). Shaping data collection congruent with experimental hypotheses. *Journal of Applied Behavior Analysis, 8,* 43–51.

Ollendick, T. H., Shapiro, E. S., & Barrett, R. P. (1981). Reducing stereotypic behaviors: An analysis of treatment procedures using an alternating-treatments design. *Behavior Therapy, 12,* 570–577.

Onghena, P. (1994). *The power of randomization tests for single-case designs.* Leuven, Belgium: Katholieke Universiteit Leuven.

Pagnoni, G., Zink, C. F., Montague, P. R., & Berns, G. S. (2002). Activity in human ventral striatum locked to errors of reward prediction. *Nature Neuroscience, 5,* 97–98.

Park., H., Marascuilo, L., & Gaylord-Ross, R. (1990). Visual inspection and statistical analysis of single-case designs. *Journal of Experimental Education, 58,* 311–320.

Park, S., Singer, G. H. S., & Gibson, M. (2005). The functional effect of teacher positive and neutral affect on task performance of students with significant disabilities. *Journal of Positive Behavior Interventions, 7,* 237–246.

Parker, R. I., & Brossart, D. F. (2003). Evaluating single-case research data: A comparison of seven statistical methods. *Behavior Therapy, 34,* 189–211.

Parker, R. I., Brossart, D. F., Callicott, K. J., Long, J. R., Garcia de Alba, R., Baugh, F. G., & Sullivan, J. R. (2005). Effect sizes in single-case research: How large is large? *School Psychology Review, 34,* 116–132.

Parker, R. I., Cryer, J., & Byrns, G. (2006). Controlling baseline trend in single-case research. *School Psychology Quarterly, 21,* 418–443.

Parker, R. I., & Hagan-Burke, S. (2007a). Single-case research results as clinical outcomes. *Journal of School Psychology, 45,* 637–653.

Parker, R. I., & Hagan-Burke, S. (2007b). Useful effect size interpretations for single-case research. *Behavior Therapy, 38,* 95–105.

Parsons, M. B., Schepis, M. M., Reid, D. H., McCarn, J. E., & Green, C. W. (1987). Expanding the impact of behavioral staff management: A large-scale, long-term application in schools serving severely handicapped students. *Journal of Applied Behavior Analysis, 20,* 139–150.

Parsonson, B. S., & Baer, D. M. (1978). The analysis and presentation of graphic data. In T. R. Kratochwill (Ed.), *Single-subject research: Strategies for evaluating change.* New York: Academic Press.

Parsonson, B. S., & Baer, D. M. (1992). The visual analysis of data and current research into the stimuli controlling it. In T. R. Kratochwill & J. R. Levin (Eds.), *Single-subject research design and analysis.* Hillsdale, NJ: Lawrence Erlbaum Associates.

Pasiali, V. (2004). The use of prescriptive therapeutic songs in a home-based environment to promote social skills acquisition by children with autism: Three case studies. *Music Therapy Perspectives, 22,* 11–22.

Patel, M. R., Piazza, C. C., Layer, S. A., Coleman, R., & Swartzwelder, D. M. (2005). A systematic evaluation of food textures to decrease packing and increase oral intake in children with pediatric feeding disorders. *Journal of Applied Behavior Analysis, 38,* 89–100.

Patten, S. B. (2006). A major depression prognosis calculator based on episode duration. *Clinical Practice and Epidemiology in Mental Health, 2.* http://www.cpementalhealth.com/content/pdf/1745-0179-2-13.pdf

Perepletchikova, F., & Kazdin, A. E. (2005). Treatment integrity and therapeutic change: Issues and research recommendations. *Clinical Psychology: Science and Practice, 12,* 365–383.

Peterson, L., Tremblay, G., Ewigman, B., & Popkey, C. (2002). The Parental Daily Diary: A sensitive measure of the process of change in a child maltreatment prevention program. *Behavior Modification, 26,* 594–604.

Phaneuf, L., & McIntyre, L. L. (2007). Effects of individualized video feedback combined with group parent training on inappropriate maternal behavior. *Journal of Applied Behavior Analysis, 40,* 737–741.

Plomin, R., McClearn, G. E., McGuffin, P., & Defries, J. C. (2000). *Behavioral genetics* (4th ed). New York: W. H. Freeman.

Pluck, M., Ghafari, E., Glynn, T., & McNaughton, S. (1984). Teacher and parent modeling of recreational reading. *New Zealand Journal of Educational Studies, 19,* 114–123.

Pohl, R. F. (Ed.). (2004). *Cognitive illusions: A handbook on fallacies and biases in thinking, judgment, and memory.* New York: Psychology Press.

Porritt, M., Burt, A., & Poling, A. (2006). Increasing fiction writers' productivity through an Internet based intervention. *Journal of Applied Behavior Analysis, 39,* 393–397.

Price, D. D., Finniss, D. G., & Benedetti, B. (2008). A comprehensive review of the placebo effect: Recent advances and current thought. *Annual Review of Psychology, 59,* 565–590.

Prince, M. (1905). *The dissociation of a personality.* New York: Longmans, Green.

Quesnel, C., Savard, J., Simard, S., Ivers, H., & Morin, C. M. (2003). Efficacy of cognitive-behavioral therapy for insomnia in women treated for non-metastatic breast cancer. *Journal of Consulting and Clinical Psychology, 71,* 189–200.

Reeve, S. A., Reeve, K. F., Townsend, D. B., & Poulson, C. L. (2007). Establishing a generalized repertoire of helping behavior in children with autism. *Journal of Applied Behavior Analysis, 40,* 123–136.

Reinhartsen, D. R., Garfinkle, A. N., & Wolery, M. (2002). Engagement with toys in two-year-old children with autism: Teacher selection and child choice. *Journal of the Association for Persons with Severe Handicaps, 27,* 175–187.

Reitman, D., Murphy, M. A., Hupp, S. D. A., & O'Callaghan, P. M. (2004). Behavior change and perceptions of change: Evaluating the effectiveness of a token economy. *Child and Family Behavior Therapy, 26,* 17–36.

Ressler, K. J., Rothbaum, B. O., Tannenbaum, L., Anderson, P., Graap, K., Zimand, E., Hodges, L., & Davis, M. (2004). Cognitive enhancers as adjuncts to psychotherapy: Use of D-cycloserine in phobic individuals to facilitate extinction of fear. *Archives of General Psychiatry, 61,* 1136–1144.

Revusky, S. H. (1967). Some statistical treatments compatible with individual organism methodology. *Journal of the Experimental Analysis of Behavior, 10,* 319–330.

Reyes, J. R., Vollmer, T. R., Sloman, K. N., Hall, A., Reed, R., Jansen, G., et al. (2006). Assessment of deviant arousal in adult male sex offenders with developmental disabilities. *Journal of Applied Behavior Analysis, 39,* 173–188.

Ricciardi, J. N., Luiselli, J. K., & Camare, M. (2006). Shaping approach responses as intervention for specific phobia in a child with autism. *Journal of Applied Behavior Analysis, 39,* 445–448.

Rice, V. H., & Stead, L. F. (2008). Nursing interventions for smoking cessation. *Cochrane Database of Systematic Reviews,* Issue 1 (Art. No. CD001188).

Riesen, T., McDonnell, J., Johnson, J. W., Polychronis, S., & Jameson, M. (2003). A comparison of constant time delay and simultaneous prompting within embedded instruction in general education classes with students with moderate to severe disabilities. *Journal of Behavioral Education, 12,* 241–259.

Riley-Tillman, T. C., & Burns, M. K. (2009). *Evaluating educational interventions: Single-case design for measuring response to intervention.* New York: Guilford Press.

Risley, T. R. (1970). Behavior modification: An experimental-therapeutic endeavor. In L. A.

Hamerlynck, P. O. Davidson, & L. E. Acker (Eds.), *Behavior modification and ideal mental health services.* Calgary, Alberta: University of Calgary Press.

Robinson, P. W., & Foster, D. F. (1979). *Experimental psychology: A small-N approach.* New York: Harper & Row.

Roediger, H. L., III, & McDermott, K. B. (2000). Distortions of memory. In E. Tulving & F. I. M. Craik (Eds.), *The Oxford handbook of memory.* New York: Oxford University Press.

Rosales-Ruiz, J., & Baer, D. M. (1997). Behavioral cusps: A developmental and pragmatic concept for behavior analysis. *Journal of Applied Behavior Analysis, 30,* 533–544.

Rosenbaum, J. E. (2009). Patient teenagers? A comparison of the sexual behavior of virginity pledgers and matched nonpledgers. *Pediatrics, 123,* e110–e120.

Rosenthal, R., & Rosnow, R. L. (2007). *Essentials of behavioral research: Methods and data analysis* (3rd ed.). Boston: McGraw-Hill.

Rusch, F. R., & Kazdin, A. E. (1981). Toward a methodology of withdrawal designs for the assessment of response maintenance. *Journal of Applied Behavior Analysis, 14,* 131–140.

Rutter, M., Yule, W., & Graham, P. (1973). Enuresis and behavioural deviance: Some epidemiological considerations. In I. Kolvin, R. MacKeith, & S. R. Meadow (Eds.), *Bladder control and enuresis: Clinics in developmental medicine* (Vol. 48/49). London: Heinemann/SIMP.

Ryan, C. S., & Hemmes, N. S. (2005). Effects of the contingency for homework submission on homework submission and quiz performance in a college course. *Journal of Applied Behavior Analysis, 38,* 79–88.

Satake, E., Maxwell, D. L., & Jagaroo, V. (2008). *Handbook of statistical methods: Single subject design.* San Diego, CA: Plural Publishing.

Savard, J., Labege, B., Gauthier, J. G., Fournier, J., Bourchard, S., Barit, J., & Bergeron, M. (1998). Combination of Fluoxetine and cognitive therapy for treatment of major depression among people with HIV infection: A time-series analysis investigation. *Cognitive Therapy and Research, 22,* 21–46.

Scherrer, M. D., & Wilder, D. A. (2008). Training to increase safe tray carrying among cocktail servers. *Journal of Applied Behavior Analysis, 41,* 131–135.

Schmidt, F. L. (1996). Statistical significance testing and cumulative knowledge in psychology: Implications for training of researchers. *Psychological Methods, 1,* 115–129.

Schnelle, J. F., Kirchner, R. E., Macrae, J. W., McNees, M. P., Eck, R. H., Snodgrass, S., et al. (1978). Police evaluation research: An experimental and cost-benefit analysis of a helicopter patrol in high-crime area. *Journal of Applied Behavior Analysis, 11,* 11–21.

Schnelle, J. F., Kirchner, R. E., McNees, M. P., & Lawler, J. M. (1975). Social evaluation research: The evaluation of two police patrolling strategies. *Journal of Applied Behavior Analysis, 8,* 353–365.

Schwartz, I. S., & Baer, D. M. (1991). Social validity assessments: Is current practice state of the art? *Journal of Applied Behavior Analysis, 24,* 189–204.

Scotti, J. R., Evans, I. M., Meyer, L. H., & Walker, P. (1991). A meta-analysis of intervention research with problem behavior: Treatment validity and standards of practice. *American Journal on Mental Retardation, 96,* 233–256.

Sechrest, L., Stewart, M., Stickle, T. R., & Sidani, S. (1996). *Effective and persuasive case studies.* Cambridge, MA: Human Services Research Institute.

Shabani, D. B., & Fisher, W. W. (2006). Stimulus fading and differential reinforcement for the treatment of needle phobia in a youth with autism. *Journal of Applied Behavior Analysis, 39,* 449–452.

Shadish, W. R., Cook, T. D., & Campbell, D. T. (2002). *Experimental and quasi-experimental designs for generalized causal inference.* Boston: Houghton Mifflin.

Shadish, W. R., & Ragsdale, K. (1996). Random versus nonrandom assignment in controlled experiments. Do you get the same answer? *Journal of Consulting and Clinical Psychology, 64,* 1290–1305.

Shadish, W. R., Rindskopf, D. M., & Hedges, L. V. (2008). The state of the science in the meta-analysis of single-case experimental designs. *Evidence-Based Communication Assessment and Intervention, 3,* 188–196.

Shapiro, E. S., Kazdin, A. E., & McGonigle, J. J. (1982). Multiple-treatment interference in the simultaneous-or alternating-treatments design. *Behavioral Assessment, 4,* 105–115.

Shapiro, M. B. (1961a). A method of measuring psychological changes specific to the individual psychiatric patient. *British Journal of Medical Psychology, 34,* 151–155.

Shapiro, M. B. (1961b). The single case in fundamental clinical psychological research. *British Journal of Medical Psychology, 34,* 255–262.

Shapiro, M. B., & Ravenette, T. (1959). A preliminary experiment of paranoid delusions. *Journal of Mental Science, 105,* 295–312.

Shoukri, M. M. (2005). *Measures of interobserver agreement.* Boca Raton, FL: Taylor & Francis.

Sideridis, G. D., & Greenwood, C. R. (1997). Is human behavior autocorrelated? An empirical analysis. *Journal of Behavioral Education, 7,* 273–293.

Sidman, M. (1960). *Tactics of scientific research.* New York: Basic Books.

Sierra, V., Solanas, A., & Quera, V. (2005). Randomization tests for systematic single-case designs are not always appropriate. *Journal of Experimental Education, 73,* 140–160.

Simon, G. E., Manning, W. G., Katzelnick, D. J., Pearson, S. D., Henk, H. J., & Helstad, C. P. (2001). Cost-effectiveness of systematic depression treatment of high utilizers of general medical care. *Archives of General Psychiatry, 58,* 181–187.

Skiba, R., Deno, S., Marston, D., & Casey, A. (1989). Influence of trend estimation and subject familiarity on practitioners' judgments of intervention effectiveness. *Journal of Special Education, 22,* 433–446.

Skinner, B. F. (1938). *The behavior of organisms.* New York: Appleton-Century-Crofts.

Skinner, B. F. (1953a). *Science and human behavior.* New York: Free Press.

Skinner, B. F. (1953b). Some contributions of an experimental analysis of behavior to psychology as a whole. *American Psychologist, 8,* 69–78.

Skinner, B. F. (1956). A case history in scientific method. *American Psychologist, 11,* 221–233.

Skinner, C. H., Skinner, A. L., & Armstrong, K. J. (2000). Analysis of a client-staff developed shaping program to enhance reading persistence in an adult diagnosed with schizophrenia. *Psychiatric Rehabilitation, 24,* 52–57.

Spirrison, C. L., & Mauney, L. T. (1994). Acceptability bias: The effects of treatment acceptability on visual analysis of graphed data. *Journal of Psychopathology and Behavioral Assessment, 16,* 85–94.

Staats, A. W., Staats, C. K., Schutz, R. E., & Wolf, M. (1962). The conditioning of textual responses using "extrinsic" reinforcers. *Journal of the Experimental Analysis of Behavior, 5,* 33–40.

Stead, L. F., Bergson, G., & Lancaster, T. (2008). Physician advice for smoking cessation. *Cochrane Database of Systematic Reviews,* Issue 2 (Art. No. CD000165).

Stewart, K. K., Carr, J. E., Brandt, C. W., & McHenry, M. M. (2007). An evaluation of the conservative dual-criterion method for teaching university students to visually inspect AB-design graphs. *Journal of Applied Behavior Analysis, 40,* 713–718.

Stricker, J. M., Miltenberger, R. G., Garlinghouse, M. A., Deaver, C. M., & Anderson, C. A. (2001). Evaluation of an awareness enhancement device for the treatment of thumb sucking in children. *Journal of Applied Behavior Analysis, 37,* 229–232.

Sundberg, M. L., Endicott, K., & Eigenheer, P. (2000). Using intraverbal prompts to establish tacts for children with autism. *The Analysis of Verbal Behavior, 17,* 89–104.

Swaminathan, H., Horner, R. H., Sugai, G., Smolkowski, L., Hedges, L., & Spaulding, S. A. (2008). Application of generalized least squares regression to measure effect size in single-case research: A technical report (Institute of Education Sciences Technical Report). Washington, DC U.S. Department of Education.

Swanson, J. M., Arnold, L. E., Vitiello, B., Abikoff, H. B., Wells, K. C., Pelham, W. E., et al. (2002). Response to commentary on the Multimodal Treatment Study of ADHD (MTA): Mining the meaning of the MTA. *Journal of Abnormal Child Psychology, 30,* 327–332.

Swoboda, C., Kratochwill, T. R., & Levin, J. R. (2009). *Conservative Dual-Criterion (CDC) method for single-case research: A guide for visual analysis of AB, ABAB, and multiple-baseline designs.* Madison: University of Wisconsin-Madison.

Tarbox, R. S. F., Wallace, M. D., Penrod, B., & Tarbox, J. (2007). Effects of three-step prompting on compliance with caregiver requests. *Journal of Applied Behavior Analysis, 40,* 703–706.

Thigpen, C. H., & Cleckley, H. M. (1954). A case of multiple personality. *Journal of Abnormal and Social Psychology, 49,* 135–151.

Thigpen, C. H., & Cleckley, H. M. (1957). *The three faces of Eve.* New York: McGraw-Hill.

Thornberry, T. P., & Krohn, M. D. (2000). The self-report method for measuring delinquency. In D. Duffee (Ed.), *Measurement and analysis of crime and justice: Criminal justice 2000* (Vol. 4). Washington, DC: National Institute of Justice.

Tiger, J. H., Bouxsein, K. J., & Fisher, W. W. (2007). Treating excessively slow responding of a young man with Asperger syndrome using differential reinforcement of short response latencies. *Journal of Applied Behavior Analysis, 40,* 559–563.

Timberlake, W., Schaal, D. W., & Steinmetz, J. E. (Eds.). (2005). Relating behavior and neuroscience: Introduction and synopsis. *Journal of the Experimental Analysis of Behavior, 84,* 305–311.

Todd, P. M., Penke, L., Fasolo, B., & Lenton, A. P. (2007). Different cognitive processes underlie human mate choices and mate preferences. *Proceedings of the National Academy of Sciences, 104,* 15011–15016.

Todman, J. B., & Dugard, P. (2001). *Single-case and small-n experimental designs: A practical guide to randomization tests.* Mahwah, NJ: Lawrence Erlbaum Associates.

Tryon, W. W. (1982). A simplified time-series analysis for evaluating treatment interventions. *Journal of Applied Behavior Analysis, 15,* 423–429.

Tufte, E. R. (2001). *The visual display of quantitative information* (2nd ed.). Cheshire, CT: Graphics Press.

Twohig, M. P., Shoenberger, D., & Hayes, S. C. (2007). A preliminary investigation of acceptance and commitment therapy as a treatment for marijuana dependence in adults. *Journal of Applied Behavior Analysis, 40,* 619–632.

Ullmann, L. P., & Krasner, L. A. (Eds.). (1965). *Case studies in behavior modification.* New York: Holt, Rinehart & Winston.

Ulman, J. D., & Sulzer-Azaroff, B. (1975). Multielement baseline design in educational research. In E. Ramp & G. Semb (Eds.), *Behavior analysis: Areas of research and application.* Englewood Cliffs, NJ: Prentice-Hall.

Van Houten, R., Malenfant, J. E. L., Zhao, N., Ko, B., & Van Houten, J. (2005). Evaluation of two methods of prompting drivers to use specific exits on conflicts between vehicles at the critical exit. *Journal of Applied Behavior Analysis, 38,* 289–302.

Van Houten, R., & Retting, R. A. (2001). Increasing motorist compliance and caution at stop signs. *Journal of Applied Behavior Analysis, 34,* 185–193.

Van Houten, R., Van Houten, J., & Malenfant, J. E. L. (2007). Impact of a comprehensive safety program on bicycle helmet use among middle-school children. *Journal of Applied Behavior Analysis, 40,* 239–247.

Velleman, P. F. (1980). Definition and comparison of robust nonlinear data smoothing algorithms. *Journal of the American Statistical Association, 75,* 609–615.

Vlaeyen, J. W. S., de Jong, J. R., Onghena, P., Kerckhoffs-Hanssen, M., & Kole-Snijders, A. M. J. (2002). Can pain-related fear be reduced? The application of cognitive-behavioral exposure in vivo. *Pain Research Management, 7,* 144–153.

Wacker, D., McMahon, C., Steege, M., Berg, W., Sasso, G., & Melloy, K. (1990). Applications of a sequential alternating treatments design. *Journal of Applied Behavior Analysis, 23,* 333–339.

Wampold, B. E. (2001). *The great psychotherapy debate: Models, methods, and findings.* Mahwah, NJ: Lawrence Erlbaum Associates.

Wannamethee, S. G., & Sharper, A. G. (1999). Type of alcoholic drink and risk of major coronary heart disease events and all-cause mortality. *American Journal of Public Health, 89,* 685–690.

Warnes, E., & Allen, K. D. (2005). Biofeedback treatment of paradoxical vocal fold motion and respiratory distress in an adolescent girl. *Journal of Applied Behavior Analysis, 38,* 529–532.

Washington, K., Deitz, J. C., White, O. R., & Schwartz, I. S. (2002). The effects of a contoured foam seat on postural alignment and upper-extremity function in infants with neuromotor impairments. *Physical Therapy, 82,* 1064–1076.

Watson, J. B., & Rayner, R. (1920). Conditioned emotional reactions. *Journal of Experimental Psychology, 3,* 1–14.

Watson, R. I. (1951). *The clinical method in psychology.* New York: Harper.

Watson, T. S., Meeks, C., Dufrene, B., & Lindsay, C. (2002). Sibling thumb sucking: Effects of treatment for targeted and untargeted siblings. *Behavior Modification, 26,* 412–423.

Wehby, J. H., & Hollahan, M. S. (2000). Effects of high-probability requests on latency to initiate academic tasks. *Journal of Applied Behavior Analysis, 33,* 259–262.

Weiss, B., Caron, A., Ball, S., Tapp, J., Johnson, M., & Weisz, J. R. (2005). Iatrogenic effects of group treatment for antisocial youth. *Journal of Consulting and Clinical Psychology, 73,* 1036–1044.

Weisz, J. R., & Kazdin, A. E. (Eds.). (2010). *Evidence-based psychotherapies for children and adolescents* (2nd ed.). New York: Guilford Press.

Weisz, J. R., Weiss, B., Han, S. S., Granger, D. A., & Morton, T. (1995). Effects of psychotherapy with children and adolescents revisited: A meta-analysis of treatment outcome studies. *Psychological Bulletin, 117,* 450–468.

Westen, D., Novotny, C. M., & Thompson-Brenne, H. (2004). The empirical status of empirically supported psychotherapies: Assumptions, findings, and reporting in controlled clinical trials. *Psychological Bulletin, 130,* 631–663.

Whalen, C., Schreibman, L., & Ingersoll, B. (2006). The collateral effects of joint attention training on social initiations, positive affect, imitation, and spontaneous speech for young children with autism. *Journal of Autism and Developmental Disorders, 36,* 655–664.

White, K. G., McCarthy, D., & Fantino, E. (Eds.). (1989). Cognition and behavior analysis. *Journal of the Experimental Analysis of Behavior, 52,* 197–198.

White, O. R. (1972). *A manual for the calculation and use of the median slope—A technique of progress estimation and prediction in the single case.* Eugene: Regional Resource Center for Handicapped Children, University of Oregon.

White, O. R. (1974). *The "split middle": A "quickie" method of trend estimation.* University of

Washington, Experimental Education Unit, Child Development and Mental Retardation Center.

White, O. R., & Haring, N. G. (1980). *Exceptional teaching* (2nd ed.). Columbus, OH: Merrill.

Wiesman, D. W. (2006). The effects of performance feedback and social reinforcement on up-selling at fast-food restaurants. *Journal of Organizational Behavior Management, 26,* 1–18.

Wilder, D. A., Atwell, J., & Wine, B. (2006). The effects of varying levels of treatment integrity on child compliance during treatment with a three-step prompting procedure. *Journal of Applied Behavior Analysis, 39,* 369–373.

Wilhelm, S., Buhlmann, U., Tolin, D. F., Meunier, S. A., Pearlson, G. D., Reese, H. E., Cannistraro, P., Jenike, M. A., & Rauch, S. L. (2008). Augmentation of behavior therapy with D-cycloserine for obsessive-compulsive disorder. *American Journal of Psychiatry, 165,* 335–341.

Wilkinson, L., and the Task Force on Statistical Inference. (1999). Statistical methods in psychology journals: Guidelines and explanations. *American Psychologist, 54,* 594–604.

Wilkinson, L., Wills, D., Rope, D., Norton, A., & Dubbs, R. (2005). *The grammar of graphics.* Chicago: SPSS Inc.

Wilson, D. D., Robertson, S. J., Herlong, L. H., & Haynes, S. N. (1979). Vicarious effects of time-out in the modification of aggression in the classroom. *Behavior Modification, 3,* 97–111.

Wolery, M., Busick, M., Reichow, B., & Barton, E. E. (2008). Comparison of overlap methods for quantitatively synthesizing single-subject data. *Journal of Special Education.* (Online document: 101177/0022466908328009).

Wolf, M. M. (1978). Social validity: The case for subjective measurement or how applied behavior analysis is finding its heart. *Journal of Applied Behavior Analysis, 11,* 203–214.

Wong, S. E., Terranova, M. D., Bowen, L., Zarate, R., Massey, H. K., & Liberman, R. P. (1987). Providing independent recreational activities to reduce stereotypic vocalizations in chronic schizophrenics. *Journal of Applied Behavior Analysis, 20,* 77–82.

Worsdell, A. S., Iwata, B. A., Dozier, C. L., Johnson, A. D., Neidert, P. L., & Thomason, J. L. (2005). Analysis of response repetition as an error-correction strategy during sight-word reading. *Journal of Applied Behavior Analysis, 38,* 511–527.

Wright, K. M., & Miltenberger, R. G. (1987). Awareness training in the treatment of head and facial tics. *Journal of Behavior Therapy and Experimental Psychiatry, 18,* 269–274.

Yasui, M., & Dishion, T. J. (2008). Direct observation of family management: Validity and reliability as a function of coder ethnicity and training. *Behavior Therapy, 39,* 336–347.

Zilboorg, G., & Henry, G. (1941). *A history of medical psychology.* New York: Norton.